This collection of articles adds greatly to our understanding of the link between economic performance and inequality, combining theory, econometrics, and case studies, and looking at both taxes and expenditures. The questions are investigated in a huge range of circumstances—both developed and developing countries, at the national and subnational levels. The IMF recognizes that its policies can have huge distributive consequences and so this book will be important not only for guiding its own work, but for scholars and policymakers seeking to further enhance our understanding of the determinants of inequality and devising policies that might reduce it.

—**Joseph E. Stiglitz**
Professor, Columbia University

This volume constitutes a definitive reference for serious students concerned with the redistributive role of the state, particularly in developing countries. Careful technical analyses back new ideas, especially on the tax side, for progressivity with minimal or no trade-off with revenue and growth: the unexploited relevance of income and property compared to indirect taxes, the centrality of such "administrative" issues as tax compliance, the still-minor role of wealth taxes, the risk of bilateral tax treaties for low-income countries. Nor are the authors naïve about the politics. Another terrific IMF contribution on how to tackle inequality within and across countries. I hope IMF operational staff pay heed.

—**Nancy Birdsall**
President and Co-Founder, Center for Global Development

In this engaging collection, leading experts address the distributional effects of an array of fiscal instruments. The revenue chapters span income, consumption, and property taxation, while the spending chapters tackle means-tested and contributory cash transfers, as well as expenditures on health and education. The authors consider the effects of fiscal policies in countries at diverse levels of economic development, and over a period of decades, with keen attention paid to recent rounds of fiscal consolidation. This vividly detailed yet accessible volume fills a void in the inequality literature, and promises to prompt lively debate about the consequences of fiscal policy.

—**Janet C. Gornick**
Director, Luxembourg Income Study (LIS) Cross-National Data Center,
Luxembourg, and Professor, Graduate Center, City University of New York

INEQUALITY and FISCAL POLICY

EDITORS

Benedict Clements, Ruud de Mooij,
Sanjeev Gupta, and Michael Keen

INTERNATIONAL MONETARY FUND

Cataloging-in-Publication Data

Joint Bank-Fund Library

Inequality and fiscal policy / edited by Benedict Clements, Ruud de Mooij, Sanjeev Gupta, and Michael Keen. – Washington, D.C. : International Monetary Fund, 2015.
  pages ;   cm

Includes bibliographical references and index.

ISBN: 978-1-51356-775-4

1. Income distribution.   2. Fiscal policy.   3. Asia – Economic conditions.   I. Clements, Benedict J. II. Mooij, Ruud A. de.   III. Gupta, Sanjeev.   IV. Keen, Michael.   V. International Monetary Fund.

HB523.I548 2015

978-1-51356-775-4 (hard cover)
978-1-51353-162-5 (paper)
978-1-51353-868-6 (PDF)
978-1-51350-999-0 (ePub)
978-1-51354-407-6 (Mobipocket)

Please send orders to
International Monetary Fund, Publication Services
P.O. Box 92780, Washington, DC 20090, U.S.A.
Tel.: (202) 623-7430   Fax: (202) 623-7201
E-mail: publications@imf.org
Internet: www.elibrary.imf.org
www.imfbookstore.org

Contents

Foreword

Excessive income inequality in many parts of the world is one of the defining issues of our time. Not only is extreme income inequality a moral and political issue, but it has important macroeconomic implications. There is growing evidence that excessive income inequality is detrimental to macroeconomic stability and economic growth.

I strongly believe that economic growth should be more inclusive and therefore more sustainable. This means improving the design of government tax and spending policies; enhancing financial inclusion, so that the poor have access to credit and financial markets; and promoting transparency and good governance, so that the doors of opportunity are open to all.

The topic of excessive inequality is relevant for the IMF in all three of its core activities—lending to support macroeconomic adjustment programs; macroeconomic surveillance, including related policy analysis; and technical assistance to build capacity, especially on government taxation and spending.

Fiscal policy is the government's most powerful tool to achieve distributional objectives. Tax and spending policies must be designed wisely to minimize any adverse effects on incentives to work, save, and invest. On the revenue side, this implies building wider, more reliable tax bases by reducing exemptions, combating tax evasion, and strengthening administration. On the expenditure side, priorities include expanding access to education and health—which will bolster equality of opportunity—and better targeting of social benefits to the poor.

I hope this book will assist policymakers in designing more equitable fiscal policies that will help generate more equitable growth.

IMF advice has been mindful of the social impact of economic policies. Social spending floors are a key feature of programs supported under the IMF Extended Credit Facility for low-income countries. Measures to protect the most vulnerable have featured in IMF-supported programs with high-income members, including in the euro area. We are also addressing equity and social issues in our regular country-level economic surveillance, whenever they are macro-critical.

This book is designed to help further integrate income inequality issues into the IMF's policy advice. I hope it will also spark further debate and research on this topic both inside and outside the IMF.

Christine Lagarde
Managing Director
International Monetary Fund

Acknowledgments

This book has been a collective endeavor and has benefited from contributions from both inside and outside the IMF. We would like to thank the contributing authors for their close collaboration and enthusiasm for the topic. The research presented here has benefited from the comments of staff in the IMF's Fiscal Affairs Department and other departments. Several chapters have also benefited from valuable comments presented at seminars hosted by other institutions.

Michael Harrup of the IMF's Communications Department efficiently managed all aspects related to the production of the book, and we are grateful for his excellent work. We also thank Muriel Jolivert and staff in the Expenditure Policy Division of the IMF's Fiscal Affairs Department for their valuable support. We are especially grateful to Maura Francese for her thoughtful analytical contributions and skillful organization of the many steps needed to bring a book to completion.

Benedict Clements
Ruud de Mooij
Sanjeev Gupta
Michael Keen
Editors

Trends in Income Inequality and the Redistributive Role of Fiscal Policy

CHAPTER 1

Fiscal Policy and Income Inequality: An Overview

BENEDICT CLEMENTS, RUUD DE MOOIJ, MAURA FRANCESE,
SANJEEV GUPTA, AND MICHAEL KEEN

INTRODUCTION

Inequality is at the forefront of the economic policy debate in much of the world. This interest comes in the wake of the sizable increases in income disparities that many have seen during the past three decades or so, combined now with the need to deal with the continuing and severe consequences of the global economic and financial crisis. Policymakers face difficult challenges in understanding how to deal with trade-offs—or exploit complementarities—between their distributional concerns and other economic policy objectives, such as achieving high rates of economic growth and sustainable public finances. The aim of this book is to present recent research results that can help them address these challenges.[1]

Research on the causes and consequences of rising inequality has flourished in recent years, taking advantage of the growing availability of large micro data sets and of data covering longer time spans for an increasing sample of countries.[2] The phenomenal success of Piketty (2014) is a reflection of, and has further stimulated, extraordinary public interest in these issues.[3] More new thinking has focused on the analysis of these developments, however, than on how governments can design redistributive policies to address them, especially in countries with limited fiscal space. A key feature of the book is its focus on the design of fiscal policies in such circumstances.

Fiscal policy can be a potent tool for achieving a government's redistributive goals. It affects household welfare through both monetary payments (taxes and transfers) and provision of in-kind benefits (for example, free education and health services). Some tax and expenditure policies used to this end can distort incentives and reduce economic efficiency. In this regard, policymakers can do much, through careful policy design, to minimize these effects. Making certain social assistance programs conditional on participation in job training, for instance, can help strengthen incentives to return to work. In some cases, redistributive policies not only help achieve equity goals but also improve efficiency, especially when they address market imperfections. The lack of access to credit by poor households, for example, is a major market imperfection that prevents poor households from borrowing to finance education. In these circumstances, government financing of education can help families overcome this hurdle while strengthening both equity and the efficient accumulation of human capital.

---

[1] Inequality is, of course, closely related to, but distinct from, poverty. For the most part, the focus of this book is on the former.

[2] These databases include, for example, the Luxembourg Income Study Database, the Organisation for Economic Co-operation and Development Income Distribution Database, The World Top Incomes Database, the Socio-Economic Database for Latin America and the Caribbean, and the European Union Statistics on Income and Living Conditions.

[3] Other important recent publications include Atkinson 2015, Bourguignon 2015, and Atkinson and Bourguignon 2015.

The fiscal tools that are available to address inequality-related concerns vary widely across countries, reflecting their differing administrative capacity. Advanced economies may be able to condition cash transfers quite finely on income, labor force participation, and other characteristics. In contrast, sophisticated means-testing is simply not an option for developing countries. One central aim of this book is to bring out this diversity of challenges by reviewing experiences in countries at quite different levels of development.

Another theme is the need to take a comprehensive view of both tax and spending programs to assess how fiscal policies affect, and are affected by, inequality. Looking at the effect of tax measures in isolation, without looking at the spending measures they help finance, would provide an imperfect guide for policymaking—a simple point that continues to be too often ignored, or respected in the breach.

The analysis presented in this book builds on and extends work undertaken at the IMF in the recent past, including a paper prepared for the IMF Executive Board on fiscal policy and inequality (IMF 2014a). Distributive issues have been an important part of IMF policy work for decades, reflecting early recognition of the social impact of macroeconomic policies (Tanzi and Chu 1998; Tanzi, Chu, and Gupta 1999). These efforts have intensified in recent years, especially in light of new evidence that extreme inequality can be damaging for macroeconomic stability and growth (Easterly 2007; Rajan 2010; Kumhof and Rancière 2011; Ostry, Berg, and Tsangarides 2014). With many governments engaged in fiscal consolidation, recent studies have also explored how fiscal adjustment can be designed to minimize any adverse effects on income distribution (Woo and others 2013). Equity issues have also been explored in the IMF's work on energy subsidies, pensions, and jobs and growth.

To set the scene for the chapters to come, the rest of this introduction provides an assessment of different approaches to measuring the effects of fiscal policy on inequality, as well as some of the key methodological challenges in assessing the distributive effects of taxes and spending. This is followed by a description of the main findings in each chapter of the volume.

KEY ISSUES FOR INEQUALITY ANALYSIS AND THE ASSESSMENT OF FISCAL POLICY

Incidence

Assessing how tax and spending policies affect inequality requires taking a view on how they affect real incomes—that is, on their incidence. Empirical studies answer this question by allocating total tax payments and the benefits of government spending across households in some way. And many do so on the basis of some simple assumptions. For instance, many assume that indirect taxes like value-added taxes (VATs) and excises are fully borne by consumers (not passed back to the profits of suppliers or wages of their employees) while personal income taxes are fully borne by employees (so have no effect on the pretax payments they receive).

Several difficult issues arise.[4] First, the tax payment allocated to a household in such a way gives a sense of the impact on real incomes, but that is different from the effect on welfare, because it ignores the deadweight loss associated with those taxes—the loss the household suffers because transactions that would otherwise have taken place no longer will. Second, and more fundamentally for this book, these assumptions often have no firm empirical basis. Basic public finance teaches, to take just one example, that taxes on commodities will be less than fully passed through to consumers in competitive markets with less than perfectly elastic supplies. And allowing for imperfect competition and links across markets, they might be more than fully passed on to consumers.

---

[4] Some of these issues are discussed in Boadway and Keen 2000. On the formalities of incidence analysis, see Kotlikoff and Summers 1987.

Faced with these ambiguities, one looks to empirical evidence. This evidence is surprisingly sparse, but what there is warns against blithe acceptance of some of the standard assumptions. Benedek and others (forthcoming) find, for instance, that while changes in the standard VAT rate may indeed be fully shifted to consumers, the benefits of reduced rates may not be. And Rothstein (2010) finds that for each $1 spent on the earned income tax credit in the United States, about 27 cents benefits the employer, not the worker. Matters are still more complex in relation to other taxes: there is a lively debate, for instance, on the extent to which the corporate tax is passed on to workers (Gravelle 2011). And the incidence of tariffs—still very important in many developing countries—can be hard to assess, not least because it will affect not only those who purchase imports, and so pay some tariffs, but also those who purchase untaxed but none-theless now more expensive domestic substitutes. Indeed, the incidence of what look like very similar taxes may well differ between advanced and developing countries, given differing eco-nomic structures and degrees of administrative capacity. They might also differ over time, given, for instance, changes in openness to trade and capital movements.

Further difficulties arise in assessing the distributional consequences of the public provision of health, education, and other services. The benefit of these services can be allocated across house-holds by valuing them at the average cost of provision, but this approach may significantly understate households' true valuations, which are arguably the more relevant in assessing distri-butional effects. The issue becomes even more complicated when the quality of service provision to different income classes varies.

Perhaps surprisingly, the topic being so old, very much remains to be learned about the inci-dence of tax and spending policies. The assumptions commonly made may be defensible as broadly reasonable in the face of substantial ignorance, but their importance and sometimes weak basis needs to be remembered. The classic treatment of Whalley (1984) remains a salutary lesson, showing how by alternative plausible assumptions the incidence of the Canadian tax system can be made to look either broadly proportional to income or highly progressive.

Dimensions of Inequality

Inequality can be viewed from many perspectives.[5] Following most of the literature, the contribu-tions in this book generally focus on inequality at the household level, measured primarily in monetary terms (annual income or consumption), and the effects of fiscal policies on these mea-sures. But many other dimensions of inequality can be of interest: inequality of opportunity, for instance, between ethnic groups; and unequal treatment of those felt to be in all relevant respects identical—"horizontal" inequity—is often a major concern. Here, however, we focus on just two other dimensions of inequality not addressed by simply comparing household incomes at a single point in time—inequality over the life cycle and gender.

Inequality over the Life Cycle and Generational Accounting

Most measures of inequality are based on a snapshot for a single year. An individual's income in a given year, however, may not be representative of his or her lifetime income. For example, a worker may experience a decline in income during a spell of unemployment. In a similar vein, the taxes an individual pays in any given year, and benefits he or she receives, may vary greatly from year to year. During his or her prime working years, for example, an individual is likely to be paying higher taxes than when in retirement and drawing a pension. Much of what appears to be government redistributive policies is the collection of taxes from individuals during their prime working years that is offset by the payment of benefits in later years to the same individu-als. In other words, on a lifetime basis, government redistribution may be much smaller than it appears to be.

---

[5] On the multidimensional nature of inequality and how to measure it, see Aaberge and Brandolini 2015.

Longitudinal data covering the entire life cycle (or at least career-long income histories) are less common than yearly household surveys, so many fewer studies of inequality over the life cycle have been undertaken. What empirical evidence there is, however, shows that, in line with expectations, lifetime inequality is significantly lower than annual income inequality. Björklund (1993), for example, shows that dispersion in lifetime incomes is 35–40 percent lower than that of annual income in Sweden. Aaberge and Mogstad (2012) find that at age 60, annual income inequality is more than twice lifetime income inequality.

The lifetime income approach is especially relevant in the analysis of the distributive effects of pension systems, since their main objective is to redistribute an individual's income across her or his lifetime to avoid a sharp drop in consumption after retirement. If the relationship between benefits and contributions is actuarially fair, computing lifetime income washes away any redistributive effect that may be attributed to pension schemes.

However, pension systems, and public policies in general, may not be distributionally neutral when they transfer resources from the working-age population to older (or younger) cohorts. Fiscal policies may then provide differing levels of net benefits to the lifetime income of individuals belonging to different age cohorts. This is especially relevant in light of the challenges posed by age-related spending in many countries. Generational accounting is a methodology (based on the intertemporal budget constraint of the government) that aims to measure the impact of taxes and spending on representative members of different generations. The focus of this analysis is to highlight which generations bear the burden of government programs and which enjoy their benefits (Kotlikoff 2002). For example, Kashiwase and Rizza (2014) use a generational approach to assess the net benefits received from the pension systems of Italy, Japan, and the United States. They find, unsurprisingly, that in Italy and Japan the net lifetime benefits received by current retirees are much higher than those of current workers and future generations, reflecting the future effects of pension reforms introduced in recent decades.

Generational accounting studies have been undertaken mainly for advanced economies, and have their limitations; for instance, the point estimates of the net tax burden for different generations can be sensitive to specific assumptions.[6] Nevertheless, this approach can provide important insights into the intergenerational implications of fiscal policies.

Gender

Differences in the earnings of men and women remain striking. Despite similar educational levels in the advanced economies, women's wages and participation in the labor market remain lower than men's, while women still bear the burden of unpaid housework (OECD 2012). Gender inequality has an important macroeconomic dimension because raising female labor force participation rates could have significant and positive effects on economic growth (Elborgh-Woytek and others 2013).

The measurement of gender inequality has raised both theoretical and empirical issues (Ponthieux and Meurs 2015). Commonly used standard inequality measures are usually based on some concept of household per capita equivalent income or well-being. Household resources are pooled together, and then equivalence scales[7] are used to derive an average income indicator. The

---

[6] For a critical assessment of generational accounting, see Haveman 1994.

[7] An equivalence scale is a set of weights, one for each household member, that measures the additional income regarded as being necessary to achieve the same level of well-being as a one-member household. The use of equivalence scales recognizes that individuals living together enjoy economies of scale, and that different demographic groups may have different needs. There are several equivalence scales (Atkinson, Rainwater, and Smeeding 1995). Some commonly used are the "old" OECD equivalence scale (which gives a weight equal to 1 to the first household member, of 0.7 to each additional adult, and of 0.5 to each child), the OECD modified scale (which gives a value of 1 to the household head, of 0.5 to each additional adult, and of 0.3 to each child), and the square root scale (in this case, household income is divided by the square root of the household size).

implicit assumption is that all the household members enjoy the same level of income. In recent decades this view of the household (based on the so-called unitary model) has been challenged. Empirical studies suggest that changes in personal income accruing to different household members (in particular, women) lead to changes in the allocation of household resources (Bourguignon and others 1993; Duflo 2003; Ward-Batts 2008). Theoretical contributions have proposed more sophisticated approaches that take into account income-sharing rules and appear to be more consistent with the data (Browning, Chiappori, and Weiss 2011).

Because of the multifaceted nature of gender inequality and data difficulties, however, few studies have been able to empirically measure gender disparities within the household in a comprehensive way. The empirical literature on gender inequality has focused instead on several outcome measures (such as labor force participation and compensation, underrepresentation in top jobs and career progression, overrepresentation in informal employment, pension income, wealth, time spent in unpaid work, and poverty risk). Taken together, these provide insights into the extent of gender economic inequality, its determinants, and policy options for reducing it.

The empirical literature suggests that gender—and motherhood—play a significant role in labor market outcomes. Having children has a significant impact on female education and employment decisions, with mothers' labor market participation being lower than men's during the prime childbearing years. However, social norms (such as early marriage) or discriminatory institutions and practices appear also to matter a great deal. For example, OECD 2012 shows that discriminatory attitudes and gender gaps in employment rates are strongly correlated. Gonzales and others (2015) find that legal restrictions (such as those on rights to inheritance and property) and impediments (for instance, to pursuing a profession or opening a bank account) are also strongly correlated with gaps in labor force participation in both advanced and developing countries.

Addressing gender equity thus requires responses on many fronts, including but by no means only fiscal. Reforming the regulatory framework to remove obstacles and discrimination can shape a favorable environment for women to exercise their full economic potential. Universal access to education and health, by fostering human capital formation for both girls and boys, can contribute to removing differences in skills and productivity and reduce wage gaps. Public spending for the provision of good-quality and affordable child care may promote mothers' return to paid employment after childbirth (Thévenon 2011). The appropriate design of income taxes can ensure that work disincentives for second earners are eased, and that work pays for all household members (Boskin and Sheshinski 1983; Apps and Rees 1999, 2007).

ORGANIZATION AND MAIN FINDINGS OF THIS BOOK

This book consists of six parts. Part I provides an overview of income inequality trends and discusses fiscal redistribution in advanced and developing countries. Part II investigates the link between personal and functional income distributions and discusses tax policy issues linked to the taxation of wealth. Part III explores the link between fiscal consolidation and inequality. Parts IV and V focus on tax and expenditure policies, respectively, and how these can be fashioned to address distributive objectives. Finally, Part VI comprises country studies addressing various aspects of the relationship between fiscal policy and income inequality.

Part I—Trends in Income Inequality and the Redistributive Role of Fiscal Policy

Chapter 2, by Benedict Clements, Vitor Gaspar, Sanjeev Gupta, and Tidiane Kinda, looks at the relevance of inequality for the work of the IMF and how economic developments have shaped this work. Two main trends have been important in this respect. First, long-term demographic and economic trends have resulted in an increase in developing countries' share in global output, which has contributed to a decline in inequality at the global level. Second, inequality has risen within many countries.

Redistributive issues are relevant for all three core activities of the IMF: support for macroeconomic adjustment, surveillance of member countries' economic policies, and technical assistance to build capacity. The authors provide a historic overview of the IMF's involvement in these issues, which began in the late 1980s and was influenced by policy design in IMF-supported adjustment programs. This experience led to greater attention to integrating social safety nets into program design and safeguarding access to basic public services in health and education. IMF-supported programs were successful in raising social spending (Clements, Gupta, and Nozaki 2013). The IMF's work in this area has deepened further since the global financial crisis, which has had significant adverse effects on growth and welfare, particularly in advanced economies. This renewed focus reflects the recognition that inequality has the potential to undermine macroeconomic stability, and calls for a careful examination of policy options and appropriate design of fiscal measures. The analytical effort has encompassed cross-country studies, country-level assessments of fiscal consolidation and inequality, and a variety of fiscal policy tools. The survey (and the examples of IMF-supported adjustment programs) presented by the authors points to an important lesson: growth and greater equality are not necessarily in conflict. With the right design, tax and spending policies can help achieve both stronger growth and greater equality of outcomes and opportunities.

The issue of the appropriate design of tax and spending policies in advanced economies is the focus of Chapter 3, by David Coady, Ruud de Mooij, and Baoping Shang. Although redistributive goals can also be achieved by other regulatory instruments (such as price controls), the primary tools for governments to reduce inequality are taxes and spending programs. Fiscal policy instruments can have an impact both in the short term (personal income taxes, for instance, immediately reduce household disposable income) and in the long term (current education spending, for instance, is likely to affect future earnings). In advanced economies, fiscal policies have indeed played a significant role in reducing market-income inequality. For example, they have, on average, reduced the Gini coefficients by about one-third (of which, approximately two-thirds is due to transfer programs and about a third is a result of progressive taxation). With regard to public expenditures, although the appropriate composition and design of spending programs varies by country, key considerations are to effectively reach households with the lowest income and avoid the creation of "poverty traps" with these programs. The latter issue can be addressed, in part, by designing benefits to minimize unfavorable behavioral effects of transfer programs (such as disincentives to work). The redistributive impact of taxation depends on the progressivity of personal income taxes, as well as the level and structure of taxes imposed on capital income and wealth. Indirect taxes generally tend to be regressive (at least when determined as a share of income, rather than expenditures, and assuming full pass-through to consumer prices) and are less suitable instruments than income taxes for pursuing redistributive objectives. Moreover, as stressed above, the distributional impact of public policies should be assessed by taking into account not only the impact of taxation but the impact of transfers and spending that it helps finance. Many advanced economies are facing a sluggish recovery from the global financial crisis. Taxes and social spending are already high. The authorities' key challenge is to ensure an appropriate design that achieves redistributive objectives at minimum cost to economic efficiency.

The design of redistributive policies in developing countries is analyzed in Chapter 4 by Francesca Bastagli, David Coady, and Sanjeev Gupta. The authors discuss the specific challenges faced by developing countries in pursuing both efficiency and equity objectives, emphasizing the importance of taking a comprehensive approach that considers the combined impacts of taxes and spending and of encompassing both design and administration issues. Fiscal redistribution is more limited in developing countries than in advanced economies because of the developing countries' lower tax and spending levels and because of the composition of revenue and outlays. On the tax side, revenue relies heavily on indirect taxation (which has limited redistributive impact). On the expenditure side, health and education account for a high share of social spending, but they affect the income distribution in the medium term; moreover, the share of social insurance spending (mainly pensions) that benefits higher-income groups is high. Enhancing redistribution therefore requires that tax ratios be increased while competing public spending needs are addressed. As to taxation, the policy strategy should aim to broaden both income and consumption tax bases and improve design to increase progressivity. Critically, tax compliance needs to be strengthened as a prerequisite, for instance, for effective taxation of personal incomes.[8] With regard to spending, priority should be given to designing well-targeted transfer programs while avoiding fiscally expensive universal price subsidy schemes. The expansion of in-kind spending could also help reduce income gaps, if that spending is focused on increasing low-income groups' access to quality services.

In Chapter 5, Ravi Kanbur discusses the developments that have occurred during the past three decades in the economics literature on poverty and income distribution. He organizes the discussion around three main issues: (1) progress in empirical evidence, (2) theoretical advances, and (3) policies. His main finding is that there has been significant continuity in the poverty and inequality domain notwithstanding significant advances in many respects. The chapter highlights the tremendous increase in the availability of empirical evidence (linked to the much greater availability of household surveys in developing countries), which has widened the range of feasible analysis and supported the efforts to document the changes in inequality observed in many countries during the past 30 years. Kanbur argues that the most prominent theoretical contributions have been in the analysis of poverty dynamics and risk, the surfacing of gender and intra-household inequality issues, and the spread of multidisciplinary approaches (which shifted attention away from focusing solely on the monetary value of consumption and income). For policy research, the chapter underlines four main topics in recent decades: conditional cash transfer programs, governance and institutions, the role of safety nets at times of acute macroeconomic crises, and the systemic importance of spillovers and global public goods. These were not entirely new topics, but nevertheless gained prominence because of the large macroeconomic shocks that hit both advanced and developing countries.

Part II—Alternative Measures of Inequality and Their Implications for Fiscal Policy

In Chapter 6, Maura Francese and Carlos Mulas-Granados study the relationship between functional and personal income distributions. The current debate on inequality is usually based on summary indicators of the distribution of personal income (such as the Gini index or the share appropriated by the top 10 percent or 1 percent). Historically, great attention was also paid to the allocation of income between the factors of production (labor and capital), and indeed the enormously influential work of Piketty (2014) is a very conscious return to this tradition. Classical economists considered the analysis of factor shares to be the principal problem of political economy; research on this topic flourished up to the 1960s. In the following decades it became a marginal issue, perhaps because of the lack of volatility in income shares. It has made a comeback in recent decades, reflecting the decline of the wage share experienced in Group of Seven countries since the 1970s, coincident with increasing inequality. The chapter uses both micro- and macroeconomic data to assess whether the decline in the labor share has been a key factor driving increases in inequality. The empirical analysis of micro data aims at recovering

---

[8] On how this might be done, see for instance IMF 2015.

marginal effects of changes in factor shares and in the dispersion of labor income on the Gini index, using a large data set of household surveys covering both advanced and emerging economies. The results indicate that the most important determinant of rising income inequality has been the growing dispersion of wages rather than the declining share of wages. These findings are confirmed by regression analysis using macroeconomic data. They reflect the fact that labor earnings are the largest component of household income and the sizable growth of top salaries—the latter being a key driver of the rising dispersion of labor income. From a policy perspective, the results suggest that to avoid undesired distributional outcomes, attention should be paid to labor market outcomes.

Chapter 7, by Luc Eyraud, analyzes recent trends in wealth inequality and examines how wealth taxation can be used as a redistributive instrument. Although income inequality remains central to the debate on distribution, the emphasis on wealth inequality has been growing. Wealth is more unevenly distributed (both across[9] and within countries[10]) than income. High wealth concentration can have detrimental effects on growth through a variety of channels: besides fostering rent-seeking behavior, high wealth concentration can affect political, social, and economic stability. The chapter shows that historically taxes on wealth have been a major source of government revenue, but they now have a minor role, accounting for less than 2 percent of GDP, on average, for Organisation for Economic Co-operation and Development (OECD) countries. For this reason they may offer some margin to increase revenue and strengthen the progressivity of tax systems. Recurrent taxes on residential properties are widely seen as relatively growth friendly,[11] being marked by a base that is fairly immobile and hard to hide (and therefore fewer adverse incentive effects are generated). Designing these taxes to be progressive is also fairly simple (for example, by providing a basic tax-free allowance). Taxes can also be levied on property transactions and transfers. The former (for example, on the sale of real estate and financial instruments) can lead to inefficiencies since they may discourage mutually beneficial transactions. Taxes on wealth transfers (through gifts or inheritances) have not proved easy to implement on a reasonably broad basis because of difficulties both technical and political, not the least being the potentially high mobility of the wealthy. These taxes have been in decline and currently generate very little revenue in most countries. Recent developments in the exchange of tax information between countries, however, may alleviate some of the difficulties that have been experienced. Many look to wealth and wealth transfer taxes to play a more important role in the future, with the latter, for instance, potentially a key instrument to limit the intergenerational transmission of inequality.

Part III—Fiscal Consolidation and Income Inequality

In Chapter 8 Davide Furceri, João Tovar Jalles, and Prakash Loungani examine the link between budget consolidation and inequality in a sample of advanced economies. After discussing available methods for identifying consolidation episodes, the authors use regression analysis to estimate impulse response functions for alternative measures of inequality (Gini indices and income shares) and run several robustness checks. Their results indicate that fiscal adjustment tends to lead to an increase in income inequality in the short and medium terms, with this finding being robust to the use of alternative measures of fiscal consolidation and inequality. The evidence discussed in the chapter is not conclusive, however, on two issues: (1) whether tax-based or expenditure-based consolidations have different effects (most other studies have found expenditure-based adjustment more unequalizing); and (2) whether the relationship between

---

[9] North America and Europe account for two-thirds of total wealth.

[10] For instance, in advanced economies, the top 10 percent owns, on average, more than half of the wealth.

[11] See Acosta-Ormachea and Yoo 2012 and Arnold and others 2011 for empirical evidence on this issue.

fiscal adjustment and inequality is symmetric. The authors' results suggest that the benefits of fiscal adjustment should be weighed against its distributional effects and underscore the need to design fiscal measures that protect the neediest. Finally, the authors highlight that the distributional impact of fiscal consolidation must be balanced against its potential longer-term benefits, since sustainable public finances and a lighter burden of interest payments may allow a reduction in distortionary taxation.

Stefania Fabrizio and Valentina Flamini provide an overview of recent evidence on the link between fiscal adjustment and inequality for both advanced and emerging economies in Chapter 9. They start from the consideration that fiscal contraction has an impact on distribution via both market and disposable income: it leads to a reduction in output and employment and therefore in earnings; it also changes the level and composition of taxes and spending. Cyclical conditions are also relevant: the effect of a fiscal contraction can be stronger in a downturn if fiscal multipliers are higher than when the economy is growing. In addition to magnitude and pace, the econometric studies reviewed in Chapter 9 indicate that the composition of consolidation packages also matters; adjustments based on spending cuts worsen inequality more than revenue-based ones. Reviewing recent adjustment experiences in Europe, the authors highlight that both expenditure- and revenue-based fiscal consolidations can be designed to mitigate adverse effects on inequality. This can be done by protecting the most progressive and efficient redistributive spending and increasing reliance on progressive revenue measures. In developing countries, where the size of the government sector is usually smaller than in advanced economies and fiscal policies less progressive, social safety nets should be strengthened to protect vulnerable households during fiscal adjustment. Some other lessons, while straightforward, are important. For example, replacing universal subsidies with targeted measures can help prevent an increase in inequality while helping reduce budget deficits.

Part IV—Tax Policy and Inequality

Chapter 10, by Ruud de Mooij, Thornton Matheson, and Roberto Schatan, focuses on tax spillovers arising from the current international tax architecture for multinational enterprises and the opportunities for tax avoidance that they create. These spillovers can matter for distribution both within countries and, more the focus here, across them, for they can be particularly important for developing countries, which are relatively more reliant on corporate income taxes and especially those from multinationals—and have fewer appealing alternative sources of revenue. Spillovers jeopardize the government's ability to raise sufficient resources to finance social programs and comprehensive redistributive policies (besides public spending for investment). Indeed, governments in developing countries themselves face the challenge of finding a balance between ensuring an attractive investment environment for multinationals and mobilizing adequate domestic resources. However, it is not just their own policies that matter, but also international tax rules set by others. Drawing on IMF (2014b), de Mooij, Matheson, and Schatan address three specific tax issues related to the international tax architecture that determine spillovers to developing countries. The first is territoriality versus worldwide taxation in more advanced economies. The authors document a shift during the past decades in advanced economies from worldwide toward territorial taxation (under which earnings from foreign subsidiaries are exempt in the residence country). Empirical evidence suggests that, as theory predicts, this shift has increased the intensity of tax competition among developing countries, pushing them toward lower corporate tax rates. The second set of issues are those around bilateral tax treaties. These treaties allocate taxing rights between the residence and source countries and can benefit investors to the extent that they eliminate double taxation and provide some certainty of tax treatment. Empirical evidence, however, is at best inconclusive as to the effect of treaties on investment. At the same time, tax treaties create a significant risk for developing countries (which are usually source countries) of a high cost in forgone government revenue. The chapter thus cautions developing countries against signing bilateral tax treaties too readily. Finally, the chapter explores ideas for a complete revision of the international rules for allocating taxable income of multinationals between different countries. In particular, instead of separating the accounts of a multinational group, accounts could be consolidated according to a harmonized rule. Subsequently, this consolidated tax base could be divided between countries through "formulary apportionment." Although such a system clearly eliminates a number of problems and spillovers associated with the current architecture, it would also create significant new challenges. And, not least, it is highly uncertain whether developing countries would see their tax bases expanded or reduced.

In Chapter 11, John Norregaard focuses on taxation of immovable property. Property taxes, especially on residential real estate, are, as noted above, widely regarded as an efficient and equitable means for raising revenue. Their potential, however, appears not to be yet fully exploited, in particular in emerging and developing countries. For them, the untapped revenue potential is estimated to be on the order of 0.5–1.0 percent of GDP over the next 5–10 years, while for many advanced economies that currently rely only modestly on these taxes, the potential is even higher, reaching 2 percent of GDP or more. After discussing the nature of property taxation in different countries, the chapter explores the economic rationale for its fuller use. Empirical evidence supports the theoretical claim that property taxation is more efficient and less distortive than most other conventional tax instruments, with recent studies confirming that it is more benign for growth. Property taxes also play a key role in intergovernmental fiscal design: given that they are borne mainly by residents, and that property values likely reflect the value of local services and amenities, local property taxes are an attractive source of revenue for local government since they are associated with lower spillover effects and increased accountability of local administrations. The chapter finally examines the obstacles that policymakers face in introducing and reforming property taxation. Political economy considerations, as well as implementation issues, play an important role. Transparency and salience of the tax, which economists regard as desirable properties, make it politically unpopular. As to implementation, successful reforms require training and careful planning of improvements to administrative infrastructure, which entails up-front investment.

Chapter 12 addresses the issues of the targeting and design of indirect taxation. In particular, Michael Keen contributes to the debate on the VAT and whether reduced tax rates on commodities that absorb a large part of poor households' budgets (such as food) are a suitable way to improve income distribution. The theoretical and empirical literature agrees that most of the dollar benefits of reduced rates are generally appropriated by better-off households. Therefore, the amount of redistribution that can be achieved by differentiating tax rates is limited, and other instruments can be deployed by governments to address distributional concerns more effectively. Thus, the issue becomes whether these better instruments to support poor households are available. Such instruments are likely to be feasible in advanced economies, in which implementation issues are less relevant and sophisticated social programs more common. For emerging and developing countries deployment of these instruments is less straightforward, and can require evaluating whether spending programs (either cash transfers or in-kind benefits such as health and education) that are not precisely targeted perform better than differentiated tax rates. Assessing the distributional case for reduced VAT rates requires understanding the distributional impact of the public spending that a higher rate could enable. The chapter also points out, however, that even when tax-spending reforms do seem superior to differentiated VAT rates, political economy considerations may still restrain governments from acting. These obstacles may reflect a suspicion that spending programs promised by governments will not always be forthcoming or that more progressive ways to finance the increase in public spending may be available. Or it may be that powerful groups understand perfectly well how raising or eliminating reduced VAT rates would act to their disadvantage.

In Chapter 13, Ian Parry explores the distributive aspects of carbon taxation, the starting point being that carbon pricing (to reduce harmful carbon emissions) needs to be front and center in policies to limit climate change. Even though carbon pricing is becoming more widespread, it remains far from the levels needed. Concerns about the impact on poor households of raising carbon taxes by a significant margin is one of the issues that complicate the political discussion around climate policy, and risks holding back effective carbon pricing. The chapter argues, however, that distributional concerns should not delay or limit the use of carbon taxes, for several reasons. First, carbon taxes are less regressive than is generally thought; second, leakages to higher-income groups from inefficiently low energy prices are sizable (they receive about 90 percent of total benefits); and third, instruments are available to compensate low-income households for the costs stemming from high energy prices. Advanced economies have numerous opportunities for such compensation by using carbon tax revenues to finance targeted tax cuts and benefit increases—though specific needs and design clearly need to be examined on a country-by-country basis. A strong case for raising carbon taxes can also be made for developing countries, including to address local pollution damage. With respect to distributional concerns, carbon taxes might actually be less regressive in developing countries than in advanced economies, since access to power grids and motor vehicle ownership is skewed toward richer households in developing countries; and given that large hard-to-tax sectors constrain the use of other taxes (such as the personal income tax), energy taxes can serve the useful purpose of broadening the tax base. Targeted compensation of those low-income households that are adversely affected is more challenging in developing countries, given the more limited spending instruments available. Nevertheless, the additional revenue from carbon taxation could allow expansion of health, education, social housing, and other programs. In sum, distributional concerns are certainly potentially important for both fairness and the politics of reform, but these issues are generally manageable and not a persuasive reason for delaying more effective carbon pricing.

Part V—Expenditure Policy and Inequality

Energy subsidies and their reform are addressed by David Coady, Valentina Flamini, and Louis Sears in Chapter 14. Building on evidence from country studies, the authors assess the magnitude of energy subsidies and estimate the welfare impact of their reform. This is an important topic for many developing countries, in which domestic consumer prices are under the government's control and do not reflect the true cost of energy. Governments see controlling prices as a viable solution to protect domestic consumers from high and volatile oil prices. The chapter shows, however, that energy subsidies are generally a very inefficient instrument for protecting poor households: on average, the richest 20 percent of the population captures more than six times as much of the benefit of fuel subsidies as does the poorest 20 percent. Withdrawing benefits would, nevertheless, result in significant welfare losses, including for disadvantaged households: estimates indicate that increasing fuel prices by $0.25 per liter would decrease household real incomes, on average, by 5.5 percent, with the impact ranging from 3.5 percent in South and Central America to 7.0 percent in the Middle East. Thus, well-targeted compensating measures are likely to be essential for making energy subsidy reform palatable to policymakers and successful in practice. Ideally, well-targeted cash transfers should be used to compensate poor households, as they have been in several successful reform episodes. Conditional cash transfers have also gained prominence in emerging and developing countries because they also help address the causes of persistent poverty (by, for example, linking eligibility for cash transfers to participation in health and education programs). When capacity constraints prevent the use of targeted cash transfers, governments can consider instead the expansion of other high-priority spending that benefits the poor, such as school meals or subsidized education, health, and mass transit.

In Chapter 15, Benedict Clements, Csaba Feher, and Sanjeev Gupta review the functioning of pension systems, with a view to highlighting the equity considerations most relevant for their design and reform. The starting point of the analysis is the recognition that pensions are a key instrument of social policy, preventing the large drop in income that would otherwise be associated with retirement. In assessing the fairness of pension systems, it is important to distinguish between objectives for horizontal equity and those for vertical equity.[12] In many cases, there will be a trade-off between these objectives. To achieve vertical equity, for instance, significant redistribution toward the poor may be required, but this course may clash with ensuring that the link between contributions and benefits is similar for all pension system participants (horizontal equity). Intergenerational equity is also an important consideration, and involves judgments about how the burden of financing the pension system—and the benefits it pays out—should be spread across successive generations. Despite the difficulties in determining a unique criterion for an equitable pension system, some clear principles emerge from international experience. The first principle is that there are a number of reforms that are clearly equity enhancing, including expanding coverage, which is the most important consideration for achieving greater vertical equity. Expansion of coverage could be fostered by removing regulatory barriers to participation and improving administrative capacity and compliance. In addition, countries could achieve more horizontal equity in their pension systems by providing equal treatment across sectors, industries, and type of contract. The second principle is that most design features and reform options will, nevertheless, require trade-offs between different equity objectives. The third principle is that pension reform occurs under political constraints, which can hinder the equal treatment of certain social groups. The fourth principle is that the consequences of different pension reform options need to be analyzed—and the goals of pension reform communicated—to achieve broad and lasting public support. The final principle is that complementary measures in areas outside pension policy are necessary to make pension reforms effective. These measures include strengthening administrative capacity to manage increases in the number of contributors, as well as labor reforms to ensure employment opportunities for older workers.

In Chapter 16, Nora Lustig provides an empirical analysis for a sample of emerging and developing countries of the redistributive impact of public spending on education and health.[13] These two items combined account for a sizable share of public spending in the countries included in the sample: education outlays range from 2.6 to 8.3 percent of GDP, and health expenditure from 0.9 to 5.2 percent. Examining their redistributive impact requires attaching a value to in-kind services provided to citizens (free—or almost free—of charge). The common methodology applied to all countries in the sample uses average cost of provision as a proxy for the value of in-kind services. Gini indices are then computed for three income definitions: (1) market income; (2) postfiscal income (market income less taxes and social contributions, plus government transfers—such as cash transfers —and minus indirect taxes); and (3) final income (postfiscal income plus the transfer value of free or subsidized public education and health). The results indicate that in more unequal countries government policies tend to redistribute more (a somewhat different conclusion from the previous literature). Education and health spending combined lower inequality by a significant amount: their contribution to the overall decline in

---

[12] Horizontal equity requires that similar conditions (in the case of pension systems, similar contribution histories) be associated with similar results (that is, similar pension benefits). Vertical equity requires considering individuals' needs when granting benefits.

[13] The countries analyzed are those included in the Commitment to Equity project: Armenia, Bolivia, Brazil, Chile, Colombia, El Salvador, Ethiopia, Guatemala, Indonesia, Mexico, Peru, South Africa, and Uruguay.

inequality (going from market to final income) is, on average, 69 percent. Education spending is pro-poor (meaning that per capita spending is higher for poor individuals) in 9 out of 13 countries, while health expenditure is pro-poor in 5 out of 13 countries. Evidence also suggests that progressivity and pro-poorness of health and education spending have increased over time. However, despite progress and the equalizing role played by education and health, less than universal access and low quality remain a concern in developing countries.

Chapter 17, by Caroline-Antonia Hummel and Mike Seiferling, reviews the literature on fiscal federalism and inequality and presents an empirical analysis of the link between decentralization and within-country inequality. The literature on fiscal federalism has addressed this question since seminal contributions published in the 1950s. The so-called first-generation theories of fiscal federalism argued that local governments should not engage in redistributive policies. "Voting with your feet" behavior would lead to unsustainable and self-defeating patterns, with rich households migrating to jurisdictions characterized by minimal levels of taxation and transfers, and poor households concentrating in areas with generous redistributive schemes. As a result, a system of decentralized redistribution would lead to lower levels of redistribution than socially desirable. The second generation of fiscal federalism studies, however, suggested that comprehensive decentralization could be more effective in reducing regional inequality than centrally mandated redistribution over the longer term. The reason is that local governments of poorer regions could take advantage of less generous welfare provisions and lower taxes to attract investment and increase growth. In this sense, decentralization could lead to a reduction in income disparities across regions, which would translate into lower inequality at the national level. Hummel and Seiferling use data for a globally representative sample of countries over a 30-year time span to test the potential links between within-country income inequality and fiscal decentralization. The authors' empirical analysis lends support to second-generation fiscal federalism theories. More specifically, their econometric results suggest that decentralization is associated with lower inequality, provided the following conditions are met: (1) the size of the government is sufficiently large; (2) decentralization of spending is comprehensive, including redistributive spending items (social expenditure, health, and education); (3) decentralization on the expenditure side is accompanied by decentralization on the revenue side (so that local governments rely primarily on their own resources); and (4) in assigning revenue sources to subnational governments, preference is given to revenue categories without strong redistributive implications.

Part VI—Country Case Studies

In Chapter 18, Ruud de Mooij discusses the equity-efficiency trade-off in the design of the tax-benefit system in the Netherlands. The author starts by reviewing key policy insights from optimal tax theory to identify the factors that determine the equity-efficiency possibility frontier. The shape of the optimal marginal tax schedule is shown to depend on a limited number of factors, such as social preference for redistribution, the concavity of utility in income, the elasticity of labor supply, and population densities along the income distribution. The optimal marginal tax schedule typically follows a U-shaped pattern, that is, high at the bottom and top of the income distribution and low in the middle. While yielding powerful messages for tax-benefit design, however, the optimal tax framework is probably oversimplified; for example, it does not allow for the heterogeneity in elasticities that characterizes the Dutch labor market. To account for this in greater detail, the chapter explores reform options in the Dutch tax-benefit system using a detailed applied general equilibrium model. The model is calibrated for the Netherlands to reflect available empirical evidence concerning the most relevant behavioral responses (such as labor supply decisions of a heterogeneous set of households). Indeed, it accounts for household heterogeneity along several dimensions, such as skills, family composition, social benefit entitlements, and age. Moreover, it allows for a rich set of labor market choices, including hours worked, voluntary nonparticipation within couples, and search behavior by the unemployed. A union bargaining model and search frictions imply that wages do not clear the labor market, which renders the extensive margin of employment more responsive through effects on reservation wages. Despite these modifications, compared with standard optimal income tax models (that is, by varying elasticities along the income distribution), results on the efficiency implications of tax reforms are largely consistent with insights from these models, yet also refine them. For instance, they show that selective in-work tax credits for low-wage and secondary earners could increase employment. But they also show that the precise design of the phase-out range of these credits is critical for employment effects. Flat-tax reforms (which lower the marginal tax rates for top incomes) tend to worsen the equity-efficiency trade-off, that is, they either reduce employment for the same amount of redistribution or increase inequality. Replacing means-tested income transfers with a basic income benefit would reduce unemployment (because it eliminates means testing, and so reduces the marginal tax burden at the bottom), but has very large adverse effects on labor supply in the densely populated middle-income groups who would face a much higher marginal tax rate.

Chapter 19, by Serhan Cevik and Carolina Correa-Caro, focuses on China, which, over the past few decades, has experienced a substantial increase in inequality (as measured by the pretax income Gini index). This trend reflects the sustained dynamics of income accruing to the richest quintile of the population, which has been significantly higher than that registered by other income groups. The aim of the chapter is to identify the determinants of income inequality, with a focus on the distributional effects of fiscal policy, using regression analysis. The authors recognize the limitations stemming from a small sample size and challenging technical issues, and devise strategies to alleviate these concerns. Their results support the hypothesis of an inverted U-shaped relationship between growth and income inequality in China (a "Kuznets curve"), which is in line with the observed pattern for the Gini index over the recent decades of rapid growth. Government spending in China appears to be associated with worsening income inequality. This finding may reflect the low public expenditure level observed in China and its composition. Spending is mainly absorbed by infrastructure investments and public administration outlays. Taxation appears to improve the distribution of household income, even if the tax-to-GDP ratio is still significantly far from levels observed in OECD countries, and it is characterized by a low degree of progressivity (as a result of the high share of revenue collected through indirect taxes). The authors argue that fiscal policy could be redesigned to have a greater redistributive effect, especially in the long term.

In Chapter 20, Chadi Abdallah, David Coady, Sanjeev Gupta, and Emine Hanedar present an empirical investigation of options for fiscal reform in India, demonstrating the potential for achieving efficient and growth-friendly fiscal consolidation while simultaneously alleviating poverty and reducing inequality. The need for consolidation in India is widely recognized. After countercyclical policies implemented in response to the economic and financial crisis, fiscal adjustment has been achieved mainly by cutting investment, without addressing structural issues that limit the space for growth-enhancing spending and other priority measures. Against this background the authors use household survey data to assess the impact of reforms on household income and its distribution. On the tax side, the chapter simulates the effects of increasing "sin taxes," that is, consumption taxes on items generating negative environmental and health externalities (fuel products, alcohol, and tobacco). On the spending side, the exercise evaluates the consequences of increasing spending on social programs.[14] The results show that increasing the

---

[14] The exercise considers, in particular, raising spending for the Public Distribution System and the Mahatma Gandhi National Rural Employment Guarantee Act programs.

sin taxes has a regressive impact: it hurts all households, but the impact (as a share of total household income) is higher for low-income groups than for high-income groups. However, reallocating part of the proceeds from tax increases to the financing of higher social spending can offset the impact of higher taxes. Under plausible simulation parameters, the chapter shows that the reform can transfer sufficient resources to make the net incidence of taxes and transfers progressive. The overall progressivity of the reform can be further enhanced by improving the targeting of the social assistance programs. Under the current setup, leakages of benefits to higher-income households are substantial; removing (or reducing) these inefficiencies would generate enough resources to make lower-income households net gainers from the reform.

Chapter 21, by Maximilien Queyranne, Dalia Hakura, and Cameron McLoughlin, discusses the challenges of designing fiscal consolidation packages in the Republic of Congo, where income inequality is high, poverty is widespread, and the room for redistributive fiscal policies, already narrow, is expected to diminish drastically in the coming years as oil reserves shrink. While public revenue and spending appear higher in Congo than in most low-income countries, the underlying structure and composition of the budget is not geared toward the reduction of inequality and poverty. High revenue reflects mainly oil-related receipts, while tax proceeds as a ratio of GDP are lower than the average for sub-Saharan African countries. Moreover, taxation is tilted toward consumption taxes, and recent reforms of the personal income tax have not improved its progressivity. As to spending, fuel subsidies absorb a large amount of resources, exceeding overall outlays for education, health, and social protection. Furthermore, as Chapter 14 shows is generally the case, these subsidies lead to overconsumption and are poorly targeted. To improve the situation, education spending has been increased in recent years. The government has also committed to move toward universal coverage in the health sector and has started implementing a conditional cash transfer program. Going forward, financing an expansion of redistributive programs will be challenging, given the expected contraction of oil-related revenues. To protect the poor from the sizable effects of these structural changes, efforts will have to be concentrated on strengthening revenue mobilization through more progressive taxation (for example, through a better-functioning personal income tax, well-designed property taxes, and limited reduced VAT rates and exemptions) and focusing on priority spending (avoiding crude across-the-board cuts). Cutting fuel subsidies gradually but deeply, and improving the efficiency of capital spending, could create fiscal space to scale up social spending.

In Chapter 22, João Pedro Azevedo, Antonio C. David, and Fabiano Rodrigues Bastos examine the links between subnational fiscal policies and inequality dynamics in Brazil, asking whether fiscal consolidation at the state level has contributed to the reduction in inequality. In the second half of the 1990s, the Brazilian fiscal federalism architecture underwent a structural break. A debt-restructuring agreement between the federal government and the states introduced tight constraints, and as a consequence public finances at the local and state level quickly improved. The literature on the effects of fiscal consolidation on income inequality, mostly based on data for OECD countries, has generally found that budget retrenchment is associated with a deterioration in distributional outcomes. To see if this is also the case in Brazil, the authors explore the empirical relationship between the Gini index for gross posttransfer income at the state level and a set of explanatory variables that include changes in the cyclically adjusted primary balance (as a share of GDP). The results suggest that, contrary to previous findings, a tighter fiscal stance in Brazilian states is not associated with an increase in inequality. Although the authors do not attempt to establish the precise mechanisms linking fiscal policy and inequality, their results are likely to reflect distinct structural characteristics of the Brazilian states compared with OECD economies: higher inequality levels, less reliance on progressive taxation, an absence of extensive social safety nets, and higher inefficiencies in the provision of public services. For this reason, they caution against mechanically extending results available for advanced economies to emerging and developing countries.

REFERENCES

Aaberge, R., and A. Brandolini. 2015. "Multidimensional Poverty and Inequality." In *Handbook of Income Distribution*, Vol. 2, edited by A. B. Atkinson, and F. Bourguignon, 141–216. Amsterdam: Elsevier.

Aaberge, R., and M. Mogstad. 2012. "Inequality in Current and Lifetime Income." Statistics Norway Research Department Discussion Paper No. 726, Statistics Norway, Oslo.

Acosta-Ormachea, S., and J. Yoo. 2012. "Tax Composition and Economic Growth." IMF Working Paper No. 12/257, International Monetary Fund, Washington.

Apps, P. F., and R. Rees. 1999. "Individual versus Joint Taxation in Models with Household Production." *Journal of Political Economy* 107 (2): 393–403.

———. 2007. "The Taxation of Couples." IZA Discussion Paper No. 2910, Institute for the Study of Labor, Bonn.

Arnold, J., B. Brys, C. Heady, Å. Johansson, C. Schwellnus, and L. Vartia. 2011. "Tax Policy for Economic Recovery and Growth." *Economic Journal* 121 (550): 59–80.

Atkinson, A. B. 2015. *Inequality: What Can Be Done?* Cambridge, Massachusetts: Harvard University Press.

———, and F. Bourguignon, eds. 2015. *Handbook of Income Distribution*, vol. 2. Amsterdam: Elsevier.

Atkinson, A. B., L. Rainwater, and T. M. Smeeding. 1995. "Income Distribution in OECD Countries." OECD Social Policy Studies No. 18, Organisation for Economic Co-operation and Development, Paris.

Benedek, D., R. de Mooij, M. Keen, and P. Wingender. Forthcoming. "Estimating VAT Pass Through." IMF Working Paper, International Monetary Fund, Washington.

Björklund, A. 1993. "A Comparison between Actual Distributions of Annual and Lifetime Income: Sweden 1951–89." *Review of Income and Wealth* 39 (4): 377–86.

Boadway, R., and M. Keen. 2000. "Redistribution." In *Handbook of Income Distribution*, Vol. I, edited by A. B. Atkinson and F. Bourguignon, 677–789. Amsterdam: Elsevier.

Boskin, M. J., and E. Sheshinski. 1983. "Optimal Tax Treatment of the Family: Married Couples." *Journal of Public Economics* 20 (3): 281–97.

Bourguignon, F. 2015. *The Globalization of Inequality.* Princeton, New Jersey: Princeton University Press.

———, M. Browning, P. A. Chiappori, and V. Lechene. 1993. "Intra Household Allocation of Consumption: A Model and Some Evidence from French Data." *Annales d'Economie et de Statistique,* 29.

Browning, M., P. A. Chiappori, and Y. Weiss. 2011. *Family Economics.* Cambridge, U.K.: Cambridge University Press.

Clements, B., S. Gupta, and M. Nozaki. 2013. "What Happens to Social Spending in IMF-Supported Programs?" *Applied Economics* 45 (28): 4022–33.

Duflo, E. 2003. "Grandmothers and Granddaughter: Old-Age Pensions and Intrahousehold Allocation in South Africa." *World Bank Economic Review* 17 (1): 1–25.

Easterly, W. 2007. "Inequality Does Cause Underdevelopment: Insights from a New Instrument." *Journal of Development Economics* 84 (2): 755–76.

Elborgh-Woytek, K., M. Newiak, K. Kochhar, S. Fabrizio, K. Kpodar, P. Wingender, B. Clements, and G. Schwartz. 2013. "Women, Work, and the Economy: Macroeconomic Gains from Gender Equity." IMF Staff Discussion Note No. 13/10, International Monetary Fund, Washington.

Gonzales, C., S. Jain-Chandra, K. Kochhar, and M. Newiak. 2015. "Fair Play: More Equal Laws Boost Female Labor Force Participation." IMF Staff Discussion Note No. 15/02, International Monetary Fund, Washington.

Gravelle, J. 2011. "Corporate Tax Incidence: A Review of Empirical Analysis and Estimates." Congressional Budget Office Working Paper 2011–01, Washington.

Haveman, R. 1994. "Should Generational Accounts Replace Public Budgets and Deficits?" *Journal of Economic Perspectives* 8 (1): 95–111.

International Monetary Fund (IMF). 2014a. "Fiscal Policy and Income Inequality." IMF Policy Paper, Washington.

———. 2014b. "Spillovers in International Taxation." IMF Policy Paper, Washington.

———. 2015. "Current Challenges in Revenue Mobilization: Improving Compliance." IMF Policy Paper, Washington.

Kashiwase, K., and P. Rizza. 2014. "Who Will Pay? The Dynamics of Pension Reform and Intergenerational Equity." In *Equitable and Sustainable Pensions. Challenges and Experience*, edited by B. Clements, F. Eich, and S. Gupta. Washington: International Monetary Fund.

Kotlikoff, L. J. 2002. "Generational Policy." In *Handbook of Public Economics*, Vol. IV, edited by A. J. Auerbach and M. Feldstein, 1873–932. Amsterdam: Elsevier.

———, and L. Summers. 1987. "Tax Incidence." In *Handbook of Public Economics*, Vol. II, edited by A. J. Auerbach and M. Feldstein, 1043–92. Amsterdam: Elsevier.

Kumhof, M., and R. Rancière. 2011. "Inequality, Leverage and Crises." IMF Working Paper No. 10/268, International Monetary Fund, Washington.

Organisation for Economic Co-operation and Development (OECD). 2012. "Closing the Gender Gap: Act Now." OECD Publishing, Paris. http://dx.doi.org/10.1787/9789264179370-en.

Ostry, J., A. Berg, and C. Tsangarides. 2014. "Redistribution, Inequality, and Growth." IMF Staff Discussion Note, International Monetary Fund, Washington.

Piketty, T. 2014. *Capital in the Twenty-First Century.* Cambridge, Massachusetts: Harvard University Press.

Ponthiueux, S., and D. Meurs. 2015. "Gender Inequality." In *Handbook of Income Distribution*, Vol. 2, edited by A. B. Atkinson and F. Bourguignon, 981–1146. Amsterdam: Elsevier.

Rajan, R. 2010. *Fault Lines.* Princeton, New Jersey: Princeton University Press.

Rothstein, J. 2010. "Is the EITC as Good as an NIT? Conditional Cash Transfers and Tax Incidence." *American Economic Journal: Economic Policy* 2 (1): 177–208.

Tanzi, V., and K. Chu, eds. 1998. *Income Distribution and High-Quality Growth.* Cambridge, Massachusetts: MIT Press.

———, and S. Gupta. 1999. *Economic Policy and Equity.* Washington: International Monetary Fund.

Thévenon, O. 2011. "Family Policies in OECD Countries: A Comparative Analysis." *Population and Development Review* 37 (1): 57–87.

Whalley, J. 1984. "Regression or Progression: The Taxing Question of Tax Incidence." *Canadian Journal of Economics* 17 (4): 654–82.

Ward-Batts, J. 2008. "Out of the Wallet and into the Purse—Using Microdata to Test Income Pooling." *Journal of Human Resources* 43 (2): 325–51.

Woo, J., E. Bova, T. Kinda, and S. Zhang. 2013. "Distributional Consequences of Fiscal Consolidation and the Role of Fiscal Policy: What Do the Data Say?" IMF Working Paper No. 13/195, International Monetary Fund, Washington.

CHAPTER 2

The IMF and Income Distribution

Benedict Clements, Vitor Gaspar, Sanjeev Gupta, and Tidiane Kinda

INTRODUCTION

Rising income inequality is front and center in the economic policy debate across the globe. Policymakers can hardly ignore trends in distribution of income and wealth across countries and among world citizens. However, they can even less afford to undervalue the importance of income distribution in their own countries. A fair and equitable distribution of income is a fundamental element of the social contract. What is the role of macroeconomic policies in this debate and how is this relevant to the work of the IMF? This chapter argues that inequality is an important issue for the IMF in all three of its core activities—lending to support macroeconomic adjustment programs; macroeconomic surveillance, including related policy analysis; and technical assistance to build capacity, especially on government taxation and spending.

Although distributive issues have been an important part of the IMF's dialogue with member countries, work on them has intensified in the wake of the global financial crisis. Observers in the field of development economics increasingly recognize that macroeconomic policies (including government tax and spending policies) have significant effects on income distribution and that inequality can have adverse political and social consequences, with the potential to undermine macroeconomic stability and sustainable growth. The chapters in this book are a testament to the rising importance of this issue in the IMF's work as we further explore the linkages between income distribution and macroeconomics.

Income distribution is a complex issue. Many different measures can be used to characterize it. Relevant questions include whether income distribution should be captured on a market basis or after adjustments for taxes and transfers, and how to analyze income distribution across and within countries. This complexity is illustrated in the discussion below.

The remainder of this chapter is structured as follows: First, to set the context for the discussion, the distribution of income across countries is briefly examined. Trends in income distribution for both the world as a whole and within countries are reviewed. The evolution of the IMF's work on distributional issues is described. Next, the focus turns to work since 2008, highlighting the deepening of the IMF's analytical and policy work on various aspects of income inequality to better serve our member countries. A final section concludes and discusses the next steps in the IMF's work on inequality.

GLOBAL TRENDS: DISTRIBUTION ACROSS AND WITHIN COUNTRIES

When the IMF started, in the mid-twentieth century, "Europe and European offshoots," in the words of Angus Maddison, accounted for almost 60 percent of world GDP and close to 20 percent of world population (Figures 2.1 and 2.2). From that point onward, their share in

The authors wish to thank Martin Muhleisen and Christoph Rosenberg for their helpful comments and suggestions. Haoyu Wang provided excellent research assistance.

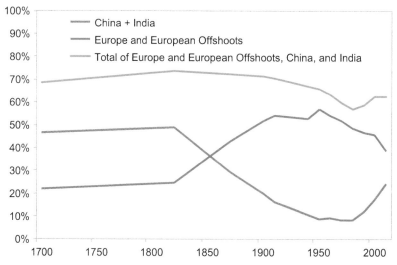

Figure 2.1 Shares of Advanced Economies (excluding Japan), China, and India in World Production, 1700–2008

Source: The Maddison Project, http://www.ggdc.net/maddison/maddison-project/home.htm, 2013 version.
Note: Advanced economies (excluding Japan) refers to Europe and European offshoots. This group comprises Australia, Austria, Belgium, Canada, Denmark, Finland, France, Germany, Greece, Ireland, Italy, the Netherlands, New Zealand, Norway, Portugal, Spain, Sweden, Switzerland, the United Kingdom, and the United States.

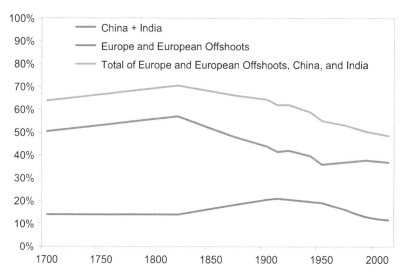

Figure 2.2 Shares of Advanced Economies (excluding Japan), China, and India in World Population, 1700–2008

Source: The Maddison Project, http://www.ggdc.net/maddison/maddison-project/home.htm, 2013 version.
Note: Advanced economies (excluding Japan) refers to Europe and European offshoots. This group comprises Australia, Austria, Belgium, Canada, Denmark, Finland, France, Germany, Greece, Ireland, Italy, the Netherlands, New Zealand, Norway, Portugal, Spain, Sweden, Switzerland, the United Kingdom, and the United States.

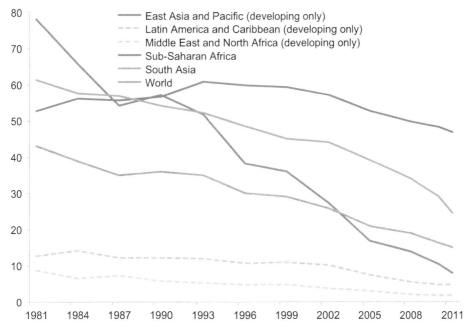

Figure 2.3   Extreme Poverty Rates by Region, 1981–2011 *(Percent)*

Sources: World Bank World Development Indicators; and IMF staff estimates.
Note: Poverty rate is defined as the fraction of the population living with less than $1.25 a day (in purchasing power parity terms).

world production declined steadily. The waning of their share in world population had started earlier. The postwar period registered some remarkable cases of convergence in GDP per capita. In Asia, the so-called Asian Tigers (Hong Kong SAR, Korea, Singapore, and Taiwan Province of China) led the way. They were joined by China and later by India. These two economies doubled their shares in world production between 1950 and 2008 and reduced their gaps with Europe and European offshoots. As a consequence of strong economic growth in China and India, and also in major transition economies, millions of people were lifted out of poverty. More generally, extreme poverty rates declined, particularly in Asia (Figure 2.3). In East Asia and South Asia, for example, extreme poverty fell from about 80 percent and 60 percent of the population in 1981, respectively, to less than 10 percent and 25 percent by 2011.

Not all regions experienced income convergence vis-à-vis Europe and European offshoots. In sub-Saharan Africa, for instance, income growth was more modest, on average, than in Asia. This hides substantial cross-country variation since a number of countries in Africa experienced periods of zero or even negative growth. The reduction in poverty rates has also been less marked in this region. In more recent years, a large share of sub-Saharan African countries have been experiencing high rates of growth, which should lead to a more rapid decline in poverty than in the past.

One striking aspect of the overall pattern of convergence in the global economy is the dominant role played by China and India—two very populous nations (Figure 2.4). After widening during a period of a hundred years, between 1850 and 1950, the income gap between China and India on one hand and Europe and European offshoots on the other has been narrowing quickly. Demographic developments suggest that Europe and European offshoots will account for a smaller share of output in the future. One reason is their lower rate of population

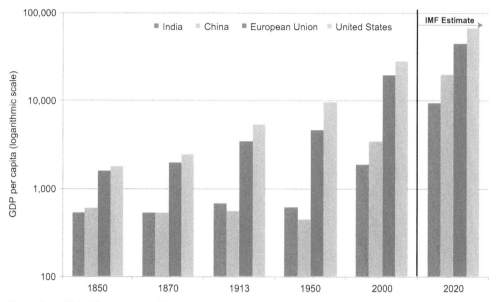

Figure 2.4 Global Convergence: GDP per Capita, 1850–2020

Sources: The Maddison Project for years before 2000; April 2015 *World Economic Outlook* and IMF staff estimates for 2020.
Note: GDP per capita in constant purchasing power parity.

and labor force growth (Lagarde and Gaspar 2014), which is contributing to a slower rate of growth of potential output (IMF 2015b).[1]

This convergence of income across economies (when using population weights) is mirrored in the decline in global inequality since the early 1990s (Bourguignon 2015; and Figure 2.5).[2] Both the Gini coefficient and the relative income gap between the top and bottom 10 percent decreased notably between 1990 and 2010.[3] Although recent revisions to the purchasing power parities highlighted complexities in measuring inequality and inherent measurement issues, related studies have confirmed a rapid decline in worldwide poverty and income inequality (Deaton and Aten 2014; Chandy and Kharas 2014).

The sharp decline of income inequality on a global scale contrasts with developments within countries. Indeed, between the 1980s and the most recent observation in the 2000s, within-country income inequality increased in three-quarters of advanced economies while it declined in the remaining advanced economies such as France, the Netherlands, and Switzerland (Figure 2.6 and Chapter 3). The dynamics of income inequality are more mixed in the developing world, where inequality increased in about half of countries, particularly in fast-growing countries such

---

[1] One interesting remark to make, when contrasting Figures 2.1 and 2.2, is that the sharp decline in the population share of China and India is not mimicked by their share in production. These countries experienced GDP per capita growth faster, on average, than the rest of the world.

[2] The convergence of income has led to calls for governance reforms of international financial institutions.

[3] Milanovic (2013) confirms a decline in global inequality, although only since the early 2000s. He attributes the falling global inequality to the fast-growing China, India, and other high-population economies.

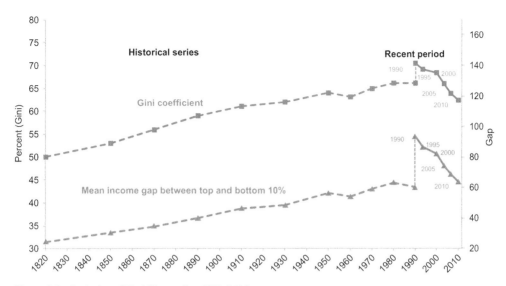

Figure 2.5   Evolution of World Inequality, 1820–2010

Source: Bourguignon (2015), Figure 1.
Note: Historical data prior to 1990 have 1990 as the base year. The data for the recent period (since 1990) have 2005 as the base year. This difference in the base year between historical and more recent periods explains much of the discontinuity between the two series in 1990.

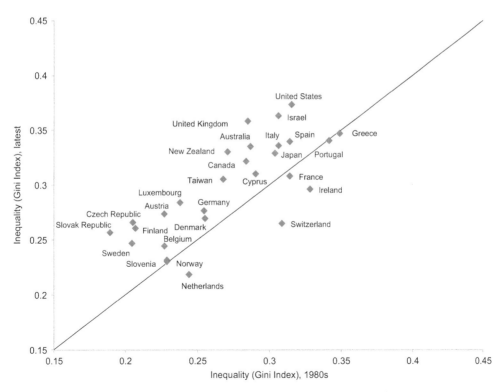

Figure 2.6   Advanced Economies: Income Inequality in the 1980s and 2000s *(Latest observation)*

Sources: European Union; Luxembourg Income Study; Organisation for Economic Co-operation and Development; World Bank; and authors' estimates.
Note: Data for the 1980s correspond to the average of the Gini index in 1980 and 1985. Latest observation corresponds to the most recent available data during the 2000s.

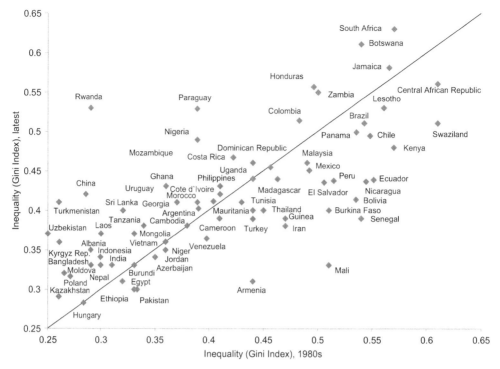

Figure 2.7   Developing Countries: Income Inequality in the 1980s and 2000s *(Latest observation)*

Sources: European Union; Luxembourg Income Study; Organisation for Economic Co-operation and Development; World Bank; and authors' estimates.
Note: Data for the 1980s correspond to the average of the Gini index in 1980 and 1985. Latest observation corresponds to the most recent available data during the 2000s.

as China and India, while it declined in others (Figure 2.7 and Chapter 4).[4] The increase in inequality reflects an array of factors, including the globalization and liberalization of factor and product markets, skill-biased technological change, increases in labor force participation by low-skilled workers, increasing bargaining power of high earners, and the growing share of high-income couples and single-parent households (Bastagli, Coady, and Gupta 2012; Alvaredo and others 2013; Hoeller, Joumard, and Koske 2014; Piketty 2014; Dabla-Norris and others 2015; Bourguignon 2015; Atkinson 2015). In advanced economies, another important factor has been changes in tax and spending policies, which are less redistributive than in the past (Chapter 3). However, there is nothing unavoidable in the play of these factors, considering that between the 1980s and the 2000s income inequality increased in many countries but declined in others.

The global financial crisis—and countries' fiscal responses to the crisis—have further heightened the focus of policymakers and the public on inequality. After the initial easing of fiscal policy in 2009, many economies have been undertaking fiscal consolidation to reduce macroeconomic risks and bring public debt ratios back to more prudent levels. These consolidation efforts have brought to the fore the importance of distribution in designing adjustment packages. Since the crisis, public support for redistribution has increased, especially in advanced economies where the crisis hit harder (Figure 2.8).

---

[4] In this chapter, developing countries refers to both middle-income and low-income countries.

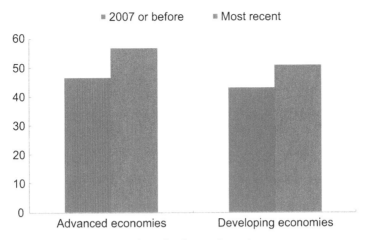

Figure 2.8 Public Support for Redistribution *(Percent)*

Source: Authors' estimates based on Integrated Values Survey data.
Note: These surveys, which include the World Values Surveys (WVS), Regional Barometers, and International
Social Surveys, ask citizens whether they favor more or less redistribution. In the WVS, respondents are
asked to indicate, on a scale from 1 to 10, whether "incomes should be made more equal" (1) or whether
the country "needs larger income differences as incentive" (10). For the purposes of this chapter, these
responses are divided into two categories: answers 1 through 5 indicate that the respondents prefer more
redistribution, and answers 6 through 10 indicate a preference for less redistribution. A similar approach is
applied to other surveys to find the share of the population that supports more redistribution. The most
recent year refers to 2008–13, with about 60 percent of the observations corresponding to 2011–13.

BEFORE THE GLOBAL CRISIS: IMF ACTIVITIES AND INCOME DISTRIBUTION

Early Focus: IMF-Supported Programs and Income Distribution

Distributional concerns first began to crop up in discussions on policy design in IMF-supported adjustment programs in the late 1980s. In particular, equity issues gained prominence with the growing awareness of the links between inequality and the economic and political sustainability of adjustment programs, particularly in developing countries. This led to the need to use social safety nets to protect vulnerable groups during structural and fiscal adjustment and to safeguard access to basic public services such as health and education during the reform process. This theme was especially relevant for transition economies, given that many of them confronted the challenge of protecting the poor while output and government revenues declined sharply in the early phases of the shift to more market-based economies.

The deepening of the IMF's engagement on structural issues in low-income countries, especially those with programs supported by the Extended Structural Adjustment Facility (ESAF), further led to greater attention to social spending during the 1990s. These programs often sought to raise both revenues and expenditures, allowing countries to achieve higher levels of social spending while maintaining macroeconomic stability (Gupta and others 2000). The Heavily Indebted Poor Countries initiative, launched in 1996 by the IMF and the World Bank, emphasized that resources from debt relief should be used to increase pro-poor spending, including on the social sectors. In IMF-supported programs, the broadening of the focus to distributional issues was reflected in the creation of the Poverty Reduction and Growth Facility in 1999 (replacing the Extended Structural Adjustment Facility), with the objectives of poverty reduction and growth figuring prominently in its lending operations for low-income economies. Education and health outlays rose more in economies with IMF-supported programs than those without. After controlling for macroeconomic conditions, the impact of IMF-supported programs, over a five-year period, is to raise education and health spending by ¾ and 1 percentage point of GDP, respectively, in low-income developing countries (Clements, Gupta, and Nozaki 2013). Protecting social spending remains a high priority for programs (Independent Evaluation Office 2014), as reflected in the rising share of programs supported by the Poverty Reduction and Growth Trust and the Extended Credit Facility; where social and other priority spending floors rose from less than 50 percent to 100 percent in 2011–13. The continued emphasis on social sectors is reflected in recent trends in spending. Take, for example, developments in health spending since 2008 in sub-Saharan African countries supported by IMF programs (Figure 2.9, panel 2).

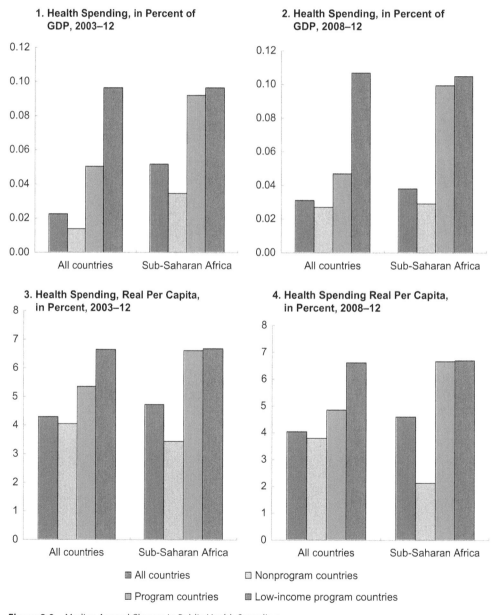

Figure 2.9 Median Annual Change in Public Health Spending

Sources: World Health Organization; IMF, Monitoring of Fund Arrangements (MONA) database; and authors' estimates.

In these countries, spending has risen by an average of about 0.1 percentage point of GDP each year. This translates into a real spending increase per capita of about 6 percent (Figure 2.9, panel 4). Figure 2.9 also demonstrates that spending has been rising at a brisker pace in countries with IMF-supported programs than in nonprogram countries.

The IMF's early work on income distribution emphasized that there need not be a trade-off between growth and distributional objectives (Tanzi and Chu 1998; Tanzi, Chu, and Gupta 1999). Rather, sound macroeconomic and structural policies were consistent with sustainable economic growth and declining poverty, and in some circumstances could contribute to reducing inequality. For instance, sound macroeconomic policies could help reduce inflation, which at high levels increases income inequality. Social spending, if well targeted, could be kept at levels consistent with fiscal sustainability and also achieve distributional objectives. Redistributive policies focusing on public expenditure can protect the poor better than tax instruments without impinging on growth. Reducing unproductive spending (such as generalized subsidies) and replacing it with targeted transfers to the poor can release resources for productive outlays on infrastructure and human capital. Enhancing the efficiency of spending on social sectors would not only improve education and health outcomes but also generate fiscal space for additional productive spending. Finally, the quality of public institutions can influence the effectiveness of distributional policies. High and rising corruption, for example, has been found to increase income inequality and poverty (Gupta, Davoodi, and Alonso-Terme 2002), and social spending can more effectively raise health and educational attainment when governance is strong.

Building institutions thus becomes important for policy formulation and implementation. For example, strengthened revenue administration can help countries ensure that taxes—including those with important distributional objectives, such as income taxes—are paid and collected as intended by governments. Improving tax administration also helps countries raise the revenues needed to finance higher levels of redistributive spending.

The IMF has been helping countries build these strong fiscal institutions through its technical assistance on revenue administration and public financial management. It also has been providing assistance on tax and expenditure policies, which often involves the analysis of policy options with important implications for income distribution. For example, any discussion of the appropriate design of an income tax system must inevitably address the distributional effects of different options for tax rates and the tax base. With respect to expenditure policies, technical assistance on energy subsidies, pension reform, and short-term spending rationalization also has important distributional consequences that are important to country authorities. A core component of much of the IMF's assistance in these areas has been to provide options on how to undertake fiscal reforms in a way that protects low-income groups. For instance, building on the IMF's technical assistance to Jordan, the country implemented a gradual and sequenced reform to contain the budgetary cost of fuel subsidies while simultaneously enhancing the government's capacity to target social assistance (Coady and others 2006).

DEEPENING OF WORK SINCE THE GLOBAL FINANCIAL CRISIS

Following the global crisis, the IMF has further deepened its analytical work on inequality issues to better inform its policy advice.

Income Inequality and Economic Growth

IMF research in recent years has taken a new perspective on this issue by examining how inequality itself—rather than the policies that redistribute income—can be harmful to growth. Berg and Ostry (2011), for example, find that countries with more unequal distributions of income experience shorter growth spells. Ostry, Berg, and Tsangarides (2014) further find that redistributive policies themselves need not have adverse effects on growth. Their analysis shows that only in extreme cases is there some evidence that redistribution may have negative effects on growth. The combined direct and indirect effects of redistribution—including the growth effects of the resulting lower inequality—are, on average, pro-growth. This result is confirmed by Dabla-Norris and others (2015). For example, increases in the income share of the bottom 20 percent are associated with higher GDP growth, while a rising share of the top 20 percent dampens growth.[5]

Many IMF member countries are now seeking to ensure that economic growth is more inclusive than in the past, that is, growth should create a high number of jobs and not lead to rising inequality.[6] Reflecting the growing interest in the theme of inclusive growth, a number of country and regional studies have been undertaken by IMF staff in this area. For instance Lee, Syed, and Wang (2013) highlight a range of policies that could help broaden the benefits of growth in China. These policies include a more progressive fiscal tax and expenditure system, higher public spending on health and education, and measures to raise labor incomes and assist vulnerable workers. Aoyagi and Ganelli (2015) highlight for Japan that full implementation of structural reforms—especially labor market reforms—is necessary to both foster growth and increase equality. Kireyev (2013) shows that better-targeted social policies and more attention to the regional distribution of spending would help reduce poverty and improve inclusiveness in Senegal.

Fiscal Policy and Income Inequality

Fiscal Policy Options to Reduce Inequality

Fiscal policy is the most potent instrument governments have to reduce income inequality.[7] At the same time, government tax and spending policies can also have powerful effects on economic incentives that can either promote efficiency and growth or diminish them. At the aggregate level, the total amount of fiscal redistribution that governments do—for example, through progressive income taxes and social welfare payments—does not appear to have an adverse effect on growth. But the design of specific tax and expenditure instruments matters, both for their effects on inequality and for their impact on economic efficiency. Good examples of efficient redistribution include a greater role for recurrent property taxes, more progressive personal income taxes, better taxation of multinational corporations, the revival of inheritance and gift taxes, expansion of low-income families' access to education and health, better targeting of social benefits, strengthened incentives to work, and the safeguarding of pensions (IMF 2014).

Fiscal Consolidation and Inequality

As noted earlier, the need for fiscal consolidation in many economies, in conjunction with rising concerns about inequality, poses a difficult challenge for policymakers. Although fiscal consolidation can help correct macroeconomic imbalances and lay the foundation for sustainable growth in the medium term, it is still likely to decrease growth in the short term and raise unemployment. Fiscal adjustments are also associated with a decline in the wage share of income, and may lead to greater wage dispersion because firms tend to lay off their less skilled workers first. All these factors contribute to an increase in the inequality of market income during fiscal consolidations. Fiscal consolidation can also affect households' disposable income through increases in taxes and cuts in government transfers, such as social benefits.

---

[5] One mechanism through which inequality can affect growth is through its effects on the financial system. Rising inequality can generate political pressure for more housing credit, which distorts lending in the financial sector (Rajan 2010).
[6] See IMF 2013a for an overview of issues related to inclusive growth and their implications for the IMF.
[7] For evidence on the effects of fiscal policies on inequality in advanced and developing economies, see also Bastagli, Coady, and Gupta (2012).

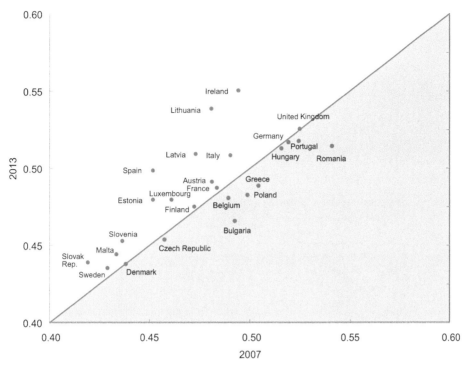

Figure 2.10   Gini Index for Market Income, 2007–2013

Source: EUROMOD statistics on Distribution and Decomposition of Disposable Income, accessed at http://www.iser.essex.ac.uk/euromod/statistics/ using EUROMOD version no. G2.0.

In this light, an important question is whether adjustments that are mostly based on tax increases, or those that rely primarily on spending cuts, are more likely to lead to an increase in inequality. Most studies covering both advanced and developing countries suggest that fiscal consolidations based on spending cuts have stronger adverse effects on income distribution; one of the reasons for this result is that spending cuts are associated with larger increases in unemployment (Woo and others 2013). Tax-based adjustments are no panacea, however, because both spending- and revenue-based consolidations are, in most cases, associated with persistent increases in inequality. This outcome, however, is not unavoidable.

Most empirical studies on fiscal consolidation and inequality have focused on the impact of adjustment episodes from the past 20 to 30 years, largely covering the period before the global financial crisis. The more recent experience with fiscal adjustments is less bleak, and underscores an important message coming from research both inside and outside the IMF: *design matters*. Fiscal adjustment need not lead to increases in inequality if it is based on measures that deliberately place a smaller share of the burden on lower-income groups. While this cannot completely offset the effects of fiscal adjustment on inequality, in many cases it can largely neutralize it.

The evidence from 27 recent fiscal consolidation episodes in advanced and emerging economies in Europe in the aftermath of the global financial crisis sheds light on this issue (see also Chapter 9).[8] In more than half of the cases, fiscal adjustments were associated with higher inequality in market incomes. This can be seen in Figure 2.10 for the countries that are above

---

[8] To assess how inequality evolved during fiscal adjustments undertaken in the aftermath of the crisis, the chapter compares the dynamic of inequality between the period before the crisis (2007) and the period after (2013). This captures most consolidation episodes, which took place from 2010, after temporary fiscal stimulus in 2008 and 2009.

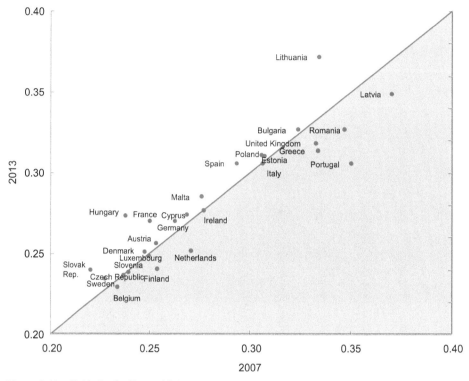

Figure 2.11   Gini Index for Disposable Income, 2007–13

Source: EUROMOD statistics on Distribution and Decomposition of Disposable Income, accessed at http://www.iser.essex.ac.uk/euromod/
statistics/ using EUROMOD version no. G2.0.

the 45 degree line. But this does not tell the whole story—in many cases, fiscal policy helped offset increases in market inequality (Figure 2.11). For instance, in Ireland, the increase in market-income inequality between 2007 and 2013 was fully offset by fiscal policy, as illustrated by the constant Gini index for disposable income. In a number of countries, such as France and Hungary, fiscal policy worsened inequality.

This is further illustrated in Figure 2.12, which shows that in two-thirds of the countries, fiscal policies were progressive and helped move Gini coefficients in a downward direction. In another one-third of cases, fiscal policies tended to raise inequality.

More detailed studies of tax and spending measures implemented during recent fiscal adjustment episodes also find that it is possible to achieve fiscal consolidation without increasing inequality.

For example, Avram and others (2013) show that in five of the nine countries they examined, adjustment measures were progressive, with upper-income groups bearing a proportionately larger share of the burden (see also Chapter 9). The different outcomes reflected the composition of the measures implemented, as well as how they were designed. Reductions in the public sector wage bill, for instance, tended to be progressive because public sector employees are often skilled and educated workers from middle- and upper-income households. In addition, some countries implemented proportionately higher cuts for higher-paid workers. These factors played a role in the progressive incidence of wage bill reductions in Greece, Portugal, Latvia, and Romania. For instance in Greece, public sector wages were capped, special allowances for civil servants reduced, and the 13th and 14th salaries abolished for high-earning workers. In Portugal, public sector pay

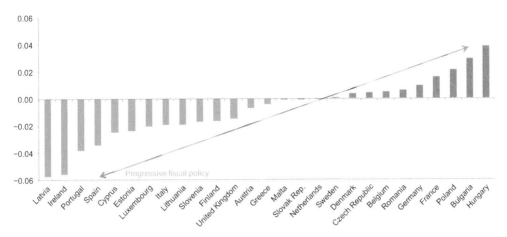

Figure 2.12   Redistributive Effect of Fiscal Policy, 2007–13 *(Effect on Gini coefficient)*

Source: EUROMOD statistics on Distribution and Decomposition of Disposable Income, accessed at https://www.iser.essex.ac.uk/files/euromod/
Statistics/WebStatistics_July1_2014_Gini_Datasets_Population_Exchangerates.xlsx using EUROMOD version No. G2.0.
Note: A negative number indicates a decline in income inequality (the Gini coefficient) due to fiscal policy. The figure measures the change in dispos-
able income (which reflects government tax and transfer programs) minus the change in market incomes. See Chapter 9 for details of the estimates.

cuts increased with wages to a maximum of 10 percent. In a similar vein, cuts in pensions in some countries were more heavily targeted to those receiving high pensions, as in Greece and Portugal. In cases in which pension cuts or freezes were more across the board, as in Estonia, they tended to aggravate inequality. Measures to raise revenues from income taxes and social security contributions tended to reduce inequality, including in Latvia, Portugal, Spain, and the United Kingdom; in the latter two countries, the effects were particularly large. But for these measures as well, design mattered. For example, reductions in the threshold for filing tax returns—which brought a larger share of workers into the tax base—tended to blunt the redistributive effect of the income tax. Increases in value-added taxes also tended to increase inequality, with the strength of the redistributive effect depending on the structure of consumption. In Spain, the poorest 10 percent of households were affected relatively more by the 5 percentage point cumulative VAT increases imposed over 2010 and 2012.

In many developing countries, reforms to reduce costly fuel subsidies while limiting their distributional impact have been a long-lasting concern. An IMF technical assistance mission to Angola suggested that a gradual and sequenced reform be implemented to contain the budgetary cost of fuel subsidies while limiting the negative impact of the reform on the welfare of lower-income groups (IMF 2015a). The reforms included a frontloaded reduction of subsidies for gasoline, which is a costly product mostly consumed by well-off households, while reduction of the subsidies for kerosene would be delayed.

In sum, recent experience suggests that a variety of distributive outcomes from fiscal consolidation measures are possible. With the right combination of measures, countries can avoid a widening of inequality while undertaking fiscal adjustment.

Labor Market Institutions, Income Inequality, and Gender Gaps

Other factors can affect inequality, such as labor market institutions. Changes in minimum wages can affect the bottom and middle of the income distribution through various channels, including their effects on the wages and employment of low-skilled workers.

Gender inequality can also have adverse macroeconomic consequences. Differences between male and female participation rates have been narrowing since 1990, but remain high in most regions (Elborgh-Woytek and others 2013). In rapidly aging economies, higher female labor force participation could boost growth by mitigating the impact of a shrinking workforce. A number of IMF country studies have highlighted sizable macroeconomic gains that could result from raising female labor force participation rates and called for policies to support female employment (for example, Loko and Diouf 2009; IMF 2012; Steinberg and Nakane 2012; Lagarde 2013; Elborgh-Woytek and others 2013; IMF 2013b). Recent country case studies also stress that enhanced social spending can help boost female labor force participation in India, Japan, and Korea (Das and others 2015; Kinoshita and Guo 2015). Rectifying the unequal legal rights of women could also boost female labor force participation rates (Gonzales and others 2015).

CONCLUSION AND NEXT STEPS

The IMF's work on income inequality has evolved in response to economic developments and the needs of its member countries. In this respect, two important developments stand out. First, developing economies' share in global economic output has risen. Second, inequality has risen in many countries. To better serve its member countries, the IMF has increased the attention it pays to distributive issues, including government tax and expenditure policies that have macroeconomic effects and influence income distribution.

IMF work on income inequality before the global crisis that began in 2008 was particularly influenced by the experience gained from IMF-supported programs. In practice, this experience led to greater attention to integrating social safety nets into adjustment programs and safeguarding access to basic public services in health and education. Other initiatives, such as the introduction of the Poverty Reduction and Growth Facility in 1999, brought growth and poverty reduction objectives to the center of program design in low-income countries, as did the Heavily Indebted Poor Countries debt-relief initiative. IMF-supported programs were successful in raising social spending, including in comparison with similar countries without programs.

The IMF has further deepened its work on inequality issues in the years since the beginning of the global financial crisis. This effort has encompassed an expansion of both cross-country analytical studies and country-level assessments of fiscal consolidation and inequality, a variety of fiscal policy instruments to achieve equity goals in an efficient manner, and the macroeconomic gains from strengthening gender equity. An important lesson is that with the right design, government tax and spending policies can help achieve both stronger growth *and* greater equality of outcomes and opportunities. For example, boosting access to basic health and education services and reducing barriers to female labor market participation can help raise growth and meet equity objectives. Even in the design of fiscal consolidation, a number of options can help reduce budget deficits without aggravating inequality. These include measures to raise revenues from income taxes and targeted (rather than across-the-board) reductions in social benefits. Measures that are good for both equity and efficiency—for example, an increase in revenues from recurrent property taxation—should also be given strong consideration when designing fiscal consolidation packages.

The IMF will continue to strengthen its analytical work on income distribution issues. These efforts will involve further cross-country analysis of the type carried out in this book on different aspects of macroeconomic policies and how they affect income distribution. Work at the country level on income distribution issues, including gender equity, will also be deepened. The approach will be selective, and will be concentrated on countries where these issues are critical. We expect considerable synergies between country-level and cross-country analysis, and we will continue to draw on the profession's work in these areas. In sum, we will continue to deepen our understanding of the nexus between income distribution and macroeconomics, with the goal of providing relevant policy advice.

REFERENCES

Alvaredo, F., A. Atkinson, T. Piketty, and E. Saez. 2013. "The Top 1 Percent in International and Historical Perspective." *Journal of Economic Perspectives* 27 (3): 3–20.

Aoyagi, C., and G. Ganelli. 2015. "Asia's Quest for Inclusive Growth Revisited." IMF Working Paper No. 15/29, International Monetary Fund, Washington.

Atkinson, A. 2015. *Inequality. What Can Be Done?* Cambridge, Massachusetts: Harvard University Press.

Avram, S., F. Figari, C. Leventi, H. Levy, J. Navicke, M. Matsaganis, E. Militaru, A. Paulus, O. Rastringina, and H. Sutherland. 2013. "The Distributional Effects of Fiscal Consolidation in Nine Countries." EUROMOD Working Paper No. EM 2/13, Institute of Social and Economic Research, University of Essex.

Bastagli, F., D. Coady, and S. Gupta. 2012. "Income Inequality and Fiscal Policy." IMF Staff Discussion Note No. 12/08, International Monetary Fund, Washington.

Berg, A. G., and D. J. Ostry. 2011. "Inequality and Unsustainable Growth: Two Sides of the Same Coin?" IMF Staff Discussion Note No. 11/08, International Monetary Fund, Washington.

Bourguignon, F. 2015. *The Globalization of Inequality*. Princeton, New Jersey: Princeton University Press.

Chandy, L., and H. Kharas. 2014. "What Do New Price Data Mean for the Goal of Ending Extreme Poverty?" Upfront blog, Brookings Institution, Washington. http://www.brookings.edu/blogs/up-front/posts/2014/05/05-data-extreme-poverty-chandy-kharas.

Clements, B., S. Gupta, and M. Nozaki. 2013. "What Happens to Social Spending in IMF-Supported Programmes?" *Applied Economics* 45 (28): 4022–33.

Coady, D., E. Moataz, R. Gillingham, K. Kpodar, P. Medas, and D. Newhouse. 2006. "The Magnitude and Distribution of Fuel Subsidies: Evidence from Bolivia, Ghana, Jordan, Mali, and Sri Lanka." IMF Working Paper No. 06/247, International Monetary Fund, Washington.

Dabla-Norris, E., K. Kochhar, F. Ricka, and N. Suphaphiphat. 2015. "Causes and Consequences of Income Inequality: A Global Perspective." IMF Staff Discussion Note No. 15/13, International Monetary Fund, Washington.

Das, Sonali, Sonali Jain-Chandra, Kalpana Kochhar, and Naresh Kumar. 2015. "Women Workers in India: Why So Few among So Many?" IMF Working Paper No. 15/55, International Monetary Fund, Washington.

Deaton, A., and B. Aten. 2014. "Trying to Understand the PPPs in ICP2011: Why Are the Results So Different?" NBER Working Paper No. 20244, National Bureau of Economic Research, Cambridge, Massachusetts.

Elborgh-Woytek, Katrin, Monique Newiak, Kalpana Kochhar, Stefania Fabrizio, Kangni Kpodar, Philippe Wingender, Benedict J. Clements, and Gerd Schwartz. 2013. "Women, Work, and the Economy: Macroeconomic Gains from Gender Equity." IMF Staff Discussion Note No. 13/10, International Monetary Fund, Washington.

Gonzales, C., S. Jain-Chandra, K. Kochhar, and M. Newiak. 2015. "Fair Play: More Equal Laws Boost Female Labor Force Participation." IMF Staff Discussion Note No. 15/02, International Monetary Fund, Washington.

Gupta, S., H. Davoodi, and R. Alonso-Terme. 2002. "Does Corruption Affect Income Inequality and Poverty?" *Economics of Governance* 3 (1): 23–45.

Gupta, S., Louis Dicks-Mireaux, Ritha Khemani, Calvin McDonald, and Marijn Verhoeven. 2000. "Social Issues in IMF-Supported Programs." IMF Occasional Paper No. 191, International Monetary Fund, Washington.

Hoeller, P., I. Joumard, and I. Koske, eds. 2014. *Income Inequality in OECD Countries: What Are the Drivers and Policy Options?* Singapore: World Scientific.

Independent Evaluation Office. 2003. *Evaluation Report: Fiscal Adjustment in IMF-Supported Programs*. Washington: Independent Evaluation Office, International Monetary Fund.

———. 2014. *Evaluation Update: Revisiting the IEO Evaluations of the IMF's Role in PRSPs and PRGF (2004) and the IMF and Aid to Sub-Saharan Africa*. Washington: Independent Evaluation Office, International Monetary Fund.

International Monetary Fund (IMF). 2008. "Reform of Quota and Voice in the International Monetary Fund—Report of the Executive Board to the Board of Governors." Washington.

———. 2010. "IMF Quota and Governance Reform—Elements of an Agreement." Washington.

———. 2012. "Fiscal Policy and Employment in Advanced and Emerging Economies." Board Paper, Washington.

———. 2013a. "Jobs and Growth: Analytical and Operational Considerations for the Fund." Board Paper, Washington.

———. 2013b. "Women at Work." *Finance and Development* (June special issue).

———. 2014. "Fiscal Policy and Income Inequality." IMF Policy Paper, Washington.

———. 2015a. "Fuel Price Subsidy Reform: The Way Forward." IMF Country Report No. 15/28, Washington.

———. 2015b. *World Economic Outlook: Uneven Growth—Short- and Long-Term Factors*. Washington, April.

Kinoshita, Y., and F. Guo. 2015. "What Can Boost Female Labor Force Participation in Asia?" IMF Working Paper No. 15/56, International Monetary Fund, Washington.

Kireyev, A. 2013. "Inclusive Growth and Inequality in Senegal." IMF Working Paper No. 13/215, International Monetary Fund, Washington.

Lagarde, C. 2013. "Dare the Difference." *Finance and Development* 50 (2).

————, and V. Gaspar. 2014. "The Fiscal Challenge of Aging Populations: A Call to Action." Paper prepared as tribute to Peter Brabeck-Letmathe.

Lee, I. H., M. Syed, and X. Wang. 2013. "Two Side of the Same Coin? Rebalancing and Inclusive Growth in China." IMF Working Paper No. 13/152, International Monetary Fund, Washington.

Loko, B., and Mame A. Diouf. 2009. "Revisiting the Determinants of Productivity Growth: What's New?" IMF Working Paper No. 09/225, International Monetary Fund, Washington.

Milanovic, B., 2013. "Global Income Inequality in Numbers: In History and Now." *Global Policy* 4 (2):198–208.

Ostry, J. D., Andrew Berg, and Charalambos G. Tsangarides. 2014. "Redistribution, Inequality, and Growth." IMF Staff Discussion Note No. 14/02, International Monetary Fund, Washington.

Piketty, T. 2014. *Capital in the 21st Century*. Cambridge, Massachusetts: Harvard University Press.

Rajan, R. 2010. *Fault Lines: How Hidden Fractures Still Threaten the World Economy*. Princeton, New Jersey: Princeton University Press.

Steinberg, C., and M. Nakane. 2012. "Can Women Save Japan?" IMF Working Paper No. 12/48, International Monetary Fund, Washington.

Tanzi, V., and K. Chu, eds. 1998. *Income Distribution and High-Quality Growth*. Cambridge, Massachusetts: MIT Press.

Tanzi, V., K-Y Chu, and S. Gupta, eds. 1999. *Economic Policy and Equity*. Washington: International Monetary Fund.

Woo, J., E. Bova, T. Kinda, and S. Zhang. 2013. "Distributional Consequences of Fiscal Consolidation and the Role of Fiscal Policy: What Do the Data Say?" IMF Working Paper No. 13/195, International Monetary Fund, Washington.

CHAPTER 3

Inequality and Fiscal Redistribution in Advanced Economies

DAVID COADY, RUUD DE MOOIJ, AND BAOPING SHANG

INTRODUCTION

A number of surveys have found increasing concern among populations about high inequality in their countries and revealed growing public support for more redistribution (IMF 2013a). A 2014 report released by the World Economic Forum's Global Agenda Councils indicates that increasing inequality tops the list of the world's most pressing threats (World Economic Forum 2014). A study by the Pew Research Center reports that a majority in all of the 44 nations it surveyed believe inequality is a big problem facing their countries (Pew Research Center 2014). There is also growing evidence that high income inequality can be detrimental to achieving macroeconomic stability and sustained growth in the long term (Easterly 2007; Ostry, Berg, and Tsangarides 2014). Others have argued that rising inequality may have been an important contributing factor to the global financial crisis (Rajan 2010; Kumhof and Rancière 2011).

Although several regulatory instruments, such as minimum wages and price controls, can be used to achieve redistributive goals, fiscal policy is the primary tool used by most governments to affect income distribution. Tax and spending policies can alter the distribution of income in both the short and medium terms. For example, in-kind benefits, such as education spending, can affect the inequality of market incomes (that is, incomes before taxes and transfers) through their impact on future earnings. Other fiscal instruments, such as income taxes and cash transfers, can directly reduce the inequality of disposable incomes (that is, incomes after direct taxes and transfers).

However, badly designed redistributive fiscal policy can have adverse implications for efficiency and growth, and can even have perverse impacts on the income distribution (IMF 2012). For example, income tax deductions, such as for mortgage interest, create distortions, and are also more likely to benefit the rich. On the transfer side, too-rapid withdrawal of means-tested benefits can involve high "tax wedges," creating strong disincentives for labor market participation and welfare dependency. The result can be a more unequal distribution of market incomes.

This chapter focuses on the design of efficient redistributive policies in advanced economies. It first describes different concepts of inequality and their trends. It then analyzes the historical role of fiscal redistribution on inequality and presents potential tax and expenditure instruments that could help achieve efficient redistribution in advanced economies.

TRENDS IN INEQUALITY

Inequality can be viewed from different perspectives, each of which can provide insights into the nature, causes, and consequences of inequality and can also have different policy implications. *Income inequality* measures the interpersonal distribution of income, capturing how individual or household incomes are distributed across the population at a particular time. In contrast, *lifetime inequality* considers inequality in incomes or earnings for an individual over his or her

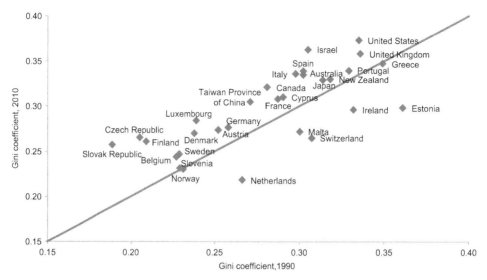

Figure 3.1 Increase in Disposable Income Inequality, 1990–2010

Sources: Eurostat; Luxembourg Income Study database; and Organisation for Economic Co-operation and Development.
Note: Disposable income is income available to finance consumption once income taxes and public transfers have been netted out. Therefore, the distributional impacts of indirect taxes and in-kind transfers are not included. The Gini coefficient ranges between 0 (complete equality) and 1 (complete inequality).

lifetime rather than for a single year. *Inequality of wealth* considers the distribution of wealth across individuals or households, which reflects not only differences in income, but also savings rates as well as bequests and inheritances. *Inequality of opportunity* focuses on the relationship between income and social mobility, in particular the extent of mobility between income groups across generations.

Income inequality. Since 1990, inequality in the personal distribution of income has increased in most advanced economies. Figure 3.1 presents Gini coefficients for disposable incomes (that is, market incomes minus direct taxes plus cash transfers)—which embody both the inequality of market-determined incomes as well as the distributional impact of income taxes and public transfers.[1] Between 1990 and 2010, the Gini for disposable income has increased in most advanced economies. More than one-third of advanced economies experienced increases in their Ginis exceeding 3 percentage points.

More recently, the public debate has focused on inequality at the top end of the income distribution, and especially so since the global economic and financial crisis. The share of total income going to top income groups has sharply increased in some countries. Since the mid-1980s, the market income shares of the richest 1 percent of the population have increased substantially in English-speaking advanced economies (Figure 3.2). For example, in the United States, the share of market income captured by the richest 10 percent surged from about 30 percent in 1980 to 48 percent in 2012, while the share of the richest 1 percent increased from 8 percent to

---

[1] The Gini coefficient ranges between 0 (denoting complete equality) and 1 (denoting complete inequality). The Gini is less sensitive to inequality at the extremes of the income distribution than many other commonly used measures. However, other inequality measures show a similar trend in overall income inequality. For instance, the ratio of the income share of the top 20 percent of the income distribution to the share of the bottom 20 percent has a correlation coefficient with the Gini of about 0.85.

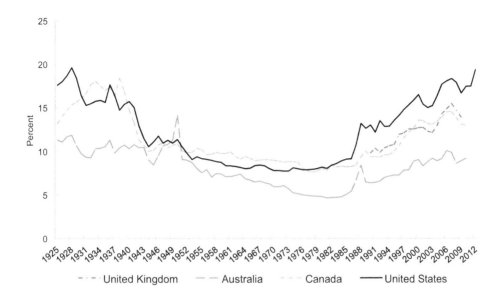

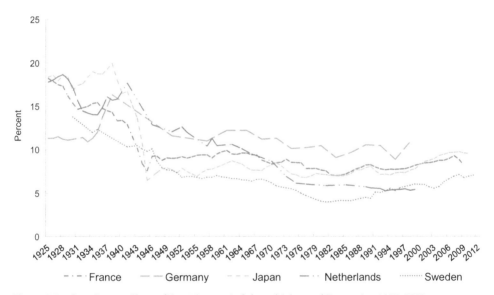

Figure 3.2   Gross Income Share of Top 1 Percent in Selected Advanced Economies, 1925–2012

Source: The World Top Incomes Database (http://g-mond.parisschoolofeconomics.eu/topincomes/).
Note: Income refers to pre-tax-and-transfer gross income. See Atkinson, Piketty, and Saez 2011 for details.

19 percent. Even more striking is the fourfold increase in the income share of the richest 0.1 percent, from 2.6 percent to 10.4 percent. The rise in the share of the highest income groups has varied substantially across countries. The increase in the share of the top 1 percent has been much less pronounced in the southern European and Nordic economies, and hardly any increases have been observed in continental Europe and Japan. These differences suggest that policies and institutions can play an important role in avoiding such increases in extreme inequality.

Lifetime income inequality. Empirical studies suggest that lifetime inequality is usually lower than inequality in any given year. This outcome occurs for two reasons. First, in many economies, individuals experience significant fluctuations in incomes from year to year. An individual who has relatively high income in one year may not necessarily have high lifetime income relative to his or her peers of the same age. Bowlus and Robin (2012) find that because of this "earnings mobility" from one year to the next, the lifetime inequality of income is about 20–30 percent lower than annual income inequality in Canada, the United Kingdom, and the United States. In France and Germany, lifetime inequality is similar to inequality of annual income. Second, lifetime incomes also tend to be less unequal because of the age-income cycle that affects the entire population: incomes tend to be lower during early working years and peak in later years, before declining again (Paglin 1975). Taking both of these factors into account, Björklund (1993) finds that the dispersion of lifetime incomes in Sweden is about 35–40 percent lower than that of annual incomes.

Wealth inequality. In advanced economies, household net wealth—financial assets and real estate minus debt—has increased substantially since the early 1970s. Assessment of trends in this area requires caution, given the limited number of economies with comprehensive data. Internationally comparable data for eight large advanced economies show that the average ratio of net household wealth to national income grew by almost 80 percent between 1970 and 2010 (Piketty and Zucman 2013). The largest increase was observed in Italy (180 percent) and the smallest increase was in the United States (21 percent). Explanations for the rapid growth in wealth include asset price booms and a significant increase in private savings.

Wealth is more unequally distributed than income. The Gini coefficient of wealth in a sample of 13 advanced economies in the early 2000s was 0.66, compared with a Gini of 0.31 for disposable incomes (Figure 3.3). The share of wealth held by the top 10 percent ranges from slightly less than half in Italy, Japan, Spain, and the United Kingdom, to more than two-thirds in Norway, Sweden, Switzerland, and the United States. In Switzerland and the United States, where wealth is most unequally distributed, the top 1 percent alone holds more than one-third of total household wealth. The inequality of wealth has risen in recent decades in several advanced economies. For instance, between the mid-1980s and early 2000s, the growth of wealth in

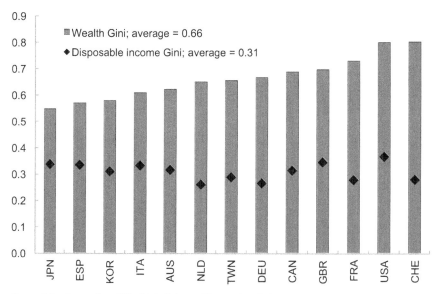

Figure 3.3   Inequality of Wealth in Selected Economies, Early 2000s

Sources: Davies and others (2008); Eurostat; Luxembourg Income Study database; and Organisation for Economic Co-operation and Development.
Note: Labels in this figure use International Organization for Standardization (ISO) country codes.

Canada and Sweden was all concentrated in the two upper deciles of the wealth distribution. During the same period, the Gini coefficients of wealth distribution in Finland and Italy rose from about 0.55 to greater than 0.6. In the United States, the Gini coefficient of wealth distribution rose from 0.80 in the early 1980s to almost 0.84 in 2007.

Nonfinancial assets make up a large share of household wealth. Survey data suggest that nonfinancial assets—such as primary residences and other real estate—represent 70–90 percent of total household gross wealth in advanced economies. Financial wealth is generally more unequally distributed than real estate; for example, Fredriksen (2012) reports that the Gini coefficient for financial wealth (on average, 0.8 for a group of seven advanced countries) exceeds that for nonfinancial wealth (0.63).

Inequality of opportunity. Income inequality can persist across generations, reflecting differences in economic opportunity. Restricted opportunities for increasing incomes can reflect a range of factors, including lack of access to education (including early childhood and tertiary education) and lack of access to certain professions or business opportunities (OECD 2011a; Corak 2013). This lack of access is in turn reinforced by low incomes. High income inequality, therefore, is both a symptom and a cause of low economic mobility, and family background is a key factor in determining the adult outcomes of younger generations.

Intergenerational income mobility is lower in countries with higher income inequality. Intergenerational earnings mobility, as measured by the elasticity between a parent's and an offspring's earnings, is low in countries such as Italy, the United Kingdom, and the United States, which have high Gini coefficients for disposable income. In contrast, mobility is much higher in the more egalitarian Nordic countries (Figure 3.4). This relationship between

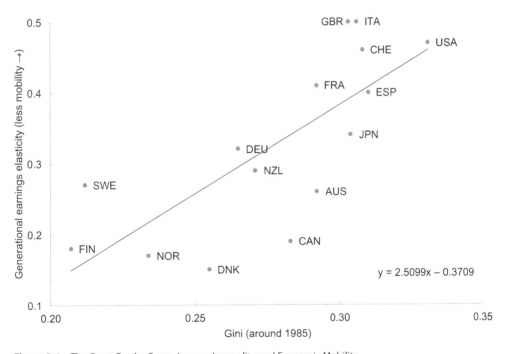

Figure 3.4   The Great Gatsby Curve: Income Inequality and Economic Mobility

Sources: Corak (2013); Eurostat; Luxembourg Income Study database; and Organisation for Economic Co-operation and Development.
Note: The intergenerational earnings elasticity estimates in the figure are the elasticity between a father's income and a son's income. The upward slope of the line suggests that countries with a high inequality of income around 1985 (high Gini coefficients) had high intergenerational earnings elasticities. A high elasticity suggests a strong relationship between a father's and a son's income and less mobility of incomes across generations. Labels in this figure use International Organization for Standardization (ISO) country codes.

income inequality and intergenerational mobility is often referred to as the "Great Gatsby Curve" (Krueger 2012). In low-mobility countries, about 50 percent of any economic advantage that a father has is passed on to his offspring, whereas in high-mobility countries this advantage falls to less than 20 percent. Evidence for Nordic countries shows that intergenerational income mobility is flat across much of the parental income distribution but rises at the top end.

Several key messages emerge from examining different aspects of inequality and their development in the past decades. First, the findings are consistent with the literature that inequality has been rising. Second, inequality of opportunity remains a major issue in advanced economies. Redistributive fiscal policies should thus first focus on addressing inequality of opportunity because such policies can potentially help reduce inequality and improve economic efficiency. Third, more attention should be paid to lifetime inequality. To the extent that market mechanisms to help households smooth income over time are absent, government could have a role in providing social insurance, which would be welfare enhancing. Fourth, the increase in wealth and inequality of wealth in many advanced economies may indicate there is more scope to increase wealth taxation, which tends to be less distortive.

ROLE OF FISCAL REDISTRIBUTION

How much has fiscal policy helped reduce income inequality? Evaluating the redistributive impact of fiscal policies requires a comparison of incomes after taxes and transfers with incomes that would exist without them. In principle, assessments of the incidence of fiscal policies should incorporate information on consumers' and producers' behavioral responses to taxes and transfers and their impact on market incomes.[2] In practice, most studies do not incorporate this aspect, since sufficient data on behavioral responses are unavailable. In these studies, the incidence of commodity taxes is typically assumed to fall on consumers, factor taxes are assumed to fall on factor suppliers (labor and capital), and transfers to beneficiaries do not lead to changes in factor supplies.[3] Despite this limitation, these studies still provide some broad picture of the redistributive role of fiscal policy by looking at the composition and overall level of taxes and spending. The evidence below is drawn from such studies.

Fiscal policy has played a significant role in reducing income inequality in advanced economies, with most of this reduction being achieved on the expenditure side through transfers. During recent decades, direct income taxes and transfers have decreased inequality in advanced economies by an average of one-third (Figure 3.5). For instance, in 2005 the average Gini for disposable income was 14 percentage points below that of the average market-income Gini. The redistributive impact of transfers accounts for about two-thirds of the decrease in the Gini. Within transfers, non-means-tested transfers (including public pensions and family benefits) account for the bulk of the redistribution (Immervoll and others 2005; Paulus and others 2009). On the tax side, personal income taxes make an important contribution to reducing inequality in a number of economies; in fact, in most economies, the redistribution achieved through income taxes is even higher than that achieved through means-tested transfers. These results are consistent with studies on poverty. Paulus and

---

[2] More about incidence analysis can be found in Boadway and Keen 2000.

[3] Although public sector support for access to finance (for example, mortgage finance and education loans) can also affect inequality, this impact is not included in these studies. Correcting market failures that strengthen access to finance can also reduce the inequality of lifetime income and of opportunity.

Figure 3.5   Redistributive Impact of Fiscal Policy in Advanced Economies, Mid-2000s

Sources: Paulus and others (2009); except for Australia, Canada, the Czech Republic, Korea, Norway, Israel, Taiwan Province of China, and the United States, for which data are from Caminada, Goudswaard, and Wang (2012).
Note: The impact on inequality of disposable income does not incorporate the redistributive impact of indirect taxes and in-kind benefits. Labels in this figure use International Organization for Standardization (ISO) country codes.

others (2009) find that fiscal policy decreases the poverty rate in 19 Organisation for Economic Co-operation and Development (OECD) countries to an average of 15 percent from an average of 30 percent, with virtually all of this decrease being achieved on the transfer side of the budget.

Social insurance and other transfers are far less redistributive when examined from the perspective of lifetime income. Pension systems, for example, redistribute income across an individual's own lifetime, with pension contributions being made during peak earning years, and benefits received during retirement when incomes are lower. Similarly, households receive more in transfers when they have children. The fiscal redistribution of incomes from the lifetime rich to the lifetime poor is thus smaller than that implied by a snapshot in any one year. For instance, Bovenberg, Hansen, and Sorenson (2012) show that about three-fourths of redistribution in Denmark involves redistribution over peoples' life cycles as opposed to redistribution from lifetime rich to lifetime poor; they also report similar magnitudes for Australia, Ireland, Italy, and Sweden from other studies.

The overall redistributive impact of fiscal policy is also influenced by the distribution of indirect taxes and in-kind transfers. Empirical evidence suggests that indirect taxes tend to be regressive or proportional to incomes (O'Donoghue, Baldini, and Mantovani 2004; Cnossen 2005). While both the value-added tax (VAT) and excise duties are found to be regressive, excise taxes are especially regressive. However, the regressivity of indirect taxes is typically much smaller when assessed against lifetime income or consumption. In-kind transfers such as education and health spending are very progressively distributed (that is, their benefits are more equally distributed than disposable incomes). On average, in-kind transfers are found to decrease the Gini coefficient by 5.8 percentage points in five European economies (Belgium, Germany, Greece, Italy, and the United Kingdom), with health (3.6 points) and education (2.2 points) accounting for virtually all of this impact (Paulus, Sutherland, and Tsakloglou 2009; Figure 3.6). In addition, expansion of access at lower levels of education can decrease earnings inequality in the medium term (De Gregorio and Lee 2002).

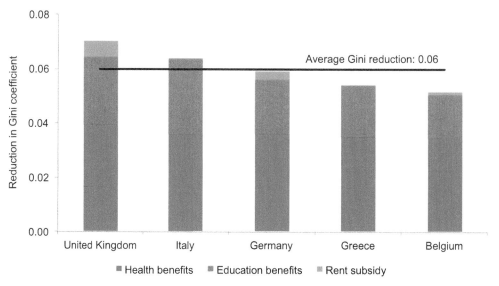

Figure 3.6   Redistributive Impact of In-Kind Spending

Source: Paulus, Sutherland, and Tsakloglou (2009).

DESIGN OF FISCAL REDISTRIBUTION

In assessing the design of fiscal redistribution, three issues are important. First, taxes and spending both matter for fiscal redistribution and should thus be evaluated jointly. For instance, an increase in regressive taxes can still be the best approach to supporting redistribution if the public expenditures they finance are highly progressive. Second, indirect effects should be taken into account. For instance, taxes and spending policies can modify market prices so that their incidence is felt elsewhere rather than by those who are directly targeted by these policies. Moreover, spending on education and health can have important dynamic effects by enhancing social mobility. Third, fiscal instruments should be compared with nonfiscal policies aimed at addressing inequality. For instance, minimum wages and rent regulations are generally designed as redistributive tools, the results of which could alternatively be achieved using fiscal instruments.

Expenditure

Social spending (social protection, education, and health) is the primary instrument used to achieve redistributive goals in most countries. This spending can be made more efficient by improving its targeting and reducing its adverse labor market effects. The appropriate mix of programs and design features will vary across economies to reflect differences in fiscal and administrative capacity.

Education

Education reforms could focus on improving access by low-income groups. Although education spending as a whole is progressive, tertiary education spending tends to be regressive. This lack of access to higher levels of education results in inequality of opportunity and perpetuates inequality across generations. A range of spending reforms focused on improving access can help enhance the distributional impact of education spending:

- *Increasing investment in lower levels of education.* The main driver behind the regressivity (or lower progressivity) of public education spending is the large share of the budget allocated to higher levels of education, which are disproportionally accessed by higher-income groups. Lack of access for lower-income groups to higher levels of education is primarily due to lack of progress through lower education levels. This situation requires improving access to, progression through, and performance in upper-secondary and tertiary education. Increasing access to early childhood education is required, especially given the substantial evidence that early education has a crucial impact on education performance at higher levels.

- *Improvements in the efficiency of education spending.* Increased spending on education at lower levels should be complemented by efforts to get better results from existing levels of spending. Inefficiencies in spending are substantial (Gupta and others 2007; Grigoli 2014).

- *Increased cost recovery in tertiary education.* Demand for tertiary education has increased rapidly and often faster than public financing capabilities. As a result, the quality of instruction in public institutions has declined and the number of private education institutions has risen (Woodhall 2007; OECD 2011b). Since much of the benefit from tertiary education accrues to graduates in the form of higher earnings and other nonmonetary benefits, a strong case can be made for financing more of this cost from tuition fees. Income-contingent student loans to cover tuition and subsistence costs allow students to begin paying off their loans once they start earning, ensuring that higher education is free at the point of use and providing insurance against the inability to repay because of low future income (Barr 2012). Increasing private financing also allows tertiary education to expand without increasing public spending.

- *Targeted conditional cash assistance.* As discussed above, targeting cash assistance to those with disadvantaged access to education, and conditioning this assistance on certain education outcomes, can help reduce income barriers to education and provide incentives for improved education achievement. Additional complementary reforms may also be necessary, such as targeted information campaigns and increasing the availability of shorter-term qualification options.

Health

Maintaining access to health care services for the poor during periods of expenditure constraint is consistent with efficient redistribution. Public health care spending is a large share of total public spending and is projected to rise by almost 3 percentage points of GDP between 2013 and 2030 (Clements, Coady, and Gupta 2012; IMF 2013b). Health care reforms to curb the growth of spending will be a necessary component of many countries' fiscal adjustment plans. Some of these reforms could take the form of an increase in cost sharing, for example, through increased copayments or a reduction in the scope of services provided by the public sector. These reforms could be designed to ensure that the poor maintain access to services, for example, by exempting them from copayments.

- *Reducing or eliminating user charges for low-income households.* Health services outside the affordable basic package could be financed by a mix of public and private mechanisms, including insurance contributions, fees, and copayments. However, out-of-pocket costs under the typical health insurance plan may still be too high for low-income households. Further improving the affordability of health care may require the reduction or elimination of user charges for certain groups. In particular, preventive care, such as immunizations, should be offered free of charge given its large social benefits. In addition, linking use of preventive care to eligibility for other social benefits could help increase coverage among low-income households.

- *Addressing supply-side barriers in less developed areas.* Since many low-income households reside in less developed areas or neighborhoods, availability of heath care facilities and health care professionals—of similar quality to those in more affluent areas—can be a major barrier to access. Overcoming this barrier may require public provision of health care as a last resort or additional incentives for service provision by private providers in these areas.

- *Improving efficiency.* Between 20 percent and 40 percent of the resources spent on health are wasted, including in advanced economies (WHO 2010). The inefficiencies in health spending suggest that there is ample room to improve health care outcomes, including for the poor, by increasing the efficiency of existing spending (Coady, Francese, and Shang 2014).

Social Protection

Appropriately designed pension reforms can perform an effective redistributive role while ensuring fiscal sustainability. Pension benefits account for about two-thirds of social protection spending and, in the absence of reforms, average pension spending is projected to rise by an additional 1½ percent of GDP by 2030 (Clements and others 2012). Pension systems play an important lifetime consumption-smoothing role by protecting the elderly from a sharp drop in consumption during retirement. Pensions account for more than half of the total redistributive impact of social transfers. At the same time, many economies will need to contain increases in pension spending in the coming decades to support fiscal consolidation. The following reform options could safeguard the redistributive role of pensions while containing the growth of spending:

- *Increasing the effective retirement age.* Gradual increases in the statutory retirement age reduce the need for other reforms that lower pension benefits and risk increasing old-age poverty (Shang 2014), and can also enhance employment and economic growth. Because lower-income groups tend to have shorter life expectancies than higher-income groups, an increase in the retirement age results in a proportionally larger reduction in their lifetime pension benefits. This outcome can be mitigated by linking pension eligibility to years of contribution instead of to a single statutory retirement age. Increases in the retirement age should also be accompanied by measures aimed at enhancing the earning opportunities for those approaching the statutory retirement age, especially the low skilled whose income potential can decline significantly as they approach retirement. In some economies, this may require strengthening of labor regulations protecting older workers, as well as retraining and adult education programs. Older workers should be protected fully by disability pensions where appropriate, and by social assistance programs to ensure that increases in retirement ages do not raise poverty rates. In addition, incentives and opportunities for early retirement (including through disability benefits) and disincentives to work beyond the statutory retirement age need to be reduced in many countries, for example, through concessional contribution rates and in-work benefits.

- *Incorporating pension incomes into a progressive income tax system.* In many countries, pensions enjoy favorable tax treatment.[4] In such cases, equalizing treatment across income sources by incorporating all pension benefits into the standard progressive income tax system can reduce the net fiscal cost of pension spending while protecting lower-income groups and lowering inequality.[5] In addition, countries that subsidize private pensions through tax relief or matching contributions should consider scaling these subsidies back

---

[4] In most countries, pension contributions are exempt from income taxation and pension benefits receive favorable tax treatment, for example, special deductions or income tax schedules based on age (IMF 2013b). Only 10 advanced and emerging economies (Austria, China, Chile, Denmark, France, Iceland, New Zealand, Poland, Russia, and Sweden) treat pensions like any other form of income, and some (notably, several emerging economies) fully exempt pension income from taxation.

[5] For instance, Moller (2012) shows that treating pensions like other forms of income in Colombia would reduce the Gini coefficient by 0.20 of a percentage point.

since these benefits accrue mostly to high-income groups and have little impact on national savings (European Commission 2008).

- *Making benefit cuts progressive.* Many parametric reforms contain spending pressures by reducing replacement rates (that is, the ratio of the average pension benefit to the average wage) over time. Where possible, these reductions should be progressive to avoid increases in poverty among the elderly. However, progressive benefit cuts require larger cuts in replacement rates for higher-income groups, and thus involve a trade-off between poverty-alleviation and consumption-smoothing objectives and may exacerbate compliance problems. If benefit cuts for lower-income groups are unavoidable, these groups need to have access to other social benefits to prevent them from falling into poverty. Addressing old-age poverty concerns through a means-tested social pension financed from general revenues would also allow the earnings-related component to achieve its broader consumption-smoothing objectives more efficiently, and it could be financed by revenue instruments that are more progressive than payroll taxes.

Family benefits can be made more efficient by greater use of means testing and by strengthening incentives to return to work. On average, in 2005 family benefits decreased the disposable-income Gini by nearly 1.5 percentage points, accounting for nearly three-quarters of the redistributive impact from total social assistance spending. These benefits include a range of transfers, such as paid maternal and paternal leave, child allowances, and child-care benefits. Parental leave schemes, for example, with a guarantee to young mothers that they can return to their previous jobs within a certain period, can help keep young mothers connected to the labor market. Child benefits facilitate consumption smoothing over the life cycle by transferring resources to families with children since children increase family needs and can also reduce second-earner incomes. These objectives can be more efficiently achieved by the following:

- *Means testing and conditioning of child benefits.* Large child allowances reduce incentives for women to enter the labor market, with detrimental effects for future earnings prospects. Linking benefits to labor force participation (including through child-care subsidies and child tax credits) can strengthen incentives to enter the labor market and decrease welfare dependency (Gong, Breunig, and King 2010; Kalb 2009; Elborgh-Woytek and others 2013). Expanding the role of means testing and including benefits in taxable income within a progressive tax schedule can make child benefits more progressive and could generate substantial savings given the very small share of these benefits that is currently means tested (Figure 3.7). Means testing also protects the consumption-smoothing role of these benefits since higher-income groups have greater consumption-smoothing opportunities.

- *Reducing the maximum duration of paid parental leave benefits.* Reducing the maximum duration in countries where paid parental leave is very long can increase incentives to return to employment. Jaumotte (2003) finds that parental leave has a positive effect on female labor supply up to a limit (20 weeks with full replacement of earnings); above this length, the marginal effect of further leave becomes negative. Appropriately designed parental leave benefits can also reduce poverty and welfare dependency, since long spells out of the workplace can have detrimental effects on future earnings potential. Capping leave benefits where they are earnings related can also increase benefit progressivity.

Countries could intensify the use of active labor market programs (ALMPs) and in-work benefits to address the work disincentives inherent in means-tested transfers. Guaranteed minimum income programs in many advanced economies aim to fill the gap between "needs" and "means." Although these programs may have only a small impact on inequality, reflecting low aggregate spending, they play a key role in addressing poverty. However, the withdrawal of benefits as individuals return to employment creates strong work disincentives, especially for

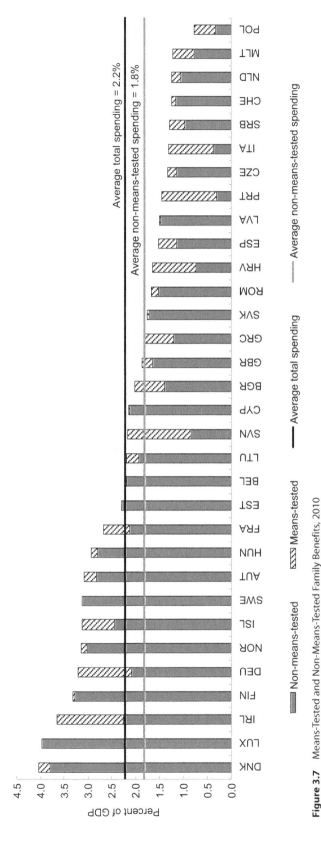

Figure 3.7 Means-Tested and Non-Means-Tested Family Benefits, 2010

Source: Eurostat.
Note: Labels in this figure use International Organization for Standardization (ISO) country codes.

low-wage workers and families with children. These disincentives can be reduced through the following:

- *Strict conditioning of eligibility for benefits on participation in ALMPs.* In most advanced economies, continued eligibility for benefits is conditioned on participation in ALMPs, including personal employment services, training, job placement, and public employment schemes. Tight activation measures are especially important for containing spending and providing incentives to work. The intensity of activation requirements should increase with unemployment duration to allow an initial period for job search, followed by assistance with job placement and access to training opportunities. Although the strictness of this conditioning has increased since the early 2000s, there is still significant room for improvement in many countries (OECD 2012).

- *Greater use of in-work benefits.* Many economies have adopted a system of in-work benefits that allows for the gradual withdrawal of benefits as earnings or employment duration increases (IMF 2012). This approach reduces the net tax on additional earnings, which can even be negative for low-income groups (Box 3.1). When combined with effective ALMPs, in-work benefits can have significant beneficial impacts on employment, inequality, and poverty. Containing the fiscal cost of in-work benefits requires that these benefits be withdrawn more rapidly as incomes increase, which may create work disincentives further up the income distribution (Box 3.1).

BOX 3.1 In-Work Benefits and Tax Credits

In-work benefits are used in many advanced economies to stimulate labor force participation and provide income support to low-income groups. In many countries these benefits take the form of tax credits, which constitute a net transfer to the individual when they exceed income tax liabilities. These benefits increase the net income gain from accepting a job relative to the alternative of being out of work and provide income support. In-work benefits are usually phased out as incomes rise, with the steepness of the phase out depending on the primary objective of the program. In countries that emphasize the labor force participation objective, benefits are usually gradually phased out with individual income (Belgium, Finland, Germany, the Netherlands, and Sweden). Minimum-hours-worked requirements are often used to prevent the provision of income support to high-skilled workers in part-time jobs. In countries that emphasize the income-support objective, benefits are often conditional on the presence of children in the household and generally phased out more steeply with family income to prevent leakage of benefits to higher-income families and reduce fiscal cost (Canada, France, Korea, New Zealand, the Slovak Republic, the United Kingdom, and the United States). However, the steep phasing out of benefits causes high marginal tax rates and creates strong adverse labor supply effects (de Mooij 2008).

Empirical studies suggest positive net employment effects from in-work credits. In the United Kingdom and the United States, evaluation studies find that programs have a positive net effect on employment, especially for single women with children (Hotz and Scholz 2003; Immervoll and Pearson 2009). Although negative labor supply effects have been found for those with income levels within the phase-out range, these effects were small (Eissa and Hoynes 2006). The aggregate effect on labor supply has been found to be quite small.

The use of in-work tax credits is most appropriate for countries with strong tax administrations based on the withholding of tax obligations. If most taxpayers are already filing tax returns, an effective withholding tax system is in place, and credits are provided on the same basis as the income tax (that is, individual or family based), the cost of administering in-work tax credits would be small. However, costs can be substantial if low-wage earners are currently not filing tax returns, there is no effective withholding system, or schemes are extended to the self-employed. In addition, it is important to ensure that the existence of other means-tested social benefits do not offset the positive work incentives from tax credits. If the earned income tax credit is based on self assessment, as in the United States, noncompliance and false claims (for example, regarding the number of qualifying children) can be a problem. Given the administrative capacity required to implement these programs, and their potentially large fiscal costs, in-work benefits are unlikely to be a viable option for many developing economies.

Unemployment benefits play a key role in protecting individuals from loss of income due to transitory or structural unemployment. However, these programs, if not well designed, can adversely affect employment incentives and outcomes (Meyer 2002; Abbring, van den Berg, and van Ours 2005; OECD 2006). By increasing work incentives, efficient benefit design can reduce spending while also decreasing income inequality, since unemployment benefits are typically below wages. The efficiency of unemployment benefits can be achieved through a number of design features, including the following:

- *Strict eligibility criteria.* Tightening eligibility rules (for example, based on past employment and contributions or mandatory participation in ALMPs) reduces fiscal costs by providing incentives to return to employment or by channeling more of the unemployed to social assistance with lower benefits.

- *Short duration.* Lowering the maximum duration of benefit eligibility can expedite the return to employment or the transition to social assistance. About a third of OECD countries have a maximum duration in excess of 12 months.

- *Declining benefit levels.* Reducing replacement rates with unemployment duration provides strong incentives to return to employment. The desired generosity of benefits can be achieved through various combinations of benefit level and duration.

Taxation

Although the primary contribution of taxation to the pursuit of equity goals is through the financing of public spending, taxes in themselves can also efficiently contribute to the achievement of redistributive goals. This depends on the progressivity of the personal income tax (PIT), the taxation of capital income and wealth concentrated among the better off, and the design of indirect taxes.

Personal Income Tax

The PIT is best equipped to tax people based on their ability to pay. Indeed, progressive PITs (usually in combination with income transfers) play a critical role in many countries in raising revenue while reflecting concerns about income inequality. The design of the PIT contains several elements:

- *Implementing progressive PIT rate structures can contribute to reducing inequality.* The median top PIT rate (based on a large group of economies across the globe) dropped from 59 percent in the early 1980s to 30 percent more recently. Since the mid 1990s, 27 countries—especially in central and eastern Europe and central Asia—have introduced flat tax systems, usually with a low marginal rate. These regimes are typically less redistributive than those with stepwise increasing PIT rates, especially for top incomes. In these and other economies with relatively low top PIT rates—or in economies in which the top PIT bracket starts at a relatively high level of income—there may be scope for more tax progressivity at the top. Note, however, that behavioral distortions impose an upper limit on how much these top PIT rates can be increased. For instance, IMF 2013b finds that revenue-maximizing PIT rates are probably somewhere between 50 percent and 60 percent—and optimal rates are probably somewhat lower than that, depending on the welfare weights assigned to the rich.

- *Increasing progressivity also requires reconsideration of tax deductions.* Many economies adopt various tax allowances in their PITs related to children, education, housing, health insurance, commuting, and charitable donations. Some of these allowances accrue disproportionately to the rich, such as deductions for mortgage interest: households with high incomes are more often homeowners, and tax relief is often granted in the form of deductions, which are worth more at higher marginal tax rates. Rationalizing mortgage interest deductibility could complement steps toward a more progressive tax system and also improve efficiency, since these deductions create their own distortions (IMF 2009). More generally, tax expenditures of this kind often result in significant revenue losses. In many countries, tax expenditures might not be subject to the same public scrutiny as ordinary public spending, especially when the government does not publish a tax expenditure review. Tax expenditures should undergo the same cost-benefit analysis as spending measures. Some, but not all, tax deductions might well be justified on the basis of their implications for equity and efficiency, such as deductions for charitable giving.

- *Reforming the PIT threshold can, in some cases, enhance tax progressivity.* A threshold—either in the form of a zero tax bracket, a basic deduction, or a general tax credit—supports tax progressivity by reducing or eliminating the tax burden on people with the lowest incomes. Thresholds vary significantly across economies. In the OECD, the median threshold is approximately 25 percent of the average wage. However, the threshold should not be too high to prevent greatly reduced revenues. Note also that tax credits are, in principle, more progressive than tax deductions, since the value of a credit does not depend on the marginal tax rate faced by the taxpayer, as does a deduction.

Capital Income Tax

Taxes on capital income can strengthen the progressivity of the tax system, but high rates can have substantial efficiency costs. Taxpayers who save and invest are generally among the better off, so even a proportional tax on capital income can increase progressivity. Moreover, capital income taxation is necessary to mitigate arbitrage in the taxation of entrepreneurial income because it is often difficult (or even impossible) to distinguish labor income from capital income earned by the owner-directors of a firm. Therefore, it is important to broadly harmonize the rates of the PIT and the combined burden of the corporate income tax (CIT) and dividend and capital gains taxation. However, capital income taxes, if too high, can have high efficiency costs because of their distortionary effects on savings and investment. Moreover, it can be administratively difficult to tax capital in light of its mobility, which leads to ample evasion and avoidance opportunities. In addition, the mobility of capital allows firms to shift a large share of the burden of these taxes onto labor. To strike the right balance between equity and efficiency, governments could consider the following options:

- *Tax different types of capital income in a neutral way.* Capital income is generally taxed at both corporate and personal levels. However, interest payments are usually deductible for the CIT (whereas returns on equity are not). In addition, some investors or investments are exempt from the PIT, and different types of capital income often face different PIT rates. As a result, interest received by individuals is often lightly taxed and dividends highly taxed, especially when compared with the taxation applied to capital gains. These differences give rise to arbitrage and lead to behavioral changes that erode the capital tax base and create economic distortions; in addition, these differences lead to horizontal inequity, that is, the unequal taxation of individuals with similar incomes and assets.

- *Consider implementing a lower effective rate on capital income than on labor income.* Several economies impose a lower overall tax rate on capital income than on labor income. For example, in dual income tax systems, capital income is separated from labor income and taxed at a uniform and relatively low rate (Cnossen 2000; Sorensen 2005). Some economies also give targeted relief for the normal return on capital through an allowance at either the corporate level (such as Belgium and Italy) or the personal level (such as Norway).

- *Adopt withholding taxes, especially if administration is weak.* Taxing capital income at the individual level can be administratively challenging, thus providing a rationale for withholding at the level of the firm, that is, through the CIT. In countries with weak tax administration, withholding taxes on interest and dividends can, to some extent, further circumvent administrative difficulties. Some Latin American countries also impose withholding taxes on capital gains.

- *Develop more effective taxation of multinational business income.* Multinational corporations use a variety of tax-planning strategies to reduce their global tax liabilities, leading to profit shifting and erosion of the tax base. The Group of 20 and the OECD have an action plan on "Base Erosion and Profit Shifting," which aims to address some of these challenges (OECD 2013). IMF (2014) explores the broader context of spillovers from the taxation of multinationals.

- *Automatically exchange information internationally.* Information sharing has been announced by the Group of 20 as the new global standard and can enable economies to more effectively impose residence-based capital income taxes by mitigating international tax evasion and avoidance (Keen and Ligthart 2005). Some progress has been made in this regard, led by the OECD's Global Forum on Transparency and Information Exchange. Unilateral measures are also proceeding, notably the U.S. Foreign Account Tax Compliance Act, which envisages penalties for noncompliance.

Wealth Taxes

Wealth taxes, especially on immovable property, are also an option for economies seeking more progressive taxation. Wealth taxes of various kinds target the same underlying base as capital income taxes, namely assets. These taxes could thus be considered a potential source of progressive taxation, especially in countries in which taxes on capital incomes (including on real estate) are low or largely evaded. The different types of wealth taxes include recurrent taxes on property or net wealth, transaction taxes, and inheritance and gift taxes. Revenue from these taxes has not kept up with the surge in wealth as a share of GDP since the early 1970s (see earlier discussion); as a result, the effective tax rate has dropped from an average of about 0.9 percent in 1970 to approximately 0.5 percent more recently. Ways to raise additional revenue from the various types of wealth taxation include the following (and are also discussed in Chapter 7):

- *Property taxes are equitable and efficient, but underutilized in many economies.* The average property tax yield in 65 economies (for which data are available) in the 2000s was about 1 percent of GDP. There is considerable scope to exploit this tax more fully, both as a revenue source and as a redistributive instrument, although effective implementation would require a sizable investment in administrative infrastructure (Norregaard 2013).

- *Recurrent taxes on net wealth generally raise little revenue.* Financial wealth is mobile and taxes are hard to enforce because they are easily evaded. Few advanced economies today have recurrent taxes on broad measures of net wealth and, where they exist, revenue is typically low. More effective exchange of information across economies could help mitigate evasion and improve the prospect for net wealth taxes to increase revenue yields. If evasion can be forestalled, wealth taxes have some appeal as an instrument to reduce wealth inequality and support equality of opportunity.

- *Taxes on inheritances and gifts could play a useful role in limiting intergenerational inequality and strengthening equality of opportunity* (Boadway, Chamberlain, and Emmerson 2010). However, where such taxes exist, rates are generally low, exemptions and special arrangements widespread, and revenue yields small. In the OECD countries, revenue has declined from 0.35 percent of GDP in 1970 to less than 0.15 percent in recent years. France and Belgium, where revenue yields are, respectively, 0.40 and 0.65 percent of GDP, illustrate that more potential from these taxes may be available.

- *Transaction taxes on property and financial assets are administratively appealing*, since transactions can often be easily observed and administered. However, such taxes are economically distortive because they impede otherwise mutually beneficial trades. Transaction taxes on real estate can thus reduce labor mobility and raise unemployment. Financial transaction taxes (FTT) have been much discussed in the aftermath of the financial crisis, including in the European Union, where 11 member states have plans to introduce broad-based FTTs. However, FTTs can have significant social costs due to cascading effects (tax levied on tax), increased costs of capital, avoidance schemes, and the potential that they would impede socially worthwhile transactions. Moreover, their distributional impact is unclear because the incidence may be shifted onto consumers (Matheson 2012).

Consumption Taxes

Consumption taxes are generally inferior for achieving redistributive objectives compared with income-related taxes and transfers. As discussed earlier in the chapter, the VAT is generally regressive in advanced economies—at least when measured as a percentage of current income rather than current consumption. Excises also tend to bear relatively more heavily on people with low incomes in advanced economies (Cnossen 2005). Regarding the design of indirect taxes, the following recommendations apply:

- *Minimize the use of exemptions or reduced VAT rates.* Exemptions or reduced rates on necessities, such as food or energy, are often used to mitigate the regressive impact of the VAT in advanced countries, given that expenditure shares of these goods are generally higher for the poor. However, such policies are blunt redistributive instruments, because the rich generally spend more in absolute terms on these goods and thus enjoy significant benefits. Advanced economies usually have access to better instruments for helping the poor and vulnerable, such as targeted transfers and progressive PIT systems. For instance, Crawford, Keen, and Smith (2010) find that elimination of reduced VAT rates in the United Kingdom, and the use of the proceeds to increase social benefits, would significantly reduce inequality while also boosting revenue.

- *Set a sufficiently high VAT registration threshold.* Small traders bear a significant compliance burden for the VAT, which they would likely partly pass on to consumers in the form of higher prices (Ebrill and others 2001). A threshold aims to reduce the compliance cost of the VAT for small traders, and the revenue forgone is typically not much higher (or may even be lower) than the cost of collection. A threshold can also strengthen the progressivity of the VAT by reducing the tax on small traders in rural areas where VAT compliance is particularly problematic.

- *Use specific excises mainly for purposes other than redistribution.* Specific excises on cigarettes, alcoholic beverages, gambling, and motor fuels should be viewed as corrective tools designed to alter individual behavior in a way that is socially desirable. For example, greater taxation of energy (including through carbon taxation) can help address carbon emissions and various local pollution externalities and generate a significant amount of revenue. Although low-income groups would suffer a decline in real incomes with rising energy prices, mitigating measures targeted to lower-income groups could be introduced to offset any undesired effects on income distribution (Metcalf 2007; Clements and others 2013). Special excises on luxury goods, such as yachts, jewelry, or perfume, typically contribute little to achieving equity objectives, raise little revenue, and add to administrative costs, with the exception of taxes on motor vehicles.

CONCLUSION

In many advanced economies, inequality has been rising and this has coincided with growing public support for income redistribution. This comes at a time when many advanced economies are facing a sluggish economic recovery from the global financial crisis, taxes and social spending are already high, and public debt remains elevated. This renders it especially important that redistributive objectives be achieved at a minimum cost to economic efficiency.

While other policy instruments such as labor market regulations can also be used to achieve redistributive goals, fiscal policy is the primary tool with which governments can affect income distribution. Indeed, fiscal policy has played a significant role in reducing income inequality in advanced economies. Direct income taxes and transfers have reduced inequality by about one-third, and in-kind transfers have lowered inequality by another 15 percent.

Redistributive tax and expenditure policies need to be carefully designed to balance distributional and efficiency objectives. Priority should be given to policies that can both reduce inequality and improve efficiency. For example, improving the access of lower-income groups to higher education and maintaining their access to health services could help improve the earnings potential for children from low-income families and reduce inequality of opportunity. Such in-kind transfers could also improve economic efficiency as these children would be more productive in their lives and make larger contributions to the economy and society. Pension systems also play an important role in helping households smooth consumption over their life spans. For long-term sustainability, pension systems need to keep retirement ages in line with life expectancy, with adequate provisions for the poor whose life expectancies could be shorter. If additional redistribution is desired by society, the revenues would need to be raised with the least distortionary effect and the transfer system targeted to keep fiscal costs low while avoiding adverse effects on employment. This includes implementing progressive PIT rate structures, reducing regressive tax exemptions, and using means testing with a gradual phasing out of benefits as incomes rise. In addition, greater use of taxes on property and energy could also be considered.

REFERENCES

Abbring, J., G. van den Berg, and J. van Ours. 2005. "The Effect of Unemployment Insurance Sanctions on the Transition Rate from Unemployment to Employment." *Economic Journal* 115 (5): 602–30.

Atkinson, A., T. Piketty, and E. Saez. 2011. "Top Incomes in the Long Run of History." *Journal of Economic Literature* 49 (1): 3–71.

Barr, N. 2012. *Economics of the Welfare State*. Oxford: Oxford University Press.

Björklund, A. 1993. "A Comparison of Actual Distributions of Actual and Lifetime Incomes: Sweden 1951–1989." *Review of Income and Wealth* 39 (4): 377–86.

Boadway, R., E. Chamberlain, and C. Emmerson. 2010. "Taxation of Wealth and Wealth Transfers." In *Dimensions of Tax Design*, edited by J. Mirrlees, S. Adam, T. Besley, R. Blundell, S. Bond, R. Chote, M. Gammie, P. Johnson, G. Miles, and J. Poterba. London: The Mirrlees Review, Institute for Fiscal Studies.

Boadway, Robin, and Michael Keen. 2000. "Redistribution." In *Handbook of Income Distribution*, Volume 1, edited by A. B. Atkinson and F. Bourguignon, 677–789. Amsterdam: Elsevier.

Bovenberg, A. L., M. I. Hansen, and P. B. Sorenson. 2012. "Efficient Redistribution of Lifetime Income through Welfare Accounts." *Fiscal Studies* 33 (1): 1–37.

Bowlus, A., and J. M. Robin. 2012. "An International Comparison of Lifetime Inequality: How Continental Europe Resembles North America." *Journal of the European Economic Association* 10 (6): 1236–62.

Caminada, K., K. Goudswaard, and C. Wang. 2012. "Disentangling Income Inequality and the Redistributive Effect of Taxes and Transfers in 20 LIS Countries over Time." LIS Working Paper No. 581, Luxembourg Income Study, Luxembourg.

Clements, B., D. Coady, F. Eich, S. Gupta, A. Kangur, B. Shang, and M. Soto. 2012. "The Challenge of Public Pension Reform in Advanced and Emerging Market Economies." IMF Occasional Paper No. 275, International Monetary Fund, Washington.

Clements, B., D. Coady, S. Fabrizio, S. Gupta, T. Alleyne, and C. Sdralevich, eds. 2013. *Energy Subsidy Reform: Lessons and Implications*. Washington: International Monetary Fund.

Clements, B., D. Coady, and S. Gupta, eds. 2012. *The Economics of Public Health Care Reform in Advanced and Emerging Economies*. Washington: International Monetary Fund.

Cnossen, S. 2000. "Taxing Capital Income in the Nordic Countries: A Model for the European Union?" In *Taxing Capital Income in the European Union—Issues and Options for Reform*, edited by S. Cnossen. Oxford: Oxford University Press.

————. 2005. *Theory and Practice of Excise Taxation: Smoking, Drinking, Gambling, Polluting, and Driving.* Oxford: Oxford University Press.

Coady, David, Maura Francese, and Baoping Shang. 2014. "The Efficiency Imperative: Public Health Spending Must Become More Efficient to Avoid Overwhelming Government Coffers." *Finance and Development* 51 (4).

Corak, M. 2013. "Income Inequality, Equality of Opportunity, and Intergenerational Mobility." *Journal of Economic Perspectives* 27 (3): 79–102.

Crawford, I., M. Keen, and S. Smith. 2010. "Value Added Taxes and Excises." In *Dimensions of Tax Design*, edited by J. Mirrlees, S. Adam, T. Besley, R. Blundell, S. Bond, R. Chote, M. Gammie, P. Johnson, G. Miles, and J. Poterba. London: The Mirrlees Review, Institute for Fiscal Studies.

Davies, J. B., S. Sandstrom, A. Shorrocks, and E. N. Wolff. 2008. "The World Distribution of Household Wealth." UNU-WIDER Discussion Paper No. 2008/03, United Nations University, Helsinki.

De Gregorio, J., and J.-W. Lee. 2002. "Education and Income Inequality: New Evidence from Cross Country Data." *Review of Income and Wealth* 48 (3): 395–416.

de Mooij, R. 2008." Reinventing the Dutch Tax-Benefit System: Exploring the Frontier of the Equity-Efficiency Trade-Off." *International Tax and Public Finance* 15 (1): 87–103.

Easterly, W. 2007. "Inequality Does Cause Underdevelopment: Insights from a New Instrument." *Journal of Development Economics* 84 (2): 755–76.

Ebrill, L., M. Keen, J. P. Bodin, and V. Summers. 2001. *The Modern VAT.* Washington: International Monetary Fund.

Eissa, N., and H. W. Hoynes. 2006. "The Hours of Work Response of Married Couples: Taxes and the Earned Income Tax Credit." In *Tax Policy and Labor Market Performance*, edited by Jonas Agell and Peter Birch Sorensen. Cambridge, Massachusetts: MIT Press.

Elborgh-Woytek, K., M. Newiak, K. Kochhar, S. Fabrizio, K. Kpodar, P. Wingender, B. Clements, and G. Schwartz. 2013. "Women, Work, and the Economy: Macroeconomic Gains from Gender Equity." IMF Staff Discussion Note No. 13/10, International Monetary Fund, Washington.

European Commission. 2008. "Privately Managed Funded Pension Provision and their Contribution to Adequate and Sustainable Pensions," The Social Protection Committee. http://ec.europa.eu/social/BlobServlet?docId=743&langId=en.

Fredriksen, K. B. 2012. "Less Income Inequality and More Growth—Are They Compatible?" Part 6, "The Distribution of Wealth." OECD Economics Department Working Paper No. 929, Organisation for Economic Co-operation and Development, Paris.

Gong, X., R. Breunig, and A. King. 2010. "How Responsive Is Female Labour Supply to Child Care Costs: New Australian Estimates." IZA Discussion Paper No. 5119, Institute for the Study of Labor, Bonn.

Grigoli, F. 2014. "A Hybrid Approach to Estimating the Efficiency of Public Spending on Education in Emerging and Developing Economies." Working Paper No. 14/19, International Monetary Fund, Washington.

Gupta, S., G. Schwartz, S. Tareq, R. Allen, I. Adenauer, K. Fletcher, and D. Last. 2007. "Fiscal Management of Scaled-Up Aid." IMF Working Paper No. 07/222, International Monetary Fund, Washington.

Hotz, V. Joseph, and John Karl Scholz. 2003. "The Earned Income Tax Credit." In *Means-Tested Transfer Programs in the United States*, edited by R. Moffitt, 141–97. Chicago: University of Chicago Press.

Immervoll, H., H. Levy, C. Lietz, D. Mantovani, C. O'Donoghue, H. Sutherland, and G. Verbist. 2005. "Household Incomes and Redistribution in the European Union: Quantifying the Equalising Properties of Taxes and Benefits." EUROMOD Working Paper EM9/05, University of Essex.

Immervoll, H., and M. Pearson. 2009. "A Good Time for Making Work Pay? Taking Stock of In-Work Benefits and Related Measures across the OECD." OECD Social, Employment and Migration Working Paper No. 81 and IZA Policy Paper No. 3, Organisation for Economic Co-operation and Development, Paris.

International Monetary Fund. 2009. "Debt Bias and Other Distortions: Crisis-Related Issues in Tax Policy." Policy Paper, Washington. www.imf.org/external/np/pp/eng/2009/061209.pdf.

————. 2012. "Fiscal Policy and Employment in Advanced and Emerging Economies." Policy Paper, Washington. http://www.imf.org/external/pp/longres.aspx?id=4668.

————. 2013a. "Fiscal Policy and Income Inequality." Policy Paper, Washington. http://www.imf.org/external/np/pp/eng/2014/012314.pdf.

————. 2013b. *Fiscal Monitor: Taxing Times.* Washington, October. www.imf.org/external/pubs/ft/fm/2013/02/pdf/fm1302.pdf.

————. 2014. "Spillovers in International Corporate Taxation." Policy Paper, Washington.

Jaumotte, F. 2003. "Female Labour Force Participation: Past Trends and Main Determinants in OECD Countries." OECD Economics Department Working Paper No. 376, Organisation for Economic Co-operation and Development, Paris.

Kalb, G. 2009. "Children, Labour Supply and Childcare: Challenges for Empirical Analysis." *Australian Economic Review* 42 (3): 276–99.

Keen, M., and J. Ligthart. 2005. "Coordinating Tariff Reduction and Domestic Tax Reform." *Journal of International Economics* 56 (2): 489–507.

Krueger, A. 2012. "The Rise and Consequences of Inequality in the United States." Paper presented to the Center for American Progress, Washington, January 12.

Kumhof, M., and R. Rancière. 2011. "Inequality, Leverage and Crises." IMF Working Paper No. 10/268, International Monetary Fund, Washington.

Matheson, T. 2012. "Security Transaction Taxes: Issues and Evidence." *International Tax and Public Finance* 19 (6): 884–912.

Metcalf, G. 2007. "A Proposal for a US Carbon Tax Swap: An Equitable Tax Reform to Address Climate Change." The Brookings Institution, Washington.

Meyer, B. 2002. "Unemployment and Workers' Compensation Programmes: Rationale, Design, Labor Supply and Income Support." *Fiscal Studies* 23 (1): 1–49.

Moller, L. C. 2012. "Fiscal Policy in Colombia: Tapping Its Potential for a More Equitable Society." World Bank Working Paper No. 67623, World Bank, Washington.

Norregaard, J. 2013. "Taxing Immovable Property: Revenue Potential and Implementation Challenges." IMF Working Paper No. 13/129, International Monetary Fund, Washington.

O'Donoghue, Cathal, Massimo Baldini, and Daniela Mantovani. 2004. "Modelling the Redistributive Impact of Indirect Taxes in Europe: An Application of EUROMOD." EUROMOD Working Papers EM7/01, EUROMOD at the Institute for Social and Economic Research, University of Essex.

Organisation for Economic Co-operation and Development (OECD). 2006. *OECD Employment Outlook: Boosting Jobs and Incomes.* Paris: OECD Publishing.

———. 2011a. *Divided We Stand: Why Inequality Keeps Rising.* Paris: Organisation for Economic Co-operation and Development. http://dx.doi.org/10.1787/9789264119536-en.

———. 2011b. *Education at a Glance 2011: OECD Indicators.* Paris: OECD Publishing. http://dx.doi.org/10.1787/eag-2011-en.

———. 2012. "Income Inequality and Growth: The Role of Taxes and Transfers." OECD Economics Department Policy Notes No. 9, Paris.

———. 2013. *Action Plan on Base Erosion and Profit Shifting.* Paris: OECD Publishing.

Ostry, Jonathan, Andrew Berg, and Charalambos Tsangarides. 2014. "Redistribution, Inequality, and Growth." IMF Staff Discussion Note 14/2, International Monetary Fund, Washington.

Paglin, M. 1975. "The Measurement and Trend of Inequality: A Basic Revision." *American Economic Review* 65 (4): 598–609.

Paulus, A., M. Čok, F. Figari, P. Hegedüs, N. Kump, O. Lelkes, H. Levy, C. Lietz, S. Lüpsik, D. Mantovani, L. Morawski, H. Sutherland, P. Szivos, and A. Võrk. 2009. "The Effects of Taxes and Benefits on Income Distribution in the Enlarged EU." EUROMOD Working Paper No. EM8/09, University of Essex.

Paulus, Alar, Holly Sutherland, and Panos Tsakloglou. 2009. "The Distributional Impact of In Kind Public Benefits in European Countries." EUROMOD Working Papers No. EM10/09, EUROMOD at the Institute for Social and Economic Research, University of Essex.

Piketty, T., and G. Zucman. 2013. "Capital Is Back: Wealth-Income Ratios in Rich Countries 1700–2010." Paris School of Economics.

Pew Research Center. 2014. "Emerging and Developing Economies Much More Optimistic than Rich Countries about the Future: Education, Hard Work Considered Key to Success, but Inequality Still a Challenge." Pew Research Center, Washington.

Rajan, R. 2010. *Fault Lines.* Princeton, New Jersey: Princeton University Press.

Shang, B. 2014. "Pension Reform and Equity: The Impact of Reducing Pension Benefits on Poverty." In *Equitable and Sustainable Pensions: Challenges and Experience*, edited by Benedict Clements, Frank Eich, and Sanjeev Gupta. Washington: International Monetary Fund.

Sorensen, P. B. 2005. "Dual Income Taxation: Why and How?" CESifo Working Paper No. 1551, Munich.

Woodhall, M. 2007. "Funding Higher Education: The Contribution of Economic Thinking to Debate and Policy Development." Education Working Paper Series No. 8, World Bank, Washington.

World Economic Forum. 2014. "Outlook on the Global Agenda 2015." World Economic Forum, Geneva.

World Health Organization (WHO). 2010. *World Health Report—Health System Financing: The Path to Universal Coverage.* Geneva: World Health Organization.

CHAPTER 4

Fiscal Redistribution in Developing Countries: Overview of Policy Issues and Options

FRANCESCA BASTAGLI, DAVID COADY, AND SANJEEV GUPTA

INTRODUCTION

The developing world has experienced sustained economic growth and poverty reduction during the past two decades. Globally, income inequality has also been on a steady downward trend driven by relatively high growth in developing countries and a decline in between-country income inequality (Pinkovskiy and Sala-i-Martin 2009). However, the persistence of high, and often rising, income inequality in many developing countries is a growing concern for policymakers and the public. In a survey of policymakers in Asia, about 70 percent of respondents answered that concerns about income inequality had increased during the past decade, and more than half disagreed with the statement that rising income inequality is acceptable so long as poverty is declining (Kanbur, Rhee, and Zhuang 2014). A public opinion survey in Latin America found that about 90 percent of the population regarded the existing income distribution in their country as unfair or very unfair (Latinobarómetro 2003). Evidence from public surveys also indicates that widening income inequality has been accompanied by growing public demand for income redistribution across the developing world (IMF 2014a).

This chapter discusses the role of fiscal policy in reducing income inequality in developing countries. The objective is to provide an overview of issues that arise in the context of designing redistributive fiscal policies rather than to provide an exhaustive review of country studies. It adds to the existing literature on fiscal redistribution in developing economies by taking a global (as opposed to regional) developing-country perspective of fiscal redistribution.[1] It discusses how tax and spending policies can be designed to minimize the trade-off between efficiency and equity objectives, emphasizing the importance of taking a comprehensive approach that considers the combined redistributive and efficiency impacts of taxes and spending, and of encompassing both design and administration issues. In practice, since existing tax and spending policies in many developing economies suffer from numerous design and implementation inefficiencies, fiscal reforms that improve the redistributive impact of fiscal policy can actually be efficiency enhancing.

The chapter is structured as follows: The available empirical evidence on the level and trends in income inequality in developing countries over recent decades is reviewed. The extent of fiscal redistribution in developing countries is discussed. How the redistributive role of fiscal policy can be enhanced in developing countries while containing any efficiency-equity trade-offs is then addressed, followed by a summary of the findings.

---

[1] For a regional perspective, see Claus, Martinez-Vazquez, and Vulovic 2014 for Asia; Cubero and Hollar 2011 for Central America; and Breceda, Rigolini, and Saavedra 2009 and Lustig, Pessino, and Scott 2014 for Latin America and the Caribbean.

TABLE 4.1

Changes in Disposable Income Inequality, 1990–2010 *(Percentage point change in Gini coefficient)*

	Large Increase (Change ≥ 5)	Medium Increase (3 ≤ Change < 5)	Small Increase (0 < Change < 3)	Small Decrease (−3 < Change ≤ 0)	Medium Decrease (−5 < Change ≤ −3)	Large Decrease (Change ≤ −5)
Latin America and the Caribbean	Paraguay	Costa Rica, Colombia	Uruguay, Honduras, Jamaica, Guatemala	Dominican Republic, Argentina	Venezuela, Mexico, Panama	Chile, Peru, El Salvador, Brazil, Ecuador, Bolivia, Nicaragua
Sub-Saharan Africa	Rwanda, Ghana, South Africa	Côte d'Ivoire, Nigeria, Tanzania	Zambia, Mozambique	Burundi, Uganda, Madagascar, Niger, Cameroon		Central African Republic, Lesotho, Ethiopia, Guinea, Kenya, Swaziland, Burkina Faso, Senegal, Mali
Asia and the Pacific	China, Sri Lanka, Lao P.D.R., Indonesia	Mongolia, Taiwan Province of China, Bangladesh	India, Nepal	Cambodia, Malaysia, Vietnam, Philippines	Thailand	
Middle East and North Africa	Turkmenistan, Kyrgyz Republic, Uzbekistan, Israel		Tajikistan, Morocco, Tunisia	Mauritania, Egypt	Pakistan	Jordan, Iran
Emerging Europe	Lithuania, Croatia, Latvia, FYR Macedonia, Slovak Republic, Czech Republic, Albania, Poland	Moldova, Belarus, Georgia, Kazakhstan	Bulgaria, Ukraine, Slovenia	Azerbaijan, Hungary	Turkey	Serbia, Estonia, Armenia

Source: Bastagli, Coady, and Gupta (2012).

INCOME INEQUALITY IN DEVELOPING COUNTRIES

Over recent decades, inequality in the distribution of per capita income has increased in many countries across the developing world. Table 4.1 reports the percentage point change in the Gini coefficient between 1990 and 2010 by country and shows that 46 countries out of the 89 developing countries for which data over this time span are available experienced an increase in inequality.[2] Some 20 countries, including large developing countries such as China, Indonesia, and South Africa, experienced increases of more than 5 percentage points. Inequality rose in most countries in Asia and the Pacific and in the Middle East and North Africa. Although average inequality fell in sub-Saharan Africa during this period, it still rose by more than 3 percentage points in more than one-fourth of these economies. Inequality also increased in more than one-third of countries in Latin American and the Caribbean, although, on average, it declined slightly. However, since 2000, the Gini coefficient has steadily declined in nearly all countries in Latin American and the Caribbean.

More striking are the persistent differences across regions. Figure 4.1 presents the most recent data available on income inequality for advanced and developing countries, clearly showing a large gap. These regional differences are much more significant than the increase in average income inequality in recent decades. Based on the data in Table 4.1, between 1990 and 2010 the average inequality in each region changed by less than 3.25 percentage points. In contrast, average inequality in the two most unequal regions (sub-Saharan Africa and Latin America and the Caribbean) remained 12 percentage points higher than the two most equal regions (emerging Europe and the advanced economies).

---

[2] In this chapter, the term "developing" countries includes emerging market European countries.

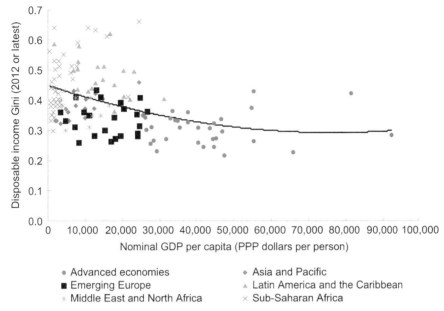

Figure 4.1   Disposable Income Inequality in Advanced and Developing Countries

Source: Authors' calculations based on data from Bastagli, Coady, and Gupta (2012).
Note: PPP = purchasing power parity.

REDISTRIBUTIVE FISCAL POLICY IN DEVELOPING COUNTRIES

The redistributive impact of fiscal policy depends not only on the *magnitude* of tax and spending but also on the *composition* of tax and spending (for example, the relative balance between indirect and direct taxes or between universal or means-tested transfers). If the combined redistributive impact of tax and spending is progressive, then the higher the level of tax and spending in a country the larger is the redistributive impact. Similarly, for a given level of tax and spending, the more that revenue collection is concentrated in redistributive taxes (for example, progressive income taxes) and the more that spending is concentrated in redistributive transfers (for example, well-targeted social transfers), the greater the redistributive impact of fiscal policy.

The evidence presented in the previous chapter clearly shows that fiscal policy has played a significant redistributive role in advanced countries, with direct income taxes and transfers reducing the income Gini coefficient by an average of about one-third, with the transfer side accounting for two-thirds of this. The potential redistributive impact of fiscal policies in developing countries is substantially reduced compared with advanced economies, reflecting differences in both the levels and the composition of tax and spending. Figure 4.2 presents the *magnitude* of tax and social spending in advanced and developing countries. Whereas average tax ratios for advanced economies exceed 30 percent of GDP, ratios in developing economies generally fall in the range 15–20 percent of GDP.[3] As a result, social spending, which includes social protection

---

[3] Although total revenue (which includes nontax revenues and external grants) is higher in all regions, the pattern across regions is similar with the exception of countries in the Middle East and North Africa, where total revenues are, on average, closer to the higher levels observed in many advanced and emerging European economies.

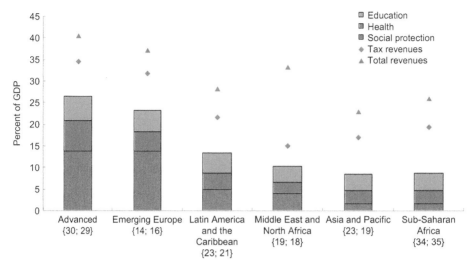

Figure 4.2   Levels and Composition of Tax Revenues and Social Spending, 2010

Source: IMF database.
Note: Numbers in brackets refer to number of countries in the {tax; spending} country samples.

spending as well as education and health spending, is also substantially lower in developing economies, but especially in Asia and the Pacific and in sub-Saharan Africa.

The redistributive implications of lower tax and spending can be seen by comparing the redistributive impact of fiscal policy in Latin America (the region with the highest average level of income inequality, and higher tax and spending levels compared with other developing countries) with the impact in advanced economies (the region with the lowest average level of income inequality).[4] The average Gini coefficients of market income for a sample of advanced and Latin American economies were 0.46 and 0.53, respectively (Figure 4.3). The corresponding coefficients for disposable income were 0.29 and 0.49, respectively. Therefore, whereas income taxes and transfers reduced the Gini by 0.17 in the sample of advanced economies, it decreased it by only 0.04 in the sample of Latin American economies. In other words, about two-thirds (0.13 out of 0.20) of the difference in average inequality of disposable income between advanced and Latin American countries is explained by differences in the redistributive impact of taxes and transfers.

The *composition* of tax and social spending in developing economies also reduces the redistributive impact of fiscal policy. On the tax side, the redistributive impact is limited by greater reliance on indirect taxes (Figure 4.4). Overall, indirect taxes tend to be either slightly progressive or slightly regressive, and therefore have only a small impact on income distribution (Chu, Davoodi, and Gupta 2004; Gemmell and Morrissey 2005; Coady 2006). Income taxes, however, have been found to be progressive (Gemmell and Morrissey 2005). Within indirect taxes, trade (mainly import) taxes also have a relatively high share, especially in low-income countries, although this share has been decreasing in recent decades. Incidence studies have typically found

---

[4] Such a comparison is not possible for other regions given the absence of comprehensive country studies of the redistributive impact of taxes and transfers.

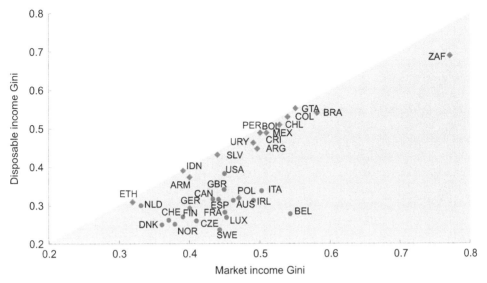

Figure 4.3 Redistributive Impact of Income Taxes and Transfers in Advanced and Developing Countries, Mid-2000s

Sources: Lustig, Pessino, and Scott (2014); Goñi, López, and Servén (2011).
Note: Diamonds denote developing countries and circles advanced economies. Data labels in the figure use International Organization for Standardization (ISO) country codes.

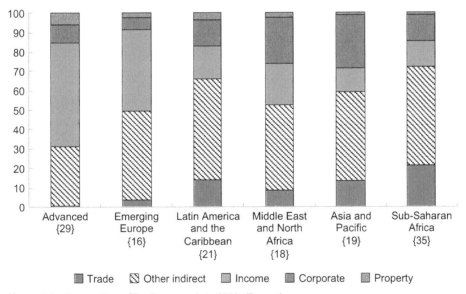

Figure 4.4 Composition of Tax Revenues, Late 2000s *(Percent)*

Source: IMF database.
Note: Numbers in brackets denote country sample size.

that import taxes are regressive,[5] while excise taxes—such as fuel, alcohol, and tobacco excises—tend to be progressive. The distributive impact of value-added taxes has been found to be mixed (Bird and Zolt 2005; Coady 2006); while Sahn and Younger (1999) find that the value-added tax is progressive in some African countries, other studies have found that it can be less progressive than the consumption taxes it has replaced, so that such reforms can be on net regressive (Munoz and Cho 2003; Hossain 1995, 2003; Tareq and others 2005). However, these studies also find that the progressivity of a value-added tax can be enhanced through the adoption of lower rates for basic goods or by setting the registration threshold high enough to exclude most small-scale enterprises, which tend to be used more intensively by lower-income groups (Jenkins, Jenkins, and Kuo 2006).[6]

Although spending on education and health can decrease income inequality and poverty in the medium term by increasing the future incomes of lower-income groups (De Gregorio and Lee 2002), it does not decrease current disposable income inequality (it may, however, free up resources for other consumption). Thus, the high share allocated to education and health spending can introduce a trade-off between lower current income inequality and lower future income inequality. However, existing benefit-incidence studies show that the redistributive impact of education and health spending in the medium term is compromised by the regressivity of this spending in many developing countries, but especially in low-income countries where access levels are much lower for poor households (Figure 4.5).[7] But increases in in-kind spending to finance the *expansion* of basic education and health services are likely to be much more progressively distributed than existing spending so that the average progressivity of spending should increase over time (van de Walle 1995).

The much lower coverage of social insurance (mainly pensions) in developing countries, especially among lower-income groups, is a key factor behind the lower redistributive impact of social spending. In most developing economies, participation in social insurance schemes is restricted to workers in the formal sector and to public sector employees. Data for the early 2000s show that the share of the population older than the legal retirement age in receipt of a pension in developing economies was, on average, about 40 percent in the Middle East and North Africa and in Latin America and the Caribbean, and about 25 percent in Asia and the Pacific and in sub-Saharan Africa, as compared with 90 percent in European economies (ILO 2010). With coverage heavily skewed toward higher-income groups, lower-income groups receive a very small share of the benefits—in more than half of a sample of developing countries with data, fewer than 10 percent of the poorest 40 percent of households received a social insurance benefit, and these households received less than 10 percent of total social insurance spending (Figure 4.6, panel 1).

Low social assistance spending in most developing economies results in low coverage of the poor and substantial leakage of benefits to the non-poor—in more than half of the countries for which data are available, fewer than half of the poorest 20 percent of households received some social assistance, and these households received less than a quarter of total assistance spending

---

[5] However, studies using general equilibrium models tend to find that import taxes on unskilled-labor-intensive goods (for example, food) are highly progressive because of large increases in unskilled wages (Hertel and Reimer 2005). However, these taxes are also extremely inefficient since they distort production and consumption decisions. In addition, they are extremely blunt redistributive instruments because they tend to benefit some poor households while hurting other poor households (Coady, Dorosh, and Minten 2009).

[6] The results from computable general equilibrium models also support the findings that excise taxes are progressive and that the distributional implications of the value-added tax depend on how basic foods are treated (see Coady 2006 for a review).

[7] In health, the progressivity of primary health care spending is dominated by the regressivity of higher-level health spending. In education, the progressivity of primary education spending is dominated by the regressivity of secondary and tertiary education spending. See Demery 2000 for more details.

1. Education

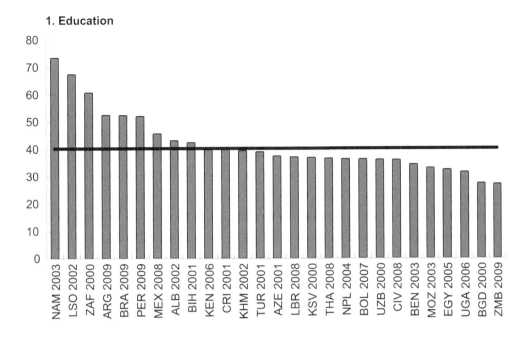

2. Health

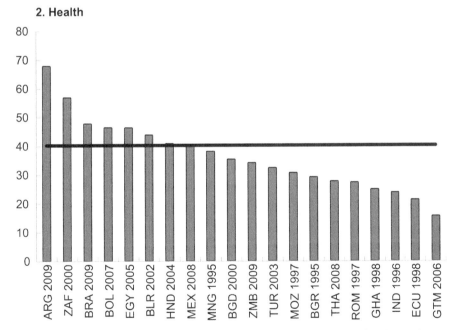

Figure 4.5   Average Benefit Incidence for Education and Health Spending *(Percent of public spending going to poorest 40 percent of households)*

Sources: Davoodi, Tiongson, and Asawanuchit (2010); Lustig and others (2011); and data provided by the World Bank.
Note: Data labels in the figure use International Organization for Standardization (ISO) country codes.

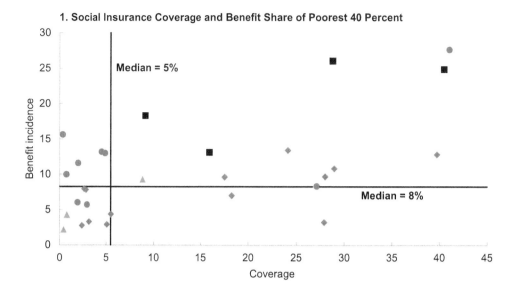

1. Social Insurance Coverage and Benefit Share of Poorest 40 Percent

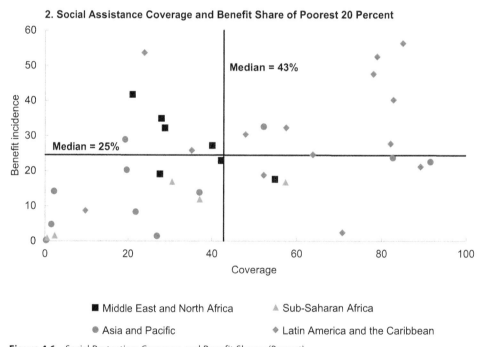

2. Social Assistance Coverage and Benefit Share of Poorest 20 Percent

■ Middle East and North Africa   ▲ Sub-Saharan Africa

● Asia and Pacific   ◆ Latin America and the Caribbean

Figure 4.6   Social Protection: Coverage and Benefit Shares *(Percent)*

Source: World Bank Aspire database.
Note: For presentational purposes, Mexico (79, 0) and Thailand (99,1) are excluded from the social insurance figure.

(Figure 4.6, panel 2). At the same time, many developing countries allocate large sums to energy subsidies by setting consumer prices below cost-recovery levels (known as pretax subsidies), although these subsidies are often not recorded in the budget (in oil producers, for example). Posttax energy subsidies, which arise when energy prices are below levels that reflect cost recovery plus an optimal tax to reflect revenue needs and the environmental cost of energy consumption, are significantly larger. Recent estimates show that subsidies are especially large in oil-exporting countries but are also large in many other developing countries (Clements and others 2013). Most of the benefit from such universal subsidies accrues to higher-income groups; a recent review of country studies finds that the top income decile receives seven times more in subsidies than the bottom decile (Arze del Granado, Coady, and Gillingham 2010). Therefore, these subsidies reinforce rather than reduce income inequality and crowd out more redistributive social spending

OPTIONS FOR ENHANCING EFFICIENT FISCAL REDISTRIBUTION IN DEVELOPING COUNTRIES

Enhancing the capability of fiscal policy to address income inequality in developing economies will require strengthening both their resource mobilization capacity their capacity to use more progressive tax and spending instruments. While many low-income countries may prioritize reducing poverty over reducing broader inequality, many middle- and lower-middle-income countries, where poverty rates have decreased substantially with economic growth, are increasingly emphasizing the need for a more inclusive growth process. At the same time, most developing economies are constrained by low tax ratios while facing increasing demand for public investments in education, health, and physical infrastructure to help stimulate or sustain economic growth. Strategies for enhancing the redistributive impact of fiscal policy therefore need to recognize these competing objectives.

The theoretical literature on the design of efficient redistributive fiscal policies in developing economies provides some basic guiding principles (Newbery and Stern 1987). First, income-based instruments, such as direct income taxation and means-tested transfers, are more efficient at achieving redistributive goals than are other policy instruments (Atkinson and Stiglitz 1976). Second, where access to such direct tax and transfer instruments is restricted (for example, because of administrative or political constraints), it may be desirable to replace these instruments with instruments that link taxes and transfers to household characteristics that are highly correlated with income (so-called tagging) such as whether a member has a disability, whether the household is headed by a female or a widow, and the number of children and elderly in the household (Akerlof 1978). Third, consumption-based indirect taxes or subsidies do not redistribute income efficiently since higher-income households typically account for a substantially greater proportion of consumption than do lower-income households (Sah 1983). However, where governments do not have access to efficient direct income-based tax and transfer instruments, consumption taxes may have a distributive role. However, because the amount of redistribution that can be achieved through differential consumption taxes and subsidies is limited, and because such taxes and subsidies distort consumption patterns, there is a high return to the development of more effective direct transfer instruments that allow indirect taxes to focus more on raising revenue to finance more efficient redistributive transfers. Fourth, corrective Pigouvian consumption taxes levied on consumption goods that generate negative social externalities (for example, reflecting pollution from the consumption of fossil fuels, or the adverse health or social impacts from alcohol or tobacco consumption) can provide a "win-win" opportunity for efficient redistribution when their consumption is highly concentrated among higher-income groups.

In summary, where administrative constraints limit the range of direct tax and transfer instruments available to a government, a mix of direct and indirect instruments is often desirable. The corollary is that there are typically substantial efficiency and equity gains to be had from the development of greater administrative capacity to effectively implement direct tax and transfer instruments. In addition, as noted earlier, the design of efficient redistribution should focus on the combined redistributive impact of taxes and spending.

Tax Reform Options

Increasing tax ratios in developing economies is a key component of any strategy for enhancing fiscal redistribution while addressing competing public spending needs.[8] Low tax ratios in developing countries have been attributed to the greater importance of sectors (such as small-scale agriculture and small-scale or informal enterprises) for which information gathering is extremely difficult since literacy is low, record-keeping is poor or nonexistent, and administrative systems are often weak (Musgrave 1969; Goode 1984).[9] As economies develop, the number of formal market transactions tends to increase, population literacy improves, and government administrative systems become more effective. These advances, in turn, enable a widening of the tax base and an expansion of the set of feasible tax instruments (Gillis 1989). These trends are reinforced by increasing demand for publicly provided goods and services.

In practice, tax structures in many developing economies have evolved in an ad hoc manner in response to various internal and external pressures, and reflect a host of historical, social, political, and economic factors. The resulting inefficiencies and inequities, reflecting both design and administration shortcomings, mean that "win-win" opportunities for increasing tax revenues while improving the efficiency and equity of the system are likely to be available. Realizing these efficiency and equity gains will require improvements in both the design and the administration of tax policy focused on broadening income and consumption tax bases by reducing exemptions and loopholes and strengthening compliance.[10] Continued reliance on a small base of compliant taxpayers to increase tax ratios is likely to exacerbate the distortionary impact of taxes and the existing inequities without raising much extra revenue.

During the past decade, many developing economies have managed significant increases in tax ratios. The median change in the tax ratio during 2000–10 ranged from slightly more than 3 percent of GDP in Asia and Pacific and Latin American and Caribbean countries to less than 2 percent in sub-Saharan Africa and about 1 percent in the Middle East (Figure 4.7). Most of the increase reflects increases in revenues from indirect taxes and corporate taxes. Tax ratios actually fell in more than half the countries in the Middle East and North Africa, a third of countries in Asia and Pacific, and in a quarter of countries in sub-Saharan Africa. However, the high degree of variation in tax ratios across developing economies at similar levels of development suggests that there is ample scope to increase tax revenues in many countries.

---

[8] This section draws on IMF 2011, which provides a detailed discussion of tax administration and design challenges in developing countries. The focus of this chapter is tax revenues. Although in some developing economies nontax revenues (primarily resource-based taxes) are important, the design of efficient fiscal regimes for taxing resource revenues is outside the scope of this chapter. For a detailed discussion of resource tax regimes, see Daniel, Keen, and McPherson 2010. For a discussion of the trade-offs faced in using resource revenues for redistribution, see Gupta, Segura Ubiergo, and Flores 2014.

[9] There is a substantial literature on the reasons behind low tax ratios in developing economies, including Ahmad and Stern 1989, Burgess and Stern 1993, Heady 2002, Keen and Simone 2004, and Gordon and Li 2009.

[10] Although taxation of wealth is typically considered to be both efficient and equitable, it is not widely used, and the effective tax rate has dropped from an average of about 0.9 percent in 1970 to about 0.5 percent in 2010. Among developing countries, only Colombia, Namibia, South Africa, and Uruguay collect more than 1 percent of GDP through recurrent property taxes. Wealth taxes include a range of options such as recurrent taxes on property or net wealth, transaction taxes, and inheritance and gift taxes. IMF 2013 discusses the scope for increasing revenues from wealth taxes. In the context of developing countries, the most promising revenue source is probably property taxes, which average about half a percent of GDP in developing countries compared with more than 1 percent in advanced economies (Bahl, Martínez-Vázquez, and Youngman 2008). However, since implementing property taxes would require a significant investment in administrative infrastructure, it is probably only feasible in the medium term (Norregaard 2013).

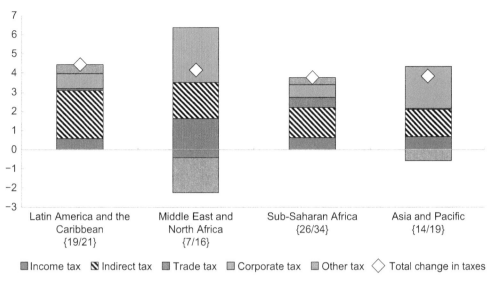

Figure 4.7   Increases in Tax Ratios in Developing Economies, 2000–10

Source: IMF staff calculations.

Note: Samples only include countries in which tax ratios increased. Numbers in brackets refer to number of countries {where tax ratio increases, in full sample}.

Personal Income Taxation

A key challenge in developing economies is to develop more effective progressive personal income tax (PIT) systems. The median income tax ratio is 7.9 percent of GDP in advanced economies, but substantially lower in developing economies, ranging from 1.9 percent in the Middle East and North Africa to about 1.6 percent in other regions. Although PIT systems in developing economies often use progressive tax schedules, narrow tax bases—due to high income tax thresholds, widespread exemptions, and the preferential treatment of capital and other income—contribute to low effective income tax progressivity.[11] In many countries, PIT revenues come mainly from wage tax withholding on large enterprises and public sector employees (Peter, Buttrick, and Duncan 2010). This situation is exacerbated by administrative systems that suffer from weak detection and enforcement capacity, thereby resulting in high levels of tax evasion, especially by high-income groups. Although distributional and administrative considerations point to the desirability of relatively high income thresholds for income tax liability, these thresholds may still be too high in some countries. For example, whereas in the OECD the median threshold is about 25 percent of per capita income, in 16 developing economies the threshold exceeds twice per capita income (Peter, Buttrick, and Duncan 2010).[12] At the same time, some developing countries do not allow for any threshold—all income groups are liable for income tax (USAID 2013).

Therefore, to increase income tax ratios, improvements will be required in both the design and implementation of income tax regimes, primarily with a focus on broadening the income tax base

---

[11] A study by Modi (1987) finds that, on average, less than 5 percent of the population in developing countries pays PIT (compared with 50 percent in advanced countries) and less than 15 percent of the income is taxable (compared with 57 percent in advanced countries).

[12] With respect to the upper end of the PIT schedule, Peter, Buttrick and Duncan (2010) find that top PIT rates start at about 18 times per capita income in upper-middle-income countries and at 83 times in low-income countries.

rather than increasing tax rates (Crandall and Bodin 2005; Kloeden 2011; Zake 2011; IMF 2011). On the design side, broadening the base will require lowering the thresholds for tax liability and for top-income tax rates where these are high, and reducing exemptions, privileges and loopholes so that all income is taxed in the same manner regardless of source to avoid distorting economic activities. On the administrative side, more active segmentation of income-tax-payers (for example, high- and middle-income groups, self-employed earners, and agriculture) will be required to address the challenges associated with collecting income taxes from these groups—many countries have already created large-taxpayer offices as part of this strategy.

Corporate Income Taxation

As a share of total revenues, corporate tax revenue is even more important in developing economies than in advanced. Despite decreasing tax rates worldwide, corporate tax revenues have actually increased as a share of GDP in developing economies since the early 1990s. However, international tax competition will present increasing challenges to developing countries in protecting corporate tax revenues (IMF 2014b).[13]

Ensuring sufficient corporate income tax revenues is desirable for raising revenue efficiently and equitably. In the short term, corporate taxation tends to be highly progressive since recipients of capital income tend to be higher-income groups. However, in the long term, the incidence of corporate taxes on wages and capital income depends on the relative mobility of capital and labor across both sectors and countries (Auerbach 2006). If capital is more internationally mobile, the incidence of corporate taxes will tend to fall more on wages to the extent that labor is immobile.[14] Empirical evidence on the long-term incidence of corporate taxes suggests that between 45 and 75 percent of the corporate tax burden falls on wages (Gentry 2007; Arulampalam, Devereux, and Maffini 2010), reducing its redistributive impact since wage earners typically have lower mean incomes than do those with capital income.

As with personal income taxation, increasing (or protecting) corporate income tax ratios will require improvements in both the design and implementation of corporate tax regimes with a focus on broadening the income tax base rather than increasing tax rates. Given administrative constraints in implementing PITs, corporate taxation can work like an income withholding tax in developing economies by taxing income before it gets distributed to corporate owners. Therefore, for efficiency reasons, it is important to harmonize PIT rates across different sources of capital income. Although the growing international mobility of capital and associated evasion and avoidance opportunities present increasing administrative difficulties for developing countries, the associated efficiency costs can be contained by setting corporate income tax rates lower than PIT rates, having a common tax treatment of different types of capital income (including reducing tax exemptions),[15] increasing the use of withholding taxes (especially where administration is weak),

---

[13] See Chapter 10.

[14] The impact on wages is reduced where the home country is large enough to affect the international rate of return on capital. Also, the taxation of "rents" (that is, above normal profits) is still likely to fall on owners of capital.

[15] Preferential tax treatment for certain types of investment has become pervasive in many developing economies, but especially in low-income countries (IMF 2013). In 1980 about 40 percent of low-income countries (LICs) in sub-Saharan Africa offered tax holidays, but this figure increased to about 80 percent by 2005. Especially pronounced has been the increase in the number of countries providing holidays through free trade zones. A number of studies have estimated the fiscal cost of corporate income tax (CIT) incentives, although care needs to be taken when comparing and interpreting these studies because of methodological differences and data limitations. Cubeddu and others (2008) put the revenue cost of CIT incentives in 15 Caribbean countries at an average of about 5.5 percent of GDP. Villela, Lemgruber, and Jorratt (2010) estimate the cost of preferential treatment under the income tax at 0.5–6.0 percent of GDP in Latin America. Raising "CIT-productivity" in LICs to the LIC median for those countries below the median was estimated by IMF 2011 to increase revenue by about 0.7 percent of GDP.

and strengthening the taxation of multinational businesses that use a variety of tax-planning strategies to reduce their global tax liabilities.

Indirect Taxation

Efficiency considerations suggest that indirect taxes should fall on final consumption (and not intermediate consumption to avoid distorting production decisions), with higher rates on goods that are less price elastic. In general, then, there is a trade-off between efficiency and equity objectives when designing indirect taxes since necessities tend to have relatively low elasticities but account for a larger share of the budgets of lower-income households. When countries have access to effective redistributive spending instruments, the design of indirect taxes should focus mainly on raising revenue efficiently, although tax administration considerations suggest that the number of rates should be minimized. However, where administrative constraints also limit the availability of effective redistributive spending instruments, lower tax rates on goods that are relatively important in the budgets of low-income households (for example, basic foods) may be warranted on distributional grounds. But, again, administrative constraints on the tax side also suggest that the number of rates should be minimized.[16] Specific excises on such goods as cigarettes, alcoholic beverages, gambling, motor fuels, and luxury goods can also raise significant revenue and increase tax progressivity while also helping to internalize consumption externalities and to promote socially desirable consumption patterns.

The gradual shift from trade taxes to broader consumption taxes in developing countries in recent decades has improved the efficiency and equity of indirect tax systems (Newbery and Stern 1987; Keen and Simone 2004).[17] As trade taxes have decreased in importance, more broad-based consumption taxes have increased. A more contentious issue has been the equity implications of replacing sales taxes with a value-added tax (VAT), which has happened in most developing countries. As seen earlier, the equity implications will depend on how the VAT is designed. Although some studies find that the VAT has been less progressive than the sales taxes they replaced, other evidence shows that the progressivity of a VAT can be enhanced by adopting lower rates for basic goods or by setting the registration threshold high enough to exclude most small-scale businesses. The relatively large administrative and compliance costs associated with the VAT, especially for small traders, also make it desirable to adopt VAT registration thresholds that exclude small businesses. Given that the standard VAT rate is already high in many countries, emphasis should be placed on reducing the use of exemptions and reduced rates by restricting them to goods that are particularly important in the budgets of lower-income households (for example, basic foods).

Social Spending

Although higher levels of social spending can enhance the redistributive impact of fiscal policy in developing economies, there is also substantial scope for improving the redistributive impact of existing spending in many countries. The importance of such improvements is further reinforced to the extent that countries find it difficult to increase tax ratios to finance higher spending in the short term. In addition, countries need to make difficult choices between increasing education

---

[16] Attempts to focus lower tax rates (or even subsidies) on a narrower set of often low-quality consumption items that are consumed mainly by lower-income groups are likely to give rise to large inefficiencies and be self-defeating. Since their budget shares will be low, the tax differentials required to provide income support will be large, giving rise to large substitution effects.

[17] Trade taxes, which are essentially a subsidy to domestic producers financed by a tax on domestic consumers, are an inefficient revenue-raising instrument since they distort both production and consumption decisions. They are also a very blunt redistributive instrument, benefiting some poor households but hurting others.

and health spending as a way of addressing income inequality and poverty in the medium term, and increasing social protection spending to address current inequality and poverty.

The relatively small redistributive impact of public transfers in most developing economies is due in large part to the limited coverage of public pension systems of lower-income groups. In addition, these pension systems often require significant financing from general government revenues, thus crowding out more redistributive social spending. Given that the primary focus of these programs is social insurance, from a redistribution perspective it is desirable to prioritize parametric reforms that put existing systems on a sound financial footing and reduce the need for financing from general revenues before scaling up program coverage. Doing so could free up resources to finance, for example, an expansion of noncontributory "social pensions" that provide a flat pension aimed at poverty reduction (Holzmann, Robalino, and Takayama 2009). Social pensions exist in a number of developing countries, including low-income countries (for example, Bangladesh, Brazil, Chile, Costa Rica, Ethiopia, India, Nepal, Madagascar, South Africa, and Thailand). Setting these pensions at a level sufficient to alleviate poverty can help reduce incentives to remain outside the formal pension system and also contain their fiscal cost.[18] If sufficient administrative capacity exists, then means testing can further contribute to containing the fiscal cost.

Many developing economies could also enhance the effectiveness of their social assistance programs by addressing key design and implementation shortcomings. Most developing economies rely on a diverse set of poverty alleviation programs, including cash transfers, food or other in-kind transfers, public workfare, fee waivers (for example, for education and health services), and price subsidies (especially for food and energy). These programs often fall short of their redistributive objectives, and their cost-effectiveness could be greatly improved by reforms to address the following shortcomings (Grosh and others 2008):

- *Fragmentation and duplication*—Many countries have a myriad of small programs with overlapping objectives spread across various ministries with little or no coordination. This increases the fixed administrative costs associated with program implementation.

- *Bad targeting*—Many of the targeting approaches used are badly designed (for example, based on weak or loosely specified tagging that is not well correlated with poverty), resulting in substantial leakage of benefits to non-poor households and increasing the fiscal cost of these programs.

- *Low coverage and benefits*—The low level of spending spread across numerous small programs with high leakage leads to low coverage of the poor and low benefit levels.

- *Reliance on costly in-kind benefits*—Some countries spend significant amounts on food distribution programs that are prone to large leakages (including from theft and wastage) and involve large overhead costs. Overhead costs can be as much as 50 percent higher than the value of the in-kind benefit to beneficiaries.

- *Reliance on universal price subsidies*—Many countries spend substantial amounts on universal price subsidies. Reflecting the overall inequality of consumption, most of the benefit from these subsidies accrues to higher-income households.

Consolidation of benefits into a smaller number of programs with clearly established objectives can help reduce the cost of these programs and improve efficiency. Together with improved

---

[18]The cost of these social pensions can be substantial. For example, spending on social pensions ranges from ½ to ¾ percent of GDP in many developing economies (Holzmann, Robalino, and Takayama 2009; Bosch, Melguizo, and Pagés 2013). South Africa's Social Grants Program includes a means-tested social pension program costing 1.3 percent of GDP. Based on a pension set at 70 percent of country-specific poverty lines, Kakwani and Subbarao (2005) estimate the cost of a universal pension for everyone older than 65 years in 15 sub-Saharan African countries to range from 0.7 percent of GDP in Madagascar to 2.4 percent of GDP in Ethiopia. Limiting the pension to only the elderly poor would approximately halve this cost for most countries.

targeting and the scaling down of price subsidies, consolidation will enhance the poverty impact of existing spending and create the fiscal space to finance the development of more effective safety net programs with expanded coverage and adequate benefit levels.[19]

Many low- and middle-income developing countries have extensive public works programs that play an important role in addressing persistent or seasonal poverty as well as protecting households from income shocks. These programs have been successfully implemented in a range of settings, including in the wake of natural disasters and economic crises as well as in postconflict states, although the precise design needs to reflect the differing administrative capacity in emerging and low-income countries (Subbarao, del Ninno, and Rodriguez-Alas 2013). Public works programs can be designed to encourage self-selection of the poor, which can reduce the fiscal costs and avoid crowding out private sector jobs. This self-selection can be achieved by setting wages below those prevailing in the market for unskilled labor so that programs will only attract those without other opportunities. This design also allows for the automatic scaling down of programs in the aftermath of a crisis as higher-wage job opportunities expand. If timed to avoid coinciding with peak employment seasons (for example, during agricultural harvests) this can prevent crowding out of private sector jobs. However, these cost-effective design features can make public works programs ineffective (or even counterproductive) at addressing severe shocks such as prolonged drought when those affected may be too weak to work (Bastagli and Holmes 2014). Even in normal times, the work requirement may exclude those incapable of work such as the physically or mentally disabled. In both these circumstances, unconditional transfers are likely to be more effective. Countries with greater administrative capacity can also enhance the developmental role of these programs by putting greater emphasis on the infrastructure and training components of these programs (these programs are often referred to as "social funds"). However, the need to allocate a greater share of resources in these programs to capital and administrative costs introduces a trade-off between addressing current poverty (through wages) and future poverty (through infrastructure development).

Turning to education and health spending, enhancing its progressivity requires that expansion be focused on increasing the access of low-income groups to quality education and health services. For education, this requires expanding enrollment and progression rates in primary and secondary education, which will eventually also help improve the progressivity of spending on higher levels of education as average education attainment increases for lower-income groups relative to the population average. But sufficient attention needs to be given to ensuring that quality education services are delivered, which will enhance future earnings capacity. At the tertiary level, increasing demand in the context of tight public finances has often resulted in a decline in the quality of instruction in public institutions and growth in private education institutions (Woodhall 2007; Hanushek and Woessmann 2011; Pritchett 2013). Since much of the benefit from tertiary education accrues to graduates in the form of higher earnings and other nonmonetary benefits, a strong case can be made for financing more of this cost from tuition fees. However, means-tested income support is still required to ensure lower-income groups can also access tertiary education services. Increasing private financing also allows tertiary education to expand in response to growing demand for skilled labor without increasing public spending.

For health, there is a growing consensus that ensuring universal access to a fiscally sustainable, publicly financed basic package of health services is required to generate substantial improvements in health outcomes and to enhance the progressivity of public health spending (Jamison and others 2013). Access to a broad package of essential health services (including primary care)

---

[19] A review of safety nets in Africa, for instance, finds that they have expanded in a number of countries (for example, Ghana, Kenya, Mozambique, Rwanda, and Tanzania) in the wake of recent economic crises and are evolving from fragmented programs to a more integrated social safety net (Monchuk 2014).

is still incomplete in many developing economies. As a consequence, the poor often forgo or delay necessary care at an early stage of illness when treatment is more cost-effective. Many households fall into poverty because of high out-of-pocket spending and many others are just one major illness away from poverty. In particular, preventive care, such as immunizations, should be offered free of charge given their large social benefits.

The recent expansion of "conditional cash transfer" programs provides a promising approach to enhancing the distributive power of public spending in developing economies while also addressing the trade-off between using income transfers to reduce current poverty and in-kind transfers (that is, education and health) to reduce future poverty. These programs typically target the poorest households, link benefits to the number of children, and condition continued eligibility on attendance of children at health clinics and school. In many countries conditional cash transfers have been used to consolidate a number of existing programs to reduce administrative costs and improve effectiveness.[20] The use of proxy means testing has helped reduce the fiscal cost of these programs without generating any significant work disincentives. The largest such programs are in Brazil (Bolsa Familia) and Mexico (Oportunidades), which in 2012 cost 0.5 percent of GDP and 0.8 percent of GDP, and covered one-quarter and one-fifth of the population, respectively.[21] These programs have had substantial impacts on poverty and inequality, as well as education and health outcomes, and can help increase investment by alleviating credit constraints (Fiszbein and Schady 2009). In addition, they indirectly affect the inequality of market incomes over time by decreasing the inequality of education outcomes.[22] However, since they require adequate administrative capacity to implement means-testing and monitor conditionality, as well as ensuring that the targeted poor populations have access to basic education and health services, they are more challenging for economies with limited administrative capacity.[23]

CONCLUSION

This chapter highlights the important role of fiscal policy in achieving distributional objectives in developing economies. Evidence from advanced countries shows that fiscal policy reduces income inequality by about one-third, and that the extent of fiscal redistribution is substantially higher if in-kind spending is included. However, the extent of fiscal redistribution is much more limited in developing economies because of their lower tax and spending levels as well as the composition of this tax and spending. Comparing average inequality levels in Latin America and the Caribbean (the region with the highest level of income inequality) with levels in advanced economies (the region with the lowest income inequality), the chapter shows that differences in the extent of fiscal redistribution can explain two-thirds of the difference in average income inequality after taxes and transfers between these regions. On the tax side, fiscal

---

[20] In Mexico, for instance, the conditional cash transfer program was financed by eliminating food subsidies. Coady and Harris (2004) estimate that, in addition to the gains from better targeting, the elimination of price subsides generated substantial efficiency gains equivalent to MEX$38 for MEX$100 pesos spent on the program.

[21] The direct impact of such transfers in Brazil and Mexico accounted for one-fifth of the decrease in the Gini between 1995 and 2004 in these two countries (Soares and others 2007).

[22] Recent studies have found that improved education outcomes, as reflected in the increase in the education level of the working population, has been the dominant factor behind decreasing income inequality in Latin America, followed by the growth in public transfers in terms of importance (Azevedo, Inchauste, and Sanfelice 2013).

[23] Many countries in sub-Saharan Africa (for example, Burkina Faso, Liberia, Madagascar, Malawi, Niger, and Tanzania) and Asia (for example, Bangladesh, Cambodia, India, Indonesia, Pakistan, and the Philippines) are first adopting these programs on a pilot basis before gradually expanding them nationwide (Fiszbein and Schady 2009; Garcia and Moore 2012; Monchuk 2014).

redistribution is limited by the heavy reliance on indirect taxes, which have little impact on income distribution. On the spending side, the high share of education and health spending (which only affect income distribution in the medium term) in total social spending, and the high share of social insurance (mainly pensions) that benefits mainly higher-income groups, limit the impact of fiscal policy on income inequality. In addition, low coverage of social assistance spending with substantial leakages to higher-income groups further reduces the extent of fiscal redistribution.

Increasing tax ratios in developing economies is a key component of any strategy for enhancing fiscal redistribution while addressing competing public spending needs. Improvements in both the design and administration of tax policy, focused on broadening income and consumption tax bases by reducing exemptions and strengthening compliance, will be required to increase tax ratios. Although the primary role of taxes is to raise revenue efficiently to finance redistributive transfers, taxes can also be progressively designed to directly contribute to the achievement of equity goals. From a design perspective, this can be accomplished by expanding personal income taxation by lowering the tax-exempt income threshold and possibly the top-income tax threshold, better integrating the corporate income tax system with the personal income tax system (with possibly a lower rate for corporate income tax), and reducing tax exemptions and preferential tax rates. On the administrative side, tax compliance can be improved by more active segmentation of income-tax-payer groups to address the different challenges associated with collecting income taxes from these groups. The limited potential for redistribution through differential consumption taxes combined with administrative considerations points to minimizing the use of exemptions and reduced rates and adoption of a registration threshold that excludes small traders. These measures will both enhance the efficiency and progressivity of taxes and increase income tax ratios to help finance greater redistributive and other public spending.

Although higher levels of social spending can enhance the redistributive impact of fiscal policy in developing economies, there is also substantial scope for improving the redistributive impact of existing spending in many countries. Competing development needs for spending and the challenges faced in increasing tax ratios mean that many developing countries will need to give priority to designing well-targeted transfer programs and avoid the use of fiscally expensive universal price subsidy schemes. With social insurance, which currently disproportionately benefits higher-income groups, priority could be given to parametric reforms that put existing systems on a sound financial footing and reduce the need for financing from general revenues. To the extent that social pensions are expanded, benefit levels can be kept low enough to reduce disincentives for contributing to formal social insurance schemes and means tested to contain fiscal costs.

The effectiveness of social assistance can be enhanced by reducing fragmentation and duplication, improving targeting and expanding coverage, and reducing universal price subsidies. The effectiveness of public works programs can be improved by the appropriate use of wage-setting practices to encourage self-selection; an emphasis on labor-intensive projects in countries in which administrative capacity is weak; and the incorporation of development objectives when administrative capacity is higher, which allows greater emphasis to be put on the infrastructure and training components of these programs. Enhancing the redistributive impact of education and health spending requires that expansion be focused on increasing access for low-income groups to quality education and health services. In this respect, the expansion of "conditional cash transfer" programs, which target the poorest households and condition transfers on accessing education and health services, provides a promising approach to enhancing the distributive power of public spending in developing economies while also addressing the trade-off between using income transfers to reduce current poverty and in-kind transfers (that is, education and health) to reduce future poverty.

REFERENCES

Ahmad, E., and N. Stern. 1989. "Taxation for Developing Countries." In *Handbook of Development Economics*, Vol. II, edited by H. Chenery and T. N. Srinivasan. Amsterdam: Elsevier Science.

Akerlof, G. 1978. "The Economics of 'Tagging' as Applied to the Optimal Income Tax, Welfare Programs, and Manpower Planning." *American Economic Review* 68 (1): 8–19.

Arulampalam, W., M. Devereux, and G. Maffini. 2010. "The Direct Incidence of Corporate Income Tax on Wages." IZA Discussion Paper 5293, Institute for the Study of Labor, Bonn.

Arze del Granado, J., D. Coady, and R. Gillingham. 2010. "The Unequal Benefits of Fuel Subsidies: A Review of Evidence for Developing Countries." IMF Working Paper No. 10/202, International Monetary Fund, Washington.

Atkinson, A., and J. Stiglitz. 1976. "The Design of Tax Structure: Direct and Indirect Taxation." *Journal of Public Economics* 6 (1–2): 55–75.

Auerbach, A. 2006. "Who Bears the Corporate Tax? A Review of What We Know." In *Tax Policy and the Economy*, Vol. 20, edited by J. Poterba. Cambridge, Massachusetts: MIT Press.

Azevedo, J., G. Inchauste, and V. Sanfelice. 2013. "Decomposing the Recent Inequality Decline in Latin America." Policy Research Working Paper No. 6715, World Bank, Washington.

Bahl, R., J. Martínez-Vázquez, and J. Youngman. 2008. *Making the Property Tax Work*. Cambridge, Massachusetts: Lincoln Institute of Land Policy.

Bastagli, F., D. Coady, and S. Gupta. 2012. "Fiscal Policy and Income Inequality." Staff Discussion Note No. 12/08 (revised), International Monetary Fund, Washington.

Bastagli, F., and R. Holmes. 2014. "Delivering Social Protection in the Aftermath of a Shock: Lessons from Bangladesh, Kenya, Pakistan and Viet Nam." ODI Research Report, Overseas Development Institute, London.

Bird, R. M., and E. M. Zolt. 2005. "Redistribution via Taxation: The Limited Role of the Personal Income Tax in Developing Countries." *UCLA Law Review* 62 (6): 1627–96.

Bosch, M., A. Melguizo, and C. Pagés. 2013. *Mejores Pensiones, Mejores Trabajos*. Washington: Inter-American Development Bank.

Breceda, K., J. Rigolini, and J. Saavedra. 2009. "Latin America and the Social Contract: Patterns of Social Spending and Taxation." *Population and Development Review* 35 (4): 721–48.

Burgess, R., and N. Stern. 1993. "Taxation and Development." *Journal of Economic Literature* 31 (June): 762–830.

Chu, K-Y., H. Davoodi, and S. Gupta. 2004. "Income Distribution and Tax and Government Social-Spending Policies in Developing Countries." In *Inequality, Growth, and Poverty in an Era of Liberalization and Globalization*, edited by Giovanni Andrea Cornia. New York: Oxford University Press.

Claus, I., J. Martinez-Vazquez, and V. Vulovic. 2014. "Government Fiscal Policies and Redistribution in Asian Countries." In *Inequality in Asia and the Pacific*, edited by R. Kanbur, C. Rhee, and J. Zhuang. Manila: Asian Development Bank; and London: Routledge.

Clements, B., D. Coady, S. Fabrizio, S. Gupta, T. Alleyne, and C. Sdralevich, eds. 2013. *Energy Subsidy Reform: Lessons and Implications*. Washington: International Monetary Fund.

Coady, D. 2006. "The Distributional Impacts of Indirect Tax and Public Pricing Reforms." In *Analyzing the Distributional Impact of Reforms: A Practitioner's Guide to Pension, Health, Labor Markets, Public Sector Downsizing, Taxation, Decentralization and Macroeconomic Modeling*, Vol. 2, edited by A. Coudouel and S. Paternostro. Washington: World Bank.

———, P. Dorosh, and B. Minten. 2009. "Evaluating Alternative Policy Responses to Higher World Food Prices: The Case of Increasing Rice Prices in Madagascar." *American Journal of Agricultural Economics* 93 (3): 711–22.

Coady, D., and R. Harris. 2004. "Evaluating Transfer Programs within a General Equilibrium Framework." *Economic Journal* 114 (October): 778–99.

Crandall, W., and J.-P. Bodin. 2005. "Revenue Administration Reforms in Selected Middle Eastern Countries, 1994–2004." IMF Working Paper No. 05/203, International Monetary Fund, Washington.

Cubeddu, L., A. Bauer, P. Berkman, M. Kandil, K. Nassar, and P. Mullins. 2008. "Tax Incentives and Foreign Direct Investment: Policy Implications for the Caribbean." In *The Caribbean: Enlarging Economic Integration*, edited by A. Bauer, P. Lashin, and S. Panth, 44–84. Washington: International Monetary Fund.

Cubero, R., and I. Hollar. 2011. "Equity and Fiscal Policy: The Income Distribution Effects of Taxation and Social Spending in Central America." *International Journal of Public Budget* 75 (March/April).

Daniel, P., M. Keen, and C. McPherson, eds. 2010. *The Taxation of Petroleum and Minerals: Principles, Problems and Practice*. New York: Routledge.

Davoodi, H. R., E. Tiongson, and S. Asawanuchit. 2010. "Benefit Incidence of Public Education and Health Spending Worldwide: Evidence from a New Database." *Poverty and Public Policy* 2 (2): 5–52.

De Gregorio, J., and J.-W. Lee. 2002. "Education and Income Inequality: New Evidence from Cross-Country Data." *Review of Income and Wealth* 48 (3): 395–416.

Demery, L. 2000. *Benefit Incidence: A Practitioner's Guide*. Poverty and Social Development Group, Africa Region. Washington: World Bank.

Fiszbein, A., and N. Schady. 2009. *Conditional Cash Transfers: Reducing Present and Future Poverty*. Washington: World Bank.

Garcia, M., and C. Moore. 2012. *The Cash Dividend: The Rise of Cash Transfer Programs in Sub-Saharan Africa*. Directions in Development. Washington: World Bank.

Gemmell, N., and O. Morrissey. 2005. "Distribution and Poverty Impacts of Tax Structure Reform in Developing Countries: How Little We Know." *Development Policy Review* 23 (2): 131–44.

Gentry, W. 2007. "A Review of the Evidence on the Incidence of the Corporate Income Tax," U.S. Department of the Treasury, Office of Tax Analysis, Paper 101, Washington.

Gillis, M., ed. 1989. *Tax Reform in Developing Countries*. Durham, North Carolina: Duke University Press.

Goñi, E., J. Lopéz, and L. Servén. 2011. "Fiscal Redistribution and Income Inequality in Latin America." *World Development* 39 (9): 1558–69.

Goode, R. 1984. *Government Finances in Developing Countries*. Washington: The Brookings Institution.

Gordon, R., and W. Li. 2009. "Tax Structures in Developing Countries: Many Puzzles and a Possible Explanation." *Journal of Public Economics* 93 (7–8): 855–66.

Grosh, M. E., C. del Ninno, E. Tesliuc, and A. Ouerghi. 2008. *For Protection and Promotion: The Design and Implementation of Effective Safety Nets*. Washington: World Bank.

Gupta, S., A. Segura Ubiergo, and E. Flores. 2014. "Direct Redistribution of Resource Revenues: Worth Considering?" Staff Discussion Paper No. 14/05, International Monetary Fund, Washington.

Hanushek, E., and L. Woessmann. 2011. "The Economics of International Differences in Educational Achievement." In *Handbook of the Economics of Education*, Vol. 3, edited by E. Hanushek, S. Machin, and L. Woessmann. Amsterdam: North Holland.

Heady, C. 2002. "Tax Policy in Developing Countries: What Can Be Learned from OECD Experience?" Unpublished, Organisation for Economic Co-operation and Development, Paris.

Hertel, T., and J. Reimer. 2005. "Predicting the Poverty Impacts of Trade Liberalization: A Survey." *Journal of International Trade and Economic Development* 14 (4): 377–405.

Holzmann, R., D. A. Robalino, and N. Takayama. 2009. *Closing the Coverage Gap: The Role of Social Pensions and Other Retirement Income Transfers*. Washington: World Bank.

Hossain, S. 1995. "The Equity Impact of the Value-Added Tax in Bangladesh." *IMF Staff Papers* 42 (June): 411–32.

———. 2003. "Poverty and Social Impact Analysis: A Suggested Framework." IMF Working Paper No. 03/195, International Monetary Fund, Washington.

International Labour Organization (ILO). 2010. *World Social Security Report 2010/11: Providing Coverage in Times of Crisis and Beyond*. Geneva: International Labour Organization.

International Monetary Fund. 2011. "Revenue Mobilization in Developing Countries." Policy Paper, International Monetary Fund, Washington.

———. 2013. *Fiscal Monitor: Taxing Times*. Washington, October. www.imf.org/external/pubs/ft/fm/2013/02/pdf/fm1302.pdf.

———. 2014a. "Fiscal Policy and Income Inequality." Policy Paper, International Monetary Fund, Washington. http://www.imf.org/external/np/pp/eng/2014/012314.pdf.

———. 2014b. "Spillovers in International Corporate Taxation." Policy Paper, Washington.

Jamison, D., L. H. Summers, G. Alleyne, K. J. Arrow, S. Berkley, A. Binagwaho, F. Bustreo, and others. 2013. "Global Health 2035: A World Converging within a Generation." *The Lancet* 382 (9908): 11–68.

Jenkins, G., H. Jenkins, and C.-Y. Kuo. 2006. "Is the Value Added Tax Naturally Progressive?" Working Paper No. 1059, Queen's University, Kingston, Ontario.

Kakwani, N., and K. Subbarao. 2005. "Aging and Poverty in Africa and the Role of Social Pensions." Social Protection Discussion Paper No. 0521, World Bank, Washington.

Kanbur, R., C. Rhee, and J. Zhuang, eds. 2014. *Inequality in Asia and the Pacific: Trends, Drivers, and Policy Implications*. Manila: Asian Development Bank; and London: Routledge.

Keen, M., and A. Simone. 2004. "Tax Policy in Developing Countries: Some Lessons from the 1990s, and Some Challenges Ahead." In *Helping Countries Develop: The Role of Fiscal Policy*, edited by Sanjeev Gupta, Ben Clements, and Gabriela Inchauste, 302–52. Washington: International Monetary Fund.

Kloeden, D. 2011. "Revenue Administration Reforms in Anglophone Africa since the Early-1990s." IMF Working Paper No. 11/162, International Monetary Fund, Washington.

Latinobarómetro. 2003 and various years. "Informe-Resumen: La Democracia y la Economía." Santiago.

Lustig, N., S. Higgins, M. Jaramillo, W. Jimenez, G. Molina, V. Paz Arauco, C. Pereira, C. Pessino, J. Scott, and E. Yañez. 2011. "Fiscal Policy and Income Distribution in Latin America: Challenging the Conventional Wisdom." Tulane Economics Working Paper No. 1124, Tulane University, New Orleans, Louisiana.

Lustig, N., C. Pessino, and J. Scott. 2014. "The Impact of Taxes and Social Spending on Inequality and Poverty in Argentina, Bolivia, Brazil, Mexico, Peru, and Uruguay: Introduction to the Special Issue." *Public Finance Review* 42 (3): 287–303.

Modi, J. 1987. "Statistical Appendix." In *Supply-Side Tax Policy: Its Relevance to Developing Countries*, edited by Ved P. Gandhi. Washington: International Monetary Fund.

Monchuk, V. 2014. *Reducing Poverty and Investing in People: The New Role of Safety Nets in Africa*. Directions in Development: Human Development. Washington: World Bank.

Munoz, S., and S. Cho. 2003. "Social Impact of a Tax Reform: The Case of Ethiopia." In *Helping Countries Develop: The Role of Fiscal Policy*, edited by S. Gupta, B. Clements, and G. Inchauste. Washington: International Monetary Fund.

Musgrave, R. 1969. *Fiscal Systems*. New Haven, Connecticut: Yale University Press.

Newbery, D., and N. Stern, eds. 1987. *The Theory of Taxation for Developing Countries*. New York: Oxford University Press.

Norregaard, J. 2013. "Taxing Immovable Property: Revenue Potential and Implementation Challenges." IMF Working Paper No. 13/129, International Monetary Fund, Washington.

Peter, K., S. Buttrick, and D. Duncan. 2010. "Global Reform of Personal Income Taxation, 1981–2005: Evidence from 189 Countries." *National Tax Journal* 63 (3): 447–78.

Pinkovskiy, M., and X. Sala-i-Martin. 2009. "Parametric Estimations of the World Distribution of Income." NBER Working Paper No. 15433, National Bureau of Economic Research, Cambridge, Massachusetts.

Pritchett, L. 2013. *The Rebirth of Education: Schooling Ain't Learning*. Baltimore: Brookings Institution Press.

Sah, R.-K. 1983. "How Much Redistribution Is Possible through Commodity Taxes?" *Journal of Public Economics* 20 (1): 89–101.

Sahn, D., and S. Younger. 1999. "Fiscal Incidence in Africa: Microeconomic Evidence." Cornell University, Ithaca, New York.

Soares, S., R. Osório, F. Soares, M. Medeiros, and E. Zepeda. 2007. "Conditional Cash Transfers in Brazil, Chile, and Mexico: Impacts upon Inequality." IPC Working Paper No. 35, International Poverty Centre, Brasilia.

Subbarao, K., C. del Ninno, and C. Rodriguez-Alas. 2013. *Public Works as a Safety Net: Design, Evidence, and Implementation*. Washington: World Bank.

Tareq, S., J. Ligthart, A. Segura-Ubiergo, N. Wandwasi, and I. Izvorski. 2005. "Bosnia and Herzegovina: Assessing the Distributional Impact of a VAT." Technical Assistance Report, Fiscal Affairs Department, International Monetary Fund, Washington.

United States Agency for International Development (USAID). 2013. "Collecting Taxes, Full Data 2012." USAID, Washington.

van de Walle, D. 1995. "Incidence and Targeting: An Overview of Implications for Research and Policy." In *Public Spending and the Poor*, edited by D. van de Walle and K. Nead. Washington: World Bank.

Villela, L., A. Lemgruber, and M. Jorratt. 2010. "Tax Expenditure Budgets: Concepts and Challenges for Implementation." Working Paper No. 179, Inter-American Development Bank, Washington.

Woodhall, M. 2007. "Funding Higher Education: The Contribution of Economic Thinking to Debate and Policy Development." Education Working Paper No. 8, World Bank, Washington.

Zake, Justin. 2011. "Customs Administration Reform and Modernization in Anglophone Africa—Early 1990s to Mid-2010." IMF Working Paper No. 11/184, International Monetary Fund, Washington.

CHAPTER 5

Poverty and Distribution: Thirty Years Ago and Now

Ravi Kanbur

INTRODUCTION

In 1987 the *IMF Staff Papers* published "The Measurement and Alleviation of Poverty: With an Application to the Impact of Macroeconomic Adjustment" (Kanbur 1987). This paper, which was written in 1985 during a stay at the IMF as a Visiting Scholar, spoke to the key analytical and policy issues of the day as I saw them. The present chapter highlights what has happened in the past three decades in the poverty and distribution discourse from an analytical and policy-oriented perspective. There is no attempt to be comprehensive. Rather, this somewhat idiosyncratic take on the literature of the past 30 years is offered as a way of sparking a discussion on where we stand and where we need to go.

The mid-1980s were the culmination of 15 years of intensive discussion on the analytical and philosophical aspects of poverty and inequality conceptualization and measurement. Publications by Tony Atkinson (1970) and Amartya Sen (1973, 1976) ignited a technical literature on inequality and poverty indices that overlapped with and complemented economists' engagement with an emerging philosophical literature on inequality and distribution. Kenneth Arrow (1973) formulated Rawls (1971) in terms that economists could relate to, and Nozick's (1974) counter also made it to economists' reading lists. In poverty measurement, the paper by Foster, Greer, and Thorbecke (1984) introduced a poverty index (the Foster-Greer-Thorbecke [FGT] measure) that has become the workhorse of empirical work because of the intuitive way in which it captures differing degrees of poverty aversion, and because it is additively decomposable—thereby allowing an easy and intuitive accounting disaggregation of national poverty into policy-salient components. Kanbur (1987) used these decomposability properties to analyze the possible effects of expenditure-switching policies on poverty, while Besley and Kanbur (1988) analyzed the targeting of food subsidies to minimize the FGT poverty index, drawing on a literature that went back to Akerlof (1978). More generally, the public economics literature on taxation and expenditure advanced rapidly on the theoretical front, with a whole range of results being derived on distributionally sensitive fiscal policies (for example, Atkinson and Stiglitz 1980; Newbery and Stern 1987).

This chapter takes up the story in the mid-1980s and brings it up to date. It considers developments in three categories: facts and empirics, concepts and theory, and policies and interventions. While issues that came to the fore particularly in the past 30 years will be addressed, there were indeed antecedents in an earlier period. Moreover, a clean categorization into empirics, theory, and policy is also not possible, and some issues cover all three to varying degrees. Finally, this treatment is clearly idiosyncratic rather than comprehensive; others will surely have different takes on the development of the literature.

An earlier version of this chapter, with a suitably different title, was written while the author was a Visiting Scholar at the Fiscal Affairs Department of the International Monetary Fund during March–April 2007. This version provides a significant update to the review taking into account developments in the last decade.

FACTS AND EMPIRICS

Just More Facts

A key difference between now and 30 years ago is quite simply the availability of more distributional data sets—for more countries, more time periods, and more dimensions.[1] The World Bank's Living Standards Measurement Survey (LSMS) website lists more than 100 surveys for more than 35 countries.[2] All of these surveys were developed after 1985. There are a host of surveys for the transition economies of Europe and central Asia dating from the 1990s, as these countries joined the market economic system. In Latin America and the Caribbean, where wage and income surveys dominated in the past and still do in the present, expenditure surveys are increasingly being conducted and becoming the norm.

Another major source of information that has expanded dramatically in the past 30 years comes from the Demographic and Health Surveys (DHS). The website[3] lists more than 300 surveys, most from the 1990s onward. Although the DHS do not collect information on household income and expenditure, they do collect information on assets, which some analysts have used to cross-correlate with health and nutrition outcomes (for example, Filmer and Pritchett 1999). In any event, the availability of health and nutrition data has spurred further work on these dimensions of poverty and human development. In particular, the new data have helped clarify and quantify the prevalence and spread of HIV/AIDS, an issue that was hardly on the policy agenda in developing countries in the mid-1980s.

Perhaps the most remarkable transformation occurred for Africa. When Kanbur 1987 was written, *no* modern household income expenditure surveys were available for African countries. Now surveys for the following countries are listed on the LSMS website: Côte d'Ivoire, Ghana, Malawi, Niger, Nigeria, South Africa, Tanzania, and Uganda. But these are just the surveys on this website, with microdata made available for public use through the LSMS project. The World Bank's PovcalNet project makes available data on various distributional aggregates for many more African countries, and for 161 countries globally.[4] The DHS website has microdata available for more than 35 sub-Saharan African countries.

Consider now the world's two most-populous countries, India and China. For India, every five years the National Sample Survey's "thick round" provides distributional data that are central to the policy and dialogue in that country. The controversy on data for the 1990s, and the role of this controversy in debates on the distributional impact of economic liberalization, shows the ongoing use that is made by researchers and policymakers of the time series data that are available for the country (Deaton and Kozel 2005). The emergence of China from its economic isolation in the 1980s also meant greater availability of distributional (and other) data for China. Data availability increased significantly in the 1990s, feeding into an intensive debate on growing inequality in China (for example, Chen and Ravallion 2007; Zhang and Kanbur 2005).

Greater availability of household surveys has allowed the application of techniques that had been developed before the mid-1980s, but which awaited appropriate micro-level data for implementation. Prominent examples include incidence analysis of public expenditure and distributional analysis of price and subsidy reform. Such application is now routine, including in the IMF

---

[1] There are many compilations of data sources; see, for example, the United Nations World Income Inequality Database (http://www.wider.unu.edu/research/Database/en_GB/database/).

[2] Living Standards Measurement Study (http://econ.worldbank.org/WBSITE/EXTERNAL/EXTDEC/EXTRESEARCH/ EXTLSMS/0,,contentMDK:21588800~menuPK:4196952~pagePK:64168445~piPK:64168309~theSitePK:3358997, 00.html).

[3] DHS Program (http://dhsprogram.com/Data/).

[4] PovcalNet web page (http://iresearch.worldbank.org/PovcalNet/).

(Coady, Dorosh, and Minten 2007). It would not have been possible before the mid-1980s. Time series of distributional data for a large number of countries have permitted intertemporal analysis of the evolution of inequality and poverty, and have fueled a debate on globalization, growth, and distribution. For instance, recent work at the IMF (for example, Ostry, Berg, and Tsangarides 2014; IMF 2014) has made use of the World Income Inequality Databases, which are explained and assessed by Jenkins (2014). Such comprehensive data sets were simply not available three decades ago.

For a smaller but still significant number of countries, household panel data are now available. Baulch (2011) provides an inventory of more than 60 panel data sets covering more than 30 developing and transition countries. Most of these data sets are from the 1990s onward. Along with these new panel data has come an interest in analysis of the policy implications of the findings of these panels, especially for income and poverty dynamics, and the high degree of risk and vulnerability faced by the poor in developing and transition economies.

Trends in Poverty and Inequality

From the vantage point of the debates of the mid-1980s, two sets of facts seemed to be important. First, a group of countries in East Asia had managed to achieve growth with equity, leading to dramatic declines in poverty. This seemed to suggest that increasing per capita income could exist simultaneously with declining or constant inequality, contrary to Kuznets's (1955) hypothesis that inequality would first increase and then decrease only after some time as per capita incomes increased. Second, in the absence of time series data, the testing of this hypothesis in the 1970s and 1980s relied on cross-country econometric regressions, with all the problems that those entail. Counter to the estimates of Ahluwalia (1976), work in the 1980s by Anand and Kanbur (1993a, 1993b) argued that there was no "Kuznets curve" to be found in the cross-country data. This became the conventional wisdom, and has been found to be largely corroborated by the literature of the 1990s and the 2000s, using more, and more recent, distributional data, as from the compilation by Deininger and Squire (1996, 1998). The result was interpreted by some as suggesting that there was no systematic relationship between growth and inequality change, so policymakers should go all out for growth, since inequality would be expected to remain constant and thus poverty would decline (Dollar and Kraay 2002). An alternative interpretation would simply have been to caution against the use of cross-country regression analysis to draw time series conclusions for any one country.

From the vantage point of today, however, East Asia, and Asia in general, tells a very different story for the past three decades. Growth rates have been at historically unprecedented highs, but inequality has risen sharply. The growth has aided poverty reduction, but at a slower pace than if inequality had not risen. One estimate suggests that at constant inequality Asian growth of the past two decades would have lifted 240 million more people out of poverty (Kanbur and Zhuang 2012). Rising inequality has also occurred in the Organisation for Economic Co-operation and Development economies, the United States in particular (Stiglitz 2013). The phenomenal response to the book on inequality by Piketty (2014) highlights the policy and public concerns to which this persistent inequality has given rise. The global trend appears to be led by fundamental forces of technological change that are favoring capital over labor and skilled labor over unskilled labor, and the forces for rising inequality are being transmitted throughout the world by the globalization of trade, investment, and migration (Kanbur 2014b). One part of the world has indeed reversed this trend and produced falling inequality. The Latin American story highlights the way in which purposive policy intervention can address global forces (Kanbur 2014b; Kanbur and Zhuang 2012). But the global forces have raised distributional concerns among policymakers and civil society, despite the reductions in poverty that have accompanied the high growth rates.

Rising inequality dissipates the impact of growth on poverty. A given growth rate applied to a high level of inequality will lead to a lower level of poverty decrease than the same growth rate applied to a lower level of inequality, even if inequality does not change with growth. In this sense, inequality is bad for poverty reduction (Ravallion 2008). But might rising inequality impede growth itself in future periods? On the face of it, if increased inequality and high growth rates have persisted for more than a decade for a significant number of countries—two decades or more for some countries—then it does seem that rising and high inequality may not be an impediment to growth. However, the time series may not be long enough to draw confident conclusions. The literature has once again had to fall back on cross-country regressions, this time of growth as a dependent variable and inequality as an independent explanatory variable. Despite ample room for agnosticism given the usual pitfalls of cross-country regressions, a consensus does seem to be developing that high inequality may be detrimental to growth.[5]

Micro and Macro Evaluation

The 1980s saw the peak, and then the decline, of two methods of distributionally oriented evaluation of government interventions. The first, on project evaluation and shadow prices, dated back to the developments in public economics of the late 1960s and the 1970s. But by the mid-1980s intellectual interest had waned, and operational interest never reached critical mass.[6] The second, on evaluation of macro policies, and their distributional consequences in particular, using computable general equilibrium models also had its day in the 1980s and the early 1990s and then faded.[7]

One empirical strategy that was prevalent in the mid-1980s and before can be argued to have been used even more intensively in the subsequent period. This strategy is the use of cross-country regressions to test hypotheses about the impact of interventions and policies on growth and distributional outcomes. Cross-country regularities were brought to the fore in the 1960s and the 1970s in the work of authors such as Adelman and Morris (1974) and Chenery and Syrquin (1975). This chapter has already referred to the Kuznets curve literature of the 1970s and 1980s. But the availability of expanded data sets for more countries, the macroeconomic focus of the "structural adjustment period" of the 1980s and the 1990s, and the revival of growth theory in the 1990s assisted in an explosion of econometric analyses using cross-country data. Indeed, cross-country regressions have in many ways been central to the development debates of the past two decades.

This literature has not been without its controversies. Much attention has focused on the impact of globalization on growth, inequality, and poverty. Many of the technical issues highlighted in the Kuznets literature of the earlier period are equally present in these debates—most prominent among them, the extent to which inference can be drawn about development processes from cross-section relationships across countries with very different structural conditions. The endogeneity of key explanatory variables, such as trade ratios or tariffs to measure openness,

---

[5] In their review, Kanbur and Lustig (2000) conclude that "the jury is still out." The World Bank's overview in World Bank (2005, 103) was also agnostic. However, a body of work later emanating from the IMF has provided support for the hypothesis that inequality impedes growth; see, for example, Ostry, Berg, and Tsangarides 2014.

[6] As Little and Mirrlees (1991, p 359) note in their own 20-year retrospective, "A battle raged in the World Bank during the 1970s about whether social prices should be used. Formally, the 'social price brigade' won, in that their guidelines on the use of distributional weights were actually incorporated in the *Operational Manual* in 1980. In practice, we believe, they were hardly ever used except in an experimental manner."

[7] Kanbur 1990b is one attempt at this type of exercise. The sheer complexity of these models was perhaps the primary reason for their failure in the analytical and the policy arenas. It was very difficult to explain the reasoning behind the outcomes, which lay somewhere in the interaction of the sometimes hundreds of equations and the crucial handful of "closure rules," and the results could be sensitive to the large number of assumed parameter values.

has also been much debated.[8] The "institutional quality" variables that have increasingly been used in these regressions are open to similar questions. However, despite the debates, the cross-country regressions approach to evaluating development policies and interventions continues to be a significant presence in the current development discourse.

However, one empirical strategy was largely absent in the mid-1980s and before, but rapidly gained prominence in the past decade. This strategy takes the "medical drugs testing" approach seriously and implements it for development interventions. The basic problem with the standard econometric approach is the difficulty of controlling for unobserved heterogeneity, which may have correlation patterns that bias the estimated results. The "randomized evaluation" methodology from pharmaceuticals testing has framed the response of a growing number of development economists, especially in the 2000s. Some have argued that this should be at the heart of what organizations like the World Bank do in the development business (Banerjee and He 2003). The movement has had an impact in the academic literature, but also in the fact that evaluation procedures are much more carefully discussed in project design. This is project evaluation of a type, then, that is very different from the type that rose to prominence in the 1970s and faded in the 1980s—the design of control groups has replaced the estimation of shadow prices. Invariably, of course, there has been a backlash. The very strength of randomized evaluation—namely, the controlling of specific conditions to isolate the impact of the intervention in question—raises questions about the generalizability of the conclusions, particularly for policy purposes. There is also the concern that the "big questions" in development are being sidelined in favor of the small detail of the design of randomization. The debate continues, and is one of the live and vital issues in development economics today.[9]

CONCEPTS AND THEORY

Poverty Dynamics and Risk

The greater availability of panel data sets has led to a greater empirical appreciation of the general "churning" that takes place around the poverty line. In rural KwaZuku-Natal in South Africa, 44 percent of the population either moved into or out of poverty during a five-year period. The number was 28 percent in rural Nicaragua during a three-year period, and similar numbers can be found for a range of countries (Chronic Poverty Research Centre 2005, Table 11.1). In countries for which panels have been developed for a period of a decade or more, the volatility of household incomes has been well documented.[10]

Leaving aside the empirical literature that has developed on the basis of these panel data sets, the issues raised by them have led to a new wave of theorizing on and conceptualization of poverty in a dynamic and risky setting. The standard snapshot view is by now relatively straightforward. There is a threshold value of well-being, and poverty is below this threshold. Various axioms capture intuitions about aggregation into a single poverty index, and from these are derived families of poverty indices, like that put forward by Foster, Greer, and Thorbecke (1984). But

---

[8] As Rodrik (2012, 141) argues, "Consider an illustration from trade policy. The estimated coefficient on import tariffs in growth regressions run for the contemporary period is typically negative (albeit insignificantly so) and rarely positive. One frequently hears the argument that we can at least draw the conclusion from this fact that import protection cannot be beneficial to growth. But once again this and similar inferences are invalid. A negative partial correlation between growth and import tariffs is not only consistent with protection being growth-enhancing, it is actually an equilibrium consequence of trade protection being used in a socially optimal fashion."

[9] See Kanbur 2006; Duflo, Glennerster, and Kremer 2007; Rodrik 2009; and Deaton 2009 for reprises of the debate. For a recent example of randomized evaluation, see Banerjee and others 2014.

[10] For example, Dercon 2004 for Ethiopia.

now consider dynamics, or risk. Suppose the individual is in poverty in one period, and out of poverty in the next. How is this individual's poverty to be assessed? One possibility is to compare the individual's present discounted value of well-being (as measured by consumption, say) to the present discounted value of the poverty line (chronic poverty). But this still leaves open the issue that an individual not in poverty by this measure is still in poverty in one of the two periods (transient poverty [Jalan and Ravallion 2000]). An alternative is to classify as chronically poor those who are poor in both periods.[11]

All of the above led to a lively literature on dynamics and poverty measurement in the 1990s. But risk and vulnerability must also be added to the measurement mix. What is the risk of income and consumption fluctuations faced by individuals and households, and how does this risk vary at different income levels? Moreover, how is individual risk to be aggregated to provide an overall level of risk for the society as a whole—what weights are to be used? Empirical issues arise in estimating risk from the fairly short runs available for panels so far (two or three observations for most, half a dozen or so for a small number), but the theoretical literature has developed quickly in response to these questions, and a range of dynamic and risk-encompassing measures of poverty are now available (for example, Ligon and Schechter 2003; Calvo and Dercon 2009; Foster 2009).

An extreme case of the variability caused by risk is mortality. What happens to standard measures of poverty when a poor person dies? All else being held constant, the measures decrease! This is surely an unacceptable property of our poverty measures, and raises a fundamental question about their axiomatic structure. All of these measures are derived assuming that the population set is unchanged. But when individuals disappear because of mortality, or new individuals appear because of birth, new rules are needed to make the disappearance or appearance commensurate with the ongoing presence of individuals. Various methods for addressing this issue have been proposed (for example, Kanbur and Mukherjee 2007), but the basic point is that while the "Sen axioms" of the 1970s served us well in helping to derive operational poverty measures, during the past decade these axioms have increasingly been questioned in the conceptual literature.

Gender and Intrahousehold Inequality

In the mid-1980s, the discourse on the systematic incorporation of gender and intrahousehold allocation into the poverty distribution was just beginning. Sen (1983) introduced the issue of gender inequality within the household and in general during the development process. The 1980s also saw the beginning of theoretical and conceptual work on intrahousehold allocation models and their application to the newly available household survey data sets.

A major data constraint in mapping out the extent and nature of intrahousehold inequality in consumption, commensurate with consumption-based measures of overall inequality and poverty, is that individual-level data on consumption are not available. Indeed, it is difficult to see how this could be done comprehensively, since a significant portion of household consumption (like the house itself) is a "public" good within the household. In any event, information, even for those items like food that are individualized, is collected at the household level. The standard practice is then to divide the monetary measure of total household consumption by the number of household members, and allocate to each individual the per capita household consumption. Sometimes (though not very often in official statistics), household size is adjusted for composition and for economies of scale. But throughout, in the absence of individual consumption data, the assumption is that real inequality within the household is not present. In a first attempt to measure the effect of ignoring household

---

[11] This perspective is advanced by Chronic Poverty Research Centre 2005.

inequality, Haddad and Kanbur (1990) use a specially collected data set with individual-level food-consumption information from the Philippines. They find that overall inequality and poverty could be understated by as much as 30 percent.

Apart from its impact on measures of inequality and poverty, neglect of intrahousehold inequality also affects policy interventions that try to target individuals within the household, such as young children or women. A model of intrahousehold allocation as a function, among other things, of overall household resources is needed. It would be fair to say that well into the 1980s the standard "unitary model" ruled the roost. The key theoretical prediction of this model, with implications for empirical testing and for policy, is that of "income pooling": the household's consumption pattern, including that of individuals in that household, depends only on the total budget constraint, not on which individual brings in what amount of resources to the budget. But from the 1980s onward, and especially in the 1990s, new theoretical models, and new types of econometric testing, began to question systematically the income-pooling hypothesis. For example, intrahousehold bargaining models were developed to highlight the implication that the resources brought to the household by an individual would partly determine how much benefit that individual could draw from the available household consumption (Manser and Brown 1980; Bourguignon and Chiappori 1992; Ghosh and Kanbur 2008). The econometric theory of testing for "collective" as opposed to unitary models using only household-level consumption data was developed and applied. And the impacts of differential sources of household income on observable individual outcomes such as anthropometrics were also tested and found to be significant (for example, Browning and Chiappori 1998; Quisumbing and Maluccio 2003). By the mid-1990s, a group of economists was already working in this area and had issued a manifesto arguing that the burden of proof would now be on those who would support the unitary model (Alderman and others 1995). Since then the theory and the evidence against the unitary model has continued to grow.

Although developed-country policy issues have also propelled these conceptual changes, and their empirical testing, development-economics issues have played a central role in motivating these analytical advances, which started slowly in the 1980s, accelerated in the 1990s, and have matured in the 2000s. These issues are surveyed and synthesized in the World Bank's *World Development Report 2012: Gender Equality and Development* (World Bank 2011).

Multidimensionality and Interdisciplinarity

What exactly is poverty? If it is the lack of an adequate standard of living, what exactly is this standard of living? In the 1980s the discussion, at least in the international agencies, was dominated by economic concepts and measurement—essentially the monetary value of goods and services consumed. Sure, there were concerns and methods for addressing at least some items of consumption for which there were no market prices (like production of food for home consumption), but the core approach and method were very clearly tied to "money metric utility."

In the 1990s this sole focus on the monetary value of consumption (or income) shifted to a systematic concern with a broader range of items, even though income and consumption retained a central role. Starting in 1990, the United Nations Development Programme's Human Development Report introduced the Human Development Index, which combined income with education and health to produce an overall index for ranking countries. Despite many technical criticisms of the index,[12] its introduction changed the terms of the debate. It brought education and health to the forefront as key independent components of assessment, not just as inputs to income enhancement, thereby cementing these dimensions of the "basic

---

[12] For an early critique, see Kanbur 1990a.

needs" approach of the 1970s. Part of the rationale for such broadening was to argue that education and health were components of the standard of living that could not be proxied by income (conceptually or empirically). Another part was that an explicit discussion of education and health also broadened the policy focus to incorporate direct interventions in these sectors rather than relying solely or primarily on instruments seen to increase incomes more directly. The development of the AIDS pandemic, not really foreseen clearly in the 1980s, also served to bring health goals to the fore. The multidimensionality wrought by the Human Development Index is seen in fuller form in the eight Millennium Development Goals of the UN system, which were signed on to by world leaders in 2000 for the period 2000–15, and their extension in discussions on the "post-2015" agenda (United Nations 2014).[13] At the time of writing, the world is looking to the post-2015 agenda under the heading of Sustainable Development Goals. Whatever the outcome of this complex process, it looks as though multidimensionality will play a larger role.

One dimension of the standard of living that has not received as much support and consensus as education and health is "voice"—the extent to which poor people participate in and influence the decisions that affect them. There are, of course, difficulties in the conceptualization and measurement of voice, or of "empowerment," another term often used to capture this constellation of concerns. And the causal, instrumental role of "democracy" and "governance" variables in growth is perhaps even less clear than the roles of education and health. However, the importance of these factors in an evaluation of development outcomes is at least implicitly recognized in the conditionality of many bilateral donors, who put a high weight on the poor having voice and accountability. As the discussion matures, and concepts and measurement are sharpened, no doubt this cluster of issues will take its rightful place in the broadening of the standard of living from narrow, income-focused approaches.[14]

Development has, of course, seen interest from many of the social science disciplines. Historically, these disciplines have largely gone their separate ways, with their own literatures, journals, and conferences. Before the mid-1980s, economics and philosophy interacted somewhat on issues of equity and social welfare. However, since the mid-1990s the amount of cross-fertilization between the disciplines in the social sciences in the study of development has increased significantly, and a lot if it has been driven by distributional concerns.

At the World Bank and in the donor agencies, the hiring of noneconomists was initially prompted by the need to assess the social and environmental consequences of infrastructure projects, such as population resettlement that accompanied dam construction (Cernea 1988, 1999). From the mid-1980s onward, however, and especially from the 1990s, the World Bank's poverty assessments were required to have a "qualitative" component that went beyond, and complemented, the standard distributional analysis from a representative household survey (Carvalho and White 1997). This requirement was replicated in other donors' reports as well, meaning that methods particular to anthropology and sociology were now part of reports that were formerly entirely economics oriented, and still continued to be primarily economics oriented.

The push toward multidimensionality has moved alongside, and is related to, the push toward greater interdisciplinarity, or at least multidisciplinarity, in the discourse on distribution and poverty. In the mid-1980s the dominant approach in the World Bank and elsewhere in

---

[13] The move to many dimensions raises the conceptual question of how poverty is to be measured when there is deprivation along many dimensions. The past decade has seen a burgeoning of a literature on this topic—see, for example, Alkire and Foster 2011.

[14] The World Bank's *World Development Report 2000/2001: Attacking Poverty* (World Bank 2000) introduced empowerment as a key dimension of the poverty discourse.

international agencies was the quantitative-economics one. A broadening has undoubtedly occurred since then. The juxtaposition of the methods of different disciplines, of household survey analysis combined with econometric analysis on the one hand, with participatory poverty analysis, unstructured interviews, and discourse analysis on the other, has led to a creative tension in these agencies and in the wider development studies community. This is an interaction that was simply not present before the mid-1980s.

Kanbur 2003b characterizes the "qualitative-quantitative" spectrum as being composed of five dimensions: (1) type of information, nonnumerical to numerical; (2) type of population coverage, specific to general; (3) type of population involvement, active to passive; (4) type of inference methodology, inductive to deductive; and (5) type of disciplinary framework, broad social science to neoclassical economics. In a subsequent paper (Kanbur and Shaffer 2007a), the divide is characterized in more fundamental epistemological terms, between the empiricist-positivist tradition and the tradition of critical hermeneutics. The latter suggests that tensions will always remain when different disciplines, and their methods, are brought to bear on the common problem of understanding poverty and distributional outcomes.

However, the greater interplay of disciplines and their methods has undoubtedly brought dividends, as shown, for example, in the compilation of studies in Kanbur and Shaffer 2007b, and in a number of other studies, all of which date from the early years of the 2000s. One example is an assessment of conditional cash transfers (discussed in the next section) in Nicaragua and Turkey. The donors required that both quantitative and qualitative methods be used. The results of the evaluation are presented and assessed by Adato (2008). The quantitative part of the assessment followed the best practice of randomized evaluation, discussed in the previous section. In Nicaragua, for example, "Out of 42 *comarcas,* 21 were randomly selected into the program, and 21 into the control group. Household and individual level data was collected in 2000, before the intervention began, in both control and treatment localities. Data on the same variables was then collected in the same households in 2002" (Adato 2008, 7). The impact of the program was then estimated through the double-difference method, to control for unobserved differences across communities and over time. For the qualitative component, however, "field researchers, with B.A. or M.A. degrees in sociology or anthropology, conducted research in two communities each (for a total of six communities in each study) over a period of 4–5 months, moving between them at different intervals. The field researchers resided with families in the communities" (Adato 2008, 9).

The quantitative analysis established that the programs were having the effects intended. However, the qualitative analysis revealed a number of features that could threaten the sustainability of the program in the long term. The targeting criteria, while performing well on their own terms, did not resonate with the population on the ground, creating tensions in the community among those receiving the transfer and those who could not understand why they were excluded. Also, having understood that transfers depended on their child falling below a certain nutritional assessment, the qualitative analysis indicated that some mothers were deliberately underfeeding to satisfy program requirements—fortunately, this led to a program redesign.

Perhaps the most radical departure in economics since the mid-1980s is the "behavioral revolution," which incorporates insights from psychology into development. Daniel Kahneman was awarded the 2002 Nobel prize in economics for his work on this topic, and the essence of the approach is captured in Kahneman (2011). This behavioral perspective has now begun to seep into development economics and into the analysis of poverty and income distribution (see, for example, Datta and Mullainathan 2014; Jäntti, Kanbur, and Pirttilä 2014a, 2014b). The inroads being made into conventional development economics are further highlighted by the fact that the World Bank's 2015 World Development Report is on this topic (World Bank 2014). One example of the value added by the behavioral perspective is a reassessment of interventions to encourage savings by introducing a range of commitment devices (Karlan 2014).

There are thus a growing number of examples of the benefits of interdisciplinarity in the analysis of poverty and distribution. These examples were simply not there when Kanbur 1987 was written. Despite the tensions, this trend is set to continue.

A lively debate had begun 30 years ago among philosophers on "legitimate" inequality. In particular, the issue was what role personal responsibility had in inequality. Dworkin (2000) is recognized as a prime mover in this debate, but other names include Cohen (2008), Arneson (2013), and Sen (2001). Roemer (1998) brought this debate squarely into the mainstream of economic analysis, and it entered the development economics discourse with the World Bank's 2006 World Development Report (World Bank 2005). There is now a vibrant literature on theory (Fleurbaey and Maniquet 2012) and an ever-growing set of papers with empirical applications (for a recent survey, see Brunori, Ferreira, and Peragine [2013]). A fruitful interdisciplinary interaction between economics and philosophy continues to occur.

Roemer's (1998) formulation is now central to the literature. He considers an outcome variable of interest (income, for instance) and distinguishes conceptually between two sets of variables to which can be attributed variation in this outcome variable across the population. The first set are "circumstances," over which the individual has no control (gender, race, parental wealth, and so forth), while the second set are labeled "effort," being variables the individual can control. At the conceptual level, variation due to circumstances is a legitimate target of redistribution—it is inequality of opportunity. How big is inequality of opportunity relative to opportunity of income? One way to quantify this is to specify the circumstance variables and, through nonparametric inequality decomposition or parametric regression analysis, attribute a portion of the variation to circumstances. The ratio of this amount to the total variation is then a measure of the inequality of opportunity. This is the method followed by Paes de Barros and others (2009), using a set of methods that are growing in use in policy circles (Brunori, Ferreira, and Peragine 2013).

These developments in the inequality literature have been criticized recently by Kanbur and Wagstaff (2014). Treating the residual variation beyond that explained by the specified circumstance variables as reflecting effort and only effort surely understates inequality of opportunity. The residual includes luck, some of which may have been taken on willingly, but other parts of ill fortune may not have been of the individual's doing. There are also unmeasured circumstance variables like innate talents, which are not the result of effort by the individual, or the individual's environment including peer effects. Finally, some of the circumstances may themselves influence effort, and this effect should also be incorporated into inequality of opportunity. Some empirical approaches to address these issues have been developed, but they are under debate. It looks as though the inequality-of-opportunity discourse will continue to be present in a way that it was not 30 years ago.

POLICIES AND INTERVENTIONS

The case can be made that none of the examples considered above, for theory and empirics, point to anything new since the mid-1980s. All of them—intrahousehold inequality, evolution of inequality, interdisciplinarity, and so on—have antecedents in the previous period. This is certainly true, and this discussion is only highlighting a tendency and a pattern, rather than an absolute break in the mid-1980s. The difficulty of delineating a sharp break is most acute in the case of policy debates and interventions, since most debates of this type are generic and eternal in nature, and most interventions have been discussed if not actually implemented at some time in the past. Trade policy, redistribution and transfers, expenditure on health and education, and others are all the subject of intense debate now, but they have surely been discussed before. However, the four issues highlighted in this section do deserve their characterization as being somewhat new to the scene, at least in comparison to the vantage point of the mid-1980s.

Conditional Cash Transfers

Conditional cash transfers (CCTs) are no exception to the maxim that there is nothing new under the sun. They existed before the mid-1980s—public works schemes for famine relief are to be found in ancient times. However, there has been an explosion of these schemes, and they have risen to prominence in the policy and analytical debate only from the 1990s onward, and especially in the 2000s. The Employment Guarantee Scheme of Maharashtra State in India dates from the early 1970s, but in recent years programs that make transfers conditional on school attendance of children and other requirements have been introduced in Bangladesh, Brazil, Mexico, Nicaragua, Turkey, and a host of African countries as well (Kakwani, Soares, and Son 2005; Das, Do, and Ozler 2004; Levy 2006).

This proliferation of CCTs is remarkable. What explains the sudden interest in them, and what lessons have been learned from their operation so far? The answer to the first part of the question is twofold—growing inequality and positive evaluation results. CCTs can be seen as a response to the rising inequality that has accompanied growth in many countries. Even where growth has reduced poverty despite rising inequality, as discussed in a previous section distributional concerns have persisted and grown. One reason may be that the increasing inequality may be picking up ground-level realities that are missed by official statistics. For example, in many countries poverty measures that emphasize the depth of poverty are falling more slowly or even rising. In many more countries the overall poverty decline is an aggregation of significant numbers of winners and losers. Although the winners outnumber the losers, and their climb out of poverty is to be celebrated, the plight of those who have become poor or whose poverty has increased cannot be ignored.[15] This suggests there is a role for redistributive policy to target the losers from economic reform and economic crisis. Furthermore, conditioning the transfer on behavior can help induce changes such as keeping children in school or increasing visits to health centers. Many governments have looked to CCTs to address the issue of increasing inequality in the context of economic reform and liberalization.

In addition to the felt need is the simple fact that evaluations of these programs have shown positive results. The evaluation of Mexico's Progresa-Oportunidades program played a key role. The designers of the program incorporated evaluation using appropriate control groups right from the start. To quote Levy (2006, 37), "Between October 1997 and November 1999, a total of 24,000 families in 506 localities were interviewed regularly. Of those localities, 320 that were incorporated in the program as of October 1997 were in the initial treatment group and 186 were in the control group, until they were incorporated in the program in late 1999." It was argued that the assignment to treatment and control was effectively random, so that randomized evaluation techniques could be implemented. The evaluation continued in similar fashion as the program was scaled up. The positive results that emerged from the evaluation were accepted by the technical community because of the methods used,[16] helping greatly in the spread of the CCT message from country to country.

Thus, CCTs are now being implemented in a large number of countries, and the evaluations are mostly positive (Fiszbein and Schady 2009). What are the lessons being learned? The previous section discussed the sometimes surprising findings of qualitative as compared with quantitative analysis. Design details matters, and for long-term sustainability these qualitative issues have to be considered. Institutional details and the monitoring and accountability of officials are always important. Generic issues that arise with achieving the objectives of any program include low

---

[15] These and other dimensions of the disconnect between official statistics and perceptions and reality on the ground are discussed in Kanbur 2010a.

[16] For an example of the technical issues discussed and addressed, see Behrman and Todd 1999. A comprehensive assessment of CCTs is provided in Fiszbein and Schady 2009.

participation and fungibility (Das, Do, and Ozler 2004). Trade-offs between coverage and leak-age, and between the specific objectives of the program and what people would like to spend the cash on, are ever present, must be handled in the design, and cannot be wished away.

Governance and Institutions

A constellation of related issues has come to the fore since the mid-1990s in a way that was not present before the mid-1980s. These issues broadly have to do with the role of institutions in the development process. Although applicable to the development process in general, they resonate particularly with poverty and distributional outcomes. If growth itself depends on the quality of institutions, then so does poverty reduction. If, furthermore, the distribution of gains from growth also depends on the nature of institutions, the importance of these factors is additionally magnified. These perspectives are well captured by Acemoglu and Robinson (2012). The litera-ture has had both macro and micro strands.

The analysis of these factors was boosted by the publication of comparable cross-country gover-nance indicators beginning in the mid- and late 1990s,[17] which fed into and played a central part in the blossoming of the cross-country growth regressions literature discussed in the previous sec-tion. It remains one-half of the "institutions versus geography" debate—is growth better explained by the favorable (or otherwise) geographical location of the country, or by the institutions that regulate economic activity, including institutions of economic policymaking? From the policy per-spective, however, the important question is—even if a relationship with the quality of institutions in a general sense is found, what specifically can be done about it? As Rodrik (2008, 100) says,

> Desirable institutions provide security of property rights, enforce contracts, stimulate entrepreneur-ship, foster integration in the world economy, maintain macroeconomic stability, manage risk-taking by financial intermediaries, supply social insurance and safety nets, and enhance voice and account-ability. But as the variety of institutional forms that prevail in the advanced countries themselves suggests…, each one of these ends can be achieved in a large number of different ways.

Therein lies the difficulty in generalizing, and finding "best practices" to transfer across coun-tries. Country and context specificity is the constant pull away from generalizations based on cross-country regressions using the sorts of indicators developed by Kaufmann, Kraay, and Mastruzzi (2008). In any event, changing deep institutions is a hard task, not easily done by simply "transferring best practice."

The more micro-oriented strand in the literature is more interdisciplinary and, not surpris-ingly, also emphasizes context specificity. It is perhaps best exemplified by the World Bank's *World Development Report 2004: Making Services Work for Poor People* (World Bank 2003). The report focuses on "the relationships of accountability—between policymakers, service providers, and citizens" (World Bank 2003, xv) and proposes that this can be done by "(i)ncreasing poor clients' choice and participation in service delivery [so] they can monitor and discipline providers… (r)aising poor citizens' voice, through the ballot box and making information widely available… [and] by rewarding the effective and penalizing the ineffective delivery of services to poor people" (World Bank 2003, 1). But once again, the question might be asked—how exactly are these three things to be done?

The past 20 years have seen a move away from policy prescriptions disembodied from the institutional context, and toward a more explicit recognition of the importance of institutional structure. This is a major difference from the mid-1980s. Indeed, Kanbur 1987 reflects the some-what technocratic tenor of the times. However, with the recognition of the importance of

---

[17] See the World Bank website http://info.worldbank.org/governance/wgi/index.aspx#home, and Kaufmann, Kraay, and Mastruzzi 2008.

institutions on the policy front, and after an initial phase of attempting to implement uniform "best practices," there is now considerable uncertainty encapsulated in the importance of context specificity of appropriate institutional design.

Macroeconomic Crises and Safety Nets

As noted earlier, most macroeconomic policy debates have a perennial feel to them. Issues of exchange rate management, fiscal balance, monetary policy, and so on were very much present in the 1980s and before. In this sense, therefore, far less is new about the macroeconomic perspective on poverty.

However, one macroeconomic issue was not as prominent as it is now. Perhaps the most striking global macroeconomic phenomena of the past three decades were the financial crises of 1997 and 2008. The first was centered on East Asia but with repercussions around the world. The implications for growth and poverty reduction were dramatic. By some estimates, the gains of a decade were wiped out overnight in countries such as Indonesia.[18] The crisis of 2008 was even more severe, leading the world into a recession that came close to matching the Great Depression of the 1930s. Except through natural disasters, such rapid reversals, such vulnerability, were not really part of the mental makeup of the mid-1980s.

The global macroeconomic crises have influenced the policy discourse. Research of the past few years, including from the IMF, has been cautious about the benefits of capital market integration, and has emphasized the need to manage the risks and to carefully sequence the opening up of capital markets (for example, Kose and others 2006). Asian countries built up significant reserves to protect themselves against outflows, and perhaps against being forced to have recourse to the IMF. The crisis of 2008 similarly caused a rethinking of financial sector deregulation on the one hand, and on austerity policies during recessions on the other.

From the point of view of poverty and distribution, however, the crises of the late 1990s and the late 2000s brought to the fore like never before the issue of safety nets and cast it in a newer, sharper, light. The discourse of the 1980s had developed a negative view of transfer schemes such as food subsidies, and broader social security schemes like pensions. It was argued, quite rightly in many cases, that these schemes represented major fiscal exposures while at the same time being poorly targeted toward the poor. A leading illustration in the 1970s, for example, was the Sri Lanka rice subsidy scheme, which was dismantled in the late 1970s and early 1980s (Anand and Kanbur 1991). However, the macroeconomic crises, together with possible negative effects on some poor of policy reform, led in the 1990s to a revisiting of transfer schemes as a response to crisis. The popularity of public works schemes to counter short-term downturns in economic activity grew. India's National Rural Employment Guarantee Act of 2004 is one of the largest in the world. True, the discourse on the rationale for these schemes mixes up the micro and the macro, but the sharp macroeconomic downturns experienced by many countries in the late 1990s and the late 2000s, and the expectation that such downturns were more likely in a globalized world economy, is a significant explanation. The consensus against safety nets has turned and, fully cognizant of the lessons of the earlier period on targeting and on implementation, and in concert with other rationales for transfers (such as keeping children in school), there is now far greater acceptance of them as policy instruments to manage distributional risk from macroeconomic and microeconomic shocks.[19] At the same time, there is a far greater appreciation of external assistance in helping countries address the poverty and inequality consequences of sharp macroeconomic downturns.[20]

---

[18] For a detailed assessment of the impact of the crisis on income and non-income dimensions of the standard of living in Indonesia, see Strauss and others 2004.

[19] See the discussion in Kanbur 2010b, 2014b.

[20] Proposals for special windows of crisis assistance have been accepted by the World Bank's soft loan window, the International Development Association (Kanbur 2012).

Global Public Goods and Distribution

The financial crises of the 1990s highlighted the linkages in the world economy and the vulnerabilities of the poor in one economy to events in other countries, perhaps very far away. Since the 1990s the policy discourse has become attuned to global public goods, or more generally cross-border public goods and the role of international public policy in providing them. The issues covered under this umbrella include greenhouse gas emissions, global forest cover, migration and refugees, financial contagion, water basin and riparian rights management, and the spread of disease.

There is nothing particularly novel at the conceptual level about these phenomena. The public economics techniques of the 1980s and earlier can be easily adapted to frame these issues. When there are cross-border externalities, there is a gain from coordination, and thus a gain to development, if some or all of the countries involved are developing countries. But the coordination mechanism itself is a public good, and a tendency to underinvest in such mechanisms will occur for the usual reasons. If the costs of this coordination can be borne by richer countries, then to the extent that the cross-border public good benefits poor countries, these resource inputs can legitimately be claimed to be development assistance.[21]

All of the above was understood 20 or more years ago. What is new is the veritable explosion of discussion, debate, and action on the design and financing of these coordination mechanisms. Particularly in the environmental arena, from the Montreal Protocol to the Kyoto agreement to the Clean Development Mechanism and carbon trading, there has been continuous concern and response to the concern during the past two decades. Indeed, the continued concern about climate change and how it and the attempts to mitigate it will affect poor countries and the poor in poor countries—the "climate justice" issue—will ensure that this policy issue stays on the agenda in the coming decades (Kanbur 2014a). Yet it was almost totally absent from the discourse 20 years ago.

CONCLUSION

This chapter adopts the "Rip Van Winkle" stratagem of asking what differences would be noticed, in the domain of poverty and distribution, by someone who fell asleep in 1985 and woke up in 2015. In one sense there is tremendous continuity—the discourse on poverty lines, poverty measurement, the inequality-growth relationship, fiscal balance, costs of inflation, public works schemes, food and energy subsidies, and so on would be very familiar to a visitor from three decades ago. But there are also discernible differences. This chapter highlights 10 such differences under three broad headings. Under facts and empirics the chapter emphasizes (1) the tremendous increase in household survey information for developing countries, particularly for Africa; (2) the sharp trend toward increasing inequality in many countries over the past 30 years; and (3) the dominance of macroeconomic cross-country regressions and the rise of microeconomic randomized evaluations, in contrast to the demise of computable general equilibrium models and project evaluation. Under concepts and theory the chapter highlights (1) poverty dynamics and risk, (2) gender and intrahousehold inequality, and (3) multidisciplinarity as distinguishing features of the past two decades. Finally, under policies and interventions the chapter picks out (1) conditional cash transfers, (2) governance and institutions, (3) macroeconomic crises, and (4) global public goods as being part of the discourse on poverty and distributional policy in a way that they were not when Kanbur 1987 was written three decades ago.

---

[21] Kanbur (2003a, 2004, 2005) explores the implications of the theory for the practical aspects of international agency operations, particularly the World Bank.

REFERENCES

Acemoglu, Daron, and James Robinson. 2012. *Why Nations Fail: The Origins of Power, Prosperity and Poverty*. New York: Crown Business.

Adato, Michelle. 2008. "Integrating Survey and Ethnographic Methods to Evaluate Conditional Cash Transfer Programs." IFPRI Discussion Paper No. 00810, International Food Policy Research Institute, Washington.

Adelman, Irma, and Cynthia Taft Morris. 1974. *Economic Growth and Social Equity in Developing Countries*. London: Oxford University Press.

Ahluwalia, Montek. 1976. "Inequality, Poverty and Development." *Journal of Development Economics* 3 (4): 307–42.

Akerlof, George. 1978. "The Economics of 'Tagging' as Applied to the Optimal Income Tax, Welfare Programs and Manpower Planning." *American Economic Review* 68 (1): 8–19.

Alderman, Harold, Pierre-Andre Chiappori, Lawrence Haddad, John Hoddinott, and Ravi Kanbur. 1995. "Unitary Versus Collective Models of the Household: Is It Time to Shift the Burden of Proof?" *World Bank Research Observer* 10 (1): 1–19.

Alkire, Sabine, and James Foster. 2011. "Counting and Multidimensional Poverty Measurement." *Journal of Public Economics* 95 (7–8): 476–87.

Anand, Sudhir, and Ravi Kanbur. 1991. "Public Policy and Basic Needs Provision in Sri Lanka." In *The Political Economy of Hunger, Volume III: Endemic Hunger*, edited by J. Dreze and A. Sen. Oxford, U.K.: Clarendon Press.

———. 1993a. "Inequality and Development: A Critique." *Journal of Development Economics* 41 (1): 19–43.

———. 1993b. "The Kuznets Process and the Inequality-Development Relationship." *Journal of Development Economics* 40 (1): 25–52.

Arneson, Richard. 2013. "Equality of Opportunity: Derivative Not Fundamental." *Journal of Social Philosophy* 44 (4): 316–30.

Arrow, K. 1973. "Some Ordinalist-Utilitarian Notes on Rawls's Theory of Justice." *Journal of Philosophy* 70 (9): 245–63.

Atkinson, A. B. 1970. "On the Measurement of Inequality." *Journal of Economic Theory* 2 (3): 244–63.

———, and Joseph Stiglitz. 1980. *Lectures in Public Economics*. Maidenhead, U.K.: McGraw-Hill.

Banerjee, Abhijit, Esther Duflo, Rachel Glennerster, and Cynthia Kinnan. 2014. "The Miracle of Microfinance? Evidence from a Randomized Evaluation." MIT Department of Economics, Cambridge, Massachusetts. http://economics.mit.edu/files/5993.

Banerjee, Abhijit, and Ruimin He. 2003. "The World Bank of the Future." *American Economic Review, Papers and Proceedings* 93 (2): 39–44.

Baulch, Bob. 2011. "Household Panel Data Sets in Developing and Transition Countries (Version 2, March 2011)." Chronic Poverty Research Centre. http://www.chronicpoverty.org/uploads/publication_files/Annotated_Listing_of_Panel_Datasets_in_Developing_and_Transitional_Countries.pdf.

Behrman, Jere, and Petra Todd. 1999. *Randomness in the Experimental Samples of PROGRESA (Education, Health and Nutrition Program)*. Washington: International Food Policy Research Institute.

Besley, Timothy, and Ravi Kanbur. 1988. "Food Subsidies and Poverty Alleviation." *Economic Journal* 98 (392): 701–19.

Bourguignon, F., and P. A. Chiappori. 1992. "Collective Models of Household Behavior: An Introduction." *European Economic Review* 36 (2/3): 355–64.

Browning, M., and P. A. Chiappori. 1998. "Efficient Intra-Household Allocation: A General Characterization and Empirical Tests." *Econometrica* 66 (6): 1241–78.

Brunori, Paolo, Francisco H. G. Ferreira, and Vito Peragine. 2013. "Inequality of Opportunity, Income Inequality and Economic Mobility: Some International Comparisons." ECINEQ Working Paper No. 2013–284, Society for the Study of Economic Inequality, Verona, Italy.

Calvo, Cesar, and Stefan Dercon. 2009. "Chronic Poverty and All That: The Measurement of Poverty over Time." In *Poverty Dynamics: Interdisciplinary Perspectives*, edited by A. Addison, D. Hulme, and R. Kanbur. Oxford, U.K.: Oxford University Press.

Carvalho, Sonia, and Howard White. 1997. "Combining the Quantitative and Qualitative Approaches to Poverty Measurement and Analysis." World Bank Technical Paper No. 366, World Bank, Washington.

Cernea, Michael. 1988. *Involuntary Resettlement in Development Projects. Policy Guidelines for World Bank Financed Projects*. Washington: World Bank.

———. 1999. "The Need for Economic Analysis of Resettlement: A Sociologist's View." In *The Economics of Involuntary Resettlement: Questions and Challenges*, edited by M. M. Cernea. Washington: World Bank.

Chen, Shaoua, and Martin Ravallion. 2007. "China's (Uneven) Progress against Poverty. *Journal of Development Economics* 82 (1): 1–42.

Chenery, Hollis, and Moises Syrquin. 1975. *Patterns of Development, 1950–1970*. Oxford: Oxford University Press.

Chronic Poverty Research Centre. 2005. *The Chronic Poverty Report, 2004–05.* Manchester, U.K.: Institute for Development Policy and Management, University of Manchester. http://www.chronicpoverty.org/uploads/publication_files/CPR1_ReportFull.pdf.

Coady, David, Paul Dorosh, and Bart Minten. 2007. "Evaluating Alternative Approaches to Poverty Alleviation in Madagascar: Rice Tariffs versus Targeted Transfers." Fiscal Affairs Department, International Monetary Fund, Washington.

Cohen, G. A. 2008. *Rescuing Justice and Equality.* Cambridge, Massachusetts: Harvard University Press.

Das, Jishnu, Quy-Toan Do, and Berk Ozler. 2004. "Conditional Cash Transfers and the Equity-Efficiency Debate." World Bank, Washington.

Datta, Saugato, and Sendhil Mullainathan. 2014. "Behavioral Design: A New Approach to Development Policy." *Review of Income and Wealth* 60 (1): 7–35.

Deaton, A. 2009. "Instruments of Development: Randomization in the Tropics, and the Search for the Elusive Keys to Economic Development." *Proceedings of the British Academy, 2008 Lectures* 162: 123–60.

———, and Valerie Kozel, eds. 2005. "Data and Dogma: The Great Indian Poverty Debate." *World Bank Research Observer* 20 (2): 177–99.

Deininger, K., and L. Squire. 1996. "A New Data Set Measuring Income Inequality." *World Bank Economic Review* 10 (3): 565–91.

———. 1998. "New Ways of Looking at Old Issues: Inequality and Growth." *Journal of Development Economics* 57 (2): 259–88.

Dercon, Stefan. 2004. "Growth and Shocks: Evidence from Rural Ethiopia." *Journal of Development Economics* 74 (2): 309–29.

Dollar, David, and Aart Kraay. 2002. "Growth Is Good for the Poor." *Journal of Economic Growth* 7 (3): 195–225.

Duflo, Esther, Rachel Glennerster, and Michael Kremer. 2007. "Using Randomization in Development Economics Research: A Toolkit." In *Handbook of Development Economics*, Vol. 4, edited by T. Paul Schults and John Strauss, 3895–62. North Holland: Elsevier Science Ltd.

Dworkin, Ronald. 2000. *Sovereign Virtue: The Theory and Practice of Equality.* Cambridge, Massachusetts: Harvard University Press.

Filmer, D., and L. Pritchett. 1999. "The Effect of Household Wealth on Educational Attainment: Evidence from 35 Countries." *Population and Development Review* 25 (1): 85–120.

Fiszbein, Ariel, and Norbert Schady. 2009. *Conditional Cash Transfers: Reducing Present and Future Poverty.* World Bank Policy Research Report. Washington: World Bank.

Fleurbaey, Marc, and Francois Maniquet. 2012. *Equality of Opportunity: The Economics of Responsibility.* Singapore: World Scientific Publishing Company.

Foster, James. 2009. "A Class of Chronic Poverty Measures." In *Poverty Dynamics: Interdisciplinary Perspectives*, edited by A. Addison, D. Hulme, and R. Kanbur. Oxford, U.K.: Oxford University Press.

———, Joel Greer, and Erik Thorbecke. 1984. "A Class of Decomposable Poverty Measures." *Econometrica* 52 (3): 761–76.

Ghosh, Suman, and Ravi Kanbur. 2008. "Male Wages and Female Welfare: Private Markets, Public Goods, and Intrahousehold Inequality." *Oxford Economic Papers* 60 (1): 42–56.

Haddad, Lawrence, and Ravi Kanbur. 1990. "How Serious Is the Neglect of Intrahousehold Inequality?" *Economic Journal* 100 (402): 866–81.

International Monetary Fund (IMF). 2014. "Fiscal Policy and Income Inequality." IMF Policy Paper, Washington. http://www.imf.org/external/np/pp/eng/2014/012314.pdf.

Jalan, Jyotsna, and Martin Ravallion. 2000. "Is Transient Poverty Different? Evidence for Rural China." *Journal of Development Studies* 36 (6): 82–99.

Jäntti, M., R. Kanbur, and J. Pirttilä. 2014a. "Poverty, Development, and Behavioral Economics." *Review of Income and Wealth* 60 (1): 1–6.

———. 2014b. "Poverty and Welfare Measurement on the Basis of Prospect Theory." *Review of Income and Wealth* 60 (1): 182–205.

Jenkins, Stephen. 2014. "World Income Inequality Databases: An Assessment of WIID and SWIID." ISER Working Paper No. 2014–31, Institute for Social and Economic Research, University of Essex. https://www.iser.essex.ac.uk/research/publications/working-papers/iser/2014-31.pdf.

Kahneman, Daniel. 2011. *Thinking, Fast and Slow.* New York: Farrar, Strauss and Giroux.

Kakwani, Nanak, Fabio Veras Soares, and Hyun H. Son. 2005. "Conditional Cash Transfers in African Countries." Working Paper No. 9, International Poverty Centre, United Nations Development Programme, Brasilia, Brazil. http://www.ipc-undp.org/publication/27379.

Kanbur, Ravi. 1987. "Measurement and Alleviation of Poverty: With an Application to the Effects of Macroeconomic Adjustment." *IMF Staff Papers* 34 (1): 60–85.

———. 1990a. "Poverty and Development: The Human Development Report and The World Development Report, 1990." In *Poverty Monitoring: An International Concern*, edited by Rolph van der Hoeven and Richard Anker. New York: St. Martin's Press.

———. 1990b. *Poverty and the Social Dimensions of Structural Adjustment in Côte d'Ivoire*. SDA Working Paper Series. Washington: World Bank.

———. 2003a. "IFI's and IPG's: Operational Implications for the World Bank." In *Challenges to the IMF and the World Bank*, edited by Ariel Bura. New York: Anthem Press.

———, ed. 2003b. *Q-Squared: Qualitative and Quantitative Methods of Poverty Appraisal*. New Delhi: Permanent Black.

———. 2004. "Cross-Border Externalities, International Public Goods, and Their Implications for Aid Agencies." In *Global Tensions: Challenges and Opportunities in the World Economy*, edited by L. Beneria and S. Bisnath. London: Routledge.

———. 2005. "Regional Versus International Financial Institutions." In *Regional Public Goods: From Theory to Practice*, edited by A. Estevadeordal, B. Frantz, and T. R. Nguyen. Inter-American Development Bank: Washington.

———, ed. 2006. "New Directions in Development Economics: Theory or Empirics?" *Economic and Political Weekly* 40 (40): 4328–46.

———. 2010a. "Globalization, Growth and Distribution: Framing the Questions." In *Equity in a Globalizing World*, edited by Ravi Kanbur and A. Michael Spence, 41–70. Washington: World Bank for the Commission on Growth and Development.

———. 2010b. "Macro Crises and Targeting Transfers to the Poor." *Journal of Globalization and Development* 1 (1): Article 9.

———. 2012. "Stress Testing for the Poverty Impacts of the Next Crisis." In *Knowing, When You Do Not Know*, edited by Ambar Narayan and Carolina Sánchez-Páramo, 50–55. Washington: World Bank.

———. 2014a. "Education for Climate Justice." The Climate Justice Dialogue. http://www.mrfcj.org/pdf/faces-of-climate-justice/Education-for-Climate-Justice.pdf.

———. 2014b. "Globalization and Inequality." In *Handbook of Income Distribution*, Vol. 2B, edited by A. B. Atkinson and F. Bourguignon. Amsterdam: Elsevier.

———, and Nora Lustig. 2000. "Why Is Inequality Back on the Agenda?" *Annual World Bank Conference on Development Economics, 1999*. Washington: World Bank.

Kanbur, Ravi, and Diganta Mukherjee. 2007. "Premature Mortality and Poverty Measurement." *Bulletin of Economic Research* 59 (4): 339–59.

Kanbur, Ravi, and Paul Shaffer. 2007a. "Epistemology, Normative Theory and Poverty Analysis." *World Development* 35 (2): 183–96.

———, eds. 2007b. *Experiences of Combining Qualitative and Quantitative Approaches in Poverty Analysis*. Special issue of *World Development* 35 (2).

Kanbur, Ravi, and Adam Wagstaff. 2014. "How Useful Is Inequality of Opportunity as a Policy Construct?" Policy Research Working Paper No. 6980, World Bank, Washington.

Kanbur, Ravi, and Xiaobo Zhang. 2005. "Fifty Years of Regional Inequality in China: A Journey through Revolution, Reform and Openness." *Review of Development Economics* 9 (1): 87–106.

Kanbur, Ravi, and Juzhong Zhuang. 2012. "Confronting Rising Inequality in Asia." In *Asian Development Outlook 2012*. Washington: Asian Development Bank.

Karlan, Dean. 2014. "Savings by and for the Poor: A Research Review." *Journal of Income and Wealth* 60 (1): 36–78.

Kaufmann, Daniel, Aart Kraay, and Massimo Mastruzzi. 2008. "Governance Matters VII: Aggregate and Individual Indicators, 1996–2007." World Bank Policy Research Paper No. 4654, World Bank, Washington. http://papers.ssrn.com/sol3/papers.cfm?abstract_id=1148386.

Kose, M. Ayhan, Eswar Prasad, Kenneth Rogoff, and Shang-Jin Wei. 2006. "Financial Globalization: A Reappraisal." *IMF Staff Papers* 56 (1): 8–62.

Kuznets, Simon. 1955. "Economic Growth and Income Inequality." *American Economic Review* 45 (1): 1–28.

Levy, Santiago. 2006. *Progress against Poverty: Sustaining Mexico's Progresa-Oportunidades Program*. Washington: Brookings Institution Press.

Ligon, E., and L. Schechter. 2003. "Measuring Vulnerability." *Economic Journal* 113 (486): C95–C102.

Little, I. M. D., and James Mirrlees. 1991. "Project Appraisal and Planning Twenty Years On." *Proceedings of the World Bank Annual Conference on Development Economics, 1990*. Washington: World Bank.

Manser, M., and M. Brown. 1980. "Marriage and Household Decisionmaking: A Bargaining Analysis." *International Economic Review* 21 (1): 31–44.

Newbery, David, and Nicholas Stern, eds. 1987. *The Theory of Taxation for Developing Countries*. Oxford: Oxford University Press.

Nozick, Robert. 1974. *Anarchy, State and Utopia*. Oxford: Basil Blackwell.

Ostry, Jonathan, Andrew Berg, and Charalambos Tsangarides. 2014. "Redistribution, Inequality and Growth." IMF Staff Discussion Note No. 14/02, International Monetary Fund, Washington. http://www.imf.org/external/pubs/ft/sdn/2014/sdn1402.pdf.

Paes de Barros, R., F. H. G. Ferreira, J. R. M. Vega, J. C. Saavedra, M. De Carvalho, S. Franco, S. Freije-Rodriguez, and J. Gignoux. 2009. *Measuring Inequality of Opportunities in Latin America and the Caribbean*. Washington: World Bank.

Piketty, Thomas. 2014. *Capital in the Twenty-First Century*. Cambridge, Massachusetts: Harvard University Press.

Quisumbing, Agnes R., and John A. Maluccio. 2003. "Resources at Marriage and Intrahousehold Allocation: Evidence from Bangladesh, Ethiopia, Indonesia, and South Africa." *Oxford Bulletin of Economics and Statistics* 65 (3): 283–328.

Ravallion, Martin. 2008. "Inequality Is Bad for the Poor." In *Inequality and Poverty Reexamined*, edited by John Micklewright and Steven Jenkins. Oxford: Oxford University Press.

Rawls, John. 1971. *A Theory of Justice*. Cambridge, Massachusetts: Harvard University Press.

Rodrik, Dani. 2008. "Second-Best Institutions." *American Economic Review* 98 (2): 100–4.

———. 2009. "The New Development Economics: We Shall Experiment, But How Shall We Learn?" In *What Works in Development? Thinking Big and Thinking Small*, edited by J. Cohen and W. Easterly. Washington: Brookings Institution Press.

———. 2012. "Why We Learn Nothing from Regressing Economic Growth on Policies." *Seoul Journal of Economics* 25 (2): 137–51.

Roemer, John E. 1998. *Equality of Opportunity*. Cambridge, Massachusetts: Harvard University Press.

Sen, Amartya K. 1973. *On Economic Inequality*. Oxford: Clarendon Press.

———. 1976. "Poverty: An Ordinal Approach to Measurement." *Econometrica* 44 (2): 219–31.

———. 1983. "Economics and the Family." *Asian Development Review* 1 (2): 14–26.

———. 2001. *Development as Freedom*, second edition. New York: Oxford University Press.

Stiglitz, Joseph E. 2013. *The Price of Inequality: How Today's Divided Society Endangers Our Future*. New York: W.W. Norton and Company.

Strauss, John, Kathleen Beegle, Agus Dwiyanto, Yulia Herawati, Daan Pattinasarany, Elan Satriawan, Bondan Sikoki, Sukamdi, and Firman Witoelar. 2004. *Indonesian Living Standards before and after the Crisis: Evidence from the Indonesia Family Life Survey*. Santa Monica, California: Rand Corporation. http://www.rand.org/pubs/monographs/MG137.html.

United Nations. 2014. "Introduction to the Open Working Group Proposal for Sustainable Development Goals," Sustainable Development Knowledge Platform, UN Department of Economic and Social Affairs, New York. http://sustainabledevelopment.un.org/sdgsproposal.

United Nations Development Programme (UNDP). 1990. *Human Development Report*. New York: Oxford University Press.

World Bank. 2000. *World Development Report 2000/2001: Attacking Poverty*. New York: Oxford University Press.

———. 2003. *World Development Report 2004: Making Services Work for Poor People*. New York: Oxford University Press.

———. 2005. *World Development Report 2006: Equity and Development*. Washington: World Bank.

———. 2011. *World Development Report 2012: Gender Equality and Development*. Washington: World Bank.

———. 2014. *World Development Report 2015: Mind, Society and Behavior*. Washington: World Bank.

Zhang, Xiaobo, and Ravi Kanbur. 2005. "Spatial Inequality in Education and Health Care in China." *China Economic Review* 16 (2): 189–204.

PART II

Alternative Measures of Inequality and Their Implications for Fiscal Policy

CHAPTER 6

Functional Income Distribution and Its Role in Explaining Inequality

Maura Francese and Carlos Mulas-Granados

INTRODUCTION

In the years preceding the global economic and financial crisis, analysts and policymakers wondered about diverging trends between aggregate measures of economic performance (such as economic growth) and stagnating wages and household incomes. Public interest in the issue of whether capital was receiving too high a share of the economic pie was also high.[1] In 2006 Ben Bernanke, the Chairman of the Federal Reserve, expressed the hope that "corporations would use some of those profit margins to meet demands from workers for higher wages," and in 2007 Germany's finance minister asked European companies to "give a fairer share of their soaring profits."[2]

Interest in these contrasting trends has deepened since the onset of the financial crisis, driven in part by the rescue of financial institutions by many governments juxtaposed with rising unemployment and inequality.[3]

A brief examination of the time series of income inequality (measured by the Gini index) and the labor share of income[4] in Group of Seven countries shows that the wage share has indeed been declining since the 1970s while inequality has been on the rise (Figure 6.1). On average, the wage share declined by 12 percent whereas income inequality increased by 25 percent in some advanced economies in barely three decades.

Although apparently correlated, these two phenomena may not be directly linked in a causal relationship. Income inequality refers to the personal distribution of income, and the labor share refers to the remuneration of employees in total factor income (value added) in a given year. The classical economists of the nineteenth century took for granted that capitalists were rich and their income was solely based on the returns to capital, while laborers were poor and relied only on wages. As the world evolved during the twentieth century, scholars working in this field acknowledged that the study of factor shares and inequality became more difficult as evidence started to show mixed realities in which "many employees earn more than capitalists, many property owners work and many workers own property" (Lydall 1968, 2).

The authors wish to thank Andrea Brandolini, Benedict Clements, and Sanjeev Gupta for their helpful comments and suggestions. They are also grateful to participants at the Fiscal Affairs Department seminar and at the 17th Banca d'Italia Workshop on Public Finance (Perugia, April 9–11, 2015) for their valuable feedback. Ryan Espiritu and Louis Sears provided excellent research assistance. The analysis in this chapter has also been published in the IMF's working paper series. This chapter should not be reported as representing the views of the IMF, its Executive Board, or its management. The views expressed in this chapter are those of the authors and do not necessarily represent those of the IMF or IMF policy.

[1] In this chapter, capital income includes both profits and rents, that is, all value added that does not accrue to labor (including self-employment).

[2] See Glyn (2009) citing Bernanke's statement reported by the *New York Times* (July 20, 2006) and Germany's finance minister's declaration reported by the *Financial Times* (February 28, 2007).

[3] The flurry of ensuing policy work and analysis even caught on at Wall Street companies like Standard and Poor's and Morgan Stanley, which released their first reports on inequality in the fall of 2014 (Rotondaro 2014).

[4] For the rest of the chapter, "labor share" of income and "wage share" of income are used as synonyms.

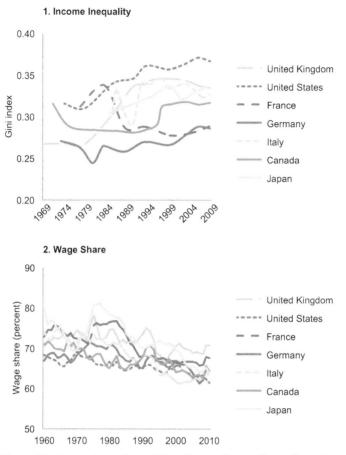

Figure 6.1 Income Inequality and Wage Share in Group of Seven Countries

Sources: Luxembourg Income Study for Canada, France, Germany, Italy, United Kingdom, and United States and Organisation for Economic Co-operation and Development for Japan (panel 1); European Commission AMECO database (panel 2).
Note: In panel 1, for the years in which the Gini coefficient is available both from the Organisation for Economic Co-operation and Development and the Luxembourg Income Study, data are in line and show similar patterns.

The analysis in this chapter tests whether the declining labor share of income has been a key driving factor for the growth in inequality. The conclusion is that it has not—the most important determinant of rising income inequality has been the growing dispersion of wages, especially at the top of the wage distribution. This finding echoes the results of Piketty (2014), who concludes that inequality of total income is closer to inequality of income from labor.

Although these results confirm previous findings in the literature, the chapter makes an important contribution by providing evidence from a wide sample of countries and simultaneously analyzing microeconomic data from household surveys and macroeconomic data from national accounts. As is well known, micro and macro data do not always perfectly match. However, this chapter finds that they reveal broadly similar trends.

The remainder of the chapter is organized as follows: the next section briefly reviews the relevant literature. The subsequent section explains how the Gini index can be decomposed and linked to factor shares and pseudo-Gini indices of the income sources, and applies this decomposition to available micro data. The vast sample of income surveys made available to researchers by the Luxembourg Income Study (LIS) data center is used for this exercise. Using 231 household surveys covering 43 countries for the period 1978–2010, the marginal effects of changes in factor shares and in the dispersion of labor and capital on the Gini index for market income are computed. The next section broadens the scope of the analysis and uses macroeconomic data for a large set of 93 countries for the period 1970–2013 to explore the aggregate effect of the labor share on income inequality. The final section presents closing remarks and the main conclusions.

REVIEW OF THE LITERATURE

The analysis of factor shares of income was considered the principal problem of political economy by classical economists such as David Ricardo. Until the 1960s this topic was given great preeminence in economic textbooks and academic research. When Kaldor (1961) famously summarized the long-term properties of economic growth, he stated that the shares of national income received by labor and capital were roughly constant over long periods. The analysis of factor income shares was the subject of 90 percent of the papers presented at the conference of the International Economic Association in 1965 (Marchal and Ducros 1968; Glyn 2009). The dominant theme was that factor shares were important for the macroeconomic performance of economies because they are linked to the potential "profit-squeeze" problem, that is, real wages growing faster than productivity (Glyn and Sutcliffe 1972; Bruno and Sachs 1985; Eichengreen 2007).

Since the 1970s, however, the analysis of factor shares has no longer been at the center of economic debate, given their lack of volatility and reflecting the fact that "the division of income could be easily explained by a Cobb-Douglas production function" (Mankiw 2007, 55). Those concerned with personal income distribution emphasized that there was no direct (or mechanical) link with factor shares, and that differences in personal income were related to differences in educational attainment (Stigler 1965; Goldfarb and Leonard 2005). In addition, a broader share of the population was starting to enjoy some kind of capital income. As home ownership, financial assets holdings, and capital-funded pensions expanded in advanced economies, the division into (pure) workers receiving only wages and (pure) capitalists and landlords receiving only profits and rents became blurred, thus contributing to the decline in attention to this theme.

Interest in the analysis of factor shares returned in the early 2000s. Atkinson (2009) cites three reasons for this growing attention: first, the analysis of factor shares is useful for understanding the link between incomes at the macroeconomic level (national accounts) and incomes at the individual or household level; second, factor shares can potentially help explain inequality in personal income (at least partly, if certain types of income are mainly received by some type of economic agents); and last they "address the concern of social justice with the fairness of different sources of income" (Atkinson 2009, 5).

Researchers returning to work in this area initially focused on explaining the shifts in the labor share (Bentolila and Saint Paul 2003), its gradual but constant decline (De Serres and others 2002; Gollin 2002), and the relationship between wages and productivity (Dew-Becker and Gordon 2005; Feldstein 2008). The perception that citizens were not fully enjoying the fruits of the long period of economic expansion of the late 1990s and early 2000s also attracted the attention of national policymakers and international organizations. The IMF (2007, 2014), the European Commission (2007), the Bank for International Settlements (Ellis and Smith 2007), and the Organisation for Economic Co-operation and Development (OECD) (2008) all published reports that documented the decline in the labor share of income and provided several explanations for this trend, mainly linked to the impact of globalization and technological change on labor skills, international capital mobility, and wage bargaining.

Since then, contributions in this field can be divided into two groups: a collection of papers that document the recent and constant decline in the labor share and seek to explain the main drivers of this decline; and another group of studies that focuses more on its consequences for economic inequality. In the first group, most researchers use survey data and focus on single countries, mainly the United States (Gomme and Rupert 2004; Harris and Sammartino 2011;

Elsby, Hobjin, and Sahin 2013); others have analyzed macroeconomic data and cross-country developments (ILO 2011, 2012). In particular, the International Labour Organization (ILO) contributions have highlighted the impact of capital mobility on the evolution of factor shares since 2000. Stockhammer's (2013) report, published by the ILO, finds a strong negative effect of financial liberalization on the wage share and documents the consequences of cutbacks in welfare payments and globalization. The available evidence on the effects of technological change on labor income shares is mixed (positive in developing economies and modestly negative in advanced ones). Karabarbounis and Neiman (2014) attribute the declining share of labor income to the decrease in the relative price of investment goods, often ascribed to advances in information technology and the computer age, which have induced firms to shift away from labor and toward capital. According to these authors "the lower price of investment goods explains roughly half of the observed decline in the labor share, even when we allow for other mechanisms influencing factor shares, such as increasing profits, capital-augmenting technology growth, and the changing skill composition of the labor force" (Karabarbounis and Neiman 2014, 61).

In the second group of studies, which mostly focus on the interplay between functional income distribution and income inequality, researchers have also worked with survey household data from single countries. Adler and Schmid (2012) find that declining labor income shares are associated with growing inequality and an increasing concentration of market income in Germany. Similarly, Jacobson and Occhino (2012a, 2012b) follow Lerman and Yitzhaki (1985) and decompose the Gini coefficient into the weighted average of the pseudo-Gini indices of labor and capital income, with the weights equal to the two income shares. Using household data for the United States, they confirm that the decline in the labor share made total income less evenly distributed and more concentrated at the top of the distribution, thus increasing income inequality in the United States. According to their results, a 1 percent decrease in the labor share of income increases the Gini coefficient in the United States by 0.15–0.33 percent. An ILO report addresses the relationship between wages and inequality using several sources, and it comes to the conclusion that "inequality starts in the labor market" (ILO 2015, xvii), meaning that developments in the distribution of wages have been key factors for inequality dynamics.

In this context, the major contribution of this chapter is that it performs a deeper empirical analysis than previous studies by using more micro and macro data sources and pooling them across a larger set of countries.

INCOME SHARES OR THE DISTRIBUTION OF INCOME? A LOOK AT HOUSEHOLD DATA

This section explores how changes in labor and capital income shares and their distribution have affected the dynamics of income inequality. The inequality measure is the Gini index, and the data source is the Luxembourg Income Study (LIS) database.

A wide set of household surveys covering a large sample of economies and spanning more than three decades is used. Thus, regularities that are supported by a broad empirical base can be sought.

The starting point is a decomposition of the Gini index that can then be applied to micro data. The decomposition analysis follows an established path in the literature (Lerman and Yitzhaki 1985; CBO 2011) and breaks down changes in the Gini index into changes in the income components and variations in their pseudo-Gini (or concentration) indices. In particular, assuming that household income (y) comes from K sources, the following relationship applies (see Annex 6.1 for details on how the decomposition is obtained):

$$G_y = \sum_{k=1}^{K} C_{y_k} s_k. \tag{6.1}$$

G_y is the Gini index for total income y, and C_{y_k} and s_k are, respectively, the pseudo-Gini (or concentration) indices and the shares of each income component (given that $y = \sum_{k=1}^{K} y_k$). Pseudo-Gini indices capture the level of "unevenness" in the distribution of each income component and are proportional to the Gini index of the income category ($C_{y_k} = \rho_k^{Gini} G_{y_k}$).[5]

As equation (6.1) indicates, the Gini index can therefore be represented as a weighted average of the pseudo-Gini indices of income components, where the weights are the income shares.

Changes in the overall Gini index occurring over a period starting at time t_0 can therefore be summarized as follows:

$$\Delta G_y = \underbrace{\sum_{k=1}^{K} \Delta s_k C_{y_k}^0}_{\substack{\text{impact of changes} \\ \text{in the income shares}}} + \underbrace{\sum_{k=1}^{K} \Delta C_{y_k} s_k^0}_{\substack{\text{impact of changes} \\ \text{in the concentration} \\ \text{of the income components}}} + \underbrace{\sum_{k=1}^{K} \Delta s_k \Delta C_{y_k}}_{\approx 0}, \tag{6.2}$$

in which the third addend can safely be assumed to be close to zero.

Given equation (6.1), it is also possible to recover the marginal impact of changes in pseudo-Gini indices:

$$\frac{\delta G_y}{\delta C_{y_k}} = s_k. \tag{6.3}$$

As to the impact of changes in the income shares, assuming that a variation in labor income (l) is compensated for by an opposite change in capital income (c), while everything else stays the same, gives the following:

$$\frac{\delta G_y}{\delta s_l} = C_l - C_c. \tag{6.4}$$

If the pseudo-Gini index of capital is higher than that of labor, an increase in the labor share reduces inequality (whereas a reduction raises the Gini index). This condition requires the Gini index for capital income to be "sufficiently" higher than that of labor.

Empirical values for the decomposition of the Gini index are computed using the LIS database; Annex 6.2 presents how the breakdown is computed.

The analysis begins by considering a small sample of advanced economies: France, Germany, the United Kingdom, and the United States. These countries are the Group of Seven members with the highest and the lowest levels of income inequality (Figure 6.1, panel 1); in addition, longer series are available for these countries, allowing developments over an extended period to be considered, which is helpful given that inequality tends to move slowly.

Table 6.1 reports the results of decomposing the change in the Gini index (according to the breakdown described in equation (6.2)) observed in these countries since the late 1970s.[6] We start by considering disposable income (market income plus transfers and minus taxes); the increase in inequality has been significant: more than 25 percent and 35 percent, respectively, in the United States and the United Kingdom, and almost 10 percent in Germany. In France, inequality is lower than in the 1970s and mid-1980s, and has been substantially stable since the

---

[5] See Annex 6.1 for a discussion of the relationship between Gini and pseudo-Gini indices and its interpretation.

[6] The results presented here are robust to using alternative decomposition measures to calculate the contribution of income components to overall inequality. See the discussion in Annex 6.1, and in particular note 28.

TABLE 6.1

Decomposition of Changes in Inequality (*Measured by the Gini index*)

		United States 1979–2013	United Kingdom 1979–2010	Germany 1978–2010	France 1978–2010
ΔG_{ynet}		0.08	0.10	0.03	−0.01
Impact of Changes in Taxation		0.01	0.00	−0.02	0.00
ΔGy		0.07	0.10	0.05	−0.01
Impact of Changes in Transfers		−0.03	−0.03	−0.03	−0.03
ΔGm		0.10	0.13	0.08	0.02
Impact of Changes in Income Shares					
Labor	$\Delta s_l(C^0_l - C^0_c)$	0.00	0.00	0.01	0.00
Impact of Changes in Pseudo-Gini Indices					
Labor	$s^0_l \Delta C_l$	0.09	0.13	0.06	0.03
Capital	$s^0_c \Delta C_c = -s^0_l \Delta C_c$	0.01	0.00	0.02	0.00
Residual		0.00	0.00	0.00	0.00
G^0_{ynet}		0.31	0.27	0.26	0.33
G_{ynet} in the Final Year		0.40	0.36	0.29	0.31
G^0_y		0.36	0.30	0.29	0.34
G_y in the Final Year		0.43	0.40	0.34	0.33
G^0_m		0.41	0.39	0.42	0.44
G_m in the Final Year		0.51	0.52	0.49	0.47
G^0_l		0.44	0.43	0.45	0.46
G_l in the Final Year		0.53	0.57	0.54	0.53
G^0_c		0.92	0.88	0.61	0.97
G_c in the Final Year		0.94	0.97	0.87	0.88

Source: Authors' calculations based on Luxembourg Income Study data.

mid-1990s with a slight pickup in recent years.[7] Looking at market income, the increase in inequality has been substantial for all four countries.

The main result of the decomposition exercise suggests that the driving factor behind growing inequality in market income has not been the decline in the labor share, but the increase in the pseudo-Gini indices, mainly that of labor income.[8] The increase in the pseudo-Gini for labor income accounts for 75 percent of the increase in inequality in Germany; more than 90 percent and 95 percent in the United States and the United Kingdom, respectively; and for 100 percent of the increase observed in France. Changes in the labor share of income appear to have made a negligible contribution to the overall increase in inequality.[9]

---

[7] The Gini index for disposable income for France published by the OECD, which covers the period 1996–2011, displays values close to those that can be computed using LIS data. For the most recent years it shows that inequality has been slightly increasing in this country.

[8] These findings are in line with others available in the literature. For example Hoeller and others (2012) also find that the main driver of market-income inequality is inequality in labor income.

[9] A comparison of these results with the CBO (2011) study on the United States shows that the overall picture is similar (for instance, the percentage increase in the Gini index for market income is similar: 23 percent vs. 21 percent) and both analyses suggest that the most relevant driving factor has been the rising unevenness of income sources. However, the contribution of shifting income composition is lower in this analysis based on the LIS data set. The CBO study finds that during the period 1979–2007, increases in the pseudo-Gini account for 80 percent of the total change in the Gini index for market income, the rest being due to the shift in income shares. If 2007 had been taken to be the final year in this chapter's analysis, the contribution of changes in income shares would have been found to be negligible (in line with what is found using 2010 as an end point), while almost all the increase in inequality would be explained by swelling income unevenness (of which 90 percent can be ascribed to the dynamics in the distribution of labor income). This difference may reflect the definitions adopted in the two studies: whereas the CBO analysis excludes business income (such as income from businesses and farms operated by their owners) from labor income, this analysis using LIS data includes earnings of the self-employed in this category (Annex 6.2).

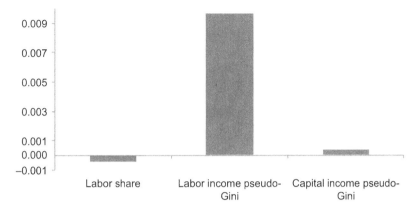

Figure 6.2   Marginal Impact on the Gini Index for Market Income of Changes in the Labor Share and Pseudo-Gini Indices for Labor and Capital

Source: Authors' calculation based on Luxembourg Income Study data.
Note: Average values across countries (43 countries; 231 observations or income surveys).

Given the wealth of data offered by the LIS database, the empirical decomposition of the Gini index for market income can be extended to a larger sample of countries (43 in total) that includes not only advanced economies (26) but also emerging ones (17). Selecting as a starting year the oldest available income survey in each country since the late 1970s, the analysis can be expanded to include a total of 231 income surveys covering the past three decades (Annex Table 6.2.1).[10]

Once the components of the Gini index are calculated, the average marginal effects of changes in the income composition and the pseudo-Gini indices for labor and capital can be calculated for each country. The results obtained from this extended sample mirror those described for France, Germany, the United Kingdom, and the United States. The main hypothesis is confirmed. The variable that has had the most sizable impact on market-income inequality (as measured by Gini coefficients) is the change in the pseudo-Gini index of labor income; increases in the unevenness of capital income also raise inequality, but by a much smaller degree given that wages represent the lion's share of market income for the vast majority of the surveyed households (see Figure 6.2 and Table 6.2, which report average marginal effects on inequality). Computed at sample average values, the analysis finds that a 10 percent increase in the pseudo-Gini index of labor income would increase the Gini index for market income by more than 9 percent.

Consistent with previous studies, the analysis finds that, on average, increases (reductions) in the wage share reduce (raise) the Gini index. In this sample, however, this effect is small but statistically significant. For the average values observed in this sample, a 10 percent decline in the labor share would increase the inequality index of market income by about 0.9 percent. This result is mostly driven by emerging market economies, and is attributable to the larger difference between the pseudo-Gini index of capital and labor income relative to advanced economies.[11] The overall magnitude and relevance of the marginal effects of changes in income shares and pseudo-Gini indices, however, are not very different in the two subsamples of countries (Figure 6.3).

---

[10] Household surveys over such a long period and covering a broad set of countries are obviously heterogeneous. Of course, pooling all the data would not be advisable. The analysis therefore proceeds by considering each survey separately (taking into account whether income and income components are recorded net or gross of taxes), then assessing the impact on inequality of the different factors for each country and finally across the entire sample.

[11] The pseudo-Gini index for capital income in emerging economies is, on average, higher (by 0.16) than in advanced economies; the difference for labor income is less than half (0.07).

TABLE 6.2

Average Effects on the Gini Index for Market Income

	All Countries	Standard Deviation	T	P > |t|
Impact of a 0.01 Change in the Share of Labor Income				
$\delta G_m / \delta s_l$	−0.0004**	0.0012	−2.2889	0.0272
Impact of a 0.01 Increase in the Pseudo-Gini Index				
$\delta G_m / \delta C_l$	0.0096***	0.0003	250.3138	0.0000
$\delta G_m / \delta C_c$	0.0004***	0.0003	9.8787	0.0000

Subsamples	Advanced Economies	Emerging Economies
Impact of a 0.01 Change in the Share of Labor Income		
$\delta G_m / \delta s_l$	−0.0001	−0.0010
Impact of a 0.01 Increase in the Pseudo-Gini Index		
$\delta G_m / \delta C_l$	0.0096	0.0097
$\delta G_m / \delta C_c$	0.0004	0.0003

Source: Authors' calculation based on Luxembourg Income Study data.
Note: Significance levels are computed using standard deviations calculated over the sample of 43 countries
(26 advanced and 17 emerging) considering the available income surveys since the late 1970s.
** $p < 0.05$; *** $p < 0.01$.

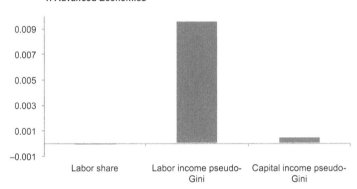

1. Advanced Economies

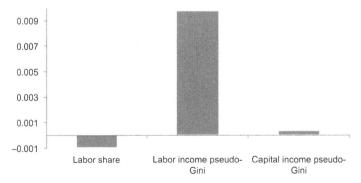

2. Emerging Economies

Figure 6.3 Advanced and Emerging Economies: Marginal Impact on the Gini Index for Market Income of Changes in the Labor Share and Pseudo-Gini Indices for Labor and Capital

Source: Authors' calculations based on Luxembourg Income Study data.
Note: Average values across countries (panel 1: 26 countries; 174 observations or income surveys; panel 2: 17 countries; 57 observations or income surveys).

A few remarks may also help qualify these findings and underscore some important aspects. As observed, the micro data analysis suggests that shifts in functional income distribution have an effect, although a small one, that depends on the difference between the unevenness of the distribution of labor and capital incomes. If the unevenness in the distribution of labor income approaches that of capital income (which has historically been higher), then how income is functionally distributed no longer matters for inequality.

The estimates obtained in the empirical exercise are affected by the weaknesses traditionally associated with income surveys, which generally underreport the extent of capital income; they also do not very accurately capture the tail of the income distribution (generally the exceptionally rich are poorly represented). This analysis therefore likely underestimates what has been happening at the top of the income scale and the relevance of developments concerning capital earnings. Recent work on the top 1 percent (or even smaller groups of very rich earners) would suggest that the share of income accruing to top earners has been increasing even more rapidly than that appropriated by other (less) rich percentiles (Alvaredo and others 2013). Even though the estimates included in this chapter may not appropriately incorporate these developments, they likely capture well the general trends.

LABOR SHARE AND INEQUALITY IN A MACRO FRAMEWORK

This section addresses the same issue (the link between functional income distribution and inequality) in a different framework. The analysis moves to a macro framework to determine whether the main findings (that the increasing inequality of labor income is more important than the declining labor share in explaining the observed increase in total income inequality) still hold. The framework also controls for simultaneous additional factors that affect the labor share and the Gini index.

To preserve continuity with the definition used in the previous section, the Gini coefficient for disposable income is now written as in equation (6.5):

$$G_{y^{net}} = C_c + \left(C_l - C_c \right) s_l + r, \tag{6.5}$$

in which r is the redistributive impact of the tax and welfare system (which is proxied by the ratio of public revenues to GDP, and social protection and health spending).[12]

From equation (6.5) an estimating equation is derived and then estimated for a sample of 93 advanced, emerging, and low-income countries. The labor share reflects underlying economic developments (mainly in the labor market) and the following specification results:

$$
\begin{cases}
G_{y^{net},it} = \alpha_i + \beta s_l + \gamma r_{it} + \varepsilon_{it} \\
s_{l,it} = a_i + \sum_{j=1}^{J} \theta_j x_{j,it} + \upsilon_{it}
\end{cases}
\tag{6.6}
$$

in which ε_{it} and υ_{it} are error terms; i and t are indices for country and time; x_j are J factors that affect the labor share of income, such as the rate of unemployment, the share of employment in the services sector, and the type and intensity of wage-setting coordination.

---

[12] The analysis on micro data (also reflecting data limitations for tax and transfers for this very wide sample of countries) allows the marginal effects on market-income inequality to be recovered. Since the Gini index for disposable income is used here as a dependent variable, the impact of the tax and transfer system must be taken into account to present a framework consistent with that of the previous section.

TABLE 6.3

Determinants of Labor Share, Fixed Effects

Labor Share	(1)	(2)	(3)	(4)	(5)
Labor Share (t–1)	0.8074***	0.7788***	0.7493***	0.8134***	0.7748***
	(62.33)	(55.78)	(42.23)	(41.4)	(36.5)
Unemployment (t–1)		−0.1974***	−0.1587***	−0.1506***	−0.1328***
		(10.28)	(6.95)	(8.33)	(6.07)
Employment Services Sector			−0.0655***	−0.0636***	−0.0697***
			(5.90)	(5.59)	(5.3)
Type of Wage-Setting Coordination				0.0887**	
				(2.28)	
Intensity of Wage-Setting Coordination					0.1976**
					(2.11)
Constant	9.8812***	13.441***	18.5677***	16.041***	18.767***
	(14.64)	(16.53)	(13.37)	(9.51)	(10.23)
Number of Observations	2,184	1,845	1,305	775	856
Number of Countries	106	83	80	31	38
R^2	0.6516	0.6824	0.6753	0.8193	0.7441

Source: Authors' calculations.

Note: Absolute value of t-statistics in parentheses.

** $p < 0.05$; *** $p < 0.01$.

The data set used in the empirical exercise (an unbalanced panel) covers a large sample of countries; the number of observations drops when control variables are added and when a structural model is used that allows simultaneous estimation of the wage share and Gini equations as in equation (6.6).[13] The period covered is from the 1970s to 2013, although the coverage for each country varies (Annex Table 6.3.1 reports the earliest and latest value for the Gini index for the countries included in the sample). The database is explained in detail in Annex 6.3. As to the estimation methodology the wage share and Gini equations are initially explored separately using panel techniques.[14] A structural model that includes simultaneously both equations (to account for the endogeneity of the wage share in the Gini equation) is then run.[15]

Table 6.3 presents the results obtained when separately estimating a wage share equation. The preferred specification (columns 4 and 5)[16] captures the effect of labor market indicators and

---

[13] The sample includes about 800 observations for the preferred specification of the wage share equation (Table 6.3, columns 4 and 5) and 350 for the preferred specification of the Gini equation (Table 6.4, columns 6 and 7). When the two equations are estimated together the sample size drops to 300 and 150 observations (Table 6.5, columns 5 and 6); the largest fall in the number of observations is caused by the addition of the variables that capture the wage-bargaining setup, which are available for a smaller number of countries. Another factor that reduces the sample size is related to the Gini coefficient being available at less than an annual frequency.

[14] We run both a fixed and a random effects model. The Breusch and Pagan Lagrange multiplier test suggests that a fixed effects model is appropriate.

[15] The model includes two linear simultaneous equations. The labor income share is treated as an observed endogenous variable in the Gini equation. The model is estimated using a (full information) maximum likelihood estimator.

[16] The first three columns of Table 6.3 report results of parsimonious specifications used as a starting point. They show that the signs and significance of coefficients are robust when explanatory variables are added. Robust standard errors are computed to determine the statistical significance of coefficients.

institutional characteristics on the labor share;[17] results are in line with those generally found in the literature (Stockhammer 2013). The wage share does not display large and erratic changes from one year to the next, and its lagged value is significant. As expected, the wage share is negatively related to unemployment: large slack in the labor market negatively affects the income share flowing to workers. With regard to structural indicators, the labor share is lower when the share of employment in the services sector is higher, since unionization is typically higher in industry and lower among service workers. The wage-bargaining framework matters: more centralized and coordinated setups (including social dialogue with government participation) are associated with higher aggregate income from work.[18]

Results for the Gini equation, when estimated separately, are reported in Table 6.4. The preferred specifications, the most complete ones, are reported in columns 6 and 7.[19] With regard to the relationship between the labor income share and the Gini index, the analysis indicates that inequality declines when the wage share increases; however, the estimated coefficient is significant only when the dispersion of labor income is not taken into account. When a proxy for the dispersion of wages (measured by the ratio of top 10 percent salaries to bottom 90 percent salaries) is added, the wage share seems to no longer matter, whereas the dispersion variable turns out to be positively (and significantly) related to inequality.[20] With regard to the other control variables, all proxies aimed at capturing the redistributive impact of public policies have the expected negative effect on the Gini index (revenues and health spending display significant coefficients, but social protection spending does not).[21]

The outcome of the estimation remains stable when equation (6.6) is estimated with a structural model that treats the labor share as an endogenous variable (Table 6.5). The dispersion of labor income remains more important than the wage share in explaining income inequality; the estimated coefficient of the wage share continues to be negative, and even though small in magnitude, it is now statistically significant. Government action keeps playing a role; government revenue (as a proxy for redistributive tax policies), social protection spending, and health expenditure all contribute significantly to reducing income inequality.[22] It is likely that the quality, efficiency, and design of public policies also has an impact on inequality. However, there are no widely available indicators that could be used in the empirical analysis to capture these effects. Finally, in line with the literature the analysis finds that economic and financial globalization lead to higher income inequality. The wage share equation indicates that control variables are no longer significant.

---

[17] Because a panel estimator is used, other country-specific factors (for example, technology) are absorbed by country effects, and this setup does not explicitly single out all determinants of the labor share or inequality (even though they are taken care of by country dummies).

[18] This is consistent with results obtained by Checci and García-Peñalosa (2010). On a smaller sample of OECD economies, they study in detail the role of market institutions on personal income distribution and conclude that greater unionization and greater wage bargaining are important factors affecting inequality.

[19] Again, the first columns of Table 6.4 report results of parsimonious specifications that were the starting point. Signs and significance of coefficients are robust when explanatory variables are added.

[20] Note that the variable that measures the ratio of the top 10 percent of salaries to the bottom 10 percent reported in Table 6.4 reflects total income dispersion. This choice guarantees a larger number of observations, which is consistent with the large data set of countries. The 10-to-90 income ratio of labor income (which would directly capture wage dispersion) is only available for OECD countries. Nonetheless, both variables (that measured on total income and that measured on labor income) are highly correlated. Estimation results are the same when the model is run using the reduced sample of OECD countries and the 10-to-90 income ratio of labor income.

[21] These results are robust to the inclusion of the unemployment rate as a control variable, as in Checchi and García-Peñalosa 2010. The inclusion of the unemployment rate in the Gini equation takes into account that labor income is nil for the unemployed. The structural model presented in Table 6.5 duly takes into account the impact of the unemployment rate; for consistency the same specification is maintained for both the fixed effects and structural model estimations.

[22] Revenue is always significant; health and social protection spending are significant when the complete set of explanatory variables is taken into account.

TABLE 6.4

Determinants of Income Inequality, Fixed Effects

Gini Disposable Income	(1)	(2)	(3)	(4)	(5)	(6)	(7)
Labor Share	-0.0008***	-0.0006	-0.0003	-0.0001	0.0000	0.0004	0.0006
	(2.70)	(1.50)	(0.69)	(0.30)	(0.02)	(1.03)	(1.21)
Dispersion of Labor Income		0.0242***	0.0203***	0.0174***	0.0173***	0.0173***	0.0161***
		(4.77)	(4.23)	(3.80)	(3.80)	(3.83)	(3.54)
Public Revenues			-0.0011***	-0.0008**	-0.0007**	-0.0008**	-0.0008**
			(3.40)	(2.28)	(2.19)	(2.39)	(2.29)
Public Social Protection Spending				-0.0011	-0.0006	-0.0009	-0.0007
				(1.24)	(0.67)	(0.98)	(0.74)
Public Health Spending					-0.0046*	-0.0055**	-0.0070***
					(1.89)	(2.25)	(2.67)
Economic Globalization						0.0007***	
						(2.80)	
Financial Globalization							0.0094**
							(2.38)
Constant	0.3847***	0.3888***	0.4158***	0.4129***	0.4231***	0.3650***	0.4051***
	(25.89)	(22.28)	(19.26)	(19.32)	(19.28)	(12.18)	(17.58)
Number of Observations	683	445	393	353	353	352	353
Number of Countries	93	84	83	71	71	70	71
R^2	0.2817	0.4626	0.6363	0.6609	0.5810	0.3756	0.4252

Source: Authors' calculations.
Note: Absolute value of t-statistics in parentheses.
* $p < 0.1$; ** $p < 0.05$; *** $p < 0.01$.

TABLE 6.5

Determinants of Labor Share and Income Inequality, Structural Model

	(1)	(2)	(3)	(4)	(5)	(6)
			Labor Share			
Labor Share ($t-1$)	0.9796***	0.9631***	0.9809***	0.9809***	0.9809***	0.9256***
	(95.44)	(87.00)	(80.56)	(80.56)	(80.56)	(33.48)
Unemployment ($t-1$)		−0.0561***	−0.0574***	−0.0574***	−0.0574***	−0.1330***
		(2.92)	(2.87)	(2.87)	(2.87)	(3.56)
Employment Services Sector			−0.0093	−0.0093	−0.0093	−0.0035
			(0.85)	(0.85)	(0.85)	(0.16)
Intensity of Wage-Setting Coordination						−0.0733
						(0.56)
Constant	0.7250	2.1850***	0.7235	0.7235	0.0723	5.6232**
	(1.43)	(3.53)	(0.91)	(0.91)	(0.91)	(2.80)
			Gini Disposable Income			
Labor Share	−0.0027***	−0.0013***	−0.0012***	−0.0013***	−0.0012***	−0.0015***
	(10.41)	(4.75)	(3.80)	(3.98)	(3.59)	(3.68)
Dispersion of Labor Income	0.1619***	0.1772***	0.1668***	0.1626***	0.1623***	0.6036***
	(14.46)	(14.95)	(13.71)	(12.84)	(12.99)	(19.38)
Public Revenues		−0.0038***	−0.0039***	−0.0040***	−0.0037***	−0.0014***
		(14.18)	(9.75)	(9.82)	(8.90)	(3.16)
Public Social Protection Spending			−0.0006	−0.0011	−0.0013	−0.0039*
			(0.79)	(1.17)	(1.42)	(1.76)
Public Health Spending				−0.0028	−0.0038*	−0.0039*
				(1.17)	(1.59)	(1.78)
Economic Globalization					0.0007**	0.0003*
					(2.72)	(1.61)
Constant	0.4628***	0.5275***	0.5386***	0.5384***	0.5671***	0.0459***
	(34.06)	(38.13)	(32.85)	(32.91)	(30.00)	(14.51)
Number of Observations	425	351	309	309	309	148
χ^2	0.08	4.93	15.66	14.58	21.38	33.39
Probability > χ^2	0.9613	0.2943	0.0157	0.0418	0.0062	0.0001

Source: Authors' calculations.
Note: Absolute value of z-statistics in parentheses.
* $p < 0.1$; ** $p < 0.05$; *** $p < 0.01$.

If the major conclusion that can be extracted from this empirical analysis is that higher income inequality is more driven by wage dispersion than by the wage share of national income, then the natural question becomes, what explains that dispersion? Although this issue is not the major focus of this chapter and could be a topic for further analysis, Table 6.6 shows the results of regressing the dispersion of wages on different factors.[23] Column 5 shows that higher financial globalization and higher unemployment levels are associated with higher dispersion of wages. In contrast, higher unionization in industry,[24] a higher share of educated workers, and higher primary government spending (as a proxy for the size of the state) are factors that help reduce the distance between higher and lower wages.

---

[23] Again, this model was estimated using both versions of income dispersion (total and wage). Results reported in Table 6.6 are those from total dispersion to guarantee a larger sample. As noted in the previous footnote, these results are very similar when the model is estimated using a subsample of OECD countries and using wage dispersion.
[24] Jaumotte and Osorio Buitron (forthcoming) also find evidence that a decline in union density—the fraction of union members in the workforce—affects inequality, in particular, that it is associated with the rise of top income shares.

TABLE 6.6

Determinants of Wage Dispersion

Dispersion of Labor income	(1)	(2)	(3)	(4)	(5)
Financial Globalization	0.0719**	0.0701*	0.037*	0.1531*	0.0788***
	(2.07)	(1.69)	(1.79)	(1.74)	(2.62)
Unemployment		0.0082*	0.0066*	0.0231**	0.0075**
		(1.65)	(1.69)	(2.05)	(2.25)
Industry Unionization			−0.0118***	−0.0235***	−0.0097***
			(2.86)	(2.72)	(3.39)
Tertiary Education				−0.0176***	−0.0086***
				(2.96)	(4.47)
Government Spending					−0.009 ***
					(5.22)
Constant	0.2295***	0.1601***	0.5643***	1.0694***	0.8488***
	(9.73)	(2.89)	(3.72)	(3.31)	(6.86)
Number of Observations	1,045	810	785	405	342
Number of Countries	142	91	90	74	67
R^2	0.004	0.006	0.017	0.062	0.257

Source: Authors' calculations.
Note: Absolute value of z-statistics in parentheses.
* $p < 0.1$; ** $p < 0.05$; *** $p < 0.01$.

CONCLUSION

This chapter analyzes the relationship between functional and personal income distribution, a topic that has returned to center stage in the academic and policy discussion. In the advanced world the wage share and inequality have shown opposite trends in recent decades: the share of factor income to labor has been declining, while inequality has risen. This chapter addresses this issue from different angles, first by analyzing what is behind widely used inequality measures based on micro data (that is, Gini indices), and second by running regression analyses on macro data.

The empirical evidence suggests that the most important determinant of income inequality is not the share of income that accrues to labor or capital, but the dispersion of labor income. This result reflects the fact that the lion's share of household income is labor earnings. It also occurs because top salaries have grown enormously, and wage dispersion has become a driving force behind income inequality. The increase in wage dispersion has been associated with growing financial globalization, a decrease in industry unionization, and a decline in the size of the state.

From a policy perspective these results suggest that to avoid unfavorable (or undesired) distributional consequences, policymakers will have to pay attention to labor market outcomes and to the dispersion of wages, including distortions induced in the labor market by different policy interventions or by changes in labor market institutions.[25] Public policies that support inclusive growth (by, for example, promoting participation in the labor market and strengthening the human capital of low-income groups) may prevent the rise in economic disparities. In addition, tax and transfer policies should be properly assessed with regard to their costs and their relative effectiveness in correcting market-income inequalities while minimizing distortions.

---

[25] These indications are also in line with findings from recent research on Latin America (the most unequal region in the world), where the recent decline in inequality appears to be mostly related to labor income developments (Lustig, Lopez Calva, and Ortiz-Juares 2015).

ANNEX 6.1. GINI COEFFICIENTS, PSEUDO-GINI (OR CONCENTRATION) INDICES, AND GINI CORRELATIONS

The Gini coefficient for income y can be written as:

$$G_y = \frac{2\operatorname{cov}\left(y, F\left(y\right)\right)}{\overline{y}} \tag{6.7}$$

or

$$\operatorname{cov}\left(y, F\left(y\right)\right) = \frac{\overline{y}G_y}{2}. \tag{6.8}$$

The Gini index captures the distance of the observed income distribution from a hypothetical condition of perfect equality in which each individual would be endowed with exactly the same income (in such a case, the Gini index would be equal to zero).[26]

If income y comes from K sources, the Gini index can be decomposed as follows (Lerman and Yitzhaki 1985; CBO 2011):

$$G_y = \sum_{k=1}^{K} \underbrace{\left[\underbrace{\frac{\operatorname{cov}\left(y_k, F\left(y\right)\right)}{\operatorname{cov}\left(y_k, F\left(y_k\right)\right)}}_{\text{Gini correlation } \rho_k^{Gini}} \underbrace{\frac{2\operatorname{cov}\left(y_k, F\left(y_k\right)\right)}{\overline{y}_k}}_{\substack{\text{Gini index for income} \\ \text{component } k}}\right]}_{\text{pseudo-Gini (or concentration) index for income component } k} \underbrace{\left[\frac{\overline{y}_k}{\overline{y}}\right]}_{\substack{\text{component } k\text{'s share} \\ \text{of total income}}} \tag{6.9}$$

$$G_y = \sum_{k=1}^{K} \underbrace{\underbrace{\rho_k^{Gini}}_{\substack{\text{Gini} \\ \text{correlation}}} \underbrace{G_{y_k}}_{\substack{\text{Gini index for income} \\ \text{component } k}}}_{\text{pseudo-Gini index for income component } k} \underbrace{s_k}_{\substack{\text{component } k\text{'s share} \\ \text{of total income}}} = \sum_{k=1}^{K} C_{y_k} s_k \tag{6.10}$$

in which the pseudo-Gini (or concentration) index is given by equation (6.11):

$$C_{y_k} = \rho_k^{Gini} G_{y_k} = \frac{2\operatorname{cov}\left(y_k, F\left(y\right)\right)}{\overline{y}_k} \tag{6.11}$$

and the Gini correlation index is given by equation (6.12):

$$\rho_k^{Gini} = \frac{\operatorname{cov}\left(y_k, F\left(y\right)\right)}{\operatorname{cov}\left(y_k, F\left(y_k\right)\right)} = \frac{2\operatorname{cov}\left(y_k, F\left(y\right)\right)}{\overline{y}_k G_{y_k}}. \tag{6.12}$$

As equation (6.10) indicates, the Gini index is a weighted average of the pseudo-Gini indices of income components, and the weights are the income shares. But what is the difference between a Gini and a pseudo-Gini index for an income component y_k? As can be seen by comparing equations (6.7) and (6.11), the difference is due to the reference ranking of individuals used in the

---

[26] A Gini index equal to 1 would be observed in the case of extreme inequality in which one individual would appropriate all available income, leaving nothing to the others.

two calculations. For the pseudo-Gini index C_{yk}, the weights attached to each individual correspond to the ranking in the distribution of total income ($F(y)$), whereas for the Gini index G_{yk}, the reference ranking would be that of the distribution of the kth income component ($F(y_k)$). The two indices would be the same if the ranking of individuals in the two distributions were the same, that is, if no reranking would take place when moving from the income component distribution to the total income distribution. It should also be noted that the higher an income component share (of total income) is, the lower the possibility of reranking (and therefore the closer C_{yk} and G_{yk} would be) (Pyatt, Chen, and Fei 1980).

BOX 6.1.1 Difference between the Gini Correlations and Correlation Coefficients

The standard (Pearson) correlation coefficient (ρ) and the Gini correlation index have the same numerator: cov(y_k,$F(y)$). But whereas the correlation coefficient denominator is the product of the standard deviations, the denominator of the Gini correlation index is half the product of the Gini coefficient and the average for the income component under consideration:

$$\rho = \frac{\text{cov}\left(y_k, F(y)\right)}{\sigma_{y_k}\sigma_{F(y)}}$$

$$\rho_k^{Gini} = \frac{\text{cov}\left(y_k, F(y)\right)}{\text{cov}\left(y_k, F(y_k)\right)} = \frac{\text{cov}\left(y_k, F(y)\right)}{\dfrac{\bar{y}_k G_{y_k}}{2}} = \frac{2\text{cov}\left(y_k, F(y)\right)}{\bar{y}_k G_{y_k}}$$

The decomposition of the Gini index presented here has been used in many empirical studies. The literature has shown, however, that it is characterized by some limitations. In particular, Shorrocks (1982, 1983) shows that there is no unique way to decompose inequality, and proposes an alternative decomposition rule that satisfies a set of desirable properties[27] and delivers contributions for each income component to inequality. The measure proposed by Shorrocks is in equation (6.13):

$$SH_k = \frac{\text{cov}\left(y_k, y\right)}{\text{var}\left(y\right)}. \tag{6.13}$$

In the framework set forth in this chapter, the contributions to inequality of each income component are instead given by equation (6.14):

$$SH_k^G = \frac{\text{cov}\left(y_k, F\left(y\right)\right)}{\text{cov}\left(y, F\left(y\right)\right)}. \tag{6.14}$$

The standard Gini decomposition in the analysis presented in this chapter is appropriate for several reasons. First, because market income is decomposed into only two exhaustive components (see Annex 6.2), the Gini decomposition is unique (Shorrocks 1982). Second, as also

---

[27] For example, symmetry (meaning that the order of the income components does not affect the decomposition results) and continuity (which requires that for each income component the results do not depend on the number of other income components).

highlighted by Lerman and Yitzhaki (1985), this approach provides an economic interpretation of the empirical results and the marginal effects of changes in the income sources (wage and capital shares) and their distributional characteristics (pseudo-Gini indices) can be derived. Finally, in this analysis, the standard Gini decomposition and the Shorrocks measure provide very similar results.[28]

ANNEX 6.2. INEQUALITY DECOMPOSITION USING THE LIS DATA SET

Bringing equations (6.1) and (6.2) to the LIS data implies singling out the empirical counterparts of total income and of income components. The reference unit in the calculations in this chapter is the household, and the income definition is the per capita equivalent income computed using the LIS equivalence scale.[29] The countries considered in the analysis are reported in Annex Table 6.2.1.

Total gross income y is defined as market income m plus transfers g:

$$y = m + g. \tag{6.15}$$

Transfer income g comprises both private transfers (such as alimony, remittances, transfers from nonprofit institutions) and public transfers (such as pensions, unemployment benefits, disability benefits). Public transfers make up the bulk of transfer income.

Gross market income m is the sum of labor[30] l and capital income c (from financial or nonfinancial types of investments):

$$m = l + c. \tag{6.16}$$

Net (or disposable) household income is obtained by subtracting taxes t from total income:

$$y^{net} = y - t. \tag{6.17}$$

Using equation (6.10), the breakdown of changes in inequality in market income over a certain period can be obtained as in equation (6.18):

$$\Delta G_m = \underbrace{\left[\Delta s_l C_l^0 + \Delta s_c C_c^0 \right]}_{\text{income shares impact}} + \underbrace{\left[s_l^0 \Delta C_l + s_c^0 \Delta C_c \right]}_{\text{concentration indices impact}} + \underbrace{\left[\Delta s_l \Delta C_l + \Delta s_c \Delta C_c \right]}_{\approx 0}, \tag{6.18}$$

in which s_l and s_c, and C_l, and C_c are, respectively, the income shares and pseudo-Gini indices for l and c, and 0 is the base year (or the initial year in the analysis, which varies depending on the country).

---

[28] If we consider the four countries whose results are summarized in Table 6.1, the standard Gini decomposition and the Shorrocks measure provide very similar assessments of the contribution of each income component to inequality. In particular, for the observed period for the United States, the average contribution of labor income to inequality is 0.94 (0.06 for capital income) using the standard Gini decomposition; the corresponding Shorrocks measure (SH) is 0.92 (0.08). For the United Kingdom, the corresponding average values are $SH_l^G = 0.97$ ($SH_c^G = 0.03$) and $SH_l = 0.95$ ($SH_c = 0.05$); for France: $SH_l^G = 0.96$ ($SH_c^G = 0.04$) and $SH_l = 0.94$ ($SH_c = 0.06$); and for Germany: $SH_l^G = 0.94$ ($SH_c^G = 0.06$) and $SH_l = 0.83$ ($SH_c = 0.17$). The results therefore confirm that the largest impact on inequality is to be expected from labor income variations.

[29] The LIS equivalence scale is defined as the square root of the number of individuals in the household.

[30] The labor income definition we use includes both wages from paid employment and income from self-employment.

Given that income shares add up to 1, it follows that $\Delta s_c = -\Delta s_l$ (changes in the labor share are absorbed by an opposite change in the capital share), so that equation (6.18) can be rewritten as in equation (6.19):

$$\Delta G_m = \underbrace{\Delta s_l \left[C_l^0 - C_c^0 \right]}_{\text{income shares impact}} + \underbrace{\left[s_l^0 \Delta C_l + s_c^0 \Delta C_c \right]}_{\text{concentration indices impact}} + \Delta s_l \underbrace{\left[\Delta C_l - \Delta C_c \right]}_{\approx 0}, \tag{6.19}$$

and the observed impact of changes in income composition on inequality will depend on the initial values of the pseudo-Gini indices for labor and capital.

The impact of transfers and taxation on inequality can be measured by equations (6.20) and (6.21), respectively:

$$\Delta G_y - \Delta G_m \tag{6.20}$$

$$\Delta G_{y_{net}} - \Delta G_y. \tag{6.21}$$

Marginal effects on income inequality can be calculated from the following equation for the Gini index for gross market income:

$$G_m = C_l s_l + C_c s_c. \tag{6.22}$$

Remembering that

$$s_c = 1 - s_l, \tag{6.23}$$

we have that at any point in time the marginal impact from a variation in market-income composition is expressed by equation (6.24):

$$\frac{\delta G_m}{\delta s_l} = C_l - C_c. \tag{6.24}$$

If the pseudo-Gini index for capital is higher than that for labor, then an increase (reduction) in the labor share reduces (raises) inequality. When considering Gini indices of the income components, this requires that

$$G_c > \frac{\rho_l^{Gini}}{\rho_c^{Gini}} G_l, \tag{6.25}$$

which implies that the Gini index for capital has to be "sufficiently" larger than the Gini index for labor.

The condition in equation (6.25) can also be written in terms of average labor and capital incomes:

$$\bar{l} > \frac{\text{cov}\left(l, F(m)\right)}{\text{cov}\left(c, F(m)\right)} \bar{c}, \tag{6.26}$$

which requires average labor income to be "sufficiently" higher than average capital income.

ANNEX TABLE 6.2.1

Countries Included in the Analysis

Australia (gross)	1981; 1985; 1989; 1995; 2001; 2003; 2008; 2010
Austria (net; gross)	1994; 1997; 2000; 2004
Belgium (net; gross)	1985; 1988; 1992; 1995; 1997; 2000
Brazil (gross)	2006; 2009; 2011
Canada (gross)	1981; 1987; 1991; 1994; 1997; 1998; 2000; 2004; 2007; 2010
China (gross)	2002
Colombia (gross)	2004; 2007; 2010
Czech Republic (gross)	1992; 1996; 2004
Denmark (gross)	1987; 1992; 1995; 2000; 2004; 2007; 2010
Egypt (net)	2012
Estonia (mixed; gross)	2000; 2004; 2007; 2010
Finland (mixed; gross)	1987; 1991; 1995; 2000; 2004; 2007; 2010
France (mixed; gross)	1978; 1984; 1989; 1994; 2000; 2005; 2010
Germany (gross)	1978; 1981; 1983; 1984; 1989; 1994; 2000; 2004; 2007; 2010
Greece (net; gross)	1995; 2000; 2004; 2007; 2010
Guatemala (gross)	2006
Hungary (net)	1991; 1994; 1999; 2005; 2007; 2009; 2012
Iceland (gross)	2004; 2007; 2010
India (net)	2004
Ireland (gross; net)	1987; 1994; 1995; 1996; 2000; 2004; 2007; 2010
Israel (gross)	1979; 1986; 1992; 1997; 2001; 2005; 2007; 2010
Italy (net; mixed)	1986; 1987; 1989; 1991; 1993; 1995; 1998; 2000; 2004; 2008; 2010
Japan (gross)	2008
Korea (gross)	2006
Luxembourg (net; gross)	1985; 1991; 1994; 1997; 2000; 2004; 2007; 2010
Mexico (net)	1984; 1989; 1992; 1994; 1996; 1998; 2000; 2002; 2004; 2008; 2010
Netherlands (gross)	1983; 1987; 1990; 1993; 1999; 2004; 2007; 2010
Norway (gross)	1979; 1986; 1991; 1995; 2000; 2004; 2007; 2010
Peru (net)	2004
Poland (net; mixed; gross)	1992; 1995; 1999; 2004; 2007; 2010
Romania (gross)	1995; 1997
Russia (net)	2000; 2004; 2007; 2010
Serbia (net)	2006; 2010; 2013
Slovak Republic (gross; net)	1992; 1996; 2004; 2007; 2010
Slovenia (net)	1997; 1999; 2004; 2007; 2010
South Africa (gross)	2008; 2010
Spain (net; gross)	1980; 1985; 1990; 1995; 2000; 2004; 2007; 2010
Sweden (gross)	1981; 1987; 1992; 1995; 2000; 2005
Switzerland (gross)	1982; 1992; 2000; 2002; 2004
Taiwan Province of China (gross)	1981; 1986; 1991; 1995; 1997; 2000; 2005; 2007; 2010
United Kingdom (gross)	1979; 1986; 1991; 1994; 1995; 1999; 2004; 2007; 2010
United States (gross)	1979; 1986; 1991; 1994; 1997; 2000; 2004; 2007; 2010; 2013
Uruguay (net)	2004

Source: Luxembourg Income Study database.

Note: Cutoff date for data is February 24, 2015. Material in parentheses indicates whether income components are recorded gross or net of taxes; definition may vary by year of survey, in which case the applicable descriptions (gross, net, or mixed) are listed. For a detailed definition of the recording method (gross, net, or mixed) of taxes, see http://www.lisdatacenter.org/.

ANNEX 6.3. DESCRIPTION OF THE DATABASE

Annex Table 6.3.1 reports the earliest and latest value for the Gini index for the countries included in the estimation sample.

The data sources for the estimation analysis are the following:

- For the disposable Gini index (a discontinuous variable observed only in some years, which vary depending on the country) data from various sources are used with the aim of covering the largest possible sample. The sources are the OECD, Eurostat, the World Bank's World Development Indicators, LIS, and the Socio-Economic Database for Latin America and the Caribbean.

ANNEX TABLE 6.3.1

Countries Considered in the Estimation and Descriptive Statistics for Inequality

Country		Earliest Observation		Latest Observation	
		Gini	Year	Gini	Year
Argentina	EME	0.46	1995	0.44	2007
Armenia	EME	0.34	2003	0.31	2008
Australia	ADV	0.28	1981	0.34	2008
Austria	ADV	0.23	1987	0.27	2011
Azerbaijan	EME	0.35	1995	0.34	2008
Belarus	EME	0.29	1995	0.27	2008
Belgium	ADV	0.23	1985	0.24	2011
Bhutan	LIDC	0.47	2003	0.38	2007
Bolivia	LIDC	0.56	1997	0.44	2009
Bosnia and Herzegovina	EME	0.36	2007	0.36	2007
Brazil	EME	0.55	2004	0.52	2008
Bulgaria	EME	0.31	1995	0.26	2012
Burkina Faso	LIDC	0.40	2003	0.40	2003
Burundi	LIDC	0.33	2006	0.33	2006
Cameroon	LIDC	0.41	1996	0.40	2001
Canada	ADV	0.32	1971	0.32	2008
Chile	EME	0.54	1996	0.51	2009
China	EME	0.36	1996	0.42	2005
Colombia	EME	0.55	2000	0.53	2009
Costa Rica	EME	0.43	1995	0.49	2009
Côte d'Ivoire	LIDC	0.37	1995	0.44	1998
Croatia	EME	0.27	1998	0.37	2011
Cyprus	ADV	0.29	1997	0.31	2012
Czech Republic	ADV	0.26	1996	0.27	2004
Denmark	ADV	0.26	1987	0.27	2012
Dominican Republic	EME	0.46	1996	0.46	1996
Egypt	EME	0.30	1996	0.31	2008
Estonia	ADV	0.36	2000	0.30	2012
Finland	ADV	0.21	1987	0.26	2012
France	ADV	0.29	1979	0.31	2012
Gabon	EME	0.41	2005	0.41	2005
Georgia	EME	0.40	2003	0.41	2008
Germany	ADV	0.27	1973	0.28	2012
Greece	ADV	0.35	1995	0.35	2012
Guatemala	EME	0.56	2002	0.53	2006
Honduras	LIDC	0.52	2001	0.58	2005
Hong Kong SAR	ADV	0.43	1996	0.43	1996
Hungary	EME	0.29	1999	0.28	2012
India	EME	0.33	2005	0.33	2005
Iran	EME	0.44	1998	0.38	2005
Ireland	ADV	0.33	1987	0.30	2011
Israel	ADV	0.34	1997	0.36	2008
Italy	ADV	0.31	1986	0.34	2012
Japan	ADV	0.30	1985	0.33	2008
Jordan	EME	0.36	1997	0.34	2008
Kazakhstan	EME	0.35	1996	0.29	2009
Kenya	LIDC	0.43	1997	0.48	2005
Korea	ADV	0.31	2006	0.31	2006
Kyrgyz Republic	LIDC	0.36	1998	0.36	2009
Latvia	ADV	0.27	1993	0.35	2012
Lesotho	LIDC	0.53	2003	0.53	2003
Lithuania	EME	0.34	1993	0.36	2012
Luxembourg	ADV	0.24	1985	0.28	2012
Macedonia, FYR	EME	0.28	1998	0.43	2009
Malta	ADV	0.30	2000	0.27	2012
Mexico	EME	0.52	1996	0.45	2010
Moldova	LIDC	0.37	1997	0.33	2010
Mongolia	LIDC	0.33	2002	0.37	2008

Country		Earliest Observation		Latest Observation	
		Gini	Year	Gini	Year
Morocco	EME	0.39	1999	0.41	2007
Mozambique	LIDC	0.47	2003	0.46	2008
Namibia	EME	0.64	2004	0.64	2004
Nepal	LIDC	0.44	2003	0.33	2010
Netherlands	ADV	0.25	1983	0.22	2012
New Zealand	ADV	0.32	1990	0.33	2008
Niger	LIDC	0.44	2005	0.35	2008
Nigeria	LIDC	0.43	2004	0.43	2004
Norway	ADV	0.22	1979	0.23	2012
Panama	EME	0.55	1997	0.50	2008
Papua New Guinea	LIDC	0.51	1996	0.51	1996
Philippines	EME	0.46	1997	0.43	2009
Poland	EME	0.26	1992	0.32	2004
Portugal	ADV	0.35	1975	0.34	2012
Romania	EME	0.28	1995	0.28	1997
Senegal	LIDC	0.41	2001	0.39	2005
Serbia	EME	0.33	2002	0.28	2009
Sierra Leone	LIDC	0.43	2003	0.43	2003
Singapore	ADV	0.42	1998	0.42	1998
Slovak Republic	ADV	0.25	1996	0.26	2012
Slovenia	ADV	0.23	1997	0.23	2004
South Africa	EME	0.57	1995	0.63	2009
Spain	ADV	0.32	1980	0.34	2012
Sri Lanka	EME	0.41	2002	0.40	2007
Sweden	ADV	0.26	1967	0.25	2011
Switzerland	ADV	0.31	1992	0.27	2012
Tajikistan	LIDC	0.33	2003	0.33	2007
Tanzania	LIDC	0.35	2000	0.38	2007
Tunisia	EME	0.41	2000	0.41	2005
Turkey	EME	0.42	1994	0.39	2008
Ukraine	EME	0.39	1995	0.26	2009
United Kingdom	ADV	0.27	1969	0.36	2011
United States	ADV	0.32	1974	0.37	2010
Uruguay	EME	0.42	1998	0.44	2005
Venezuela	EME	0.46	1997	0.39	2007

Sources: See text of this annex.
Note: ADV = advanced economy; EME = emerging market economy; LIDC = low-income and developing countries.

- For the wage share, the main data source is the ILO database. When available, the adjusted wage share is used. For many countries, longer time series for wage shares are also published in the European Commission's Annual Macroeconomic Database (AMECO). For these countries, the two data sets display similar patterns, and AMECO data can be used to extrapolate developments over a longer time period.

- The unemployment rate is taken from the IMF *World Economic Outlook*.

- The employment rate in the services sector comes from the ILO.

- For the variables capturing the wage setting setup we use the Institutional Characteristics of Trade Unions, Wage Setting, State Intervention and Social Pacts data set, 1960–2011 (produced by Jelle Visser, Amsterdam Institute for Advanced Labour Studies). The variables used (ictwss_Coord and ictwss_Type) capture the following aspects: coordination of wage-setting, and the type, or the modality or mechanism through which coordination of wage-bargaining behavior is produced. The higher the value of the variable the higher the degree of coordination or centralization of the wage-bargaining framework.

- The dispersion of labor income is measured as the ratio of total income of the top 10 percent to the bottom 10 percent, and data are taken from the World Bank's World Development Indicators.

- The ratios of public revenue, social protection spending, and health expenditures to GDP are taken from the IMF *World Economic Outlook*; Eurostat; OECD; the World Health Organization; the United Nations Educational, Scientific and Cultural Organization; CEPALSTAT; the Asian Development Bank; the World Bank; and the IMF International Financial Statistics.

- Economic globalization is measured as a score based on actual flows and trade restrictions, and the data are drawn from the KOF Index of Globalization (Dreher, Gaston, and Martens 2008).

- Financial globalization is proxied by the log of total foreign assets and liabilities divided by GDP, which is computed from data from updated and extended versions of the data set constructed by Lane and Milesi-Ferretti (2007).

REFERENCES

Adler, M., and K. D. Schmid. 2012. "Factor Shares and Income Inequality: Empirical Evidence from Germany 2002–2008." University of Tuebingen Working Paper No. 34, University of Tuebingen.

Alvaredo, F., A. B. Atkinson, T. Piketty, and E. Saez. 2013. "The Top 1 Percent in International and Historical Perspective." *Journal of Economic Perspectives* 27 (3): 3–20.

Atkinson, A. B. 2009. "Factor Shares: the Principal Problem of Political Economy?" *Oxford Review of Economic Policy* 25 (1): 3–16.

Bentolila, S., and G. Saint Paul. 2003. "Explaining Movements in the Labor Share." *Contributions to Macroeconomics* 3 (1): 1–31.

Bruno, M., and J. Sachs. 1985. *The Economics of Worldwide Stagflation*. Cambridge, Massachusetts: Harvard University Press.

Checchi, D., and C. García-Peñalosa. 2010. "Labour Market Institutions and the Personal Distribution of Income in the OECD." *Economica* 77 (37): 413–50.

Congressional Budget Office (CBO). 2011. "Trends in the Distribution of Household Income Between 1979 and 2007." CBO Study Pub. No. 4031, Congress of the United States, Washington.

De Serres, A., S. Scarpetta, and C. Maisonneuve. 2002. "Sectoral Shifts in Europe and the United States: How They Affect Aggregate Labor Shares and the Properties of Wage Equations." OECD Economics Department Working Paper No. 326, OECD, Paris.

Dew-Becker, I., and R. J. Gordon. 2005. "Where Did the Productivity Growth Go? Inflation Dynamics and the Distribution of Income." *Brookings Papers on Economic Activity* 36 (2): 67–127.

Dreher, A., N. Gaston, and P. Martens. 2008. *Measuring Globalisation—Gauging Its Consequences*. (Updated KOF Index of Globalization). New York: Springer Science and Business Media.

Eichengreen, B. 2007. *The European Economy since 1945*. Princeton, New Jersey: Princeton University Press.

Ellis, L., and K. Smith. 2007. "The Global Upward Trend in the Profit Share." Working Paper No. 231, Bank for International Settlements, Basel.

Elsby, M. W., B. Hobjin, and A. Sahin. 2013. "The Decline of the US Labor Share." *Brookings Papers on Economic Activity* 47 (2): 1–63.

European Commission. 2007. "The Labour Income Share in the European Union." In *Employment in Europe*. European Commission Directorate-General for Employment, Social Affairs and Equal Opportunities.

Feldstein, M. 2008. "Did Wages Reflect Growth in Productivity?" *Journal of Policy Modeling* 30 (4): 591–94.

Glyn, A. 2009. "Functional Distribution and Inequality." In *Oxford Handbook of Economic Inequality*, edited by W. Salverda, B. Nolan, and T. M. Smeeding. Oxford: Oxford University Press.

———, and R. Sutcliffe. 1972. *British Capitalism, Workers and the Profits Squeeze*. Harmondworth: Penguin Books.

Goldfarb, R. S., and T. C. Leonard. 2005. "Inequality of What among Whom? Rival Conceptions of Distribution in the 20th Century." *Research in the History of Economic Thought and Methodology* 23: 75–118.

Gollin, D. 2002. "Getting Income Shares Right." *Journal of Political Economy* 110 (2): 458–74.

Gomme, P., and P. Rupert. 2004. "Measuring Labor's Share of Income." Federal Reserve Bank of Cleveland, Policy Discussion Paper No. 7.

Harris, E., and F. Sammartino. 2011. "Trends in the Distribution of Household Income between 1979 and 2007." Congressional Budget Office, Washington.

Hoeller, P., I. Joumard, M. Pisu, and D. Bloch. 2012. "Less Income Inequality and More Growth—Are They Compatible? Part 1. Mapping Income Inequality Across the OECD." OECD Working Paper No. 924, Paris.

International Labour Organization (ILO). 2011. "The Labour Share of Income: Determinants and Potential Contribution to Exiting the Financial Crisis." In *World of Work Report 2011: Making Markets Work for Jobs*. Geneva: ILO.

———. 2012. *Global Wage Report 2012/13: Wages and Equitable Growth*. Geneva: ILO.

———. 2015. *Global Wage Report 2014/15: Wage and Income Inequality*. Geneva: ILO.

International Monetary Fund (IMF). 2007. *World Economic Outlook*. Washington, April.

———. 2014. "Fiscal Policy and Income Inequality." IMF Board Paper, International Monetary Fund, Washington.

Jacobson, M., and F. Occhino. 2012a. "Behind the Decline in Labor's Share of Income." Federal Reserve Bank of Cleveland.

———. 2012b. "Labor's Declining Share of Income and Rising Inequality." Federal Reserve Bank of Cleveland.

Jaumotte, F., and C. Osorio Buitron. Forthcoming. "Union Power and Inequality." IMF Staff Discussion Note, International Monetary Fund, Washington.

Kaldor, N. 1961. "Capital Accumulation and Economic Growth." In *The Theory of Capital*, edited by F. A. Lutz and D. C. Hague. New York: St. Martins Press; London: Macmillan.

Karabarbounis, L., and B. Neiman. 2014. "The Global Decline of the Labor Share." *Quarterly Journal of Economics* 29 (1): 61–103.

Lane, P. R., and G. M. Milesi-Ferretti. 2007. "The External Wealth of Nations Mark II: Revised and Extended Estimates of Foreign Assets and Liabilities, 1970–2004." *Journal of International Economics* 73 (November): 223–50.

Lerman, R. I., and S. Yitzhaki. 1985. "Income Inequality Effects by Income Source: A New Approach and Applications to the United States." *Review of Economics and Statistics* 67: 151–56.

Lustig, N., L. F. Lopez Calva, and E. Ortiz-Juares. 2015. "Deconstructing the Decline in Inequality in Latin America." In *Proceedings of IEA Roundtable on Shared Prosperity and Growth*, edited by K. Basu and J. Stiglitz. New York: Palgrave-Macmillan.

Luxembourg Income Study (LIS) Database, http://www.lisdatacenter.org (multiple countries; computations on microdata completed by February 24, 2015). Luxembourg: LIS.

Lydall, H. F. 1968. *The Structure of Earnings*. Oxford: Clarendon Press.

Mankiw, N. G. 2007. *Macroeconomics*, 6th edition. New York, Worth.

Marchal, J., and B. Ducros. 1968. *The Distribution of National Income*. London: Macmillan.

Organisation for Economic Co-operation and Development (OECD). 2008. *Growing Unequal? Income Distribution and Poverty in OECD Countries*. Paris: OECD.

Piketty, T. 2014. *Capital in the Twenty-First Century*. Cambridge, Massachusetts: Harvard University Press.

Pyatt, G., C. N. Chen, and J. Fei. 1980. "The Distribution of Income by Factor Components." *Quarterly Journal of Economics* 95 (3): 451–73.

Rotondaro, V. 2014. "Wall Street Is Worried about Inequality?" National Catholic Reporter website, October 14. http://ncronline.org/blogs/ncr-today/wall-street-worried-about-inequality.

Shorrocks, A. F. 1982. "Inequality Decomposition by Factor Components." *Econometrica* 50 (1): 193–211.

———. 1983. "The Impact of Income Components on the Distribution of Family Incomes." *Quarterly Journal of Economics* 98 (2): 311–26.

Stigler, G. 1965. "The Influence of Events and Policies on Economic Theory." *Essays in the History of Economics*. Chicago: University of Chicago Press.

Stockhammer, E. 2013. "Why Have Wage Shares Fallen? A Panel Analysis of the Determinants of Functional Income Distribution." ILO Working Paper No. 470913, International Labour Organization, Geneva.

CHAPTER 7

The Wealth of Nations: Stylized Facts and Options for Taxation

Luc Eyraud

INTRODUCTION

This chapter analyzes trends in wealth inequality across advanced and developing economies and examines how wealth taxation can be used as a redistributive instrument.

That income inequality has increased in many economies since the 1970s is generally accepted, although it is less known that the wealth gap has been growing too (Piketty 2014). The rise in wealth inequality might have negative macroeconomic implications, an idea that has recently entered the arena of public debate. There is a growing sense that wealth inequality can be detrimental to growth because it fosters rent-seeking behaviors (by potentially reducing the work effort of the better off), generates political and economic instability that reduces investment, deprives the poor of their ability to accumulate human capital (when access to financial markets is limited and education needs to be partly funded from asset sales), and impedes the social consensus required to adjust to shocks (Alesina and Rodrik 1994; Deininger and Olinto 2000; Morck, Stangeland, and Yeung 2000; Bagchi and Svejnar 2013).

To contain the rise in wealth inequality, a number of fiscal instruments exist to affect capital accumulation and asset price dynamics. Both tax and spending policies can be used to alter the distribution of wealth. For example, the provision of social housing reduces home ownership and can dampen real estate prices. A range of wealth taxes, such as those levied on immovable property, can be a source of progressive taxation. In addition, instruments that reduce the inequality of disposable income have an indirect effect on wealth distribution through their impact on capital formation.

This chapter is structured as follows. The next section describes trends in the size and distribution of household wealth in the world during the past 30 years. The subsequent section discusses how wealth taxes can be used for redistributive purposes while minimizing efficiency costs.

STYLIZED FACTS ON HOUSEHOLD WEALTH IN THE WORLD

Household wealth can be defined in different ways. In a broad sense, wealth encompasses any store of value—measured as the present value of all future income, including pension rights and human capital. Given data limitations, this chapter relies on the narrower concept of "net worth," which is the value of assets held by households less the value of their liabilities. In general, statistical databases define nonfinancial assets as dwellings and land; financial wealth includes currency and deposits, securities, and net equity of households in life insurance and pension funds (Ynesta 2008).

Even this narrow concept is not without its measurement problems. Wealth estimates are derived from microeconomic studies (household survey and tax data) that are subject to significant sampling errors and underreporting at both tails of the distribution. In addition, data harmonization is still limited despite efforts to produce cross-country wealth databases and surveys.

TABLE 7.1

Selected Advanced Economies: Households and Nonprofit Institutions Serving Households' Net Financial Wealth *(Percent of GDP, 1980–2012)*

	1980	1990	1999	2002	2007	2012
Canada	105.3	101.2	172.7	142.4	168.2	167.2
France	NA	NA	137.8	119.7	137.4	139.4
Germany	NA	NA	98.6	94.9	120.6	126.5
Greece	NA	NA	223.3	105.3	96.5	63.0
Ireland	NA	NA	NA	74.5	50.2	86.3
Italy	NA	NA	213.7	200.4	189.3	177.8
Japan	95.8	156.6	200.2	209.3	227.0	262.3
Portugal	84.2	102.2	161.5	125.1	124.9	134.4
Spain	82.2	76.4	126.5	93.5	94.0	81.5
United Kingdom	NA	135.0	259.4	164.2	175.7	190.4
United States	205.4	205.3	292.3	218.8	273.6	282.0

Sources: National data; Organisation for Economic Co-operation and Development; and IMF staff estimates and calculations.
Note: NA = data not available.

TABLE 7.2

Selected Advanced Economies: Households' Net Wealth (Financial and Nonfinancial) *(Percent of GDP, 1995–2011)*

	1995	1999	2002	2008	2010	2012
Canada[1]	300.6	337.3	314.7	333.1	383.4	392.2
France	NA	337.1	359.9	472.7	508.9	513.4
Germany	NA	301.3	304.8	339.2	359.2	366.8
Ireland	NA	NA	294.8	342.7	329.3	283.9
Italy	439.8	486.6	495.3	551.0	559.5	545.2
Japan	461.1	475.9	454.3	451.8	464.2	479.9
Portugal	351.2	363.0	331.7	330.8	330.4	325.7
Spain	NA	NA	488.5	591.5	580.0	512.5
United Kingdom	359.7	464.0	422.2	415.3	480.4	483.6
United States[1]	381.8	447.3	401.4	388.6	423.6	435.9

Sources: National data; Organisation for Economic Co-operation and Development; and IMF staff estimates and calculations.
Note: NA = data not available.
[1] Includes durable goods.

Mindful of these caveats, this section presents some stylized facts on trends in households' net wealth across advanced and developing countries.[1]

Size and Evolution of Household Wealth

Advanced Economies

In most advanced economies, household net wealth is high and growing. After a steady decline throughout much of the twentieth century due to the adverse shocks of the two World Wars and the stock market crash of 1929, household wealth-income ratios have been rising rapidly since the early 1970s (Piketty 2014), with a swift acceleration during the new-economy boom of the 1990s (Tables 7.1 and 7.2). This increase has been particularly pronounced in Europe.

---

[1] In this chapter, wealth data are extracted from household balance sheets produced by national statistics institutes and central banks. If data are incomplete (in particular regarding nonfinancial assets), household surveys are sometimes used to fill in the gaps. For countries with both balance sheet and survey data, precedence is given to balance sheet data, which generally take into account broader data sources, including tax registers.

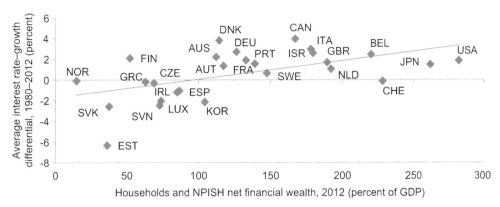

Figure 7.1   Selected Advanced Economies: Interest Rate–Growth Differential and Households and NPISH Net Financial Wealth

Sources: Organisation for Economic Co-operation and Development; and IMF staff estimates and calculations.

Note: NPISH = nonprofit institutions serving households. Data labels in the figure use International Organization for Standardization (ISO) country codes.

In the United States, wealth has increased at a slower pace, marked by two significant corrections during the financial crises of 2002 and 2008. Japan has followed a more idiosyncratic path, with stronger wealth accumulation during the 1980s, followed by a decline in the early 1990s after the bursting of the asset price bubble. In most countries, the global financial crisis severely affected the net wealth of households, but after a steep decline in 2008, most wealth ratios bounced back to their previous levels.

Today, households' net wealth ranges between three and six times GDP in most advanced economies. These are high levels by historical standards. Based on long-term series constructed for four large advanced economies (France, Germany, the United Kingdom, and the United States), Piketty and Zucman (2014) show that wealth-to-income ratios are returning to the high values observed in Europe in the nineteenth century.

Abstracting from country-specific developments, the sharp increase in wealth accumulation during the past 40 years was driven by a series of common factors (De Bonis, Fano, and Sbano 2013; ECB 2013). First, the growth slowdown following the 1973 oil shock raised the interest rate–growth differential, mechanically inflating the wealth-to-output ratio.[2] Figure 7.1 shows this differential and subsequent household financial wealth are strongly correlated in advanced economies. Second, valuation effects also played a major role. Asset prices grew rapidly during the period: the new economy boosted financial asset values in the 1990s, whereas the 2000s saw a sharp acceleration in real asset prices, reflecting in some cases the formation of property market bubbles (Figure 7.2). Finally, in some countries, private savings have increased over time as a result of structural factors, including population aging; the financial deregulation of the 1980s, which increased households' participation in financial markets; and the development of funded pension systems.

Global Trends

The availability of household balance sheet data is more limited for emerging markets and low-income countries. Credit Suisse (2013), which collects and reports data at a global level, finds that household wealth has increased in all regions of the world since the early 2000s. Global

---

[2] Slower growth affects both the numerator and the denominator of the wealth-to-income ratio, but the effect on the stock of wealth is smaller than on the flow of income (see discussion in Piketty 2014).

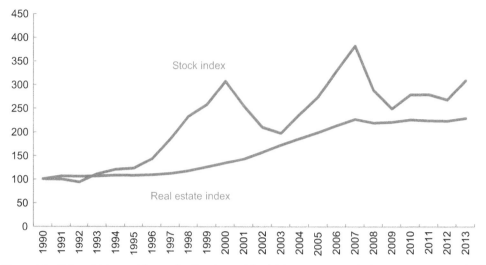

Figure 7.2 Selected Advanced Economies: Housing and Stock Prices, 1990–2013 *(Index, 1990 = 100, unweighted average)*

Sources: IMF, International Financial Statistics; and Organisation for Economic Co-operation and Development Economic Outlook.

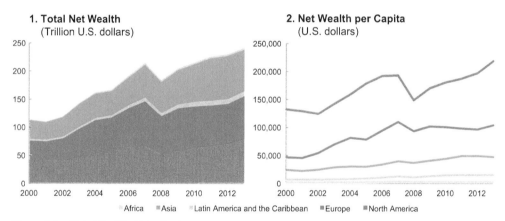

Figure 7.3 Global Net Wealth by Region

Source: Credit Suisse (2013).
Note: "Asia" includes Asia and the Pacific, China, and India.

household net wealth rose by about 110 percent between 2000 and 2013, while net wealth per adult rose by 80 percent. Household wealth declined significantly during the financial crisis in 2007–08, but recovered subsequently and exceeded its precrisis level from 2012 onward.[3] This trend was observed in all regions of the world and in most countries, with the exception of some European countries (Figure 7.3).

Today, wealth is unequally distributed across regions. Both North America and Europe account for about one-third of global wealth, while 20 percent is held in the Asia-Pacific region.

---

[3] The overall picture is nonetheless distorted by valuing wealth in U.S. dollars, given that the dollar depreciated against most major currencies during the period, accounting for part of the rise in dollar-denominated wealth. Holding exchange rates constant, the rise in global wealth would be less significant. Under this assumption, Credit Suisse (2013) estimates that net wealth per adult increased by about 50 percent during the period.

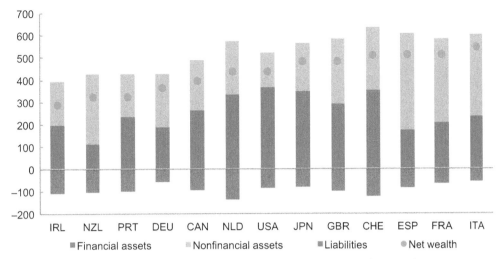

Figure 7.4 Selected Advanced Economies: Composition of Net Wealth *(Percent of GDP, 2012)*

Sources: National data; Organisation for Economic Co-operation and Development; and IMF staff estimates.
Note: Data labels in the figure use International Organization for Standardization (ISO) country codes.

The rest of the world (China, India, Latin America, and Africa) owns the remaining 16 percent of total household wealth despite hosting 60 percent of the adult population.

Wealth Composition

The composition of household portfolios varies widely across countries (Figure 7.4). In general, nonfinancial assets represent more than half of total wealth.[4] Spain and New Zealand are among the advanced economies with the highest share of real assets (more than 70 percent of gross assets at the end of 2012). The United States is an outlier with financial assets representing about 70 percent of the total.

Many factors can explain the cross-country differences in wealth composition (ECB 2013). In general, the share of financial assets is higher in countries with private pension systems, a large public housing sector (which discourages home ownership), a high level of financial development, and smaller households (large households tend to accumulate more real estate assets). Differences in risk tolerance, taxation, and valuation effects also influence the composition. For instance, the Swedish tax reform of 1991, which reduced capital income taxation with the introduction of a flat rate, had a lasting impact on the portfolio composition, increasing the share of financial assets (Klevmarken 2006).

In emerging market and low-income economies, household balance sheet data are generally not available. Based on survey data, it seems that the share of nonfinancial assets is even larger than in advanced economies. This share apparently exceeds 80 percent in some countries, such as India and Indonesia (Credit Suisse 2013).

---

[4]This section's findings are based on national account (administrative) data, but it is noteworthy that survey data generally report an even higher share of nonfinancial assets. This result may be due to several factors, including differences in asset coverage; difficulties in self-assessing financial assets (leading individuals to underestimate their value in surveys); low response rate and underreporting, which are more pronounced for financial assets; and accounting rules (in particular regarding the reporting of self-employed business assets).

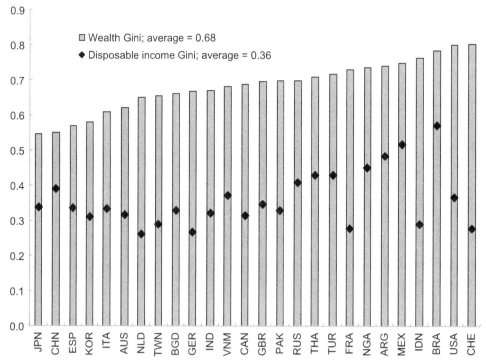

Figure 7.5   Inequality of Wealth and Income

Sources: Davies and others (2008); Luxembourg Income Study; Organisation for Economic Co-operation and Development; Socio-Economic Database for Latin America and the Caribbean (CEDLAC and the World Bank).
Note: Data labels in the figure use International Organization for Standardization (ISO) country codes.

Wealth Distribution

Wealth is very concentrated within countries (Davies and others 2010; Bonesmo Fredriksen 2012). Household wealth is much more unequally distributed than income. The Gini coefficient of wealth in a sample of 26 advanced and developing economies in the early 2000s was 0.68, compared with a Gini of 0.36 for disposable incomes (Figure 7.5). The main reason for this discrepancy is that high-income individuals have higher saving rates and thus accumulate wealth faster than do poorer households, and they generally hold riskier assets with higher yields.

However, there are important country differences. The share of wealth held by the top 10 percent ranges from slightly less than half in Chile, China, Italy, Japan, Spain, and the United Kingdom, to more than two-thirds in Indonesia, Norway, Sweden, Switzerland, and the United States. In Switzerland and the United States, where wealth is most unequally distributed, the top 1 percent alone holds more than one-third of total household wealth.

In most countries, the lowest 50 percent of households in the wealth distribution generally hold only a very small fraction of total net wealth (Figure 7.6). In Denmark, this share is even negative, reflecting few incentives for the middle and lower classes to accumulate assets in a country with strong social security and public housing programs.

From the beginning of the twentieth century until the 1970s, wealth inequality declined dramatically in most countries for which long time series of wealth distribution are available (Davies and others 2008). This trend has reversed in the past three decades, with wealth inequality rising in most advanced economies.[5] For instance, between the mid-1980s and early 2000s, the growth

---

[5] There are very few emerging markets with wealth distribution series allowing comparison over time. Among those is China, where wealth inequality has risen at a strong pace.

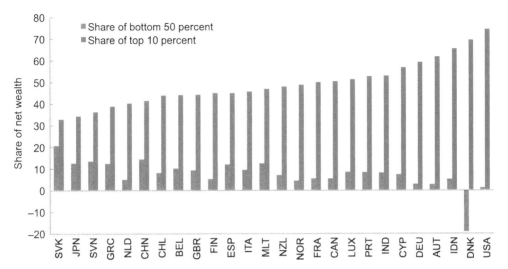

Figure 7.6 Shares of Net Wealth Held by Bottom 50 Percent and Top 10 Percent

Sources: Credit Suisse (2013); and Statistics Norway.
Note: Data labels in the figure use International Organization for Standardization (ISO) country codes.

of wealth in Canada and Sweden was all concentrated in the two upper deciles of the wealth distribution. During the same period, the Gini coefficients of wealth distribution in Finland and Italy rose from about 0.55 to greater than 0.6 (Ballarino and others 2012). In the United States, the Gini coefficient for wealth, after rising steeply between 1983 and 1989 from 0.80 to 0.83, remained stable until 2007, and then increased sharply to 0.87 during the financial crisis (Wolff 2014). Wealth inequality has risen for a number of reasons. The stock market boom of the 1990s was particularly beneficial to rich households who own higher proportions of stocks, bonds, and other financial products than poor households do. Tax reforms, including lower marginal tax rates on top incomes and lower taxes on all forms of capital, also played a role in the widening of wealth disparities during the period (Bonesmo Fredriksen 2012).

TAXING WEALTH TO REDUCE INEQUALITY

There are several quite different types of taxes on wealth. These taxes can be grouped into two broad categories: those that apply to wealth holdings—immovable property tax and net wealth tax (NWT)—and those that apply to wealth transfers, which is further divided into transaction taxes (levied when the asset is sold) and gift and inheritance taxes (levied when the asset is given). Their base is generally the gross value of assets but some taxes bear on net wealth (assets minus liabilities).

This section discusses the prospects of raising additional revenue and reducing inequality using the various types of wealth taxation. It explores how such policies could be designed, looking at taxes on residential property, inheritance, capital transactions, and net wealth.

General Considerations on Wealth Taxation and Inequality

Taxes levied on wealth, especially on immovable property, can be used for redistributive purposes. These taxes, of various kinds, target the same underlying base as capital income taxes, namely assets. Because wealth is concentrated among the better off, even a small proportional tax on the capital stock can increase progressivity. Wealth taxes can thus be considered a potential source of progressive taxation.

Recently these taxes have featured prominently in the public debate on fiscal policy. They are often perceived to be key policy instruments for spreading the burden of fiscal adjustment more equally among taxpayers. In many countries, wealth taxes are also politically more acceptable to the median voter (compared with other consolidation measures).

A natural question that arises is whether wealth taxes are redundant with capital income taxes since, at least for income-generating assets, an annual tax on the capital stock is roughly equivalent to taxing capital income from that wealth at a higher rate.[6] However, the two forms of taxation are not strictly equivalent, and wealth taxes are likely to have stronger distributional effects in certain circumstances:

- *Comprehensiveness.* A wealth tax may be more encompassing than a capital income tax because it also taxes assets that are not associated with monetary payoffs, such as works of art (while these assets increase their owners' welfare). By the same token, the wealth tax is useful when only part of the periodic increase in wealth is taxed by the capital income tax, in particular if there are exemptions or if capital gains are not realized.

- *Difficulties in observing the base.* Taxing net wealth may be more convenient for assets whose income is not readily observable. For example, taxing the value of owner-occupied housing (net of mortgage debt) is a way of taxing its imputed return, given that homeowners pay no tax on imputed rents.

- *Policy design constraints.* Wealth taxation may be a supplement to capital income taxation if capital income taxation is constrained by policy design. For instance, in a dual income tax system in which capital income is taxed at a low flat rate, wealth taxation may be used to achieve redistributive objectives.[7]

The redistributive properties of wealth taxes come at a cost. Capital taxes, if too high, can have high efficiency costs because of their distortionary effects on savings and investment (see "A Menu of Options for Wealth Taxation" later in this chapter). Moreover, taxing capital can be administratively difficult in light of its mobility, with the risk of creating ample evasion and avoidance opportunities. Another issue is that the mobility of capital allows firms to shift a large share of the burden of these taxes onto labor or consumers, thereby affecting the distributional consequences. The following sections analyze these trade-offs for various types of wealth taxes.

Revenues from Wealth Taxes

Although wealth taxes can, in themselves, contribute to achieving redistributive goals, an important contribution of wealth taxation to the pursuit of equity goals is through the financing of spending measures. Therefore, a key question is how much wealth can taxes generate. In this regard, there seems to be room to raise additional revenue from them.

For governments in search of fiscal space, household wealth is a buoyant tax base that is still relatively untapped despite its rapid accumulation since the 1990s. During recent decades,

---

[6] If A is the asset value at the beginning of the year and i is the nominal return on this asset (taking the form of dividends, interest, or capital gains), the capital income on the asset will be iA. Imposing a tax rate t on capital income each year is equivalent to imposing an annual tax rate of $T=it/(1+i)$ on the asset itself (note that the formula discounts the capital income by $[1+i]$ to value the receipts of both taxes at the same point in time). This equivalence also shows that a wealth tax implicitly imposes a lower tax on the returns of high-yield assets, at least in the short term, compared with a capital income tax. Indeed, the tax rate on returns is $T(1+i)/i$ (which declines when i increases), with the equivalence being the two taxes written as $((Ai)/(1+i)) \times (T(1+i)/i) = A \times T$.

[7] A counterargument is that the rationale for a low uniform tax rate on capital income is to reduce tax evasion and avoidance by wealthy taxpayers. It is likely that a wealth tax would also be subject to similar design constraints.

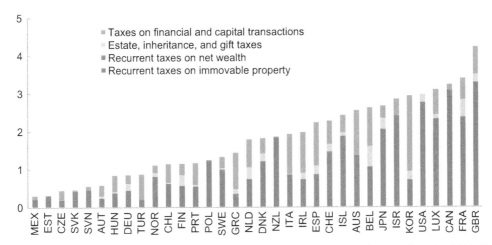

Figure 7.7   Taxes on Wealth in Organisation for Economic Co-operation and Development Countries, 2000–12
(Percent of GDP)

Source: Organisation for Economic Co-operation and Development Revenue Statistics.
Note: Data labels in the figure use International Organization for Standardization (ISO) country codes.

revenue from wealth taxes has not kept up with the surge in wealth as a share of GDP and, as a result, the effective tax rate on wealth has dropped from an average of about 0.9 percent in 1970 to approximately 0.5 percent today in advanced economies. This is not a new phenomenon: wealth taxes were a major source of revenues in the nineteenth century, but have trended downward ever since.

Today, wealth taxes yield little revenue in most countries (Figure 7.7). On average, they amount to slightly less than 2 percent of GDP in the Organisation for Economic Co-operation and Development (OECD)—of which about half comes from taxes on immovable property and one-fourth from transaction taxes. Other types of wealth taxes generate negligible revenue, except the wealth tax in Luxembourg. Somewhat surprisingly, Anglo-Saxon countries show the highest burdens from wealth taxes, while Scandinavian countries are in the lower ranks.

Nonetheless, the long-term declining trend of wealth taxes may have come to a halt. Since the onset of the financial crisis, there have been numerous reform initiatives to raise more revenues from real estate in both advanced and emerging market economies (Norregaard 2013). Governments also eye the stock of financial assets held by the private sector. Recent examples include the haircut of uninsured bank deposits in Cyprus in 2013 and the plan to introduce a financial transaction tax in 10 European countries. Comprehensive taxes on wealth are returning as well. Although many countries repealed their NWT in the past 20 years, both Iceland and Spain reintroduced it as a temporary measure during the crisis.

A Menu of Options for Wealth Taxation

The prospect of raising additional revenue from the various types of wealth taxation and their role in reducing inequality is summarized in the following discussion.

Taxes on Residential Property

Property taxes in the form of recurrent taxes levied on land and buildings are widely seen as an attractive revenue source (Norregaard 2013). These taxes are generally considered to be more efficient than others, primarily because the tax base is less mobile and hard to hide, resulting in fewer adverse effects on resource allocation. These efficiency properties are enhanced when the

TABLE 7.3

Property Tax Revenues *(Percent of GDP, except where noted otherwise)*				
	1970s	1980s	1990s	2000s
OECD countries	1.24	1.31	1.44	2.12
(number of countries)	(16)	(18)	(16)	(18)
Developing countries	0.42	0.36	0.42	0.60
(number of countries)	(20)	(27)	(23)	(29)
Transition countries	0.34	0.59	0.54	0.68
(number of countries)	(1)	(4)	(20)	(18)
All countries	0.77	0.73	0.75	1.04
(number of countries)	(37)	(49)	(59)	(65)

Source: Bahl and Martinez-Vazquez (2008).

tax—mainly borne by residents—functions as a "benefit tax"[8] financing local government services: if perceived as payment for services, the tax should be fully neutral with respect to labor supply, investment, and savings decisions. In addition, to the extent that increases in property taxes are fully capitalized in property prices, with resulting one-off losses for present owners, the tax increase should not affect the rate of return for new owners and could therefore be neutral to investment behavior.

For these reasons, property taxes are considered to be a potentially stable revenue source and—by requiring little international tax coordination—attractive to economies that are otherwise exposed to tax competition for mobile tax bases. At the macroeconomic level, studies on the growth hierarchy of taxes have generally found taxation of immovable property to be more benign for economic growth than are other forms of taxation, in particular compared with direct taxes (Arnold 2008).

The equity implications of property taxation are a contentious issue. Norregaard (2013) reviews the main elements of the debate. Some evidence indicates that the burden of property taxes is borne by the owners of capital and land. Because these owners are predominantly higher-income individuals, property taxation is generally found to be progressive. It is important that property taxes can be made more progressive through a basic allowance or by varying the rate with the value of the property. The use of market values (as opposed to taxation based on square footage) is also likely to maximize fairness of the property tax because market values broadly reflect the capitalized benefits provided by local services that are financed by the tax.

Turning to revenue potential, property taxes are widely seen to be an underexploited revenue source. The average yield of property taxes in 65 economies (for which data are available) in the 2000s was about 1 percent of GDP, but in developing economies it averaged only half that (Table 7.3). Especially outside Anglo-Saxon countries, scope to raise more revenue is readily evident, though effective implementation of a property tax requires sizable up-front investment in administrative infrastructure, particularly in emerging market economies.

Taxes on Inheritances and Gifts

Taxes on estates, inheritances, and gifts[9] (IGT) can play a useful role in limiting the intergenerational transmission of inequality, which is high in many economies (Boadway, Chamberlain, and Emmerson 2010). IGT can also reduce inequality by enhancing the progressivity of the tax system, given that these taxes are only paid by the better off. Some also take the view that correcting

---

[8] According to the "benefit principle" of taxation, people should be taxed in proportion to the marginal benefits they receive from government goods and services.

[9] An estate tax is one levied on the value of assets at death; an inheritance tax is levied on the recipients.

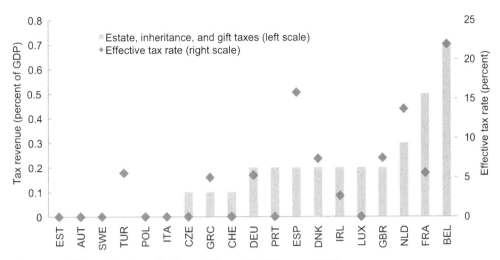

Figure 7.8 Effective Inheritance Tax Rates in Europe, 2012 *(Percent of GDP)*

Sources: AGN International–Europe (2013); and Organisation for Economic Co-operation and Development.

Note: Effective tax rates are based on taxes paid by the estate of a married individual who died on January 1, 2013, leaving a spouse and two children. The gross value of the estate is assumed to be €2.6 million. Data labels in the figure use International Organization for Standardization (ISO) country codes.

for advantages or disadvantages arising from circumstances beyond an individual's control—such as being born into a wealthy family—is a proper function of the tax system. In this regard, IGT can equalize opportunities.

Not all bequests on death are accidental; therefore, taxes on inherited wealth are likely to affect the saving decisions of both the donee and the donor, which may create an efficiency cost. Inheriting may reduce the effort of the donee to both save and work (the "Carnegie effect"). The effect of the tax on the donor's savings, which depends on the donor's motives for giving, is more ambiguous.[10] The tax may discourage savings because the cost of making a net bequest (the foregone consumption) increases; but greater savings are required to achieve any net target. The empirical evidence is mixed, suggesting that the overall effect on the donor's savings may be negative but small (Mirrlees and others 2011).[11]

IGT currently raise little revenues. Where the taxes exist, rates are generally low, exemptions and special arrangements widespread, and revenue yields small (Figure 7.8). In the OECD, revenue has been declining over time from 0.35 percent of GDP in 1970 to less than 0.15 percent today. These taxes may have the potential to raise more revenue, as illustrated by, for example, France and Belgium, where revenue yields are, respectively, 0.5 percent and 0.6 percent of GDP. In addition, the potential tax base is large. Although there is little consensus on the relative importance of inherited versus life-cycle wealth, survey-based evidence suggests that inherited wealth could account for at least 20 percent of total wealth in the United States (Davies and

---

[10] There will be no impact, for instance, on the behavior of donors who accumulate wealth simply for their own enjoyment and, failing to annuitize it, die before they have spent it all, or on the accumulation of wealth in excess of a normal rate of return.

[11] Kopczuk (2013) reviews the evidence, which is more informative about shorter-term responses to incentives—one macabre distortion being to the timing of death (Kopczuk and Slemrod 2003)—than it is about longer-term effects on capital accumulation. Theoretical results on optimal bequest taxation differ widely. Fahri and Werning (2010) find that it is optimal to subsidize bequests (because donors do not take full account of the social benefit to the recipients). In a different setting, Piketty and Saez (2012) find the optimal rate to be positive, and in some cases, substantial. For a general discussion, with an eye to practicalities of implementation, see Boadway, Chamberlain, and Emmerson (2010).

BOX 7.1 Real Estate Transaction Taxes

By discouraging transactions on the real estate market, transaction taxes have far-reaching consequences:

- The reduced market liquidity may increase price volatility, although both theory and empirical evidence are mixed (Andrews 2010).

- Transaction costs are likely to raise the elasticity of demand with respect to pretax prices, which may inflate housing prices and mitigate their response to supply shocks.[1]

- Transaction costs create incentives for buyers and sellers to collude and partly evade the tax by arranging a lower price for the property and a corresponding separate payment, either informal or formal (for the fixtures and fittings); this eases the distortions but undermines habits of tax compliance.

- Finally—and perhaps most important—theoretical and empirical studies show that transaction costs create lock-in effects[2] in the housing market and have negative effects on residential and job mobility, thereby impeding labor market matching and increasing structural unemployment (Oswald 1996, 1999; van Ommeren and van Leuvensteijn 2005; Caldera Sánchez and Andrews 2011).

---

[1] This result holds under the assumption that supply and demand functions are linear and the tax is ad valorem. The demand function can be written as $Y^d = -\alpha P(1+t) + \beta$, with P denoting the pretax price and t the ad valorem tax paid by the buyer. By definition, t raises the elasticity of Y^d to P. Increasing the slope of the demand curve (in absolute terms) raises the equilibrium price. Another implication is that a translation of the supply curve (due to new construction) results in a smaller decline in pretax prices.

[2] The "lock-in effect" describes a reduction in the frequency of house sales.

Shorrocks 2000; Wolff and Gittleman 2011), equivalent to more than 100 percent of GDP. By comparison, the present value of IGT revenues over 30 years is less than 10 percent of GDP.[12] In addition, the share of inherited wealth is likely to rise in the future because the baby boomers are reaching the inheritance-giving age group.

Transaction Taxes

Transaction taxes—primarily on the sale of real estate and financial instruments—typically account for one-quarter of wealth tax revenues in the OECD. They are administratively appealing, since transactions can often be fairly easily observed (stamp duty on the sale of shares in the United Kingdom, for instance, is one of the cheapest, per pound collected, of all taxes), and there are strong incentives for compliance when legal title is contingent on payment. Changes in ownership happen relatively infrequently and can be fairly easy for tax administrations to keep track of—especially when the purchaser has clear interest in ensuring that the necessary legal requirements reflecting the ownership change are completed (Thuronyi 1996). In some low-income and emerging market economies with constraints on the ability to administer taxes, transaction taxes have distinct practical advantages.

It may also be argued that those taxes are user charges to finance the costs to the state of maintaining ownership records and of regulating transactions and asset markets. The revenues raised, however, do not seem to outweigh their efficiency costs. Transaction taxes are inherently inefficient, in that they impede otherwise mutually beneficial trades and thereby hinder the efficient allocation of assets.

As discussed in Box 7.1, taxes on real estate transactions, for example, have been shown to impact labor mobility adversely and to raise unemployment (van Ommeren and van Leuvensteijn 2005). Although some argue that transaction taxes can help reduce asset price volatility, the effect is uncertain in both principle and practice (because the tax leads to a thinner market).

Financial transaction taxes (FTT) have been much discussed recently, including in the European Union where 10 member states have plans to introduce a broad-based FTT. Yet, FTTs can have significant social costs because of their cascading effects (tax levied on tax), and can increase the cost of capital, encourage avoidance schemes, and potentially impede socially

---

[12] Based on annual revenues of 0.13 percent of GDP (corresponding to the OECD average, as well as the 2011 U.S. revenues) and a nominal discount rate of 5 percent.

TABLE 7.4

			Progressive Tax Rate Schedule:
	Survey Year	1 Percent Tax on Wealthiest 10 Percent of Households[1]	1 Percent on Top 10 Percent and Additional 1 Percent on Top 5 Percent[2]

Potential Revenues from Recurrent Net Wealth Taxes *(Percent of GDP)*

	Survey Year	1 Percent Tax on Wealthiest 10 Percent of Households[1]	Progressive Tax Rate Schedule: 1 Percent on Top 10 Percent and Additional 1 Percent on Top 5 Percent[2]
Austria	2010	0.7	1.2
Belgium	2010	0.9	1.5
Cyprus	2010	2.3	3.7
Finland	2009	0.4	0.7
France	2010	0.6	1.0
Germany	2010	0.7	1.2
Greece	2009	0.4	0.6
Italy	2010	0.8	1.3
Luxembourg	2010	1.0	1.8
Malta	2010	0.9	1.5
Netherlands	2009	0.3	0.5
Portugal	2010	0.8	1.3
Slovak Republic	2010	0.3	0.4
Slovenia	2010	0.3	0.5
Spain	2008	0.7	1.2
Unweighted Average		0.7	1.2

Sources: Household Finance and Consumption Network (2013); and IMF staff estimates.
Note: Tax base excludes private pensions and business equity.
[1] Tax applies only to portion of wealth that is above the 90th percentile.
[2] The 1 percent (2 percent) tax applies only to net wealth above the 90th (95th) percentile.

worthwhile transactions. Moreover, their distributional impact is unclear given that the incidence may be shifted onto consumers (Matheson 2012).

Recurrent Taxes on Net Wealth

Few advanced economies today have recurrent taxes on broad measures of net wealth (assets less liabilities) and, where they exist, revenue is typically low.[13] They have been declining in Europe since the mid-1990s (repealers include Austria, Denmark, Finland, Germany, the Netherlands, and Sweden). Within Europe, only France, Iceland, Norway, Spain, and Switzerland still have recurrent NWTs. But this may be changing: Iceland and Spain reintroduced the tax during the financial crisis, and it is now being actively discussed elsewhere. The top marginal rate of current NWTs is generally less than 2 percent, while revenues are less than 1 percent of GDP (except for Luxembourg and Switzerland, where the wealth tax yields 1.5–2.0 percent of GDP a year).

The renewed interest in NWTs in the public debate arises primarily from the potential revenue they could generate. Even with large allowances, gains may be substantial (although subject to considerable uncertainty related, for instance, to the valuation of assets) because private wealth is very large and concentrated. In the sample of advanced economies for which balance sheet data are available, net wealth of households amount, on average, to 400 percent of GDP, with the top 10 percent wealthiest households owning about half of total net wealth. A 1 percent tax on these households' net wealth could, theoretically, raise up to 2 percent of GDP per year—thereby doubling the amount of revenue from all wealth taxes.

Based on household-level data, Table 7.4 presents some simulations using the Eurosystem's Household Finance and Consumption Survey (Household Finance and Consumption Network

---

[13] Recurrent taxes on net wealth are different from one-off "capital levies." The latter come along with significant risks of economic distortions and have almost never successfully raised revenue (Eichengreen 1989; Keen 2013).

2013). In a sample of 15 European economies, a 1 percent *progressive* tax on the net wealth of the top 10 percent of households could raise about 1 percent of GDP per year.[14] Calculations using the Luxembourg Wealth Study database point to broadly similar numbers (IMF 2013).[15]

Some efficiency arguments also favor an NWT. A modest tax may induce individuals to real-locate their assets from less to more productive uses, to offset the additional tax (for instance, by turning idle land into productive income-yielding uses). The large tax base would also ensure that rates are low. In addition, wealth taxes may raise revenues from appreciated assets, in light of the fact that very often capital gains are either not taxed until assets are sold or even not taxed at all (including at the time of the owners' death as in the United States).

However, the scope for higher NWTs is limited by three major constraints: The first is that the revenue potential of NWTs may be difficult to realize. The modern history of recurrent wealth taxes is not encouraging. NWTs have high administration costs. Practical problems arise in ascertaining wealth ownership, assigning it to particular taxpayers, and valuing ownership interests. Relief and exemptions—for land, for instance, and family-owned businesses—creep in, creating avoidance opportunities, as do complex aspects of the legalities (in dealing with trusts, for instance). Financial wealth is mobile, and so, ultimately, are people, thus generating tax com-petition that largely explains the erosion of these taxes.

Substantial progress likely requires enhanced international cooperation to make it harder for the very well-off to evade taxation by placing funds elsewhere and simply failing to report as their own tax authorities in principle require. Curbing the practice of relocating assets to avoid taxation requires that countries be able and willing to exchange information about the incomes and assets of one another's residents. Significant progress has been made since the G20 reinvigorated efforts in this area, led by the OECD's Global Forum on Transparency and Information Exchange for Tax Purposes, to the point that 1,000 or so information exchange agreements are now in place. And automatic exchange of information, rather than simply on request, is now becoming the global standard. Unilateral measures offering reciprocal exchange of information are also proceed-ing, notably the U.S. Foreign Account Tax Compliance Act of 2010; these measures, unlike work to date in the Global Forum, envisage penalties for noncompliance. Although these initiatives face difficulties that should not be underestimated, over the longer term they have the potential to make much fairer tax systems.

The second major issue with NWTs is the risk of discouraging capital accumulation. The layering of the NWT on top of the existing capital income tax could indeed result in high effec-tive marginal rates, particularly at lower real rates of return and at higher inflation rates (Figure 7.9).[16] In advanced economies, withholding taxes on dividends and interest are, on aver-age, levied at 20 percent. For an investor earning a 5 percent real return on assets, a 1 percent NWT effectively doubles the 20 percent capital income tax to 40 percent; in the presence of 2 percent inflation, the tax on the real return would rise to 67 percent in the short term (if infla-tion is not anticipated, and the pretax real rate of return declines) and 48 percent in the medium term (once nominal pretax rates of return have adjusted). Facing lower returns, investors may shift from savings to consumption, which would negatively affect domestic investment and

---

[14] The simulations are based on a progressive tax schedule: households with net wealth above the 90th percentile benefit from an exemption amounting to the threshold value (i.e., the tax is levied on the portion of net wealth exceeding this value).

[15] The Luxembourg Wealth Study sample includes Canada, Germany, Italy, Japan, the United Kingdom, and the United States.

[16] Suppose that an asset of value A is subject to a wealth tax at rate T and generates a nominal rate of return of $i=r+\pi$ (where r is the real rate of return and π the inflation rate) that is taxed at rate t. Total tax paid is then $TA+t(r+\pi)A$. (To simplify the calculations, the formula does not include the present value of the capital income tax.) Therefore, the effec-tive tax rate on real returns is, on the horizontal axis in Figure 7.9: $\tau \equiv t+ (T/r)+ (\pi/r)$. With zero inflation, $\tau \equiv t+ (T/i)$.

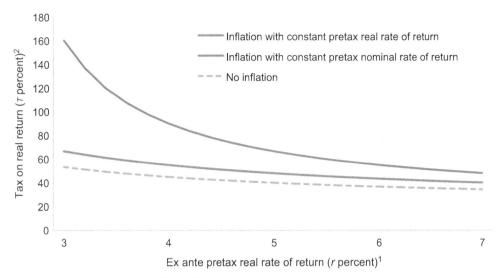

Figure 7.9   Impact of a 1 Percent Wealth Tax on the Taxation of Real Returns of Investors

Source: Author's calculation.
[1] Ex ante = before negative effect of unanticipated inflation on the real rate of return.
[2] Tax on real return combines the capital income tax (t = 20 percent) and the wealth tax (T = 1 percent). Inflation is assumed to be 2 percent per year.

growth. They may also look for opportunities abroad and expatriate.[17] In addition, assets with low returns (and, even more so, assets that do not generate income) would effectively be taxed at rates exceeding 100 percent, possibly infringing property rights.

Third, if a taxpayer's assets do not generate recurrent income (for instance, land and businesses that do not pay dividends), the NWT can also create illiquidity problems—an effect compounded by the fact that assets without cash flow are difficult to borrow against. Forcing taxpayers to sell assets to pay a wealth tax is, in most cases, unfair and not desirable. Liquidity concerns are particularly acute in low-income countries, where the population may not have sufficient cash or access to financial institutions to pay recurrent wealth taxes.[18] Nonetheless, liquidity problems can be mitigated by making payment more flexible, for instance, by allowing the tax to be paid over several years.

CONCLUSIONS

Household wealth is very unequally distributed—even more so than income: in advanced economies, the top 10 percent own, on average, more than half of the wealth. Arguably, household wealth is a better indicator of ability to pay than annual income—and indeed taxes on wealth and transfers have historically been a major source of revenue. Now, however, they yield very little— less than 2 percent of GDP, on average, in the OECD.

This chapter shows that wealth tax instruments have substantial untapped revenue potential and can strengthen the progressivity of the tax system, since wealth is concentrated among the

---

[17] This problem is less severe when the initial level of capital income taxation is low or if the NWT is progressive with a generous allowance. Households below the threshold do not face a disincentive to save. And the NWT does not discourage innovation and risk taking in the early phase of wealth accumulation. Only wealthy households with high saving rates would face disincentives to accumulate wealth.

[18] In these countries, transaction taxes and inheritance taxes present some advantages because the transfer of assets generates revenues that provide the basis for taxation.

better off. There are, in fact, several types of taxes on wealth with quite different trade-offs between efficiency and equity:

- *Recurrent taxes on residential property*, which account for about one-half of wealth tax totals, are widely seen as an attractive and underexploited revenue source: the base is fairly immobile and hard to hide, the tax comes at the top of the hierarchy of long-term growth friendliness, and it can be made progressive through a basic allowance or by varying the rate with the value of the property.

- *Taxes on wealth transfers—on estates, inheritances, and gifts*—raise very little: rates are low, and exemptions and special arrangements create multiple avoidance opportunities. The primary appeal of inheritance taxes is in limiting the intergenerational transmission of inequality and perhaps also in equalizing opportunities. In revenue terms, the yield in the countries with the highest returns, about half a percent of GDP, suggests some potential.

- *Transaction taxes—primarily on the sale of real estate and financial instruments*—typically account for one-quarter of the wealth tax revenue. They are administratively appealing, since transactions can often be fairly easily observed, and the incentives for compliance are strong when legal title is contingent on payment. But transaction taxes are inherently inefficient, in that they impede otherwise mutually beneficial trades; those on real estate transactions, for example, have been shown to adversely affect labor mobility.

- *Recurrent taxes on net wealth* (assets less liabilities) have been declining in Europe since the mid-1990s. But this may be changing: Iceland and Spain reintroduced the tax during the financial crisis, and it is now being actively discussed elsewhere. The revenue potential is subject to considerable uncertainty but is in principle sizable. Little hard evidence is available on the likely behavioral impact, a primary risk being that of discouraging capital accumulation. In addition, financial wealth is mobile, and so, ultimately, are people—generating tax competition and evasion that largely explains the erosion of these taxes. Substantial progress will likely require enhanced international cooperation to make it harder for the very well-off to evade taxation by placing funds elsewhere and simply failing to report to their own tax authorities as required.

REFERENCES

Accessing Global Knowledge (AGN) International. 2013. "Tax Surveys." AGN International, London. www.agn-europe.org/tax/index.html.

Alesina, A., and D. Rodrik. 1994. "Distributive Politics and Economic Growth." *Quarterly Journal of Economics* 109 (2): 465–90.

Andrews, Dan. 2010. "Real House Prices in OECD Countries: The Role of Demand Shocks and Structural and Policy Factors." OECD Economics Department Working Paper No. 831, OECD Publishing, Paris.

Arnold, J. 2008. "Do Tax Structures Affect Aggregate Economic Growth? Empirical Evidence from a Panel of OECD Countries." OECD Economics Department Working Paper No. 643, OECD Publishing, Paris.

Bagchi, S., and J. Svejnar. 2013. "Does Wealth Inequality Matter for Growth? The Effect of Billionaire Wealth, Income Distribution, and Poverty." IZA Discussion Paper No. 7733, Institute for the Study of Labor, Bonn.

Bahl, R. and J. Martinez-Vazquez. 2008. "The Determinants of Revenue Performance." In *Making the Property Tax Work*, edited by R. Bahl, J. Martínez-Vázquez, and J. Youngman. Cambridge, Massachusetts: Lincoln Institute of Land Policy.

Ballarino, G., M. Braga, M. Bratti, D. Checchi, A. Filippin, C. Fiorio, M. Leonardi, E. Meschi, and F. Scervini. 2012. "Gini Country Report: Growing Inequalities and Their Impacts in Italy." Amsterdam Institute for Advanced Labour Studies, Amsterdam.

Boadway, R., E. Chamberlain, and C. Emmerson. 2010. "Taxation of Wealth and Wealth Transfers." In *Dimensions of Tax Design*, edited by J. Mirrlees, S. Adam, T. Besley, R. Blundell, S. Bond, R. Chote, M. Gammie, P. Johnson, G. Miles, and J. Poterba. London: The Mirrlees Review, Institute for Fiscal Studies.

Bonesmo Fredriksen, K. 2012. "Less Income Inequality and More Growth: Are They Compatible? Part 6. The Distribution of Wealth." OECD Economics Department Working Paper No. 929, OECD Publishing, Paris.

Caldera Sánchez, Aida, and Dan Andrews. 2011. "To Move or Not to Move: What Drives Residential Mobility Rates in the OECD?" OECD Economics Department Working Paper No. 846, OECD Publishing, Paris.

Credit Suisse. 2013. *Global Wealth Databook 2013*. Zurich: Credit Suisse Research Institute.

Davies, J. B., S. Sandstrom, A. Shorrocks, and E. N. Wolff. 2008. "The World Distribution of Household Wealth." UNU-WIDER Discussion Paper No. 2008/03, United Nations University, Helsinki.

———. 2010. "The Level and Distribution of Global Household Wealth." *Economic Journal* 121 (March): 223–54.

Davies, J. B., and A. Shorrocks. 2000. "The Distribution of Wealth." In *Handbook of Income Distribution*, edited by Anthony B. Atkinson and François Bourguignon, 605–76. Amsterdam: North Holland.

De Bonis, R., D. Fano, and T. Sbano. 2013. "Household Wealth in the Main OECD Countries from 1980 to 2011: What Do the Data Tell Us?" Money and Finance Research Group Working Paper No. 82, Marche Polytechnic University, Ancona, Italy.

Deininger, K. W., and P. Olinto. 2000. "Asset Distribution, Inequality, and Growth." Policy Research Working Paper No. 2375, World Bank, Washington.

Eichengreen, B. 1989. "The Capital Levy in Theory and Practice." NBER Working Paper No. 3096, National Bureau of Economic Research, Cambridge, Massachusetts.

European Central Bank (ECB). 2013. "The Eurosystem Household Finance and Consumption Survey, Results from the First Wave." Statistical Paper Series No. 2, April, Frankfurt, European Central Bank.

Fahri, E., and I. Werning. 2010. "Progressive Estate Taxation." *Quarterly Journal of Economics* 125 (2): 635–73.

Household Finance and Consumption Network. 2013. HFCS data set. Eurosystem, European Central Bank, Frankfurt. http://www.ecb.europa.eu/home/html/researcher_hfcn.en.html.

International Monetary Fund. 2013. "Taxing Times." *Fiscal Monitor*. Washington, October.

Keen, M. 2013. "Once and for All—Why Capital Levies Are Not the Answer," IMF Blog. http://blog-imfdirect.imf.org.

Klevmarken, N. A. 2006. "On Household Wealth Trends in Sweden over the 1990s." In *International Perspectives on Household Wealth*, edited by E. N. Wolff. Northampton, Massachusetts: Edward Elgar Publishing Ltd.

Kopczuk, W. 2013. "Taxation of Intergenerational Transfers and Wealth." In *Handbook of Public Economics*, Vol. 5, edited by A. Auerbach, R. Chetty, M. Feldstein, and E. Saez. Amsterdam: North Holland.

———, and J. Slemrod. 2003. "Dying to Save Taxes: Evidence from Estate Tax Returns on the Death Elasticity." *Review of Economics and Statistics* 85 (2): 256–65.

Matheson, T. 2012. "Security Transaction Taxes: Issues and Evidence." *International Tax and Public Finance* 19 (6): 884–912.

Mirrlees J., S. Adam, T. Besley, R. Blundell, S. Bond, R. Chote, M. Gammie, P. Johnson, G. Myles, and J. Poterba. 2011. *Tax by Design: The Mirrlees Review*. Oxford, U.K.: Oxford University Press.

Morck, R., D. Stangeland, and B. Yeung. 2000. "Inherited Wealth, Corporate Control, and Economic Growth: The Canadian Disease?" In *Concentrated Corporate Ownership*, edited by Randall Morck, 319–69. Chicago: University of Chicago Press.

Norregaard, J. 2013. "Taxing Immovable Property: Revenue Potential and Implementation Challenges." IMF Working Paper No. 13/129, International Monetary Fund, Washington.

Oswald, Andrew J. 1996. "A Conjecture on the Explanation for High Unemployment in the Industrialized Nations: Part I." Warwick University Economic Research Paper No. 475, Coventry, U.K.

———. 1999. "The Housing Market and Europe's Unemployment: A Non-Technical Paper." Unpublished, University of Warwick, Coventry, U.K.

Piketty, T. 2014. *Capital in the Twenty-First Century*. Cambridge, Massachusetts: Harvard University Press.

———, and E. Saez. 2012. "A Theory of Optimal Capital Taxation." NBER Working Paper No. 17989, National Bureau of Economic Research, Cambridge, Massachusetts.

Piketty, T., and G. Zucman. 2014. "Capital Is Back: Wealth-Income Ratios in Rich Countries 1700–2010." *Quarterly Journal of Economics* doi: 10.1093/qje/qju018.

Thuronyi, V. ed. 1996. *Tax Law Design and Drafting*, Vol. 1. Washington: International Monetary Fund.

van Ommeren, J., and M. van Leuvensteijn. 2005. "New Evidence of the Effect of Transaction Costs on Residential Mobility." *Journal of Regional Science* 45 (4): 681–702.

Wolff, E. N. 2014. "National Report Card: Wealth Inequality." Stanford Center on Poverty and Inequality, Stanford, California.

———, and M. Gittleman. 2011. "Inheritances and the Distribution of Wealth or Whatever Happened to the Great Inheritance Boom?" Working Paper No. 1300, European Central Bank, Frankfurt.

Ynesta, I. 2008. "Households' Wealth Composition across OECD Countries and Financial Risks Borne by Households." *OECD Journal: Financial Market Trends* 2008 (2): 1–25.

PART III

Fiscal Consolidation and Income Inequality

Fiscal Consolidation and Inequality in Advanced Economies: How Robust Is the Link?

Davide Furceri, João Tovar Jalles, and Prakash Loungani

> *[We need a] fiscal policy that focuses not only on efficiency, but also on equity, particularly on fairness in sharing the burden of adjustment, and on protecting the weak and vulnerable.*
>
> Christine Lagarde (2012)

INTRODUCTION

Fiscal policy played a key role in the response to the global financial crisis. At its onset, many Group of 20 countries implemented comprehensive support packages, mainly based on expenditure hikes, to try to stave off the crisis. Combined with the decline in tax revenues (as incomes fell), the increase in social spending (particularly unemployment benefits), and the costs of financial bailouts of banks and companies, the net result was a sharp rise in government debt. Public debt rose, on average, from 70 percent of GDP in 2007 to slightly more than 100 percent of GDP in 2014—its highest level in 50 years (IMF 2014b).

Concerned about the long-term sustainability of public finances, many governments across the world have begun implementing budgetary consolidation measures. The effects of such fiscal consolidations on output remain a matter of some debate, revolving in part around the measurement of fiscal consolidation. Using the cyclically adjusted primary balance (CAPB), some work suggests that fiscal consolidation could be expansionary (for example, Alesina and Perotti 1995; Alesina and Ardagna 2010, 2012).[1] In contrast, using a narrative approach to measuring consolidation, Guajardo, Leigh, and Pescatori (2014) argue that consolidations are contractionary.

In addition to the aggregate effects of fiscal consolidations, the distributional impacts are also starting to receive attention. Many studies suggest that fiscal consolidation episodes are usually associated with increases in income inequality (Roe and Siegel 2011; Ball, Leigh, and Loungani 2013; Ball and others 2013; Bova and others 2013; Agnello and Sousa 2014; Agnello and others 2014).

The authors are grateful to Branko Milanovic for comments on related work and for providing his data on Gini coefficients. Thanks also go to Vitor Gaspar, Sanjeev Gupta, Ben Clements, Maura Francese, Patrick Petit, Estelle Liu, Jan Babecký, Andre Brandolini, Teresa Ter-Minassian, Pietro Tomasino, Petya Koeva Brooks, Giovani Callegari, and Thomas Warmedinger for their useful comments, suggestions, and advice. The authors are equally thankful to participants present in the FAD seminar series and in the Banca d'Italia Perugia Conference. The opinions expressed herein are those of the authors and do not necessarily reflect those of the IMF, its member states, or its policy.

[1] In neoclassical models, fiscal policy affects economic activity by means of wealth effects, intertemporal substitution, and distortions. If consolidation measures remove uncertainty with respect to fiscal sustainability (signaling tax cuts in the future and raising discounted disposable income), hence boosting confidence, then the negative impact on output may be limited or even give rise to an "expansionary fiscal contraction."

This chapter examines the robustness of the link between fiscal consolidation and inequality. This relationship is important for several reasons. First, as noted above, the aggregate effects of fiscal consolidation appear to depend on how consolidation is measured. Are the distributional effects also sensitive to the measurement of consolidation? Second, the measurement of inequality is also the subject of some controversy. Many studies use the Standardized World Income Inequality Database (SWIID). But there are concerns about this data set because of the extensive use of interpolation and other assumptions to fill in missing data (Jenkins 2014). Thus, this chapter examines how robust the consolidation-inequality link is to the use of alternate measures of inequality. A third contribution of the chapter is to revisit the issues of whether spending-based and tax-based consolidations have different effects on inequality and whether the consolidation-inequality link is symmetric (that is, do fiscal *expansions* lower inequality?). Fourth, a number of technical robustness checks are carried out that confirm the validity of this chapter's findings. Finally, in general, the distributional effects of consolidation must be balanced against the potential longer-term benefits that consolidation can confer as interest rates decline and the lighter burden of interest payments permits cuts in distortionary taxes. It should be recognized that there is scope for improving the targeting and efficiency of public programs and that, in this case, fiscal adjustments would not unavoidably run into such a trade-off between efficiency and equity.

The remainder of this chapter is organized as follows: First, the definitions and sources of the data are detailed, then the econometric methodology is presented. The main empirical findings are analyzed, followed by a conclusion and a discussion of some policy considerations.

DATA

Inequality and Income Shares

Many studies use the SWIID because it provides long time series of Gini coefficients for a large group of countries. However, problems with comparability of data across years and countries, and with the imputation methodology used, have long been noted (Atkinson and Brandolini 2001) and have recently been confirmed in a comprehensive assessment by Jenkins (2014).

In light of such concerns, this analysis tests the robustness of the consolidation-inequality link using several measures of distributional outcomes. They comprise (1) the Gini coefficient for disposable income (both gross and net concepts), taken from SWIID; (2) the shares of wages and profits in GDP, obtained from the Organisation for Economic Co-operation and Development (OECD) Analytical Database; (3) the Gini coefficient for disposable income retrieved from the OECD Stats; and (4) the combined "all the Ginis" index compiled by Milanovic (2014) by merging several sources.[2]

Fiscal Consolidation Episodes

The literature addressing the identification of fiscal episodes is vast and has, for a long time, relied on changes in the CAPB. Some caveats surrounding this approach have been highlighted recently. In particular, the CAPB approach could bias empirical estimates toward finding evidence of non-Keynesian effects (Afonso and Jalles 2014). Many nonpolicy factors, such as price fluctuations, influence the CAPB and can lead to erroneous conclusions about the presence of fiscal policy changes.[3] In addition, even when the CAPB accurately measures fiscal actions, these actions

---

[2] This data set is publicly available at the following website: http://econ.worldbank.org/WBSITE/EXTERNAL/ EXTDEC/EXTRESEARCH/0,,contentMDK:22301380~menuPK:64214916~pagePK:64214825~piPK:64214943~the SitePK:469382,00.html.

[3] For example, a stock price boom raises the CAPB by increasing capital gains tax revenue, and also tends to coincide with an expansion in private domestic demand (Morris and Schuknecht 2007).

include discretionary responses to economic developments, such as fiscal tightening to restrain rapid domestic demand growth.

With these considerations in mind, an alternative "narrative approach" is considered, which relies on the identification of fiscal episodes based on concrete policy decisions. The episodes are identified by looking at IMF and OECD historical reports and by checking what countries intended to do when the reports were published.[4] This policy-action-based approach makes use of descriptive historical facts that usually depict what happened to the deficit in a particular period but do not go into the details of policymakers' intentions and discussions or congressional records. Proponents of this approach argue that the estimated size of the fiscal measures during the identified episodes have the advantage of not being affected by the cycle (since their construction is bottom up), can minimize identification problems,[5] and are unlikely to embody risks of reverse causation (Guajardo, Leigh, and Pescatori 2014). However, the narrative approach could also have some drawbacks: it largely relies on judgment calls, and it may not entirely eliminate endogeneity problems (that is, fiscal policy reacting to output performance and not the other way around).

The analysis that follows thus relies on both the narrative and CAPB-based approaches. For the narrative approach, the analysis uses the publicly available data set compiled by Devries and others (2011), which uses the policy-action-based method for 17 advanced economies between 1978 and 2009.[6] For the CAPB-based approach, the analysis relies on the following:

- Alesina and Ardagna (1998), who adopt a fiscal episode definition that allows some stabilization periods to last only one year. More specifically, they define a fiscal episode to be a change in the CAPB that is at least 2 percentage points of GDP in one year or at least 1.5 percentage points, on average, in the past two years.

- Giavazzi and Pagano (1996), who decrease the probability of fiscal adjustment periods that last only one year by using a limit of 3 percentage points of GDP for a single year consolidation. They propose using the cumulative changes in the CAPB that are at least 5, 4, or 3 percentage points of GDP in, respectively, four, three, or two years, or 3 percentage points in one year.

- Afonso (2010), who defines the occurrence of a fiscal episode as being when either the change in the CAPB is at least one-and-a-half times the standard deviation (from the panel sample of 17 countries) in one year, or when the change in the CAPB is at least one standard deviation, on average, in the past two years.

Table 8.1 reports the fiscal episodes identified according to the four alternative methods. The number of fiscal contractions ranges from 29 in Afonso's (2010) approach, to 43 in Alesina and Ardagna's (1998) approach. In Devries and others' (2011) narrative approach, the magnitude of the fiscal consolidation episode ranges between 0.1 percent and about 5 percent of GDP, with an average of about 1 percent of GDP. Moreover, it reports many more years in which fiscal contractions take place (171 years against an average of 70 for the CAPB approaches). For fiscal consolidations, the average duration of the reported episodes is, on average, 1.7 years for the CAPB approaches and about 3.8 years for the narrative approach. Finally, the three CAPB-based methods agree with the total number of years from the narrative approach about 50 percent of the time.

---

[4] Note, however, that this approach differs from the one used by Romer and Romer (2010), who identify exogenous tax policy changes by carefully analyzing U.S. congressional documents.

[5] However, as Jorda and Taylor (2013) argue, fiscal shocks may not be exogenous and can be predicted.

[6] The countries are Australia, Austria, Belgium, Canada, Denmark, Finland, France, Germany, Ireland, Italy, Japan, the Netherlands, Portugal, Spain, Sweden, the United Kingdom, and the United States.

TABLE 8.1

Fiscal Episodes Based on the Change in the CAPB and on the Narrative Approach

Country	Narrative Approach Devries and others (2011)	Alesina and Ardagna (1998)		Giavazzi and Pagano (1996)		Afonso (2010)	
			CAPB Approaches				
	Contractions	Expansions	Contractions	Expansions	Contractions	Expansions	Contractions
Australia	1985–88, 1994–99	1975, 2009	1987–88	2009	1987–88	2009	1987–88
Austria	1980–81, 1984, 1996–97, 2001–02	1976, 2004	1984, 1997, 2001, 2005	1976, 2004	1997	2004	1984, 1997, 2001, 2005
Belgium	1982–87, 1990–97	1981, 2005, 2009	1982–85, 1993, 2006	1981, 2005, 2009	1982–87	1981, 2005, 2009	1982–85
Canada	1984–97	1977, 2001–02, 2009	1981, 1986–87, 1996–97	1975, 1977–78, 2002, 2009	1987, 1996–98	1975, 2009	1987, 1996–97
Denmark	1983–86, 1995	1975–76, 1982, 1990–91, 1994, 2009–10	1983–86	1975–76, 1982, 1991, 2010	1983–87	1975–76, 1982, 1991, 2010	1983–86
Finland	1992–97	1978–79, 1987, 1991–92, 2009–10	1976–77, 1981, 1984, 1988, 1996–97, 2000–01	1979–80, 1991–93, 2010	1976–77, 1997–98, 2000–01	1978–79, 1987, 1991–92, 2010	1976–77, 1996–97, 2000–01
France	1987–92, 1995–2000	2009–10		2009–10		2009–10	
Germany	1982–84, 1991–2000, 2003–07	1975, 1990–91, 2001–02		1975, 1991, 2001–03		1975, 1990–91, 2001–02	
Ireland	1982–88, 2009	1974–75, 1978–79, 1995, 2001–02, 2007–09	1976–77, 1983–84, 1988, 2010	1975, 1979, 2001–03, 2007–10	1976–77, 1983–86, 1988–89, 2010	1974–75, 1978–79, 2001–02, 2007–09	1976–77, 1983–84, 1988, 2010
Italy	1991–98, 2004–07	1981, 2001	1977, 1982–83, 1992–93	2001	1977, 1982–83, 1992–94	1981, 2001	1977, 1982–83, 1992–93
Japan	1980–83, 1997–98, 2003–07	1975, 1994–95, 1998, 2009–10	1998–99, 2005–06	1993–95, 1998, 2009–10	1998–2000, 2005–07	1993–94, 1998, 2009–10	1999–2000, 2006–07
Netherlands	1981–88, 1991–93, 2004–05	2001–02, 2009–10	1991, 1993	2002, 2010	1991, 1993	2002, 2009–10	1991
Portugal	1983, 2000–07	1978–79, 1985, 1990, 1993, 2005, 2009–10	1977, 1983–84, 1986, 1988, 1992, 1995, 2006	1978–80, 2005, 2009–10	1977, 1983–84, 1986	1978–79, 1993, 2005, 2009–10	1977, 1983–84, 1986, 1988, 1992
Spain	1983–84, 1989–97	2008–09	1986, 1987, 2010	2008–10	1987	2008–09	1987
Sweden	1984, 1993–98	1974, 1979, 1991–93, 2002–03, 2010	1976, 1983–84, 1987, 1996–97	1974, 1979–80, 1991–94, 2002–03	1984, 1987, 1996–99	1974, 1979, 1991–93, 2002	1984, 1987, 1996–97
United Kingdom	1980–82, 1994–99	1972–73, 1990, 1992–93, 2001–02, 2009–10	1981, 1997–98, 2000	1972–75, 1992–94, 2001–04, 2009–10	1981–82, 1997–2000	1972–73, 1992–93, 2001–03, 2009–10	1981, 1997–98
United States	1980–81, 1985–98	2001–02, 2007–08		2001–02, 2007–10		1974, 2001–02, 2007–08	
Years with Episodes	171	95	79	95	73	78	59
Average Duration (years)	3.8	1.6	1.5	2.0	2.1	1.6	1.6

Source: All measures computed by the authors except for the Devries and others (2011) column.
Note: See chapter text for definitions. CAPB = cyclically adjusted primary balance.

METHODOLOGY

To estimate the distributional impact of fiscal consolidation episodes in the short and medium terms, the exercise follows the method proposed by Jorda (2005), which consists of estimating impulse response functions directly from local projections. For each period k, equation (8.1) is estimated using annual data:

$$G_{i,t+k} - G_{i,t} = \alpha_i^k + Time_t^k + \sum_{j=1}^{l} \gamma_j^k \Delta G_{i,t-j} + \beta_k D_{i,t} + \varepsilon_{i,t}^k, \tag{8.1}$$

in which $k = 1, \ldots, 8$ and G represents one of the measures of distributional outcomes; $D_{i,t}$ is a dummy variable equal to 1 for the starting date of a consolidation episode in country i at time t and is 0 otherwise; α_i^k are country fixed effects; $Time_t^k$ is a time trend; and β_k measures the distributional impact of fiscal consolidation episodes for each future period k. Since fixed effects are included in the regression, the dynamic impact of consolidation episodes should be interpreted as being compared with a baseline country-specific trend. In the main results, the lag length (l) is set at 2, even if the results are extremely robust to different numbers of lags included in the specification (see robustness checks and sensitivity presented in the next section). Equation (8.1) is estimated using the panel-corrected standard error estimator (Beck and Katz 1995).

Impulse response functions are obtained by plotting the estimated β_k for $k = 1, \ldots, 8$, with confidence bands computed using the standard deviations of the estimated coefficients β_k. Although the presence of a lagged dependent variable and country fixed effects may, in principle, bias the estimation of γ_j^k and β_k in small samples (Nickell 1981), the length of the time dimension mitigates this concern.[7] Reverse causality is addressed by estimating the distributional effect in the years that follow a fiscal consolidation episode. In addition, robustness checks for endogeneity confirm the validity of the results.[8]

An alternative way of estimating the dynamic impact of fiscal consolidation episodes is to estimate an autoregressive distributed lag (ARDL) equation of changes in inequality and consolidation episodes and to compute the impulse response functions from the estimated coefficients (Romer and Romer 1989; Cerra and Saxena 2008). However, the impulse response functions derived using this approach tend to be sensitive to the choice of the number of lags, thus making the impulse response functions potentially unstable. In addition, the significance of long-lasting effects with ARDL models can be driven simply by the use of one-type-of-shock models (Cai and Den Haan 2009). This is particularly true when the dependent variable is highly persistent, as in this analysis. In contrast, the approach used here does not suffer from these problems because the coefficients associated with the lags of the change in the dependent variable enter only as control variables and are not used to derive the impulse response functions, and because the structure of the equation does not impose permanent effects. Finally, confidence bands associated with the estimated impulse response functions are easily computed using the standard deviations of the estimated coefficients, and Monte Carlo simulations are not required.

EMPIRICAL RESULTS

Gini Coefficient for Disposable Income

The impacts of fiscal consolidation (using Devries and others' [2011] narrative approach to identifying episodes) on the four alternative definitions of the Gini index are shown in Figure 8.1.

---

[7] The finite sample bias is on the order of 1/T, where T in the sample is 32.

[8] For time-series properties of the underlying data, stationarity tests (not shown) confirm the need to use first differences in equation (8.1) to avoid unit root issues. Moreover, cross-section dependence tests (not shown) reject the null of cross-sectional independence for the homogeneous panel of countries under scrutiny in this study.

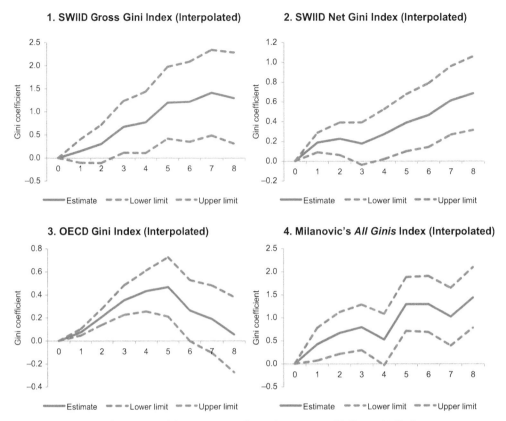

Figure 8.1 Impact of Fiscal Consolidation on Inequality: A Comparison of Different Gini Indices

Source: Authors' calculations.

Note: Dashed lines show one-standard-error confidence bands. SWIID = Standardized World Income Inequality Database.

Each panel shows the estimated impulse response function and the associated one-standard-error bands (dotted lines). The horizontal axes measure years after the start of the fiscal consolidation episode.[9]

In general, fiscal consolidation is followed by a persistent rise in income inequality.[10] The Gini index increases by an average (across different proxies) of about 0.2 units (corresponding to a Gini index point) in the short term (one year after the occurrence of the consolidation episode) and by nearly 0.9 units in the medium term (eight years after the occurrence of the consolidation episode).[11] The short-term response is consistent with Agnello and Sousa (2014), who find that fiscal consolidations lead to an increase in the Gini of about 0.3 units. A possible explanation for why persistent impulse response functions could be observed relates to the composition of the

---

[9] In what follows, the chapter uses a sample of 17 advanced economies, which gives a maximum of 608 observations between 1978 and 2009.

[10] Bear in mind that the analysis does not distinguish between structural and temporary fiscal shocks and that there is no proxy that captures the characteristics of the shock (that is, whether the shock is realized through changes in progressive or regressive budget items; that is, two fiscal adjustments with opposite distributional characteristics—such as one raising progressive taxation and the other increasing more regressive taxation—are treated identically).

[11] The scale of the Gini index (and therefore of the impulse response function's vertical axis) goes from 0 to 100 as is standard practice in the literature.

fiscal adjustment, discussed below. For example, permanent cuts to social assistance benefits can structurally reduce the distributional impact of government spending. Another explanation could be labor market changes triggered by macroeconomic developments or public policies (for example, a rise in unemployment during times of fiscal retrenchment would affect the market-income channel). However, further work is needed on the channels that lead to these outcomes, in particular the permanent versus temporary effects of fiscal adjustments.

The results of several additional robustness checks are shown in Figure 8.2. These results are shown for one particular measure of inequality, the SWIID net Gini index, but similar findings hold for the other measures as well. First, equation (8.1) is reestimated by including time fixed effects to control for specific time shocks, such as those affecting world interest rates. The results for this specification remain statistically significant and broadly unchanged (Figure 8.2, panel 2).

As shown by Teulings and Zubanov (2013), a possible bias introduced by estimating equation (8.1) using country fixed effects is that the error term of the equation may have a non-zero expected value, due to the interaction of fixed effects and country-specific arrival rates of consolidation episodes. This would lead to a bias in the estimates that is a function of k. To address this issue and check the robustness of the findings, equation (8.1) is reestimated by excluding country fixed effects from the analysis. The results reported in Figure 8.2, panel 3 suggest that this bias is negligible (the difference in the point estimate is small and not statistically significant).

Estimates of the impact of consolidation on inequality could be biased because of endogeneity, given that unobserved factors influencing the dynamics of the Gini coefficient may also affect the probability of the occurrence of a consolidation episode. In particular, a significant deterioration

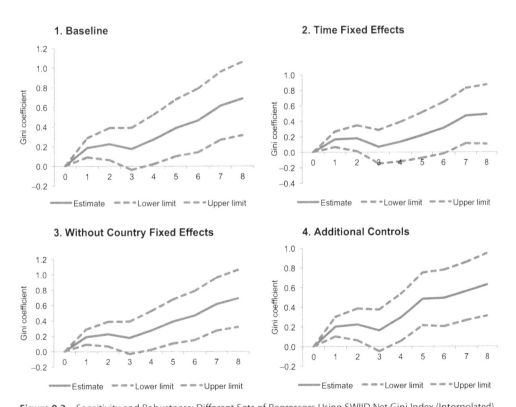

Figure 8.2 Sensitivity and Robustness: Different Sets of Regressors Using SWIID Net Gini Index (Interpolated)

Source: Authors' calculations.
Note: Dashed lines show one-standard-error confidence bands.

TABLE 8.2

Panel Estimations of Different Gini Indices				
Specification	SWIID Gini Index, Gross	SWIID Gini Index, Net	OECD Gini Index	Milanovic's *All Ginis* Index
Baseline	1.332**	0.585**	0.595***	1.491***
	(0.646)	(0.297)	(0.185)	(0.418)
Robustness				
Time Fixed Effects	0.672	0.241	0.598***	1.822***
	(0.631)	(0.293)	(0.195)	(0.544)
Without Country Fixed Effects	1.392**	0.564*	0.453*	1.478***
	(0.640)	(0.301)	(0.263)	(0.459)
Additional Controls	0.915	0.487	0.685***	1.729***
	(0.699)	(0.313)	(0.219)	(0.476)

Source: Authors' calculations.

Note: The dependent variable is the fifth year forward difference of the corresponding inequality proxy as identified in the first row. The coefficients presented in the table denote the estimates of the consolidation episode (narrative approach). Each entry corresponds to an independent regression in which nonrelevant regressors (including a constant term) are omitted for reasons of parsimony. Robust standard errors are in parentheses.

$* \, p < 0.1; ** \, p < 0.05; *** \, p < 0.01.$

in economic activity, which would affect unemployment and inequality, may lead to an increase in the public debt ratio via automatic stabilizers, and therefore increase the probability of consolidation. To address this issue, equation (8.1) is augmented to control for (1) contemporaneous and past crisis episodes (banking, debt, and currency crises); (2) change in economic activity (proxied by real GDP growth); and (3) change in the total unemployment rate. The results of this exercise are reported in Figure 8.2, panel 4 and confirm the robustness of the previous findings.[12]

As an additional sensitivity check, equation (8.1) is reestimated for different lags (*l*) of changes in the Gini coefficient. The results confirm that previous findings are not sensitive to the choice of the number of lags (results are available upon request).

Finally, as noted earlier, another concern is that the different Gini alternatives use interpolations to fill in gaps in the inequality data.[13] Although interpolations increase the number of observations, they also add some concerns about data quality. This analysis, therefore, uses raw data and panel regressions are estimated with the fifth year forward difference of the relevant Gini index as the dependent variable. The results are very robust (Table 8.2). Moreover, these results are also robust to a number of more technical checks as shown Table 8.2, including the inclusion of time fixed effects, the exclusion of country fixed effects, and the inclusion of a different set of control variables in the estimated regressions.

The Role of the Composition of Consolidation Packages: Spending Based versus Tax Based

Does the composition of fiscal consolidation (spending based versus tax based) matter for inequality? The literature demonstrates a broad consensus that tax-based consolidations are typically more contractionary than spending-based ones, particularly in the medium term (Alesina

---

[12] It is important to note that the sample contains both large and small open economies. Large economies are relatively rarely hit by fiscal shocks. Small economies, however, are almost continuously hit by shocks and some of these (spending cuts, for instance) are not always exogenous but are the result of other external shocks. Although we use the narrative approach, we are aware that the current identification strategy should be subjected to improvements in future research.

[13] The use of interpolated data (as opposed to "raw" data) is necessary because Jorda's (2005) local projection estimator is sensitive to data gaps.

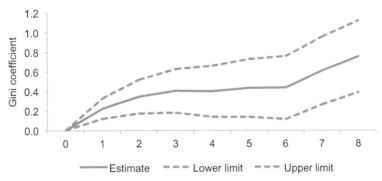

1. Standard Definition, Spending Based

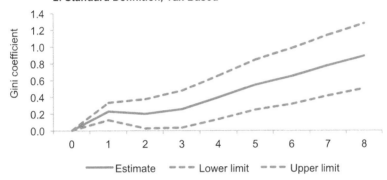

2. Standard Definition, Tax Based

Figure 8.3 Composition of Fiscal Adjustments Using SWIID Net Gini Index (Interpolated): Tax versus Spending Based

Source: Authors' calculations.
Note: Dashed lines show one-standard-error confidence bands.

and Ardagna 2010; IMF 2010a). In normal times, spending cuts tend to be more successful than tax increases at enhancing economic growth (Alesina and Perotti 1995; Alesina and Ardagna 2012) because spending cuts are generally perceived to be more credible by economic agents (Hernandez de Cos and Moral-Benito 2012).[14] At the same time, however, most of the direct redistributive impact of fiscal policy in advanced economies has been achieved through the expenditure side of the budget—especially non-means-tested transfers (Bastagli, Coady, and Gupta 2012). Therefore, whether tax-based or spending-based consolidations are more harmful for income inequality is not clear a priori.

To evaluate whether the composition of the consolidation package matters, equation (8.1) is separately estimated for tax-based and spending-based adjustments, by constructing starting dummies of tax- and spending-consolidation episodes (in the Devries and others 2011 data set, the average magnitude of both spending- and tax-based consolidations is about 1 percent of GDP). The results presented in Figure 8.3 for a selected measure of income inequality, the

---

[14] The majority of the empirical literature also supports the view that expenditure-driven consolidations increase the likelihood of success of the adjustment episode (see, for example, Giavazzi and Pagano 1996; McDermott and Wescott 1996; Alesina and Ardagna 1998; Giavazzi, Jappelli, and Pagano 2000). There is also evidence that consolidations, particularly reductions in public expenditure, can contribute to reducing sovereign debt spreads, and therefore the cost of servicing sovereign debt (Akitoby and Stratmann 2006).

SWIID net Gini index (though results are consistent across alternative proxies), show that spending- and tax-based programs have similar effects in the short and medium terms. This result, however, has to be treated with caution given that most past fiscal adjustments have involved both spending cuts and tax increases. To address this issue, following Guajardo, Leigh, and Pescatori 2014, equation (8.1) is separately estimated for (1) episodes in which tax-based adjustments have been larger than spending-based adjustments and (2) episodes in which spending-based adjustments have been larger than tax-based adjustments. These correspond to an alternative definition of tax- and spending-based consolidations. The results obtained with this exercise (available upon request) suggest that spending-based consolidations tend to have larger effects. In particular, the short-term effect of fiscal consolidations on income inequality is about 0.24 percent after one year for spending-based consolidations and 0.09 percent for tax-based ones.[15] The medium-term effect after eight years is about 1.05 percent and about 0.13 percent, respectively, for spending-based and tax-based consolidations. At this point it is important to go back to the issue of persistence and mention that labor market indicators such as the unemployment rate do display some hysteresis given that they do not return to their initial levels after a fiscal adjustment that is mainly tax driven (see IMF 2014a, p. 24, for details).

Wages versus Profit and Rent Income

Another way to assess the distributional effects of fiscal consolidation measures is to examine their effects on different types of income. The traditional categories that make up total income are wages, profits, and rents, harkening back to times when the roles of workers, capitalists, and landlords were fairly distinct. Although these distinctions have eroded somewhat, the split between wages and other forms of income is a starting point for describing how income is divided between Main Street and Wall Street. To assess the effects of fiscal consolidations on the distribution of income between wage earners and others, equation (8.1) is estimated for the share of wage income in GDP and the share of profits in GDP.

The results of this empirical exercise are reported in Figures 8.4 and 8.5, respectively, for wages and profits. The results suggest that fiscal consolidation measures typically reduce the slice of the pie going to wage earners and increase the slice of the pie going to profit recipients. These findings are consistent with the results presented in panels 4, 5, and 6 of these two figures, which suggest that fiscal consolidations have a larger negative effect on the level of inflation-adjusted wage income than on the level of inflation-adjusted profit and rent incomes. Moreover, as before, spending-based adjustments seem to be the most detrimental, at least as far as wage incomes are concerned. In the case of profits, the distinction does not matter much as evidenced by confidence bands above and below the horizontal axis. Future work could consider adjusting the wage share to take into account the incomes of the self-employed (see Gollin 2002) and examining how fiscal consolidations affect the private wage share, since many of these episodes are likely to include measures that directly contain the wage bill for the public sector.

Narrative Approach versus CAPB-Based Methods for Identifying Fiscal Episodes

So far the results have been based on use of Devries and others' (2011) narrative approach data set. What if the "traditional" method of identifying fiscal episodes using changes in the CAPB were to be used? Taking the three alternative approaches detailed above and estimating equation (8.1)

---

[15] This approach is also imperfect. Indeed, to properly differentiate between spending- and tax-based consolidations, one should consider episodes characterized by only spending- or tax-based adjustments. Doing so, however, would dramatically reduce the number of "pure" spending- and tax-based consolidations in the sample.

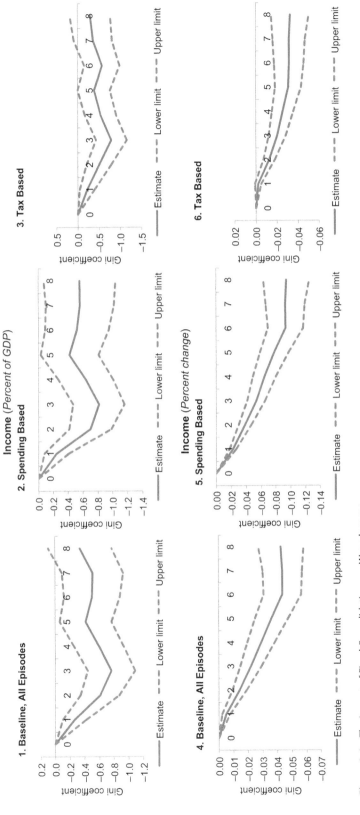

Figure 8.4 The Impact of Fiscal Consolidations on Wage Income

Source: Authors' calculations.

Note: Dashed lines show one-standard-error confidence bands.

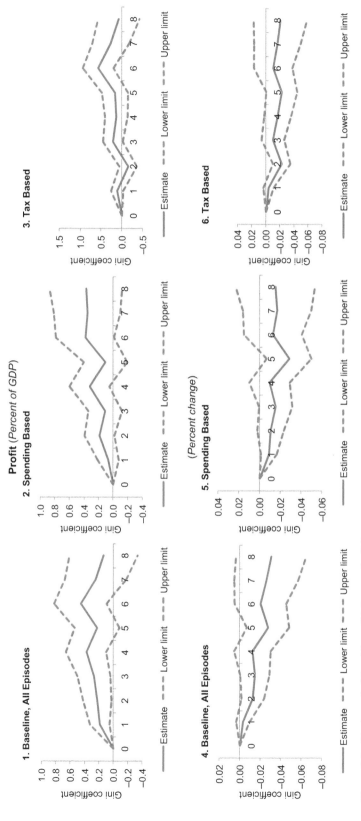

Figure 8.5 The Impact of Fiscal Consolidations on Profit Income

Source: Authors' calculations.

Note: Dashed lines show one-standard-error confidence bands.

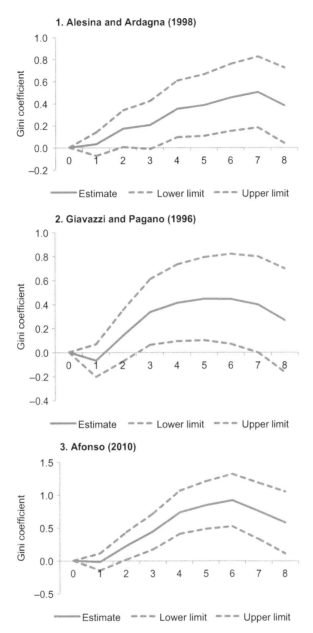

Figure 8.6 CAPB-Based Identification of Fiscal Adjustments: A Comparison of Three Methods

Source: Authors' calculations.
Note: Dashed lines show one-standard-error confidence bands.

for the SWIID net Gini index (though results are consistent across alternative proxies) gives the impulse response functions displayed in Figure 8.6. In general, fiscal consolidations are still found to lead to an increase in income inequality irrespective of the approach under scrutiny.

Picking one approach, say Afonso's (2010), the previous results are invariant to the choice of the dependent variable, that is, the source of the Gini index employed (results available upon request).[16]

---

[16] Using either Giavazzi and Pagano 1996 or Alesina and Ardagna 1998 instead does not qualitatively change the results.

What about Fiscal Expansions?

A final aspect is the following: to what extent is there symmetry in the results when considering a fiscal expansion instead of a fiscal consolidation? In this case, only the CAPB-based methods can provide a tentative answer. Reestimating equation (8.1) and constructing a figure analogous to Figure 8.6, where now $D_{i,t}$ denotes the starting year of a fiscal expansion episode, yields the impulse response functions displayed in Figure 8.7. The results seem to suggest that fiscal

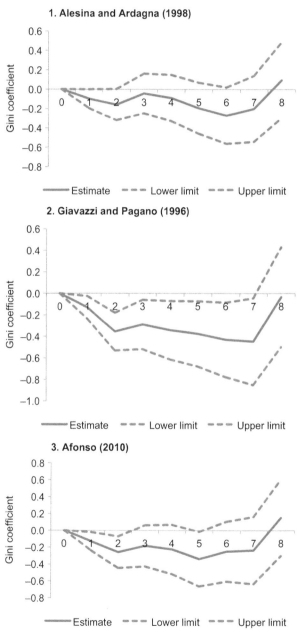

Figure 8.7 CAPB-Based Identification of Fiscal Expansions: A Comparison of Three Methods

Source: Authors' calculations.
Note: Dashed lines show one-standard-error confidence bands.

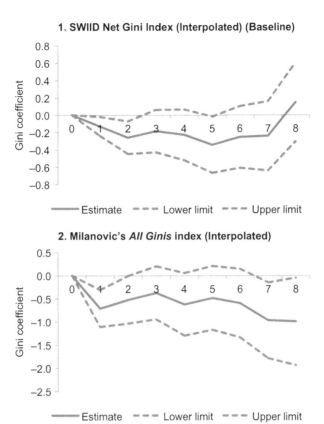

Figure 8.8 Fiscal Expansions: Afonso (2010) Method on Different Inequality Proxies

Source: Authors' calculations.
Note: Dashed lines show one-standard-error confidence bands.

expansions lower inequality, but the impact is generally short lived, dissipating after two to three years. This finding holds when using the SWIID net Gini index as well as Milanovic's *All Ginis* index (see Figure 8.8).

CONCLUDING REMARKS AND POLICY CONSIDERATIONS

This analysis finds, for a sample of 17 OECD countries for the period 1978–2009, that fiscal consolidations tend to lead to an increase in income inequality in the short and medium terms. Typical fiscal consolidations lead to an increase in income inequality on the order of 0.2–1.0 units (corresponding to a Gini index point) in the short and medium terms. This finding is robust to the use of alternate measures of consolidation (in particular, the traditional methods of identifying fiscal episodes based on changes in the CAPB) and to the use of alternate measures and sources of inequality data. The main finding is also robust to a vast array of technical checks such as inclusion of time fixed effects, the exclusion of country fixed effects, and the inclusion of different sets of control variables. The analysis also finds that more work is needed to sort out, among other things, the differences between tax-based and spending-based fiscal adjustments and whether the consolidation-inequality link is symmetric. This is particularly relevant when focusing on specific case studies in recent experience. Although the time span covered in this study ends in 2009, in Portugal, for example, the large tax increase in 2012 did not result in significant deterioration of the Gini coefficient in subsequent years. In Iceland, the massive austerity plan introduced in the aftermath of the global financial crisis, which successfully culminated in today's balanced budget, led to a visible improvement in the degree of progressivity of the tax system.

Ultimately, the findings of this chapter do not suggest that countries should not undertake fiscal consolidation. The results do suggest, however, that the benefits of fiscal adjustments should be weighed against their likely distributional impact. Many governments assign some weight to distributional outcomes and, as discussed in other chapters of the book, may have the flexibility to design the consolidation in a way that mitigates at least some of the distributional impacts. History shows that fiscal plans succeed when they permit "some flexibility while credibly preserving the medium term consolidation objectives" (Mauro 2011, 256).[17]

As noted in IMF 2013, the results about the impact of consolidation on equity "strengthens the case for better targeting of both spending and revenue measures." Specifically, the paper notes that "equity considerations suggest that a larger share of the adjustment burden could be borne by the rich, which could be achieved through revenue measures targeted at the higher income segments of the population. Revenue increases can therefore be an important component of consolidation packages, even in countries where the adjustment should focus on the expenditure side, as in a number of European countries. However, better targeted spending can also help achieve equity objectives, though there may be a trade-off between growth and equity concerns when choosing consolidation measures" (IMF 2013, 35).

All in all, this chapter's results bolster the IMF's general fiscal policy advice to advanced economies. At the onset of the Great Recession, the IMF played a key role in making the case for—and helping coordinate through the auspices of the Group of 20—a coordinated global fiscal stimulus (Spilimbergo and others 2008). Since many governments entered the crisis with high debt-to-GDP ratios, attention turned to consolidation once financial conditions started to stabilize. But cognizant of the adverse impact of fiscal consolidation on growth (IMF 2010c), the policy stance has been to support "a case-by-case assessment of what is an appropriate pace of consolidation" and to emphasize the need "to make fiscal policy more growth-friendly" (Lipton 2013). The results here strengthen that policy stance by suggesting that not only does consolidation lower aggregate incomes in the economy, but it adds to the pain of those most likely to benefit from income redistribution.

REFERENCES

Afonso, A. 2010. "Expansionary Fiscal Consolidations in Europe: New Evidence." *Applied Economics Letters* 17 (2): 105–9.

———, and J. T. Jalles. 2014. "Assessing Fiscal Episodes." *Economic Modeling* 37 (February): 255–70.

Agnello, L., V. Castro, J. T. Jalles, and R. M. Sousa. 2014. "The Impact of Income Inequality and Fiscal Stimuli on Political (In)stability." Unpublished, Organisation for Economic Co-operation and Development, Paris.

Agnello, L., and R. M. Sousa. 2014. "How Does Fiscal Consolidation Impact on Income Inequality?" *Review of Income and Wealth* 60 (4): 702–26.

Akitoby, B., and T. Stratmann. 2006. "Fiscal Policy and Financial Markets." IMF Working Paper No. 06/16, International Monetary Fund, Washington.

Alesina, A., and S. Ardagna. 1998. "Tales of Fiscal Adjustments." *Economic Policy* 13 (27): 489–545.

———. 2010. "Large Changes in Fiscal Policy: Taxes versus Spending." In *Tax Policy and the Economy*, Volume 24, edited by J. R. Brown. Cambridge, Massachusetts: National Bureau of Economic Research.

---

[17] For instance, plans could specify that unemployment benefits would be shielded from cuts in the event of slower growth than assumed in the plan.

————. 2012. "What Makes Fiscal Adjustments Successful?" Unpublished.

Alesina, A., and R. Perotti. 1995. "Fiscal Expansions and Adjustments in OECD Economies." *Economic Policy* 10 (21): 207–47.

Atkinson, A. B., and A. Brandolini. 2001. "Promise and Pitfalls of the Use of 'Secondary' Datasets: Income Inequality in OECD Countries as a Case Study." *Journal of Economic Literature* 34 (3): 771–99.

Ball, L., D. Furceri, D. Leigh, and P. Loungani. 2013. "The Distributional Effects of Fiscal Consolidation." IMF Working Paper No. 13/151, International Monetary Fund, Washington.

Ball, L., D. Leigh, and P. Loungani. 2013. "Okun's Law: Fit at Fifty?" NBER Working Paper No. 18668, National Bureau of Economic Research, Cambridge, Massachusetts.

Bastagli, F., D. Coady, and S. Gupta. 2012. "Income Inequality and Fiscal Policy." IMF Staff Discussion Note No. 12/08, International Monetary Fund, Washington.

Beck, N. L., and J. N. Katz. 1995. "What to Do (and Not to Do) with Time-Series Cross-Section Data." *American Political Science Review* 89 (3): 634–47.

Bova, E., J. Woo, T. Kinda, and S. Zhang. 2013. "Distributional Consequences of Fiscal Consolidation and the Role of Fiscal Policy: What Do the Data Say?" IMF Working Paper No. 13/195, International Monetary Fund, Washington.

Cai, X., and W. J. Den Haan. 2009. "Predicting Recoveries and the Importance of Using Enough Information." CEPR Discussion Paper No. 7508, Center for Economic and Policy Research, Washington.

Cerra, V., and S. Saxena. 2008. "Growth Dynamics: The Myth of Economic Recovery." *American Economic Review* 98 (1): 439–57.

Devries, P., J. Guajardo, D. Leigh, and A. Pescatori. 2011. "A New Action-Based Dataset of Fiscal Consolidation." IMF Working Paper No. 11/128, International Monetary Fund, Washington.

Giavazzi, F., T. Jappelli, and M. Pagano. 2000. "Searching for Non-Linear Effects of Fiscal Policy: Evidence from Industrial and Developing Countries." *European Economic Review* 44 (7): 1259–89.

Giavazzi, F., and M. Pagano. 1996. "Non-Keynesian Effects of Fiscal Policy Changes: International Evidence and the Swedish Experience." *Swedish Economic Policy Review* 3 (1): 67–103.

Gollin, D. 2002. "Getting Income Shares Right." *Journal of Political Economy* 110 (2): 458–74.

Guajardo, J., D. Leigh, and A. Pescatori. 2014. "Expansionary Austerity: New International Evidence." *Journal of the European Economic Association* 12 (4): 949–68.

Hernandez de Cos, P., and E. Moral-Benito. 2011. "Endogenous Fiscal Consolidations." Banco de España Working Paper No. 1102, Banco de España, Madrid.

International Monetary Fund (IMF). 2010a. "From Stimulus to Consolidation: Revenue and Expenditure Policies in Advanced and Emerging Economies." IMF Departmental Paper No. 10/3, International Monetary Fund, Washington.

————. 2010b. "Large Changes in Fiscal Policy: Taxes versus Spending." In *Tax Policy and the Economy,* Volume 24, ed. by J. R. Brown. Cambridge: National Bureau of Economic Research.

————. 2010c. "Will It Hurt? The Macroeconomic Effects of Fiscal Consolidation." Chapter 3 in *World Economic Outlook*, Washington, October.

————. 2012. "What Makes Fiscal Adjustments Successful?" Unpublished, Washington.

————. 2013. "Reassessing the Role and Modalities of Fiscal Policies in Advanced Economies." IMF Policy Paper, Washington.

————. 2014a. *Fiscal Monitor: Back to Work—How Fiscal Policy Can Help*. Washington, October.

————. 2014b. *Fiscal Monitor: Public Expenditure Reform—Making Difficult Choices.* Washington, April.

Jenkins, S. 2014. "World Income Inequality Databases: An Assessment of WIID and SWIID." IZA Discussion Paper No. 8501, Institute for the Study of Labor, Bonn.

Jorda, O. 2005. "Estimation and Inference of Impulse Responses by Local Projections." *American Economic Review* 95 (1): 161–82.

————, and A. M. Taylor. 2013. "The Time for Austerity: Estimating the Average Treatment Effect of Fiscal Policy." Federal Reserve Bank of San Francisco Working Paper 2013/25.

Lagarde, C. 2012. *China Daily*, December 27.

Lipton, D. 2013. "Bellwether Europe 2013." Speech, April 25.

Mauro, P. 2011. *Chipping Away at the Public Debt: Sources of Failure and Keys to Adjustment in Public Debt.* Hoboken, New Jersey: Wiley.

McDermott, C., and R. Wescott. 1996. "An Empirical Analysis of Fiscal Adjustments." *IMF Staff Papers* 43 (4): 725–53.

Milanovic, B. 2014. "The Return of 'Patrimonial Capitalism': A Review of Thomas Piketty's *Capital in the Twenty-First Century*." *Journal of Economic Literature* 52 (2): 519–34.

Morris, R., and L. Schuknecht. 2007. "Structural Balances and Revenue Windfalls: The Role of Asset Prices Revisited." ECB Working Paper No. 737, European Central Bank, Frankfurt.

Nickell, S. 1981. "Biases in Dynamic Models with Fixed Effects." *Econometrica* 49 (6): 1417–26.

Roe, M. J., and J. I. Siegel. 2011. "Political Instability: Effects on Financial Development, Roots in the Severity of Economic Inequality." *Journal of Comparative Economics* 39 (3): 279–309.

Romer, C., and D. Romer. 1989. "Does Monetary Policy Matter? A New Test in the Spirit of Friedman and Schwartz." *NBER Macroeconomics Annual* 4: 121–70.

———. 2010. "The Macroeconomic Effects of Tax Changes: Estimates Based on a New Measure of Fiscal Shocks." *American Economic Review* 100 (3): 763–801.

Spilimbergo, A., S. Symansky, O. Blanchard, and C. Cottarelli. 2008. "Fiscal Policy for the Crisis." IMF Staff Position Note No. 08/01, International Monetary Fund, Washington.

Teulings, C. N., and N. Zubanov. 2013. "Is Economic Recovery a Myth? Robust Estimation of Impulse Responses." *Journal of Applied Econometrics* 29 (3): 497–514.

CHAPTER 9

Fiscal Consolidation and Income Inequality

STEFANIA FABRIZIO AND VALENTINA FLAMINI

INTRODUCTION

Fiscal adjustment, by its very nature, affects income inequality. It does so through the direct effect of tax increases and government spending cuts on disposable income as well as the macroeconomic effects of the adjustment on market income and employment. Given the significant adjustments undertaken by many economies after the initial response to the global financial crisis—against the background of increased inequality—the interest of policymakers worldwide in this theme has intensified. With many economies still needing more fiscal adjustment to meet their medium-term fiscal targets (IMF 2014a), the issue has taken center stage in the policy debate of many countries.

This chapter, which draws upon work in IMF 2014b, provides an overview of recent evidence on fiscal adjustment and income inequality in both advanced and developing economies. It makes several contributions to the literature. First, it provides evidence of how the social environment and support for redistribution have changed in recent years. Second, it shows that, when it comes to the redistributive effect of fiscal adjustment, the composition and design of the fiscal consolidation measures matter. In fact, both revenue- and expenditure-based adjustments can be designed to mitigate the adverse effect of the consolidation on inequality. Finally, the chapter provides policy advice about specific measures that policymakers in advanced and developing countries could consider to mitigate the impact of fiscal adjustment on inequality.

The rest of this chapter is structured as follows. To set the background for the current debate, the next section presents evidence on the recent evolution of the social environment and public support for income redistribution worldwide, including in countries undertaking fiscal adjustment. The subsequent section reviews how fiscal consolidation affects inequality in advanced economies and examines the recent experiences of a number of European countries. The chapter then turns to the distributional incidence of fiscal consolidation in developing countries and why in general it differs from the experience in advanced economies. The final section concludes by setting out options for equitable fiscal consolidation.

FISCAL CONSOLIDATION AND THE SOCIAL CONTEXT

The legacy of the global crisis has been challenging for many countries that have begun to adjust public finances in a fragile macroeconomic environment. These countries have made important fiscal efforts in the past few years, but uncertainties are still widespread. Specifics, of course, vary across countries. In advanced economies, fiscal adjustment following the financial crisis has stabilized the average debt-to-GDP ratio. Nevertheless, this ratio is expected to remain at historic highs (and exceed 100 percent by 2020), and countries will have to continue to reduce it to safer levels. In developing countries, debt ratios and deficits remain generally moderate, although, on average, above precrisis levels, and fiscal risks are on the rise.

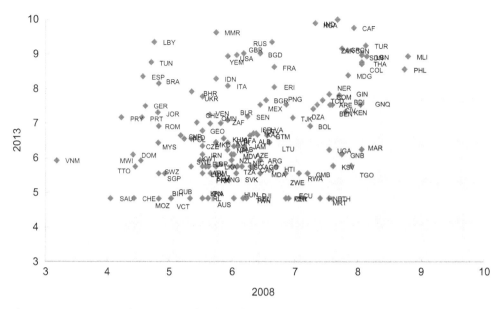

Figure 9.1 Domestic Conflict in Advanced and Developing Economies *(Logarithm)*

Source: IMF staff calculations based on Banks and Wilson (2014).

Note: Data for 2012 or 2011 are used when data for 2013 are not available. Data labels in the figure use International Organization for Standardization (ISO) country codes.

The task of fiscal consolidation has been made more difficult by the intensification of social tensions. Between 2008 and 2013, domestic conflict increased worldwide (in 90 out of 139 countries for which data are available), including in countries that underwent fiscal consolidation (Figure 9.1).[1] This account is in line with the findings of Vegh and Vuletin (2014), who go a step further and show that the recent fiscal adjustment in the euro area countries has aggravated social outcomes, specifically unemployment and domestic conflict.

With intensified social tensions, public support for income redistribution has also increased. International public surveys such as the World Value Survey, regional barometers, and international social surveys monitor public support for redistribution in both advanced and developing countries by asking citizens whether they favor more or less redistribution. Evidence from these surveys indicates that since 2008 support for redistributive policy has grown in 34 out of 41 advanced and developing economies, including in countries that underwent fiscal consolidation (Figure 9.2).

This intensification of social tensions and the greater support for redistribution have stirred a lively debate about the potential impact of fiscal policy on inequality. This debate has become relevant given that sizable and prolonged fiscal consolidation requires public support to be politically sustainable (Cournède and others 2013; IMF 2014b). At the present juncture, a key priority for policymakers is to understand the distributional impact of tax and spending adjustment policies and to design them in a way that does not increase inequality. Indeed, a broad consensus that the burden of adjustment is being shared fairly is essential for generating the public support required for successful and sustainable fiscal consolidation.

---

[1] As a measure of domestic social tensions, this chapter uses the variable "weighted conflict measures" from the Cross-National Time-Series database (Banks and Wilson 2014), which captures various dimensions of domestic conflict, including assassinations, strikes, guerrilla warfare, government crises, purges, riots, revolutions, and antigovernment demonstrations.

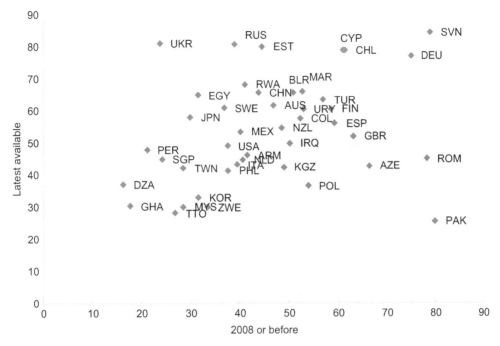

Figure 9.2 Public Support for Redistribution in Advanced and Developing Economies *(Index)*

Source: Integrated World Values Survey, 1981–2014 (http://www.worldvaluessurvey.org/WVSDocumentationWV6.jsp).
Note: The survey variable ranges between 1 (income should be made more equal) and 10 (we need larger income differences as incentives for individual effort). The data points in the figure are country averages of responses less than or equal to 5, which indicate support for different degrees of redistribution. Data labels in the figure use International Organization for Standardization (ISO) country codes.

FISCAL CONSOLIDATION AND INCOME INEQUALITY IN ADVANCED ECONOMIES

Fiscal policy affects inequality through its impact on the distribution of both market and disposable income. Fiscal consolidation typically leads to a short-term reduction in output and employment, which often leads to a decline in wages.[2] This decline tends to increase market-income inequality, given the relatively high share of wages in the incomes of lower-income groups (Jenkins and others 2011). Increasing unemployment also tends to widen wage inequality, since wages for unskilled workers fall relative to wages for skilled workers as employers hoard skilled labor (Mukoyama and Sahin 2006). For example, considering 42 episodes of fiscal consolidation from 1945 to 2012 in advanced countries, evidence suggests that as unemployment went up, on average, from 7½ to almost 10 percent, the Gini index also increased, by more than 1 percent, on average (Figure 9.3). The duration and magnitude of these effects depend on the size of automatic stabilizers, as well as on the growth response and its impact on employment. If multipliers are particularly high during downturns (Jordà and Taylor 2013), fiscal contraction can have a strong effect on employment. These effects may be long-lasting if a prolonged period of slow growth has adverse effects on the supply side of the economy (Aghion, Hemous, and Kharroubi 2009).[3] However, labor market regulations that increase labor supply can help accelerate the

---

[2] If fiscal consolidation is postponed and macroeconomic imbalances are not addressed, a reduction in growth and employment may still occur.
[3] This effect can operate through the labor market as the number of long-term unemployed rises and individuals lose human capital.

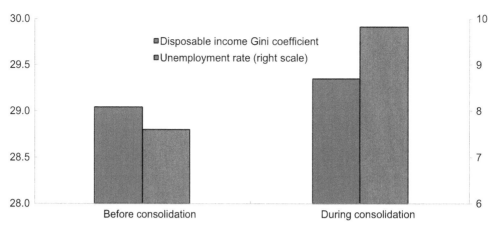

Figure 9.3 Unemployment Rates and Gini Coefficients during Periods of Fiscal Consolidation *(Percent)*

Sources: Solt (2014); Eurostat; and IMF, *World Economic Outlook*.
Note: Fiscal adjustment episodes are defined as in Escolano and others 2014 based on changes in cyclically adjusted primary balances in countries with positive primary gaps. The sample covers 91 episodes across 49 advanced and developing economies between 1945 and 2012.

decline in unemployment as economic growth resumes and avoid persistently high unemployment (Bastagli, Coady, and Gupta 2012).

In addition to its magnitude, the composition and pace of fiscal consolidation influence its impact on inequality. Beyond its effects on market incomes, fiscal adjustment affects the level and composition of taxes and spending items and thus disposable incomes. Income inequality tends to increase the more fiscal adjustment relies on raising regressive taxes and on cutbacks in progressive spending. Econometric studies find that fiscal consolidations based on spending cuts worsen inequality by more than revenue-based ones (Box 9.1). Frontloaded adjustments can have especially strong effects on social welfare if they are implemented when unemployment is already high (Blanchard and Leigh 2013).

Evidence from recent fiscal consolidation episodes, however, suggests that a progressive mix of adjustment measures can significantly help offset the adverse effects of adjustment on inequality, though the consolidation may still lead to reduced incomes in the short term, reflecting its impact

---

BOX 9.1 Fiscal Consolidation and Inequality: A Brief Review of the Empirical Literature Based on Econometric Analysis

There is a broad consensus in the regression-based research that adjustments based on spending cuts have larger effects on income inequality than those based on tax hikes. A number of econometric studies assess how fiscal consolidation affects income inequality both through its impact on market-income inequality (through rising unemployment and wage inequality) and disposable incomes (through changes in taxes and spending). Woo and others (2013) find that spending cuts are significantly associated with an increase in inequality, whereas tax increases have a negative but statistically insignificant effect. Ball and others (2013) show that both spending- and tax-based fiscal consolidation have typically led to a significant and persistent increase in inequality, decline in wage income and in the wage share of income, and increases in long-term unemployment, although spending-based consolidations tend to worsen inequality more than tax-based ones. Agnello and Sousa (2012) find that income inequality significantly rises during periods of fiscal consolidation. However, although spending-driven austerity plans are detrimental to income distribution, tax increases may have an equalizing effect. Finally, Mulas-Granados (2005) finds that expenditure-based adjustments have a greater effect on inequality than do revenue-based ones, but are less detrimental to short-term growth, unemployment, and inflation.

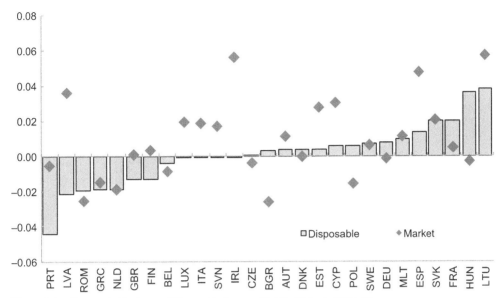

Figure 9.4 Changes in Market- and Disposable-Income Gini Coefficients, 2007–13

Source: EUROMOD statistics on Distribution and Decomposition of Disposable Income, accessed at http://www.iser.essex.ac.uk/euromod/statistics/ using EUROMOD version No. G2.0.

Note: An increase in the Gini coefficient indicates an increase in inequality. The Gini coefficient for market income is estimated based on disposable-income micro data by adding back (in the case of taxes) or deducting (in the case of benefits) each income component, using the EUROMOD microsimulation model. Estimates for market-income Gini in 2007 and 2013 are based on European Union Statistics on Income and Living Conditions 2008 (income reference period: 2007) and European Union Statistics on Income and Living Conditions 2010 (income reference period: 2009), respectively. For the latter, market-income updates from the income reference period to later years are based on a combination of updating factors. For more information on the exact updating factors used for each country, please refer to the Country Reports (https://www.iser.essex.ac.uk/euromod/resources-for-euromod-users/country-reports). Changes between years and tax-benefit components are not necessarily statistically significant. Data labels in the figure use International Organization for Standardization (ISO) country codes.

on output and employment. Comparing changes in the Gini index for market and disposable income during 27 recent consolidation episodes in advanced economies and emerging Europe suggests that, in more than half of these economies, market-income inequality increased during these periods. However, in almost all these cases, fiscal policy mitigated the increase in market-income inequality, leading to either a decrease in disposable-income inequality or an offsetting of the worsening of market inequality (Figure 9.4). It should be noted, however, that the reported Gini indices do not single out policy developments that occurred during this period that were not aimed at fiscal consolidation. The next section focuses on the redistributive effect of fiscal consolidation measures only in selected European economies.

RECENT EXPERIENCE IN SELECTED EUROPEAN COUNTRIES

The magnitude, composition, and design of recent fiscal consolidation packages implemented in nine European countries since the global financial crisis varied substantially. The timing also varied across countries, with Estonia, Lithuania, Latvia, Portugal, and the United Kingdom starting to consolidate in 2009; Greece, Spain, and Romania in 2010; and Italy in 2011. The impact of fiscal adjustments on overall disposable income between 2008 and 2012 ranged from 2 percent to more than 15 percent, contributing to reductions in living standards of the population (Figure 9.5; Box 9.2).[4] Public sector pay reductions were significant in Greece, Latvia, Portugal,

---

[4] Only measures adopted for fiscal consolidation purposes are considered.

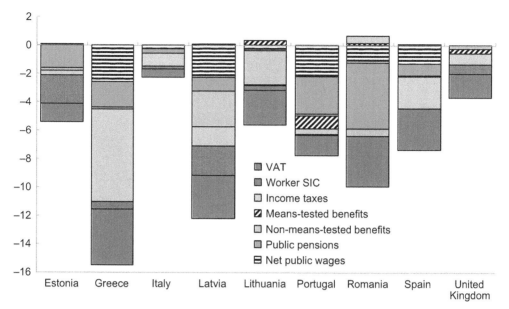

Figure 9.5 Aggregate Effect and Composition of Simulated Fiscal Consolidation Measures, 2008–12
(Percent of total household disposable income)

Source: Avram and others (2013).

Note: The aggregate impact of the value-added tax is calculated as the unweighted average of the percentage impact across household disposable income quantiles and is likely to overestimate the aggregate impact. SIC = social insurance contribution; VAT = value-added tax.

Romania, and Spain. Public pension cuts or a freeze in benefits were prevalent in Romania, Portugal, and to a lesser extent, Spain. Changes in pension indexation were adopted in Estonia. Reductions in means-tested benefits were large in Portugal and the United Kingdom, while reductions in untargeted benefits were sizable in Lithuania and Latvia. Direct tax hikes played a major role in Greece (with an important base-broadening component) and Spain,[5] and increases in worker social insurance contributions played a role in Latvia and Estonia. Increases in value-added tax (VAT) rates were adopted in all nine countries.

The direct distributional outcome reflects the composition and design of the consolidation package. Microsimulation studies indicate that these fiscal adjustments relied in most cases on measures that had a direct progressive impact on disposable income (Callan and others 2012; Avram and others 2013; Koutsampelas and Polycarpu 2013). These studies focus exclusively on the direct impact of spending- and tax-consolidation measures on household disposable income and consumption, and do not capture the interactions between policies and market-income dynamics, which can play a crucial role, especially in times of major changes, in market incomes.[6] Furthermore, although the specific consolidation measures considered account for the bulk of the fiscal consolidation in most countries, cuts in spending on public services and employment, or other spending not directly affecting household income, are not captured.

The analysis of the distributional impact of the fiscal adjustment packages suggests that both revenue and spending measures can be designed in ways that reduce their burden on lower-income groups. Simulations show that five countries (Greece, Latvia, Portugal, Romania, and Spain) implemented progressive measures between 2008 and 2012, with households in the

---

[5] Changes in property taxes were only simulated for Italy and Greece. However, property taxes are present in the other countries and are taken into account for the calculation of household disposable income.

[6] This is a crucial assumption because taxes and benefits affect market income and are, in turn, affected by it.

BOX 9.2 Distributional Impact of Fiscal Adjustment Measures in Nine European Countries, 2008–12

Recent microsimulation studies simulate the direct impact on disposable income of specific consolidation measures adopted during the period 2008–12 (see Annex 9.1 for a discussion of the methodology).

The results suggest the following:

- The overall progressivity of the consolidation package in *Greece* has been driven by progressive public sector pay cuts, pension cuts, and direct taxation. Public sector wages were capped, special allowances for civil servants reduced, and the 13th and 14th months of pay abolished for high-earning workers. The poorest 10 percent of the population was hit relatively harder by the introduction of self-employed and liberal professions social insurance contribution requirements.

- The progressive incidence in *Spain* was also due to public sector pay cuts and changes in income taxation, although the poorest 10 percent of households were relatively harder hit by the 5 percentage point cumulative value-added tax increases imposed in 2010 and 2012. The public sector pay cut averaged 5 percent but increased with wages up to 9.7 percent, and was followed by a freeze and the elimination of the 14th month of pay.

- Moderately progressive public sector wage and pension cuts also drove the overall mildly progressive effect of consolidation in *Italy*, although the scale of the average household income loss was very limited as the result of narrow targeting of the implemented measures, which by design only affected a small part of the population. Public sector wages above €90,000 and €150,000 per year were cut by 5 and 10 percent, respectively.

- In *Portugal*, the overall progressive incidence was due to progressive cuts in public wages and pensions, which offset the regressive cuts in means-tested social transfers that negatively affected households in the bottom decile. Public sector pay cuts increased with wages to a maximum of 10 percent in 2011, and were followed by a suspension of the 13th and 14th months of pay in 2012. Benefit reductions included a decrease of the amount and tightening of the eligibility conditions for family benefits. The suspension of the 13th and 14th months of pay was reversed in 2013 (after the period under consideration in the analysis).

- The moderately regressive path observed in *Lithuania* was the result of the regressivity of VAT increases, which more than offset the progressivity of public sector pay cuts (involving basic wage rates, coefficients, and bonuses).

- In *Romania*, the overall progressivity was driven mostly by public sector pay cuts and real pension reductions for middle-class and rich pensioners. Large losses from real pension cuts occurred because high inflation eroded the real value of pensions that had been frozen as part of the consolidation plan. The part of the population receiving the minimum pension was not affected by the latter measure because the minimum pension was not indexed to inflation even before the pension reform. These large reductions in public pension benefits, coupled with no policy changes in income tax and social contributions, resulted in a net increase in the income of the richest households, because taxable pensions and benefits shrank.

- Progressive reductions in public sector pay, which decreased the average wage by about 9.5 percent, and nonpension benefits more than offset regressive cuts in public pensions and drove the overall progressivity in *Latvia*.

- The overall regressive effect observed in *Estonia* was driven by a change in the indexation of public pensions as pensioners are prevalently in low-income groups, although means-tested social assistance was made more generous and lessened the impact on the incomes of the poorest.

- In the *United Kingdom*, the overall incidence was progressive, due to higher taxes, especially on the richest 1 percent of the population. Losses to households in the bottom half of the income distribution were due to cuts in benefits to families with children, including some sharper means testing.

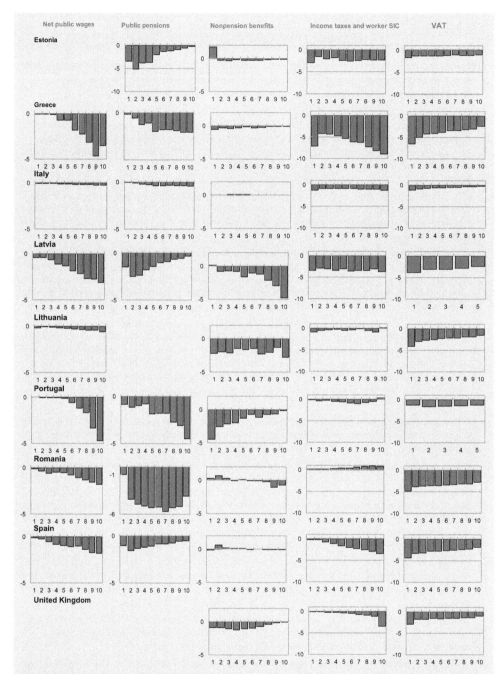

Figure 9.2.1 Change in Household Disposable Income by Type of Measure and Income Group, 2008–12 (*Percentage*)

Source: Avram and others (2013).
Note: Income quantiles are derived based on equivalized household disposable income in 2012 in the absence of fiscal consolidation measures. Other rankings could give different distributional effects. SIC = social insurance contribution; VAT = value-added tax. Missing panels indicate that a particular country did not implement consolidation-related changes of the relevant type.

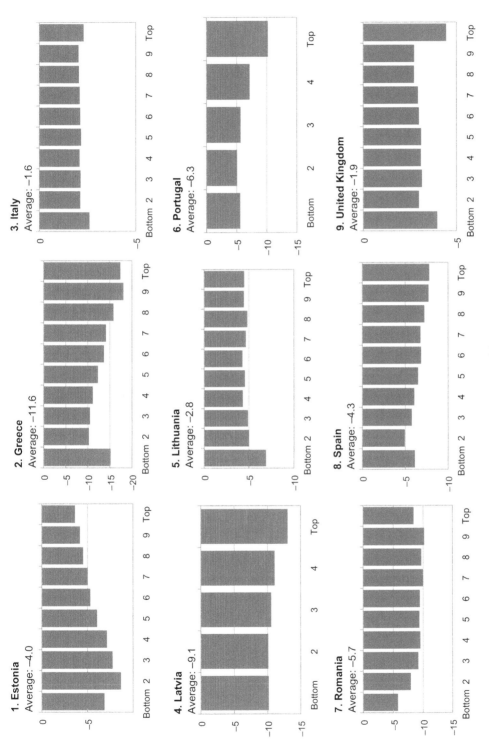

Figure 9.6 Change in Household Disposable Income Due to Simulated Fiscal Consolidation Measures, 2008–12
(Percentage of household disposable income)

Source: Avram and others (2013).
Note: Bars refer to the impact of changes in cash payments, direct taxes, social insurance contributions, and value-added tax as a percentage of each income quantile's total household disposable income. Income quantiles are derived based on equivalized household disposable income in 2012 in the absence of fiscal consolidation measures. Other rankings could give different distributional effects.

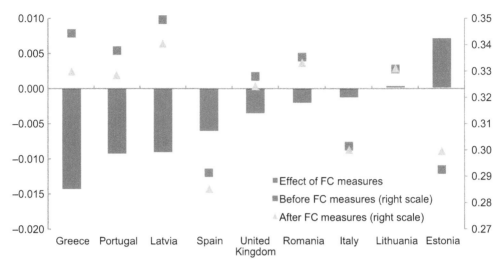

Figure 9.7 Simulated Impact of Fiscal Consolidation Measures on Gini Index, 2012
(Simulated disposable Gini coefficient indices and their difference)

Source: Based on information from Avram and others (2013).
Note: The effect of fiscal consolidation measures equals the difference between Gini coefficients before and after the fiscal consolidation measures (bars). Unlike the Gini coefficients in Figure 9.4, the coefficients reported here reflect the simulated effects of only the consolidation measures adopted during 2008–12 that directly affect disposable income and were not reversed before mid-2012. Estimates of Gini for disposable income before and after fiscal consolidation measures are conditional on the same distribution of market income. FC = fiscal consolidation.

richest quantiles bearing most of the adjustment cost (Figure 9.6).[7] In other countries, the impact of the adjustment tended to be less redistributive and smaller in size (Italy and the United Kingdom). In contrast, for two economies (Lithuania and Estonia), those in the poorest deciles suffered relatively larger reductions of their incomes. In Greece, there was also a larger drop in incomes of the poorest 10 percent of the population, but the overall effect was progressive given that the second through fourth deciles experienced smaller decreases in their incomes while the eighth through tenth income deciles experienced larger drops. The simulated effects of the fiscal consolidation measures on the Gini for disposable income are shown in Figure 9.7; they suggest that fiscal measures have a direct positive effect on disposable income inequality in seven out of nine countries. In particular, the analysis suggests the following:

- Public sector wage reductions were progressive, given that public sector employees usually earn more than do inactive people such as the unemployed and pensioners, and hence are positioned higher up in the income distribution, and because the cuts were generally structured to have a greater impact on higher-income workers.

- Cuts in untargeted benefits were largely progressive, whereas reductions in means-tested benefits were regressive.

- Proportional reductions in pensions across all beneficiaries proved to be strongly regressive because pensioners in the lower-middle-income groups lost a greater share of their total

---

[7] Box 9.2 discusses specifics of the measures and simulation results in the nine economies. Results for Ireland and Cyprus are also available but only capture the aggregate effect of fiscal measures on inequality, and do not include the effect of VAT increases. The results for Ireland indicate that the aggregate effect of tax and social benefit measures, as well as reductions in the public wage bill, was to decrease the incomes of the bottom 10 percent by about 5 percent, and of the top 10 percent by about 13 percent, during 2009–12 (Callan and others 2012). Results for Cyprus indicate that tax and payroll contribution increases implemented in 2012 reduced the incomes of households in the bottom 20 percent by less than 0.1 percent and those of the top 20 percent by about 2 percent (Koutsampelas and Polycarpou 2013).

income. In economies where pension freezes or cuts (or both) were targeted to high pensions, the overall effect was progressive.

- Increases in income tax and social contributions proved to be mostly progressive. However, the design of some of the changes in the income tax, such as decreases in the tax-free threshold, reduced the progressivity of income taxation.

- Increases in VAT rates were regressive, with the relative degree of regressivity depending on the relationship between the VAT structure and consumption patterns of different income groups.

Changes in property taxes were implemented in Greece, Italy, Latvia, Lithuania, Portugal, Romania, and Spain, but they could not be modeled for most countries because of data limitations. However, their design suggests that they were conceived to be, in general, progressive, with reduced rates and exemptions applied to vulnerable populations. Property taxes are generally found to be a relatively growth-friendly and equitable source of revenue (Chapter 11).

FISCAL CONSOLIDATION AND INCOME INEQUALITY IN DEVELOPING ECONOMIES

Although less evidence is available on the distributional incidence of fiscal policy in developing economies, the low levels of both taxes and spending suggest that the incidence is limited for these countries (Chapter 4). Furthermore, a larger share of revenues derives from indirect taxes, which tend to be less progressive than direct taxation. In addition, social spending is, in general, much lower than in advanced economies, which substantially reduces the redistributive effects of fiscal policy. The coverage of social benefits, that is, the percentage of poor households that receive benefits, is generally very low. Also, social spending in developing economies is often not well targeted and in some cases actually increases inequality. With the exception of emerging Europe, in developing economies the poorest 40 percent of the population receives less than 20 percent of the benefits of social protection spending. Many developing countries use energy subsidies as a form of social assistance, which disproportionately benefits upper-income groups. In-kind social spending in developing economies is also not well targeted and exacerbates inequality because the poor often lack access to key public services.

Since government spending in developing economies is often regressive, spending cuts undertaken as part of fiscal adjustment could actually enhance equality. Inequality and unemployment may even decline in the longer term if fiscal adjustment helps bring down inflation—which is damaging to the poor—or corrects macroeconomic imbalances that are hindering growth (Easterly and Fisher 2001; Agenor 2002; Albanesi 2007).

In this respect, fiscal consolidations can have adverse effects on inequality in the short term, but their long-term effects are often positive. Evidence from 27 past episodes of large fiscal adjustment in 19 economies shows that fiscal consolidation is associated with increased unemployment in the near term (Figure 9.8).[8] By the end of these adjustment episodes, however, unemployment had declined to close to its preadjustment levels, and income inequality also declined.[9] In general, the results also hold at the regional level.

---

[8] The sample includes Algeria, Belize, Brazil, Bulgaria, Chile, El Salvador, Hungary, Jamaica, Jordan, Kazakhstan, Mexico, Moldova, Panama, Russia, South Africa, Suriname, Trinidad and Tobago, Turkey, and Venezuela.

[9] Successful fiscal adjustments are also beneficial in the longer term because they reduce public debt ratios and create the fiscal space for countercyclical policy responses to external shocks. This can help dampen the effects of these shocks on unemployment.

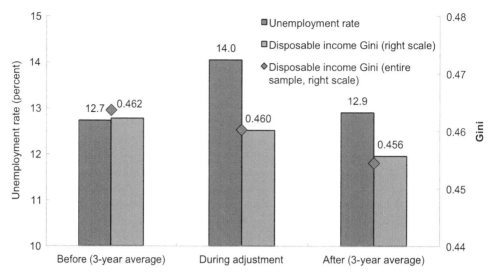

Figure 9.8   Unemployment Rates and Gini Coefficients during Large Fiscal Adjustments in Developing Economies

Sources: Solt (2014); IMF, *World Economic Outlook*; Tsibouris and others (2006); and IMF staff calculations.
Note: Data for both unemployment and Gini coefficients are available for 27 episodes in 16 countries. The entire sample for Gini coefficients includes 68 episodes in 41 countries.

However, the impact of fiscal consolidation could be longer lasting if the country experiences an economic recession during the adjustment period. In 12 out 27 episodes of fiscal consolidation, countries experienced an economic recession, defined as a contraction of GDP in at least one year during the adjustment period. As shown in Figure 9.9, the experiences of the two country groups were quite different during the consolidation periods. Countries that had an economic recession during fiscal adjustment episodes experienced, on average, a larger increase in unemployment during the consolidation period than did the other countries. Furthermore, although unemployment declined after the adjustment, it remained at significantly higher levels than before the adjustment for the countries that had a recession, suggesting that fiscal consolidation may not fully correct the macroeconomic imbalances that hindered growth if such imbalances are structural in nature. It is also remarkable that, after the adjustment period, inequality was lower compared with the preadjustment period for both country groups.

CONCLUSION

Both expenditure- and revenue-based fiscal adjustments can be designed to mitigate their adverse effects on inequality. Although the appropriate pace of fiscal adjustment depends on the state of the economy, the state of public finances, and the extent of market pressures, the analysis in this chapter suggests that the progressivity of consolidation efforts, as well as their macroeconomic impact, depends on the specific composition and design of the measures. Governments should consider protecting the most progressive and efficient redistributive spending during fiscal adjustment to minimize the effects of the adjustment on inequality. They should improve the targeting of spending and broaden the scope of spending cuts to decrease untargeted subsidies, military spending, and public sector wages, which will reduce the need for cuts in social transfers. For example, energy subsidies, which exacerbate inequality (see Chapter 14) and hold back growth, should be avoided and replaced with better targeted instruments (Clements and others 2013).

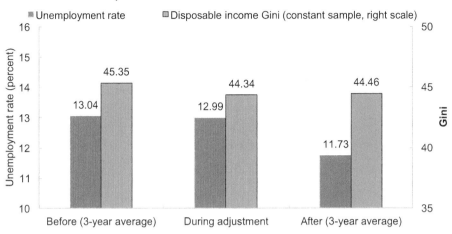

1. Economic Expansion

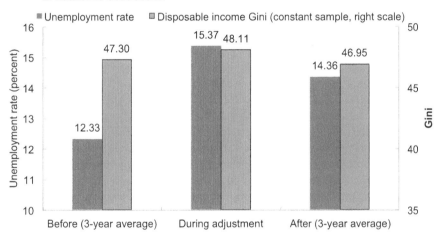

2. Economic Contraction

Figure 9.9   Unemployment Rates and Gini Coefficients during Large Fiscal Adjustments in Developing Economies that Experienced Economic Contraction and Expansion during the Consolidation Period

Sources: Solt (2014); IMF, *World Economic Outlook*; Tsibouris and others (2006); and IMF staff calculations.
Note: "Economic contraction" countries are those that had at least a year of GDP contraction during a period of fiscal consolidation. The two groups include 12 episodes of economic contraction in 9 countries (panel 1) and 15 episodes of economic expansion in 14 countries (panel 2).

In advanced economies, greater reliance on progressive revenue measures can also prevent the need for large cuts in social transfers, though room to increase revenue may be limited if taxes are already high (Baldacci, Gupta, and Mulas-Granados 2012). Progressive tax measures should also be considered, such as reductions in regressive tax expenditures and greater taxation of wealth and property. Spending measures should be designed to reduce labor market distortions. For example, linking child benefits to labor market participation can strengthen incentives for women to enter the labor market and decrease welfare dependency (Elborgh-Woytek and others 2013). Pension reforms should safeguard the distributive role of pensions by making benefit cuts progressive to protect low-income pensioners (IMF 2014b). Finally, expanding active labor markets programs, such as job-search support, targeted wage subsidies, and training programs, can help accelerate the decline in unemployment as economic growth resumes.

In developing economies, social insurance and social assistance programs often cover only a small share of the population (see Chapter 4). To prevent short-term increases in inequality, social safety nets should be strengthened to protect vulnerable households during fiscal adjustments. Replacing widespread universal subsidies with targeted social spending (see Chapter 14) can also help prevent a surge in inequality during the adjustment. Fiscal consolidations may nevertheless need to include revenue measures to be sustainable (Gupta and others 2005; Bevan 2010). Increasing the efficiency and equity of the tax system through greater reliance on progressive taxation can also help mitigate the impact of tax measures on inequality.

ANNEX 9.1. EUROMOD SIMULATIONS: A BRIEF DESCRIPTION OF THE METHODOLOGY

This annex provides a brief description of the methodology and main assumptions used by the EUROMOD model for simulating the redistributive effects of fiscal consolidation policies (see Avram and others 2013).

The analysis focuses on the fiscal consolidation measures implemented after the 2008 economic downturn and up to mid-2012[10] that were explicitly introduced for austerity reasons to cut the public deficit or stem its growth.[11] It looks at first-round effects of changes in cash payments and direct personal taxes and contributions that have a direct impact on income distribution—including reductions in cash benefits and public pensions, increases in direct taxes and contributions paid by households, and public sector pay cuts[12]—plus indirect tax increases. The analysis does not consider increases in employer-paid contributions, cutbacks in public services, reductions in public expenditure or increase in taxes that cannot be allocated to households, and cuts in public sector employment. This also leaves aside the potentially larger effects on income inequality from labor market developments and financial, macroeconomic, and political disarray.

For the simulations, household survey data collected before the global crisis are considered, with market incomes adjusted by source, in line with actual changes in average levels between the period when the data were collected and 2012. The counterfactual scenario, which would be the absence of fiscal consolidation measures, assumes the continuation of precrisis tax and benefit policies, indexed according to standard practices and official assumptions or law.[13]

The analysis makes use of EUROMOD, the European Union tax-benefit microsimulation model, developed by the University of Essex Institute for Social and Economic Research. This is a static model, that is, the simulations of taxes and benefits do not capture the potential behavioral reactions of individuals, and sociodemographic characteristics are assumed to be fixed over time. The model calculates the static effects of the tax-benefit system on household incomes in a comparable manner across countries. This allows an assessment to be made of the effects of consolidated tax-benefit policies and how tax-benefit policy reforms may affect income distribution. Simulations are based on individual microdata from Eurostat, national versions of the European Union Statistics on Income and Living Conditions (EU-SILC), and the Family Resources Survey for the United Kingdom.

Market incomes and information on other personal and household characteristics (for example, age and marital status) come from the microdata, and cash benefit entitlements, direct personal

---

[10] The starting point of the changes varies across countries because countries began consolidating in different years.

[11] The removal of temporary fiscal stimulus measures is not considered as part of the fiscal consolidation packages if those reforms were originally presented as temporary. Since the aim is to quantify the effect of fiscal consolidation on 2012 incomes, measures that were reversed before mid-2012 are also not considered.

[12] Public sector pay cuts are measured net of any reduction in income tax and social contributions.

[13] Such indexation is not the same across countries.

tax and social insurance contribution liabilities, and indirect tax payments are estimated on the basis of the tax-benefit system in place and information available in the underlying data sets. Disposable incomes are derived by applying the estimated cash benefit entitlements and direct personal tax and social insurance contribution liabilities to market incomes. Posttax incomes are obtained by deducting the proportion of disposable income paid in indirect taxes. Income quintiles are derived based on equivalized household disposable income in 2012 in the absence of fiscal consolidation measures.[14] The distributional effect of tax and benefit changes is calculated by comparing final incomes after policy changes with incomes under a no-policy-change scenario.[15]

REFERENCES

Agenor, P. R. 2002. "Business Cycles, Economic Crises, and the Poor." *Journal of Economic Policy Reform* 5 (3): 145–60.

Aghion, P., D. Hemous, and E. Kharroubi. 2009. "Credit Constraints, Cyclical Fiscal Policy and Industry Growth." CEPR Discussion Paper No. 7359, Centre for Economic Policy Research, London.

Agnello, L., and R. M. Sousa. 2012. "How Does Fiscal Consolidation Impact on Income Inequality?" Banque de France Working Paper No. 382, Banque de France, Paris. http://ssrn.com/abstract=2060097 or http://dx.doi.org/10.2139/ssrn.2060097.

Albanesi, S. 2007. "Inflation and Inequality." *Journal of Monetary Economics* 54 (4): 1088–114.

Avram, S., F. Figari, C. Leventi, H. Levy, J. Navicke, M. Matsaganis, E. Militaru, A. Paulus, O. Rastringina, and H. Sutherland. 2013. "The Distributional Effects of Fiscal Consolidation in Nine Countries." EUROMOD Working Paper No. EM 2/13, Institute of Social and Economic Research, Essex University, Essex.

Baldacci, E., S. Gupta, and C. Mulas-Granados. 2012. "Reassessing the Fiscal Mix for Successful Debt Reduction." *Economic Policy* 27 (71): 365–406.

Ball, L., D. Furceri, D. Leigh, and P. Loungani. 2013. "The Distributional Effects of Fiscal Austerity." IMF Working Paper No. 13/151, International Monetary Fund, Washington.

Banks, A. S., and K. A. Wilson. 2014. Cross-National Time-Series Data Archive. Databanks International. Jerusalem, Israel. http://www.databanksinternational.com.

Bastagli, F., D. Coady, and S. Gupta. 2012. "Income Inequality and Fiscal Policy." IMF Staff Discussion Note No. 12/08, International Monetary Fund, Washington.

Bevan, D. 2010. "Fiscal Implications of the Global Economic and Financial Crisis for Low-Income Countries." Department of Economics paper prepared for the U.K. Department for International Development, Oxford University, Oxford, U.K. http://www.dfid.gov.uk/r4d/PDF/Outputs/EcoDev_misc/60740-Fiscal-Implications-Bevan-03-10.pdf.

Blanchard, O., and D. Leigh. 2013. "Fiscal Consolidation: At What Speed?" Vox website, May. http://www.voxeu.org/article/fiscal-consolidation-what-speed.

Callan, T., C. Keane, M. Savage, and J. R. Walsh. 2012. "Distributional Impact of Tax, Welfare and Public Sector Pay Policies: 2009–2012." ESRI Working Paper, The Economic and Social Research Institute, Dublin.

Clements, B., D. Coady, S. Fabrizio, S. Gupta, T. Alleyne, and C. Sdralevich, eds. 2013. *Energy Subsidy Reform: Lessons and Implications.* Washington: International Monetary Fund.

Cournède, B., A. Goujard, Á. Pina, and A. de Serres. 2013. "Choosing Fiscal Consolidation Instruments Compatible with Growth and Equity." OECD Economic Policy Paper No. 7, Organisation for Economic Co-operation and Development, Paris.

Easterly, W., and S. Fisher. 2001. "Inflation and the Poor." *Journal of Money, Credit and Banking* 33 (2): 160–78.

Elborgh-Woytek, K., M. Newiak, K. Kochar, S. Fabrizio, K. Kpodar, P. Wingender, B. Clements, and G. Schwartz. 2013. "Women, Work, and the Economy: Macroeconomic Gains from Gender Equity." IMF Staff Discussion Note No. 13/10, International Monetary Fund, Washington.

Escolano, J., L. Jaramillo, C. Mulas-Granados, and G. Terrier. 2014. "How Much Is a Lot? Historical Evidence on the Size of Fiscal Adjustments." IMF Working Paper No. 14/179, International Monetary Fund, Washington.

Gupta, S., B. Clements, E. Baldacci, and E. Tiongson. 2005. "What Sustains Fiscal Consolidations in Emerging Market Countries?" *International Journal of Finance and Economics* 10 (4): 307–21.

---

[14] It is essential to note that other rankings could give different distributional effects.

[15] See Sutherland and Figari 2013, Sutherland 2007, and Lietz and Mantovani 2007 for further technical and methodological information.

International Monetary Fund. 2014a. *Fiscal Monitor: Back to Work—How Fiscal Policy Can Help.* Washington, October. http://www.imf.org/external/pubs/ft/fm/2014/02/fmindex.htm.

———. 2014b. "Fiscal Policy and Income Inequality." IMF Policy Paper, International Monetary Fund, Washington.

Jenkins, S., A. Brandolini, J. Micklewright, and B. Nolan. 2011. *The Great Recession and the Distribution of Household Income.* Milan: Fondazione Rodolfo Debenedetti.

Jordà, Ò., and A. M. Taylor. 2013. "The Time for Austerity: Estimating the Average Treatment Effect of Fiscal Policy." Paper presented at the NBER Summer Institute, Cambridge, Massachusetts, July.

Koutsampelas, C., and A. Polycarpu. 2013. "Austerity and the Income Distribution: The Case of Cyprus." EUROMOD Working Paper No. EM 4/13, University of Essex, Colchester.

Lietz, C., and D. Mantovani. 2007. "A Short Introduction to EUROMOD: An Integrated European Tax-Benefit Model." In *Research in Labor Economics*, Vol. 25, *Micro-Simulation in Action: Policy Analysis in Europe Using EUROMOD*, edited by O. Bargain. Bingley, U.K.: Emerald Publishing Group.

Mukoyama, T., and A. Sahin. 2006. "Costs of Business Cycles for Unskilled Workers." *Journal of Monetary Economics* 53 (8): 2179–93.

Mulas-Granados, C. 2005. "Fiscal Adjustments and the Short-Term Trade-Off between Economic Growth and Equality." *Revista de Economia Publica* 172 (1/2005): 61–92.

Solt, F. 2014. The Standardized World Income Inequality Database. V14. http://hdl.handle.net/1902.1/11992.

Sutherland, H. 2007. "EUROMOD: The Tax-Benefit Microsimulation Model for the European Union." In *Modeling Our Future: Population Ageing, Health and Aged Care, International Symposia in Economic Theory and Econometrics,* Vol. 16, edited by A. Gupta and A. Harding, 483–88. Amsterdam: Elsevier.

———, and F. Figari. 2013. "EUROMOD: The European Tax-Benefit Microsimulation Model." *International Journal of Microsimulation* 6 (1): 4–26.

Tsibouris, G., M. A. Horton, M. J. Flanagan, and W. S. Maliszewski. 2006. "Experience with Large Fiscal Adjustments." IMF Occasional Paper No. 246, International Monetary Fund, Washington.

Vegh, C. A., and G. Vuletin. 2014. "Social Implications of Fiscal Policy Responses during Crises." NBER Working Paper No. 19828, National Bureau of Economic Research, Cambridge, Massachusetts.

Woo, J., E. Bova, T. Kinda, and S. Zhang. 2013. "Distributional Consequences of Fiscal Consolidation and the Role of Fiscal Policy: What Do the Data Say?" IMF Working Paper No. 13/195, International Monetary Fund, Washington.

PART IV

Tax Policy and Inequality

International Corporate Tax Spillovers and Redistributive Policies in Developing Countries

RUUD DE MOOIJ, THORNTON MATHESON, AND ROBERTO SCHATAN

INTRODUCTION

Mobilizing domestic resources is recognized to be one of the key factors in meeting the development objectives of low-income countries, including reducing poverty and inequality (see, for example, Chapter 4). Financing social programs and comprehensive redistributive policies, as well as public investment in infrastructure, education, and health care, depend in the first place on an adequate taxation system capable of generating sufficient resources. Frequently, international businesses constitute a key group of taxpayers in developing countries and therefore are an important source of revenue.

At the same time, another essential element for development and poverty reduction in developing countries is a healthy business climate, capable of attracting foreign direct investment (FDI). FDI is critical for developing countries to become integrated into the global economy and to speed up productivity and income growth. Empirical evidence consistently shows positive correlations between FDI and economic growth in developing countries—although causality remains a contentious issue in this research. And although taxation is perhaps not the main factor weighing on multinational corporations' FDI decisions, evidence suggests it does matter significantly (de Mooij and Ederveen 2008). Excessive levels of taxation on international businesses, even if aimed at maximizing domestic resource mobilization, can dissuade foreign investors and hamper development.

Thus, there is an important trade-off between mobilizing domestic resources from international business and creating an attractive investment climate for FDI. Both are important for addressing poverty and reducing inequality, but the goals of attracting FDI and funding social development programs may clash, so pushing too hard for one may undo the other. Finding the right balance is a key challenge for all countries, but particularly so for developing countries for two reasons. First, revenue mobilization in developing countries typically relies more heavily on corporate income taxes (CIT) than it does in advanced countries (Figure 10.1)—and a relatively large part of these CIT revenues in developing countries often comes from multinationals. Second, international spillovers from global corporate tax practices are likely to weigh especially heavily on developing countries. For example, the very low tax burden imposed by some tax haven countries enables multinationals seeking to reduce their global tax liabilities to engage in tax planning, causing base erosion and profit shifting away from both developed and developing countries. Developing countries are particularly susceptible to this form of base erosion, however, due to their more limited administrative capacity.

This chapter draws heavily on IMF 2014.

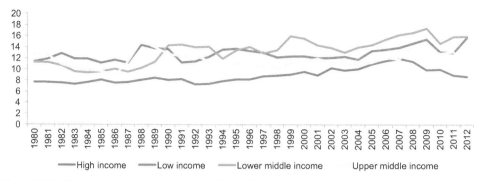

Figure 10.1 Corporate Income Tax Revenue as a Share of Total Revenue by Country Income Group *(Percent)*

Source: IMF staff estimates.

Note: Total tax revenue excluding social contributions (data on which are incomplete); resource-rich countries are excluded because of divergences in the reporting of taxes on natural resources. Figure shows medians, with countries ranked by income per capita each year and divided into four equal-sized groups.

Spillovers to developing countries raise two important policy issues: (1) the international tax rules adopted elsewhere (including in advanced countries), which determine the magnitude of spillovers to developing countries; and (2) the tax rules set by developing countries themselves to cope with spillovers. This chapter focuses on the first issue: the rules of the international tax architecture that influence the revenue-raising ability of developing countries. Advanced economies have an important responsibility with regard to this issue. This chapter does not address the second issue in any detail, other than to note that developing countries should try to design policies that strike a proper balance between protecting their tax base and maintaining a competitive business climate. For instance, well-designed anti-avoidance measures can be critical to securing a reasonable revenue take from multinationals. International guidelines for anti-avoidance measures are currently being discussed under the Base Erosion and Profit Shifting initiative of the Group of 20 and Organisation for Economic Co-operation and Development (OECD).

In discussing spillovers from the international tax architecture, this chapter focuses on three issues that are particularly relevant for revenue mobilization in developing countries:

- *Territoriality versus worldwide taxation.* The system for avoiding international double taxation adopted by major capital-exporting countries (mostly advanced economies) can provide incentives for net capital-importing countries (mostly developing countries) to engage in tax competition.

- *Bilateral tax treaties (BTTs).* Although aimed at attracting FDI, treaties often reallocate taxation of foreign investment income from the host country to the home country by, for example, lowering withholding tax rates on dividends, interest, and royalties. This treatment reduces revenues in developing countries, which are usually net capital importers.

- *Separate accounting with arm's-length pricing versus consolidation with formulary apportionment.* The current international tax system allocates taxable income of a multinational on the basis of separate accounts of subsidiaries in each country, with intracompany transactions valued on the basis of "arm's-length" pricing. An alternative principle—currently applied only within countries with subnational business taxes to allocate tax bases across localities—would be to consolidate multinational profits and divide them among jurisdictions according to factors such as the share of domestic sales, payroll, assets, and employment in each country.

The rest of this chapter is organized as follows: First, the current international tax architecture and its associated spillovers are discussed. Then the three design features outlined above and their implications for developing countries are explored in more detail.

TAXATION OF MULTINATIONAL ENTERPRISES

Current Practice and Key Concepts

The current international corporate income tax framework that defines and divides the international corporate tax base has evolved during the past century with little explicit coordination, other than through bilateral treaties that govern only a subset of relevant matters.[1] Taxing rights are based on identifying, on the one hand, the *source* of profits and, on the other hand, the *residence* of corporate taxpayers.

- *Source* refers—very loosely—to where investment is made and income generated, and is traditionally determined largely by the physical presence of labor, capital, or both. Certain thresholds of contact (proxies for the creation of value)—said to create a *permanent establishment*—must be met for a foreign-resident company to become liable to pay tax to the country deemed the source of profit.

- *Residence* means the place where the company receiving the income is deemed to have its primary location, with common tests for this being where the company is incorporated (applicable, for example, in the United States) or from where it is effectively managed (in most other countries).

Double taxation, that is, taxation by both source and residence countries, is typically avoided. Under *territorial* taxation, tax on business profits is levied only in the source country. By contrast, assertion in domestic law of the right to tax profits from any geographic source based on a company's domestic residence is generally referred to as *worldwide taxation*. In that case, double taxation is avoided by the residence country's granting to the company a *foreign tax credit* for income and withholding taxes paid in the source country. Foreign tax credits can be offered either in domestic law or in applicable *bilateral tax treaties*, or both. The result is that the residence country tax is limited to the excess of its *effective tax rate* over that of the source country.

A key issue in assessing any international tax arrangement is how it divides the rights to tax between source and residence countries. The allocation of rights is especially important for developing countries, because flows for them are commonly very asymmetric: with some exceptions (such as China), they are usually source countries—that is, the recipients of capital inflows—not investors in business activities outside their borders. The current architecture allocates taxing rights to the source country through rules regarding permanent establishments, so might seem to favor source countries. Looking deeper, however, the network of bilateral double taxation treaties based on the OECD model[2] significantly constrains the source country's rights.

The determination of source itself relies on the allocation of earnings to particular entities within corporate groups. The core allocation rule for this purpose is the *arm's-length principle* of valuing transactions within multinationals at the prices that would be agreed to by unrelated parties—which, given current guidelines, leaves considerable scope for manipulation by multinationals to shift their tax bases

---

[1] These bilateral treaties are informed by guidelines produced by the OECD and, with somewhat less impact, the United Nations. Some regional agreements also have considerable effect, notably in the European Union, where directives and decisions of the Court of Justice reflecting the principle of nondiscrimination among member states have a major impact.
[2] The United Nations model allocates somewhat more rights to the source country by, for instance, not prescribing maximum withholding tax rates and providing for source taxation of royalties. Lennard (2009), Lennard and Yaffar (2012), and Lang and Owens (2014) elaborate on the differences between the two models.

away from high-tax (often source) countries. At issue here are deeper notions as to the fair international allocation of income tax revenue and powers across countries. Arrangements that seem to contradict broad perceptions of fairness, even if those are imperfectly articulated, may increasingly give rise to unilateral domestic measures to change them, with a consequent risk that uncoordinated defensive measures will even further undermine the coherence of the international tax system.

The allocation of income between residence and source countries is further complicated by the widespread use of conduit entities—notably, financing subsidiaries—in low-tax (or no-tax) jurisdictions. Multinationals often use these entities, in conjunction with various provisions of national tax codes and tax treaties, to strip income out of both residence *and* source countries.

Spillovers

The current architecture as just outlined gives rise to spillovers—the impact that one jurisdiction's tax rules or practices have on others not party to the underlying decisions. Fiscal externalities of this kind can arise from many aspects of national tax systems, but the focus in this chapter is on cross-border effects arising through taxation at the corporate level.

- The *corporate tax base* may be affected as taxable profits in any one geographical location change to reflect both real responses (through investment and the like) and profit-shifting responses (loosely speaking, alterations of where profits are booked only for tax purposes). This channel, holding constant the tax policy of the affected country, is referred to as *base spillovers*.

- *Corporate tax rates* may also be affected, since the best response to reduced foreign tax rates abroad may be to reduce national tax rates, too. These *strategic spillovers*—tax competition in its broadest sense—are often accused of creating a race to the bottom that lowers the global CIT take.

The effects of base and strategic spillovers are closely related. Decisions about the location of real activities, for instance, may be influenced by the associated opportunities for profit shifting. Spillovers can also arise from several aspects of national tax policies. Most obviously, they can arise from differences in headline statutory CIT rates, since these rates create incentives to shift taxable profits between countries. The decline in CIT rates across the globe since 1980 may thus be a manifestation of strategic spillovers (Figure 10.2), along with more narrowly defined *preferential regimes* that offer targeted tax incentives to attract FDI or particular types of income (such as royalties).

The form and severity of spillovers depend on the structure of the international tax framework. For instance, the tax rate levied in source countries would not matter for corporate decisions under a pure system of worldwide taxation in which such income was fully subject to tax, without deferral, by the residence country.[3] The company would then simply pay the residence country rate on all its earnings, wherever they arose. Addressing spillover problems thus inevitably raises issues concerning not just particular tax arbitrage opportunities under current arrangements, but the wider architecture itself.

The effects of spillovers are not zero sum, but can create a collective inefficiency—and national interests can diverge sharply. This situation is clearest in relation to profit shifting, that is, moving taxable income from a high-tax jurisdiction to a low-tax one to reduce total tax payments. Since the company's purpose in doing so is to reduce its total tax payments, the collective revenue of the countries affected must fall, but revenue in the low-tax country will likely increase (provided that its tax rate is above zero). Similar effects arise more broadly from factors other than such straight income-shifting techniques. Noncooperative policymaking in the presence of

---

[3] This assumes that the tax rate in the residence country is equal to or higher than that of the source country.

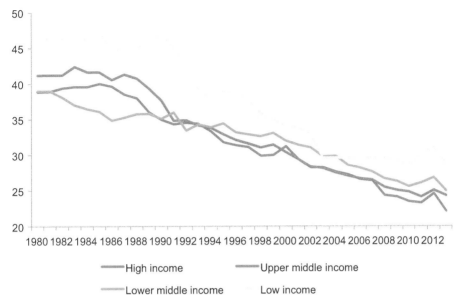

Figure 10.2   Corporate Income Tax Rates, 1980–2013 *(Percent)*

Source: IMF staff estimates.
Note: Figure shows medians, with countries ranked by income per capita each year and divided into four equal-sized groups.

externalities can result in outcomes that, from the collective perspective, are inefficient but from which some countries or jurisdictions nonetheless gain.

Recent evidence for a large number of countries suggests that both base and strategic spillovers are important (IMF 2014; Crivelli, de Mooij, and Keen, forthcoming). In particular, a reduction in the CIT rate in other countries is found to exert a significant and large impact on a country's own tax base, both through real capital and profit-shifting effects. Moreover, tax reductions in one set of countries are found to induce a significant same-way strategic reaction in other countries, exemplifying the process of tax competition. Both spillovers are also found to be considerably larger for developing countries than for advanced economies. Hence, international tax design in advanced economies as well as in tax havens will have a noticeably greater impact on tax revenue in developing countries than elsewhere. This finding warrants analysis of the key international tax design considerations from the perspective of developing countries.

KEY ISSUES FOR DEVELOPING COUNTRIES

The Trend toward Territoriality

Worldwide taxation was once predominant among capital-exporting countries. Under these rules, dividends distributed by foreign corporate subsidiaries are subject to CIT in the home country. CIT and withholding taxes paid in the host country are at least deductible against home-country tax liability, but more often a full tax credit is granted.[4] The home-country tax liability on "active"

---

[4] Depending on "pooling" rules, excess credits may be used to offset other foreign taxes paid.

income[5] is generally deferred until the foreign earnings are repatriated, allowing them to accumulate offshore without this additional layer of taxation. Foreign subsidiaries of parent companies in high-tax worldwide jurisdictions may thus have an incentive to reinvest rather than repatriate earnings, even if the pretax rate of return in the host country is lower than that in the home country.

Most OECD countries have moved their systems closer to territorial taxation principles, under which active earnings distributed by foreign subsidiaries are exempt from home-country taxation.[6] Since the 1980s, 17 OECD countries—including, in 2009, the United Kingdom, Japan, and New Zealand—have altered their international tax regimes to adopt territoriality as the main principle.[7] Territorial tax systems now account for roughly twice as much outbound FDI as worldwide systems (Table 10.1).[8] The major policy considerations driving the trend toward territoriality are the desire to avoid discouraging domestic multinationals from repatriating foreign earnings or encouraging them to reincorporate in lower-tax jurisdictions, and to level the playing field for them when they bid for assets in foreign markets.

The additional layer of home-country taxation under a worldwide system tends to equalize the tax burden on outbound investment across host countries with different tax rates: earnings from low-tax countries are subject to a higher tax upon repatriation than earnings from higher-tax countries, which generate more foreign tax credits. This system protects host countries from international tax competition. Furthermore, when a country that is a major capital exporter operates a worldwide tax system, its FDI recipients can set their CIT rates at or just below that country's CIT rate without undermining their attractiveness as investment locations. When capital exporters adopt territoriality, however, this layer of protection is stripped off, exposing host countries to additional pressure to cut their CIT, their withholding tax rates, or both.

Empirical evidence indicates that the choice between worldwide and territorial systems has a significant effect on cross-border investment patterns. Matheson, Perry, and Veung (2013) find evidence consistent with territoriality's spurring tax competition by making multinationals more sensitive to host-country tax rates: in a country-level bilateral panel regression of outward FDI from the United Kingdom, the coefficient on host-country tax rates becomes more negative after adoption of territoriality in 2009. There is also evidence that territoriality increases earnings repatriation: adoption of territoriality by the United Kingdom and Japan resulted in an immediate surge in dividend repatriation in both countries (Egger and others 2012; Hasegawa and Kiyota 2013). It remains to be seen whether these dividend surges were temporary or whether territoriality results in a permanently higher level of repatriation.

Increased dividend repatriation may result in a lower level of FDI by multinationals headquartered in jurisdictions adopting territoriality.[9] However, a reduction in effective tax rates may also spur outbound investment. For example, Smart (2011) shows that conclusion of a tax treaty providing for territorial taxation increased Canadian FDI in the treaty partner by an average of

---

[5] Generally, active income excludes dividends, interest, rents, royalties, and sales commissions or margins from companies in which the parent does not have at least some minimum ownership stake, often 10 percent.

[6] However, even under territoriality distributions of financial flows other than dividends, such as interest and royalties, are subject to taxation in the home country, usually with a credit for foreign withholding taxes paid. So-called portfolio dividends from minority shareholdings are usually also subject to home-country taxation.

[7] The distinction between worldwide and territorial taxation is not always pure; for example, Canada's domestic law prescribes a worldwide system but exempts foreign dividends through bilateral tax treaties; Germany subjects 5 percent of dividend repatriations to domestic CIT to offset domestic CIT deductions taken to generate foreign income; and countries with worldwide taxation often permit deferral of domestic tax on foreign earnings until those earnings are distributed back to the parent company.

[8] The use of conduit entities in low-tax jurisdictions, which are usually territorial, undoubtedly produces some double counting of these flows.

[9] Egger and others (2012) find a reduction in outward investment by British parent companies and a rise in the efficiency of their foreign affiliates beginning in 2009. The measure of efficiency is the sales-to-fixed-assets ratio.

TABLE 10.1

Outward Foreign Direct Investment Stock by Tax Regime, 2012

Country	Year of Adoption	Outward Foreign Direct Investment Stock (million US$)	Percent of Global Foreign Direct Investment Stock	Percent of Domestic GDP
		Territorial systems		
United Kingdom	2009	1,808,167	7.7	74
Germany	2001	1,547,185	6.6	46
France	1979	1,496,795	6.3	57
Hong Kong SAR		1,309,849	5.6	509
Switzerland	1940	1,129,376	4.8	177
Japan	2009	1,054,928	4.5	18
Belgium	1962	1,037,782	4.4	214
Netherlands	1914	975,552	4.1	126
Canada	1951	715,053	3.0	40
Spain	2000	627,212	2.7	46
Italy	1990	565,085	2.4	28
Australia	1991	424,450	1.8	27
British Virgin Islands		433,588	1.8	47,335
Singapore		401,426	1.7	148
Sweden	2003	406,851	1.7	78
Denmark	1992	229,470	1.0	74
Austria	1972	215,364	0.9	54
Norway	2004	216,083	0.9	43
Luxembourg	1968	171,468	0.7	301
Finland	1920	142,313	0.6	57
Cayman Islands		108,030	0.5	3,306
Total		15,207,686	63.7	
		Worldwide systems		
United States		5,191,116	22	33
China		509,001	2.2	6
Russia		413,159	1.8	21
Ireland		357,626	1.5	171
Brazil		232,848	1.0	10
Taiwan Province of China		226,093	1.0	47
Korea		196,410	0.8	17
Mexico		137,684	0.6	12
India		118,167	0.5	6
Total		7,636,358	31.4	

Sources: PricewaterhouseCoopers; UNCTADstat.
Note: Blank spaces in the "Year of Adoption" column indicate that the year of adoption is not known.

79 percent.[10] Shifting to territoriality may also spur outward investment by increasing the competitiveness of domestic companies in bidding for foreign assets.[11] The economic benefit of leveling the playing field among international bidders is that it ensures that assets fall into the hands of the owner most likely to maximize their productivity.

Tax Treaties

Another aspect of international taxation that may erode developing countries' corporate tax revenues is negotiation of bilateral tax treaties (BTTs). Developing countries are increasingly negotiating BTTs, primarily with OECD countries but also among themselves (Figure 10.3). Tax

---

[10] However, this result does not control for the possibility that FDI to nontreaty countries was rechanneled through treaty countries to avoid repatriation tax.

[11] Investigating the impact of the United Kingdom's and Japan's conversions to territoriality, Feld and others (2013) show that the shift increased Japan's foreign acquisitions by almost 32 percent and the United Kingdom's by almost 4 percent. The greater impact in Japan is due to its higher CIT rate. If the United States were to adopt territoriality while maintaining its current CIT rate, the authors estimate that its foreign acquisitions would rise by 17 percent.

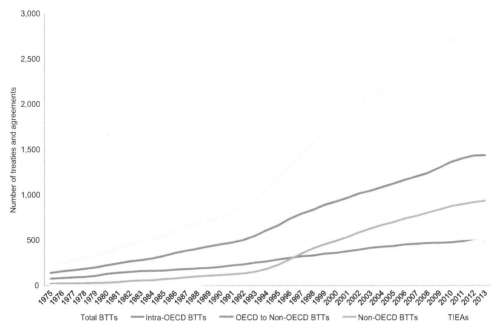

Figure 10.3 Growth of Bilateral Tax Treaties and Tax Information Exchange Agreements

Source: *International Bulletin for Financial Documentation* tax research platform (www.ibfd.org).
Note: BTT = bilateral tax treaty; OECD = Organisation for Economic Co-operation and Development; TIEA = tax information exchange agreement.

TABLE 10.2

Domestic Law versus Treaty Withholding Tax Rates, 2011

Income Level	Dividends	Participating Dividends	Interest	Royalties	Number of Countries
		Domestic Law Withholding Tax Rates			
All Countries	15.9	9.1	15.9	15.7	151
High Income	17.7	8.9	15.3	14.6	45
Non-OECD	6.4	5.7	9.8	9.3	14
Upper Middle Income	13.5	11.9	16.7	16.3	46
Lower Middle Income	13.8	12.6	16.3	17.0	35
Low Income	13.0	10.6	16.2	16.8	25

Income Level	Dividends	Participating Dividends	Interest	Royalties	Average Number of Treaties
		Treaty Withholding Tax Rates			
All Countries	12.5	7.8	9.1	9.0	31
High Income	12.0	6.9	8.1	8.0	60
Non-OECD	7.9	4.9	7.9	8.0	32
Upper Middle Income	11.5	8.0	10.8	10.1	31
Lower Middle Income	12.7	9.8	11.0	10.7	23
Low Income	12.4	9.9	12.3	10.0	8

Source: IBFD database.

treaties usually reallocate taxing rights over foreign investment income from the host country to the home country, chiefly by lowering withholding tax (WHT) rates on cross-border financial distributions such as dividends, interest, and royalties (Table 10.2). Since developing countries are usually net capital importers with little if any outbound investment, they stand to lose significant revenue from the lower WHTs negotiated in tax treaties. For example, it has been estimated that Dutch treaties cost their developing-country treaty counterparts at least €770 million in revenue each year, while U.S. tax treaties cost their developing-country counterparts at least $1.7 billion.[12]

The chief motivation for developing countries to negotiate tax treaties is the belief that BTTs stimulate inward investment. If treaties create enough net new foreign investment to offset their costs in lowered revenue on existing investments and treaty negotiation costs, then the treaties could be worthwhile. However, existing evidence on treaty costs and benefits for developing countries is at best inconclusive.

Tax treaties typically have a number of different provisions that could either stimulate or suppress foreign investment. In addition to lowering WHT rates, BTTs ensure foreign investors of fair tax treatment on par with domestic firms, provide for adjudication in case of disputes, and alleviate double taxation by coordinating definitions of the corporate tax base and ensuring foreign tax credits. Although these factors could stimulate investment, treaties also provide for the bilateral exchange of information between tax authorities, which, if effective, could increase the effective tax rate on inbound investment. BTTs are also quite costly to negotiate, requiring high levels of legal expertise and other expenses, so countries with limited resources are well advised to weigh their costs and benefits carefully.

To date, studies of the impact of BTTs on FDI show mixed results. Four studies using bilateral country-level data for developed countries find either no impact from treaty presence or a negative one (Blonigen and Davies 2004, 2005; Egger and others 2006; Louis and Rousslang 2008). Two studies find some positive impact for certain subsets of countries (Millimet and Kumas 2007; Neumayer 2007), and two studies of data sets including developing countries show a positive impact of treaties on FDI (Di Giovanni 2005; Barthel, Busse, and Neumayer 2009). Studies using firm-level data find that treaties have a positive effect on entry, though not on marginal activity (Davies, Norback, and Tekin-Koru 2009; Egger and Merlo 2011). Use of micro-data alleviates concerns about reverse causality, since BTT negotiation may be driven by past investment activity.

The above studies all represent the influence of tax treaties using a dummy variable, so the positive and negative effects of tax treaties on FDI cannot be distinguished. A study by Blonigen, Oldenski, and Sly (2011) attempts to separate positive and negative treaty effects by interacting the treaty dummy with industry effects, capturing the extent to which firms in a particular sector are likely to experience increased taxes due to information exchange.[13] The authors find that presence of a tax treaty increases average foreign affiliate sales by 45 percent, while the interacted term capturing information exchange reduces them by 28 percent. The authors also find that presence of a BTT roughly doubles the entry rate of new foreign affiliates.

There are as yet no empirical studies of the revenue impact of tax information exchange agreements (TIEAs), which have exploded in popularity since the global economic and financial crisis (Figure 10.3). These stand-alone agreements contain the same information-exchange language included in modern tax treaties but without the other provisions.[14] Blonigen, Oldenski, and Sly's (2011) finding suggests that multinationals do expect TIEAs to increase their tax burden, but whether they effectively enhance revenues is still undocumented. Given developing countries' limited administrative capacity, it is particularly unclear whether TIEAs will help them mobilize revenue from multinational enterprises.

---

[12] McGauran (2013) and estimates of the authors (which take into account dividends and interest only).

[13] The authors use the percentage of industry inputs that are homogeneous goods with readily ascertainable arm's-length prices as a proxy for vulnerability to audit resulting from tax information exchange.

[14] Several theory papers model countries' decisions to engage in information exchange; Keen and Ligthart (2006) summarize this literature and review the political economy of information exchange.

Countries operating worldwide regimes may offer *tax sparing* to their treaty partners, under which multinationals benefiting from host-country tax incentives receive tax credits for the taxes they would have paid in the absence of those incentives. Japan traditionally offered these terms to many of its Asian treaty partners—and China still does—whereas the United States does not. Empirical evidence supports the effectiveness of tax-sparing agreements in stimulating FDI,[15] although this benefit is probably offset by the complications and distortions that tax incentives introduce (along with lower revenues). If the trend toward territoriality among capital exporters continues, tax sparing will likely wane in importance.

Research clearly shows that FDI responds negatively to tax rates (de Mooij and Ederveen 2008). However, reduced WHT rates may not significantly lower the overall tax burden on FDI: although many countries now exempt corporate foreign earnings (that is, dividends from foreign subsidiaries in which the parent holds a minimum ownership stake), most still subject portfolio dividends as well as interest and royalties to domestic income tax, usually allowing a tax credit for foreign income taxes paid (including WHTs). Thus, unless the home-country tax rates are less than those of the host country, treaty reduction of WHTs may only redistribute tax revenues from host to home country without reducing them. Studies of the impact of WHTs on FDI, which do not control for other treaty factors, indicate that they do influence FDI flows as well as financing (Egger and others 2006, 2009; Barrios and others 2012; Huizinga, Laeven, and Nicodeme 2008; Arena and Roper 2010).

Comparison of domestic law and tax treaty WHTs for countries with different income levels shows that the higher cost of reducing WHT rates for developing countries affects BTT provisions (Table 10.2). Richer countries, on average, set higher WHT rates on dividends in their domestic law and reduce them significantly by treaty. They also tend to offer significant tax relief for participating dividends in their domestic law. (A notable exception to this pattern is non-OECD high-income countries, many of which are low-tax conduit jurisdictions or oil-rich countries with very low domestic law WHTs.) By contrast, lower-income countries tend to set more moderate WHT rates on dividends in their domestic laws but do not reduce them as much, either for participating dividends or for tax treaties. Because they are more reliant on CIT revenue (and have weaker PIT revenue) than are wealthier countries, developing countries may be less concerned about double taxation of dividends.

Whereas high-income countries, on average, set WHTs on interest and royalties—which, unlike dividends, are deductible for CIT purposes—at the same level as dividend WHTs, developing countries are likely to set these rates higher than dividend WHTs. This policy likely reflects their concern about the use of interest and royalty payments for transfer pricing, either cross border or into untaxed sectors of the economy (such as free trade zones). Given these countries' generally weaker tax administrations, interest and royalty WHTs perform an important function in protecting their corporate tax bases. However, their rates are often substantially reduced by tax treaty, especially for royalties, indicating a need for caution in treaty negotiation.

Empirical studies show that treaty WHTs are indeed influenced by the income levels of the negotiants, as well as by the size of their economies and the level and asymmetry of FDI flows. Chisik and Davies (2004) and Rixen and Schwarz (2009) show that domestic law rates, which form the starting point for negotiation, relate positively to treaty WHT rates. Bilateral FDI flows are also important: because net capital importers stand to lose from lower WHT rates, treaties between countries with asymmetrical FDI flows usually reduce rates less than treaties between symmetric countries. Similarly, since larger markets are likely to attract more investment,

---

[15] Both Hines (1998) and Azemar and Delios (2007) find that tax-sparing provisions have a positive impact on Japanese outward FDI flows. Similarly, Davies, Norback, and Tekin-Koru (2009), studying Swedish firm-level data, show that inclusion of a tax-sparing agreement in a BTT increases affiliate production, sales, and exports (though not entry).

negotiated rates correlate negatively with the aggregate GDP of each partner, and WHT rates are increasing in the difference between signatories' GDP levels.

The need for caution in treaty negotiation is compounded by the practice of *treaty shopping*, whereby investor countries channel funds to a host country through an entity established in a third country with which the host country has a highly favorable tax treaty. Though a country may negotiate many treaties, the majority of its inward investment often flows through just a small number of treaty partners—usually those with very low WHT rates and an otherwise advantageous tax and regulatory regime. In this manner, a treaty with one country can effectively become a "treaty with the world." *Limitation of benefit* clauses, such as those included in U.S. treaties, deny treaty benefits to entities that lack substantial economic or ownership ties to the treaty jurisdiction. These may offer some protection against this practice; however, most developing countries will have neither the bargaining power to impose such clauses nor the administrative capacity to enforce them.

Formulary Apportionment

The shortcomings of the current international framework for taxing corporate income and increasing public awareness of the cross-border leakage of corporate tax revenue have led to widespread calls for fundamental international corporate tax reform. Therefore, some observers have pressed for an approach in which a multinational enterprise's tax base is established on a unitary basis—that is, consolidated across the entire corporate group—and this base is allocated across jurisdictions by formula, according to varying combinations of the shares of sales, assets, payroll, or employees located in each. In the view of some, formulary apportionment can be especially attractive for developing countries because capacity limitations currently leave them particularly vulnerable to profit shifting.

The primary appeal of unitary taxation is that it dispenses with the need to value intragroup transactions, and so eliminates direct opportunities to shift profits through transfer pricing and other devices. And, by then allocating the base using proxies to substantial activities, it may align tax payments more closely with economic fundamentals.[16] The use of formulary apportionment to allocate the tax base across jurisdictions is long established at the subnational level, and the European Commission has also proposed a Common Consolidated Corporate Tax Base for the European Union. This suggests that formulary apportionment has at least some merit in taxing firms operating across highly integrated economies.[17]

Significant issues arise, however, in relation to the weights used in the formula, which will determine the new allocation of the tax base across jurisdictions.[18] Rough estimates can be made, for instance, of the impact for some countries of reallocating the taxable income of U.S. multinationals using the factors commonly discussed: sales, assets, payroll, and employees (Figure 10.4). These estimates point to large and systematic redistributive effects on tax bases: advanced economies generally gain tax base regardless of the factor used, while conduit countries lose base; developing countries gain base only if head-count employment is heavily weighted.

Precise definitions in determining the weights are critical, however. For instance, whether sales are measured on a destination basis (that is, by residence of the purchaser) or an origin basis

---

[16] See several papers produced by the International Centre for Tax and Development (www.ictd.ac), including, notably, Durst 2013.

[17] In various forms, formulary apportionment is used at the subnational level in Canada, Germany, Japan, Switzerland, and the United States.

[18] A separate set of questions concerns the impact on aggregate revenue; unitary taxation in itself tends to reduce this impact, since consolidation allows greater offset of losses in one part of a corporate group against profits in others (Devereux and Loretz 2008).

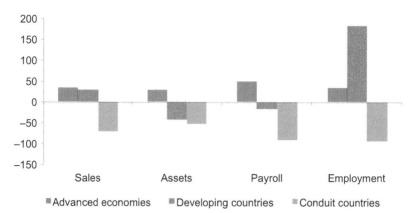

Figure 10.4 Reallocation of Taxable Income of U.S. Multinational Enterprises, Using Alternative Factors *(Percentage change)*

Source: IMF staff calculations based on U.S. Department of Commerce, Bureau of Economic Analysis, data.
Note: The figure shows the weighted averages for three country groups, using current taxable income as weights.

(residence of the seller) matters greatly, as does whether they include or—more in the spirit of the unitary approach, but further from accounting practice—exclude sales to other members of the corporate group. Moreover, valuation and avoidance issues still exist under formulary apportionment, for example, with respect to the valuation of assets.

Also, spillovers will not disappear under formulary apportionment. This method would simply present firms with different real and profit-shifting opportunities compared with the current system: these opportunities would focus on the factors entering the apportionment rule rather than on local profitability and intragroup transactions. For example, if assets are used as the basis for the apportionment, there is an incentive to locate assets in low-tax jurisdictions. This creates evident scope for production inefficiency. The incentive to attract whatever factors are given high weight in the formula could be strong under formulary apportionment, since the revenue gain from attracting such factors is not from a marginal increase in some local tax base—as it is under territoriality—but from being allocated a greater share of the group's overall profit. Tax competition can, for this reason, become even more severe than under territorial taxation.

Practical issues make formulary apportionment less simple than it may seem. A definition of the corporate group is required, for instance, and current forms of income allocation will remain necessary (with all the problems that now entails) if formulary apportionment applies only up to some water's edge. Distinct forms of distortion can also arise, potentially providing artificial incentives to merge or spin off. Whether these difficulties are greater than those under present arrangements is unclear, but they are certainly not trivial.

Whatever its merits in principle, prospects for adoption of international formulary apportionment seem remote. A substantial legal and institutional infrastructure has been built around current arrangements, so that movement toward international formulary apportionment would likely involve considerable disruption.

CONCLUSION

Mobilizing domestic revenue to address inequality concerns in developing countries requires that tax systems be designed to strike the right balance between raising revenue from multinational corporations and creating an attractive investment climate. Managing this trade-off is a challenging task, especially in light of spillovers from international corporate tax design, which appear to be particularly relevant for developing countries.

Substantial international coordination to address spillovers from international taxation has proved difficult to achieve. Some see little if any case for coordination, for political reasons. However, even if all agreed that spillovers cause collective harm, identifying and securing agreement on appropriate measures of coordination is likely to be highly problematic. This set of circumstances largely leaves countries to design their own policies under the given international architecture.

Because of spillovers, developing country governments' ability to effectively raise revenue from multinational corporations depends, apart from their own tax rules, on the international rules adopted by advanced countries. This chapter explores three such issues and the spillovers they create for developing countries: the choice between worldwide and territorial taxation in advanced countries, the design of BTTs concluded with developing countries, and the choice between separate accounting with arm's-length pricing versus unitary taxation with formulary apportionment.

The international trend among major capital-exporting countries to move from worldwide to territorial taxation systems has been found to exacerbate tax competition among capital importers, imposing downward pressure on CIT rates and bases. This tax competition particularly harms developing countries because they are usually capital importers and depend more heavily on CIT revenues than do richer countries.

BTTs provide benefits to investors, such as lower WHT rates, tax base harmonization, certainty about basic fiscal principles, and protection against double taxation. However, the empirical evidence about whether BTTs stimulate investment in developing countries is ambiguous. Moreover, treaty negotiation carries high costs in both government resources and forgone revenue, especially from reduction or elimination of WHTs. For these reasons, developing countries should approach treaty negotiation with extreme caution.

The proposal for formulary apportionment might address some spillovers under current arrangements, including spillovers to developing countries. However, such a system has its own difficulties, involves significant risk of distortion, and may not benefit developing countries. Although prospects for widespread adoption of formulary apportionment are remote, new approaches might nevertheless be introduced incrementally where the current arm's-length approach is particularly problematic.

REFERENCES

Arena, Matteo, and Andrew Roper. 2010. "The Effect of Taxes on Multinational Debt Location." *Journal of Corporate Finance* 16 (5): 637–54.

Azémar, Céline, and Andrew Delios. 2007. "The Tax Sparing Provision Influence: A Credit versus Exempt Investors Analysis." University of Glasgow, Glasgow, Scotland.

Barrios, Salvador, Harry Huizinga, Luc Laeven, and Gaetan Nicodeme. 2012. "International Taxation and Multinational Firm Location Decisions." *Journal of Public Economics* 96 (11–12): 946–58.

Barthel, Fabian, Matthias Busse, and Eric Neumayer. 2009. "The Impact of Double Taxation Treaties on Foreign Direct Investment: Evidence from Large Dyadic Panel Data." *Contemporary Economic Policy* 28 (3): 366–77.

Blonigen, Bruce, and Ronald Davies. 2004. "The Effects of Bilateral Tax Treaties on US FDI Activity." *International Tax and Public Finance* 11 (5): 601–22.

———. 2005. "Do Bilateral Tax Treaties Promote Foreign Direct Investment?" In *Handbook of International Trade*, Volume 2. *Economic and Legal Analyses of Trade Policy and Institutions*, 526–46. Malden, Massachusetts: Blackwell.

Blonigen, Bruce, Lindsay Oldenski, and Nicholas Sly. 2011. "Separating the Opposing Effects of Bilateral Tax Treaties." NBER Working Paper No. 17480, National Bureau of Economic Research, Cambridge, Massachusetts.

Chisik, R., and R. Davies. 2004. "Asymmetric FDI and Tax-Treaty Bargaining: Theory and Evidence." *Journal of Public Economics* 88 (6): 1119–48.

Crivelli, Ernesto, Ruud de Mooij, and Michael Keen. Forthcoming. "Base Erosion, Profit Shifting and Developing Countries." IMF Working Paper.

Davies, Ronald, Pehr-Johan Norback, and Ayca Tekin-Koru. 2009. "The Effect of Tax Treaties on Multinational Firms: New Evidence from Microdata." *The World Economy* 32 (1): 77–110.

de Mooij, Ruud, and Sjef Ederveen. 2003. "Corporate Tax Elasticities: A Reader's Guide to Empirical Findings." *Oxford Review of Economic Policy* 24 (4): 680–97.

Devereux, Michael, and Simon Loretz. 2008. "The Effects of EU Formula Apportionment on Corporate Tax Revenues." *Fiscal Studies* 29 (1): 1–33.

Di Giovanni, Julian. 2005. "What Drives Capital Flows? The Case of Cross-Border M&A Activity and Financial Deepening." *Journal of International Economics* 65 (1): 127–49.

Durst, Michael C. 2013. "Tax Management Transfer Pricing Report." Bureau of National Affairs.

Egger, Peter, Simon Loretz, Michael Pfaffmayr, and Hannes Winner. 2006. "Corporate Taxation and Multinational Activity." CESifo Working Paper No. 1773, Munich.

———. 2009. "Bilateral Effective Tax Rates and Foreign Direct Investment." *International Tax and Public Finance* 16 (6): 822–49.

Egger, Peter, and Valeria Merlo. 2011. "Statutory Corporate Tax Rates and Double-Taxation Treaties as Determinants of Multinational Firm Activity." *FinanzArchiv* 67 (2): 145–70.

———, M. Ruf, and G. Wamser. 2012. "Consequences of the New UK Tax Exemption System: Evidence from Micro-Level Data." CESifo Working Paper No. 3942, Munich.

Feld, L., M. Ruf, U. Scheuering, U. Schreiber, and J. Vogt. 2013. "Effects of Territorial and Worldwide Corporation Tax Systems on Outbound M&As." CESifo Working Paper No. 4455, Munich.

Hasegawa, M., and K. Kiyota. 2013. "The Effect of Moving to a Territorial Tax System on Profit Repatriations: Evidence from Japan." Research Institute of Economy, Trade and Industry Discussion Paper No. 13-E-047, Ministry of Economy, Trade, and Industry, Tokyo.

Hines, James. 1998. "'Tax Sparing' and Direct Investment in Developing Countries." NBER Working Paper No. 6728, National Bureau of Economic Research, Cambridge, Massachusetts.

Huizinga, Harry, Luc Laeven, and Gaetan Nicodeme. 2008. "Capital Structure and International Debt Shifting." *Journal of Financial Economics* 88 (1): 80–118.

International Monetary Fund. 2014. "Spillovers in International Corporate Taxation." Washington.

Keen, Michael, and Jenny Ligthart. 2006. "Information Sharing and International Taxation: A Primer." *International Tax and Public Finance* 13 (1): 81–110.

Lang, Michael, and Jeffrey Owens. 2014. "The Role of Tax Treaties in Facilitating Development and Protecting the Tax Base." WU International Taxation Research Paper No. 2014–03, University of Economics and Business, Vienna.

Lennard, Michael. 2009. "The UN Model Tax Convention as Compared with the OECD Model Tax Convention—Current Points of Difference and Recent Developments." *Asia-Pacific Tax Bulletin* 29 (February): 4–11.

———, and Armando Yaffar. 2012. "An Introduction to the Updated UN Model (2011)." *Bulletin for International Taxation* 66 (November): 590–97.

Louis, Henry, and Don Rousslang. 2008. "Host-Country Governance, Tax Treaties and US Direct Investment Abroad." *International Tax and Public Finance* 15 (3): 256–73.

Matheson, T., V. Perry, and C. Veung. 2013. "Territorial vs. Worldwide Corporate Taxation: Implications for Developing Countries." IMF Working Paper No. 13/205, International Monetary Fund, Washington.

McGauran, Kattrin. 2013. "Should the Netherlands Sign Tax Treaties with Developing Countries?" Stichting Onderzoek Multinationale Ondernemingen (SOMO), Amsterdam.

Millimet, Daniel, and Abdullah Kumas. 2007. "Reassessing the Effects of Bilateral Tax Treaties on US FDI Activity." Unpublished, Southern Methodist University, Dallas, Texas.

Neumayer, Eric. 2007. "Do Double Taxation Treaties Increase Foreign Direct Investment to Developing Countries?" *Journal of Development Studies* 43 (8): 1501–19.

PricewaterhouseCoopers. 2013. "Evolution of Territorial Tax Systems in the OECD." April 2.

Rixen, Thomas, and Peter Schwarz. 2009. "Bargaining over the Avoidance of Double Taxation: Evidence from German Tax Treaties." *FinanzArchiv* 65 (4): 442–71.

Smart, M. 2011. "Repatriation Taxes and Foreign Direct Investment: Evidence from Tax Treaties." Unpublished, University of Toronto.

CHAPTER 11

Taxing Immovable Property: Revenue Potential and Implementation Challenges

JOHN NORREGAARD

INTRODUCTION

Property taxes are widely regarded as an efficient and equitable means of raising revenue, but this revenue potential is largely untapped in many countries.[1] Property taxes generally yield relatively modest revenue, particularly in developing countries and emerging market economies, but there are also large disparities across countries that signal popular opposition as well as technical constraints in their administration—but also the possibility for enhanced utilization. The differences of opinion on property taxation are probably starker than on most other taxes. Although economists tend to strongly favor increased reliance on property taxes owing to their attractive economic properties, there is widespread popular and hence political resistance to their increased use, stemming in part from their transparency and relatively limited scope for tax avoidance and evasion.[2]

Increased use of property taxes could conceivably help ease problems with taxes levied on mobile bases. Much policy debate in recent years has focused on the revenue losses and efficiency costs stemming from levying taxes on highly mobile tax bases in a globalized setting. For example, tax competition, aggressive tax planning, and the use of tax havens to shelter income have eroded tax bases and invited the introduction of a plethora of often costly policy and administrative measures to safeguard national tax bases and powers.[3] Less attention has—until recently—been directed at the alternative policy route of meeting revenue objectives by strengthening "immobile" tax sources such as, in particular, taxes on immovable property.

Property taxation is now the subject of strong and renewed interest around the globe. This new interest clearly manifests itself in numerous reform initiatives recently adopted or considered in different countries (Box 11.1) and in a rich recent literature focusing primarily on developing and transition economies (for example, Bahl, Martinez-Vasquez, and Youngman 2008, 2010).

The author is grateful to Michael Keen, Victoria Perry, Ruud de Mooij, Dora Benedek, Russell Krelove, Mario Mansour, Thornton Matheson, Martin Grote, Selcuk Caner, Peter Mullins, Victor Thuronyi, Riel Franzsen, and Lawrence Walters for constructive comments on an earlier draft. Tarun Narasimhan and Kelsey Moser contributed with highly competent research assistance, including the compilation of the underlying data set on property tax revenue and the regression analyses reported in Box 11.2.

[1] Although a distinction should be made between taxation of business and residential properties in respect of both their economic effects and revenue potential, with potentially very different distributional effects and with business property in many countries being subject to (often much) higher tax levels than residential property.

[2] Cabral and Hoxby (2012) suggest that the salience of the tax can explain differences in the level of property taxes across areas.

[3] These measures include, for example, transfer pricing provisions, a multitude of exchange of information arrangements (such as the European Commission's interest directive and the Global Forum), controlled foreign company legislation, and thin capitalization provisions.

BOX 11.1   Recent Property Tax Reforms and Plans

Africa

Egypt adopted a new real estate law with a rate of 10 percent applied to estimated rental income, effective 2009 but with delayed application until 2012.

Liberia reformed the rate structure of the real property tax, effective 2011, and is contemplating further reform measures to strengthen property rights and the revenue potential of the real property tax.

Namibia starting in 2002 gradually introduced a central government land tax on the value of agricultural land (with a basic rate of 0.75 percent) to supplement the existing municipal tax on urban property, with the primary aim of encouraging efficient use of agricultural land.

Asia and Pacific

Cambodia introduced a new property tax in 2011, based, in principle, on assessed market values of land and buildings. The tax is being piloted in a limited number of urban areas.

China decided to introduce residential property taxation starting in 2011, in part aimed at reining in speculation and strong price appreciation in the property sector, and in part to address the country's widening wealth gap and provide local governments with a significant revenue source. Pilot projects are under way in two cities, Shanghai and Chongqing, to be followed in due course by other cities.

Hong Kong SAR introduced in early 2013 a special property transaction tax (the buyer's stamp duty) at 15 percent of the transaction price, covering nonlocal buyers and all corporate buyers, aimed at curbing speculation and high property price appreciation.

Singapore increased stamp duties on certain home buyers, which, together with a broader set of measures, is aimed at curbing property price increases and preventing an asset price bubble.

Vietnam adopted in June 2010 a new area-based tax on nonagricultural land (excluding housing) and is considering further reform in this arena.

Central Asia

Kyrgyz Republic introduced a property tax for companies and individuals on top of the existing land tax, effective January 1, 2009.

Europe

Croatia introduced in 2013 an ad valorem property tax at a uniform tax rate of 1.5 percent, to replace existing utility fees and the second home tax.

Greece adopted in late 2011 a new square-meter tax at varying specific rates, collected via electricity bills; this tax was later replaced by a succession of new reform measures.

Ireland abolished the residential property tax in 1997 (leaving the local rates on commercial property as the only recurrent property tax). A new market-value-based property tax came into effect in 2013 to replace the annual household charge of €100 put in place on January 1, 2012, as part of a broader fiscal package.

Latvia implemented reform measures in 2010 by introducing a residential property tax on buildings to complement the existing land tax, and additional measures are being considered.

Serbia is considering an in-depth modernization of its property tax system to replace the system of taxes based on property rights in tandem with a planned land privatization reform.

Latin American and the Caribbean

El Salvador is one of the few Latin American countries (together with Paraguay and Costa Rica) at present without an immovable property tax, but is considering introducing one.

Several *Caribbean* countries are contemplating introducing or strengthening property taxes, in part because their highly open economies are exposed to regional tax competition.

The revived interest may have different motivations in different country groupings. For example, the devolution of fiscal powers to strengthen local democracy is a driving force in some transition economies, while in many developing countries the lead motives are revenue mobilization and the provision of incentives for better land use. Property taxation (along with taxation of capital more generally) has also played an important role in the recent discussion of increasing income inequality and its causes in both developed and developing countries—a debate that received strong impetus with the publication of *Capital in the Twenty-First Century* (Piketty 2014).

This chapter provides the case for, and ways to overcome obstacles to, strengthening or (re)introducing property taxes. The next section discusses the nature of property taxes and their yield in different countries, and is followed by a section that presents the economic rationale for increased use of the tax. The obstacles, both political and administrative, facing policymakers when reforming property taxes are then examined. Finally, the contours of an action plan for the implementation of property tax reform are presented.

PROPERTY TAXATION—CONCEPTS AND YIELD

Although generally associated with the notion of recurrent (annual) taxes on immovable property, property taxes in practice encompass a variety of levies on the use, ownership, and transfer of property. Each of these taxes has very different objectives and varying yields. According to standard international tax classifications,[4] property taxes encompass recurrent taxes on immovable property, measured gross of debt, and levied on proprietors or tenants; recurrent taxes on net (of debt) wealth; taxes on estates, inheritances, and gifts; financial and capital transaction taxes on the issue or transfer of securities and checks, or sale of immovable property; and other recurrent or nonrecurrent taxes on property. Recurrent taxes on immovable property are the key focus of this chapter; however, the remainder of this section presents information on the broader concept of property taxes.

How much do immovable property taxes generally yield? Because of deficient data coverage and quality, summarizing the importance of and trends in property taxes on a global scale is not a straightforward exercise, and information on levels and trends is sensitive to the choice of data sources, periods, and regions analyzed. Data are particularly scarce for developing and transition economies—not least with regard to consistent time series—whereas data for Organisation for Economic Co-operation and Development (OECD) countries are comprehensive. The data set compiled for the purposes of this chapter covers generally the period 1990–2012. The data for 2012 are reproduced in Annex Tables 11.1.1 and 11.1.2, while available data for selected OECD and Latin American countries for 2013 are presented in Annex Table 11.1.3. This section presents information about key features of property taxes across countries, focusing first on their composition and then on levels and trends. It also discusses the importance of property taxes for local governments, and the issue of how much an immovable property tax could potentially yield.

The Broader Concept of Property Taxes

Depending on their policy objectives, countries differ substantially with regard to their use of the various property tax sources. Some countries emphasize the provision of a stable and substantial source of revenue for subnational governments through immovable property taxes, while others prioritize raising general revenues (by using mainly capital transfer taxes),[5] or enhancing the

---

[4]The main ones being the IMF's Government Finance Statistics and the OECD's Revenue Statistics.
[5]Capital transfer taxation is a buoyant tax handle in some countries (including in some non-OECD countries, such as South Africa), but is also generally acknowledged to generate potentially large efficiency costs, and may, furthermore, have negative spillover effects on the working of immovable property tax systems, as discussed later in this chapter.

TABLE 11.1

Composition of General Government Property Taxes, Selected OECD Countries, 2012

	New Zealand	Poland	United States	Germany	Greece	Luxembourg
Recurrent Taxes on Immovable Property	98.0	98.5	95.9	49.2	57.0	2.8
Recurrent Taxes on Net Wealth	0.0	0.0	0.0	2.8	11.2	74.9
Estate, Inheritance, and Gift Taxes	0.0	1.5	4.1	17.6	2.5	5.9
Taxes on Financial and Capital Transactions	2.0	0.0	0.0	30.3	20.8	16.4
Other	0.0	0.0	0.0	0.0	8.5	0.0
Total	100.0	100.0	100.0	100.0	100.0	100.0
Total (percent of GDP)	2.1	1.2	2.9	0.9	1.9	2.7

Source: OECD, *Revenue Statistics*.

progressivity and fairness of the overall tax system (by relying on taxes on net wealth or inheritances and gifts).[6] The property tax structure for the few countries presented in Table 11.1 reflects the large variety among OECD countries in the weights attached to these different policy objectives. Countries such as New Zealand, Poland, and the United States (together with Canada, Japan, and the United Kingdom, not shown) levy property taxes mainly on immovable property, whereas Germany uses a variety of sources including inheritance and capital transfer taxes. Greece is also using a variety of sources, but by tapping mainly property and property transfers as tax bases (as do Italy, Korea, and the Netherlands). In contrast, Luxembourg (together with Switzerland and Norway) is among the few remaining OECD countries that continue to raise significant revenue from the taxation of net wealth. Among developing, emerging market, and transition economies, the recurrent immovable property tax is the only property tax source in Azerbaijan, Georgia, Mongolia, and Ukraine. All countries covered by the data set raise revenue from immovable property on a recurrent basis (Annex Tables 11.1.1 and 11.1.2).

According to available data sources, property taxes are far from being a mainstay of the revenue systems in developed, developing, and transition economies. Bahl and Martinez-Vasquez (2008) emphasize that the average revenue raised from property taxes is modest in all three main country groupings, but seemingly with a slightly upward trend since the 1970s (Table 11.2). The data also suggest that reliance on property taxation (similar to most other taxes) is strongly related to economic development, with the average revenue ratio to GDP in OECD countries being triple that of developing countries. These data, however, cover total property tax revenue and thus not only taxes on immovable property.

More recent and detailed data with wider country coverage suggest that, at least for developed countries, total property tax yields have been broadly stable since the mid-1960s. Figure 11.1 shows that for OECD countries—the only group for which accurate and detailed time series exist—the average revenue ratio has been broadly stable at slightly less than 2 percent of GDP

---

[6] Net wealth and inheritance and gift taxes may rest on a sound rationale in their importance for redistribution from the wealthy (particularly if exemption levels are high enough to exclude the life-cycle savings of all but the wealthy), and as a useful backup to personal income taxes. But they may also discourage savings by the people to whom they apply, and— because of the mobility of their bases—taxation may induce people to move wealth abroad. They also require fairly sophisticated tax administrations, and some countries have scaled back or eliminated net wealth taxes in recent years, while others have chosen not to introduce them in the first place (for example, Mexico, the United Kingdom, and the United States have no net wealth taxation).

TABLE 11.2

Levels of and Trends in Property Tax Revenues *(Percent of GDP)*

	1970s	1980s	1990s	2000s
OECD	1.24	1.31	1.44	2.12
(number of countries)	(16)	(18)	(16)	(18)
Developing	0.42	0.36	0.42	0.60
(number of countries)	(20)	(27)	(23)	(29)
Transition	0.34	0.59	0.54	0.68
(number of countries)	(1)	(4)	(20)	(18)
All	0.77	0.73	0.75	1.04
(number of countries)	(37)	(49)	(59)	(65)

Source: Bahl and Martinez-Vazquez (2008).

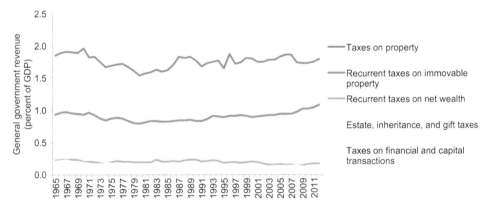

Figure 11.1   Property Taxes in OECD Countries as a Share of GDP, 1965–2012 *(Percent of GDP)*

Source: OECD, *Revenue Statistics.*

since 1965, albeit with a slight dip during the 1970s and recovery thereafter. The figure also shows that recurrent taxes on immovable property, at roughly half the total, constitute by far the largest subcomponent, also with a broadly stable revenue ratio of about 1 percent of GDP during this period (although little is known about the relative importance of the policy changes and property prices underlying this trend). Similar data for transition economies and developing countries are not readily available.

In contrast, when measured as a share of total general government tax revenue, the yields of property taxes in OECD countries have declined. The decline took place during the late 1960s and 1970s, with the share stabilizing thereafter, and is mainly a reflection of the trend in immovable property taxes (Figure 11.2). This decline is the result of buoyant income and consumption taxes and, in particular, social security contributions during this period.[7]

---

[7]This fairly recent decline in reliance on property taxes reflects in some cases a continuation of a much longer and stronger trend: for the United States, for example, Wallis (2001) reports that although the property tax in 1902 constituted 73 percent of all local government revenues, and 68 percent of combined local and state revenues, these shares had dropped to 40 percent and 18 percent, respectively, by 1992.

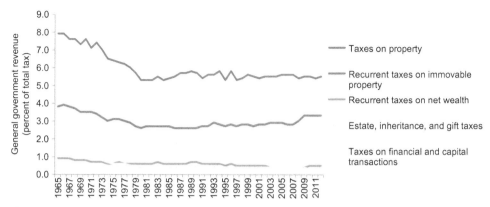

Figure 11.2 Property Taxes in OECD Countries as a Share of Total Tax Revenue, 1965–2012 *(Percent of total tax revenue)*

Source: OECD, *Revenue Statistics.*

Tax Revenue Raised from Recurrent Taxes on Immovable Property

Reliance on immovable property taxation is broadly (albeit imperfectly) correlated with country income levels. The data for 2012 were compiled for OECD and a sample of non-OECD (developing, emerging market, and developed) countries and then classified into high-income and middle- and low-income countries.[8] The average yield from immovable property taxes in high-income countries, 1.06 percent of GDP, is more than three times the average level of 0.32 percent of GDP in middle-income countries[9] (which, in turn, is 0.27 percent for lower-middle-income and 0.36 percent for upper-middle-income countries).[10] Figure 11.3 presents the correlation between immovable property tax revenue as a percentage of GDP and per capita income levels.

As is evident, cross-country variation in immovable property tax collection increases sharply with income level. Among the high-income countries, reliance on immovable property taxes varies from close to nil in Croatia and Luxembourg to heavy reliance (revenue equivalent to 2 percent of GDP or more) on this source in Canada, France, Israel, Japan, New Zealand, the United Kingdom, and the United States. In contrast, more middle-income countries rely only modestly on immovable property taxes, such as El Salvador, Peru, Tunisia, Moldova, and Mongolia. In this group, Bulgaria, Georgia, and South Africa stand out by relying on immovable property taxes to an important extent (close to or greater than 1 percent of GDP). The difference between high-income and middle-income countries with regard to the dispersion of yield ratios is striking and abundantly clear from Figure 11.4.

Although the immovable property tax may not have a central position in the overall revenue systems of most countries, it frequently contributes significantly to the financing of local

---

[8] Using the World Bank's income classification, see Annex Tables 11.1.1 and 11.1.2. Unfortunately, the sample included only one low-income country (Afghanistan).

[9] Albeit with large variations within both groups.

[10] Annex Tables 11.1.1 and 11.1.2 also show that the yield of immovable property taxes, on average, represents 3½ percent of total taxes in high-income countries compared with about 1.4 percent in middle-income countries.

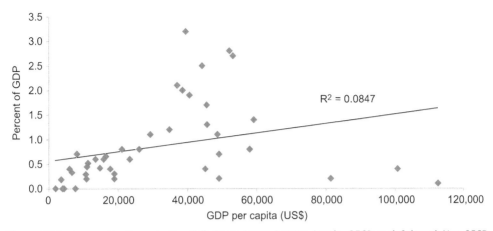

Figure 11.3 Immovable Property Tax Collections across Income Levels, OECD and Selected Non-OECD Countries, 2012

Sources: OECD, *Revenue Statistics,* and IMF, *Government Finance Statistics.*

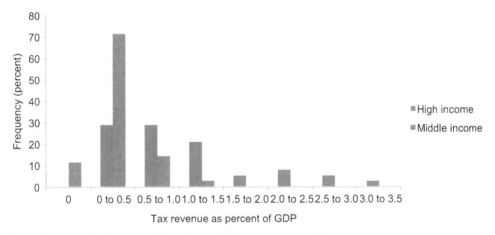

Figure 11.4 Distribution of Yields from Immovable Property Taxes, 2012

Sources: OECD, *Revenue Statistics,* and IMF, *Government Finance Statistics.*

governments. Hence, one defining aspect of property taxes is their assignment predominantly to lower levels of government, indicating that increased reliance on this source of revenue involves important issues of intergovernmental fiscal design. Annex Tables 11.1.1 and 11.1.2 shed some light on this particular role of immovable property taxes for high-income and middle-income countries: the penultimate columns show, for example, that the share of the immovable property tax in total local taxes is 100 percent in Australia and the United Kingdom, with an average of 38.3 percent in high-income countries, and slightly less (35.9 percent) in middle-income countries; and the last column of each of the two tables demonstrates that all of the immovable property tax revenue collected by government accrues solely to local governments in the majority of both high-income and middle-income countries.

Decentralization in itself may provide incentives for increased revenue mobilization from property taxation. Bahl and Martinez-Vazquez (2008) provide empirical evidence of "reverse causation" in the sense that the demand for property taxation is driven by the level of decentralization. This finding supports the notion that increased reliance on property taxation ideally should be part of a clearly formulated strategy for strengthened decentralization (an issue beyond the scope of this chapter). But the fact that developing, emerging market, and transition economies broadly are less decentralized than advanced economies may help explain the fairly modest reliance on property taxes in these countries.[11]

How much could the immovable property tax potentially yield? Absent accurate estimates of tax capacity and tax effort in this particular area,[12] a benchmark for revenue collections—admittedly simplistic—reflects the average revenue ratios of the best performers in each income group.[13] For high-income countries, that would yield a collection potential of about 2.7 percent of GDP when based on the five best performers; the similar target in middle-income countries would be a much lower 0.9 percent of GDP. If these simple benchmarks are applied to the other countries in each group, the potential average revenue increase among this group of 33 high-income countries would be 1.9 percent of GDP, while 30 middle-income countries could raise, on average, an additional 0.7 percent of GDP.[14] This exercise suggests the availability of substantial untapped revenue potential from the property tax in many countries, although the net gain in some countries would be tempered by the need to scale back the use of distortive property transfer taxes (discussed below).

Key Determinants of the Level of Recurrent Property Taxes

Preliminary regression analyses suggest that the level of economic development (as measured by GDP per capita) and urbanization play substantial roles in determining the level of recurrent property taxes across countries and over time (Box 11.2). But countries' openness, as measured by relative trade volumes, as well as their legal origin may also play important roles in determining property tax revenue. It also appears that, as countries develop and grow richer, property-tax-to-GDP ratios tend to increase.

THE CASE FOR PROPERTY TAXATION

Efficiency Considerations in Favor of Property Taxation

Considerations of economic efficiency strongly underpin the case for exploiting property taxes to their fullest potential. Their well-known efficiency-enhancing properties derive mainly from the immobility of the tax base, which, when accompanied by efficient and accurate valuation systems, entails clear benefits in different respects as outlined in this section. Recurrent taxes levied

---

[11] However, a large number of transition economies have implemented decentralization reforms, including devolution of political decision making—a key element of which has been the strengthening of property taxes, typically with some local autonomy to set tax rates (Bahl 2009).

[12] The data deficiencies do not allow empirical estimations of *tax capacity* for property taxes, defined as potential tax collections in individual countries as determined by a variety of structural attributes (Pessino and Fenochietto 2010). *Tax effort* then measures actual collections relative to estimated tax capacity.

[13] Although tax effort is not necessarily lower in middle-income than in high-income countries, the well-established positive relationship between a country's ability to collect taxes and its development level (von Haldenwang and Ivanyna 2010) would support the hypothesis that tax capacity is generally higher in high-income countries. Combining this hypothesis with an assumption that countries—within each income group—with the highest property tax ratios also exhibit the highest tax effort provides the rationale for the simple calculations made here.

[14] Bahl and Martinez-Vazquez (2008) conduct simulation experiments for developing countries based on improved collection and assessment ratios, and also arrive at significant potential for improved property tax collection.

BOX 11.2 What Determines the Level of Property Tax Revenues?

Based on panel data for 64 countries generally covering the period 1990–2010, two regression models are applied to test the significance of variables that could potentially affect the levels of per capita revenues from recurrent property taxes across countries and over time. A priori, the level of development (or wealth) as measured by GDP per capita, the degree of urbanization, openness of economies as measured by trade, corruption levels, and cultural or legal heritage are examples of such potentially important variables. The results reported here are preliminary.

Between-Effects Model. This exercise tests the cross-sectional effects of various variables on recurrent immovable property tax revenues. The main variables of interest are the level of development (or wealth) of the country measured by GDP per capita in U.S. dollars (*GDP PC*), the level of urbanization as measured by the proportion of the population living in urban conglomerations of more than 1 million people (*P*), the openness of the economy measured as imports plus exports as a share of GDP (*O*), and the country's legal heritage as reflected by a variety of dummy variables.

To capture cross-sectional effects (that is, the average effects over time in each country), a between-effects model is applied:

$$ln\left(\bar{R}\right)_i = 0.54ln\left(\overline{GDP\,PC}\right)_i + 0.65ln\left(\bar{P}\right)_i + 0.68ln\left(\bar{O}\right)_i + 1.3AS_i - 16.3 + \mu_i. \tag{11.2.1}$$

In equation (11.2.1), *R* represents recurrent immovable property revenue per capita in country *i* expressed as a function of GDP per capita, urbanization, openness, and a dummy variable (*AS*) with value 1 if the country is Anglo-Saxon in origin.

All explanatory variables shown are significant in the between-effects model with a *p*-value of less than 0.05 (a dummy variable for Commonwealth countries turned out to be insignificant). The implication is that the cross-sectional or by-country effect of development, urbanization, openness to trade, and legal heritage is positive and significant with respect to general government recurrent immovable property revenue per capita, in support of a priori expectations.

Fixed-Effects Model. The between-effects model does not account for variations in any of these variables over time. For this purpose, the fixed-effects model is used. It accounts for the over-time effects on the per capita level of recurrent immovable property taxes for each country:

$$ln\left(R\right)_{it} = 0.29ln\left(GDP\,PC\right)_{it} + 1.7ln\left(P\right)_{it} - 4.6 + \alpha_i + u_{it}. \tag{11.2.2}$$

Because the legal origin dummy variables do not vary over time, they are dropped from the model. It is worth noting that the coefficient of the openness measure, while positive, is not statistically significant in the fixed-effects model, and therefore is not included. The possible implication is that countries that change their policies to institute openness in trade over time do not also experience an increase in immovable property revenues, but countries with generally open trade policies over time experience larger recurrent immovable property revenues overall than do countries with a lesser degree of openness. Thus, the conclusion is that countries tending to be more open also tend to rely more on recurrent immovable property tax revenue, but one policy decision does not necessarily follow the other. This concept might be worth exploring in future research.

Furthermore, the analysis explores whether the supposed effect of development on recurrent immovable property revenue is meaningful. Because increases in recurrent immovable property tax revenue per capita following from increases in GDP per capita may be purely descriptive, it is worth examining whether GDP per capita squared is significant in recurrent immovable property revenue per capita:

$$R_{it} = 1.34e^{-12}\left(GDP\,PC\right)_{it} + 1.09e^{-17}\left(GDP\,PC\right)^2_{it} + 2.3e^{-7} + \alpha_i + u_{it}. \tag{11.2.3}$$

The coefficient of GDP per capita in U.S. dollars is now statistically insignificant, while the coefficient of GDP per capita in U.S. dollars squared is statistically significant with a *p*-value of 0.02, suggesting that the effect on immovable property tax revenue of an increase in development is exponential. This model therefore suggests that an improvement in a country's level of development over time (as measured by GDP per capita) will result in an increase in the share of recurrent immovable property tax revenue as a percentage of GDP.

In summary, the preliminary statistical experiments conducted here suggest that economic development (or wealth) combines with the degree of urbanization in explaining an important part of the variation across countries and over time in property tax revenue per capita; that the degree of openness and legal origin may well constitute important additional explanatory factors; and that as countries develop, the probability is that the property-tax-to-GDP ratio gradually increases. Data limitations do not allow an analysis of the possible impact of corruption.

on land and buildings are generally considered to be more efficient than other types of taxes because their impact on the allocation of resources in the economy is less adverse—they do not affect decisions to supply labor and to invest (including in human capital) and innovate. The immobility argument must be qualified, though, because only land is truly immobile; capital invested in structures (or "improvements"), particularly nonresidential structures, is indeed mobile, and a higher property tax can conceivably drive capital to lower-taxing jurisdictions.[15] In particular, if a newly introduced (or an increase in an existing) property tax is fully capitalized in property prices, present property owners would suffer a one-off loss in wealth, while new property owners would not be affected: once introduced (or increased), property taxes do not affect the rate of return and are therefore considered neutral to investment behavior.[16] This quality follows from the fact that the property tax, to the degree that it is a tax on accumulated wealth, does not alter future behavior.

International evidence suggests that immovable property taxation may be more benign than other tax instruments with respect to its effect on long-term growth. In recent studies, in part based on a broad review of the literature, OECD (2008, 2010) establishes a "tax and growth ranking" that shows that recurrent taxes on immovable property (residential property in particular) are the least distortive tax instrument because they reduce long-term GDP per capita the least, followed by consumption taxes (and other property taxes), personal income taxes, and finally corporate income taxes as the most harmful for growth. Hence, a revenue-neutral growth-oriented tax reform would involve shifting part of the revenue base from income taxes to taxes on consumption and immovable property.

Property taxes are considered good local taxes but raise intergovernmental issues. In addition to its considerable revenue potential, the property tax is generally considered an ideal source for local governments by virtue of being borne mainly by residents, with few spillovers. Also, property values to some degree reflect services supplied by local governments, strengthening the argument that it is reasonable for this base to be tapped to finance local activities. It is also considered to be a stable and predictable revenue source (see discussion in "The Cyclical Resilience of Property Tax Revenues"). Furthermore, the immovable nature of its base, which may be especially appealing at a time when other tax bases become increasingly mobile, renders the property tax particularly useful as a benefit tax at the local level, with rate differentials across jurisdictions providing the price signals required to induce improved resource allocation and hence economic efficiency in a multilevel government setting. Allocative efficiency is, though, conditional on a number of supporting assumptions, including some degree of local autonomy over rate-setting on at least one key tax such as the property tax as well as efficient equalization of tax capacity across jurisdictions.[17] Also, through the political accountability that its transparency induces, the property tax may improve the quality of the overall public finance system. In short, the property tax very well fits the criteria for a good local tax (Bahl 2009).

However, the use of property taxes on business raises particular problems and requires attention. Taxing an important factor of production will—if the benefit tax principle is not strictly

---

[15] However, present low levels of taxation, particularly in developing countries, render this distortion less of a concern (Bahl 2009).

[16] If a property asset yields US$1,000 in untaxed return and the discount rate is 5 percent, its market price in a competitive market will be US$20,000. If a tax of 20 percent is introduced, the (net-of-tax) return will fall to US$800, and the market price to US$16,000 assuming an unchanged discount rate. The (net-of-tax) rate of return will thus remain unchanged at 5 percent for new buyers. This, in principle, also applies to business properties, although the effect may be more complex if other taxes are affected (for example, if the tax is deductible for corporate income tax purposes).

[17] A "pure" benefit tax would, in principle, prevent tax competition among local governments. However, to avoid potentially harmful tax competition among local governments, particularly as the tax applies to business property, a number of countries often set narrow bands for allowable property tax rates.

adhered to—raise costs disproportionately on businesses that use relatively more property as a factor input. To some degree, this imbalance explains why countries apply special relief to agriculture through full or partial exemptions or lower tax rates.

Strengthening property taxation could also help reduce the dependency of local governments on transfers, thereby enhancing economic efficiency by improving local accountability. However, bolstering local finances—for example, through a broadening of property taxation—would not necessarily improve the overall fiscal balance. However, in the majority of intergovernmental fiscal systems that cover vertical fiscal imbalances by transfers to subnational governments, a broad-based strengthening of local property taxation could be compensated for by scaling back transfers (or shared taxes), thereby improving the overall fiscal balance with a simultaneous—and possibly efficiency-enhancing—strengthening of local fiscal autonomy. Conversely, large fiscal transfers to local governments have been found to work as a disincentive for local governments to devote resources to improving revenue raising from property taxation. Reduced fiscal transfers could help address this disincentive.

Property taxes can promote efficient use of land, thereby further stimulating development and growth. By imposing a "tax cost" on land ownership or use that to some degree may be independent from the actual use of the land (particularly if market-price valuation is applied), property taxes provide an important incentive for property owners to secure more efficient use of land and buildings (for example, OECD 2008).[18] This is an important consideration in many countries, and lies behind the use of property taxes to promote development, especially in the agricultural sector, in many developing countries (the agricultural land tax in Namibia being one clear example). If better land use is the driving motive, a pure site (land) tax on land value would offer the best tax design since—being independent from actual land use—such a tax would maximize incentives to apply the land to its optimal use.

Property taxes could conceivably reduce efficiency costs generated by other parts of the tax system. In many developed countries, owner-occupied housing receives favorable tax treatment compared with other forms of investment. This tax bias is generated through exemptions for imputed rent and capital gains combined with full or partial deductibility for interest costs. This treatment may—in addition to adding to mortgage debt levels and housing prices, and perhaps their volatility—distort capital flows and lead to overinvestment in housing (OECD 2008; IMF 2009). In these circumstances, although not first-best, raising taxes on immovable property could conceivably reduce the tax bias in favor of housing and improve efficiency and growth. This could induce an outflow of capital from residential property toward more profitable uses (OECD 2010).

In a similar vein, increased property taxes may help reduce reliance on distorting property transfer taxes.[19] Capital transfer taxes, which are popular in many countries as a buoyant tax handle, may reduce turnover of property and hence distort the allocation of this important component of capital. Furthermore, a key tenet in the optimal tax literature is that taxes of this nature impose efficiency costs through resource misallocations to the extent that their incidence rests on business inputs. For these reasons, some countries (for example, Ireland and Portugal) have considered replacing transfer taxes—totally or partially—with recurrent immovable property taxes, and the IMF's Fiscal Affairs Department tax policy advice has supported a move away from property transaction taxes.

---

[18] Some countries apply the tax to counter speculation in land that lies idle or to induce land development.

[19] Although the use of capital transfer taxes raises broader tax policy issues, such as whether a capital gains tax is in place, the issue of better balancing transfer taxes with recurrent taxes on property is pertinent in many countries, and therefore mentioned here as an important policy objective. The additional problems for valuation of property that may be induced by the use of property transfer taxes are discussed in the section titled "Issues of Policy Design and Implementation."

Property taxes may also potentially be effective in countering speculative housing price booms and house price volatility. Examples of countries using property taxation (including transaction taxes) in this respect include China and Singapore (Box 11.1). However, whether property taxes represent an efficient tool in this regard remains on open empirical question. To the extent that property taxes are predominantly capitalized in housing prices (driven by the net present value of future taxes), property taxes may at best have a one-off effect on price levels (and not on sustained house price inflation), and countercyclical use of property taxes to reduce house price volatility may not be efficient (a notion further complicated by its use mainly as a local government revenue source).[20] It also appears that factors other than tax were dominant in driving the precrisis house price bubble and subsequent bust, although tax biases may have accentuated the crisis (Keen, Klemm, and Perry 2010); and nontax policy instruments such as limits on loan-to-value and debt-to-income ratios may in some cases be more effective than tax measures.[21]

Property taxation in small and highly open economies, particularly those exposed to intensive tax competition, could be considered a means of rendering tax systems more resilient to external shocks. This resilience would come from exploiting an immobile tax base in a period of globalization.[22]

Finally, but not exclusively related to economic efficiency, a particular advantage of higher reliance on taxes on immovable property is the absence of any need to improve international tax coordination as a prerequisite for their efficient use.

Equity Considerations: Are Property Taxes Fair?

Perhaps somewhat surprisingly for a tax as ancient as the property tax, its implications for fairness is a long-standing and contentious issue—and will probably remain so.[23] The equity case for broader use of property taxes rests on the notion that they are generally assumed to be progressive—an assumption that is still not underpinned by a clear consensus.[24] The so-called new view—now about 40 years old—that property taxes are borne mainly by owners of capital and landowners appears to have some support. Studies based on this view find generally that property taxes are progressive because land and capital are owned predominantly by higher-income individuals.[25] The different views on the issue are summarized in Box 11.3.

Fairly limited work has been done to formally model property tax incidence under conditions compatible with those in developing and transition economies. It has been argued that key assumptions of the model underlying the new view, such as full capital mobility and a fixed supply of land, typically are not met in these countries, and that the predictions of the new view therefore do not hold. Based on simulations with a computable general equilibrium model

---

[20] Property transfer taxes could conceivably help dampen price volatility, but the effect is ambiguous and could be counterproductive when lower transaction volumes lead to higher volatility.

[21] The use of tax and other policy measures in controlling house price boom-busts are discussed in Rabanal and others 2011, which provides insights into the pros and cons as well as the implementation challenges of various policy tools—tax and nontax—that can be used to contain the damage to the financial system and the economy from real estate boom-bust episodes.

[22] There is, for example, renewed interest in strengthening property taxation in a number of countries in the Caribbean region as well as in the Baltic countries.

[23] A brief account of historical property tax events in selected countries, including the United Kingdom and the United States, is provided by Youngman (2008), who refers to the property tax revolts in the United Kingdom in 1990 (introduction, and subsequent repeal, of the poll tax) and in the United States in 1978 (California's Proposition 13), when unpopular value-based taxes were replaced with politically more palatable alternatives.

[24] The incidence in developing and transition economies may be even less clear than in developed countries because capital markets are less developed and ownership rights are often ill defined.

[25] The different incidence views are discussed by Sennoga, Sjoquist, and Wallace (2008), who also address the limitations to the new view and the benefit view when applied to developing and transition economies.

BOX 11.3 Views on the Incidence of Property Taxation

According to the *old (or traditional) view*, the property tax combines a tax on highly mobile capital and immobile land, with the tax on capital being shifted fully to renters, consumers, and labor, while the tax on land is borne by landowners. Incidence studies based on this view, which put the emphasis on the shifting of the tax, generally find that the property tax is regressive.

In contrast, the *new view* (attributed to Mieszkowski [1972]) assumes that capital is in fixed supply, but perfectly mobile across sectors and geography. The tax on capital is seen as a combination of a basic (or average) tax rate applied to all capital (which capital owners cannot escape since it is levied on a fixed supply of capital) plus a local differential that varies across jurisdictions—thus working as an incentive for capital to reallocate among jurisdictions until net after-tax rates of return are equalized. Incidence studies adopting this view find that the property tax is progressive (or at least not as regressive as under the old view) because land and capital are owned by higher-income individuals.

The *benefit view* provides an alternative, but not necessarily mutually exclusive, view of property tax incidence, and argues that the property tax is a benefit tax equal to the benefits received from the public services funded by the tax. The property tax thus acts as a price for local public goods, and individuals will choose the locations that offer services best in line with their preferences (the so-called Tiebout effect). By being, in essence, a user charge for local public services, the property tax is inherently fair based on the benefit principle. It has also been argued that property values capitalize the benefits provided, and hence that a tax on values represents a fair burden-sharing arrangement. By seeing the tax as a price for services received, the benefit view has the important implication that immovable property taxes are efficient taxes that do not interfere with the savings, investment, and labor supply decisions of individuals and companies.

It follows from the discussion that the relevance of each of these views may differ across countries depending on, among other factors, the degree to which property taxes actually reflect benefits received or are perceived to do so.

tailored to more accurately represent the conditions in developing and transition economies, Sennoga, Sjoquist, and Wallace (2008) find that the burden of property taxes imposed on capital and land is borne by the owners of capital and land and is not significantly influenced by the assumptions regarding the mobility of capital. Hence, the property tax is progressive, with the burden borne predominantly by middle- and high-income earners. Since wealth and the earnings of high-income individuals can be hard to tax in these countries, a property tax—appropriately administered—could address vertical equity concerns in these countries.

Adoption of a specific incidence view is needed to interpret distributional data. Data on the distribution of the property tax burden are rare, but Table 11.3 provides an example for Denmark that demonstrates some of the problems involved. The table provides a decile distribution of taxpayers with per capita averages of gross income, disposable income, and property taxes within deciles—as well as share of ownership (that is, the share of individuals in each income bracket who own immovable property) and effective tax rates. The data reflect actual tax liabilities from tax returns, that is, amounts to be paid by property owners within each decile. But the legal obligation to pay the tax does not necessarily provide an accurate reflection of its final, effective incidence, in the same manner as the obligation on traders to pay the value-added tax is not an accurate reflection of who ultimately carries the burden of the value-added tax. When observed through the prism of the new view, the property tax in Denmark appears regressive for the first two deciles— presumably because the populations in these deciles typically are quite heterogeneous[26]— and becomes progressive from the third decile up. This result occurs in part because property

---

[26]These deciles would include, for example, pensioners with low income but valuable property and the newly self-employed with low income. Some countries address these particular problems by allowing property tax deferrals until ownership of a property changes.

TABLE 11.3

Denmark: Distribution of Property Taxes as a Share of Income *(Danish kroner, except as noted)*								
	Income	Class	Gross Income per Taxpayer	Average Disposable Income	Income tax	Property Taxes	Share of Ownership	Effective Tax Rate (percentage of gross income)	Effective Tax Rate (percentage of disposable income)
1	0	113,428	89,565	69,048	20,517	1,626.30	24.1	1.82	2.36
2	113,429	138,115	164,905	126,443	38,462	1,442.20	35.6	0.87	1.14
3	138,116	158,776	197,779	148,168	49,611	1,297.30	35.6	0.66	0.88
4	158,777	180,075	232,593	169,020	63,572	1,653.00	50.5	0.71	0.98
5	180,076	201,050	268,323	190,154	78,169	2,096.50	63.6	0.78	1.10
6	201,051	223,192	303,807	211,524	92,283	2,481.00	72.2	0.82	1.17
7	223,193	248,191	342,851	234,962	107,889	3,012.50	78.6	0.88	1.28
8	248,192	280,693	390,598	263,325	127,273	3,600.30	83.1	0.92	1.37
9	280,694	332,653	460,238	303,837	156,401	4,619.80	88.1	1.00	1.52
10	332,654	+	740,659	457,278	283,380	8,206.90	93.0	1.11	1.79
Average			319,132	217,376	101,756	3,003.60	62.5	0.94	1.38

Source: Ministry for Economic Affairs and the Interior, Denmark.

ownership, as shown in the table, increases strongly over the deciles; however, application of the new view assumes that renters are not carrying any of the property tax burden, which may not be an accurate assumption.

Finally, it is generally assumed that the use of market values, by securing a minimum of variation in effective tax rates across property owners, will maximize fairness of the property tax, particularly to the extent that market values broadly reflect the capitalized benefits provided by local services that are financed by the tax. In contrast, alternative approaches, such as area-based taxation (for example, specific square meter taxes) unrelated to actual property values (or related only imperfectly so), typically entail variations in effective tax rates across properties, which may violate equity considerations.

The Cyclical Resilience of Property Tax Revenues

Although the property tax may be an efficient and fair tax, high cyclical volatility could render it less appropriate as a local tax. The deep 2008–10 recession and the high growth period that preceded it provide a unique background for studies of the cyclical sensitivity of the property tax—especially because of the crucial role of the housing market in that recession. Figure 11.1 for OECD countries—displaying basically a flat revenue ratio during the boom years leading into the recession—appears to indicate a low cyclical sensitivity of property taxation. This low tax buoyancy of immovable property during a period of very rapid asset price appreciation from the early to mid-2000s seems at first surprising.

However, recent empirical research for the United States has cast more light on the issue of the cyclical volatility of property taxes (in particular, Lutz, Molloy, and Shan 2010; Lutz 2008). As in many other countries, state and local government revenues in the United States dropped steeply following the most severe housing market contraction since the Great Depression; for example, state and local tax revenues fell by almost 5.5 percent in 2009—only the second year (along with 2002) since the Great Depression that state and local government tax revenues had fallen in nominal terms. However, the fall was driven by sharp declines in receipts from the individual income tax and the sales tax (of 17 percent and 7.5 percent, respectively) while, in sharp contrast, property tax revenues held up remarkably well, growing more than 5 percent in both 2008 and 2009, thereby serving as a significant buffer for the decline in other tax sources

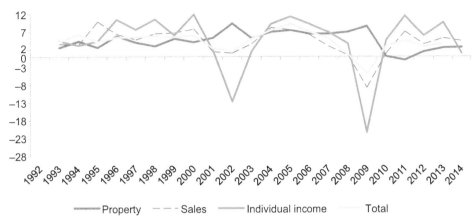

Figure 11.5   State and Local Tax Revenues, United States, 1993–2014 *(Percent change)*

Sources: Property, sales, individual income tax data from US Census Bureau, *Quarterly Summary of State and Local Tax Revenue*; total tax revenues from OECD, *Revenue Statistics*.

(Figure 11.5), although property tax revenue stopped growing in subsequent years. Figure 11.5 also illustrates that property taxes generally tend to be less volatile than other tax sources—long seen as one of the primary virtues of the property tax.[27]

The resilience of property tax revenue is, according to recent research, in part attributable to two factors. Using both time-series data and micro-level panel data from individual governments, Lutz (2008) estimates that the elasticity of property tax revenue with respect to home prices equals 0.4, indicating that policymakers tend to offset as much as 60 percent of house price changes by moving the effective tax rate in the opposite direction of the house price change (Figure 11.6). In other words, during the house price boom, local governments tended to spend part of the "rent" on popular rate reductions, while during the recession budgetary pressures forced them to raise property tax rates (possibly reflecting the relative ease with which base and rates can be adjusted as compared with other taxes). Furthermore, house price changes have an effect on property taxes only after a lag of about three years, reflecting three basic features of the tax: (1) assessments take place in a backward-looking manner because the current year's taxes are based on the assessed property value in the previous year; (2) assessed values often lag market values, in some cases by design or legal mandate and, in others, because of poor administration (which may be intentional, particularly in jurisdictions that elect their assessor); and (3) most states have a cap or other limit on increases in revenues or taxable assessments (or even in rates). These factors would, during periods of rapid house price growth, prevent revenues from growing at the same pace as market values, and could create a stock of untaxed appreciation.

---

[27]This is particularly important for local governments, which are less able to absorb revenue shocks than are central governments with more revenue sources at their disposal. However, it also suggests that the property tax may be less powerful as an automatic stabilizer than other taxes illustrated here.

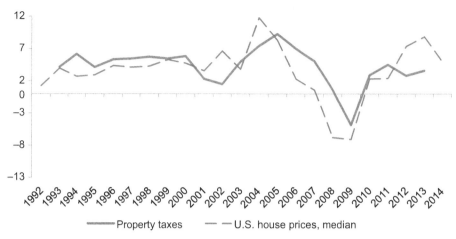

Figure 11.6 Property Tax Revenues and House Values, United States, 1993–2014 *(Percent change)*

Source: U.S. Census Bureau, *Quarterly Summary of State and Local Tax Revenue.*

ISSUES OF POLICY DESIGN AND IMPLEMENTATION

Several policy aspects and administrative challenges explain the dismal revenue productivity of immovable property taxes in many countries. Two policy variables and three administrative variables determine the yield of any property tax, as reflected in the basic revenue equation, which also provides a good structure for the ensuing discussion:

$$R = B \times t \times C \times V \times E. \tag{11.1}$$

The equation expresses collected revenue (R) as the product of the legally defined tax base at actual prices (B), the average tax rate (t), the ratio of properties actually covered in the tax roll relative to all properties (C), the ratio of assessed to actual value of property in the roll (V), and the level of enforcement measured as actual collections as a share of liabilities or invoices (E). In an ideal world, C, V, and E would each take on the value of 1 but very rarely (if ever) do so in practice. These variables are discussed in turn in what follows.

Policy and Administrative Issues

Property Tax Base

There are numerous approaches to defining and measuring the property tax base (B), which can be classified broadly along three basic dimensions. The first dimension is the approach to *assigning value* to property. These approaches can be grouped into (1) market-price-based methods, encompassing valuation based on rental values or capital (market) values, and (2) area-based methods (see Box 11.4 for brief definitions; the practical issues are discussed under valuation (V) below). A second key dimension relates to the *property components* included in the base (land only, buildings [or other improvements] only, or combinations of the two). The final key distinction relates to the *use of the property*, since different uses can be treated

BOX 11.4 Property Valuation Systems[1]

Rental value systems are used in many countries (particularly former British colonies) and define the tax base as the rent that can reasonably be expected in a fair market transaction. These systems are used in countries as diverse as India, Nigeria, Malaysia, and Trinidad. Although simple in concept, rental systems have serious practical challenges: a scarcity of data on actual rent payments makes base assessment difficult; some properties are rarely in the rental market (for example, owner-occupied housing, industrial property, vacant land); and some countries operate rent control systems. Estimates of the base may rely on rent surveys for different areas, often combined with expert judgment; estimated capital values of the property (from sales data or based on construction costs), converted to rental equivalent; or estimated (net) profit for the property. Rental values typically reflect the present use of the property, and may, therefore, not reflect the best alternative use of the property—with the lack of incentives that entails.

Capital value systems define the base as the market value of the property (land and improvements or structures) in an open market. This is the system used in most Organisation for Economic Co-operation and Development and Latin American countries, and there seems to be a shift toward this method. Many jurisdictions value land and buildings separately (Botswana, some Brazilian cities), while others base the assessment on the total value of the property (Cyprus, South Africa). Also conceptually straightforward, this system avoids some of the problems of the rental value system (for example, the value of vacant land, reflecting its value in best alternative use), and it may be the most equitable method—particularly to the extent that property value reflects the benefits of public investment. Key problems include, again, scarcity of data on market transactions and underdeclaration of such prices (for example, due to high property transfer taxes as discussed in the "Property Valuation" section in the main text). Valuations may be provided by expert assessors, who are often in short supply, and administrative costs can be high.

Land (or site) value systems tax the market value of land alone. This system is used in a variety of countries (Australia, Denmark, Estonia, Jamaica, Kenya, and New Zealand). Apart from raising revenue, it could be argued that the land value tax provides the strongest incentive for the most efficient use of land, although, because of the smaller base, the nominal tax rate must be higher to yield a given amount of revenue. This tax also entails lower administrative costs than a capital value tax. The system suffers from the same type of administrative shortcomings as the capital value tax, in addition to the complexities of assessing just the land in highly urbanized areas.

Area-based systems comprise the simplest methods. Such systems tax each parcel at a specific rate per unit area of land and per unit area of structures. It is used in many central and eastern European countries and a number of developing countries (such as, in different forms, in Nigeria and Vietnam). It is a simple, transparent, and fairly easily administered system, which allows imposition even in countries or localities with no—or only an embryonic—property market. The system ranges from a "pure" form based only on physical area, to hybrid forms that aim to better proxy capital value by also using other inputs such as zoning and indicators of quality (as used in a variety of forms in, for example, Chile, Indonesia, Poland, and Serbia), which are more complicated and often involve a significant amount of judgment. Other disadvantages include that it is generally not considered a fair tax, owing to potentially sharp differences in effective tax rates, and its buoyancy may be limited since it may not trace market price developments very well.

---

[1] A good discussion of valuation methods is provided in Bahl 2009.

differently for tax purposes, such as residential versus business property, or urban versus agricultural land.[28] The specific property base definition adopted depends in part on the objective of the tax (such as financing local governments, securing better use of land, or financing urban development), and in part on the depth of local property markets and administrative capacity in individual countries.

---

[28] Tax on agricultural land may in some cases be a substitute for agricultural income tax.

TABLE 11.4

Region	Number of Countries	Land Value	Capital Improved Value	Land and Improvements	Improvement Only	Annual Rental Value	Area	Flat Rate
Africa	25	1	8	3	4	7	11	6
Caribbean	13	4	4	2	0	8	5	0
Asia	24	2	6	2	0	11	11	0
Oceania	7	6	2	0	0	4	0	0
Western Europe	13	0	9	0	0	6	0	0
Eastern Europe	20	1	6	0	0	0	15	0
Central and South America	16	2	14	1	0	1	0	0
North America	3	0	3	0	0	0	0	0
Total	121	16	52	8	4	37	42	6

Source: Bell and Bowman (2011).

Although all property ideally should be subject to property taxation, a particularly urgent issue in many developing countries is the need to better capture the rapidly growing base of urban property to finance infrastructure. According to United Nations projections, Africa's urban population will more than double between 2000 and 2030, creating an urgent need for local tax structures that can grow in tandem with the need for urban infrastructure (AfDB, OECD, and UNDP 2010). Property taxes are considered to be a natural candidate since they are progressive, administratively feasible, and scale up automatically with urban expansion. Similarly, global demographic forecasts indicate that the world's urban population will double from 3 billion in 2000 to 6 billion in 2050, with nearly all growth occurring in developing countries. Most affected cities will see their populations grow several-fold over the next few decades, and will need to plan for future expansion and identify financing for needed arterial road networks and other basic infrastructure. One proposed strategy that may work well in developing countries with some large (and growing) cities but that are still heavily agrarian may be to introduce a combination of a capital value system for urban locales and an area-based system for more rural districts (Bahl 2009, 12).

The diversity across regions in the methods used for measurement of the property tax base is evident from Table 11.4. The table illustrates the relatively widespread use of area-based approaches among African, Asian, and transition economies.

Regardless of the method adopted to measure it, the property tax base is often porous, corroded by multiple exemptions and varieties of relief. The list of exemptions and special treatment is often long and frequently costly in revenue forgone. Typical exemptions include government property (roads, railroads, and pipelines, and central government property in local jurisdictions, for example) as well as merit uses such as schools and religious establishments. Many countries also use the property tax for broader social policy purposes, and—in addition to the use of basic property tax thresholds to protect the poor—a particularly costly (and regressive) exemption is that provided for owner-occupied housing in many countries.[29]

Property tax incentives for businesses have also escalated in some countries.[30] Some countries provide special relief depending on family structure. In Serbia, for example, owner-occupiers receive a 40 percent tax reduction, increased by 10 percentage points for each

---

[29] Bahl (2009, 5) refers, for example, to a study of Punjab province in Pakistan where bringing owner-occupied housing fully into the tax net would triple the level of provincial property tax revenues.

[30] Kenyon, Langley, and Paquin (2012) provide a good account of the use of property tax incentives for business in the United States, with a critical assessment of their effectiveness in promoting economic development.

member of the household up to a ceiling of 70 percent—potentially, contrary to intentions, rendering the tax regressive. In Uganda, in addition to the standard exemptions for government-owned property as well as property used for religious purposes, civil servants (police, military), unemployed persons, peasants, and people living in poverty unable to earn the minimum income are also exempt (Ecorys 2010). Many countries also provide tax preferences (including tax deferrals) to pensioners. Agriculture is another segment that generally receives very favorable property tax treatment, either by outright exemption (partly or fully, such as in Nicaragua, Guinea, and Tunisia [Bird and Slack 2005]) or by special treatment leading to a negligible liability (such as in Serbia). Perhaps an exception with regard to taxation of agricultural land is Namibia, where the central government land tax is designed mainly to encourage better land use. And few countries, if any, undertake systematic tax expenditure budgeting pertaining to the property tax to determine the true budgetary costs of the tax relief offered. The bottom line is that taxes frequently are paid on a base that bears little resemblance to the true level of property values, and yields could be substantially enhanced by scaling back excessive exemptions and relief.[31]

Tax Rate

Similarly, the tax rate—(t) from equation (11.1)—can be structured in different ways. If capital value is the base, a flat or progressive rate is normally applied, although, as noted above, progressivity in some countries is secured through a basic property deduction. A flat rate is typically applied if the base is rental value; under area-based taxes the norm is a specific flat rate plus a given amount per unit of area (square meter or hectare of land, buildings—or both, such as in Vietnam). Tax rate levels and structures, including for different types of properties, also vary substantially across countries (and across jurisdictions within countries). In Namibia the central government applies tax on agricultural land at a basic rate of 0.75 percent of estimated market value while urban municipalities apply very modest rates to local property.[32] Serbia uses a progressive rate structure, set by local governments, starting at 0.4 percent up to a maximum of 3 percent, while Cambodia is considering a uniform 0.1 percent tax. In the Kyrgyz Republic, a dual rate system (0.35 and 1.0 percent) is applied depending on the type of property. In many countries the authority to set rates is assigned to local governments, often within a fairly narrow band or below a ceiling set by law. In Uganda, for example, rates are determined by municipalities but with a maximum of 2 percent of rateable value. In other countries rates are set by a higher level government.

A simple, transparent, and hence fairly uniform rate structure has critical advantages. It minimizes administrative complexity and the risk of tax avoidance or evasion through misclassification of properties. It also minimizes the risk of misallocation of capital because different types of capital are not taxed at different tax rates. The use of reduced tax rates for residential properties may be politically convenient, but could lead to overinvestment in this type of property, and may reduce the accountability of local elected officials.[33] Reduced rates obviously also will have a detrimental impact on the revenue yield. If the main reason for low rates is to protect the poor, a better solution would be to use a basic threshold for the taxation of residential property. In practice, many countries tend to tax business property at higher rates (sometimes at much higher rates) than residential and agricultural property.

---

[31] Bahl 2009 estimates the revenue costs of exempting government property as equivalent to about 12 percent of collections in India's 36 largest cities. Many countries, such as Kenya and Canada, charge a payment in lieu of property taxes on government property and nonprofit uses of property (Bahl 2009).

[32] In Windhoek, for example, the rates are 0.0734 percent of the site value, and 0.0379 percent of the house (improvement) value.

[33] Particularly in developing countries, where the place of residence is often the same as the place of business, levying different rates can be administratively difficult.

Coverage Ratio

Any viable property tax administration must ensure that almost all land and improvements are included in the tax register and that efficient methods are in place to keep it up to date—(C) from equation (11.1). A significant administrative problem, particularly in developing and transition economies, is the low ratio of parcels or properties in the tax register. In Kenyan municipalities, for example, coverage ranges between 30 and 70 percent, and in Chile a large share of new construction has not been included (Bahl 2009). In Serbia, according to some estimates, between 40 and 50 percent of real estate was previously not in the property register, although the situation seemed to improve significantly following the devolution of administration of the property tax to local governments in 2007 (USAID 2010). Possible reasons for these past administrative weaknesses in Serbia include lack of effective office and field control, lack of enforcement of sanctions for not filing, and the fact that a large number of properties fell below the threshold for the property tax. In contrast, in Latvia according to one measure, more than 98 percent of properties are included in the tax register, although this measure could be somewhat distorted because of the privatization process. Apart from the obvious direct revenue consequences, low coverage may have a significant indirect impact by adversely affecting the perception of the tax's fairness and thereby property tax compliance.[34]

Property Valuation

Valuation is a major administrative problem, particularly, but not exclusively, in many developing countries and transition economies—(V) in equation (11.1). A number of reasons cause this problem: a lack of trained valuators,[35] generally weak administrative capabilities, and a "thin" or underdeveloped property tax market that generates insufficient transactions to provide a continuous flow of input to the valuation system (often combined with a lack of reliable data on the sales values of properties that are exchanged).

A key issue in this regard is the relative merits of decentralized versus central valuation systems.[36] Although there appears to be broad consensus that the legal framework for property taxation should be uniform and centrally determined, arguments both for and against making the actual valuation a central or local task can be made. A frequent argument emphasizes the usefulness of local knowledge about the nature of property markets and sales conditions, as well as the need to provide a strong incentive for local administrations to keep coverage and values up to date. In many countries (such as Vietnam), local councils are charged with keeping the valuation rolls. In several Latin American countries where the property tax is a local revenue source (Guatemala and Mexico, for instance) these administrative responsibilities have gradually shifted to local governments, and in Brazil responsibility for property tax administration rests solely with local governments (Bahl 2009). Conversely, a lack of qualified local assessors and the tendency of local valuation officers to be subject to political pressures to delay or minimize updates would favor a centralized valuation system based on a critical mass of technical expertise (such as those used in, for example, Denmark, Latvia, Lithuania, and Uruguay). In many countries local and central governments share the responsibility, and in others a payment system for valuation services across levels of government is used. Although there is no single "correct" way of organizing the valuation function, it would seem that the case for local responsibility is strongest where the property tax is an important local revenue source.

---

[34] Comprehensive and accurate registration of property, and thereby close to complete coverage of the property tax base, is a cornerstone of successful property tax reform, and is, in turn, crucially dependent on the sharing of data between key players (cadastral agency, property registry, courts, tax authorities, geodetic institutes, and others).

[35] Often because of lack of appropriate training programs or a significant gap in compensation between the public and private sectors.

[36] Or more generally, the system applied for the upkeep of the cadastre, including coverage, titling, and valuation.

These valuation problems frequently lead to value assessments for tax purposes that are much lower than market values.[37] Low assessment ratios (assessed tax base relative to actual market value) seem to be typical under any of the standard valuation methods presented in Box 11.4. Bahl (2009) reports dramatic underassessments in many developing countries, with assessment ratios in the range of 25–50 percent in selected Indian cities (rental value), and a wider range of 10–90 percent in selected Latin American cities (market value). Serbia provides another striking example: for taxpayers keeping business books, the tax base is the book value of the property, which generally is well below market value; an analysis conducted in one municipality shows that the book value for 83 percent of the properties was less than 50 percent of the market value (and for 31 percent of properties it was less than 10 percent of market value) (USAID 2010). Valuation problems are, however, not limited to developing and transition economies, but can also pose significant challenges in developed countries, such as Germany,[38] although the valuation mechanisms in place in OECD countries generally are fairly advanced. Once a valuation system is in place, updating it on a regular basis is essential: if valuation updates fall behind, it may be hard politically to "catch up" as demonstrated by the German example.

The use of property transfer taxes may exacerbate other valuation problems, with adverse implications that go beyond their efficiency costs (see "Efficiency Considerations in Favor of Property Taxation"). Transfer taxes, often in the form of stamp duties, are popular in many (including developing) countries, for a variety of reasons.[39] But significant transaction taxes on property may lead to serious tax evasion by providing a strong incentive for collusion between buyers and sellers to undervalue properties when they are sold, thereby also automatically undermining property transactions as a key source of information on up-to-date market values for the cadastre. In addition, by reducing the overall volume of property transactions, they reinforce valuation problems by thinning the market.[40]

High transaction costs may also adversely affect economic performance by discouraging labor mobility. Significant transaction taxes are found in a number of countries, such as the 15 percent real estate transaction taxes in Senegal, the 15 percent Droits d'Enregistrement in the Central African Republic, and the transfer duty rates of 8 percent for individuals with high-value property and 12 percent for companies in Namibia. A stamp duty has long been in place in the United Kingdom, now with a maximum rate of 7 percent. The drawbacks referred to above explain why some countries have considered reducing transaction taxes as an integral component of property tax reform. Transfer taxes could, alternatively, be replaced by capital gains taxes on property, the inherent self-checking mechanism of which (with opposite interests for buyers and sellers in declaring high sales values) could reduce or eliminate the incentive for underdeclaration.

[37] Which in some countries is adjusted for through increases in tax rates—a second-best solution in view of the continuous changes in relative property values.

[38] In a June 2010 judgment, Germany's Federal Fiscal Court ruled that the continued failure to conduct a general revaluation of real property violated the equality principle of the German constitution, and that a reassessment of property values was necessary. The problem was that the German property valuation system had relied on assessments dating back to 1964 for states in the former West Germany and to 1935 for states in the former East Germany. It was up to the German municipalities to implement the decision (*Tax Notes International* 2010).

[39] The transfer tax is an easy tax handle, with high compliance due to property buyers' desire to acquire proper legal ownership documents; revenues collected can be very high with low administrative costs, in part because there are many fewer taxpayers than under a recurrent property tax; and the tax may be progressive.

[40] Another means of avoiding a property transaction tax is to register property in closed corporations such that, in the case of transfers, the object of the sale may not be the property itself, but the shares in the company (or interest in a trust) that holds the property. This would also deprive the cadastre of important market price information.

Property Tax Enforcement

Enforcement of the property tax is frequently very weak resulting in modest collection ratios—(E) in equation (11.1). Dismal collection ratios (actual collections as a percentage of liability or invoices) are found in a multitude of countries (for example, 15 percent in FYR Macedonia, 50 percent in the Philippines, 60 percent in Kenya, and 70 percent in Croatia). In Latin America the collection ratios are generally 75 percent or above (Bahl 2009). Low collection ratios may result from the tax being collected by local authorities who may have a political interest in not pursuing effective collections, and from minimal expected penalties. Furthermore, if transfers from the center cover a large portion of local expenditures, adverse incentives for efficient local tax enforcement may be created.[41]

Addressing Administrative Complexities

These administrative complexities (C, V, and E) must be addressed in any property tax reform if the immovable property tax is to produce a higher yield.[42] One underlying problem is that, in contrast to income taxes and the value-added tax, the property tax cannot—or can only with significant difficulty—be self-assessed, that is, property owners cannot place an assessed value on their own property (the city of Bogota provides an interesting exception; see Box 11.5).[43] Thus, relatively high administrative (as opposed to compliance) costs are incurred because of demanding information and record-keeping requirements and the need for an efficient valuation system. As noted, a particular problem in virtually all developing countries is the shortage of qualified property assessors or valuators.

The administrative complexities, if not properly addressed, may also reinforce each other, resulting in a high cost-to-revenue ratio for property taxes. It is readily evident from equation (11.1) that a combination of low coverage, valuation, and enforcement ratios will exacerbate each other, thus reinforcing their adverse impact on yield.[44] Also, upgrading the administrative infrastructure necessary for an effective property tax often requires a significant up-front investment for establishment of registration procedures and a cadastre, introduction of information technology systems, and training programs. The recent wave of reform initiatives (Box 11.1) seem, however, to indicate that these up-front costs are not a decisive obstacle to reform. Unfortunately, information on the cost of administering property taxes is generally extremely scarce.[45]

These administrative obstacles may appear daunting, but a rich arsenal of different ways to value and tax property is available, providing a flexible means of adapting the tax and its administration to widely differing country circumstances (Mikesell and Zorn 2008). Although an efficient and accurate cadastre is a *sine qua non* of property taxation, a variety of valuation techniques can be used to measure the tax base, ranging—as discussed above—from simple unit land taxes

---

[41] Remedial measures—proposed or adopted—to strengthen enforcement include moving collection points to banks, rewarding improved enforcement with higher transfers, and linking property tax payments to the provision of utility services.

[42] See Bahl and Martinez-Vasquez 2008 for a good discussion.

[43] Although elements of self-assessment (or self-identification) are found in Hungary, Thailand, and the Philippines (Bird and Slack 2005).

[44] A simple example may clarify this point: if both coverage and valuation ratios are at about 0.7 in a given country—not unrealistic assumptions in many developing countries—the total yield of the property tax could potentially double through an aggressive program to widen coverage and update values, and—importantly—these actions are *within the existing legal and regulatory framework*.

[45] Estimates for Latvia indicate that administrative costs at the municipal level exceed 10 percent of revenues in about half of the local governments, and reach up to 36 percent (in addition to the costs incurred at the central government agency involved). However, these seemingly high ratios are affected not only by "high" administrative costs, but also by very low tax rates, and hence may not provide a generally applicable cost estimate.

BOX 11.5 The Self-Assessment Approach in Bogota City

Until the property tax reform of 1993, the property tax in Bogota city was levied only on the less than 50 percent of total property owners who were included in the cadastral base. Furthermore, the cadastral valuations were outdated, with property values about 20–30 percent of their market values. With the 1993 reform, the city (as the only municipality in the country) introduced a self-assessment scheme, forcing taxpayers to declare the properties they owned and their values, substantially improving the extent of information available about the city's real estate properties. The statute established that declared land values could not be less than the highest of the following three benchmarks: (1) 50 percent of the commercial value; (2) the cadastral valuation; or (3) the previous year's self-assessment, indexed to inflation. The 50 percent provision was repealed in 1994 on the grounds that it was impossible to assign a market value to every property in the city unless a transaction had occurred. To further enhance compliance, the self-assessed values were used as the basis for calculating capital gains on property under the income tax (applying, however, to only a minority of property owners). The existence of an autonomous cadastral organization in the city was considered instrumental in implementing the self-assessment reform in Bogota City.

The reform led to the inclusion of a large number of previously informal properties in the cadastral base, and resulted in a doubling of tax filings in one year. It also brought taxable values closer to market values, and property tax revenues in real terms grew by 77 percent in 1994. The new scheme also resulted in a sustained increase in the number of properties paying the tax throughout the following decade.

In the late 1990s, however, property values dropped significantly as a result of the economic recession, and in many cases the minimum legal value determined by self-assessment became higher than the market value. The national government responded with legislation in 2000 leading to the elimination of the self-assessment provision and the introduction of a price index (the Urban and Rural Property Valuation Index), intended to update cadastral values that are not adjusted by the Cadastre Office in field activities. The index is calculated as the average increase in property prices estimated by the same office. This caused a further increase in the number of taxpayers declaring the cadastral value, from 72 percent in 2000 to 85 percent in 2002.

Subsequent valuation improvements based on substantially increasing the coverage of cadastral updating processes led to a historical record in the number of updated properties, and produced a ratio between the cadastral valuation and commercial value of about 81 percent in 2004.

(Vietnam, Nigeria) and taxation of estimated rental value to full-fledged market-value based systems. Many developing countries apply different property taxes to urban and rural property (Brazil, Namibia), taxing land and buildings in urban areas and only land in rural areas, while other countries exempt (partly or fully) agricultural land (Nicaragua, Guinea, Tunisia). To mitigate the impact of property taxes on low-income households and to substantially simplify tax administration by excluding low-value property from the tax net, some countries only tax property over a certain threshold (measured in area or, as in Serbia, value).

Reformers can also draw on the vast experience with the use of property taxes in many developed countries (or their regions)[46] as well as in some developing countries, and software tools, such as computer-assisted mass appraisal systems (Box 11.6), are widely available and have the potential to be applied in developing countries (Eckert 2008). Similarly, multiple options are available for the allocation between central and local authorities of the range of different responsibilities in the administration of the property tax; Martinez-Vazquez and Rider (2008) map the actual allocation of these responsibilities in a number of developed, emerging market, and developing countries.

Political Economy Considerations

Political economy considerations have also played important roles for the working of the property tax in many countries. By virtue of being a very transparent tax on an immobile base—the very features that make it a good tax—it is also a very politically unpopular tax. Furthermore, the

---

[46] Such as, for example, in Denmark, Sweden, Northern Ireland, Spain, and Canadian provinces.

BOX 11.6 Computer-Assisted Mass Appraisal (CAMA) Systems

The basic idea behind CAMA systems is to estimate a price index for a class of real estate, such as residential properties or business properties, from a representative sample of sold properties in the entire population (also called a hedonic price index). This index relates sales prices to the physical and location features of the sold properties (for example, property use and quality plus zoning). The index is then applied to the register of properties to revalue the entire universe of unsold properties. In developing countries with limited data on real estate markets, CAMA methods can make use of scarce price data to value entire classes of properties much more efficiently than traditional appraisal methods can. Also, recent improvements in spatial analyses using geographic information systems and low-level satellite technology have reduced the amount of data that needs to be collected from on-site inspections, resulting in a significant cost reduction for setting up an accurate fiscal cadastre.

In CAMA systems, the taxable value is determined by using the capital (improved) market value of the property.[1] More specifically, capital market value would typically be estimated through the use of statistical techniques that assume that average or typical price-setting patterns and relationships can be estimated using samples of recently sold properties. The estimated statistical relationships between values and property attributes can then be used to estimate the market value of all properties in the same property class. This method typically involves the following steps:

Step 1: Gather market sales data for properties that were sold recently and include in the analysis sales price and property attributes. Data need to be cleaned to make sure that only data from arm's-length property transactions are captured and that transactions have no special conditions attached.

Step 2: Using this sample of recently sold properties, estimate the relationship between property attributes and the realized sales price using standard regression analysis methods.

Step 3: Collect attribute data for each land parcel, including land or site area, building area, and building quality.

Step 4: By using the established relationships (coefficients) from Step 2, calculate the estimated sales price of each property.

Step 5: Calculate the taxable value from the estimated market value if the two differ as the result of property tax policies (exemptions or thresholds and the like).

Step 6: Apply the approved tax rate to the taxable value to derive the tax liability.

---

[1] See, for example, UN-Habitat 2011, 83, for a detailed discussion.

---

property tax may, when looked at in isolation, run counter to politically and socially motivated objectives of stimulating home ownership, realizing the beneficial externalities from owner occupation.[47] Opposition to the property tax has in a number of countries led to capping of the year-to-year growth of individual property tax liabilities.[48] A problem with capping is that, by driving a wedge between tax liability and the market value, the tax may be transformed to something other than a real property tax, with subsequent consequences for economic efficiency, revenue raising, and fairness.[49]

Increased use of property taxes also raises complex issues of intergovernmental fiscal design, involving, among other components, transfer systems. Particularly in many transition economies, democratization underpinned by decentralization programs has made the property tax an increasingly

---

[47] See IMF 2009, which also illustrates the point that property taxation is only one element in determining effective tax rates on property, interest deductibility and (non)taxation of imputed rent and capital gains being others.

[48] A well-known case in the United States was "Proposition 13," an amendment to the Constitution of California enacted in 1978, which capped both property value increases (at 2 percent per year) and the tax rate (at 1 percent), but capping is now in force in most U.S. states (Lutz, Molloy, and Shan 2010). Capping is also in place in other cities and countries, such as Bogota, Buenos Aires, and Latvia.

[49] Ihlanfeldt (2011) discusses the potentially adverse impact of capping on housing and labor market mobility, and tests for these effects in Florida.

important instrument of local government financing (Bahl 2009). The use of taxes on business property also raises particular issues that require attention, among them preventing costs from being increased disproportionately for businesses that use relatively more property as a factor input.

By virtue of not being directly proportional to income, property taxes are also frequently considered to be unfair. This issue has been addressed in different manners, for example, by taxing property whose value is only above a certain threshold, or by exempting sectors characterized by a high frequency of low-income earners, such as agriculture in developing countries.

A STRATEGY FOR REFORM

The administrative and political economy challenges discussed above are not trivial, and require resolute action and careful planning. Foremost among these challenges, reforms require strong political will to introduce, enforce, and maintain a property tax—political will that must address the variety of policy and administrative challenges discussed in this chapter, and often in the face of strong popular opposition. These challenges cannot be resolved overnight but must be addressed through a medium- and long-term reform strategy that has to be carefully calibrated to fit the particular circumstances of individual countries.[50] In particular, reform approaches cannot simply be copied from successful developed countries. It is also important to realize that successful reform of immovable property taxation, with its promising revenue potential, requires up-front investment in training and creation (or upgrading) of the necessary administrative infrastructure, most importantly in the form of a comprehensive and accurate cadastre or register for tax purposes.

Common elements of a reform strategy would ideally involve the following:[51]

- An in-depth diagnostic analysis that carefully maps present capabilities and identifies policy and administrative weaknesses, combined with policy decisions on the future role of property taxes, particularly as part of a broader decentralization strategy.

- Development of specific tax policy design, with particular focus on the definition of the base, the rate structure, and exemption policy. The key objective should be simplicity with a minimum of exemptions and other relief, for ease of administration and maximum fairness. Regular costing of tax relief—revenue forgone—is essential.

- Detailed planning of administrative reform, carefully adjusted to individual country circumstances, involving in particular (1) improved coverage of the cadastre or tax register; (2) better valuation, including procedures for regular updating; (3) improved record keeping based on close coordination between the agencies involved; (4) improved collection rates through strong enforcement and low compliance costs; and (5) clear decisions on the allocation of responsibilities between the central and local governments with regard to how these core administrative tasks are carried out.

- Reduction or phasing out of property transfer taxes, to possibly be replaced by either the recurrent property tax under reform, or (where administratively feasible) a capital gains tax on property.

- Finally, to prevent property tax systems from falling back into disrepair, development of a monitoring device based on quantitative performance indicators. These indicators would ideally include regular assessments of coverage of the tax register, valuation performance, and collection efficiency.

---

[50] A particular timing issue in this respect is that the government that endures the pain of initializing reform may not be the government that reaps the benefits of reform.

[51] See Bahl 2009 for a discussion. These elements are broadly applicable to both developed and developing countries engaged in property tax reform.

CONCLUSION

In summary, efficiency and equity considerations combine to provide a strong case for exploring ways to further strengthen the role of property taxes, and in particular recurrent taxes on immovable property. Although careful planning of necessary improvements to the basic administrative infrastructure is clearly required to carry out successful reforms in this area, there is clear scope for assigning a more prominent role to immovable property taxes in the medium to longer term. Data deficiencies preclude accurate estimates of their potential role, but it would not seem unrealistic to target a revenue raising potential of about 0.5–1 percent of GDP in the next 5–10 years for many developing and emerging economies, but with a much larger potential of about 2 percent of GDP or even higher for many developed countries that today rely only modestly on taxation of immovable property.

ANNEX 11.1. SUPPLEMENTARY TABLES

ANNEX TABLE 11.1.1

Property Taxes in High-Income Countries, 2012

Country or Economy	OECD	GDP per capita, US$	Taxes on Property General Government		Recurrent Taxes on Immovable Property General Government		Local Government	
			% of GDP	% of Taxes	% of GDP	% of Taxes	% of Local Taxes	% of General Property Taxes
Australia	Yes	67,863	2.40	8.60	1.40	5.20	100.00	64.29
Austria	Yes	46,620	0.60	1.30	0.20	0.50	14.80	100.00
Belgium	Yes	43,551	3.30	7.50	1.30	2.90	58.00	92.31
Canada	Yes	52,489	3.30	10.60	2.80	9.30	90.30	92.86
Chile	No	15,302	0.91	4.26	0.61	2.85	41.75	97.70
Croatia	No	13,077	0.24	0.72	0.01	0.04	0.50	100.00
Czech Republic	Yes	18,699	0.50	1.50	0.20	0.70	55.80	100.00
Denmark	Yes	56,476	1.80	3.80	1.30	2.80	10.50	100.00
Estonia	Yes	17,109	0.30	1.00	0.30	1.00	7.90	100.00
Finland	Yes	47,159	1.20	2.80	0.60	1.50	6.60	100.00
France	Yes	42,415	3.80	8.50	2.50	5.60	42.90	100.00
Germany	Yes	42,569	0.90	2.40	0.40	1.20	14.70	100.00
Greece	Yes	22,347	1.90	5.60	1.10	3.20	79.50	100.00
Hong Kong SAR	No	36,589	2.74	20.24	0.65	4.83	n.a.	n.a
Iceland	Yes	42,505	2.50	7.10	1.60	4.70	17.60	100.00
Ireland	Yes	48,434	1.90	7.00	1.00	3.60	93.80	100.00
Israel	Yes	33,397	2.70	9.00	2.20	7.40	94.80	100.00
Italy	Yes	33,915	2.70	6.30	1.50	3.40	13.80	66.67
Japan	Yes	46,531	2.70	9.10	2.10	7.00	28.50	100.00
Korea	Yes	24,454	2.60	10.60	0.70	3.00	16.60	100.00
Latvia	No	13,886	0.76	2.73	0.76	2.73	14.22	100.00
Lithuania	No	14,171	0.29	1.06	0.26	0.96	9.95	98.71
Luxembourg	Yes	103,806	2.70	7.10	0.10	0.20	4.90	100.00
Netherlands	Yes	49,158	1.10	3.00	0.70	1.90	52.40	100.00
New Zealand	Yes	38,376	2.10	6.20	2.00	6.10	90.40	100.00
Norway	Yes	99,249	1.20	2.90	0.30	0.80	5.20	100.00
Poland	Yes	12,732	1.20	3.90	1.20	3.80	30.00	100.00
Portugal	Yes	20,065	1.20	3.90	0.70	2.30	33.70	100.00
Russia	No	14,079	1.11	3.62	1.11	3.63	15.63	21.00
Singapore	No	54,007	1.06	7.52	1.06	7.51	n.a.	n.a.
Slovak Republic	Yes	16,912	0.40	1.60	0.40	1.60	52.10	100.00
Slovenia	Yes	22,519	0.60	1.80	0.50	1.40	12.80	100.00
Spain	Yes	28,294	2.00	6.30	1.00	3.20	33.40	100.00
Sweden	Yes	54,829	1.00	2.40	0.80	1.80	2.70	50.00
Switzerland	Yes	79,344	1.80	6.60	0.20	0.60	2.80	50.00
United Kingdom	Yes	38,781	3.90	11.90	3.20	9.70	100.00	50.00
United States	Yes	51,450	2.90	11.80	2.80	11.40	72.40	96.43
Uruguay	No	14,792	2.01	7.35	0.74	2.70	58.02	83.60
Average		**38,893**	**1.75**	**5.78**	**1.06**	**3.50**	**38.30**	**90.65**

Sources: OECD, *Revenue Statistics*, for OECD countries and for Latin American countries; and IMF, *Government Finance Statistics*.
Note: n.a. = not applicable; OECD = Organisation for Economic Co-operation and Development.

ANNEX TABLE 11.1.2

Property Taxes in Middle- and Low-Income Countries, 2012

Country or Economy	OECD	World Bank Income Group	GDP per capita, US$	Taxes on Property — General Government % of GDP	Taxes on Property — General Government % of Taxes	Recurrent Taxes on Immovable Property — General Government % of GDP	Recurrent Taxes on Immovable Property — General Government % of Taxes	Recurrent Taxes on Immovable Property — Local Government % of Local Taxes	Recurrent Taxes on Immovable Property — Local Government % of General Property Taxes
Afghanistan	No	L	680	0.24	2.94	0.21	2.58	0.40	0.13
Albania	No	UM	4,321	0.19	0.83	0.19	0.83	n.a.	n.a.
Argentina	No	UM	14,698	2.64	8.96	0.36	1.21	n.a.	n.a.
Armenia	No	LM	3,035	0.41	1.82	0.24	1.06	47.60	100.00
Azerbaijan	No	UM	7,439	0.27	1.74	0.27	1.74	96.23	6.90
Belarus	No	UM	6,721	0.98	2.68	0.36	1.00	3.35	100.00
Bosnia and Herzegovina	No	UM	4,353	0.33	0.84	0.31	0.80	10.57	87.46
Brazil	No	UM	11,281	2.10	5.89	0.50	1.42	25.48	97.22
Bulgaria	No	UM	7,049	1.37	4.90	0.90	3.21	63.58	100.00
Colombia	No	UM	7,938	2.04	10.38	0.59	3.00	29.11	100.00
Costa Rica	No	UM	9,753	0.36	1.69	0.27	1.26	40.08	95.51
Dominican Republic	No	UM	5,903	0.81	6.05	0.36	2.68	n.a.	n.a.
El Salvador	No	LM	3,780	0.08	0.53	0.00	0.00	n.a.	n.a.
Georgia	No	LM	3,523	0.88	3.45	0.88	3.45	63.91	100.00
Guatemala	No	LM	3,336	0.19	1.47	0.19	1.46	100.00	100.00
Hungary	Yes	UM	12,544	1.20	3.20	0.40	1.20	18.40	100.00
Indonesia	No	LM	3,591	0.35	2.69	0.35	2.69	0.00	0.00
Jamaica	No	UM	5,339	0.29	1.07	0.19	0.71	n.a.	n.a.
Mauritius	No	UM	8,832	1.45	6.69	0.07	0.33	38.60	98.49
Mexico	No	UM	10,129	0.29	1.48	0.20	1.04	59.26	66.50
Moldova	No	LM	2,046	0.34	1.03	0.09	0.26	1.87	100.00
Mongolia	No	LM	3,635	0.15	0.58	0.15	0.58	4.95	100.00
Morocco	No	LM	2,949	1.75	5.65	0.35	1.15	36.59	100.00
Nicaragua	No	LM	1,753	0.10	0.50	0.00	0.00	n.a.	n.a.
Panama	No	UM	9,833	0.73	3.89	0.33	1.79	n.a.	n.a.
Paraguay	No	LM	3,737	0.29	1.61	0.27	1.50	49.80	100.00
Peru	No	UM	6,323	0.37	1.99	0.19	1.00	32.14	100.00
Romania	No	UM	7,929	0.70	2.41	0.67	2.31	67.17	100.00
Serbia	No	UM	5,292	0.66	1.68	0.44	1.12	9.19	100.00
South Africa	No	UM	7,314	1.42	5.07	1.16	4.12	97.81	100.00
Thailand	No	UM	5,390	0.45	2.28	0.20	1.04	13.36	100.00
Tunisia	No	UM	4,198	0.52	1.77	0.07	0.25	14.94	85.25
Turkey	Yes	UM	10,531	1.20	4.20	0.20	0.90	10.10	100.00
Uzbekistan	No	LM	1,721	1.27	3.97	0.70	2.19	n.a.	n.a.
Venezuela	No	UM	10,109	0.02	0.15	0.00	0.00	n.a.	n.a.
Yemen	No	LM	1,368	0.01	0.11	0.00	0.00	n.a.	n.a.
Average			**6,066**	**0.73**	**2.95**	**0.32**	**1.38**	**35.94**	**86.06**

Sources: OECD, *Revenue Statistics*, for OECD countries and for Latin American countries; and IMF, *Government Finance Statistics*.

Note: L = low income; LM = lower-middle income; n.a. = not applicable; OECD = Organisation for Economic Co-operation and Development; UM = upper-middle income.

ANNEX TABLE 11.1.3

Property Taxes in Selected OECD and Latin American Countries, 2013

Country or Economy	OECD	World Bank Income Group	GDP per capita, US$	Taxes on Property — General Government % of GDP	% of Taxes	Recurrent Taxes on Immovable Property — General Government % of GDP	% of Taxes	Local Government % of Local Taxes	% of General Property Taxes
Argentina	No	UM	14,709	2.88	9.24	0.42	1.35		
Austria	Yes	H	49,039	0.70	1.70	0.20	0.50	14.90	100.00
Belgium	Yes	H	45,538	3.50	7.90	1.30	2.90	58.00	92.31
Brazil	No	UM	11,173	2.02	5.66	0.52	1.45	26.08	96.91
Canada	Yes	H	52,037	3.20	10.50	2.80	9.10	89.40	92.86
Chile	No	H	15,776	0.81	4.02	0.60	2.96	41.31	98.50
Colombia	No	UM	8,031	2.14	10.63	0.70	3.48	32.23	100.00
Costa Rica	No	UM	10,528	0.40	1.79	0.29	1.29	40.15	94.44
Czech Republic	Yes	H	18,871	0.50	1.40	0.20	0.70	55.90	100.00
Denmark	Yes	H	59,129	1.80	3.80	1.40	2.90	10.80	100.00
Dominican Republic	No	UM	5,882	0.88	6.29	0.40	2.87	n.a.	n.a.
El Salvador	No	LM	3,835	0.08	0.52	0.00	0.00	n.a.	n.a.
Estonia	Yes	H	18,852	0.30	1.00	0.30	1.00	7.20	100.00
Finland	Yes	H	49,055	1.30	2.90	0.70	1.50	6.60	100.00
France	Yes	H	44,099	3.80	8.50	2.50	5.70	44.10	100.00
Germany	Yes	H	44,999	0.90	2.50	0.40	1.20	14.60	100.00
Guatemala	No	LM	3,475	0.19	1.44	0.19	1.42	100.00	99.46
Hungary	Yes	UM	13,388	1.30	3.40	0.60	1.60	20.10	83.33
Iceland	Yes	H	45,416	2.50	7.10	1.70	4.70	17.90	100.00
Ireland	Yes	H	48,608	2.20	7.70	1.10	3.90	93.30	81.82
Israel	Yes	H	36,926	2.70	8.90	2.10	7.00	94.80	100.00
Italy	Yes	H	34,715	2.70	6.30	1.20	2.90	14.30	83.33
Japan	Yes	H	38,468	2.70	n.a.	2.00	n.a.	28.20	100.00
Korea	Yes	H	25,975	2.50	10.30	0.80	3.10	17.40	87.50
Luxembourg	Yes	H	112,473	2.90	7.30	0.10	0.20	4.90	100.00
New Zealand	Yes	H	40,516	2.00	6.10	1.90	6.00	89.90	100.00
Nicaragua	No	LM	1,831	0.11	0.58	0.00	0.00	n.a.	n.a.
Norway	Yes	H	100,579	1.20	3.00	0.40	0.90	5.50	75.00
Panama	No	UM	10,876	0.84	4.41	0.45	2.36	n.a.	n.a.
Paraguay	No	LM	4,281	0.27	1.62	n.a.	n.a.	n.a.	n.a.
Peru	No	UM	6,541	0.35	1.90	0.32	1.77	62.06	100.00
Portugal	Yes	H	20,995	1.10	3.30	0.80	2.30	32.80	100.00
Slovak Republic	Yes	H	17,706	0.40	1.50	0.40	1.50	51.50	100.00
Slovenia	Yes	H	23,317	0.70	1.90	0.60	1.50	12.70	83.33
Spain	Yes	H	29,150	2.10	6.60	1.10	3.30	32.90	100.00
Sweden	Yes	H	58,014	1.10	2.50	0.80	1.90	2.60	50.00
Switzerland	Yes	H	81,276	1.80	6.60	0.20	0.60	2.80	50.00
Turkey	Yes	UM	10,721	1.40	4.60	0.20	0.80	9.50	100.00
United Kingdom	Yes	H	39,372	4.10	12.30	3.20	9.70	100.00	50.00
United States	Yes	H	53,001	2.80	11.10	2.70	10.60	71.80	96.30
Uruguay	No	H	16,421	1.88	6.93	0.66	2.43	57.65	83.56
Venezuela	No	UM	7,576	0.02	0.17	0.00	0.00	n.a.	n.a.
Average			**31,742**	**1.60**	**5.02**	**0.88**	**2.73**	**38.97**	**91.39**

Source: OECD, *Revenue Statistics*, for OECD countries and for Latin American countries.
Note: H = high income; LM = lower-middle income; n.a. = not applicable; OECD = Organisation for Economic Co-operation and Development; UM = upper-middle income.

REFERENCES

African Development Bank, Organisation for Economic Co-operation and Development, and United Nations Development Programme (AfDB, OECD, and UNDP). 2010. *African Economic Outlook 2010*. Côte d'Ivoire: AfDB; Paris: OECD; New York: UNDP.

Bahl, Roy. 2009. "Property Tax Reform in Developing and Transition Countries." Fiscal Reform and Economic Governance project, USAID, Washington.

———, and Jorge Martinez-Vazquez. 2008. "The Determinants of Revenue Performance." In *Making the Property Tax Work*, edited by Roy Bahl, Jorge Martinez-Vasquez, and Joan Youngman. Cambridge, Massachusetts: Lincoln Institute of Land Policy

———, and Joan Youngman, eds. 2008. *Making the Property Tax Work*. Cambridge, Massachusetts: Lincoln Institute of Land Policy.

———. 2010. "Challenging the Conventional Wisdom on the Property Tax." Lincoln Institute of Land Policy, Cambridge, Massachusetts.

Bell, Michael, and John H. Bowman. 2011. *Implementing a Local Property Tax When There Is No Market: The Case of Commonly Owned Land in Rural South Africa*. Cambridge, Massachusetts: Lincoln Institute of Public Policy.

Bird, Richard M., and Enid Slack. 2005. "Land and Property Taxation in 25 Countries: A Comparative Review." *DICE* 3 (3): 34–42.

Cabral, Marika, and Caroline Hoxby. 2012. "The Hated Property Tax: Salience, Tax Rates, and Tax Revolts." NBER Working Paper No. 18514, National Bureau of Economic Research, Cambridge, Massachusetts.

Eckert, Joseph K. 2008. "Computer-Assisted Mass Appraisal Options for Transitional and Developing Countries." In *Making the Property Tax Work*, edited by Roy Bahl, Jorge Martinez-Vasquez, and Joan Youngman. Cambridge, Massachusetts: Lincoln Institute of Land Policy.

Ecorys. 2010. "Taxation in Africa." Ecorys, Rotterdam.

Ihlanfeldt, Keith R. 2011. "Do Caps on Increases in Assessed Values Create a Lock-In Effect? Evidence from Florida's Amendment One." *National Tax Journal* 64 (1): 8–25.

International Monetary Fund (IMF). 2009. "Debt Bias and Other Distortions: Crisis-Related Issues in Tax Policy." Fiscal Affairs Department, Washington.

Keen, Michael, Alexander Klemm, and Victoria Perry. 2010. "Tax and the Crisis." *Fiscal Studies* 31 (1): 43–79.

Kenyon, Daphne A., Adam H. Langley, and Bethany P. Paquin. 2012. "Rethinking Property Tax Incentives for Business." Policy Focus Report, Lincoln Institute of Land Policy, Cambridge, Massachusetts.

Lutz, Byron. 2008. "The Connection between House Price Appreciation and Property Tax Revenues." Finance and Economics Discussion Series, Federal Reserve Board, Washington.

———, Raven Molloy, and Hui Shan. 2010. "The Housing Crisis and State and Local Government Tax Revenue: Five Channels." Federal Reserve Board, Washington.

Martinez-Vazquez, Jorge, and Mark Rider. 2008. "The Assignment of the Property Tax: Should Developing Countries Follow the Conventional Wisdom?" Working Paper 08–21, International Studies Program, Georgia State University, Atlanta, Georgia.

Mieszkowski, Peter. 1972. "The Property Tax: An Excise Tax or a Profits Tax?" *Journal of Public Economics* 1 (1): 73–96.

Mikesell, John L., and C. Kurt Zorn. 2008. "Data Challenges in Implementing a Market Value Property Tax: Market and Market-Informed Valuation in Russia, Ukraine, and the Baltic States." In *Making the Property Tax Work*, edited by Roy Bahl, Jorge Martinez-Vasquez, and Joan Youngman. Cambridge, Massachusetts: Lincoln Institute of Land Policy.

Organisation for Economic Co-operation and Development (OECD). 2008. "Tax and Economic Growth." Economic Department Working Paper No. 620, OECD, Paris.

———. 2009. *Revenue Statistics 1965–2008*. Paris: OECD.

———. 2010. "Tax Policy Reform and Economic Growth." OECD Tax Policy Studies No. 20, OECD, Paris.

———. 2014. *Revenue Statistics 1965–2013*. Paris: OECD.

Pessino, Carola, and Ricardo Fenochietto. 2010. "Determining Countries' Tax Effort." Hacienda Publica Spanola, Instituto de Estudios Fiscales.

Piketty, Thomas. 2014. *Capital in the Twenty-First Century*. Cambridge, Massachusetts: Harvard University Press.

Rabanal, Pau, Christopher W. Crowe, Giovanni Dell'Ariccia, and Deniz Igan. 2011. "How to Deal with Real Estate Booms: Lessons from Country Experiences." IMF Working Paper No. 11/91, International Monetary Fund, Washington.

Sennoga, Edward B., David L. Sjoquist, and Sally Wallace. 2008. "Incidence and Economic Impacts of Property Taxes in Developing and Transitional Countries." In *Making the Property Tax Work*, edited by Roy Bahl, Jorge Martinez-Vasquez, and Joan Youngman. Cambridge, Massachusetts: Lincoln Institute of Land Policy.

Tax Notes International. 2010. "Tax Court Calls for New Property Valuations," Tax Analysts, Falls Church, Virginia, August 30.

UN-Habitat. 2011. *Land and Property Tax—A Policy Guide*. Nairobi, Kenya: United Nations Human Settlements Programme.

United States Agency for International Development (USAID). 2010. "Tax Policy in Serbia—Looking Forward." USAID Sega Project, Belgrade.

von Haldenwang, Christian, and Maksym Ivanyna. 2010. "Assessing the Tax Performance of Developing Countries." Discussion Paper, Deutsches Institut für Entwicklungspolitik and German Development Institute.

Wallis, John Joseph. 2001. "A History of the Property Tax in America." In *Property Taxation and Local Government Finance*, edited by Wallace Oates, 123–47. Cambridge, Massachusetts: Lincoln Institute of Land Policy.

Youngman, Joan. 2008. "The Property Tax in Development and in Transition." In *Making the Property Tax Work*, edited by Roy Bahl, Jorge Martinez-Vasquez, and Joan Youngman. Cambridge, Massachusetts: Lincoln Institute of Land Policy.

CHAPTER 12

Targeting and Indirect Tax Design

MICHAEL KEEN

INTRODUCTION

This short paper considers a perennial concern in the design of indirect taxation: whether a reduced rate of value-added tax (VAT) (or sales tax more generally) on commodities that account for a particularly large part of the spending of the poor—"food" is the classic example[1]—can make good sense as a way of addressing equity concerns. Reduced rates of this kind are indeed widely seen as an important and valuable way to temper a regressive impact of the VAT. Analysts often respond, however, that most of the benefit of reduced indirect tax rates commonly accrues to the better-off, making this a very poorly targeted way of pursuing equity objectives. But that response cannot be the end of the argument: in less advanced economies in particular, it may not be obvious that the government has any better ways to protect the poor available to it. So the aim here is to take the argument one step further, by asking: How well targeted do public spending measures have to be for the poor to be best served not by taxing at a differentially low or zero rate those goods or services that account for an especially large part of their budget, but by instead taxing those items more heavily than that and using the proceeds to increase that public spending?

WHEN ARE THE POOR BEST SERVED BY A REDUCED RATE?

A core issue in VAT design is the question of whether the applicable rate should be the same for all goods and services—a "uniform" rate structure—or whether it should vary across them. The most prominent question in practice is whether items that are especially important to the poor should be taxed at a differentially low or zero rate (or even subsidized). The professional consensus, it is fair to say, has been in favor of uniformity. While such "expert opinion," as Bird and Gendron (2007, 222) warn, "is biased ... by the particular experience of the experts in question," there is in this case a substantial body of thought and, to a lesser extent, empirical evidence behind the standard view. It has, in any event, proved increasingly influential: as Table 12.1 shows, the proportion of VATs which were introduced with a single rate has increased markedly over time, to a point at which uniformity, on introduction at least, has become the norm.

The many conceptual and practical arguments for and against various forms of differentiation in commodity taxation have been extensively reviewed elsewhere.[2] The discussion here leaves aside efficiency concerns to focus only on the distributional concern raised above, the question

This chapter is an edited version of parts of Michael Keen, "Targeting, Cascading, and Indirect Tax Design," *Indian Growth and Development Review*, Vol. 7, No. 2 (2014), pp. 181–201, ©2014 Emerald Group Publishing Limited. Reprinted with the kind permission of Emerald Group Publishing Limited. The author is grateful to David Coady, Kavita Rao, three referees, and a co-editor of *IGDR* for very helpful comments on the original paper.

[1] As Cnossen (2012, 9) puts it, "The most contentious issue under any VAT is the treatment of food."
[2] A relatively nontechnical account, and references, can be found, for instance, in Crawford, Keen, and Smith (2010).

TABLE 12.1

VATs with a Single Rate at Time of Introduction

	Number of New VATs	Percentage with a Single Rate at Introduction
Before 1990	48	25
1990–1999	75	71
1999–2011	31	81

Source: IMF data.

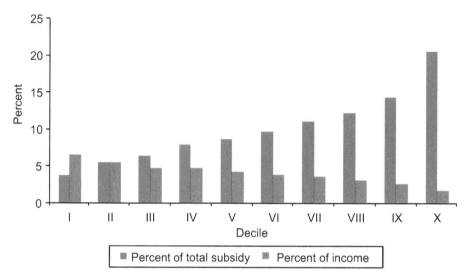

Figure 12.1 Distributional Impact of Zero-Rating in Mexico

Source: OECD (2007).

being: If some good—"food" is the archetypal example—accounts for a larger share of the expenditure of the poor than of the rich, should it on these grounds be taxed at a lower rate than the generality of commodities?

A Common but Incomplete Argument

The starting point is a simple and clear lesson from theory: the amount of redistribution that can be achieved by differentiating rates of indirect taxation will generally be quite limited. This is because the variation across households in the share of income spent on particular goods is generally just not great enough to make this an effective way to distinguish between poor and rich.[3] Put somewhat differently, even though the poor may spend a large *proportion* of their income on (say) food, the rich are likely to spend more on food in *absolute* terms—so most of the revenue foregone by taxing it at a low or zero rate effectively accrues to the rich, not the poor. Figure 12.1 illustrates this for the case of Mexico, which has extensive zero-rating of food and other items. The red bars confirm that the implicit subsidy is indeed greatest, relative to income, for the lowest income deciles—because zero-rated commodities account for a larger part of their income. The blue bars show, however, that the share of the total revenue foregone by zero rating is higher at higher levels of income—because the richer spend a larger amount on zero-rated commodities. And the latter effect is strikingly large: for each $100

---

[3] The theoretical argument here is elaborated in Sah (1983); see also Box 7.4 of Ebrill and others (2001).

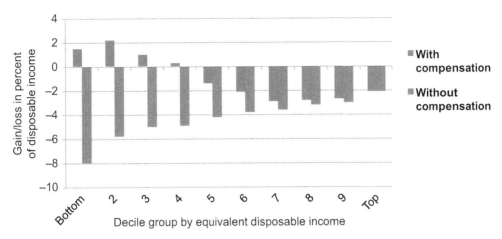

Figure 12.2   Removing Zero-Rating in the U.K., with and without Compensation

Source: Crawford, Keen, and Smith (2010).
Note: Figures based on unifying VAT at 17.5 percent in 2005–06; compensation is by a 15 percent rise in means-tested social assistance and tax credits (which costs around half of the revenue gained from eliminating zero-rating).

foregone by zero-rating, less than $5 benefits the poorest 10 percent of the population, and more than $20 benefits the top 10 percent.

The argument against reduced VAT rates on equity grounds all too often stops here. But it is not enough to show that this is a poorly targeted way to help the poorest: if a reduced rate is the only way to protect the poor, then, costly though it may be, it may nevertheless be judged optimal policy. The issue is whether better instruments for helping the poor are available.

When Are Spending Instruments Better?

Intuition suggests, and theory confirms, that the equity argument for differential rates of commodity taxation grounds is weaker the more sophisticated are the other instruments that the government can deploy to address its distributional concerns.[4] The question then is whether the government does indeed have at its disposal a rich enough set of instruments to achieve its distributional aims by these other means.

Income-Related Benefits

There is little doubt that advanced economies generally do. Take, for instance, the U.K. which, like Mexico, zero-rates a large part of consumption, including most foods. If these items were instead to be charged at the standard VAT rate, this would generate the regressive pattern of losses shown by the red bars in Figure 12.2, the reason being the same as that behind the red bars in Figure 12.1: the proportion of income spent on food and other zero-rated items decreases with the level of income, so the loss from taxing these commodities, as a proportion of income, is higher at lower income levels. But the U.K. also has a comprehensive system of means-tested (that is, income-related) transfers, and the blue bars show that by using part of

---

[4] The formal hint of this is that the restrictions on preferences (assuming these to be identical across individuals) known to be sufficient for uniformity to be optimal when the government can deploy a fully nonlinear income tax are weaker than those needed when it can only deploy only a linear income tax: weak separability between commodities and leisure (in the sense of time spent not in paid work) together with linear Engel curves in the latter case, weak separability alone in the former (Deaton 1979; Atkinson and Stiglitz 1976).

the revenue raised by eliminating zero-rating to increase these benefits, the losers from eliminating zero-rating can be more than compensated, while the government still enjoys a substantial net revenue gain.[5]

Less Finely Targeted Public Spending

What though of less advanced countries, in which such precise means-testing is not available? How well targeted must be public spending—whether in some simple form of cash transfers or the direct provision of goods and services—if it is to provide a more effective way of helping the poor than a reduced VAT rate? The examples above (and others) suggest that the "leakage" to the non-poor of the benefits from a reduced VAT rate may be so great that even spending measures that are not very finely targeted on the poor may be a better way of helping them. But just how badly targeted must these spending instruments be if reduced commodity tax rates are to be the better way to help the poor?

To address this as sharply as possible, suppose that the sole objective of policy is the maximin one of maximizing the welfare of the poorest individual, labeled p. Suppose too that the only tax instruments available are commodity taxes, and that the revenue from these is the sole source of finance for a single item of public spending, the aggregate amount of which is denoted by G. Suppose that some fixed proportion S^h of this spending goes to the benefit of each household h. In this simple framework (the details being in Annex 12.1),[6] starting from some arbitrary initial pattern of taxes and spending, the overall effect a small increase in the tax rate on some commodity k, the proceeds from which are used to increase public spending, is to increase the welfare of the poorest individual p if and only if[7]

$$\theta_k^p < \lambda^p S^p \left(\frac{1 + \Gamma_k}{1 - \Gamma_G} \right),$$ (12.1)

where $\theta_k^p \equiv C_k^p / \sum_h C_k^h$ is the proportion of all consumption of commodity k accounted for by the poorest; λ^p is the money-equivalent valuation that p places on an additional \$1 of public spending allocated to its benefit; Γ_k reflects the indirect effect on revenue of an increase in the tax on commodity k (the effect, that is, resulting from induced changes in consumption); and Γ_G is the impact that an increase in public spending has, through its effect on commodity demands, on tax revenue.[8]

---

[5] While the focus here is on equity concerns, reforms of the type just described also raise important efficiency considerations because compensating some (but not all) consumers for the effect of an increased VAT rate will generally affect incentives to provide paid work. Here things quickly become complex, with effects arising from both the VAT reform itself and the compensating reform of the direct tax-transfer system. If the compensation through the latter were exact for everyone, overall incentives to work would be expected to be largely unchanged. (For the case in which all have identical preferences, weakly separable in the manner of the Atkinson-Stiglitz [1976] result cited earlier, Laroque [2005] and Kaplow [2006] show that welfare and incentives would be entirely unchanged, and that government revenue would increase—so that a subsequent direct tax reduction could ensure that the movement toward uniformity is Pareto-improving.) Where means-testing is used only to protect the poorest, however, as envisaged in the U.K. example, the associated withdrawal of these additional benefits over some range will mean, for at least some, a lesser marginal incentive to undertake more paid work. Apps and Rees (2013) elaborate on this point in the Australian context.

[6] The analysis here is closely related to several treatments of optimal tax and transfer design. Coady (2004), in particular, explores the poverty impact of a range of social support measures in a framework similar to the present.

[7] The analysis abstracts from the costs of administration and compliance (and, potentially, wider governance problems) associated with both public spending and rate differentiation. These will be important in practice, but their relative magnitude is likely to be very context-specific. Given this, and since their broad analytical implications are straightforward, their inclusion here would be straightforward but add few insights.

[8] It is assumed throughout that $\Gamma_G < 1$, so that increased public spending does not pay for itself.

Understanding condition (12.1)—determining whether a "tax-and-spend" strategy is desirable for the poorest—is the main task in the rest of this section.[9] The condition may look somewhat convoluted, but in fact builds easily on the intuition above. It simply compares the targeting effectiveness of a reduced rate on commodity k to that of the public spending that such a rate cut implicitly foregoes.

The left hand side of (12.1) is straightforward. What matters for the targeting effectiveness of a reduced rate on k is simply the proportion of that commodity which is consumed by the poorest. This is in line with the intuition above, since that is the quantity (corresponding to the blue bars in Figure 12.1, for example) which determines what proportion of the implicit subsidy associated with a reduced tax rate actually benefits them. Experiences such as those of Mexico and the United Kingdom cited earlier warn that a broadly-based low rate can be a very poorly targeted way to help the poorest: θ_k^p in those cases is very low. In many practical contexts, however, it is possible to find goods whose consumption is strongly concentrated among the poor (θ_k^p is high)—these are often low quality variants of things that all consume in some form, such as bread. The case for a reduced rate or even subsidy on such an item is then correspondingly higher (as recently analyzed by Chander [2011]).[10] Even then, however, the extent of the redistribution that can be achieved in this way may be limited, both because consumption of such items by the better off may not be negligible and because the benefit to the poorest cannot exceed the cost of providing such goods free of charge (since a larger subsidy means a cash subsidy that would attract the better off, too). Nonetheless, even those advocating very broad-based VATs commonly accept the exemption of narrowly defined items with distinct significance to the poorest.

The right hand side of (12.1) is more complex. Here it is useful to proceed in steps. For this, suppose, for the moment, that increasing the price of k has no effect on the demand for any taxed good (so that $\Gamma_k = 0$) and neither does an increase in public spending (so that also $\Gamma_G = 0$). Then condition (12.1) reduces to $\theta_k^p < \lambda^p S^p$.

Given this, it helps fix ideas to start with the case in which public spending is in the form of cash transfers, in amounts that may differ across households. In this case, $1 of public spending allocated to the benefit of any household means $1 of cash received, so that $\lambda^p=1$. Condition (12.1) then becomes a simple comparison between the targeting effectiveness of a reduced tax rate (measured by θ_k^p) and that of the cash transfers (measured by S^p, the proportion of transfers received by the poor).

One particular structure of cash transfers that provides a useful benchmark is that in which commodity tax revenue is simply returned (at least at the margin) as an equal per capita cash payment to all H individuals in the population. This may seem far-fetched, but it is notable that the Islamic Republic of Iran has recently done precisely this (including by setting up bank accounts for more than sixty million people) in order to address the distributional consequences of drastically reducing petroleum subsidies.[11] In this case $S^p = 1/H$, and the condition (12.1) becomes the requirement that $C_k^p < (\sum_h C_k^h)/H$: increasing the tax rate on k and spending the proceeds as a poll subsidy benefits the poorest so long as their consumption of k is less than the average per capita consumption in the whole population—a very weak condition indeed, requiring no more than a positive income elasticity of demand for k.

---

[9] This condition, it should be noted, does not speak directly to the uniformity issue. Indeed, some departure from uniformity will be desirable unless, when evaluated at some uniform tax structure, the inequality in (12.1) becomes an equality for all k; and it will be in the direction of a lower rate on k if and only if the inequality is reversed.

[10] Besley and Coate (1991) is the classic treatment of the public provision of low quality private goods as a way to ease self-selection constraints on redistribution.

[11] The point is also illustrated by the simulation analysis of VAT reform in Mexico in Abramovsky, Attanasio, and Phillips 2015.

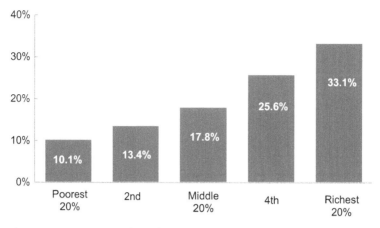

Figure 12.3   Distribution of Benefits of Curative Health Care

Source: Mahal and others (2007).

To the extent that cash transfers can be targeted in a way more progressive than a uniform poll-subsidy, the case against an especially low rate on commodities important in the budgets of the poor is of course even stronger. For many emerging economies, increasing experience with cash transfer schemes and the potential for proxy means-testing[12] is making this increasingly feasible—a point stressed in the Latin American context by Barreix, Bès, and Roca (2012), who also demonstrate the substantial reduction in poverty that could in principle be achieved by eliminating reduced rates and transferring to the poorest a sufficient amount of the proceeds as compensation. The key issue, of course, is that of designing transfer schemes sufficiently well targeted to do this.[13]

While some form of targeting of cash transfers is likely to be possible in many countries, the precision with which this can be achieved is likely to remain limited in many lower income countries. For them, the main alternative to supporting the poor by rate differentiation is likely to be through the public provision of goods or services, such as basic health and education and infrastructure.

In such cases, G in condition (12.1) must be interpreted as some such form of spending. Some guidance in understanding how this affects the case for rate differentiation is provided by empirical studies that aim to quantify the distributional aspects of public spending by allocating costs incurred to specific recipient groups: in effect, that is, estimating the S^h. Figure 12.3 shows the results, for instance, of such a study of the allocation of spending on curative health care in India. The overall pattern is regressive, in the sense that the better off benefit from a disproportionately large share of the spending. In this case, only 10 percent of the spending goes to the benefit of the poorest 20 percent. To see the implications, suppose, to keep the numbers simple, that the total population size is 100, and total curative health care spending is $100; so the poorest 20 people (all identical) benefit from spending of $10. Then $S^p = 0.1$. Suppose too for the moment that each of them values this at precisely its per capita cash value, 50 cents, so that again $\lambda^p = 1$. Then the right of (12.1) is $\lambda^p S^p = 0.1$, and the tax-and-spend strategy is preferred to a rate reduction if and only if the poorest 20 percent account for less than 10 percent of all zero-rated consumption. This too is far from implausible. Indeed in one of the few empirical studies that

---

[12] This uses correlates of income or need to construct indicators on which transfers might be based: see, for instance, Castañeda (2005) on experience with such a scheme in Colombia.

[13] It is worth noting that while biometric cards containing only personal identifiers can be useful in ensuring that benefits are delivered to intended recipients, additional information is needed to deliver benefits more finely targeted than a poll subsidy.

looks at the joint effect of a uniform VAT and the public spending it might finance, Muñoz and Cho (2004) find that the poorest 40 percent in Ethiopia would benefit from adoption of a uniform rate VAT, the proceeds of which are used to scale up spending on basic education and health.

All this, however, may still understate the case against differentially low rates. For the value that the poorest recipients place on public spending allocated to their benefit may well exceed the cash cost involved, so that $\lambda^p > 1$. Continuing the example of the previous paragraph, if the poorest 20 people each valued their enjoyment of the $10 allocated to them not at its cost of 50 cents but at $1, so that $\lambda^p = 2$ then $\lambda^p S^p = 2 \times 0.1 = 0.2$. In this case, the tax-and-spend strategy is the best way to support the poor under the very weak condition that their per capita consumption is below the population-wide average.

It remains to consider the roles played by Γ_k, the indirect revenue impact of increasing the tax on k, and by Γ_G, the revenue impact of public spending itself. We take them in turn.

For the former, the lesson is simply that the case for the tax-and-spend strategy is strengthened to the extent that increasing the tax rate on good k changes consumption in such a way as to increase overall revenue, perhaps by inducing strong substitution towards other taxed goods. The magnitude and even sign of this effect will be sensitive both to patterns of behavioral response and the pre-existing tax system. In the absence of cross price effects, for instance, it is easily seen that Γ_k reduces to the product of the initial tax rate on k (in ad valorem form) and the (absolute value of the) own-price elasticity of the aggregate demand for commodity k. If, for example, the tax rate on k is initially 15 percent and the price elasticity of demand −0.1, the comparison becomes that between θ_k^p and $\lambda^p S^p$ (0.985). Importantly, a lower own-price elasticity in itself strengthens the case for the tax-and-spend strategy, because it implies a higher revenue gain from increasing the tax rate, and hence a larger increase in public spending. Clearly though the indirect revenue impact is likely to be highly context-specific and general speculation is dangerous.

The significance of Γ_G is similar. To the extent that increased public provision changes commodity demands in such a way as to increase tax revenue, so that $\Gamma_G > 0$, this strengthens the case for an increased tax on commodity k. Again, however, the sign of this term is ambiguous: increased public spending on health or education, for instance, presumably enhances the capacity to work and so tends, in due course, to increase tax revenue; but it may also weaken the incentive to work in order to pay for privately-provided substitutes for what is now more fully provided by the public sector.

The framework underlying condition (12.1) is of course very rudimentary. It does not capture, for instance, forms of public spending that make receipt of benefit conditional on some particular actions (such as participation in a work program, or sending children to school); nor does it fully capture potential complexities arising from the interplay between public and private provision of health and education services. It does, however, point toward the kinds of targeting and incentive concerns that need to be addressed in the joint design of tax and spending systems.

It should also be noted that a range of practical concerns often blunt the impact of subjecting to VAT items that loom large in the budgets of the poorest. Typically, charging VAT is only compulsory for firms beyond some minimum size (in terms of turnover), meaning that smaller firms will escape the tax on their own value added (though of course continuing to be charged VAT, without credit or refund, on their own purchases). To the extent that the poor tend to buy from smaller retailers, the prices they face are thus likely to be less affected by the VAT than might at first sight appear.[14] In the case of the Dominican Republic, for which data identifying where purchases are made are available, Jenkins, Jenkins, and Kuo (2006) find that this effect can indeed substantially reduce the regressivity of the VAT. Simple noncompliance with the VAT is likely to have a similar effect.

---

[14] Even if the tax benefit is retained by small retailers rather than passed on to their customers, the distributional impact is still benign if those retailers are themselves of relatively low income.

CONCLUDING

The lessons from this discussion are easily summarized: assessing the distributional case for reduced VAT rates requires understanding the distributional impact of the public spending that a higher rate could enable—and even poorly targeted spending may be a better way to support the poor than a reduced rate.

The formalities, importantly, have been cast in the maximin terms of protecting the interests of the very poorest. In practice, the harsh truth always arises that there will be some who cannot be fully protected against reforms of the kind considered here. Not all entitled to some benefit may actually receive it, and it will be hard, for instance, to compensate the childless, healthy, and poor aged, for instance, by increased spending on health care and education. Practical policymaking must almost inevitably recognize that reform will result in some uncompensated losers, and look to some wider good.

What ultimately stands out, however, is the singular difficulty not of explaining the case for combined tax-spending reforms of the kind considered above—the essence is often fully understood by policymakers—but of persuading governments to adopt them. This is presumably because they believe they cannot carry their support base with them. That, in turn, may reflect a suspicion that the spending gains that policymakers promise will offset the pain of the increased tax may not always be forthcoming, or lasting. Or there may be a perception that there are other and even more progressive ways in which to finance that same increase in public spending—by paying for a reduction in the tax on k by raising that on some other commodity, for instance; the same issue still arises, however, once maximal progressivity has been achieved in these other financing instruments. Or it may simply be that the richer and more powerful groups understand very well how reduced VAT rates act to their particular advantage. It remains unclear whether the failure of policymakers to act on arguments demonstrating that reduced rates are dominated, in equity terms, by other policies is due to weaknesses of the policymaking process or to some political naiveté of arguments like those above, which further thought and work might overcome.[15]

---

[15] There has recently been some resurgence, for example, of the notion that increased use of earmarking might be useful in this respect (Ghana, which has earmarked increased VAT rates to increased health and education expenditure, being a case in point). For references, and a somewhat skeptical assessment, see Keen 2013.

ANNEX 12.1. DERIVATION OF EQUATION (12.1)

Suppose there are H individuals, the typical member having preferences described by an indirect utility function $V^h (Q^1, \ldots, Q^M, w, Y, g^h)$ defined over the consumer prices Q_i of M commodities, wage rate w (assumed or normalized to be untaxed and unchanging), lump-sum income Y (very possibly zero), and the amount of public spending $g^h = S^h G$ going to their benefit. This spending is financed only by commodity tax revenue, so that $G = \sum_{i=1}^{M} T_i \sum_{h=1}^{H} C_i^h$, where T_i is the tax on i (in ad valorem form) and C_i^h is h's consumption of commodity i.

Assuming all producer prices to be unchanged, the effect on p's welfare of an arbitrary change in T_k and G is given, using Roy's identity, by

$$dV^p = -V_Y^p C_k^p + V_g^p S^p dG, \tag{12.1.1}$$

the subscripts to V^p indicating derivatives. Perturbing the government's budget constraint gives

$$dG = \left(\sum_{h=1}^{H} C_k^h + \sum_{i=1}^{M} T_i \sum_{h=1}^{H} (\partial C_i^h / \partial Q_k) \right) dT_k \\ + \left(\sum_{i=1}^{M} T_i \sum_{h=1}^{H} (\partial C_i^h / \partial G) S^h \right) dG. \tag{12.1.2}$$

Solving (12.1.2) for dG and substituting into (12.1.1) gives (12.1) of the main text, where $\lambda^p \equiv \left(V_g^p / V_Y^p \right)$, $\Gamma_k \equiv \sum_{i=1}^{M} T_i \sum_{h=1}^{H} (\partial C_i^h / \partial Q_k) / \sum_{h=1}^{H} C_k^h$ and $\Gamma_G \equiv \sum_{i=1}^{M} T_i \sum_{h=1}^{H} (\partial C_i^h / \partial G) S^h$.

REFERENCES

Abramovsky, Laura, Orazio Attanasio, and David Phillips. 2015. "Value Added Tax Policy and the Case for Uniformity: Empirical Evidence from Mexico." Institute for Fiscal Studies Working Paper W15/08, Institute for Fiscal Studies, London.

Atkinson, Anthony B., and Joseph E. Stiglitz. 1976. "The Design of Tax Structure: Direct versus Indirect Taxation." *Journal of Public Economics* 6 (1–2): 55–75.

Apps, Patricia, and Ray Rees. 2013. "Raise Top Tax Rates, Not the GST." Legal Studies Research Paper 13/45, University of Sydney.

Barreix, Alberto, Martin Bès, and Jerónimo Roca. 2012. "Solving the Impossible Trinity of Consumption Taxes: Personalized VAT." Unpublished, Inter-American Development Bank, Washington.

Besley, Timothy, and Stephen Coate. 1991. "Public Provision of Private Goods and the Redistribution of Income." *American Economic Review* 81 (4): 979–84.

Bird, Richard, and Pierre-Pascal Gendron. 2007. *The VAT in Developing and Transitional Countries.* Cambridge, U.K.: Cambridge University Press.

Castañeda, Tarsicio. 2005. "Targeting Social Spending to the Poor with Proxy-Means Testing: Colombia's SISBEN System." Social Protection Discussion Paper No. 0529, World Bank, Washington.

Chander, Parkash. 2011. "Public Provision of Private Goods in Developing Countries." Unpublished, National University of Singapore.

Coady, David. 2004. "Designing and Evaluating Social Safety Nets: Theory, Evidence and Policy Conclusions." Food Consumption and Nutrition Division Discussion Paper No. 172, International Food Policy Research Institute, Washington.

Cnossen, Sijbren. 2012. "Introducing a Modern GST in India: Need for Further Debate." *Tax Notes International* 66 (13): 1267–83.

Crawford, Ian, Michael Keen, and Stephen Smith. 2010. "VAT and Excises." In *Dimensions of Tax Design: The Mirrlees Review,* edited by James Mirrlees and others, 275–362. Oxford, U.K.: Oxford University Press for Institute for Fiscal Studies.

Deaton, Angus. 1979. "Optimally Uniform Commodity Taxes." *Economics Letters* 2: 357–61.

Ebrill, Liam, Michael Keen, Jean-Paul Bodin, and Victoria Summers. 2001. *The Modern VAT*. Washington: International Monetary Fund.

Jenkins, Glenn P., Hatice P. Jenkins, and Chun-Yan Kuo. 2006. "Is the VAT Naturally Progressive?" Working Paper No. 1059, Economics Department, Queens University, Kingston, Ontario.

Kaplow, Louis. 2006. "On the Undesirability of Commodity Taxation Even When Income Taxation Is Not Optimal." *Journal of Public Economics* 90 (6–7): 1235–50.

Keen, Michael. 2013. "Taxation and Development—Again." In *Studies of Critical Issues in Taxation and Development*, edited by Clemens Fuest and George Zodrow, 13–41. Cambridge, Massachusetts: MIT Press.

Laroque, Guy R. 2005. "Indirect Taxation Is Superfluous under Separability and Taste Homogeneity: A Simple Proof." *Economics Letters* 87: 141–44.

Mahal, Ajay, Abdo S. Yazbeck, David H. Peters, and G. N. V. Ramana. 2007. *The Poor and Health Service Use in India*. Washington: World Bank.

Muñoz, Sonia, and Stanley Sang-Wook Cho. 2004. "Social Impact of a Tax Reform: The Case of Ethiopia." In *Helping Countries Develop: The Role of Fiscal Policy*, edited by Sanjeev Gupta, Benedict Clements, and Gabriela Inchauste, 353–84. Washington: International Monetary Fund.

Organisation for Economic Co-operation and Development (OECD). 2007. "Putting Public Finances on a Firmer Footing." Chapter 2 in *OECD Economic Survey: Mexico 2007*. Paris: Organisation for Economic Cooperation and Development.

Sah, Raj K. 1983. "How Much Redistribution Is Possible through Commodity Taxes?" *Journal of Public Economics* 20: 89–101.

CHAPTER 13

Carbon Tax Burdens on Low-Income Households: A Reason for Delaying Climate Policy?

Ian Parry

INTRODUCTION

Without strong measures to mitigate carbon dioxide (CO_2) and other greenhouse gases, global temperatures are projected to rise by about 3–4°C over preindustrial levels by the end of this century, with serious risks of catastrophic outcomes.[1]

Carbon taxes, or similar pricing instruments,[2] should be front and center in climate change mitigation. These instruments do the following:

- Exploit the full range of emissions mitigation opportunities (shifting to cleaner fuels, reducing energy use, and so on), so long as they are directly targeted at emissions[3]

- Achieve CO_2 reductions at lowest cost to the economy, so long as revenues are used productively, most obviously (for advanced countries) to lower the burden of broader taxes on labor and capital

- Promote only those emissions reductions for which environmental benefits outweigh the costs, so long as tax rates are aligned with, albeit contentious, environmental damage assessments

- Can involve a practical extension of motor fuel excises (long established in most countries and among the easiest of taxes to administer) to other fuel products[4]

- Are in many countries' own self-interest because of domestic environmental co-benefits—for example, reduced air pollution deaths (for example, Parry, Veung, and Heine, forthcoming)

- Require international coordination over one main parameter—a price floor.

Although carbon pricing schemes are emerging in many regions and countries (Figure 1 in World Bank 2014), little over one-tenth of global greenhouse gas emissions in 2013 were formally priced, and most prices are far below what is needed.[5] Clearly the politics of carbon taxes

---

The author is grateful to Steve Clark, Terry Dinan, Tarun Narasimhan, and Ruud de Mooij for help with this chapter.

[1] Including much higher warming from feedbacks in the climate system, dramatic sea level rises from collapsing ice sheets, dramatic local climate change from changing ocean currents, and so on.

[2] The discussion in this chapter focuses on carbon taxes, though the distributional incidence of their emissions trading analogs (with allowance auctions) is equivalent for the same emissions coverage, prices, and revenue use.

[3] For the United States a carbon tax is about five times as effective at reducing CO_2 as a comparable tax on electricity or incentives for renewable power generation (Figure 3.1 in Parry and others 2014).

[4] In the United States, a tax on the carbon content of fossil fuels need only involve monitoring about 1,500–2,000 taxpayers (Calder 2015).

[5] Prices in the largest program, the European Union (EU) Emissions Trading Scheme, have been below the equivalent of US\$10 per ton in recent years, substantially less than estimated environmental damages, or levels (if globally applied) consistent with aggressive long-term climate stabilization (see below).

BOX 13.1 Some Prior Literature on Carbon Tax Incidence

There have been several country case studies of carbon and energy tax incidence (mostly before revenue recycling), and some recent cross-country comparisons of energy tax incidence, but not much cross-country assessment of carbon tax incidence. This box provides a quick flavor of some of this literature.

Most work on energy tax incidence focuses on motor fuels, a recent example being Sterner 2012. He finds that these taxes are generally more regressive in the United States than in Europe (primarily because of higher vehicle ownership rates among lower-income households in the United States). And when incidence is measured using consumption expenditure (arguably a better measure—see text) rather than annual income, motor fuel taxes are often progressive, at least across low- to middle-income groups. Poterba (1991) finds similar results for the United States: the burden-to-income ratio for the bottom income quintile is 5.3 times that for the top income quintile with incidence based on annual income, but only 1.5 times that for the top income quintile with incidence based on expenditure.

Casler and Rafiqui (1993) look at a range of taxes on electricity, coal, natural gas, gasoline, and other refined petroleum products for the United States, finding that the tax-burden-to-income ratio overall for the lowest income quintile is only modestly larger than for the top income quintile (in part because indirect price effects are less regressive than the direct price effects). In a similar study, Bull, Hassett, and Metcalf (1994) show that incidence effects of energy taxes are even less regressive with incidence based on consumption. Metcalf (1999) demonstrates that similar energy tax packages can be made distributionally neutral overall for broad income groups (under income and consumption incidence measures) through targeted income and payroll tax reductions.

With regard to country-specific analyses of carbon pricing, U.S. applications include Dinan 2015; Hassett, Mathur, and Metcalf 2009; Morris and Mathur 2015; Parry and Williams 2010; and Rausch, Metcalf, and Reilly 2011, with most focusing on neutralizing adverse distributional effects through revenue recycling. Before recycling, the burden-to-income ratio for low-income households is roughly three to five times that for high-income households, or about 1.5 times as high, based on income and consumption incidence measures, respectively. The two big direct items are motor fuels and electricity, with the budget share for electricity falling most rapidly with higher income. Similar analyses for other countries include Australia (Cornwell and Creedy 1997), Denmark (Wier and others 2005), and Sweden (Brännlund and Nordström 2004).

With regard to cross-country assessments, an early study by Smith (1992), covering a variety of countries and focusing on income-based incidence, finds that carbon and energy taxes are moderately regressive for most countries, but more so for the United Kingdom and Ireland (where, because of colder climates, heating and electricity needs are greater). A study of European countries (measuring incidence against expenditure) by OECD (2014) finds that transportation taxes are generally progressive; heating fuel taxes are regressive, but only slightly so; and electricity taxes are more regressive.

are not easy, and at the heart of this is the potential impact on vulnerable (or politically influential) groups. Most debate has surrounded low-income households (the focus of this chapter) as well as trade-exposed, energy-intensive firms (which is beyond the scope).[6]

Having a sense of the distributional incidence of carbon taxes across households is critical to informing policy dialogue and aiding in designing accompanying measures—either to protect low-income households or alter the overall distributional equity of the fiscal reform. Policies perceived as broadly fair in this regard are not only desirable for their own sake (more so, given recent trends toward greater inequality in after-tax incomes—see Immervoll and Richardson 2011) but also may have a better chance of being enacted and sustained.

This chapter takes stock of methods for estimating household incidence and applies them, albeit crudely, across advanced countries (where data are more available)—Box 13.1 provides some discussion of the rather limited previous literature on carbon tax incidence.

---

[6] For some discussion of competitiveness impacts, and transitory policies to address them, see, for example, Böhringer, Carbone, and Rutherford 2012; and Fischer, Morgenstern, and Richardson 2015.

The main theme of the discussion is that, for several reasons, distributional concerns should not hold up carbon taxes:

- *Carbon taxes are less regressive (disproportionately burdening low-income groups) than they might first appear*. Although the poor generally spend a greater share of their annual income on electricity,

  - ➢ This is less true for transportation and heating fuels and other consumer products whose prices increase indirectly from higher energy costs

  - ➢ Regressive effects are less pronounced when incidence is measured against household consumption (arguably a better measure of household well-being than income)

  - ➢ Cross-country calculations suggest the incidence of carbon taxes can be anything from moderately regressive, to proportional, to moderately progressive.

- *Undercharging for carbon damages is a highly inefficient way to help low-income households*, because the vast majority of benefits (typically about 90 percent) leak away to higher-income groups. Targeted measures are much more effective.

- *There are ample opportunities for compensating low-income households in advanced countries through targeted fiscal and spending adjustments and combining carbon taxes with other progressive measures* (for example, reducing tax preferences for the wealthy), though the specifics will vary across countries (with the extent of inequality, parameters of the fiscal system, and other factors). The focus should be the distributional impact of the whole policy package, not just the component that raises energy prices.

A second theme of the chapter (though one already receiving much emphasis in the literature) is that *diverting carbon tax revenues from the general budget for compensation involves significant costs*. Reasonably accurate estimates of burdens on vulnerable groups are therefore important for gauging appropriate compensation levels. And, insofar as possible, compensation instruments that enhance economic efficiency (for example, targeted tax cuts or tax credits that strengthen incentives for work effort) should be used instead of instruments that do not (for example, transfer payments).

The chapter is organized in two main parts. The first deals with conceptual and measurement issues, while the second gives some very broad quantitative sense of the incidence effects of carbon taxes across advanced countries (prior to recycling) and discusses options for simultaneous adjustments to the broader tax and benefit system. The last section provides concluding remarks.

CONCEPTUAL AND MEASUREMENT ISSUES

The economic burden or incidence of a tax refers to whose economic welfare is reduced by this tax and by how much. Economic incidence is quite different from formal or legal incidence—for example, fuel suppliers may remit carbon tax payments to the government, but bear little incidence if the charge is mainly reflected in higher prices for fuel users. The point in the fossil fuel supply chain at which carbon taxes are levied is largely irrelevant for the ultimate incidence of the tax.

This section presents the most basic analytical model of carbon tax incidence, discusses the measurement of key factors determining incidence, considers some complicating factors, and emphasizes the importance of using carbon tax revenue efficiently.

Basic Model of Carbon Tax Incidence

Consider a static model with the following assumptions (which are relaxed later):

- The carbon tax burden is fully passed forward into consumer prices
- Co-benefits (for example, better local air quality) from carbon pricing are ignored
- Incidence is measured before adjustments in the broader tax and benefit system.

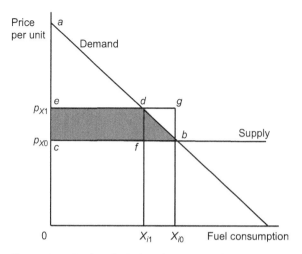

Figure 13.1 Burden of a Fuel Tax for a Household Group

Note: The red trapezoid indicates the burden (loss of consumer surplus) to a household group from the increase in price (caused by a carbon tax) for a particular fuel.

In this setting, carbon tax incidence for a particular household group reflects their loss of consumer surplus, aggregated across all consumer products whose prices rise in response to the higher energy costs caused by the carbon tax.

Consider first a tax on the carbon content of a single fuel, denoted by X, directly consumed by households (for example, gasoline or residential natural gas). Households are classified into $i = 1\ldots N$ income groups, where I_i (defined more carefully below) is average income for group i. The fuel demand curve for group i (taken to be linear over the relevant range) is shown in Figure 13.1, where the height of this curve at any point reflects the benefit to fuel users from an extra unit of consumption.

The fuel supply curve is perfectly elastic (that is, fuel is produced competitively under constant returns) with p_{X0} denoting the per unit production cost or supply price. As drawn in Figure 13.1, there is no preexisting fuel tax, so p_{X0} is also the initial (precarbon tax) price to fuel users (preexisting taxes are discussed below). Initial fuel consumption for household group i is X_{i0}, and consumer surplus—benefits to fuel users (the area under the demand curve integrated between the origin and X_{i0}) less payments to fuel suppliers—is area abc.

Suppose a carbon tax is introduced, increasing the fuel user price to p_{X1}, where $p_{X1} - p_{X0}$ equals the tax rate per ton of CO_2 times the fuel's emissions factor (CO_2 per unit of X). Fuel consumption falls to X_{i1} and consumer surplus falls by trapezoid $edbc$, consisting of the first order loss $edfc$, caused by paying a higher price on consumption (the tax payment), plus dbf, or benefits from forgone consumption $X_{i0} - X_{i1}$ net of what households would have paid for that consumption.

The consumer surplus loss or tax burden for group i, denoted B_i, can be written as in equation (13.1):

$$B_i = \left(p_{X1} - p_{X0}\right)X_{i0}\left(1 - \frac{X_{i0} - X_{i1}}{2X_{i0}}\right) \approx \left(p_{X1} - p_{X0}\right)X_{i0}. \qquad (13.1)$$

This approximation, equal to rectangle $egbc$ in Figure 13.1, is reasonable for the relatively modest changes in fuel use from carbon taxes likely to be implemented in the near term.[7]

---

[7] For example, the approximation overstates the loss of consumer surplus by only 5 percent when fuel use is reduced by 10 percent.

Expressing the burden relative to group i's income is given by equation (13.2):

$$\frac{B_i}{I_i} \approx \frac{\left(p_{X1} - p_{X0}\right)}{p_{X0}} \frac{p_{X0} X_{i0}}{I_i} . \qquad (13.2)$$

This is the proportionate fuel price increase (the same for all households) times group i's budget share for the fuel. In this highly simplified case, tax incidence is regressive if fuel budget shares are higher for lower-income groups; proportional if all groups have the same budget share; and progressive if higher-income groups have higher budget shares. Alternatively, p_{X0} could be cancelled from equation (13.2), but data at the household level are generally reported on product expenditures $(p_{X0} X_{i0})$, rather than on physical consumption units (X_{i0}).

More generally, a carbon tax directly increases consumer prices for several energy products (electricity, heating and transportation fuels) and indirectly for goods in general (by raising the costs of intermediate energy inputs). The formula in (13.2) readily generalizes to the case of multiple consumer price increases, so the burden to income approximation is simply equation (13.3):

$$\frac{B_i}{I_i} \approx \sum_{j=1}^{M} \left(\frac{p_{X1}^j - p_{X0}^j}{p_{X0}^j}\right)\left(\frac{p_{X0}^j X_{i0}^j}{I_i}\right), \qquad (13.3)$$

in which superscript j indexes a consumer product j, and there are $j = 1...M$ product groupings. The price increase for a particular product such as cars, for example, will reflect the CO_2 tax times embodied carbon, that is, CO_2 emissions per vehicle from the electricity and fuels used in the manufacture of component parts and assembly.

For advanced countries (see below), carbon taxes appear to be regressive because lower-income households have a relatively high propensity to spend out of current income, and energy products tend to be, albeit weak, necessities,[8] though incidence is less regressive when the full range of products whose prices increase are taken into account.

Measurement Issues: A Quick Look

Previous studies (such as those in Box 13.1) have measured incidence effects of carbon taxes (or broader environmental and energy taxes), using formulas like that in equation (13.3), or more sophisticated versions of it (for example, incorporating behavioral responses). Implementing equation (13.3) requires three main pieces of data: price impacts and, by household group, income and product expenditures.

Price Impacts

Absolute price increases for energy products directly consumed by households are easily calculated by the tax rate times the CO_2 emissions factors for the respective fuels. These factors are essentially fixed for motor fuels and natural gas, and vary very little across countries,[9] though CO_2 emissions rates per unit of electricity—available by country from the

---

[8] Meta analyses by Espey (1998) and Espey and Espey (2004) put median income elasticities for transport fuels and electricity at 0.83 and 0.92, respectively, in advanced countries, though there is considerable variation across studies. Unfortunately, not much is known about how income elasticities vary by income class, which would provide a more refined sense from this information of how budget shares for energy products vary across the income distribution.
[9] See, for example, the spreadsheet tool at www.imf.org/external/np/fad/environ/data/data.xlsx (based on data from the International Institute for Applied Systems Analysis).

International Energy Agency (IEA)—obviously vary with a country's power generation fuel mix. Proportionate price increases can be obtained using baseline price data, which are available from IEA for advanced countries and estimated for other countries by Clements and others (2013). Direct effects on energy prices account for about two-thirds of the total estimated burden of a carbon tax for the United States, and likely somewhat more than this for other advanced countries (see below).

Input/output tables can be used to estimate the indirect impacts of carbon taxes on the prices of other consumer products. These tables provide, for different industries, the value of outputs for final and intermediate products, and inputs—both energy (fuels, electricity) and non-energy (labor, capital, raw materials, and so on). Dividing fuel and electricity purchases by fuel prices, and applying emissions factors, the embodied CO_2 per dollar for each intermediate product, and ultimately each final product, can be inferred, and multiplied by the CO_2 tax to give the proportionate price increases.[10]

One complication is that the CO_2 emissions factor for power generation, and embodied carbon in various non-energy consumer products, will fall somewhat in response to carbon pricing as firms adopt energy-saving technologies, power generators switch to cleaner fuels, and so on, though (for similar reasoning as noted above) it may be reasonable to ignore this dampening effect on consumer prices for the scale of carbon taxes considered here.

Incidence Relative to Income or to Expenditure?

The appropriate definition of income against which tax burdens, including carbon tax burdens, should be measured for different household groups is somewhat unsettled. Annual income is problematic given that many people with low annual income (for instance, students, retirees with high accumulated savings, people temporarily laid off or on maternity leave) are not poor in a life-cycle context, yet they contribute greatly to disparities in annual income across households.[11] This problem is partly (though, because of constraints on consumption smoothing across the lifecycle, not fully) alleviated by measuring incidence against annual consumption expenditure rather than income. Incidence studies based on expenditure suggest that the potentially regressive impacts of energy or carbon taxes are much less pronounced (Poterba 1991; Hassett, Marthur, and Metcalf 2009).[12]

Household Expenditures

Spending by household income groups on energy and non-energy products is often available from household expenditure surveys. Many advanced countries routinely conduct these surveys;[13] the World Bank's Living Standards Measurement Study compiles them for approximately 40 developing countries; various other developing countries (for example, Bangladesh, Cambodia, India) administer surveys themselves. There are some concerns about the accuracy of the surveys (collecting data from thousands of households is difficult and costly), including the ability of households to remember or accurately record their expenditures, the design of the survey instrument, and data collection or entry (see Xu and others 2007).

---

[10] Input/output tables are available for 40 countries at www.wiod.org/new_site/database/wiots.htm (see Timmer and others 2015).

[11] Up to one-half of the inequalities in annual income across households might be attributed to variations in income over their life cycle rather than differences between life-cycle income (Lillard 1977).

[12] Regressive impacts would be milder still if a measure of lifetime income were used instead of expenditure (Walls and Hanson 1999).

[13] For example, the United States carries out the Consumer Expenditure Survey annually, the United Kingdom the Living Costs and Food Survey annually, and Eurostat the Household Budget Surveys every five years for every EU member country.

Some Further Considerations

This subsection discusses the possible passback of carbon taxes in lower supply prices and the incidence implications of co-benefits from carbon pricing.

Passback of Carbon Taxes in Lower Supply Prices

Some minor fraction of the burden of carbon taxes may be passed backward in lower producer prices, to the extent that fuel supply curves are upward sloping in the medium to longer term (for example, due to scarce inputs or long-lived, sector-specific capital). To the extent this reduces the net-of-tax return to capital, some of the carbon tax burden is borne by owners of capital (in lower equity values or dividends) with progressive effects because the better off earn a relatively high share of their income from capital (Metcalf and others 2008). But if, as seems plausible even for large economies like the United States, net-of-tax returns to capital are largely determined in world markets, the burden of lower supply prices will tend to be borne by labor in the form of lower wages. The incidence implications here, which depend on whether pollution-intensive industries disproportionately employ low- or high-wage workers; and on substitution elasticities between labor, capital, and polluting inputs and so on; become difficult to estimate (Fullerton and Heutel 2011). On balance, studies for the United States suggest that the passback of carbon taxes reduces the regressivity of carbon taxes (Rausch, Metcalf, and Reilly 2011), though the empirical effects are model specific.

Co-Benefits

Carbon pricing can produce significant environmental co-benefits, for example, reduced air pollution from coal combustion and externalities like congestion from motor vehicles, at least until these other externalities are fully priced through other policies. Co-benefit estimates can be quite large, averaging $57.5 per ton of CO_2 across the top 20 emitters (Parry, Veung, and Heine, forthcoming), though with substantial cross-country variation (due to sharp differences in population exposure to pollution, for instance).

Suppose, not unreasonably, that peoples' valuation of air pollution and other externality benefits is roughly proportional to income (OECD 2012). Then the distribution of local air pollution co-benefits across income groups within a country may be progressive if exposure risks decline with income (because the wealthy reside in areas with cleaner air). Vehicle externality benefits (largely borne by motorists as a group) are also progressive (though to a lesser extent) given that miles driven generally rise by less than proportional to income (Pickrell and Schimek 1997). These effects are not definitive, however—for example, reduced air pollution might positively affect local property values, with adverse effects for low-income renters.

Implications and Importance of Revenue Recycling

Accounting for the use of carbon tax revenues is critical because it is the overall incidence of the policy change, including accompanying adjustments to the broader tax and social safety net system, that matters, not just the component reflecting higher energy prices. This subsection discusses how revenue recycling might affect distributional incidence and underscores the potentially high opportunity costs to diverting substantial revenues to compensation schemes.

Recycling and Incidence

Extending equation (13.3), the burden-to-income ratio for household i, accounting for recycling benefits, is given by equation (13.4):

$$\frac{B_i}{I_i} \approx \sum_{j=1}^{M} \frac{\left(p_{X1}^j - p_{X0}^j\right)}{p_{X0}^j} \frac{p_{X0}^j X_{i0}^j}{I_i} - \alpha_i, \tag{13.4}$$

in which α_i is household group i's gain (approximated by the first order transfer) from broader tax and benefit adjustments as a proportion of their income. Clearly, the regressivity of the tax could be reduced if this gain were larger as a fraction of income for low-income households than for high-income households.

Unfortunately, accurate estimates of the distributional benefits from alternative adjustments of tax and benefit schedules through carbon tax recycling are not presently available for most countries. These schedules are typically complex (with numerous tax brackets subject to different marginal rates, various means-tested tax credits and benefits, and so on) so microsimulation data sets (readily available, for example, for the United States and the United Kingdom, but less so for other countries) are really needed to run individual household incomes (which can be heterogeneous) through these schedules to compute net tax liabilities, before aggregating over household samples within a broad income category.

Even these data-based fiscal incidence studies involve inaccuracies in that they do not typically account for behavioral responses to tax and benefit changes, nor the complicated ways in which relative prices (for example, for labor and capital) might be affected, with second-round implications for household burdens (Boadway and Keen 2000). Computable general equilibrium models can incorporate these effects, though the results are typically sensitive to structural and parameter assumptions, and these models cannot take advantage of the highly disaggregated data reflecting intricate details of the tax and benefit systems used in data-based studies.

One further point relates to the potential compensation for low-income households through automatic indexing of transfer and other benefit programs to higher general price levels, which is considered in some incidence studies. For example, in the United States, indexing of social security payments to seniors and federal income taxes to the consumer price level, and food purchase vouchers for low-income households to food prices, would offset about 10 percent of the burden of a carbon tax on the bottom income quintile according to Dinan 2015.[14]

Costs from Revenue Diversion

The key point from the literature on interactions between environmental taxes and the broader fiscal system is the critical importance of efficient revenue use—most obviously cutting other distortionary taxes on labor, capital, and consumption—for containing policy costs and improving social welfare (for example, Goulder and others 1999). The point is even more valid in light of public finance literature (Feldstein 1999; Saez, Slemrod, and Giertz 2012), underscoring that broader taxes significantly distort not only the *level* of economic activity (by reducing the returns to work effort and capital accumulation) but also its *composition* (by promoting informality and excessive spending on tax-preferred goods like housing and fringe benefits).

Figure 13.2 underscores the point with illustrative calculations of the efficiency costs of a carbon tax (excluding environmental benefits), expressed as a percentage of GDP, for a representative, large-emitting economy, under plausible, though very crude, assumptions about the price-responsiveness of emissions and the efficiency costs of broader taxes. The main point is that with revenue recycling, the efficiency costs of carbon taxes that reduce emissions by about 20 percent or less (that is, CO_2 taxes up to about $60 per ton) are very small, and perhaps even slightly negative,[15] while deadweight

---

[14] Only about 40 percent of U.S. households in the bottom income quintile receive social security benefits, and 20 percent receive food purchase vouchers. Moreover, indexing of benefits would only provide full compensation for a particular household if all (rather than a fraction) of its income was from benefits, and if its budget shares for energy were representative of (rather than higher than) those of the average household (because the average household determines the formula for calculating cost-of-living increases in response to higher energy prices).

[15] The negative cost result differs from the standard implication of Diamond and Mirrlees (1971), that swapping product taxes for broader income taxes will, under neutral assumptions, increase efficiency costs. The reason is that Diamond and Mirrlees do not incorporate distortions from the broader fiscal system, beyond those in factor markets. See Parry and Bento 2000 for more explanation.

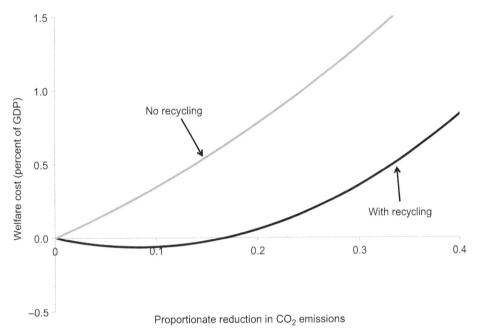

Figure 13.2   Illustrative Cost of a Carbon Tax, with and without Revenue Recycling

Source: Based on formulas in Parry and Williams 2010.
Note: The figure assumes a CO_2 intensity of 0.5 tons per $1,000 of GDP (about average for the top 20 CO_2-emitting countries—see Parry, Veung, and Heine, forthcoming); each successive $3 per ton increase in the CO_2 tax reduces emissions by 1 percent; and a marginal efficiency cost of $0.3 per extra dollar of revenue raised from broader taxes, with 60 percent and 40 percent of this due to distortions in the level of, and composition of, economic activity, respectively. Costs with recycling are moderately negative over some range, which differs from the general tax results derived in Diamond and Mirlees 1971, due to the inclusion here of additional distortions (affecting the composition of economic activity) from the broader fiscal system, beyond those in factor markets (affecting only the level of economic activity).

costs are substantial—0.75 percent of GDP for a 20 percent emissions reduction—when carbon tax revenues are returned lump sum or in other ways that do not increase economic efficiency.

A key implication is the potentially high opportunity costs from diverting revenues from the general budget to compensation schemes that do not enhance economic efficiency. Avoiding unnecessary compensation is therefore important and, where possible, compensation measures should be used that promote economic efficiency (for example, targeted reductions in personal income and payroll taxes, and earned income tax credits, all of which increase returns from formal work effort).

Summary

A first-pass assessment of carbon tax incidence in many different countries, before revenue recycling, can be obtained based on CO_2 emissions factors, energy prices, input/output tables (to measure indirect consumer price effects), and expenditure patterns for household income groups. Although there are complicating factors (for instance, behavioral responses, changes in producer prices, co-benefits from carbon pricing), it is difficult to make general statements about how they affect overall incidence, even directionally. Broader adjustments to the tax and benefit system that accompany carbon taxes need to be integrated into incidence analyses, while making transparent that revenue diversion from the general budget for compensation involves significant costs, for example, by reducing opportunities to cut other taxes that distort economic activity.

BOX 13.2 Carbon Tax Incidence in Developing Countries

This box makes three broad points about carbon tax incidence in developing countries.

First, carbon taxes might be less regressive in developing countries than in advanced countries if access to the power grid and vehicle ownership is skewed toward higher-income groups (though low-income households are affected by diesel fuel taxes indirectly through higher bus fares). Some suggestive evidence to back up this possibility comes from incidence studies of petroleum product subsidies, which are largely concentrated in the Middle East and North Africa. According to Figure 3.12 in Clements and others (2013), on average, the bottom income quintile receives only 3 percent of the benefits from gasoline subsidies, 7 percent from diesel fuel subsidies, and 4 percent from liquefied petroleum gas subsidies.

Second, the case for including carbon taxes as part of the fiscal system could be stronger in developing countries than in advanced countries if large informal sectors constrain the revenue bases of broader fiscal instruments such as personal income taxes and value-added tax. Carbon and more general energy taxes can help broaden the tax base into the informal sector (Bento, Jacobsen, and Liu 2012).

Third, however, targeted compensation for low-income households can be more challenging, at least if many people are not formally registered as taxpayers or benefit recipients. Besides strengthening social safety nets, use of carbon tax revenues for broader spending on health, education, housing, job programs, clean fuel alternatives, and so on may be needed to maintain equity objectives in light of higher energy prices, though this likely involves greater leakage of program benefits to the non-poor.

INCIDENCE ACROSS ADVANCED COUNTRIES: A BROAD PICTURE

The subsections here pull together various data sources to paint a very broad picture of overall carbon tax incidence for advanced countries, before and after revenue recycling. Box 13.2 provides some brief remarks for developing countries.

Incidence before Recycling

The discussion starts with the first-order, economy-wide burden of a CO_2 tax using an illustrative tax rate of $35 per ton[16] and the impacts of the tax on various prices for both energy and other products. These results are then matched to data on household budget shares.

Economy-Wide Incidence

Figure 13.3 shows, for selected advanced countries in 2012 (and ignoring behavioral responses), the first-order burden of the $35 CO_2 tax—the tax revenue as a percentage of GDP, decomposing the tax that would be paid by primary fuels.[17]

The tax burdens vary from less than 0.5 percent of GDP in Denmark, France, Norway, Sweden, and Switzerland—countries where there is relatively little use of coal in particular, but also natural gas—to more than 1.5 percent of GDP in the Czech Republic, Korea, and Poland—which are all relatively heavy coal users.

Price Impacts

Figure 13.4 provides some flavor of the direct impacts of a $35 per ton CO_2 tax on household energy prices in advanced countries. Specifically, it shows (assuming full pass through and

---

[16] This figure is based on the central case of US IAWG (2013). If applied to leading CO_2-emitting countries, this starting price would be broadly consistent with keeping long-term, mean projected warming to about 2.5°C (Nordhaus 2013, 228).

[17] The CO_2 tax is superimposed on top of any existing CO_2 pricing (for example, about $10 per ton for covered emissions in the EU trading system).

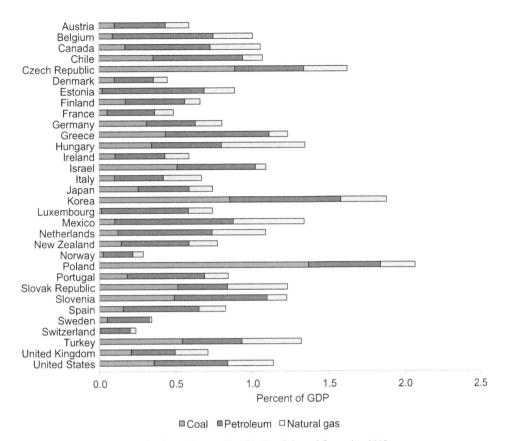

Figure 13.3 First-Order Burden from a $35 per Ton CO_2 Tax, Selected Countries, 2012

Sources: IEA (2014); IMF (2015).

Note: Figure shows the first-order burden of a CO_2 tax (excluding behavioral responses), that is, the tax rate times current emissions, expressed as a percentage of GDP, and decomposed according to the contribution of different primary fuels to CO_2 emissions.

calculated as discussed above) the percentage increase in energy prices for 2012 (or thereabouts) for residential electricity, natural gas, gasoline, and diesel.

The absolute price increases for natural gas, gasoline, and diesel are essentially uniform for each fuel across countries (given uniform emissions factors), though proportionate price increases are larger in countries with relatively low energy prices. For example, household natural gas prices increase by about 20 percent in Canada, Mexico, and the United States (where supply costs and taxes are low), but less than 6 percent in Chile, Denmark, Greece, Japan, and Sweden (where supply costs are higher and, for Denmark and Sweden, specific taxes are levied in addition to value-added tax). Similarly, gasoline and diesel prices increase by more than 8 percent in Mexico and the United States (where fuel taxes are relatively low), but these prices rise by less than 5 percent in most other cases (the percentage increase in diesel prices is a bit larger than for gasoline because of the higher emissions factor and, in many cases, lower tax rate for diesel).

The absolute price increase differs substantially for electricity, from more than US$0.025 per kilowatt hour (kWh) in Estonia, Greece, and Israel (where power generation is fossil-fuel intensive) to about US$0.0025 per kWh or less in France, Norway, Sweden, and Switzerland (where there is little reliance on fossil-fuel generation). Percent price increases exceed about 15 percent in Estonia, Israel, Mexico, Korea, and the United States, while they are less than 2 percent in France, Norway, Sweden, and Switzerland.

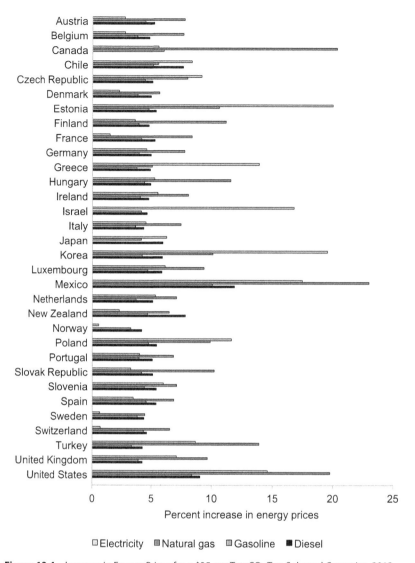

Figure 13.4 Increase in Energy Prices for a $35 per Ton CO₂ Tax, Selected Countries, 2012

Sources: IEA (2014); Parry and others (2014).
Note: All data are for 2012, aside from the CO₂ emissions factors (from IEA), which were available for 2011. Price increases
are calculated by the CO₂ emissions factor for each fuel, times $35 per ton, divided by the baseline household price.

With regard to the indirect impacts of carbon taxes on the prices of other consumer products, for the United States, Morris and Mathur (2015) estimate these price effects for a CO_2 tax of $15 per ton in 2010. The prices of other products rise, but in most cases by a fairly modest percentage compared with energy price increases. For example, some consumer prices (clothing and health, for instance) rise by less than 0.5 percent, and others (for example, mass transit, household supplies) by between 0.5 and 1 percent, though in some cases (such as auto purchases and parts, air and transit travel) price increases are somewhat more significant at between 1 and 2 percent.

Figure 13.5 shows the contribution of direct and indirect price effects to the burden of a carbon tax, expressed relative to income and consumption, as borne by different income quintiles in

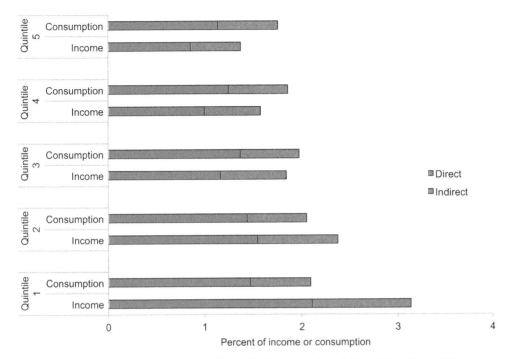

Figure 13.5   Direct and Indirect Burden of a Carbon Tax by Income Quintile in the United States, 2010

Source: Morris and Mathur (2015).
Note: Calculations are a simple average over data for income deciles.

the United States. Burdens from indirect price effects are smaller than those from the direct price effects and smaller in relative terms for lower-income groups (the size of the indirect burden relative to the direct burden falls from 54 percent for the top income quintile to 42 percent for the bottom income quintile for the consumption-based measure). Therefore, accounting for indirect effects moderately increases progressivity.

Speaking very loosely, the increases in non-energy consumer products in other advanced economies might be expected to either follow a pattern broadly similar to those in Morris and Mathur 2015 for countries like Estonia, Korea, and Mexico (where proportionate increases in electricity prices are broadly similar to those for the United States) or to rise more moderately in the majority of cases (where proportionate increases in electricity prices are less pronounced than in the United States). In the latter cases, this moderate rise implies an even smaller burden from indirect price effects relative to the burden from direct price effects.

Cross-Country Incidence

A consistent, cross-country database of carbon tax incidence is not available from previous studies, because these studies either have an individual-country focus or look at the incidence of energy taxes (see Box 13.1). Here the chapter crudely extrapolates carbon tax incidence for advanced countries as follows:

The analysis starts with data, by income quintile, on the share of consumption paid in electricity, heating, and motor fuel taxes, reported in OECD 2014. These figures are divided by tax rates (from IEA 2014) and multiplied by the absolute energy price increases underlying Figure 13.4 (as a proxy for heating by natural gas) to give the burden by quintile of the direct impacts on energy prices of a $35 per ton CO_2 tax. Finally, burdens from indirect price increases are inferred

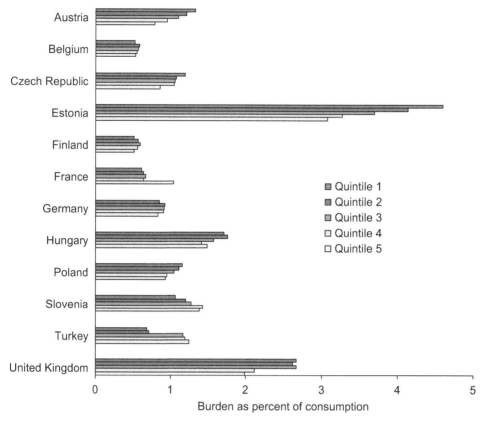

Figure 13.6   Carbon Tax Incidence by Income Quintiles before Revenue Recycling, Selected Countries, 2012

Source: Author's calculations using OECD 2014 and IEA 2014.

using, by quintile, the ratio of burdens from indirect and direct price increases from Figure 13.5 (for consumption), after scaling these ratios by the proportionate increase in electricity prices in other countries relative to those in the United States.[18]

The result, for selected countries, is shown in Figure 13.6. Cross-country differences reflect differences in carbon-tax-induced energy price impacts (relatively high for Estonia and the United Kingdom and low for Belgium and France—see Figure 13.4) and initial budget shares for energy. The main point is that, within countries, effects vary from moderately regressive (for example, in Austria, the Czech Republic, Estonia, Poland, the United Kingdom), to roughly proportional (Belgium, Finland, Germany), to moderately progressive (Slovenia, Turkey).

Incidence after Recycling

This section considers distributional impacts from the use of carbon tax revenues, first if used for reductions in other energy excises (on electricity and vehicles) and then for adjustments to the broader tax and benefit system.

---

[18] This latter adjustment does not substantially alter overall incidence patterns, given that the indirect burdens are minor relative to direct burdens.

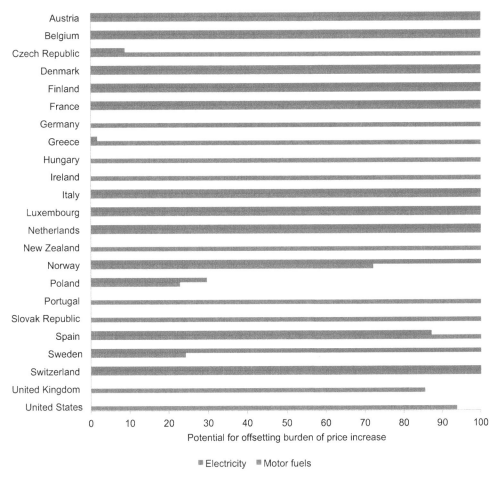

Figure 13.7 Burden of Higher Household Energy Prices that Could Be Offset by Lowering Other Energy Taxes, Advanced Countries, 2010

Sources: IEA (2014); IMF (2011).

Note: For electricity, the bars show the proportion of the increase in residential electricity prices from a $35 per ton CO_2 tax that could be offset by lowering a preexisting excise tax on residential electricity consumption. For motor fuels, the bars show the proportion of the increase in motor fuel prices from the same carbon tax that could be offset (on an annualized basis) by lowering excises on vehicle sales.

Reducing Other Energy Taxes

One possibility for offsetting, in a transparent way, some of the carbon-tax-induced burden on households from higher energy prices might be to lower preexisting taxes on energy that the carbon tax makes redundant on climate grounds. The main targets here are excises on residential electricity consumption, and on vehicle sales, that are applied across many advanced countries.[19]

Figure 13.7 shows, for a selection of advanced countries, what portion of the increase in residential electricity prices, and motor fuel prices (weighting across gasoline and diesel fuel prices) induced by a $35 per ton CO_2 tax could be offset by lowering preexisting excises, where they apply. For 11 out of 23 countries, the burden on households from higher electricity prices could be completely neutralized by offsetting reductions in electricity excises, or put another way, current excises exceed (often by well over 100 percent) the impact of carbon taxes on residential

---

[19] These taxes are imposed in addition to taxes (value-added or similar general sales taxes) on consumer goods in general.

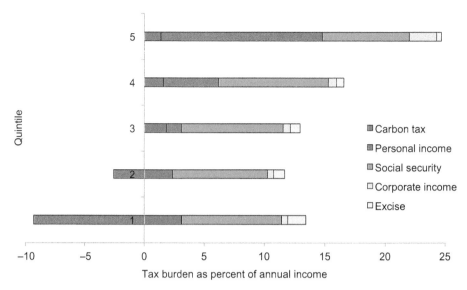

Figure 13.8 Share of Federal Taxes by Income Quintile, United States, 2009

Sources: CBO (2012); and Figure 13.6.
Note: Carbon tax burden is for 2010.

electricity prices.[20] And in 18 cases, the burden of higher motor fuel prices could be neutralized, on an annualized basis, by lowering excises on motor vehicle sales.

However, many countries have little scope for offsetting the burden of higher natural gas prices on households, or the indirect impacts on the prices of other consumer products, by cutting preexisting excises. And of course, scaling back electricity and vehicle excises will moderately offset some of the emissions reductions from carbon taxes and reduce, quite substantially, the net revenues from the carbon tax—potentially in proportion to the share of residential electricity and motor fuels in total CO_2 emissions.[21]

Adjusting the Broader Tax and Benefit System

The distributional impacts of potential adjustments to the broader tax and benefit system accompanying a carbon tax will depend on country specifics, such as the underlying distribution of pretax income and rates and brackets in personal income tax schedules; therefore, the discussion here offers only some general remarks, along with some statistics for the United States.

Figure 13.8 shows the share of income from various federal taxes, and a prospective carbon tax, in the United States by income quintile. Payroll taxes are approximately proportional up to the top income quintile, where they become regressive (because of the cut-off beyond which the marginal tax rate drops to zero). In contrast, the personal income tax is quite progressive, because of tax credits at the bottom end (making the average tax burden negative), tax allowances, and rising marginal rates. Less important with regard to tax burdens are excises that are regressive and corporate income taxes that are progressive at the upper end (though accurately measuring the incidence of this tax is difficult; see below).

---

[20] For many EU countries, cutting electricity excises would not conflict with the EU Energy Tax Directive, given that it imposes a relatively modest floor tax on electricity equivalent to about US 0.07 cents per kWh.
[21] The burden of higher energy prices might also be offset by introducing "subsistence" thresholds for energy consumption below which no tax is paid. Although this measure is progressive, it is similar to using revenues for lump-sum transfers (see the discussion below), which yields no efficiency gains.

With regard to personal income taxes, a proportional reduction in marginal tax rates will perform well on efficiency grounds (improving incentives for work effort and savings, and reducing incentives for tax sheltering) but will have regressive effects. In contrast, raising personal income tax thresholds benefits low-income households disproportionately relative to their income, though the tax reduction (the increase in the threshold times the household's marginal tax rate) is larger in absolute terms for higher-income households. Extending tax credits (for child care, for instance) is a bit better in this regard because the value of the credit is the same for all taxpayers. Better still (for targeting low-income households) is expanding earned income tax credits, which phase out as income rises. None of these measures reach all low-income households, however, because some of them do not pay income tax. Moreover, the economic efficiency gains from these tax reductions are smaller than from cuts in marginal tax rates—they promote labor force participation and shifting from informal to formal work effort, both of which depend on average tax rates, but not hours worked on the job or shifting from tax-preferred to ordinary spending, both of which depend on marginal tax rates. Efficiency gains from cutting payroll rates are likely to be somewhat smaller than those for cutting income tax rates because there are fewer exemptions and deductions for payroll taxes (for example, fringe benefits are exempt but mortgage interest is not).

The burden of corporate income taxes largely falls on labor in countries with globally integrated capital markets (where the net-of-tax return to capital cannot be pushed down below that available in other countries). Although the burden across workers at different earnings levels is unclear, capital and skills may be complementary so that cutting corporate income taxes benefits high-wage workers disproportionately. Cutting capital taxes likely produces the biggest source of efficiency gains, given the international mobility of the tax base, though in large part at the expense of welfare losses in other countries suffering the capital flight; indeed, tax theory (Kanbur and Keen 1993) suggests that other countries will respond by cutting their own capital taxes, thereby dampening efficiency gains in the domestic economy.

Compared with tax systems, benefit programs potentially offer a far more efficient means for redistributing to lower-income households. The drawback of most benefit programs (for example, social security, unemployment, housing, family-dependent benefits) is that they do not increase economic efficiency. Nonetheless, at least for the United States, only a minor fraction of the 10 percent or so of carbon tax revenues needed to keep the bottom income quintile whole (40 percent, or 4 percent of carbon tax revenue, according to Dinan 2015) need come from these types of instruments.

Finally, in addition to recycling carbon tax revenues in tax cuts and benefit increases, numerous other accompanying fiscal adjustments could alter the incidence of a fiscal package containing a carbon tax, most obviously scaling back tax expenditures that disproportionately benefit the better off. For example, cutting relief for pension contributions, estates transferred at death, state and local income taxes, mortgage interest, charitable giving, capital gains and dividends, could all have progressive effects (CBO 2013).

Summary

The general theme of the above discussion is that distributional concerns are potentially manageable. For one thing, the energy price impacts of carbon taxes may not be that regressive, at least if incidence is measured against household consumption, and may be proportional, or even progressive in some countries. For another, there are numerous opportunities in advanced countries to compensate low-income households by recycling carbon tax revenues in targeted tax cuts and benefit increases and to combine carbon taxes with other progressive measures, though the specifics need to be carefully examined on a country-by-country basis. Failing to charge for carbon damages is, in fact, a very inefficient distributional policy because the vast majority of benefits leak away to higher-income groups, or put another way, only a small fraction of the carbon tax revenues are needed to compensate low-income households. Even for this group, a large portion of the compensation could take the form of tax cuts and earned income tax credits (that have some efficiency benefits) rather than transfer payments (that do not). With regard to the recycling of other revenues, policymakers typically need to trade off efficiency and distributional objectives (tax reductions with higher efficiency gains tend to be more regressive) though there is always scope for other adjustments (for example, reforming tax preferences) to promote distribution neutrality in a broad fiscal package.

CONCLUSION

The general message of this chapter is that, although distributional concerns are potentially important for both fairness and the politics of reform, they should not hold up the establishment of a robust price on CO_2 emissions.

   This discussion concludes by noting a couple of carbon pricing schemes that seem needlessly costly. One is emissions trading systems in which allowances are given away for free to existing emitters. Not only does this policy forgo large economic efficiency gains from recycling revenues in other tax reductions, it does nothing to improve distributional outcomes across households—in fact, it may greatly worsen them by transferring windfall profits to wealthy households via higher equity values for firms receiving free allowances (Dinan and Rogers 2002; Parry 2004). The other scheme, "tax and dividend," also forgoes large efficiency benefits, by returning 100 percent of carbon tax revenues to households in equal lump-sum transfers. As emphasized above (for the United States), only about 10 percent of revenues are needed to compensate bottom income quintiles, and only a minor portion of this need take the form of instruments (like transfer payments) that do not increase economic efficiency.

REFERENCES

Bento, Antonio, Mark Jacobsen, and Antung A. Liu. 2012. "Environmental Policy in the Presence of an Informal Sector." Discussion paper, Cornell University, Ithaca, New York.

Boadway, Robin, and Michael Keen. 2000. "Redistribution." In *Handbook of Income Distribution*, edited by A. Atkinson and F. Bourguignon. Amsterdam: North Holland.

Böhringer, C., J. C. Carbone, and T. F. Rutherford. 2012. "Unilateral Climate Policy Design: Efficiency and Equity Implications of Alternative Instruments to Reduce Carbon Leakage." *Energy Economics* 34 (Supplement 2): S208–S217.

Brännlund, Runar, and Jonas Nordström. 2004. "Carbon Tax Simulations Using a Household Demand Model." *European Economic Review* 48 (1): 211–33.

Bull, Nicholas, Kevin Hassett, and Gilbert Metcalf. 1994. "Who Pays Broad-Based Energy Taxes? Computing Lifetime and Regional Incidence." *Energy Journal* 15 (3): 145–64.

Calder, Jack. 2015. "Administration of a US Carbon Tax." In *Implementing a US Carbon Tax: Challenges and Debates*, edited by I. Parry, A. Morris, and R. Williams, 38–61. New York: Routledge.

Casler, Stephen D., and Aisha Rafiqui. 1993. "Evaluating Fuel Tax Equity: Direct and Indirect Distributional Effects." *National Tax Journal* 46 (2): 197–205.

Clements, Benedict, David Coady, Stefania Fabrizio, Sanjeev Gupta, Trevor Alleyene, and Carlo Sdralevich, eds. 2013. *Energy Subsidy Reform: Lessons and Implications*. Washington: International Monetary Fund.

Congressional Budget Office (CBO). 2012. *The Distribution of Household Income and Federal Taxes, 2008 and 2009*. Washington: Congressional Budget Office.

———. 2013. *The Distribution of Major Tax Expenditures in the Individual Income Tax System*. Washington: Congressional Budget Office.

Cornwell, Antonia, and John Creedy. 1997. "Measuring the Welfare Effects of Tax Changes Using the LES: An Application to a Carbon Tax." *Empirical Economics* 22 (4): 589–613.

Diamond, Peter A., and James A. Mirrlees. 1971. "Optimal Taxation and Public Production I: Production Efficiency, and II: Tax Rules." *American Economic Review* 61: 8–27, 261–78.

Dinan, Terry. 2015. "Offsetting a Carbon Tax's Burden on Low-Income Households." In *Implementing a US Carbon Tax: Challenges and Debates*, edited by I. Parry, A. Morris, and R. Williams, 38–61. New York: Routledge.

———, and Diane Lim Rogers. 2002. "Distributional Effects of Carbon Allowance Trading: How Government Decisions Determine Winners and Losers." *National Tax Journal* 55 (2): 199–222.

Espey, M. 1998. "Gasoline Demand Revisited: An International Meta Analysis of Elasticities." *Energy Economics* 20 (3): 273–95.

Espey, J. A., and M. Espey. 2004. "Turning on the Lights: A Meta Analysis of Residential Electricity Demand Elasticities." *Journal of Agricultural and Applied Economics* 36 (1): 65–81.

Feldstein, Martin. 1999. "Tax Avoidance and the Deadweight Loss of the Income Tax." *Review of Economics and Statistics* 81 (4): 674–80.

Fischer, Carolyn, Richard Morgenstern, and Nathan Richardson. 2015. "Carbon Taxes and Energy Intensive Trade Exposed Industries: Impacts and Options." In *Implementing a US Carbon Tax: Challenges and Debates*, edited by I. Parry, A. Morris, and R. Williams, 159–77. New York: Routledge.

Fullerton, Don, and Garth Heutel. 2011. "Analytical General Equilibrium Effects of Energy Policy on Output and Factor Prices." *The B.E. Journal of Economic Analysis & Policy* 10 (2): 1–26.

Goulder, Lawrence H., Ian W. H. Parry, Roberton C. Williams, and Dallas Burtraw. 1999. "The Cost-Effectiveness of Alternative Instruments for Environmental Protection in a Second-Best Setting." *Journal of Public Economics* 72 (3): 329–60.

Hassett, K., A. Mathur, and G. Metcalf. 2009. "The Incidence of a US Carbon Tax: A Lifetime and Regional Analysis." *Energy Journal* 30 (2): 155–78.

International Energy Agency (IEA). 2014. *World Energy Statistics and Balances*. Paris: International Energy Agency.

International Monetary Fund (IMF). 2011. "Promising Domestic Fiscal Instruments for Climate Finance." Background Paper for the Report to the G20 on "Mobilizing Sources of Climate Finance," International Monetary Fund, Washington. www.imf.org/external/np/g20/pdf/110411b.pdf.

———. 2015. World Economic Outlook Database. International Monetary Fund, Washington. www.imf.org/external/pubs/ft/weo/2014/02/weodata/index.aspx.

Immervoll, Herwig, and Linda Richardson. 2011. "Redistribution Policy and Inequality Reduction in OECD Countries: What Has Changed in Two Decades?" IZA Discussion Paper No. 6030, Institute for the Study of Labor, Bonn, Germany.

Kanbur, Ravi, and Michael Keen. 1993. "Jeux Sans Frontiers: Tax Competition and Tax Coordination When Countries Differ in Size." *American Economic Review* 83: 877–92.

Lillard, L. A. 1977. "Inequality: Earnings versus Human Wealth." *American Economic Review* 67 (2): 42–53.

Metcalf, Gilbert E. 1999. "A Distributional Analysis of Green Tax Reforms." *National Tax Journal* 52: 665–81.

———, J. F. Holak, H. Jacoby, S. Paltsev, and J. Reilly. 2008. "Analysis of US Greenhouse Gas Tax Proposals." NBER Working Paper No. 13980, National Bureau of Economic Research, Cambridge, Massachusetts.

Morris, Adele, and Aparna Mathur. 2015. "The Distributional Burden of a Carbon Tax: Evidence and Implications for Policy." In *Implementing a US Carbon Tax: Challenges and Debates*, edited by I. Parry, A. Morris, and R. Williams, 38–61. New York: Routledge.

Nordhaus, William D. 2013. *The Climate Casino: Risk, Uncertainty, and Economics for a Warming World*. New Haven, Connecticut: Yale University Press.

Organisation for Economic Co-operation and Development (OECD). 2012. *Mortality Risk Valuation in Environment, Health and Transport Policies*. Paris: Organization for Economic Cooperation and Development.

———. 2014. *The Distributional Incidence of Energy Taxes*. Paris: Organization for Economic Cooperation and Development.

Parry, Ian W. H. 2004. "Are Emissions Permits Regressive?" *Journal of Environmental Economics and Management* 47 (2): 364–87.

———, and Antonio M. Bento. 2000. "Tax Deductions, Environmental Policy, and the 'Double Dividend' Hypothesis." *Journal of Environmental Economics and Management* 39 (1): 67–96.

Parry, Ian W. H., Dirk Heine, Shanjun Li, and Eliza Lis. 2014. *Getting Energy Prices Right: From Principle to Practice*. Washington: International Monetary Fund.

Parry, Ian W. H., Chandara Veung, and Dirk Heine. Forthcoming. "How Much Carbon Pricing Is in Countries' Own Interests? The Critical Role of Co-Benefits." *Climate Change Economics*.

Parry, Ian W. H., and Roberton Williams. 2010. "What Are the Costs of Meeting Distributional Objectives for Climate Policy?" *B.E. Journal of Economic Analysis and Policy* 10 (2, Symposium): Article 9.

Pickrell, Don, and Paul Schimek. 1997. "Trends in Personal Motor Vehicle Ownership and Use: Evidence from the Nationwide Personal Transportation Survey." In *Proceedings from the Nationwide Personal Transportation Survey Symposium*, October 29–31. No. 17 of Searching for Solutions: A Policy Discussion Series. Washington, DC: U.S. Federal Highway Administration, 85–127.

Poterba, James M. 1991. "Is the Gasoline Tax Regressive?" In *Tax Policy and the Economy*, edited by David Bradford, 5. Cambridge, Massachusetts: National Bureau of Economic Research.

Rausch, S., G. E. Metcalf, and J. M. Reilly. 2011. "Distributional Impacts of Carbon Pricing: A General Equilibrium Approach with Micro-Data for Households." *Energy Economics* 33 (S1): S20–S33.

Saez, Emmanuel, Joel Slemrod, and Seth H. Giertz. 2012. "The Elasticity of Taxable Income with Respect to Marginal Tax Rates: A Critical Review." *Journal of Economic Literature* 50 (1): 3–50.

Smith, Stephen. 1992. "The Distributional Consequences of Taxes on Energy and the Carbon Content of Fuels." *European Economy*, Special Edition No. 1: *The Economics of Limiting CO_2 Emissions*, 241–68.

Sterner, T. 2012. "Distributional Effects of Taxing Transport Fuel." *Energy Policy* 41: 75–83.

Timmer, M. P., E. Dietzenbacher, B. Los, R. Stehrer, and G. J. de Vries. 2015. "An Illustrated User Guide to the World Input–Output Database: The Case of Global Automotive Production." *Review of International Economics*. doi: 10.1111/roie.12178.

United States Interagency Working Group on Social Cost of Carbon (US IAWG). 2013. *Technical Support Document: Technical Update of the Social Cost of Carbon for Regulatory Impact Analysis under Executive Order 12866*. Washington: Interagency Working Group on Social Cost of Carbon, United States Government.

Walls, Margaret, and Jean Hanson. 1999. "Distributional Aspects of an Environmental Tax Shift: The Case of Motor Vehicles Emissions Taxes." *National Tax Journal* 52 (1): 53–65.

Wier, Mette, Katja Birr-Pedersen, Henrik Klinge Jacobsen, and Jacob Klok. 2005. "Are CO_2 Taxes Regressive? Evidence from the Danish Experience." *Ecological Economics* 52 (2): 239–51.

World Bank. 2014. *State and Trends of Carbon Pricing*. Washington: World Bank.

Xu, Ke, Frode Ravndal, David Evans, and Guy Carrin. 2007. "Assessing the Reliability of Household Expenditure Data: Results of the World Health Survey." Discussion Paper No. 5, World Health Organization, Geneva.

PART V

Expenditure Policy and Inequality

The Unequal Benefits of Fuel Subsidies Revisited: Evidence for Developing Countries

DAVID COADY, VALENTINA FLAMINI, AND LOUIS SEARS

INTRODUCTION

The negative economic and environmental effects of fuel subsidies are widely recognized.[1] But these subsidies are also undesirable from an equity perspective since they exacerbate income inequalities and are not a cost-effective approach to protecting the poor. Their adverse impact on inequality arises through two channels. First, the benefits of fuel subsidies are distributed in proportion to household energy consumption, and the consumption baskets of higher-income households are typically more energy intensive than those of lower-income households. Second, public expenditures on energy subsidies crowd out more redistributive public spending or require financing through regressive taxation. Yet governments in developing countries remain reluctant to remove them because of the adverse impact of higher fuel prices on household real incomes, in particular of lower-income households who are least able to absorb the cost of higher fuel prices. Assessing the magnitude of the income loss from fuel price increases and its distribution across income groups is therefore a key input into designing more cost-effective policies to protect the most vulnerable social groups and gaining political and public support for reducing subsidies.

This chapter reviews evidence from country studies that estimate the welfare impact of fuel price increases on households. It does so by extending the cross-country evidence reviewed by Arze Del Granado, Coady, and Gillingham (2012) to include more recent studies for a larger number of countries. Arze Del Granado, Coady, and Gillingham (2012) cover estimates of welfare impacts for 20 countries from Africa, Asia, the Middle East, and Latin America undertaken between 2005 and 2009. This chapter extends the survey to 32 countries up to 2014. In some instances, more recent studies for countries already covered became available so the number of new studies reviewed is larger than the number of countries added to the sample. The analysis provides up-to-date cross-country empirical evidence indicating that a very large share of benefits from universal price subsidies goes to high-income households, further reinforcing existing inequalities in income and consumption. These results can also be used to approximate the welfare impact of fuel subsidies in future country studies for which the data necessary for the analysis are not available.

The chapter is structured as follows: First, it presents evidence on the fiscal importance of energy subsidies. It describes recent trends in international oil prices, the extent to which these changes have been passed through to domestic fuel prices in various regions, and the resulting

---

[1] These negative effects include the following: (1) their high fiscal cost crowds out high-priority public spending and private investment; (2) they dilute incentives for improving energy efficiency, thus magnifying the macroeconomic and fiscal impacts of volatile international prices; (3) they result in excessive environmental costs, including local and global pollution as well as traffic congestion and accidents; and (4) they can lead to illegal and disruptive cross-country smuggling and domestic shortages.

fiscal implications. It then briefly outlines the methodology used to estimate the welfare impact of fuel price increases aimed at reducing the fiscal cost of fuel subsidies. The empirical results of the survey are presented by looking at the magnitude, composition, and distribution of the welfare impact of fuel subsidy reform. An overview is provided of issues that need to be addressed when designing an energy subsidy reform strategy, with an emphasis on safety net measures to protect the poor.

TRENDS IN INTERNATIONAL OIL PRICES AND DOMESTIC PASS-THROUGH

Fuel subsidies arise in many developing countries because domestic consumer prices for fuel products are directly controlled by governments and are only adjusted on an ad hoc basis in an attempt to protect domestic consumers from high and volatile oil prices. International price increases are perceived as temporary and therefore not passed onto domestic consumers. But if international price increases are sustained, the domestic price increases required to eliminate subsidies quickly become more politically challenging, resulting in policy inertia and escalating subsidies.

After the mid-2000s, international oil prices started to increase steadily before increasing more sharply during 2007 and the first half of 2008 (Figure 14.1). Across all developing regions, many countries failed to pass these increases on to domestic consumers. For instance, more than half of developing countries passed on less than two-thirds of the increase in international diesel prices to domestic consumers during this period. The pass-through was especially low in the Middle East and North Africa region, where half of the countries passed through less than 13 percent of international price increases (Table 14.1). Incomplete pass-through led to a substantial increase in subsidies in many countries, particularly in countries in the Middle East and North Africa as well as in developing Asia. The resulting fiscal cost was substantial, with the combined cost for diesel, gasoline, and kerosene exceeding 3 percent of GDP on an annualized basis in more than half of developing countries. The total fiscal cost would be even higher if subsidies to other energy products, such as liquefied petroleum gas (LPG) and electricity, were included (Clements and others 2013).

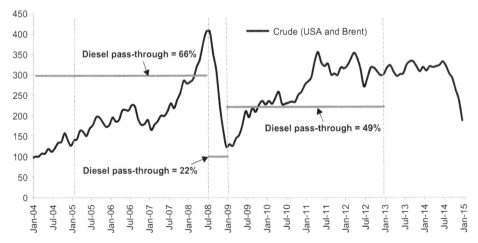

Figure 14.1 International Oil Prices and Domestic Pass-Through, 2000–14 *(Index, January 2000 = 100)*

Sources: IMF, *World Economic Outlook*, April 2015; U.S. Energy Information Administration; IMF staff estimates.
Note: Pass-through is defined as the increase in domestic prices divided by the increase in international prices in U.S. dollars.

TABLE 14.1

Diesel Price Pass-Through and Net Taxes in Developing Countries, 2004–12

	End-2004–Mid-2008	Mid-2008–End-2008	End-2008–End-2012	End-2013–End-2014
Pass-through (Percent)				
Developing Economies {118}	66	22	49	11
Developing Asia {28}	65	12	54	40
Latin America and the Caribbean {32}	51	28	83	12
Middle East and North Africa {19}	13	1	10	0
Sub-Saharan Africa {39}	85	38	35	0
Fiscal cost (Percent of GDP)				
Developing Economies {118}	1.92	−3.14	1.74	−0.88
Developing Asia {28}	1.43	−4.68	2.24	−0.89
Latin America and the Caribbean {32}	2.50	−2.98	1.27	−0.80
Middle East and North Africa {19}	1.93	−3.44	3.20	−1.89
Sub-Saharan Africa {39}	2.15	−3.42	1.50	−0.92

Net-tax (US$/liter)	End-2004	Mid-2008	End-2008	End-2012	End-2014
Developing Economies {118}	0.10	−0.08	0.33	0.22	0.37
Developing Asia {28}	−0.11	−0.37	0.17	0.05	0.16
Latin America and the Caribbean {32}	0.09	−0.08	0.29	0.22	0.29
Middle East and North Africa {19}	−0.14	−0.78	−0.12	−0.36	0.07
Sub-Saharan Africa {39}	0.27	0.14	0.54	0.32	0.47

Sources: Deutsche Gesellschaft für Internationale Zusammenarbeit (GIZ); International Energy Agency; U.S. Energy Information Agency; IMF staff estimates.

Note: Pass-through is defined as the increase in domestic prices divided by the increase in international prices in U.S. dollars. Fiscal cost refers to the increase in fuel subsidies or decrease in tax revenues for gasoline, diesel, and kerosene, based on changes in end-of-period prices and annualized cost. Net taxes per liter are defined as unit taxes minus unit subsidies; a negative value indicates prevalence of subsidies. Numbers in brackets refer to the size of the sample of countries in each group. Sample size for end-2013–end-2014 is significantly lower than previous periods, totaling 102 developing countries rather than 118.

After peaking in mid-2008, international prices plummeted during the following six months. As prices began to fall, many countries passed through very little of the decline to consumers in an attempt to recoup past revenue losses. During this period, pass-through fell below 15 percent in more than half of the developing countries, and was below 1 percent in most of the Middle East and North Africa region. As a result, fuel tax levels increased and subsidies decreased. For instance, by end-2008 the median net tax per liter in sub-Saharan Africa was four times higher than at midyear, unit subsidies in Middle East and North Africa countries shrank by 85 percent, while median net taxes in developing Asia and Latin America and the Caribbean turned positive (Table 14.1). However, the relief was short-lived because international oil prices rebounded sharply beginning in early 2009—by April 2011 international prices had almost reached the peak levels seen in mid-2008. Again, taxes fell and subsidies increased during the next few years, and the fiscal costs associated with controlled prices escalated, wiping out much of the fiscal gain accrued during the second half of 2008.

The decline in international prices in late 2014–early 2015 has presented countries with another opportunity to adopt a permanent solution to the burden of energy subsidies. However, transforming this temporary respite into a permanent solution will require advance planning and foresight on the part of policymakers. In this respect, knowledge of the magnitude and distribution of the impact of fuel price increases on real household incomes is crucial to designing measures to mitigate the impact on the poor, which, in turn, is important for making reforms politically feasible and durable.

METHODOLOGY

The impact of increasing domestic fuel prices on the welfare of households arises through two channels.[2] First, households face the direct impact of higher prices for fuels consumed for cooking, heating, lighting, and personal transport. Second, an indirect impact is felt through higher prices for other goods and services consumed by households as higher fuel costs are reflected in increased production costs and consumer prices. The magnitude of these impacts depends on the importance of cooking, lighting, heating, and personal transport costs in total household consumption, as well as on the fuel intensity of other goods and services consumed by households. The distribution of the impacts across different income groups will depend on the relative importance of these factors across income groups. For example, if the consumption baskets of higher-income groups are relatively more fuel intensive than those of lower-income groups, the impact on higher-income groups will be relatively large.

Direct Impact

Evaluating the direct impact requires survey data on household expenditures that include detailed information on fuel consumption. These data can be used to calculate the budget share for each fuel product for each household, that is, total household expenditure on each fuel product divided by total household consumption. All of the studies in this review use such data to calculate the direct impact of fuel price increases on households. The budget share for a given fuel provides an estimate of the welfare impact of a doubling of the fuel price absent any demand response. For example, if the budget share for gasoline is 0.05 (the household allocates 5 percent of its total consumption budget to gasoline), a doubling of the price of gasoline will result in a decrease in welfare for the household equivalent to a 5 percent decrease in real income. Given the underlying assumption of no demand response, these welfare impacts should be interpreted as short-term impacts or upper bounds on longer-term impacts.

Indirect Impact

Most of the country studies evaluate the indirect impact of higher fuel prices by estimating the impact on the prices of other goods and services, which requires a price-shifting model. The model used in these studies is based on that presented in Coady and Newhouse 2006, which assumes that increases in fuel production costs are fully passed forward onto the domestic prices of goods and services. Estimating these price increases requires information on the production structure of the economy, for example, an input/output table describing the share of different inputs in the production cost structure. Recent household survey data are often available, but not so for input/output tables, which are often more outdated. A key implication is that the fuel cost shares across sectors will tend to underestimate (overestimate) current shares if prices have increased (decreased) in the meantime. Therefore, the impact of fuel price increases on economy-wide prices, and the resulting welfare losses, will be underestimated (overestimated).

The approach used to estimate the indirect impact on the prices of other goods and services implicitly assumes that goods are nontraded, that domestic production technologies exhibit constant returns to scale, and that demand is completely price inelastic (Chapter 3 of Newbery and Stern 1987). The nontraded assumption is arguably less problematic in the present context since much of the indirect impact of fuel price increases comes from the higher cost of domestic transport for distributing goods and services within a country, and this component of all goods and services is inherently nontraded. The full pass-through of higher production costs to domestic

---

[2] For a more detailed discussion, see Coady and Newhouse 2006. An online IMF course on evaluating the magnitude and welfare impact of energy subsidies is available at https://www.edx.org/course/energy-subsidy-reform-imfx-esrx-0.

consumer prices is also facilitated by the fact that the prices of all imported goods are also likely to be similarly affected by higher international fuel prices. However, the assumption of demand inelasticity means that estimates should again be interpreted as short-term impacts or upper bounds on long-term impacts. Once the impact of higher domestic fuel prices on the prices of other goods and services is estimated, these estimates are multiplied by the household budget share for each of these consumption categories (taken from a household survey) to get the welfare impact of each price change. These welfare impacts are then aggregated to estimate the total indirect welfare impact of fuel price increases for each household.

Total Impact

The total impact of fuel price increases is then calculated as the sum of the direct and indirect impacts. The distribution of the impact across households in different parts of the income distribution is estimated by calculating the average impact for households in different income groups. Consistent with most studies of poverty and inequality, households are allocated to welfare quintiles based on a measure of consumption per capita or per adult equivalent (that is, consumption adjusted for different needs reflecting different household demographic composition). The distribution of the welfare impact from a price increase is classified as progressive (regressive) if the percentage welfare loss increases (decreases) with household consumption. Whether lower fuel prices are seen as an effective approach to protecting the welfare of low-income households will depend on the share of the total benefit from low fuel prices that accrues to lower-income households. Effective targeting requires that a high proportion of benefits accrue to lower-income households; if a substantial proportion of benefits leak to higher-income households, it is likely that more cost-effective approaches to social protection are possible.

WELFARE IMPACT OF FUEL PRICE INCREASES

As in Arze Del Granado, Coady, and Gillingham 2012, this chapter reviews country studies that were conducted mainly by staff at the IMF and World Bank following a comparable methodology,[3] and recalculates the welfare impact based on a common price increase of $0.25 per liter.[4] The recalculation is done by scaling welfare impacts proportionally to reflect different initial retail price levels across countries. Annex Table 14.1.1 presents the list of all case studies used in this review, as well as their source data and author institution. The adjustment factors used to convert the original into the common price increase of $0.25 per liter are presented in Annex Table 14.1.2. In many countries higher fuel prices also lead governments to increase electricity tariffs if electricity uses fuel as an input. Since the most recent country reports reviewed in this chapter do not include information on electricity tariff reforms, this chapter does not provide additional evidence on the welfare impact and distribution of higher electricity tariffs and only reports results from the original article for ease of reference.

Magnitude and Composition of Welfare Impact

The total (direct plus indirect) impact on households of a $0.25 per liter increase in fuel prices is sizable, and the indirect portion accounts for a substantial share of this impact. On average, such

---

[3] Not all fuel products were covered in all studies, either reflecting the focus of the study or availability of data in the household survey, but in most countries the main fuel products were covered.

[4] The choice for a common price increase is arbitrary and innocuous. To put the magnitude of this price increase in perspective, between December 2003 and June 2008 international fuel prices increased by about $0.8 per liter. Between end-2006 and mid-2008, a period of sharply rising prices, fuel prices increased by about $0.5 per liter. The welfare impact of any specific price increase can be calculated by scaling accordingly.

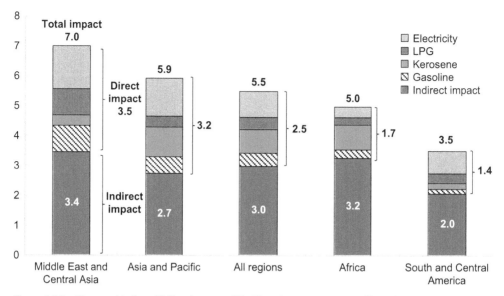

Figure 14.2 Direct and Indirect Welfare Impacts of Fuel Price Increases *(Percent of household total consumption)*

Source: Authors' calculations based on results from reviewed studies.
Note: LPG = liquefied petroleum gas.

an increase in fuel prices results in a 5.5 percent decline in household real incomes, with the impact ranging from 3.5 percent in South and Central America to 7.0 percent in the Middle East (Figure 14.2). Annex Table 14.1.3 presents country- and product-specific results.

The welfare impact is higher in the Middle East and Central Asia, where retail fuel prices are comparatively low (Figure 14.3, panel 1). Because the simulated price increase is the same across regions, differences in the magnitude of its impact can be expected to reflect a volume effect due to higher consumption of fuels where retail prices are low. In general, data show an inverse relationship between retail prices of diesel and gasoline and consumption of these products as a share of national income. For instance, in panel 2 of Figure 14.3, advanced economies and emerging countries in Europe, which have higher average retail prices, tend to display low consumption of diesel and gasoline. In contrast, countries in the Middle East and Central Asia have lower average prices and higher consumption of fuels. This difference is consistent with higher energy prices providing stronger incentives for improving energy efficiency.

Although, on average, the indirect impact accounts for 55 percent of the total impact, its share differs substantially across regions. Whereas the indirect effect is 65 and 60 percent of the total impact in sub-Saharan Africa and South and Central America, respectively, it is less than 50 percent in Asia and Pacific and in the Middle East and Central Asia. In all cases it is a sizable component of the total impact, reflecting the fact that a high proportion of total fuel consumption is for intermediate use. Therefore, it is important for any evaluation of the welfare impact of fuel price changes to incorporate this indirect effect.

The magnitude of the indirect impact on households depends on the fuel intensity of their consumption. Figure 14.4 presents data on the average budget share for food, transport, and "other" goods and services (excluding direct fuel consumption). It also presents the estimated effect of the simulated fuel price changes on the prices of each of these categories, as well as the aggregate indirect welfare impact across each of these categories. Transport expenditures include household use of privately and publicly provided public transport services (that is public and privately owned buses, taxis, and other forms of public transport). The indirect effect is

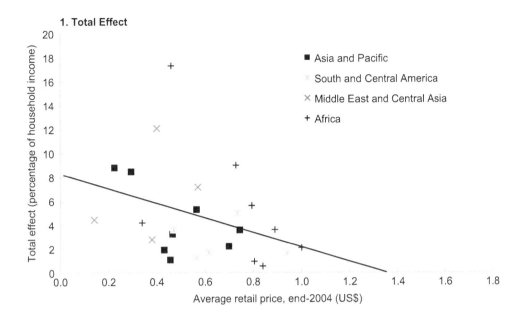

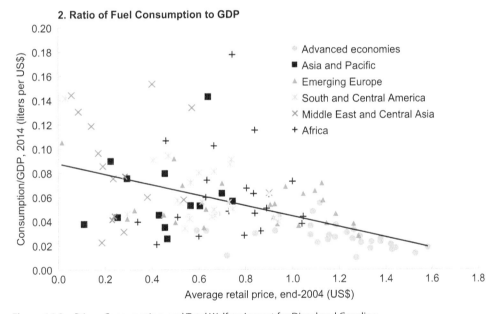

Figure 14.3 Prices, Consumption, and Total Welfare Impact for Diesel and Gasoline

Source: Authors' calculations based on results from reviewed studies.

calculated as a budget-share weighted average of price changes across these consumption categories. On average, the slightly lower budget share for "other" compared with food is offset by the greater fuel intensity of "other" goods and services, as reflected in its higher price effect. As a result, on average, higher prices of "other" goods account for slightly less than 50 percent of the indirect impact on households and higher food prices for about 40 percent. Although transport services absorb, on average, only 4.1 percent of household budgets, the relatively large price effect (reflecting the relatively high energy intensity of these services) means that it accounts for

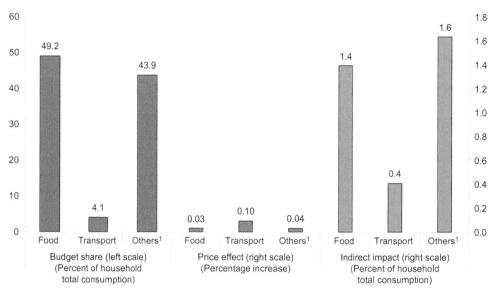

Figure 14.4   Composition of Indirect Impact

Source: Authors' calculations based on results from reviewed studies.
[1] Category "Others" excludes fuel products directly consumed by households for cooking, lighting, and transport. Hence, budget shares do not add
to 100, but to 100 minus households' share of direct consumption in fuels.

about 12 percent of the indirect impact. Annex Table 14.1.4 presents a breakdown of the indirect
welfare impact by country.

The composition of the direct effect also differs across regions. For example, kerosene is relatively important in Africa because of the low level of household access to electricity. Kerosene is
much less important in the Middle East and in South and Central America because access to
electricity is more extensive. However, low-income household access to certain fuels can mean
that the estimates in Annex Table 14.1.3 for each fuel may substantially underestimate the impact
on households with access. For example, if only half of households have access to electricity, the
impact on electricity users will be double that presented in the table. In practice, this issue is often
especially important for electricity and LPG.

Distribution of Welfare Impact

The total, direct, and indirect welfare impacts are approximately distributionally neutral, with the
percentage decrease in welfare being very similar across income groups (Figure 14.5). However,
substantial variation across products is hidden for the direct effect. The impacts for gasoline and
electricity are strongly progressive, but the kerosene impact is strongly regressive. The distribution
of the impact of LPG seems to differ across regions. On average, the simulated impact of the
increase in LPG prices is progressive, but is very regressive in the Middle East and Central Asia
region. Annex Table 14.1.5 presents the distribution of the direct and indirect welfare impacts
across income groups, disaggregated by region and country.

Since the distribution of the total impact of fuel price increases is approximately neutral, significantly higher total consumption levels of well-off households mean substantial leakage of
benefits to higher-income groups. Therefore, maintaining low fuel prices results in a badly targeted subsidy. Figure 14.6 presents the shares of the total benefits that each income group would
receive from subsidized fuel prices, separately for the total, direct, and indirect welfare impact as
well as for the direct benefit for gasoline, LPG, and kerosene. On average, the top income

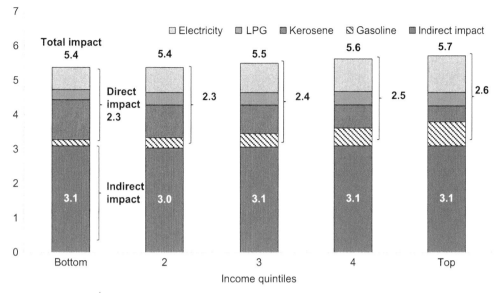

Figure 14.5   Distribution of Welfare Impact by Income Group *(Percent of household total consumption)*

Source: Authors' calculations based on results from reviewed studies.
Note: LPG = liquefied petroleum gas.

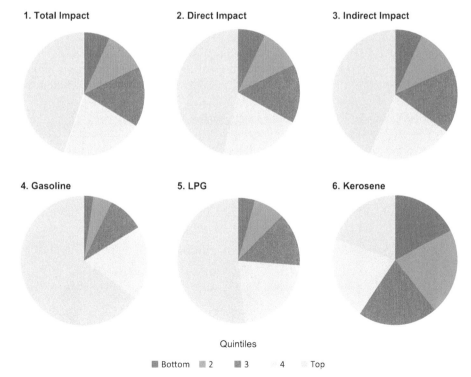

Figure 14.6   Distribution of Subsidy Benefits by Income Group *(Percent of total subsidy benefit)*

Source: Authors' calculations based on results from reviewed studies.
Note: LPG = liquefied petroleum gas. The indirect impact is the welfare impact of higher prices of goods and services due to an increase in the price of diesel.

quintile receives more than six times more in total subsidies than the bottom quintile. The concentration of subsidy benefits in the hands of the top income groups is even more pronounced for gasoline and LPG, where the top income quintile receives 27 and 12 times that of the bottom quintile, respectively. Although the poorest households receive a much higher share of kerosene subsidies than for other fuel subsidies, there is still substantial leakage of kerosene subsidies to higher-income groups. Annex Table 14.1.6 presents the shares of the total benefits that each income group would receive from subsidized fuel prices, disaggregated by region.

The substantial leakage of subsidy benefits to the top income groups means that universal fuel subsidies are an extremely costly approach to protecting the welfare of poor households. For example, if we take the poorest 40 percent of households to be the target "poor" group, the cost to the budget of transferring one dollar to this group via gasoline subsidies is about 14 dollars. This occurs because nearly 93 out of every 100 dollars of gasoline subsidy "leaks" to the top three quintiles. These leakages are higher in Africa and in Asia and Pacific, where poor households' access to gasoline and LPG is comparatively lower than in other regions (Figure 14.7, Annex Table 14.1.6). Even for kerosene, this cost-benefit ratio is about 3 dollars.

Such high leakage of subsidy benefits means that there is likely to be a high return to developing more cost-effective ways of protecting the real incomes of poor households. For example, if 15 out of every 100 dollars allocated to a safety net program is absorbed by administrative costs and 80 percent of the remaining 85 dollars in beneficiary transfers reaches the poor (or 68 percent of the total budget), then the cost-benefit ratio for such a program is 1.5 dollars, which is substantially lower even than for kerosene subsidies. In addition, the extent of protection that can be given to the poor via kerosene subsidies without severely disrupting fuel markets is very limited. Relatively low kerosene prices result in substitution of kerosene for diesel (legally or illegally) and often lead to shortages for rural households and smuggling to neighboring countries with higher prices.

For electricity, varying tariff levels according to consumption levels can mitigate the impact of energy price increases on poor households, but this approach to protecting low-income households is often less effective than believed. A large proportion of poor households do not benefit from lower lifeline tariffs because many do not have access to electricity and many with larger family sizes (driven by the number of children) consume at levels above "lifeline thresholds." Moreover, to the extent that lifeline subsidies are financed by higher tariffs for larger electricity consumers, poor households that consume large amounts of electricity could actually be worse off as a result. In practice, therefore, nonlinear electricity pricing (that is, block tariff structures with a lower lifeline tariff) are a very crude way of protecting poor households and can come with important negative side effects.

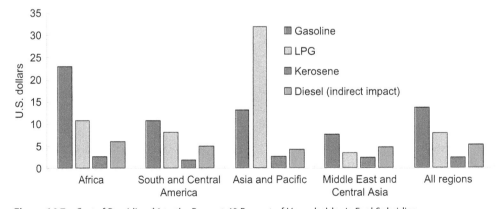

Figure 14.7   Cost of Providing $1 to the Poorest 40 Percent of Households via Fuel Subsidies

Source: Authors' calculations based on results from reviewed studies.
Note: LPG = liquefied petroleum gas.

PROTECTING LOW-INCOME HOUSEHOLDS

Although higher-income groups capture most of the benefits from lower fuel prices, subsidy reform can still result in a sizable reduction in the real incomes of low-income households and thus increased poverty. Therefore, well-targeted measures to mitigate the impact of energy price increases on the poor are critical for building public support for subsidy reform. Some approaches in different country contexts are discussed below. Box 14.1 discusses additional measures that can help promote successful subsidy reform.

BOX 14.1 Reforming Fuel Subsidies: Lessons from International Experience

International experiences with energy subsidy reform suggest a number of barriers to successful reform, including (1) lack of information regarding the magnitude and shortcomings of subsidies; (2) lack of government credibility and administrative capacity; (3) concerns regarding the adverse impact on the poor; (4) concerns regarding the adverse impact on inflation, international competitiveness, and volatility of domestic energy prices; (5) opposition from specific interest groups benefiting from the status quo; and (6) weak macroeconomic conditions (Clements and others 2013).

Many countries that have successfully reformed energy subsidies have incorporated specific measures into their subsidy reform strategies to overcome these barriers. While there is no single recipe for success, analysis of international reform experiences suggests the following six reform ingredients can help address reform barriers and increase the likelihood that reforms will achieve their objectives, thus helping to avoid policy reversals:

- *Develop a comprehensive reform plan*—The reform plan should have clear objectives. It should identify specific measures that will achieve these objectives, and include a timeline for implementing and assessing these measures. A comprehensive plan will incorporate many of the measures discussed in this box. Designing and executing such a reform plan therefore needs careful advance planning.

- *Develop an effective communication strategy*—An extensive public communication campaign can help generate broad political and public support and help prevent misinformation and should be undertaken throughout the reform process. Transparency is a key component of a successful communication strategy.

- *Appropriately phase and sequence price increases*—Phasing in price increases and sequencing them differently across energy products may be desirable. The appropriate phasing and sequencing of price increases will depend on a range of factors, including the magnitude of the price increases required to eliminate subsidies, the economy's fiscal position, the political and social context in which reforms are being undertaken, and the time needed to develop an effective social safety net and communication strategy. However, gradual reform can create additional reform challenges, including lower budgetary savings in the short term, distortion in consumption patterns due to sequencing of reform by energy product, and the risk that opposition may build up over time.

- *Improve the efficiency of energy state-owned enterprises (SOEs)*—Improving the efficiency of SOEs (refineries, distribution companies, and so on) can reduce the fiscal burden of the energy sector. Energy producers often receive substantial budgetary resources—consisting of both current and capital transfers—to compensate for inefficiencies in production, distribution, and revenue collection. Improvements in efficiency can strengthen the financial position of these enterprises and reduce the need for such transfers. It will also help assure consumers that price increases are not simply being used to protect inefficient and poorly governed producers.

- *Implement targeted mitigating measures*—Well-targeted measures to mitigate the impact of energy price increases on the poor are critical for building public support for subsidy reforms. The degree to which compensation should be targeted is a strategic decision that involves trade-offs between fiscal savings, capacity to target, and the need to achieve broad acceptance of the reform. Subsidy reform involving SOE restructuring may require temporary, sector-specific social measures to support employees and enterprises.

- *Depoliticize energy pricing*—Successful and durable reforms require a depoliticized mechanism for setting energy prices. Establishing an automatic pricing formula for fuel products that links domestic energy prices to international energy prices can help distance the government from the pricing of energy and make it clearer that domestic price changes reflect changes in international prices that are outside the government's control. Price-smoothing rules can help prevent large price increases. How much smoothing the government chooses to implement will depend on its preference between lower price volatility and higher fiscal volatility.

Targeted cash transfers or near-cash transfers are typically the preferred approach to compensation. Cash transfers give beneficiaries the flexibility to purchase the level and type of energy that best suits their needs, and at a time and place of their choosing. They also remove the need for governments to be directly involved in the distribution of subsidized energy to households, which is often extremely costly and prone to abuse (Grosh and others 2008). Targeted cash transfers were used to protect poor households in several successful subsidy reform episodes. For example, Armenia successfully introduced a targeted cash transfer program during its electricity reform, which helped poor beneficiaries maintain real consumption in the face of higher electricity bills. Indonesia's nonconditional cash transfer program, which covered 35 percent of the population, was an important component of its successful strategy in overcoming social and political opposition to fuel subsidy reforms. Its experience also suggests that such programs need good preparation and monitoring to effectively assist the poor.

Conditional cash transfer programs that link eligibility for benefits to household investments in the education and health status of family members can both protect poor households from poverty and enhance their human capital base to break the intergenerational transmission of poverty. The expansion of these programs throughout emerging and low-income economies has greatly increased the capacity of these economies to protect poor households from price and other shocks while simultaneously addressing the root causes of persistent poverty (Fiszbein and Schady 2009; Garcia and Moore 2012; Monchuk 2014).

If cash transfers are not feasible, as is the case in many low-income countries, other programs can be expanded while administrative capacity is being developed. These efforts should focus on existing programs that can be expanded quickly, possibly with some improvements in the effectiveness of targeting (for instance, school meals, public works, reductions in education and health user fees, subsidized mass urban transport, subsidies for water and electricity connection costs). Scaling up such programs should be done in conjunction with a more gradual approach to removing subsidies, for example, delaying fuel price increases for products (such as kerosene) that are used more by lower-income groups.

This approach has been used in a number of countries. Gabon, Ghana, Niger, Nigeria, and Mozambique expanded targeted social spending programs to protect lower-income households from fuel price increases. To alleviate the impact of its subsidy reform on the poor, Morocco expanded existing social programs (providing support to school-age children and helping the poor with medical expenses) and introduced new programs to support low-income widows and physically disabled individuals, in addition to providing support for the public transportation sector to mitigate the cost of higher fuel prices and limit fare increases. The Philippines maintained electricity subsidies for indigent families, provided college scholarships for low-income students, and subsidized loans to convert engines used in public transportation to less costly LPG (World Bank 2008).

In the context of electricity reforms, Armenia, Brazil, Kenya, and Uganda kept their lower lifeline tariffs for electricity fixed and concentrated tariff increases on households with higher electricity consumption levels. Kenya subsidized connection costs in place of electricity price subsidies, which helped expand coverage to poor households and those in remote and rural areas. The rural electrification program helped increase the number of connections from 650,000 in 2003 to 2 million as of 2014 with a fund for connection fee payments financed by donors.

Even after removing current subsidies, many countries will be reluctant to make the big jump to complete price deregulation because of the concern that increasing and volatile international prices will adversely affect poor and middle-income households. As a result, although a number of countries have successfully undertaken subsidy reforms, in many cases subsidies have reemerged during periods of sharp or prolonged increases in international prices (for example, in Gabon, Ghana, Indonesia, and Jordan). For such countries, an attractive interim solution may be to adopt an automatic pricing mechanism that includes some formal built-in domestic price smoothing (Coady and others 2012). A number of countries (including Chile, Peru, and Mauritius, as well as countries in sub-Saharan Africa) already have adopted such mechanisms. This approach essentially shares international price volatility between domestic consumers and the budget. By allowing both price increases and decreases, but capping these changes, full pass-through of international price movements to domestic consumers is ensured over the medium term while these consumers are protected from sudden sharp increases and an escalating subsidy bill is avoided. Successful implementation of an automatic pricing mechanism can facilitate the transition to a liberalized pricing regime by getting the public accustomed to frequent changes in domestic energy prices. Also, by demonstrating the government's willingness to steer clear of subsidies and the associated market disruption, private sector confidence and investment in the energy sector—which is crucial for growth—can be renewed, paving the way for a more permanent solution through complete price deregulation. South Africa, the Philippines, and Turkey have successfully implemented automatic pricing mechanisms for fuel products, in the latter two cases during their transitions to liberalized fuel pricing. India liberalized gasoline and diesel prices in 2010 and 2014, respectively.

CONCLUSIONS

This chapter revisits the issue of distribution of benefits from fuel subsidies in developing countries and updates and expands the results of a previous meta study by Arze del Granado, Coady, and Gillingham (2012). The results reinforce the previous finding that fuel subsidies are badly targeted, mainly benefiting higher-income groups, and are fiscally costly. But the withdrawal of subsidies can have a sizable impact on household welfare, including that of lower-income groups. The analysis finds that a $0.25 per liter increase in fuel prices decreases household real incomes by, on average, 5.5 percent. Approximately half of this impact comes through the indirect effect on the prices of other goods and services consumed by households.

The distribution of this welfare impact is approximately neutral, with the magnitude of the welfare loss being similar across income groups. However, reflecting the underlying unequal distribution of aggregate consumption, the richest 20 percent of households captures, on average, more than six times more in fuel subsidies than the poorest 20 percent, making universal fuel subsidies a very inefficient policy instrument for protecting poor households from fuel price increases. The benefits of gasoline subsidies are the most regressively distributed, with more than 83 percent of total benefits accruing to the richest 40 percent of households. Although the consumption of kerosene is more evenly distributed across income groups, a substantial amount of kerosene subsidies still goes to high-income households.

Given the adverse impact of subsidy reform on poor households, it is important that mitigating measures be implemented to protect these households. The chapter discusses alternative strategies that can be used to achieve this end. Ideally, well-targeted cash transfers should be used to protect poor households. If such programs are not available, alternative approaches can be used, such as temporarily maintaining universal subsidies on commodities that are more important in the budgets of the poor; expanding existing safety net programs, possibly with some improvements in targeting; and increasing high-priority spending that benefit the poor, such as in health, education, and infrastructure. If countries are reluctant to fully pass through sharp increases in international fuel prices, they should consider adopting an automatic pricing mechanism with built-in price smoothing to protect households while ensuring full pass-through in the medium term.

ANNEX 14.1. SUPPLEMENTARY TABLES

ANNEX TABLE 14.1.1

Year of Data and Report, and Author Institution

	Year of Report	Year of Household Survey	Year of Input-Output Matrix	Author Institution
Africa				
Angola	2014	2008/2009	2014	IMF
Cameroon	2007	2001	2001	IMF
Gabon	2006	2005	2001	IMF
Central African Republic	2006	2003	2001	IMF
Senegal	2008	2005	2006	IMF
Ghana	2005	1999	1993	IMF
Kenya	2010	2006	n.a.	World Bank
Mali	2006	2001	1998	IMF
Congo	2008	2005	2005	IMF
Burkina Faso	2008	2003	2007	IMF
Madagascar	2007	2005	n.a.	World Bank
Madagascar	2014	2010	n.a.	IMF
South Africa	2014	2010	2010	World Bank
Uganda	2010	2005/2006	n.a.	World Bank
South and Central America				
Bolivia	2009	2007	n.a.	IMF
Peru	2008	2007	1994	IMF
El Salvador	2009	2005	n.a.	IMF
Honduras	2006	2004	2004	IMF
Paraguay	2011	2006	2006	IMF
Asia and Pacific				
Bangladesh	2006	2000	1993	IMF
Bangladesh	2010	2005	n.a.	World Bank
Sri Lanka	2006	1999	2001	IMF
Cambodia	2010	2003/2004	n.a.	World Bank
India	2010	2004/2005	n.a.	World Bank
India	2013	2010	2004	IMF
Indonesia	2014	2012	2011	World Bank
Malaysia	2009/2013	2005	2005	IMF/Universiti Utara Malaysia
Pakistan	2010	2004/2005	n.a.	World Bank
Philippines	2007	2003	n.a.	IMF
Thailand	2010	2006	n.a.	World Bank
Vietnam	2010	2006	n.a.	World Bank
Middle East and Central Asia				
Jordan	2005	2002/2003	1998	IMF
Jordan	2011	2008/2009	2006	IMF
Lebanon	2008	2004	n.a.	IMF
Sudan	2012	2009	n.a.	IMF
Yemen	2013	2006	2009	IMF

Source: Authors' survey of the literature.
Note: n.a. = not available.

ANNEX TABLE 14.1.2

Adjustment Factors by Country Study and Fuel Product

	Gasoline	Kerosene	Diesel	LPG
Angola	0.32	0.69	0.48	0.54
Bangladesh	0.22	0.33	n.a.	n.a.
Bangladesh	0.54	0.86	0.86	0.70
Bolivia	0.54	0.71	0.52	0.53
Burkina Faso	0.29	0.57	0.40	0.35
Cambodia	0.40	0.62	0.55	0.47
Cameroon	0.40	0.92	0.48	0.44
Central African Republic	0.24	0.45	0.27	0.26
Congo, Republic of	0.30	0.49	0.45	0.37
El Salvador	0.38	n.a.	0.41	0.39
Gabon	0.29	0.59	0.38	0.34
Ghana	0.96	1.42	1.02	0.99
Honduras	0.36	0.53	0.47	0.42
India	0.28	1.23	0.46	0.37
India	0.28	1.23	0.46	0.37
Indonesia	0.53	0.94	n.a.	n.a.
Jordan	0.53	1.25	1.29	0.91
Jordan	0.53	1.25	1.29	0.91
Kenya	0.19	0.24	n.a.	n.a.
Lebanon	0.35	0.67	0.72	0.54
Madagascar	0.27	0.42	0.32	0.30
Malaysia	0.41	0.45	n.a.	n.a.
Mali	0.36	0.59	0.58	0.47
Pakistan	0.26	0.26	n.a.	n.a.
Paraguay	0.17	n.a.	0.23	n.a.
Peru	0.27	0.27	0.27	0.27
Philippines	0.66	0.81	0.82	1.04
Senegal	0.25	0.28	0.28	0.27
South Africa	0.24	0.38	0.27	n.a.
Sri Lanka	0.33	0.95	0.88	0.61
Sudan	0.34	0.48	0.51	0.86
Thailand	0.18	0.22	n.a.	n.a.
Uganda	0.16	0.21	n.a.	n.a.
Vietnam	0.22	0.24	n.a.	n.a.
Yemen	0.43	0.54	n.a.	0.54

Source: Authors' calculations based on results from reviewed studies.
Note: LPG = liquefied petroleum gas; n.a. = not available.

ANNEX TABLE 14.1.3

Direct and Indirect Welfare Impacts of Fuel Price Increases *(Percent of household total consumption)*

	Direct by Product				Direct	Indirect	Total
	Gasoline	Kerosene	LPG	Electricity			
Africa (average)	0.3	0.9	0.2	0.4	1.7	3.2	5.0
Cameroon	0.2	1.4	0.1	0.5	2.3	1.3	3.6
Gabon	0.2	0.3	0.5	1.2	2.2	3.5	5.6
Central African Republic	0.0	0.6	0.0	0.0	0.7	2.8	3.5
Senegal	0.1	0.3	0.3	0.4	1.0	1.1	2.1
Ghana	0.6	5.0	0.1	n.a.	5.6	11.7	17.3
Mali	0.4	0.9	n.a.	0.3	1.5	1.4	2.9
Congo, Republic of	0.0	0.9	0.0	0.3	1.3	7.7	9.0
Burkina Faso	0.5	0.6	0.0	0.2	1.3	0.7	2.0
Madagascar	0.0	0.8	n.a.	0.2	1.0	n.a.	1.0
Angola	1.1	0.6	0.2	n.a.	1.9	2.2	4.2
Kenya	0.0	0.5	n.a.	n.a.	0.5	n.a.	0.5
Madagascar	0.1	0.3	n.a.	n.a.	0.4	n.a.	0.4
South Africa	0.8	0.0	n.a.	n.a.	0.8	0.1	0.9
Uganda	0.0	0.3	n.a.	n.a.	0.4	n.a.	0.4
South and Central America (average)	0.2	0.2	0.3	0.8	1.4	2.0	3.5
Bolivia	0.3	n.a.	0.5	n.a.	0.7	2.9	3.6
Peru	0.1	0.1	0.3	0.5	0.9	0.7	1.7
El Salvador	0.2	0.1	0.3	1.1	1.7	n.a.	1.7
Honduras	0.1	0.4	0.2	0.7	1.4	3.5	5.0
Paraguay	0.2	n.a.	n.a.	n.a.	0.2	1.1	1.3
Asia and Pacific (average)	0.6	1.0	0.4	1.3	3.2	2.7	5.9
Bangladesh	0.1	0.9	0.1	0.7	1.7	1.5	3.2
Sri Lanka	0.2	1.0	0.3	1.1	2.7	2.6	5.3
Cambodia	n.a.	0.3	0.4	1.5	2.2	n.a.	2.2
India	0.2	1.8	0.4	1.1	3.6	n.a.	3.6
Indonesia	0.7	4.1	0.2	3.8	8.8	n.a.	8.8
Bangladesh	0.0	0.3	n.a.	n.a.	0.3	n.a.	0.3
India	0.1	1.0	0.0	n.a.	1.1	1.4	2.5
Malaysia	2.7	n.a.	n.a.	0.3	3.0	5.5	8.5
Pakistan	0.3	0.1	n.a.	n.a.	0.3	n.a.	0.3
Philippines	0.1	0.3	1.0	0.4	1.9	n.a.	1.9
Thailand	1.1	n.a.	n.a.	n.a.	1.1	n.a.	1.1
Vietnam	0.7	0.1	n.a.	n.a.	0.8	n.a.	0.8
Middle East and Central Asia (average)	0.9	0.4	0.9	1.4	3.5	3.4	7.0
Jordan	0.9	0.7	1.1	3.0	5.7	6.3	12.1
Lebanon	1.9	n.a.	0.8	2.4	5.1	2.0	7.1
Jordan	1.1	0.2	0.7	0.2	2.2	3.6	5.8
Sudan	0.1	0.1	n.a.	0.1	0.3	2.4	2.8
Yemen	0.3	0.4	0.9	n.a.	1.7	2.7	4.4
All regions (average)	**0.4**	**0.8**	**0.4**	**0.9**	**2.5**	**3.0**	**5.5**
Only regions with indirect effect	0.5	0.8	0.3	0.7	2.4	3.0	5.4

Source: Authors' calculations based on results from reviewed studies.
Note: LPG = liquefied petroleum gas; n.a. = not available.

ANNEX TABLE 14.1.4

Composition of Indirect Impact *(Percent of household total consumption)*

	Direct By Product				Direct	Indirect	Total
	Gasoline	Kerosene	LPG	Electricity			
Africa (average)	0.3	0.9	0.2	0.4	1.7	3.2	5.0
Cameroon	0.2	1.4	0.1	0.5	2.3	1.3	3.6
Gabon	0.2	0.3	0.5	1.2	2.2	3.5	5.6
Central African Republic	0.0	0.6	0.0	0.0	0.7	2.8	3.5
Senegal	0.1	0.3	0.3	0.4	1.0	1.1	2.1
Ghana	0.6	5.0	0.1	n.a.	5.6	11.7	17.3
Mali	0.4	0.9	n.a.	0.3	1.5	1.4	2.9
Congo, Republic of	0.0	0.9	0.0	0.3	1.3	7.7	9.0
Burkina Faso	0.5	0.6	0.0	0.2	1.3	0.7	2.0
Madagascar	0.0	0.8	n.a.	0.2	1.0	…	1.0
Angola	1.1	0.6	0.2	n.a.	1.9	2.2	4.2
Kenya	0.0	0.5	n.a.	n.a.	0.5	…	0.5
Madagascar	0.1	0.3	n.a.	n.a.	0.4	…	0.4
South Africa	0.8	0.0	n.a.	n.a.	0.8	0.1	0.9
Uganda	0.0	0.3	n.a.	n.a.	0.4	…	0.4
South and Central America (average)	0.2	0.2	0.3	0.8	1.4	2.0	3.5
Bolivia	0.3	n.a.	0.5	n.a.	0.7	2.9	3.6
Peru	0.1	0.1	0.3	0.5	0.9	0.7	1.7
El Salvador	0.2	0.1	0.3	1.1	1.7	n.a.	1.7
Honduras	0.1	0.4	0.2	0.7	1.4	3.5	5.0
Paraguay	0.2	n.a.	n.a.	n.a.	0.2	1.1	1.2
Asia and Pacific (average)	0.6	1.0	0.4	1.3	3.2	2.7	5.9
Bangladesh	0.1	0.9	0.1	0.7	1.7	1.5	3.2
Sri Lanka	0.2	1.0	0.3	1.1	2.7	2.6	5.3
Cambodia	n.a.	0.3	0.4	1.5	2.2	n.a.	2.2
India	0.2	1.8	0.4	1.1	3.6	n.a.	3.6
Indonesia	0.7	4.1	0.2	3.8	8.8	n.a.	8.8
Bangladesh	0.0	0.3	n.a.	n.a.	0.3	n.a.	0.3
India	0.1	1.0	0.0	n.a.	1.1	1.4	2.5
Malaysia	2.7	n.a.	n.a.	0.3	3.0	5.5	8.5
Pakistan	0.3	0.1	n.a.	n.a.	0.3	n.a.	0.3
Philippines	0.1	0.3	1.0	0.4	1.9	n.a.	1.9
Thailand	1.1	n.a.	n.a.	n.a.	1.1	n.a.	1.1
Vietnam	0.7	0.1	n.a.	n.a.	0.8	n.a.	0.8
Middle East and Central Asia (average)	0.9	0.4	0.9	1.4	3.5	3.4	7.0
Jordan	0.9	0.7	1.1	3.0	5.7	6.3	12.1
Lebanon	1.9	n.a.	0.8	2.4	5.1	2.0	7.1
Jordan	1.1	0.2	0.7	0.2	2.2	3.6	5.8
Sudan	0.1	0.1	n.a.	0.1	0.3	2.4	2.8
Yemen	0.3	0.4	0.9	n.a.	1.7	2.7	4.4
All regions (average)[1]	**0.4**	**0.8**	**0.4**	**0.9**	**2.5**	**3.0**	**5.5**
Only countries with indirect effect[2]	0.5	0.8	0.3	0.7	2.4	3.0	5.4

Source: Authors' calculations based on results from reviewed studies.

Note: … = information not available in the country study; n.a. = not available. LPG = liquefied petroleum gas.

[1]Category "others" excludes fuel products directly consumed by households for cooking, lighting, and transport. Hence, budget shares do not add to 100, but to 100 minus household's share of consumption in fuel products. The price effect is the proportionate increase in prices resulting from a $0.25 per liter increase in fuel prices. The indirect impact is the product of budget shares and the price impact.

[2] Jordan's report did not disaggregate transport from other nonfood expenditures.

ANNEX TABLE 14.1.5

Distribution of Welfare Impact by Income Group *(Percent of household total consumption)*

	Bottom	2	3	4	Top	All Households
			Consumption Quintiles			
Africa						
Total Impact	4.7	4.8	4.8	5.0	5.3	5.0
Total Direct Impact	1.7	1.6	1.6	1.6	1.9	1.7
Gasoline	0.1	0.1	0.2	0.3	0.5	0.3
Kerosene	1.3	1.1	0.9	0.7	0.5	0.9
LPG	0.1	0.2	0.2	0.3	0.3	0.2
Electricity	0.2	0.3	0.3	0.4	0.6	0.4
Indirect Impact	3.0	3.1	3.2	3.4	3.4	3.2
South and Central America						
Total Impact	3.8	3.7	3.9	4.1	3.9	3.5
Total Direct Impact	1.1	1.3	1.5	1.7	1.6	1.4
Gasoline	0.0	0.1	0.1	0.3	0.4	0.2
Kerosene	0.4	0.3	0.1	0.1	0.0	0.2
LPG	0.2	0.3	0.4	0.4	0.3	0.3
Electricity	0.4	0.6	0.8	0.9	0.9	0.8
Indirect Impact	2.7	2.4	2.4	2.4	2.3	2.0
Asia and Pacific						
Total Impact	4.1	4.7	5.0	5.3	5.5	5.9
Total Direct Impact	2.3	2.7	3.0	3.3	3.6	3.2
Gasoline	0.3	0.4	0.5	0.6	0.8	0.6
Kerosene	1.3	1.2	1.1	1.0	0.6	1.0
LPG	0.0	0.2	0.3	0.4	0.6	0.4
Electricity	0.7	0.9	1.1	1.3	1.6	1.3
Indirect Impact	1.8	2.0	2.0	2.0	1.9	2.7
Middle East and Central Asia						
Total Impact	8.7	7.7	7.5	7.1	6.7	7.0
Total Direct Impact	3.9	3.6	3.6	3.4	3.1	3.5
Gasoline	0.4	0.7	1.0	1.1	1.2	0.9
Kerosene	0.6	0.4	0.4	0.3	0.2	0.4
LPG	1.2	1.0	0.8	0.7	0.5	0.9
Electricity	1.7	1.4	1.4	1.3	1.2	1.4
Indirect Impact	4.8	4.1	3.9	3.7	3.6	3.4
All Regions						
Total Impact	5.4	5.4	5.5	5.6	5.7	5.5
Direct Impact	2.3	2.3	2.4	2.5	2.6	2.5
Gasoline	0.2	0.3	0.4	0.5	0.7	0.4
Kerosene	1.1	1.0	0.8	0.7	0.4	0.8
LPG	0.3	0.3	0.4	0.4	0.4	0.4
Electricity	0.7	0.7	0.8	0.9	1.1	0.9
Indirect Impact	3.1	3.0	3.1	3.1	3.1	3.0

Source: Authors' calculations based on results from reviewed studies.
Note: LPG = liquefied petroleum gas. Indirect impact is not available by quintile for all countries.

ANNEX TABLE 14.1.6

Distribution of Subsidy Benefits by Income Group *(Percent of total subsidy benefit)*

	Consumption Quintiles					All Households
	Bottom	2	3	4	Top	
Africa						
Total Impact	7.1	10.7	14.9	20.8	46.5	100
Total Direct Impact	7.7	10.6	14.2	19.8	47.6	100
Gasoline	1.5	2.9	6.3	16.2	73.1	100
Kerosene	14.0	21.2	19.2	20.4	25.2	100
LPG	2.7	6.5	11.7	22.4	56.6	100
Indirect Impact	6.2	10.1	14.8	21.5	47.4	100
South and Central America						
Total Impact	6.0	10.7	16.3	23.2	43.8	100
Total Direct Impact	5.2	9.9	15.3	22.0	47.4	100
Gasoline	3.0	6.3	11.5	23.2	56.0	100
Kerosene	29.2	25.2	20.5	16.9	8.1	100
LPG	3.4	8.7	16.0	24.2	47.8	100
Indirect Impact	7.5	12.6	18.1	23.7	38.2	100
Asia and Pacific						
Total Impact	6.3	10.4	14.9	22.4	46.0	100
Total Direct Impact	6.2	10.3	14.6	21.7	47.3	100
Gasoline	2.5	5.2	9.0	17.0	66.4	100
Kerosene	17.1	20.6	22.0	22.2	18.1	100
LPG	0.3	2.9	8.0	18.6	70.2	100
Indirect Impact	10.0	13.6	17.0	22.4	37.2	100
Middle East and Central Asia						
Total Impact	8.6	12.8	17.2	22.4	39.0	100
Total Direct Impact	9.5	13.4	16.9	21.7	38.5	100
Gasoline	4.3	8.8	13.5	20.4	53.0	100
Kerosene	18.2	20.5	22.0	21.9	17.5	100
LPG	11.9	15.8	19.3	22.7	30.3	100
Indirect Impact	8.5	12.7	16.9	22.1	39.7	100
All Regions						
Total Impact	7.0	11.0	15.6	21.9	45.0	100
Direct Impact	7.1	10.8	14.9	20.9	46.2	100
Gasoline	2.4	5.0	9.0	18.2	65.0	100
Kerosene	17.5	21.4	20.6	20.7	19.7	100
LPG	4.4	8.3	13.5	22.0	51.9	100
Indirect Impact	7.2	11.3	16.0	22.1	43.3	100

Source: Authors' calculations based on results from reviewed studies.
Note: LPG = liquefied petroleum gas. Indirect impact is not available by quintile for all countries.

REFERENCES

Arze Del Granado, F. J., D. Coady, and R. Gillingham. 2012. "The Unequal Benefits of Fuel Subsidies: A Review of Evidence for Developing Countries." *World Development* 40 (11): 2234–48.

Clements, B., D. Coady, S. Fabrizio, S. Gupta, T. Alleyne, and C. Sdralevich, eds. 2013. *Energy Subsidy Reform: Lessons and Implications*. Washington: International Monetary Fund. http://www.elibrary.imf.org/page/energys ubsidylessons.

Coady, D., J. Arze del Granado, L. Eyraud, H. Jin, V. Thakoor, A. Tuladhar, and L. Nemeth. 2012. "Automatic Fuel Pricing Mechanisms with Price Smoothing: Design, Implementation, and Fiscal Implications." Technical Notes and Manuals No. 12/03, International Monetary Fund, Washington. http://www.imf.org/external/pubs/ft/tnm/2012/tnm1203.pdf.

Coady, D., and D. Newhouse. 2006. "Evaluating the Distribution of the Real Income Effects of Increases in Petroleum Product Prices in Ghana." In *Analyzing the Distributional Impacts of Reforms: Operational Experience in Implementing Poverty and Social Impact Analysis*, edited by A. Coudouel, A. Dani, and S. Paternostro. Washington: World Bank.

Fiszbein, A., and N. Schady. 2009. *Conditional Cash Transfers: Reducing Present and Future Poverty*. Washington: World Bank.

Garcia, M., and C. Moore. 2012. *The Cash Dividend: The Rise of Cash Transfer Programs in Sub-Saharan Africa*. Washington: World Bank.

Grosh, M. E., C. del Ninno, E. Tesliuc, and A. Ouerghi. 2008. *For Protection and Promotion: The Design and Implementation of Effective Safety Nets*. Washington: World Bank.

Monchuk, V. 2014. *Reducing Poverty and Investing in People: The New Role of Safety Nets in Africa*. Washington: World Bank.

Newbery, D., and N. Stern, eds. 1987. *The Theory of Taxation in Developing Countries*. Washington: Oxford University Press for World Bank.

World Bank. 2008. "Philippines Quarterly Update." Washington. http://documents.worldbank.org/curated/en/2008/11/11962976/philippines-quarterly-update.

CHAPTER 15

Equity Considerations in the Design of Public Pension Systems

Benedict Clements, Csaba Feher, and Sanjeev Gupta

INTRODUCTION

Public pension systems are key instruments of social policy: they prevent poverty after retirement and limit the difference between pre- and postretirement consumption levels, thereby influencing income distribution (Figure 15.1). Public pension spending is also one of the largest items in advanced and emerging economies' budgets (Figure 15.2); the financing of public pensions can require high taxes and constrain other public expenditures. Pension spending is projected to increase more in the future, rising another 1 and 1¾ percent of GDP in advanced and emerging economies, respectively, between 2014 and 2030 on a weighted average basis (IMF 2015). These schemes influence workers' behavior toward labor supply, tax compliance, and savings. If designed well, they can improve welfare and equity—but design shortcomings can also impose an unnecessary fiscal burden and welfare losses on current and future generations. The unavoidable trade-offs between the size and redistributive features of these systems versus other public expenditures and fiscal sustainability present governments with difficult policy choices.

To address the impact of aging on pension systems' long-term fiscal sustainability, advanced and European transition economies introduced various parametric and structural pension reforms during the past 25 years. But sustainability issues still remain in light of demographic developments, including rising life expectancy. In contrast, emerging economies outside Europe, along with low-income countries, face different problems: low pension coverage, special occupational schemes relying heavily on budget transfers, or promises leading to large pension deficits despite favorable demographic conditions. Fiscal constraints and equity objectives cannot be considered in isolation. This chapter provides an overview of equity considerations in the design and reform of pension systems.

The main findings from economic theory and international experience, further elaborated in this chapter, are the following:

First, although the choice of policy objectives and the actual design of old-age income support systems are fraught with difficult choices, certain policies are unequivocally equity enhancing. Most important among these are the expansion of coverage and the uniform treatment of economic sectors (for example, the inclusion of farmers in mandatory social insurance) and types of employment (for example, permitting part-time and informal workers to participate in pension insurance schemes).

Second, design features and reforms entail trade-offs between intergenerational and intragenerational redistribution objectives; fiscal constraints and fairness; the resources allocated to public pensions and to other expenditures; and primary objectives (that is, consumption smoothing and prevention of old-age poverty) and externalities (such as labor supply responses to high social security contributions). It is crucial that policymakers be aware of these trade-offs,

The authors would like to thank Mauricio Soto and Baoping Shang for their insightful comments.

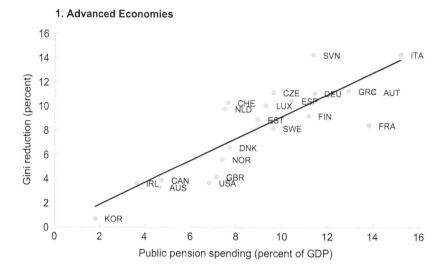

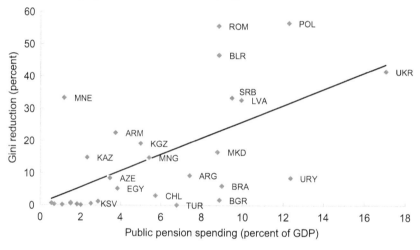

Figure 15.1 Public Pension Spending and Its Impact on Inequality

Source: IMF staff calculations.

Note: Data labels in the figure use International Organization for Standardization (ISO) abbreviations.

have a clear policy stance to be communicated to the population, and be familiar with the welfare and fiscal consequences of particular design features.

Third, pension policy is formulated under various constraints (fiscal, political, administrative, and the economy's level of market development) that may require policymakers to settle for second-best options.

Finally, pension policy cannot fully compensate the elderly for inequities suffered before retirement; indeed, pension policy can only be successful if its objectives and instruments are aligned with other welfare systems and are supported by labor market regulations and public education and health policies.

The remainder of the chapter is structured as follows: First, pension systems' basic objectives and instruments are discussed. Next, an overview of pension systems' equity features is presented, followed by the introduction of the most common types of public pension arrangements. The chapter's final sections present the equity impact of various pension reform options, followed by conclusions.

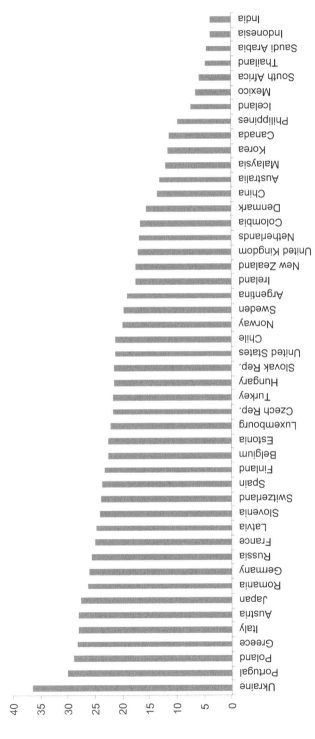

Figure 15.2   Public Pension Expenditures *(Percent of general government expenditures)*

Sources: IMF (2015); and IMF staff calculations.

PENSION SYSTEMS' POLICY OBJECTIVES

Public pension systems—and, in a broader sense, old-age income support—have two basic objectives: to protect participants against income poverty and to limit the decline in consumption after retirement. These objectives can be achieved through savings and insurance schemes as well as welfare transfers. Earnings or contributions to the system are important determinants of benefits in insurance schemes, but old-age welfare payments are typically unrelated to a given worker's employment history, earnings, and contributions. Thus, although earnings-related benefits can provide for consumption smoothing, discretionary social welfare payments are better suited to poverty alleviation. Although both objectives are important, fiscal constraints or societal preferences may lead governments to partially or fully forgo one of them as part of their pension policy. In these cases, consumption smoothing may be delegated to privately managed financial sector providers on a voluntary or mandatory basis, while poverty alleviation may become part of social assistance outside the pension system (Figure 15.3).

In developed economies and most European emerging economies, mandatory pension schemes reach near-universal coverage of the elderly population (Figure 15.4), aiming at both poverty alleviation and consumption smoothing. The distributional impact of these schemes is significant: in the absence of public pensions, poverty among the elderly would be four times as high in European Union member states than what is observed today (Clements, Eich, and Gupta 2014). Developed economies' main instrument for achieving both policy objectives is mandatory participation in social insurance schemes, requiring affiliates to forgo a share of their labor income in exchange for savings and social insurance entitlements. Exceptions exist, however; in Australia, Denmark, Israel, Mexico, the Netherlands, and New Zealand, the state only provides a universal or targeted basic pension approximately corresponding to the poverty-alleviation objective, while encouraging contributions to regulated pension savings or insurance schemes. This arrangement results in lower public pension expenditures and pension benefits as well as greater individual choice regarding intertemporal savings and consumption patterns. At the same time, if voluntary participation in contributory pension schemes is limited—for instance, because of myopia, income poverty, or labor informality—the pressure to increase the basic pension or to augment it with additional social transfers may rise.

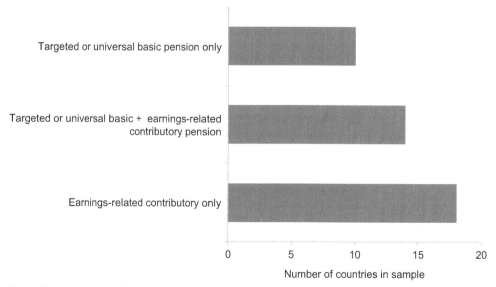

Figure 15.3   Structure of Public Pension Schemes in 41 OECD and Selected Non-OECD Countries

Source: Organisation for Economic Co-operation and Development (OECD) (2013).
Note: Argentina, Australia, Austria, Belgium, Brazil, Canada, China, the Czech Republic, Denmark, Estonia, Finland, France, Germany, Greece, Hungary, Iceland, India, Indonesia, Ireland, Israel, Italy, Japan, Korea, Luxembourg, Mexico, the Netherlands, New Zealand, Norway, Poland, Portugal, Russia, Saudi Arabia, the Slovak Republic, Slovenia, South Africa, Spain, Sweden, Switzerland, Turkey, the United Kingdom, the United States.

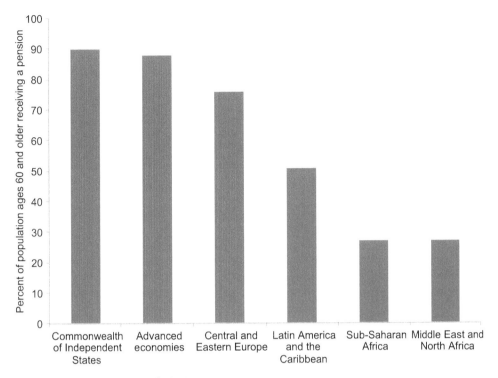

Figure 15.4   Pension Coverage by Region

Source: International Labour Organization (2014).

Low-income countries are typically younger demographically and have higher levels of informality in the labor market. Mandatory pension coverage is often limited to civil servants, public employees, the armed forces, members of the judiciary, and legislators (Bloom and McKinnon 2013). The total cost of these schemes today is relatively small, but they will need to expand to accommodate population aging and the disappearance of traditional intrafamily and communal income support mechanisms.

THE CONCEPT OF EQUITY IN PENSION SYSTEMS

There is no universally applicable, "correct" answer to what makes a pension system equitable. One way to assess whether a pension system is equitable is to determine how closely the distribution of retirement benefits reflects income distribution in active working years. A system paying benefits strictly based on contribution performance may be viewed as equitable since it treats every dollar of contribution in the same way. A flat, general revenue–financed basic pension can be viewed as equitable, too, because it redistributes in favor of people with low lifetime incomes and insufficient pension entitlements or savings. These two approaches are captured by the concepts of vertical and horizontal equity (Table 15.1).

With regard to intragenerational equity, *horizontal equity* requires that similar contributions result in similar benefits, whereas *vertical equity* requires consideration of individuals' needs (McDaniel and Repetti 1993). A horizontally equitable pension scheme will promise the same total pension benefit to people who have made similar contributions; in other words, it will provide similar internal rates of return—the theoretical interest rate that equates lifetime contributions to expected pension benefits discounted to the time of retirement (Santos and Domínguez 2011). A life-expectancy-adjusted, uniform internal rate of return across the income distribution

TABLE 15.1

Factors of Equity in Public Pension Systems

	Horizontal Equity	Vertical Equity
Intragenerational Equity	Strong contribution-benefit link along the entire income distribution; uniform internal rate of return within cohorts	Contribution-benefit link weak for low-income scheme members; internal rate of return negatively correlated with contribution performance
Intergenerational Equity	Same relationship between lifetime contributions and benefits for subsequent cohorts; uniform rate of return for subsequent cohorts	Internal rates of return negatively correlated with affluence; better-off generations receive lower relative benefits and may reduce underfunding

Source: Authors.

is horizontally equitable, whereas vertical equity requires internal rates of return that are differentiated according to income or other characteristics.

Intergenerational equity within a pension scheme refers to the manner in which the internal rate of return on contributions compares across generations: intergenerational equity requires that the burden of financing the pension system and the benefits to be paid out be spread fairly across successive generations. It is important to recognize, however, that what this kind of fairness means may be subject to different interpretations. On the one hand, it could be argued that it would be fair to shift a larger absolute burden onto successive generations, because they are expected to have higher real incomes than preceding generations. This approach would reduce the internal rate of return realized by later generations and can be interpreted as seeking intergenerational vertical equity. On the other hand, fairness could be interpreted as meaning that all generations should face the same relative burden so that the proportion of income that will have to be transferred to the state to finance the pension system remains stable.

The question of intergenerational equity also arises when major paradigmatic shifts happen in the pension system. The introduction and later expansion of pay-as-you-go, defined-benefit pension schemes in postwar Europe and the United States was one such case (Figure 15.5). Early

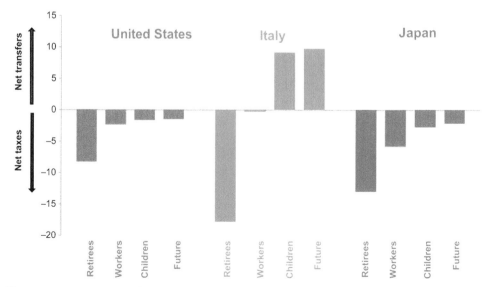

Figure 15.5 Intergenerational Equity in Public Pension Schemes *(Percent of lifetime income)*

Source: Clements, Eich, and Gupta (2014).

TABLE 15.2

Pension System Design Features and Equity Characteristics

	Horizontal Equity	Vertical Equity
Intragenerational Equity	Uniform scheme rules, gender-specific annuities, linear accrual schedules, no minimum vesting or eligibility criteria	Universal coverage, minimum pension provisions, progressive adjustments to the calculation base, progressive income taxation of pensions, benefit ceilings
Intergenerational Equity	Full funding, benefits adjusted to longevity changes, stable income tax system	Inflation-indexed minimum pensions, means-tested basic pensions, debt financing of pension deficits

Source: Authors.

retiree generations often reaped a windfall while the cost of actuarial imbalances was (and still is) borne by subsequent generations of taxpayers and beneficiaries[1] (Clements, Eich, and Gupta 2014). Similarly, in a shift from an unfunded to a funded pension system, as occurred in several Latin American and European emerging economies, the transition requires financing the legacy liabilities of the prereform system.[2]

THE IMPACT OF PENSION DESIGN FEATURES ON EQUITY

Intragenerational equity is affected by numerous factors (Table 15.2) but coverage stands out as one of the most important features. Partial versus universal coverage results from two factors: eligibility and willingness to participate. Eligibility to participate is a crucially important design feature, because, as opposed to other determinants of income redistribution within the pension system, it is a matter of equal opportunity to partake in the benefits of a pension system, whatever the system's internal distributional characteristics may be. Partial eligibility to participate may result from the exclusion of certain forms of employment (such as part-time and informal employment) and types of employers (small enterprises and the self-employed) from social security. Partial coverage may also result from the incapacity or unwillingness to participate because of low per capita incomes, large informal sectors, or limited monetization. Weak enforcement may also undermine coverage when data administration, collection, or enforcement capacity is inadequate (Auerbach, Genoni, and Pagés 2007).

Today, low coverage is a problem typical of low-income and non-European emerging economies. This situation may change, however. In European transition economies, where labor market informality, inactivity, and unemployment rates have grown significantly in comparison with the pretransition era of notional full employment, the share of the elderly meeting minimum eligibility conditions will decline in the coming decades (Schwarz and Arias 2014). If governments wish to protect everyone against old-age poverty—including people without sufficient contribution histories—then the contributory principle of the system will become weaker, potentially undermining contribution compliance at higher income levels. Contributions will become increasingly viewed as net lifetime taxes instead of actuarially fair insurance premiums.

---

[1] The case of Italy demonstrates the impact of pension reforms on intergenerational equity: In the early 1990s, and then in the 2000s, the retirement age was increased, reducing the benefit-receipt period and total pension wealth. Contribution rates were increased and a solidarity tax was imposed on high pensions. Furthermore, the manner in which new pensions are calculated relates lifetime contributions much more closely to benefits then the prereform system did.

[2] Transition costs emerge because pension liabilities mature over a very long horizon while contribution revenues start to decline as soon as a funded reform becomes effective. The revenue shortfall may be financed by higher current taxes, additional debt (higher future taxes), or lower public expenditures in other areas. Regardless of the chosen financing strategy, the level or distribution of lifetime taxes paid and services or transfers received will be different from what they would have been before the reform.

BOX 15.1 Actuarial Balance, Actuarial Fairness, Actuarial Neutrality

A pension system's distributional features are also closely linked to how assets and liabilities compare at the individual's, the cohort's, or the entire scheme's level. A pension scheme is actuarially balanced if its total liabilities equal its assets, regardless of the time period being assessed. An actuarially fair scheme matches expected pension entitlements to lifetime contributions, whereas actuarial neutrality implies that the marginal net benefit earned by working one year longer remains constant (Queisser and Whitehouse 2006). An actuarially balanced scheme is equitable in an intergenerational sense but being in actuarial balance does not necessarily imply actuarial fairness or neutrality. Likewise, a system that is actuarially fair does not need to be either neutral or balanced; indeed, the actuarial imbalances of most public defined-benefit schemes are the result of benefits that were actuarially unfair, that is, overly generous, compared with contributions made. Actuarial imbalances may contribute to intergenerational inequity, while the lack of actuarial fairness may impose horizontal inequity in exchange for greater vertical equity for members of the same generation.

In addition to coverage, the other main systemic features influencing equity are regulatory homogeneity, actuarial fairness, risk sharing, mode of financing, and taxation of benefits. Regulatory homogeneity refers to the extent to which the system differentiates between schemes and schemes' members according to sector, gender, length of service, and age-earning profiles. For the concept of actuarial fairness, please refer to Box 15.1. Risk sharing is the manner in which the risk of underfunding expected benefits is distributed between beneficiaries and the underwriter of pension promises. Mode of financing refers to the difference between the incidence of revenues and benefits.

If a system consists of several schemes (for instance, specialized by economic sector or geographic region), their regulations are homogeneous if the horizontal and vertical equity characteristics are similar across the schemes. Homogeneity does not ensure either actuarial fairness or fiscal sustainability; it simply implies that people with similar characteristics are treated similarly (in an actuarially fair or unfair manner). For instance, if private sector employee pensions are based on lifetime average wages while the public sector scheme uses final salaries to establish benefits, then the system is heterogeneous, reducing horizontal equity across schemes and their members. Similarly, if farmers pay lower contributions in return for entitlements similar to the entitlements received by nonagricultural workers (as in Austria, Finland, France, Germany, Poland, and Moldova), the heterogeneity of the internal rates of return on contributions translates into horizontal inequity across people belonging to different schemes (Choi 2009).

At the level of individuals, if a system is actuarially fair, it is horizontally equitable, too, and provides no intentional, ex ante redistribution across members who have varying characteristics; redistribution is constrained to the type of ex post redistribution that is implicit to annuities. In defined-contribution schemes,[3] redistribution is limited to what the payout products can accommodate. If benefits are paid as a lump sum or as phased withdrawals, then payouts are determined by the individual's account balance at retirement, which, in turn, is defined by the amount and timing of contributions and the net investment returns earned. If annuities are competitively and fairly priced, and there are no regulations enforcing ex ante redistribution among annuitants to impose vertical equity, there will be little room for additional redistribution across, for instance, people of different genders, retirement account balances, or marital status.

The most common divergence from actuarial fairness is with regard to gender. Women, on average, live longer than men but their contribution histories tend to be shorter because of child rearing and other unpaid services they provide within the household (Clements, Eich, and Gupta 2014). Women also tend to earn lower wages. These factors—lower average wages, shorter service histories, and pension entitlements paid out over a longer period of retirement—would lead to

---

[3] Strictly speaking, this only holds for defined-contribution schemes that operate without performance guarantees.

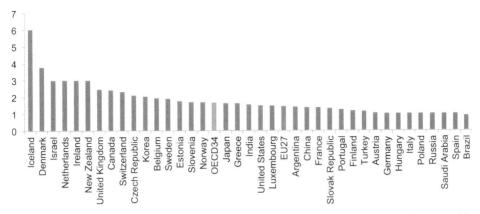

Figure 15.6 Vertical Equity in Public Pension Systems *(Ratio of income replacement rates for low and high earners)*

Source: Organisation for Economic Co-operation and Development (2013).
Note: EU27 = the 27 members of the European Union (before Croatia joined in 2013); OECD34 = the 34 members of the OECD. The figure compares two theoretical workers who earn 50 percent and 150 percent, respectively, of the economy-wide average wage throughout their lives, and shows how much higher the low earner's replacement rate is compared with that of the high earner. Note that the replacement rates compare both workers' pensions to their own wages; thus, low earners' higher replacement rates will still translate into lower absolute pension levels.

monthly pensions significantly below men's. However, public pension systems may compensate for these circumstances through higher pension accrual rates, recognition of noncontributory years spent at home with children as service time, and the disregarding of women's longer life expectancy at retirement. These measures improve women's welfare and imply sacrificing horizontal equity for the sake of vertical equity.

Pension rules may also diverge from actuarial fairness and horizontal equity in other ways. In defined-benefit schemes, income does not enter directly into the pension formula but goes through some adjustment to form the basis of benefits. The adjustment involves valorizing past earnings to wage levels observed at retirement and compressing the distribution of the pension calculation base. The result of these progressive pension calculation rules is that higher earners realize a lower return on their contributions than do low earners (Figure 15.6). It is important to note that compressing the distribution of benefits (relative to the distribution of the contribution base) may not, in itself, make the system internally more redistributive—improved vertical equity would require that at least part of the savings thus achieved be reallocated to low earners to increase their pension levels.

With regard to risk sharing, a pension scheme can be defined benefit or defined contribution. In a defined-contribution scheme, the risk that assets will prove insufficient to generate expected retirement wealth is borne by the individual contributor; in defined-benefit schemes this risk is borne by the scheme sponsor or underwriter (Broadbent and Palumbo 2006). The underwriter for private schemes is the sponsoring employer or the financial intermediary underwriting the pension insurance policy. For public schemes, it is the community of current and future taxpayers as represented by the state. If the incidence of these incremental taxes or reduced services differs from that of pension benefits, then publicly managed, underfunded, defined-benefit schemes redistribute income from current or future taxpayers to current pensioners. In countries with large occupational pension sectors (such as Denmark, the Netherlands, the United Kingdom, the United States, and others), explicit or implicit government guarantees may also exist. Because these guarantee schemes are funded by contributions from the pension industry but may enjoy an ultimate state guarantee, guarantees issued to private pension schemes might imply redistribution across schemes, as well as across scheme members and taxpayers outside the schemes.

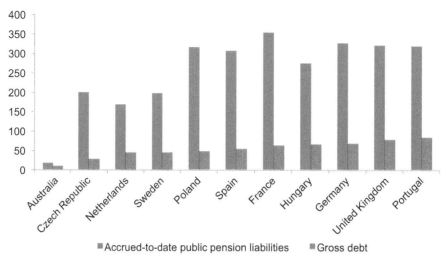

Figure 15.7   Public Debt versus Implicit Pension Liabilities *(Percent of GDP)*

Source: van der Wal (2014).

Defined-benefit schemes permit more redistribution (or divergence from horizontal equity) because these schemes do not record financial assets; instead they record information that at the time of retirement is translated into cash benefits according to rules that may or may not be actuarially fair. The "price" at which past contributions buy retirement benefits is set by the legislature at the time of retirement and with as much regard for horizontal and vertical equity as social policy objectives require. From a public policy perspective, defined-benefit schemes, and within those, universal coverage public schemes, are more accommodating of vertical equity considerations. Privately underwritten defined-benefit schemes (such as pension insurance products offered by insurance companies or occupational pension schemes underwritten by employers) have less room for intergenerational redistribution than do publicly managed defined-benefit social insurance schemes. There are various reasons for this, including the funding requirements for privately managed defined-benefit schemes, smaller risk pools, limited access to additional resources, and the accounting differences between public and private schemes.

With regard to the mode of financing, a pension scheme may be fully funded or pay-as-you-go financed. Pay-as-you-go schemes are extreme cases of underfunding: they function without reserves or with reserves that are dwarfed by the scheme's accrued liabilities (Figure 15.7). Defined-contribution schemes are fully funded, by definition, while defined-benefit schemes can function fully funded or underfunded (pay-as-you-go with or without reserves). Whether a defined-benefit scheme is fully funded or pay-as-you-go financed is immaterial from an intergenerational equity perspective as long as the scheme's resources are sufficient to meet its current obligation.[4] If, however, the scheme's current resources are insufficient, then expenditure- or revenue-side adjustment measures become necessary, leading to intergenerational redistribution, typically toward earlier from later generations.

Taxation can alter a pension system's equity characteristics significantly. Pensions are deferred compensation and should be treated similarly to other income, but they rarely are (Figure 15.8). Taxes may be levied at the contribution, accumulation, or payout phase, but the choice of when

---

[4]Theoretically, pay-as-you-go contribution rates can be established at their long-term equilibrium level with reserves built up when the system is young (has few pensioners compared with contributors), and drawn down as the system matures.

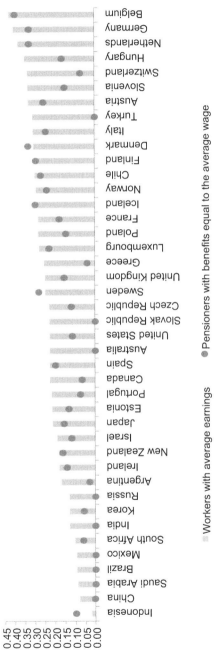

Figure 15.8 Effective Tax Rates Levied on Workers and Pensioners

Source: OECD (2013).

to tax pension wealth has distributional consequences, depending on the progressivity of income tax schedules. Since the early 1970s, a discernible trend has emerged toward subjecting social insurance benefits, including pensions, to income taxation, although concessions remain widespread. In the majority of Organisation for Economic Co-operation and Development countries, tax allowances and tax relief, such as deductions from the taxable income base or lower tax rates (for instance, in Australia, Canada, Chile, Estonia, Ireland, and others), are extended to pension benefits. In the United States, between 15 and 50 percent of public pension income is tax free, depending on the recipient's total income (OECD 2013).

The equity impact of taxation of pensions depends on whether the personal income tax regime is progressive and whether tax rules change between the contribution period and retirement period. If the income tax rate is flat and the rate remains unchanged over time, the choice of when to tax pensions is immaterial from an equity perspective. A progressive income tax regime can help compress the benefit distribution relative to the distribution of gross incomes although the extent of compression will be typically higher if the tax is levied when the contribution-liable income is earned[5] rather than when it is paid out in the form of pensions. Total lifetime taxes will be lower if pensions are taxed at the payout phase, and the individual's welfare may also improve, depending on how the progressivity in the tax system and the higher marginal utility of marginal income in old age compare.

EQUITY IN COMMON TYPES OF PENSION SCHEMES

The most common arrangement among public pension schemes is a combination of universal coverage, pay-as-you-go financing, and earnings-related, defined-benefit pension benefits. These schemes tend to provide significant intragenerational redistribution to ensure vertical equity while their reforms, which aim to improve fiscal sustainability in the face of aging populations, lead to intergenerational redistribution. Intragenerational redistribution is partly intentional, such as in the case of redistribution in favor of women; partly unintentional but in line with social policy preferences (for instance, from single to married people or to people with children); and partly unintentional and undesired, such as the channeling of pension wealth from less educated to more educated people (on account of the latter's higher life expectancy). With regard to fiscal sustainability, the liabilities of these schemes are not automatically adjusted to be commensurate with their assets (expected revenues). Thus, unless the benefit rules and contribution rates were established at their long-term equilibrium, the combination of a no-policy-change scenario with aging will result in a worsening financial position, necessitating intergenerational redistribution from future workers to those of today.

With regard to adequacy, these schemes can perform well and provide people who have low lifetime earnings or short contribution histories (or both) with benefits high enough to meet poverty alleviation objectives. Being able to do so is a direct consequence of these schemes' ability to diverge from actuarially fair horizontal equity. Defined-benefit schemes typically involve redistribution both within and between cohorts, but the size of the redistribution is difficult to assess given the multiple nonlinearities introduced by minimum benefits, contribution ceilings, and the compression of benefit distributions through partial recognition or indexation of contribution histories. The extent of redistribution also depends on whether it is measured on an individual or household level (Gustman and Steinmeier 2000) and whether the income position of households is established based on actual or potential earnings.

Notional defined contribution (NDC) and point systems are both strictly earnings related and provide benefits that reflect relative contribution performance and life expectancy at retirement

---

[5] Technically, this would mean that income tax is payable on total income, without deducting pension contributions.

within (point systems) as well as across (NDC) cohorts. NDC schemes are relatively new and were first introduced in Latvia, Poland, and Sweden, then followed by others such as those in Italy and the Kyrgyz Republic. NDC systems have equity features similar to those of traditional defined-contribution schemes; at the same time, however, they do not observe the same asset-liability matching constraints and allow for more government intervention to ensure fiscal sustainability. Because assets and returns are notional, governments can adjust credited returns; however, once contributions and notional returns are credited to individual accounts they become fixed monetarily, allowing little room for ex post revaluation of entitlements for the sake of reducing unfunded liabilities. A pure NDC scheme imposes no interpersonal redistribution across the members of the same cohort but may imply intergenerational redistribution, depending on how notional rates of return and annuity factors are changed, by the government, over time.[6] Point systems (as in Germany and France) record relative contribution performance within cohorts but leave room for policymakers to decide how much a point is worth in monetary terms, from cohort to cohort, depending on fiscal or other considerations. Thus, point systems can maintain intragenerational horizontal equity while allowing expenditure-side adjustments for the sake of intergenerational equity.[7]

Fully funded defined-contribution arrangements are common among privately managed voluntary pension schemes but were relatively rare among mandatory, universal schemes before the structural pension reforms of the 1990s and 2000s in Latin America (for instance, in Bolivia, Chile, Colombia, El Salvador, Mexico, Panama, and Peru) and Eastern Europe (for instance, in Bulgaria, Croatia, Estonia, Hungary, Poland, and the Slovak Republic). Under this arrangement, there is usually no ex ante interpersonal redistribution, either within or between cohorts, at least during the accumulation period. This basic model may be altered if rate-of-return guarantees are issued by an entity separate from the scheme's members. If a horizontally equitable pension scheme is defined as one that imposes neither net taxes nor transfers, then a defined-contribution scheme is a perfectly equitable design from an interpersonal perspective. It is also important to note, however, that these schemes may not be able to address vertical equity considerations and meet the poverty alleviation function of public pension schemes. This shortcoming is especially the case in countries with large informal sectors and low pension coverage. Thus, such schemes may need to be supplemented with welfare transfer programs to reduce poverty among the elderly (as, for instance, has been done in Chile, Israel, El Salvador, Mexico, and Paraguay).

Noncontributory basic pension schemes are traditionally viewed as part of the pension system although conceptually they are closer to conditional welfare transfers (with age used as a proxy for incapacity to generate labor income) or guaranteed minimum income schemes. These schemes are operated with vertical equity and, in particular, poverty alleviation, in mind. The incidence of benefits and the sources financing them are weakly related. Noncontributory schemes are the most transparent approach to redistribution aiming at vertical equity; they can also create the political economy conditions for making contributory schemes horizontally more equitable and imposing hard budget constraints on them. Eligibility and the targeted income level play an important role in this regard. Age, usually augmented by residence criteria to forestall benefit tourism, is the defining eligibility criterion of these pension benefits, which either are universally available ("basic pensions," as in Estonia, Ireland, and the Netherlands) or may be targeted to the low-income elderly, with eligibility based on the level of other pension income or total income. Targeting may be achieved by ex ante means testing (for example, in Belgium, Denmark,

---

[6] In an NDC regime, the only instruments available for adjusting the growth of future pension liabilities are the credited returns and the annuity factors.

[7] Governments, in practice, can and do adjust pension parameters in line with fiscal constraints. The design of the public system determines the relative ease and transparency of revenue- and expenditure-side adjustments.

and Korea) or by self targeting; in the latter case, a tax claw-back progressively reduces net benefit receipts as total taxable income rises (as in Australia).

Two policy constraints apply to benefit levels: first, basic pensions should be sufficient to keep retirees out of poverty in the absence of any other income—otherwise the pension system cannot meet its social policy objective; second, they should not provide strong disincentives for participating in contributory arrangements and voluntarily saving for old age. These two considerations also suggest that caution must be exercised when introducing noncontributory basic pensions. In particular, in countries in which the contributory scheme's benefit distribution is compressed around the minimum pension or the contributory minimum pension falls close to the basic pension level, a noncontributory scheme may aggravate noncompliance and harm the fiscal sustainability of contributory social insurance schemes (Holzmann, Robalino, and Takayama 2009). Under such conditions, basic pensions may ultimately crowd out contributory public schemes as compliance falls in response to highly different internal rates of return on contributions.[8]

THE IMPACT OF PENSION REFORMS ON EQUITY

In an ideal case, longevity-adjusted implicit returns on contributions are homogeneous, contribution histories are long, contributions are high enough to ensure that benefit levels are adequate to prevent poverty, and fiscal considerations pose no constraints to meeting pension obligations. In reality, no contributory public pension scheme meets this description. Fiscal sustainability, and the goals of equal treatment of all contributions (horizontal equity) and protection of the vulnerable against poverty (vertical equity) mutually constrain each other. In the presence of fiscal constraints, prioritizing poverty alleviation requires heterogeneous returns—that is, it requires intragenerational redistribution to improve vertical equity. The same fiscal constraints combined with uniform returns to contributions along the entire income distribution may result in inadequate benefits for low earners, leading to poverty or higher social transfers outside the pension system. Horizontally equitable benefits that are adequate even for low earners can lead to overgenerous pensions and unsustainably high pension expenditures. As a consequence of demographic aging these trade-offs become more pronounced, forcing governments to initiate pension reforms.

Pension reforms fall into three broad categories: parametric, structural, and paradigmatic. Parametric reforms maintain the system's objectives and main instruments but adjust its parameters such as retirement ages, benefit calculation rules, and pension indexation. Structural reforms keep the system's objectives (intended coverage, the relative importance of poverty alleviation, and consumption smoothing) mostly unchanged but modify the main channels of achieving them by altering the division of responsibilities across the state, the private sector, and the individual, or amending the nature of the system's constituent elements (such as introducing mandatory funded pension schemes or shifting the poverty alleviation function into a separate scheme). Paradigmatic reforms amend the system's basic objectives by perhaps introducing universal coverage, establishing a poverty alleviation pillar in a system that previously only aimed at horizontal equity, or substantially revising the extent of mandated intertemporal and interpersonal redistribution (the size of the system).

Parametric Reforms

Parametric adjustments are the most common reform, intended to enhance the system's long-term fiscal viability, modify its distributional characteristics, or address its unintended externalities—but without changing the system's objectives or structure. With the exception of

---

[8] For further discussion, please see Schwartz and Arias 2014.

changing pension indexation rules and the tax treatment of benefits, both of which affect the current stock of beneficiaries, parametric reforms typically focus on future retirees' eligibility and benefit levels, influencing intergenerational equity. Parametric measures may alter retirement ages, contribution rates and bases, and benefit calculation rules, as well as the valorization of past earnings (in defined-benefit schemes) and the indexation of pensions.

Retirement age increases have been among the most common reforms since the early 1990s as a response to the dual challenge of declining labor force participation rates among older segments of the population and the increasing share of elderly people. Practically all OECD countries have increased retirement ages, and many have also tightened early retirement opportunities to close the gap between statutory and effective retirement ages. The equity impact of later retirement is determined by the actuarial fairness of the retirement age increase, whether the labor market can accommodate the marginal labor supply of older workers, and whether equity is viewed as a matter of pension wealth (the total value of all benefit payments) or the level of periodic (monthly) pension benefits.

The impact of retirement age increases on total pension wealth is indirectly related to income. Since lifetime income and wealth are strongly correlated with life expectancy, a change in the retirement age implies redistribution from less to more well-off beneficiaries. Although this redistribution can be partly compensated for by progressive benefit calculation rules, retirement age increases intensify intragenerational redistribution on a pension wealth basis. At the same time, if the marginal labor supply can be accommodated, *monthly* pensions will increase on account of longer service periods (Rawdanowicz, Wurzel, and Christensen 2013). This effect does not benefit all contributors to the same extent, however, because better educated people have a higher probability of late-career employment and their age-earning profiles make it more likely that their additional earnings will increase their average wage entering the pension formula. Retirement age increases should, therefore, be supplemented by measures that improve, through continuing education and training, older workers' productivity, and by regulations that reduce age discrimination and allow for flexible working conditions (Heywood and Siebert 2009).

Less generous benefit indexation influences a pension system's intergenerational equity features by changing the relationship between total benefits received and contributions made. In theory, indexation rules can be amended without changing overall pension wealth—total benefits received are similar whether combining less generous indexation with higher accrual rates (higher first pensions) or increasing lower pensions at a higher rate. Leaving pension wealth unchanged does not imply that total lifetime welfare remains unchanged, however; that depends on individuals' intertemporal consumption preferences and their subjective discount rates. Indexation of public pensions can have an unintended distributional impact on households' total income, too: the poorer the pensioner household, the higher the share of public pension benefits in total income (Brown and Weisbenner 2013). If the real value of benefits does not increase (as occurs under price indexation) while alternative sources of old-age income (such as private pensions, returns on savings, and assets) increase, lower indexation will have a greater negative impact on total old-age income at the lower end of the benefit distribution.

Reforms that reduce average starting pensions can also alter systems' equity characteristics. Longer benefit assessment periods, especially calculating benefits based on lifetime earnings instead of on final salary, improve horizontal equity. High earners' age-earning profiles are not only higher but the profiles' steepness is also greater than that of lower earners. Thus, high earners' pensions are higher relative to their own career average wage than are lower earners' pensions. Increasing the minimum contributory period for eligibility has ambiguous welfare consequences, depending on the labor supply response of people with service lengths between the old and the new criteria. Stricter eligibility criteria may reduce coverage. However, the system's horizontal equity for its eligible members may increase—longer contribution histories would make it possible to move away from accrual schedules that reward short contribution histories with relatively higher replacement rates.

Modifying the accrual schedule's shape and the average replacement alters both vertical and horizontal equity. A uniform downward shift of the accrual schedule has no impact on horizontal equity. At the same time, it may reduce vertical equity and require compensating antipoverty measures within or outside the pension system to meet a government's antipoverty objectives. Conversely, a uniform upward shift of the accrual schedule, by virtue of providing a larger segment of contributors with an adequate benefit, will permit greater horizontal equity without increasing poverty among pensioners with low career earnings. The shape of the accrual schedule—whether marginal years of contribution are rewarded with lower, equal, or higher marginal replacement rates—can be an instrument of redistribution from people with different contribution histories. Moving from concave to linear and then to convex accrual schedules reduces the system's capacity for ensuring vertical equity; at the same time, it provides stronger incentives for people to work longer.

Structural Reforms

Structural reforms maintain the extent of the mandate (the amount of present consumption forgone for the sake of retirement income) but change the mode of financing, risk sharing, or the distribution of the underfunding risk. Recent structural reforms have focused mostly on partially privatizing public pension schemes and on changing the risk-sharing characteristics of the system. The introduction of mandatory, privately managed defined-contribution schemes (as in Bulgaria, Croatia, Hungary, Poland, Romania, and others) increased the systems' overall horizontal equity by strengthening the link between contributions and future benefits. These reforms also reduced vertical equity and exposed people with short contribution histories and low career earnings to the risk of old-age poverty, especially among those people with little or no pretransition contribution histories. Structural reforms, similarly to parametric ones, can improve a system's intergenerational equity by gradually reducing unfunded pension liabilities and the portion of future cohorts' tax burdens that are financing the funding gap accumulated in the past.

Another common type of structural reform is the introduction of uniformity into pension schemes and the treatment of different types of labor contracts, such as urban versus rural residents and formal versus informal employment. Such efforts are under way in China, Japan, Thailand, and a number of other African and South Asian countries where the workers outside the public sector are either not covered by mandatory pension schemes or the schemes' regulations are significantly different. These reforms improve horizontal equity and can have positive indirect effects on labor mobility and compliance.

Paradigmatic Reforms

Paradigmatic reforms change pension systems' basic objectives. The most common type of paradigmatic reform is the expansion of partial coverage to explicitly target the entire population, as in China, India, Nepal, and Thailand, for instance. This type of reform may involve making contributory schemes universally accessible or introducing noncontributory social pensions that aim to reduce old-age poverty. These reforms are typical in low-income countries and non-European emerging economies where previous pension systems only covered civil servants, public employees, and urban dwellers employed in the formal sector. In theory, governments may also decide to give up the consumption-smoothing objective of a pension system in the face of fiscal constraints and focus, instead, solely on poverty alleviation. The fiscal cost of terminating contributory schemes that have large legacy liabilities keeps governments from reducing earnings-related schemes to a basic pension; at the same time, economic crises (for example, hyperinflation, loss of the revenue base because of war or civil strife) may compel policymakers to pursue such marked paradigm shifts, as was the case in Georgia and Kosovo.

An important issue regarding paradigmatic changes is the dialectic nature of reforms: the compounded impact of parametric and structural reforms may amount to a major paradigm shift. For instance, compressing the benefit distribution because of fiscal constraints (upper limit) and poverty alleviation objectives (lower limit) may result in a quasi-flat benefit structure that is incompatible with earnings-related contributory financing. Likewise, making all components of a pension system strictly related to earnings (regardless of the choice of defined-benefit or defined-contribution risk sharing) while constraining total pension spending for reasons of fiscal sustainability can make achievement of the poverty alleviation objective impossible.

CONCLUSIONS AND POLICY IMPLICATIONS

Historic, economic, and social contexts determine the interpretation of equity that is acceptable in a given society. Despite the absence of a universally applicable "mix" of horizontal and vertical equity or levels of inter- and intragenerational redistribution, policymakers need to be aware of the equity impacts of pension system design features; otherwise they will be unable to efficiently select the means of achieving their policy objectives. Despite these difficulties in determining what constitutes an equitable pension system, some clear principles emerge from international experience.

First, some policies are clearly equity enhancing. Expanding coverage—or keeping coverage from declining—is the most important of the policies contributing to improved vertical equity. Coverage can be directly increased by dismantling regulatory barriers to participation, introducing administrative structures that make it easy to register and comply, providing financial incentives through the tax treatment of contributions or targeted matching contributions, ensuring that explicit and implicit pension contracts are honored, and finally, by expanding the obligation to participate. Factors beyond pension policy, such as better control over informality, or higher transparency of public finances, can also help improve coverage. In Eastern European emerging economies, where informality has undermined compliance and fiscally driven parametric reforms may have devalued pension promises, efforts to maintain compliance are necessary. Equal treatment of economic sectors, industries, types of contracts, ethnic groups, and so on can unequivocally improve horizontal equity. Homogeneity of pension rules across schemes with similar characteristics can equalize internal rates of return, provide the same level of protection against poverty, and reduce labor market distortions arising from the existence of different schemes.

Second, most design features and reform options require trade-offs. In a fiscally constrained policy space, the trade-off is between horizontal and vertical equity. Under circumstances of broad and deep poverty requiring significant redistribution toward the poor to achieve vertical equity, the trade-off is between horizontal equity and fiscal cost. If there is a manifest social preference for a strong contribution-benefit link, then the choice is between fiscal cost and the extent of poverty alleviation. Making benefit indexation less generous, for instance, to address fiscal constraints, will leave consumption smoothing unchanged but may compromise a system's ability to provide poverty indexation. Likewise, introducing a noncontributory minimum pension to cover people without other pension entitlements will either increase total pension expenditures or will require that contributory pension benefits be reduced. This will compress the total benefit distribution around the basic pension and reduce the system's horizontal equity. Another example of policy trade-offs is permitting women to retire earlier than men: ensuring that their benefits are adequate despite their shorter contribution periods will reduce horizontal equity or increase pension expenditures. Similar choices are unavoidable in the design or reform of pension systems; therefore, the gains and losses inherent in these policy choices need to be carefully analyzed.

Third, pension policy is not made on the basis of pure economic analysis but under political constraints. Sociocultural circumstances and traditions may hinder the equal treatment of certain social groups, including women; a society's self-image as a meritocracy may stand in the way of redistribution toward people with insufficient contribution histories; powerful groups—such as the armed forces, high ranking civil servants, and legislators—may be disinterested in reforms that reduce their privileges; and resistance from older workers to partially revising their pension entitlements may necessitate slowing down reforms. Likewise, the available instruments to achieve the preferred policy objectives may be constrained, too, by limited administrative capacity and financial market development. The absence of a sufficiently developed domestic capital market, for example, can hinder the development of a competitive and efficient private pension sector; the lack of electronic databases of past contributions may prevent the transformation of a defined-benefit scheme into an NDC one; and the absence of reliable death and residence registries may hamper efforts to exercise effective control over benefit uptake.

Fourth, the fiscal and welfare consequences of various reform options need to be analyzed, and the goals of pension policy should be communicated, to achieve broad and lasting support for the policy direction chosen. Pension policies take years, even decades, to fully implement, and their reversals are costly both fiscally and to the credibility of structural reforms. Transparency of pension finances, and their consequences for intergenerational equity, should be ensured by the development and regular publication of indicators capturing public pension systems' long-term financial position and the impact of reforms on future pension spending and revenues.

Finally, pension policy effectiveness hinges, to a large extent, on other policy areas. These areas include, among others, labor regulations, access to and quality of public education and health care, and tax policy and administration. Retirement age increases need to be accompanied by policies promoting late-career employment; the expansion of contributory pension schemes is only feasible if tax administration capacity can accommodate the expansion; improving women's labor force participation rates and, consequently, their pension coverage and average benefits cannot happen without flexible work arrangements and access to affordable child care facilities. Welfare in old age is a reflection of individuals' working careers, income, and assets; their decisions regarding the intertemporal reallocation of consumption; and the social policies, including pension regulations, that may alter the welfare consequences of preretirement life events. Public pension systems can lessen the consequences of inequities suffered in education and the labor market caused by ethnic, gender, or other discrimination. But the pension system cannot, in itself, be expected to correct all these ills. Indeed, a pension system's ability to prevent poverty and a marked drop in consumption is a gauge not only of the system's success but of the effectiveness and integrity of a variety of public policies.

REFERENCES

Auerbach, Paula, Maria Eugenia Genoni, and Carmen Pagés. 2007. "Social Security Coverage and the Labor Market in Developing Countries." IZA Discussion Paper No. 2979, Institute for the Study of Labor, Bonn.

Bloom, David E., and Roddy McKinnon. 2013. "The Design and Implementation of Public Pension Systems in Developing Countries: Issues and Options." IZA Policy Paper No. 59, Institute for the Study of Labor, Bonn.

Broadbent, John, and Michael Palumbo. 2006. "The Shift from Defined Benefit to Defined Contribution Pension Plans—Implications for Asset Allocation and Risk Management." Paper prepared for the Working Group on Institutional Investors, Global Savings and Asset Allocation established by the Committee on the Global Financial System.

Brown, Jeffrey R., and Scott J. Weisbenner. 2013. "The Distributional Effects of the Social Security Windfall Elimination Provision." *Journal of Pension Economics and Finance* 12 (4): 415–34.

Choi, Jongkyun. 2009. "Pension Schemes for the Self-Employed in OECD Countries." Employment and Migration Working Paper No. 84, OECD Publishing, Paris.

Clements, Benedict, Frank Eich, and Sanjeev Gupta, eds. 2014. *Equitable and Sustainable Pensions: Challenges and Experience.* Washington: International Monetary Fund.

Gustman, Alan L., and Thomas L. Steinmeier. 2000. "How Effective Is Redistribution under the Social Security Benefit Formula?" NBER Working Paper No. 7597, National Bureau of Economic Research, Cambridge, Massachusetts.

Heywood, John S., and W. Stanley Siebert. 2009. "Understanding the Labour Market for Older Workers." IZA Discussion Paper No. 4033, Institute for the Study of Labor, Bonn.

Holzmann, Robert, David A. Robalino, and Noriyuki Takayama, eds. 2009. *Closing the Coverage Gap: The Role of Social Pensions and Other Retirement Income Transfers.* Washington: World Bank.

International Labour Organization. 2014. *World Social Protection Report 2014–15: Building Economic Recovery, Inclusive Development and Social Justice.* Geneva: International Labour Organization.

International Monetary Fund. 2015. *Fiscal Monitor: Now Is the Time—Fiscal Policies for Sustainable Growth,* Washington, April.

McDaniel, Paul R., and James R. Repetti. 1993. "Horizontal and Vertical Equity: The Musgrave/Kaplow Exchange." *Florida Tax Review* 1 (10): 607–22.

Organisation for Economic Co-operation and Development (OECD). 2013. *Pensions at a Glance.* Paris: OECD Publishing.

Queisser, Monika, and Edward Whitehouse. 2006. "Neutral or Fair? Actuarial Concepts and Pension-System Design." OECD Social, Employment and Migration Working Paper No. 40, OECD Publishing, Paris.

Rawdanowicz, Lukasz, Eckhard Wurzel, and Ane Katherine Christensen. 2013. "The Equity Implications of Fiscal Consolidation." OECD Economics Department Working Paper No. 1013, OECD Publishing, Paris.

Santos, Tania, and Immaculada Domínguez. 2011. "Financial Solvency of Pension Systems in the European Union." International Conference on Economic Modeling – EcoMod2011 Proceedings, University of Azores, Portugal.

Schwarz, Anita, and Omar S. Arias, eds. 2014. *The Inverting Pyramid: Pension Systems Facing Demographic Challenges in Europe and Central Asia.* Washington: World Bank.

van der Wal, Dirk. 2014. "The Measurement of International Pension Obligations." DNB Working Paper No. 424, De Nederlandsche Bank, Amsterdam.

CHAPTER 16

The Redistributive Impact of Government Spending on Education and Health: Evidence from Thirteen Developing Countries in the Commitment to Equity Project

Nora Lustig

INTRODUCTION

Two key indicators of a government's (or society's) commitment to equalizing opportunities and reducing poverty and social exclusion are the share of total income devoted to social spending and how equalizing and pro-poor this spending is (Lindert 2004; Barr 2012). Typically, redistributive social spending includes cash benefits[1] and benefits in kind such as spending on education and health.[2] This chapter examines the level, redistributive impact, and pro-poorness of government spending on education and health for 13 developing countries from the Commitment to Equity (CEQ) project:[3] Armenia, Bolivia, Brazil, Chile, Colombia, El Salvador, Ethiopia, Guatemala, Indonesia, Mexico, Peru, South Africa, and Uruguay.[4]

The author is very grateful to Nancy Birdsall, Benedict Clements, Jean-Yves Duclos, Sanjeev Gupta, Sean Higgins, Peter Lindert, and Stephen Younger for their helpful comments and suggestions. She is also very grateful to Luis Munguia and Yang Wang for their excellent research assistance. All errors and omissions are the author's sole responsibility.

[1] "Cash" benefits typically include cash transfers and near-cash transfers such as school feeding programs and free uniforms and textbooks. Depending on the analysis, cash benefits also include consumption subsidies (for example, on food) and energy consumption and housing subsidies. The studies included here include cash and near-cash transfers as well as (in most cases) consumption subsidies. Housing subsidies are not included.

[2] Social spending as a category frequently includes spending on pensions funded by contributions. Following Lindert 1994, this analysis does not include them. Strictly speaking, one should include the subsidized portion of these pensions as part of redistributive social spending (for example, the portion of contributory pensions that is paid out of general revenues and not from contributions). However, estimates of these subsidies are hard to produce. As an alternative, the results for the scenario in which contributory pensions are treated as a government transfer and part of social spending are available upon request. Noncontributory pensions (also known as social or minimum pensions) are treated as any other cash transfer.

[3] Led by Nora Lustig since 2008, the CEQ project is an initiative of the Center for Inter-American Policy and Research (CIPR) and the Department of Economics, Tulane University, the Center for Global Development and the Inter-American Dialogue. For more details, visit www.commitmentoequity.org.

[4] The selected countries are not meant to be a representative sample of the developing world. The analysis is based on the country studies that have been undertaken and fully completed under the CEQ project as of January 2015. Because the project first started in Latin America, countries from this region make up nine of the thirteen. The authors of the country studies are Armenia (Younger and Khachatryan 2014), Bolivia (Paz Arauco and others 2014), Brazil (Higgins and Pereira 2014), Chile (Ruiz-Tagle and Contreras 2014), Colombia (Melendez 2014), El Salvador (Beneke, Lustig, and Oliva 2014), Ethiopia (Hill, Tsehaye, and Woldehanna 2014), Guatemala (Cabrera, Lustig, and Morán 2014), Indonesia (Afkar, Jellema, and Wai-Poi forthcoming), Mexico (Scott 2014), Peru (Jaramillo 2014), South Africa (Inchauste and others 2014), and Uruguay (Bucheli and others 2014). Note that updated figures posted on the CEQ website may differ from those in the chapter; overall results and conclusions remain intact.

This chapter makes two important contributions. First, results are comparable across countries because the 13 studies apply a common methodology. Second, because the fiscal incidence analysis is comprehensive, the contribution of in-kind benefits (in the form of education and health care services) to the overall reduction in inequality can be estimated. In particular, the analysis addresses the following questions: Does government spending on education and health increase with per capita income and income inequality across the countries included here? Do more unequal societies redistribute more? What is the contribution of spending on education and health to the overall reduction in inequality? How pro-poor is spending on education (total and by level) and health? Information from administrative accounts and the fiscal incidence estimates generated in the country studies is used to answer these questions.

Examining the redistributive impact and pro-poorness of education and health spending requires attaching a value to the benefit to an individual of attending a public school or receiving health care in a public facility for free (or almost free). Conceptually, attaching a value to in-kind benefits—free government services—is complex (for example, Lambert 2001). One frequently used (and imperfect) approach is to value services at the average cost of provision.[5] This is the method used here. Such an approach ignores the fact that consumers may value services quite differently from what they cost. Given the limitations of available data, however, the cost-of-provision method is the best for now.[6]

To calculate the contribution of spending on education and health to the overall reduction in inequality, estimates are also needed of the incidence of other fiscal interventions: direct and indirect taxes, direct transfers, and indirect subsidies. This analysis uses the fiscal incidence results analyzed by Lustig, Pessino, and Scott (2014) and Lustig (forthcoming).[7] The fiscal incidence method is described in detail by Lustig and Higgins (2013) and follows what is known as the "accounting approach."[8]

The progressivity and pro-poorness of education and health spending are determined based on the size and sign of the relevant concentration coefficient. In keeping with generally accepted convention, spending is regressive when the concentration coefficient is *higher* than the market-income Gini. Spending is progressive when the concentration coefficient is *lower* than the market-income Gini. Spending is pro-poor when the concentration coefficient is not only lower than the market-income Gini, but also has a negative value.[9] A negative concentration coefficient implies that *per capita* spending tends to be higher the poorer the individual.[10] When the concentration coefficient equals zero, per capita spending is the same across the distribution: spending is neutral in absolute terms. By definition, government spending that is pro-poor (or neutral in absolute terms) is also progressive. However, not all government spending that is progressive is pro-poor.

The findings can be summarized as follows. Total social spending—cash transfers plus education and health spending—as a share of GDP is high by historical standards and it increases with gross national income (GNI) per capita. Health spending as a share of GDP increases with GNI

---

[5] This approach goes back quite a long time. See, for example, Meerman 1979; Selowsky 1979; Demery and others 1995; Demery, Dayton, and Mehra 1996; and Sahn and Younger 2000.

[6] By using averages, the method also ignores differences across income groups and regions: for example, governments may spend less (or more) per pupil or patient in poorer areas of a country. Some studies in the CEQ project adjusted for regional differences. For example, Brazil's health spending was based on region-specific averages.

[7] See the country-specific sources in footnote 4.

[8] As with any standard fiscal incidence analysis, the studies do not incorporate behavioral, life-cycle, or general equilibrium effects. However, the fiscal incidence of taxes and benefits is not generated by a mere mechanical application of statutory rates; the analysis incorporates assumptions regarding economic incidence, tax evasion, informality, and the reach of transfer programs.

[9] Implicit in the rankings is the assumption that concentration curves do not cross.

[10] This does not need to happen at every income level. A concentration coefficient will be negative as long as the concentration curve lies above the diagonal.

per capita while education spending does not. Spending on primary education as a share of GDP is roughly the same at different GNI per capita levels. Spending on secondary education as a share of GDP, however, rises with income per capita. The share of spending on tertiary education declines with GNI per capita. Social spending and spending on education and health as a share of GDP increase with market income (before taxes and transfers) inequality.

Do more unequal countries redistribute more? Results suggest that the answer is yes. Consistent with the prediction of the Meltzer-Richard median voter hypothesis (Meltzer and Richard 1981), more unequal countries reduce inequality by more whether that inequality is measured in absolute (percentage points) or relative (in percent) terms. This is an interesting result, not least because it differs from what has been found by historical research (Lindert 2004) and some of the contemporary studies (Luebker 2014). This result is not just driven by the fact that richer countries (in this sample) tend to be more unequal and, because they are richer, these countries also have more capacity to raise revenues and afford higher levels of spending. Regressing the change in the Gini on the Gini before redistribution shows that the coefficient is positive (albeit not always significant), even if GNI per capita is controlled for.

What contribution does spending on education and health make to the overall reduction in inequality? The overall reduction in inequality is defined as the difference between the market-income Gini and the Gini obtained after direct and indirect taxes, cash transfers, subsidies, and in-kind transfers in education and health.[11] In the literature, this is called the redistributive effect of the net fiscal system.[12] Education and health spending (combined) lowers inequality by a significant amount, and its marginal contribution to the overall decline in inequality is, on average, 69 percent.

How progressive and, especially, pro-poor is spending on education (total and by level) and health? Total spending on education is pro-poor in nine countries, and education spending per capita is roughly the same across the income distribution in three. Only in Ethiopia, by far the poorest and most equal country, is education spending progressive but not pro-poor. Spending on preschool, primary, and secondary education is pro-poor except in Ethiopia. Spending on tertiary education is regressive in three countries and progressive but not pro-poor in ten. Health spending is pro-poor in five countries. Of the remaining eight, health spending per capita is roughly equal across the income distribution in three and progressive (but not pro-poor) in five. There is some evidence that the progressivity and pro-poorness of education and health spending has increased over time.

The chapter is organized as follows: First, the patterns of spending on education and health are analyzed with respect to income per capita and market-income inequality. A brief description of the fiscal incidence methodology is then provided. The impact of education and health spending on the overall decline in inequality is considered. Finally, the progressivity and pro-poorness of education and health spending are examined.

PER CAPITA INCOME, INEQUALITY, AND SOCIAL SPENDING

Education and Health Spending and Per Capita Income

Does government spending on education and health increase with per capita income and income inequality across the countries included here? Figure 16.1 shows primary spending,[13] total social spending, spending on education, and spending on health as a share of GDP on the vertical axis

---

[11] In the CEQ project, this is called "final income."

[12] In the absence of reranking, this is identical to the Reynolds-Smolensky index for the net fiscal system. The redistributive effect can be measured using other inequality indicators such as the Theil index or varieties of the "Kuznetz ratio." Results for the latter are available upon request.

[13] Primary spending equals total government spending minus interest payments on domestic and external public debt.

1. Primary and Social Spending/GDP versus GNI/Capita

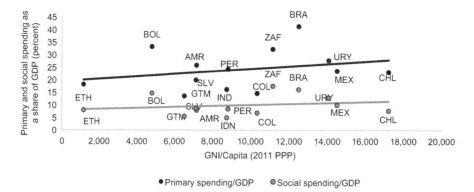

2. Education Spending/GDP versus GNI/Capita

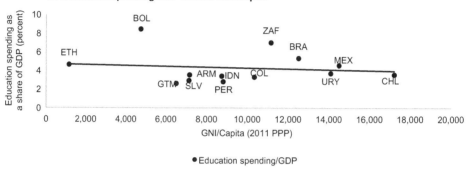

3. Health Spending/GDP versus GNI/Capita

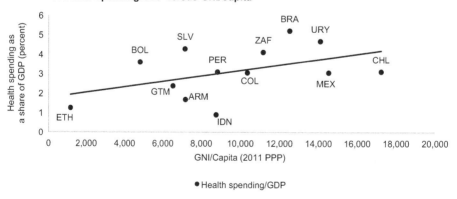

Figure 16.1   Primary, Social, Education, and Health Spending and GNI per Capita, circa 2010

Source: Author's calculations based on Armenia: Younger and Khachatryan (2014); Bolivia: Paz Arauco and others (2014); Brazil: Higgins and Pereira (2014); Chile: Ruiz-Tagle and Contreras (2014); Colombia: Melendez (2014); El Salvador: Beneke, Lustig, and Oliva (2014); Ethiopia: Hill, Tsehaye, and Woldehanna (2014); Guatemala: Cabrera, Lustig, and Morán (2014); Indonesia: Afkar, Jellema, and Wai-Poi (forthcoming); Mexico: Scott (2014); Peru: Jaramillo (2014); South Africa: Inchauste and others (2014); and Uruguay: Bucheli and others (2014).

Note: GNI = gross national income; PPP = purchasing power parity. Primary spending equals total government spending minus interest payments on domestic and external public debt. Social spending is defined as the sum of direct transfers and public spending on education and health (contributory and noncontributory). It does not include housing subsidies. Direct transfers here do *not* include contributory pensions. The spending shares and GNI per capita figures correspond to the year of the household survey: Armenia, 2011; Bolivia, 2009; Brazil, 2009; Chile, 2009; Colombia, 2010; El Salvador, 2011; Ethiopia, 2011; Guatemala, 2010; Indonesia, 2012; Mexico, 2010; Peru, 2009; South Africa, 2010–11; Uruguay, 2009. The data labels in the figure use International Organization for Standardization (ISO) abbreviations. Note that the numbers included in this section are those provided by the authors of the individual studies based on government statistics. The numbers do not necessarily match those found in "bulk" databases such as the World Bank's World Development Indicators database, those of the IMF, the OECD's Social Expenditure Database (SOCX), or databases of other institutions that form part of the United Nations system broadly defined. Definitions of categories may vary too.

and GNI per capita (in purchasing power parity) on the horizontal axis for the 13 countries. Note that social spending is defined as the sum of direct transfers and public spending on education and health (contributory and noncontributory). It does not include housing subsidies. Also, direct transfers here do *not* include contributory pensions from the government social insurance program. In all the analysis presented here, contributory pensions are treated as part of market income. In an alternative specification, the analysis assumes that contributory pensions are a direct government transfer. The results are very similar so are not included here.[14]

Total social spending and spending on public health as a share of total income rise with GNI per capita (Figure 16.1). This result is consistent with what has been found in the literature on the evolution of the welfare state.[15] The share of spending on education, however, has a negative slope. This result is mainly driven by Bolivia, an outlier in the bunch; if Bolivia is removed, the slope becomes slightly positive. If disaggregated by educational level, spending on primary education is roughly the same at different levels of GNI per capita. Spending on secondary education, however, rises with income per capita, and spending on tertiary education declines.[16]

Both the size of the total budget (measured here by primary spending as a share of GDP) and social spending are quite heterogeneous across countries. Brazil, South Africa, and, in particular, Bolivia (given its lower-middle-income status) stand out as countries with relatively large governments and more fiscal resources devoted to social spending. However, these three countries are not the ones that devote the largest shares of their budgets (measured by primary spending) to spending on education and health. Colombia, with 43 percent of its budget allocated to education and health, is the leader of this group. In Brazil, in contrast, education and health spending comprises only 25 percent of primary spending, one of the lowest shares allocated to these two items in this sample of countries. Armenia has the lowest share of spending on education and health, allocating just one-fifth of its budget. Bolivia and South Africa allocate 36 percent and 34 percent of their budgets, respectively, to education and health spending.

The composition of social spending also exhibits quite a bit of heterogeneity, with some governments devoting larger shares to education and others to health (Figure 16.2). For example, El Salvador spends a larger share of GDP on health (4.3 percent) than on education (2.9 percent), but Indonesia spends close to nothing on health (0.9 percent).

One interesting fact is that Ethiopia—a low-income country and by far the poorest and most equal of the 13—devotes more than 7 percent of its GDP to social spending. This contrasts starkly with how much redistributive spending occurred in the now developed world when it was as poor as Ethiopia is today. Based on Angus Maddison's (Maddison 2010) estimates, Western Europe was as poor as today's Ethiopia (in per capita 1990 Geary-Khamis international dollars) somewhere around the seventeenth century. According to Lindert (2004, 7), by the end of the eighteenth century, today's rich countries spent close to nothing on social programs:

> In 1776, . . . the modern age of social spending had not yet dawned. People paid hardly any taxes for the social programs that take such a large tax bite from paychecks today. Most poor people received negligible help from anybody. The elderly received no public pensions, mainly because few people survived to be elderly and average working incomes were too low to support many dependents. Most children did not go to school, and parents had to pay for those who did.

---

[14] The analysis in which contributory pensions are considered a government transfer is available upon request.

[15] For example, see Lindert 1994, 2004 and the work cited therein.

[16] Keeping in mind all the caveats of a single-variable regression and the small size of the sample, the elasticity of social spending with respect to income per capita equals 1.14; the elasticities for education and health are 0.98 and 1.44, respectively. The coefficients are significant for $p < 0.01$. Note that this regression uses a sample of 17 countries for which data on social spending were available. In addition to the 13 analyzed in this chapter, the regression includes Costa Rica, Ecuador, Jordan, and Sri Lanka.

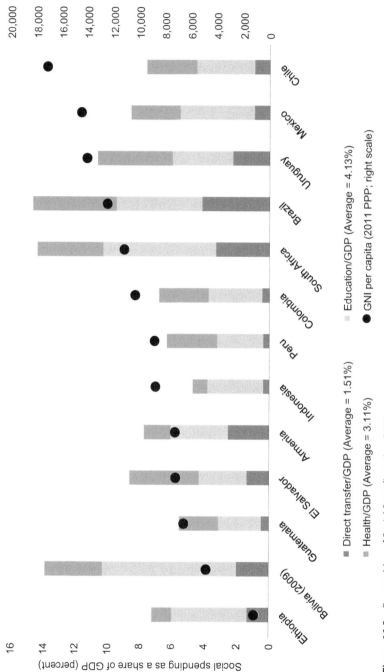

Figure 16.2 Composition of Social Spending, circa 2010

Source: Author's calculations based on Armenia: Younger and Khachatryan (2014); Bolivia: Paz Arauco and others (2014); Brazil: Higgins and Pereira (2014); Chile: Ruiz-Tagle and Contreras (2014); Colombia: Melendez (2014); El Salvador: Beneke, Lustig, and Oliva (2014); Ethiopia: Hill, Tsehaye, and Woldehanna (2014); Guatemala: Cabrera, Lustig, and Morán (2014); Indonesia: Afkar, Jellema, and Wai-Poi (forthcoming); Mexico: Scott (2014); Peru: Jaramillo (2014); South Africa: Inchauste and others (2014); and Uruguay: Bucheli and others (2014).

Note: GNI = gross national income; PPP = purchasing power parity. Social spending here is defined as the sum of direct transfers and public spending on education and health (contributory and noncontributory). It does not include housing, food, energy, or any other subsidies. Direct transfers here do not include contributory pensions. The spending shares and GNI per capita figures correspond to the year of the household survey: Armenia, 2011; Bolivia, 2009; Brazil, 2009; Chile, 2009; Colombia, 2010; El Salvador, 2011; Ethiopia, 2011; Guatemala, 2010; Indonesia, 2012; Mexico, 2010; Peru, 2009; South Africa, 2010–11; Uruguay, 2009. The data labels in the figure use International Organization for Standardization (ISO) abbreviations.

Around 2010, the ratio of public education spending to GDP ranges from 2.6 percent in Guatemala to 8.3 percent in Bolivia. Ethiopia, the poorest country in the sample, devotes 4.6 percent of its GDP to education. The countries that spend the least are Guatemala, Peru, and El Salvador, at 2.6, 2.8, and 2.9 percent of GDP, respectively. According to Angus Maddison's estimates, in 1990 international dollars, El Salvador's GDP per capita in 2008 was similar to that of the United States in 1880, and Guatemala's and Peru's were similar to the United States' around 1900. The United States, a pioneer in public education, devoted 0.74 percent of GDP in 1880 and 1.24 percent in 1900 (Appendix C in Lindert 2004). That is, the three lowest spenders on public education in this chapter spent more than twice the amount spent by the United States when it was approximately equally poor. Sweden was as rich as today's El Salvador around 1910, at which time Sweden spent 1.26 percent of GDP on public education, or about half as much as El Salvador today.

Government spending on health circa 2010 ranges from 0.9 percent of GDP in Indonesia to 5.2 percent in Brazil; the figure for Ethiopia is 1.25 percent. When the United States (around 1900) was as rich as Indonesia in the early twenty-first century (2008), it spent about 0.17 percent of GDP in government subsidies for health care (Table 1D in Lindert 1994). When the United States was as rich as Brazil was in 2008, it spent 0.4 percent.[17]

Lindert argues that the three main forces behind the rise of tax-based social spending from the late nineteenth century onward can be "linked to three other great social transformations: the transition to fuller democracy, the demographic transition. . . , and the onset of sustained economic growth" (Lindert 2004, 20). The fact that social spending is comparatively higher in the 13 developing countries analyzed here indicates that the (socially, politically, and economically) acceptable floor has been raised. One clear difference is that all 13 countries have universal suffrage whereas when present-day rich countries were equally poor, women were not allowed to vote (or there were restrictions to their vote). Thus, this chapter's findings are consistent with one of Lindert's explanatory variables for the rise in tax-based social spending, that is, fuller democracy. However, the world experienced another change during the twentieth century: the rise in domestic and external government borrowing and in official and private foreign aid. Ethiopia, for example, receives about 3 percent of GDP in grants.

Social Spending and Inequality

One of the most important findings in Lindert's (2004) path-breaking work is that both across countries and over time, resources devoted to the poor are lower in the nations in which poverty and inequality are greater. As shown in Figure 16.3, total social spending and spending on education and health as a share of GDP increase with income inequality (measured here by the Gini coefficient). This would seem to contradict earlier findings discussed by Lindert. Are the results mainly driven by South Africa? If South Africa is removed from the analysis, total social spending's line becomes flatter, education spending's line becomes horizontal, and health spending's line stays more or less the same.[18] In addition, a larger share of resources devoted to

---

[17] The United States in about 1925 was as rich as Brazil in 2008. The health spending figure corresponds to 1920 (Lindert 1994).

[18] South Africa's market-income Gini may appear higher than in other sources such as the World Bank World Development Indicators (POVCAL) database, which shows a Gini equal to .6502 for 2012 (http://iresearch.worldbank. org/PovcalNet/index.htm?2). However, published inequality figures use expenditures (such as in the World Bank's World Development Indicators) or disposable income, and not market income. In the CEQ study for South Africa (Inchauste and others 2015), the Gini for per capita disposable household income is 0.6944, in line with other sources. For example, Leibbrandt and others (2010, Table 2.6) show a Gini of 0.70 for 2008.

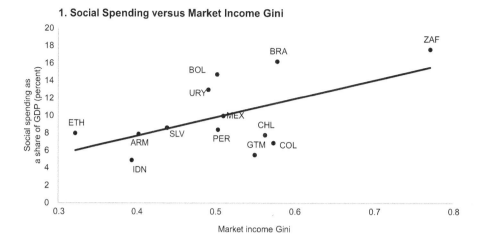

1. Social Spending versus Market Income Gini

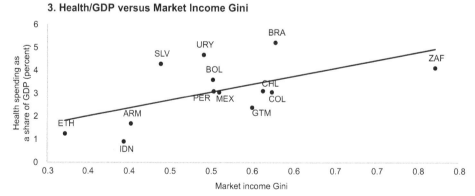

2. Education/GDP versus Market Income Gini

3. Health/GDP versus Market Income Gini

Figure 16.3 Social Spending and Income Inequality, circa 2010

Source: Author's calculations based on Armenia: Younger and Khachatryan (2014); Bolivia: Paz Arauco and others (2014); Brazil: Higgins and Pereira (2014); Chile: Ruiz-Tagle and Contreras (2014); Colombia: Melendez (2014); El Salvador: Beneke, Lustig, and Oliva (2014); Ethiopia: Hill, Tsehaye, and Woldehanna (2014); Guatemala: Cabrera, Lustig, and Morán (2014); Indonesia: Afkar, Jellema, and Wai-Poi (forthcoming); Mexico: Scott (2014); Peru: Jaramillo (2014); South Africa: Inchauste and others (2014); and Uruguay: Bucheli and others (2014).

Note: The spending shares and the Gini coefficients correspond to the year of the household survey: Armenia, 2011; Bolivia, 2009; Brazil, 2009; Chile, 2009; Colombia, 2010; El Salvador, 2011; Ethiopia, 2011; Guatemala, 2010; Indonesia, 2012; Mexico, 2010; Peru, 2009; South Africa, 2010–11; Uruguay, 2009. The Gini coefficients for Ethiopia and Indonesia are calculated using expenditure per capita; for the rest of the countries, they are calculated using income per capita. The data labels in the figure use International Organization for Standardization (ISO) abbreviations.

education and health does not indicate that governments are spending more resources on the poor. This will depend on the distribution of this spending, a question turned to below.

FISCAL INCIDENCE ANALYSIS: METHODOLOGICAL HIGHLIGHTS

Fiscal incidence analysis is used to assess the distributional impacts of a country's taxes and transfers.[19] Essentially, fiscal incidence analysis consists of allocating taxes and public spending (social spending in particular) to households or individuals so that incomes before taxes and transfers can be compared with incomes after taxes and transfers. Transfers include both cash transfers and benefits in kind such as free government services in education and health care.

In general, fiscal incidence exercises are carried out using household surveys, as is done here.[20] As with any fiscal incidence study, this analysis starts by defining the basic income concepts. Three are used here: market, postfiscal, and final income.[21] *Market income*[22] is total current income before direct taxes, equal to the sum of gross (pretax) wages and salaries in the formal and informal sectors (also known as earned income), income from capital (dividends, interest, profits, rents, and so on) in the formal and informal sectors (excluding capital gains and gifts), consumption of own production,[23] imputed rent for owner-occupied housing, private transfers (remittances and other private transfers such as alimony), and retirement pension benefits from the contributory social insurance system.[24] *Postfiscal income* is defined as market income minus direct personal income taxes on all income sources (included in market income) that are subject to taxation and all contributions to social security (except for the portion going toward pensions), plus direct government transfers (mainly cash transfers but can include food transfers and free textbooks and school uniforms) and indirect subsidies, minus indirect taxes (for example, value-added tax, sales tax, and the like). *Final income* is defined as postfiscal income plus government transfers in the form of free or subsidized services in education and health valued at average cost of provision minus copayments or user fees, when they exist.[25]

---

[19] This section is based on Lustig and Higgins 2013.

[20] The surveys used in the country studies are the following: Armenia: Integrated Living Conditions Survey, 2011 (I); Bolivia: Encuesta de Hogares, 2009 (I); Brazil: Pesquisa de Orçamentos Familiares, 2009 (I); Chile: Encuesta de Caracterización Social (CASEN), 2009 (I); Colombia: Encuesta de Calidad de Vida, 2010 (I); El Salvador: Encuesta De Hogares De Propositos Multiples, 2011 (I); Ethiopia: Ethiopia Household Consumption Expenditure Survey and Ethiopia Welfare Monitoring survey, 2011 (C); Guatemala: Encuesta Nacional de Ingresos y Gastos Familiares, 2010 (I); Indonesia: Survei Sosial-Ekonomi Nasional, 2012 (C); Mexico: Encuesta Nacional de Ingreso y Gasto de los Hogares, 2010 (I); Peru: Encuesta Nacional de Hogares, 2009 (I); South Africa: Income and Expenditure Survey and National Income Dynamics Study, 2010–2011 (I); Uruguay: Encuesta Continua de Hogares, 2009 (I). The letters "I" and "C" indicate that the study used income or consumption data, respectively. For more details, see the country studies cited in the introduction. The references to each study are provided in note 4.

[21] The surveys for Ethiopia and Indonesia do not have income data, so the incidence analysis is based on the assumption that consumption equals disposable income.

[22] Market income is sometimes called primary or original income.

[23] Except for Bolivia and South Africa, whose data on auto-consumption (also called own-production or self-consumption) were not considered reliable.

[24] One area in which there is no agreement is how pensions from a pay-as-you-go contributory system should be treated. Arguments exist in favor of either treating contributory pensions as part of market income because they are deferred income or as a government transfer, especially in systems with a large subsidized component. Since this is an unresolved issue, the country studies were done for a benchmark case in which contributory pensions are part of market income and a sensitivity analysis in which pensions are classified under government transfers. These are available upon request.

[25] To avoid exaggerating the effect of government services on inequality, the totals for education and health spending in the studies reported here were scaled down so that their proportion to disposable income in the national accounts is the same as that observed using data from the household surveys.

Once these income concepts are generated, households are ranked by per capita market income. Next, inequality and poverty indicators are calculated for the three income concepts. Given that the valuation of government services at cost of provision is not equivalent to "cash," poverty levels are not calculated for final income. If not free, it is unlikely that the poor would be willing to pay for these services at their cost. With the inequality indicators in hand, the contribution of government spending on education and health to the fiscal-policy-induced change in inequality can be calculated. Having allocated the education and health benefits to individuals, indicators of fiscal progressivity, such as cumulative shares, concentration coefficients, and Kakwani indices for spending on education (total and by level) and health (total and, when possible, by contributory and noncontributory systems, for example) can be calculated. The method applied here to value the benefit to an individual of going to a public school or receiving health care in a public facility is equivalent to using a simple binary indicator of whether the individual uses the government service.[26]

An important limitation in monetizing benefits at the average cost of provision is that all who use a service or participate in a program implicitly receive the same benefits, which is obviously not correct. This approach is likely to introduce "a systematic bias in the results. Viewed from the supply side, the poor probably attend lower-quality schools and receive lower-quality healthcare" (Sahn and Younger 2000, 331). In fact, the quality of education and health care may be lower even when governments spend more in per capita terms, such as in poor remote areas that are more costly to reach.

The fiscal incidence analysis used here is point in time and does not incorporate behavioral or general equilibrium effects. That is, no claim is made that the original or market income equals the true counterfactual income in the absence of taxes and transfers. It is a first-order approximation. However, the analysis is not a mechanically applied accounting exercise. The incidence of taxes is the economic rather than statutory incidence. It is assumed that individual income taxes and contributions by both employees and employers, for instance, are borne by labor in the formal sector, and consumption taxes are fully shifted forward to consumers. For consumption taxes, the analyses take into account the lower incidence associated with own-consumption, rural markets, and informality.

REDISTRIBUTIVE EFFECT AND THE MARGINAL CONTRIBUTION OF EDUCATION AND HEALTH SPENDING

To measure the impact of fiscal interventions on inequality—that is, the redistributive effect—this analysis compares the Gini coefficient for final income with the Gini for market income. Figure 16.4 shows that the reduction in inequality ranges from 17.5 Gini points in South Africa to 2.3 Gini points in Ethiopia, and that its absolute value rises with GNI per capita.[27]

According to Lindert (2004, 15),

> History reveals a "Robin Hood paradox," in which redistribution from rich to poor is least present when and where it seems most needed. Poverty policy within any one polity or jurisdiction is supposed to aid the poor more, . . . the greater the income inequality. Yet over time and space, the pattern is usually the opposite.

While there are exceptions to this general tendency, the underlying tendency itself is unmistakable, both across the globe and across the past three centuries.

---

[26]This is, of course, only true within a level of education. A concentration coefficient for total nontertiary education, for example, calculated as the sum of the different spending amounts by level is not equivalent to the binary indicator method.
[27]It should be noted, however, that for Ethiopia and Indonesia—due to the characteristics of the household surveys—the Gini coefficient is measured using consumption per capita while income per capita is used for the rest. A well-known fact is that consumption is less unequally distributed than income.

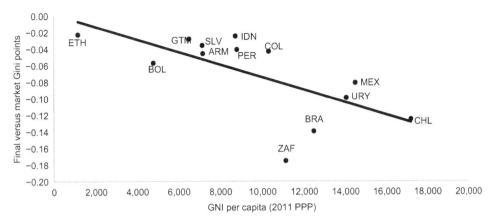

Figure 16.4   Redistributive Effect and GNI Per Capita, circa 2010

Source: Author's calculations based on Armenia: Younger and Khachatryan (2014); Bolivia: Paz Arauco and others (2014); Brazil: Higgins and Pereira (2014); Chile: Ruiz-Tagle and Contreras (2014); Colombia: Melendez (2014); El Salvador: Beneke, Lustig, and Oliva (2014); Ethiopia: Hill, Tsehaye, and Woldehanna (2014); Guatemala: Cabrera, Lustig, and Morán (2014); Indonesia: Afkar, Jellema, and Wai-Poi (forthcoming); Mexico: Scott (2014); Peru: Jaramillo (2014); South Africa: Inchauste and others (2014); and Uruguay: Bucheli and others (2014).
Note: GNI = gross national income; PPP = purchasing power parity. The Gini coefficients correspond to the year of the household survey: Armenia, 2011; Bolivia, 2009; Brazil, 2009; Chile, 2009; Colombia, 2010; El Salvador, 2011; Ethiopia, 2011; Guatemala, 2010; Indonesia, 2012; Mexico, 2010; Peru, 2009; South Africa, 2010–11; Uruguay, 2009. The Gini coefficients for Ethiopia and Indonesia are calculated using expenditure per capita; for the rest of the countries, they are calculated using income per capita. The data labels in the figure use International Organization for Standardization (ISO) abbreviations.

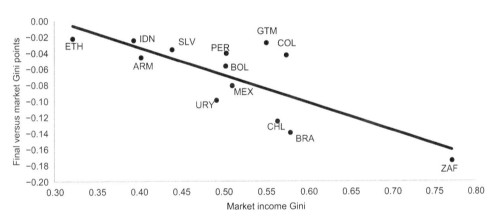

Figure 16.5   Redistribution and Market-Income Gini, circa 2010

Source: Author's calculations based on Younger and Khachatryan (2014); Paz Arauco and others (2014); Higgins and Pereira (2014); Ruiz-Tagle and Contreras (2014); Melendez (2014); Beneke, Lustig, and Oliva (2014); Hill, Tsehaye, and Woldehanna (2014); Cabrera, Lustig, and Morán (2014); Afkar, Jellema, and Wai-Poi (forthcoming); Scott (2014); Jaramillo (2014); Inchauste and others (2014); and Bucheli and others (2014).
Note: The Gini coefficients for Ethiopia and Indonesia are calculated using expenditure per capita; for the rest of the countries, they are calculated using income per capita. The data labels in the figure use International Organization for Standardization (ISO) abbreviations.

As discussed in Lustig (forthcoming), and in contrast to Lindert's (2004) findings, no "Robin Hood" paradox is apparent in this group of 13 developing countries. On the contrary, redistribution from rich to poor is greater in countries where inequality before fiscal interventions is higher (Figure 16.5), a result that seems consistent with the prediction of the Meltzer and Richard 1981 median-voter hypothesis. The redistributive effect ranges from 17.5 Gini points in South

Africa—the country with the highest market-income inequality—to 2.3 Gini points in Ethiopia—the country with the lowest market-income inequality. This result is robust even if South Africa is removed (an outlier in size of redistribution measured in percentage points). The result is also robust if the redistributive effect is measured as a percentage change instead of Gini points. Preliminary estimates suggest that the result that more unequal countries tend to redistribute more does not occur because more unequal countries tend to be richer and therefore have higher capacity to raise revenues and afford higher levels of spending. Regressing the change in the Gini (in percentage points) on GNI per capita and the market-income Gini shows that the coefficient for market-income Gini is 0.257,[28] that is, it is positive and significant even if GNI per capita is controlled for.[29] The coefficient for GNI per capita is significant but small: 0.000004.[30] The regression-based results, however, are not robust to removing South Africa. The coefficient for the market-income Gini is still positive, but it is no longer significant (Lustig forthcoming).

What is the contribution of public spending on education and health to the decline in final income inequality? Several ways can be used to calculate the contribution of a particular fiscal intervention to the change in inequality (or poverty): the marginal contribution, the sequential contribution, and the total contribution. The marginal contribution of spending on education and health to the reduction in final income inequality is calculated by comparing the inequality indicators with this type of spending included and without it, that is, as the difference between the final income and the postfiscal Gini coefficients.[31] This method is equivalent to asking the question, what if the government had not spent at all on education and health?[32]

The results are shown in Table 16.1. The marginal contribution of public spending on education and health as a proportion of the total reduction in inequality (that is, final income versus market income) ranges from as low as 12 percent in Ethiopia to as high as 100 percent in Bolivia and Guatemala.[33] The simple average is 69 percent.

THE PROGRESSIVITY AND PRO-POORNESS OF GOVERNMENT SPENDING ON EDUCATION AND HEALTH

When analyzing the impact of fiscal interventions on living standards, it is useful to distinguish between the net benefits in cash and the benefits received in the form of free government services in education and health. The cash component is measured by postfiscal income, equal to market income plus direct cash transfers, minus direct taxes (mainly personal income taxes), minus indirect taxes (mainly consumption taxes), plus indirect subsidies. The level of postfiscal income will tell whether the government has enabled an individual to be able to purchase private goods and services above what his or her original market income would have allowed. In

---

[28] This regression should be viewed with caution—because the Gini coefficients are measured with error, and the error is likely to be smaller the richer the country, the coefficient may be biased.

[29] The coefficient is significant for $p < 0.05$.

[30] The coefficient is significant for $p < 0.10$.

[31] Note that because of path dependency, adding up the marginal contributions of each intervention will not equal the total change in inequality. Clearly, adding up the sequential contributions will not equal the total change in inequality either. An approach that has been suggested to calculate the contribution of each intervention in a way that the contributions add up to the total change in inequality is to use the Shapley value. The studies analyzed here do not do that.

[32] In this particular instance, the marginal and sequential contributions are equivalent. The *marginal contribution* should not be confused with the *marginal incidence*, the latter being the incidence of a small change in spending. The marginal contribution is *not* a derivative.

[33] When the marginal contribution of education and health spending equals 100 percent it means that the other fiscal interventions combined had no effect on inequality.

TABLE 16.1

Contribution of Spending on Education and Health to the Overall Redistributive Effect, circa 2010

	Armenia (2011)	Bolivia (2009)	Brazil (2009)	Chile (2009)	Colombia (2010)	El Salvador (2011)	Ethiopia (2011)	Guatemala (2010)	Indonesia (2012)	Mexico (2010)	Peru (2009)	South Africa (2010)	Uruguay (2009)
Gini of Market Income	0.4030	0.5030	0.5788	0.5637	0.5742	0.4396	0.3217	0.5509	0.3942	0.5107	0.5039	0.7712	0.4920
Gini of Postfiscal	0.3744	0.5028	0.5455	0.5251	0.5673	0.4294	0.3019	0.5508	0.3911	0.4809	0.4892	0.6946	0.4590
Gini of Final Income	0.3569	0.4460	0.4390	0.4381	0.5309	0.4036	0.2991	0.5227	0.3694	0.4294	0.4630	0.5961	0.3926
Marginal Contribution of Spending on Education and Health													
Difference between Final and Postfiscal	−0.0175	−0.0568	−0.1065	−0.0869	−0.0364	−0.0258	−0.0028	−0.0281	−0.0217	−0.0515	−0.0262	−0.0985	−0.0663
As a Share of Difference between Final and Market (percent)	38	100	76	69	84	72	12	100	88	63	64	56	67

Source: Author's calculations based on Armenia: Younger and Khachatryan (2014); Bolivia: Paz Arauco and others (2014); Brazil: Higgins and Pereira (2014); Chile: Ruiz-Tagle and Contreras (2014); Colombia: Melendez (2014); El Salvador: Beneke, Lustig, and Oliva (2014); Ethiopia: Hill, Tsehaye, and Woldehanna (2014); Guatemala: Cabrera, Lustig, and Morán (2014); Indonesia: Afkar, Jellema, and Wai-Poi (forthcoming); Mexico: Scott (2014); Peru: Jaramillo (2014); South Africa: Inchauste and others (2014); and Uruguay: Bucheli and others (2014).

Note: Year of survey in parentheses. The Gini coefficients for Ethiopia and Indonesia are calculated using expenditure per capita; for the rest of the countries, they are calculated using income per capita. For methodology, see Lustig and Higgins 2013 and text.

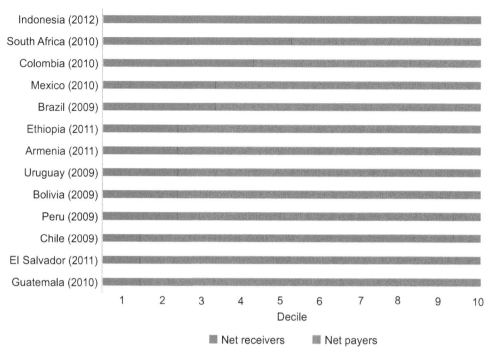

Figure 16.6 Net Payers to and Net Receivers from the Fiscal System by Decile, circa 2010

Source: Author's calculations based on Armenia: Younger and Khachatryan (2014); Bolivia: Paz Arauco and others (2014); Brazil: Higgins and Pereira (2014); Chile: Ruiz-Tagle and Contreras (2014); Colombia: Melendez (2014); El Salvador: Beneke, Lustig, and Oliva (2014); Ethiopia: Hill, Tsehaye, and Woldehanna (2014); Guatemala: Cabrera, Lustig, and Morán (2014); Indonesia: Afkar, Jellema, and Wai-Poi (forthcoming); Mexico: Scott (2014); Peru: Jaramillo (2014); South Africa: Inchauste and others (2014); and Uruguay: Bucheli and others (2014).

Note: Year of the survey in parentheses. The data for Ethiopia and Indonesia are calculated using expenditure per capita; for the rest of the countries, they are calculated using income per capita.

principle, it would be desirable for the poor—especially the extremely poor—to be net receivers of fiscal resources in cash so that poor individuals can buy and consume the minimum amounts of food and other essential goods imbedded in the selected poverty line.

Lustig (forthcoming) shows that in Chile, El Salvador, and Guatemala, on average, net receivers include individuals in the bottom decile only (Figure 16.6). In Armenia, Bolivia, Ethiopia, Peru, and Uruguay, only the bottom 20 percent is composed of net receivers in cash, on average.

Using the purchasing-power-parity (PPP) US$2.50 per day international poverty line, the extreme poor are net payers, on average, in Armenia, El Salvador, Ethiopia, Guatemala, and Peru. In Ethiopia, the poor are net payers even when using the lower international poverty line of PPP US$1.25 per day. Using the PPP US$2.50 per day international poverty line, the incidence of postfiscal income poverty (after direct cash transfers, direct taxes, and net indirect taxes) is higher than market-income poverty in Armenia, Bolivia, Brazil, Colombia and Ethiopia (in Ethiopia, this result occurs with the $1.25 poverty line as well). Governments must raise taxes to function, and those taxes may make the poor poorer even if the taxes and taxes net of cash transfers and subsidies are progressive (that is, equalizing). If the number of poor people made poorer by the fiscal system exceeds the number of poor people who escape poverty because of net transfers, the postfiscal income headcount ratio will be higher than the market-income one. However, even if poverty indicators show a reduction, it is still possible to find that a significant proportion of the postfiscal poor were impoverished by the fiscal system. Higgins and Lustig (2015), for example, find that for some poverty lines, roughly 40 percent of the postfiscal poor were impoverished by fiscal policy in Brazil. Significant fiscal impoverishment occurred even though the fiscal system overall is found to be progressive (that is, equalizing) and poverty-reducing.

To what extent are the poor—especially in the countries in which they are net payers or in which postfiscal income poverty is higher (or both)—benefiting from government spending on education and health? This analysis measures the progressivity of public spending on education and health using concentration coefficients (also called quasi-Ginis).[34]

In keeping with conventions, spending is defined to be regressive whenever the concentration coefficient is higher than the market-income Gini. When this occurs, the benefits from that spending as a share of market income *tend* to rise with market income.[35] Spending is progressive whenever the concentration coefficient is lower than the market-income Gini. This means that the benefits from that spending as a share of market income tend to fall with market income. Within progressive spending, spending is defined as neutral in absolute terms—spending per capita is the same across the income distribution—whenever the concentration coefficient is equal to zero. Spending is defined as pro-poor whenever the concentration coefficient is not only lower than the Gini but its value is also negative. Pro-poor spending implies that *per capita* government spending on the transfer *tends* to fall with market income.[36] Any time spending is pro-poor or neutral in absolute terms, by definition it is progressive. The converse, of course, is not true.[37]

Use of the concentration coefficient to determine the progressivity of transfers, however, has one important drawback. A concentration coefficient may indicate that spending is progressive, for example, even if the concentration curve crosses the Lorenz curve for market income. To check whether there are crossings, concentration curves (or cumulative concentration shares) should be compared. For a benefit that is globally regressive, the concentration curve will lie everywhere *below* the market-income Lorenz curve. For globally progressive transfers, the concentration curve will lie everywhere *above* the market-income Lorenz curve. When the cumulative concentration curve coincides with the diagonal, spending per capita is the same across the income distribution, or neutral in absolute terms. In the case of pro-poor spending, the concentration curve lies everywhere *above* the diagonal.

The above classification is summarized in Figure 16.7. In the results presented below, there are no crossings (at the decile level) so broadly no ambiguity is introduced when relying just on the concentration coefficients. With regard to total spending on education and health, the conclusions are the same whether the analysis relies on the concentration shares (concentration curves) or the concentration coefficients.

A clarification is in order. In the analysis presented here, households are ranked by per capita market income, and no adjustments are made to household size because of differences in composition by age and gender. In some analyses, the pro-poorness of education spending, for example, is determined using children—not all members of the household—as the unit of analysis.

---

[34] A concentration coefficient is calculated analogously to the Gini coefficient. Let p be the cumulative proportion of the total population when individuals are ordered in increasing income values using market income, and let $C(p)$ be the concentration curve, that is, the cumulative proportion of total program benefits (of a particular program or aggregate category) received by the poorest p percent of the population. Then, the concentration coefficient of that program or category is defined as $2\int_0^1 (p - C(p))dp$.

[35] "Tend" because for global regressivity (progressivity) to occur it is not a necessary condition for the share of the benefit to rise (fall) at each and every income level. When the share rises (falls) at every income level, the benefit is regressive (progressive) *everywhere*. Whenever a benefit is *everywhere* regressive (progressive), it will be *globally* regressive (progressive), but the converse is not true.

[36] This case is also sometimes called progressive in absolute terms.

[37] Care must be taken not to infer that any spending that is progressive (regressive) will automatically be equalizing (unequalizing). Once one leaves the world of a single fiscal intervention, it is no longer possible to infer whether the impact of a specific intervention is inequality increasing or inequality reducing by just looking at the level and progressivity (or lack thereof) of the intervention in question (Lambert 2001, 277–78).

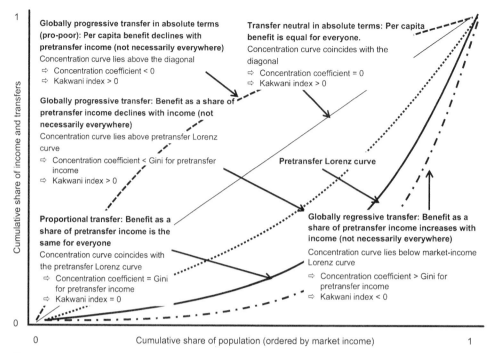

Figure 16.7 Progressivity of Transfers: A Diagrammatic Representation

Because poorer families have, on average, a larger number of children, the observation that concentration curves are pro-poor is a reflection of this fact. It does not mean that poorer families receive more resources per child.

Education

The cumulative concentration shares for education spending as a whole are shown in Table 16.2. As can be observed, education spending is pro-poor or neutral in absolute terms in all countries with the exception of Ethiopia where the richest 20 percent captures 35 percent of education spending.[38] Education spending is the most pro-poor (measured by the cumulative share accruing to the bottom 20 percent) in Brazil, Peru, and Uruguay.

Progressivity by education level is now examined. Table 16.3 shows the concentration coefficients for education disaggregated by level. Total education spending is pro-poor in all countries except Bolivia, Guatemala, and Indonesia, where it is approximately neutral in absolute terms, and Ethiopia, where it is very progressive but only in relative terms. Preschool tends to be pro-poor in all countries for which data are available (and preschool is provided), particularly so in South Africa. Primary school is pro-poor in all countries except for Ethiopia, where it is neutral in absolute terms. For secondary school, the pattern is quite heterogeneous. It is roughly neutral in absolute terms in El Salvador and Mexico; progressive only in relative terms in Ethiopia, Guatemala, Indonesia, and Uruguay; and pro-poor in the rest. Government spending on tertiary

---

[38] Given that Ethiopia is the poorest country and has a high rural population, this is not surprising. Education and health coverage in today's middle-income countries was low among the rural poor when the countries were poorer.

TABLE 16.2

Distribution of Market Income and Cumulative Concentration Shares of Education Spending by Decile, circa 2010 (Percent)

Decile	Armenia (2011) Market Income	Armenia (2011) Education	Bolivia (2009) Market Income	Bolivia (2009) Education	Brazil (2009) Market Income	Brazil (2009) Education	Chile (2009) Market Income	Chile (2009) Education	Colombia (2010) Market Income	Colombia (2010) Education	El Salvador (2011) Market Income	El Salvador (2011) Education	Ethiopia (2011) Market Income	Ethiopia (2011) Education
1	1.2	13.7	0.7	10.0	0.7	15.7	1.0	12.4	0.9	12.4	1.8	12.5	3.0	6.5
2	4.3	25.5	2.8	19.9	2.4	29.1	3.3	24.8	2.8	24.4	5.0	25.3	7.9	15.3
3	9.1	36.8	6.3	30.0	5.0	41.1	6.3	36.9	5.7	35.8	9.2	37.4	13.8	23.5
4	15.2	47.0	11.0	40.6	8.5	52.1	10.2	47.7	9.5	46.3	14.5	48.9	20.8	31.3
5	22.7	58.6	17.1	50.6	13.2	61.4	15.1	58.2	14.2	56.9	21.0	60.3	28.7	38.9
6	31.6	67.7	24.7	60.5	19.4	70.2	21.1	68.1	20.2	66.7	28.8	70.5	37.6	46.8
7	42.3	75.9	34.2	72.0	27.4	78.2	28.8	77.4	27.9	77.2	38.3	79.8	47.7	55.7
8	55.2	84.6	46.1	83.1	38.4	85.9	38.9	86.1	38.3	86.6	50.3	88.2	59.5	65.4
9	71.5	93.5	62.8	92.6	54.7	92.7	53.7	94.2	53.6	94.8	66.7	95.6	73.9	77.9
10	100.0	100.0	100.0	100.0	100.0	100.0	100.0	100.0	100.0	100.0	100.0	100.0	100.0	100.0

Decile	Guatemala (2010) Market Income	Guatemala (2010) Education	Indonesia (2012) Market Income	Indonesia (2012) Education	Mexico (2010) Market Income	Mexico (2010) Education	Peru (2009) Market Income	Peru (2009) Education	South Africa (2010) Market Income	South Africa (2010) Education	Uruguay (2009) Market Income	Uruguay (2009) Education
1	1.3	10.1	3.1	9.4	1.1	11.5	1.2	13.8	0.1	10.6	1.2	14.4
2	3.4	20.5	7.3	19.3	3.5	22.7	3.5	26.7	0.3	22.1	3.6	27.0
3	6.3	30.7	12.1	28.8	7.0	34.0	6.9	39.5	0.7	33.2	7.1	38.0
4	10.2	40.8	17.7	38.3	11.5	45.1	11.4	51.6	1.6	44.6	11.7	48.3
5	15.1	51.1	24.2	48.4	17.1	56.3	17.1	62.9	3.1	54.8	17.5	57.8
6	21.4	59.8	31.9	58.6	24.1	67.0	24.4	72.6	5.8	64.2	24.9	66.7
7	29.5	69.9	41.1	68.4	32.9	76.7	33.6	81.0	10.3	73.1	34.2	75.1
8	40.3	80.7	52.6	78.4	44.3	85.7	45.4	89.3	18.6	81.3	46.3	83.9
9	56.6	90.7	68.2	88.9	60.6	93.9	61.7	96.0	36.3	89.8	63.3	92.9
10	100.0	100.0	100.0	100.0	100.0	100.0	100.0	100.0	100.0	100.0	100.0	100.0

Source: Author's calculations based on Armenia: Younger and Khachatryan (2014); Bolivia: Paz Arauco and others (2014); Brazil: Higgins and Pereira (2014); Chile: Ruiz-Tagle and Contreras (2014); Colombia: Melendez (2014); El Salvador: Beneke, Lustig, and Oliva (2014); Ethiopia: Hill, Tsehaye, and Woldehanna (2014); Guatemala: Cabrera, Lustig, and Morán (2014); Indonesia: Afkar, Jellema, and Wai-Poi (forthcoming); Mexico: Scott (2014); Peru: Jaramillo (2014); South Africa: Inchauste and others (2014); and Uruguay: Bucheli and others (2014).

Note: Year of survey in parentheses. The data for Ethiopia and Indonesia are calculated using expenditure per capita; for the rest of the countries, they are calculated using income per capita. For methodology, see Lustig and Higgins 2013 and country studies sources.

TABLE 16.3

Concentration Coefficients and Budget for Education Spending by Level, circa 2010

	Armenia (2011)		Bolivia (2009)		Brazil (2009)		Chile (2009)		Colombia (2010)		El Salvador (2011)		Ethiopia (2011)	
	CC/Gini	Budget Share (percent)	CC/Gini	Budget Share (percent)	CC/Gini	Budget Share (percent)	CC/Gini	Budget Share (percent)	CC/Gini	Budget Share (percent)	CC/Gini	Budget Share (percent)	CC/Gini	Budget Share (percent)
Education	**-0.1075**	**44.7**	**-0.0184**	**59.4**	**-0.1539**	**36.2**	**-0.1129**	**45.6**	**-0.1033**		**-0.1388**	**31.2**	**0.1831**	**48.7**
Preschool	-0.0508	3.6	-0.2065	1.4	-0.3263	2.0	-0.2246	5.0	-0.2708		-0.2028	2.7	n.a.	n.a.
Primary	-0.1765	10.2	-0.2544	24.5	-0.3113	16.1	-0.1896	22.3	-0.3125	61.5	-0.2208	22.1	-0.0280	21.5
Secondary School	-0.1383	17.4	-0.1153	6.0	-0.2121	2.6	-0.1395	11.9	-0.1704	47.9	0.0189	3.9	0.2774	12.7
Lower Secondary	-0.1806	12.1												
Upper Secondary	-0.0412	5.3												
Tertiary	0.2461	2.2	0.2974	26.2	0.4367	5.6	0.2924	6.4	0.2854	13.5	0.4369	2.4	0.4098	14.6
Market-Income Gini	**0.4030**		**0.5030**		**0.5788**		**0.56**		**0.5742**		**0.4396**		**0.3217**	

	Guatemala (2010)		Indonesia (2012)		Mexico (2010)		Peru (2009)		South Africa (2010)		Uruguay (2009)	
	CC/Gini	Budget Share (percent)	CC/Gini	Budget Share (percent)	CC/Gini	Budget Share (percent)	CC/Gini	Budget Share (percent)	CC/Gini	Budget Share (percent)	CC/Gini	Budget Share (percent)
Education	**-0.0099**	**45.1**	**0.0234**	**68.3**	**-0.0866**	**52.2**	**-0.1689**	**44.1**	**-0.1102**	**48.6**	**-0.1103**	**34.8**
Preschool	-0.1004	5.0	n.a.	n.a.	-0.2426	6.0	-0.2486	3.8	-0.4467	17.2	-0.4296	13.7
Primary	-0.1806	24.0	-0.0772	22.2	-0.2499	18.1	-0.3445	16.8	-0.4305		-0.1223	8.9
Secondary School	0.0256	10.2	0.0028	36.4	0.0850	18.7	-0.2009	14.7	-0.1200	13.0	-0.2623	5.4
Lower Secondary	-0.0148	7.6	-0.0306	27.5	-0.1625	10.9					0.0966	3.5
Upper Secondary	0.1505	2.5	0.1064	8.9	0.0232	7.8					0.3130	7.6
Tertiary	0.5866	6.0	0.4788	9.8	0.3193	9.5	0.2542	8.8	0.4698	11.1		
Market-Income Gini	**0.5509**		**0.3942**		**0.5107**		**0.5039**		**0.7712**		**0.4920**	

Source: Author's calculations based on Armenia: Younger and Khachatryan (2014); Bolivia: Paz Arauco and others (2014); Brazil: Higgins and Pereira (2014); Chile: Ruiz-Tagle and Contreras (2014); Colombia: Melendez (2014); El Salvador: Beneke, Lustig, and Oliva (2014); Ethiopia: Hill, Tsehaye, and Woldehanna (2014); Guatemala: Cabrera, Lustig, and Morán (2014); Indonesia: Afkar, Jellema, and Wai-Poi (forthcoming); Mexico: Scott (2014); Peru: Jaramillo (2014); South Africa: Inchauste and others (2014); and Uruguay: Bucheli and others (2014).

Note: Year of survey in parentheses. CC = concentration coefficient; n.a = not available. Budget as a share of social spending. The concentration coefficients for total spending on education for Chile were calculated as the weighted average of spending by level with their respective budget shares as weights. The Gini coefficient for Ethiopia and Indonesia are calculated using expenditure per capita; for the rest of the countries, they are calculated using income per capita. For methodology, see Lustig and Higgins 2013 and country studies.

education is regressive in Ethiopia, Guatemala, and Indonesia; distribution neutral in El Salvador and Uruguay (roughly); and progressive to various degrees in the rest, but never pro-poor. Compared with their respective levels of market-income inequality, spending on tertiary education is most progressive in South Africa, followed by Colombia and Chile.

What narratives can be extrapolated from the distributional patterns of education spending just described? As a low-income country with a large rural population (more than 80 percent of the total), it is not surprising that education spending in Ethiopia is not "pro-poor." Of the 13 countries, Ethiopia is likely to have the biggest challenges in coverage of education at all levels, including the most basic ones. The Ethiopian government spends a higher share of social spending on tertiary education than do other countries. Public spending on tertiary education, in general, is aimed more toward growth than toward redistributive purposes. A critical mass of tertiary-educated citizens can also be important for strengthening local democratic institutions and for the ability to deliver public services in education and health to the population at large.

In the large middle-income countries of Brazil and South Africa and also in Uruguay, a pattern emerges. Spending on preschool and primary education is highly pro-poor (large negative concentration coefficients) whereas spending on tertiary education tends to be more "pro-rich." One possible explanation is that the middle classes and the rich opt out of public schooling at lower levels because of their poor quality and benefit later from the free high-quality tertiary education that the publicly educated children cannot access because they lack the preparation and skills.

Health

Table 16.4 shows the cumulative concentration shares for government health spending. It shows that health spending benefits the poorest 20 percent in Chile, Colombia, and Uruguay more, while it benefits the richest 20 percent in El Salvador, Ethiopia, Guatemala, Indonesia, and Peru relatively more. Using the concentration coefficients, health spending is pro-poor in Brazil, Chile, Colombia, South Africa, and Uruguay; roughly neutral in absolute terms in Armenia, Bolivia, and Mexico; and progressive in only relative terms in the rest (Table 16.5). Compared with their market-income inequality, the lowest progressivity is found in El Salvador, Ethiopia, Indonesia, and Peru (see the Kakwani coefficients). For Ethiopia once again, the pattern may be due to the large share of rural population, which makes providing access to health services more challenging.

Table 16.6 summarizes the results regarding the pro-poorness of government spending on education (total and by level) and health. Spending on education is more pro-poor in Armenia, Brazil, Chile, Colombia, Mexico, Peru, and Uruguay because a larger share of the education budget is allocated to education levels (especially primary and, in middle-income countries, secondary) that are progressive in absolute terms: that is, pro-poor. For Ethiopia, the results should not be read as a lack of commitment on the part of the government to equalizing opportunities and reducing poverty and social exclusion. With a Gini coefficient of about 0.3, Ethiopia is a very equal country to begin with. Because it is a low-income country, almost the entire population lives under the middle-income international poverty line of US$4 a day and 80 percent of the population lives in rural areas (Hill, Tsehaye, and Woldehanna 2014). When today's middle-income countries were poorer, as indicated above, their spending on education and health was much less progressive and often not pro-poor. In fact, as discussed, judged by the share of total income devoted to social spending, Ethiopia appears quite committed to social progress: its level of spending is much higher than today's rich countries' levels of spending were when their income per capita levels were as low as Ethiopia's is today.

TABLE 16.4

Distribution of Market Income and Cumulative Concentration Shares of Health Spending by Decile, circa 2010 (Percent)

Decile	Armenia (2011) Market Income	Health	Bolivia (2009) Market Income	Health	Brazil (2009) Market Income	Health	Chile (2009) Market Income	Health	Colombia (2010) Market Income	Health	El Salvador (2011) Market Income	Health	Ethiopia (2011) Market Income	Health
1	1.2	8.2	0.7	9.6	0.7	10.5	1.0	23.9	0.9	15.7	1.8	7.2	3.0	8.9
2	4.3	19.8	2.8	19.8	2.4	21.8	3.3	43.7	2.8	30.9	5.0	15.0	7.9	17.8
3	9.1	30.5	6.3	33.6	5.0	33.4	6.3	59.7	5.7	44.4	9.2	23.3	13.8	26.4
4	15.2	39.4	11.0	43.6	8.5	45.6	10.2	73.7	9.5	57.0	14.5	32.3	20.8	35.8
5	22.7	48.5	17.1	53.8	13.2	57.4	15.1	86.3	14.2	68.0	21.0	41.7	28.7	44.5
6	31.6	58.3	24.7	64.6	19.4	69.0	21.1	95.0	20.2	78.3	28.8	51.3	37.6	54.7
7	42.3	70.8	34.2	74.3	27.4	80.8	28.8	100.0	27.9	86.4	38.3	61.9	47.7	64.3
8	55.2	79.8	46.1	82.9	38.4	90.3	38.9	102.2	38.3	92.5	50.3	73.3	59.5	74.4
9	71.5	90.5	62.8	91.5	54.7	97.2	53.7	102.1	53.6	97.1	66.7	86.0	73.9	85.6
10	100.0	100.0	100.0	100.0	100.0	100.0	100.0	100.0	100.0	100.0	100.0	100.0	100.0	100.0

Decile	Guatemala (2010) Market Income	Health	Indonesia (2012) Market Income	Health	Mexico (2010) Market Income	Health	Peru (2009) Market Income	Health	South Africa (2010) Market Income	Health	Uruguay (2009) Market Income	Health
1	1.3	5.6	3.1	7.3	1.1	9.1	1.2	5.7	0.1	10.2	1.2	12.4
2	3.4	12.0	7.3	15.5	3.5	18.4	3.5	12.0	0.3	20.6	3.6	24.4
3	6.3	18.8	12.1	23.9	7.0	27.8	6.9	18.9	0.7	31.2	7.1	36.1
4	10.2	27.3	17.7	33.3	11.5	37.5	11.4	27.1	1.6	42.0	11.7	47.2
5	15.1	36.6	24.2	42.8	17.1	47.3	17.1	36.5	3.1	53.1	17.5	57.8
6	21.4	47.4	31.9	52.5	24.1	57.5	24.4	46.6	5.8	64.2	24.9	67.6
7	29.5	58.4	41.1	62.8	32.9	67.8	33.6	58.2	10.3	75.3	34.2	76.8
8	40.3	71.3	52.6	73.0	44.3	78.1	45.4	70.6	18.6	85.9	46.3	85.2
9	56.6	85.2	68.2	85.2	60.6	89.0	61.7	85.1	36.3	95.0	63.3	93.0
10	100.0	100.0	100.0	100.0	100.0	100.0	100.0	100.0	100.0	100.0	100.0	100.0

Source: Author's calculations based on Armenia: Younger and Khachatryan (2014); Bolivia: Paz Arauco and others (2014); Brazil: Higgins and Pereira (2014); Chile: Ruiz-Tagle and Contreras (2014); Colombia: Melendez (2014); El Salvador: Beneke, Lustig, and Oliva (2014); Ethiopia: Hill, Tsehaye, and Woldehanna (2014); Guatemala: Cabrera, Lustig, and Morán (2014); Indonesia: Afkar, Jellema, and Wai-Poi (forthcoming); Mexico: Scott (2014); Peru: Jaramillo (2014); South Africa: Inchauste and others (2014); and Uruguay: Bucheli and others (2014).

Note: Year of survey in parentheses. Budget as a share of social spending as defined here. The data for Ethiopia and Indonesia are calculated using expenditure per capita; for the rest of the countries, they are calculated using income per capita. The concentration shares for Peru do not include spending on contributory health programs, while the concentration coefficient in Table 16.5 does. For methodology, see Lustig and Higgins 2013 and country studies sources.

TABLE 16.5

Concentration Coefficients and Budget for Health Spending by Level, circa 2010

	Armenia (2011)		Bolivia (2009)		Brazil (2009)		Chile (2009)		Colombia (2010)		El Salvador (2011)		Ethiopia (2011)	
	CC/Gini	Budget Share (percent)	CC/Gini	Budget Share (percent)	CC/Gini	Budget Share (percent)	CC/Gini	Budget Share (percent)	CC/Gini	Budget Share (percent)	CC/Gini	Budget Share (percent)	CC/Gini	Budget Share (percent)
Health	0.0075	21.3	−0.0447	25.9	−0.1188	35.5	−0.4800	40.1	−0.2433	28.4	0.1178	44.0	0.0773	20.4
Market-Income Gini	0.4030		0.5030		0.5788		0.56		0.5742		0.4396		0.3217	
Kakwani	0.3955		0.5477		0.6976		1.0437		0.8175		0.3218		0.2444	

	Guatemala (2010)		Indonesia (2012)		Mexico (2010)		Peru (2009)		South Africa (2010)		Uruguay (2009)	
	CC/Gini	Budget Share (percent)	CC/Gini	Budget Share (percent)	CC/Gini	Budget Share (percent)	CC/Gini	Budget Share (percent)	CC/Gini	Budget Share (percent)	CC/Gini	Budget Share (percent)
Health	0.1775	41.2	0.1111	23.1	0.0356	35.1	0.1798	48.3	−0.1026	28.6	−0.1020	44.0
Market-Income Gini	0.5509		0.3942		0.5107		0.5039		0.7712		0.4920	
Kakwani	0.3733		0.2831		0.4751		0.3241		0.8738		0.5940	

Source: Author's calculations based on Armenia: Younger and Khachatryan (2014); Bolivia: Paz Arauco and others (2014); Brazil: Higgins and Pereira (2014); Chile: Ruiz-Tagle and Contreras (2014); Colombia: Melendez (2014); El Salvador: Beneke, Lustig, and Oliva (2014); Ethiopia: Hill, Tsehaye, and Woldehanna (2014); Guatemala: Cabrera, Lustig, and Morán (2014); Indonesia: Afkar, Jellema, and Wai-Poi (forthcoming); Mexico: Scott (2014); Peru: Jaramillo (2014); South Africa: Inchauste and others (2014); and Uruguay: Bucheli and others (2014).

Note: Year of survey in parentheses. CC = concentration coefficient. Budget as a share of social spending as defined here. The Gini coefficient for Ethiopia and Indonesia are calculated using expenditure per capita; for the rest of the countries, they are calculated using income per capita. For methodology, see Lustig and Higgins 2013 and country studies sources.

TABLE 16.6

Progressivity and Pro-poorness of Education and Health Spending: Summary of Results

	Education Total			Preschool			Primary			Secondary			Tertiary				Health		
	Pro-poor CC is negative	Same per capita for all; CC = 0	Progressive CC positive but lower than market income Gini	Pro-poor CC is negative	Same per capita for all; CC = 0	Progressive CC positive but lower than market income Gini	Pro-poor CC is negative	Same per capita for all; CC = 0	Progressive CC positive but lower than market income Gini	Pro-poor CC is negative	Same per capita for all; CC = 0	Progressive CC positive but lower than market income Gini	Pro-poor CC is negative	Same per capita for all; CC = 0	Progressive CC positive but lower than market income Gini	Regressive CC positive AND higher than market income Gini	Pro-poor CC is negative	Same per capita for all; CC = 0	Progressive CC positive but lower than market income Gini
Armenia (2011)	+				+		+			+					+			+	
Bolivia (2009)		+		+			+			+					+			+	
Brazil (2009)	+			+			+			+					+		+		
Chile (2009)	+			+			+			+					+		+		
Colombia (2010)	+			+			+			+					+		+		
El Salvador (2011)	+			+			+				+				+*				+
Ethiopia (2011)			+	n.a.				+				+				+			+
Guatemala (2010)		+		+			+				+					+			+
Indonesia (2012)		+		n.a.			+				+					+			+
Mexico (2010)	+			+			+			+					+			+	
Peru (2009)	+			+			+			+					+				+
South Africa (2010)	+			+			+			+					+		+		
Uruguay (2009)	+			+			+			+					+*		+		

Sources: Tables 16.3 and 16.5.

Note: Year of survey in parenthesis. CC = concentration coefficient; n.a. = not applicable. If the concentration coefficient is greater than or equal to −0.05 but not higher than 0.05, it was considered equal to 0.

*CC is almost equal to market-income Gini coefficient.

CONCLUSION

This chapter analyzes the level, redistributive impact, and pro-poorness of government spending on education and health in 13 developing countries that are part of the Commitment to Equity project: Armenia, Bolivia, Brazil, Chile, Colombia, El Salvador, Ethiopia, Guatemala, Indonesia, Mexico, Peru, South Africa, and Uruguay. In particular, it addresses the following four questions: Does government spending on education and health increase with per capita income and income inequality? Do more unequal societies redistribute more? What is the contribution of spending on education and health to the overall reduction in inequality? How pro-poor is spending on education and health?

Social spending as a share of GDP ranges from 17.6 percent in South Africa to 4.9 percent in Indonesia. Government spending on education ranges from 2.6 percent of GDP in Guatemala to 8.3 percent in Bolivia; and spending on health ranges from 0.9 percent of GDP in Indonesia to 5.2 percent in Brazil.[39] Spending levels are generally higher than what today's rich countries spent when they were as poor as some of the lowest spenders in this sample are today. Clearly, forces must have been at play that led the developing world to devote more resources to social spending. One key difference is universal suffrage. When today's rich countries were as poor as today's developing countries, women and other groups were not universally allowed to vote.

Social spending as a share of total income increases with GNI per capita. Health spending increases with GNI per capita but education spending does not, a result mainly driven by Bolivia. Spending on primary education is roughly the same at different GNI per capita levels. Spending on secondary education, however, rises with income per capita and spending on tertiary education declines, a result that requires further research. Social spending and spending on education and health increase with market-income (pretaxes and transfers) inequality.

Measuring the redistributive impact and pro-poorness of education and health spending requires attaching a value to the benefit to an individual of using free public education and health services. Here, education and health services are valued at average cost of provision. Individuals were allocated the average cost of provision based on usage of the service. A well-known limitation of such an approach is that it ignores the fact that consumers may attach a value to services that is quite different from what the services cost. Given the limitations of available data, however, the cost-of-provision method is the best for now. To calculate the redistributive effect and pro-poorness of education and health spending, household income per capita is calculated after the values for education and health transfers are added to income net of direct taxes, indirect taxes, direct transfers, and indirect subsidies. The new Gini coefficient was compared with the Gini for market income. To assess the pro-poorness of education and health spending, the analysis uses concentration coefficients and cumulative shares.

Education and health spending lowers inequality by a significant amount, and its marginal contribution to the overall decline in inequality is, on average, 69 percent. There is no "Robin Hood" paradox in the countries covered here. On the contrary, redistribution from rich to poor is more present in countries in which inequality before fiscal interventions is higher.

Total spending on education is pro-poor in all countries except Bolivia, Guatemala, and Indonesia, where it is approximately neutral in absolute terms, and Ethiopia, where it is progressive only in relative terms. Preschool tends to be pro-poor in all countries for which there are data, particularly so in South Africa. Primary school is pro-poor in all countries except Ethiopia in which it is neutral in absolute terms. For secondary school, the pattern is quite heterogeneous. It is roughly neutral in absolute terms in El Salvador and Mexico; progressive only in relative terms in Ethiopia, Guatemala, Indonesia, and Uruguay; and pro-poor in the rest. Government

---

[39] Data are for about 2010.

spending on tertiary education is regressive in Ethiopia, Guatemala, and Indonesia; distribution neutral in El Salvador and (almost so in) Uruguay; and progressive to various degrees in the rest. Compared with their respective levels of market-income inequality, spending on tertiary education is most progressive in South Africa, followed by Colombia and Chile. Health spending is pro-poor in Brazil, Chile, Colombia, South Africa, and Uruguay; roughly neutral in absolute terms in Armenia, Bolivia, and Mexico; and progressive in only relative terms in El Salvador, Ethiopia, Guatemala, Indonesia, and Peru. Compared with their market-income inequality, the lowest progressivity is found in Ethiopia, Indonesia, El Salvador, and Peru.

Although a comparison of the evolution of the progressivity of education and health spending over time is beyond the scope of this chapter, it is interesting to note that spending on education and health appears to have become more pro-poor. Based on the data reported by Tanzi (2008), the share of education and health spending accruing to the bottom 20 percent for most Latin American countries was lower around 2000 than around 2010.[40] Although the studies used by Tanzi are not strictly comparable with those reported here, this result seems to indicate that the pro-poorness of government spending on education and health in Latin America has increased during the past decade. Another example of this trend can be found in South Africa. Comparing the results in this chapter with those by Sahn and Younger (2000),[41] spending on secondary education and health became pro-poor whereas it was not before.[42]

In spite of this progress, given that in Bolivia, El Salvador, Ethiopia, Guatemala, and Peru the poor are, on average, net payers to the fiscal system or postfiscal income poverty is higher than market-income poverty, the fact that spending on education, health, or both is not pro-poor is of great concern. Less-than-universal access to and inability to use free (or quasi-free) government services in education and health for the poor, especially the extremely poor, however, should be of concern even if spending is pro-poor by the measures conventionally used and even if the poor are net receivers from the fiscal system in cash terms (total taxes paid minus direct transfers and subsidies). Governments should emphasize universalizing access to free services for those who cannot afford private schools and private medical services. A subject for further research is an examination of access to and usage of government services in education and health by income group, and an assessment of to what extent coverage for the poor is not universal.

Guaranteeing access to and facilitating usage of public education and health services for the poor, however, is not enough. As long as the quality of schooling and health care provided by the government is low, distortive patterns (for example, mostly the middle classes and the rich benefiting from free tertiary education),[43] such as those observed in Brazil, South Africa, and Uruguay, will be a major obstacle to the equalization of opportunities. However, with the existing information, one cannot disentangle to what extent the progressivity or pro-poorness of education and health spending is a result of differences in family composition (that is, the poor have more children and, therefore, poor households receive higher benefits in the form of basic education transfers) or frequency of illness (that is, the poor have worse health than the nonpoor) from the "opting-out" of the middle classes and the rich. This is another topic for further research.

---

[40] Compare Tables 16.2 and 16.4 with Tables 4 and 5 in Tanzi 2008.

[41] Compare results in Tables 16.3 and 16.5 with Table 1 in Sahn and Younger 2000 (335).

[42] In Sahn and Younger 2000, the concentration curves crossed the 45-degree line. That is, the null hypothesis that per capita income was the same for all could not be rejected.

[43] Among the reasons for this outcome is the fact that children of poor households tend to drop out of high school more, and the rich children who receive enough quality (often private) education are better equipped to pass the entrance examination.

REFERENCES

Afkar, Rythia, Jon Jellema, and Matthew Wai-Poi. Forthcoming, "Fiscal Policy, Redistribution, and Inequality in Indonesia." In Gabriela Inchauste and Nora Lustig (eds.), *The Distributional Impact of Fiscal Policy: Experience from Developing Countries*.

Barr, Nicholas. 2012. *Economics of the Welfare State*. Oxford, U.K.: Oxford University Press.

Beneke, Margarita, Nora Lustig, and José Andrés Oliva. 2014. *El impacto de los impuestos y el gasto social en la desigualdad y la pobreza en El Salvador*. CEQ Working Paper No. 26, Center for Inter-American Policy and Research and Department of Economics, Tulane University, and Inter-American Dialogue; and CEQ Master Workbook: El Salvador.

Bucheli, Marisa, Nora Lustig, Máximo Rossi, and Florencia Amábile. 2014. "Social Spending, Taxes and Income Redistribution in Uruguay." *Public Finance Review* 42 (3): 413–33.

Cabrera, Maynor, Nora Lustig, and Hilcías Morán. 2014. *Fiscal Policy, Inequality and the Ethnic Divide in Guatemala*. CEQ Working Paper No. 20, Center for Inter-American Policy and Research and Department of Economics, Tulane University, and Inter-American Dialogue; and CEQ Master Workbook: Guatemala, August 27.

Demery, Lionel, Shiyan Chao, Rene Bernier, and Kalpana Mehra. 1995. "The Incidence of Social Spending in Ghana." Poverty and Social Protection Discussion Paper No. 82, World Bank, Washington.

Demery, Lionel, Julia Dayton, and Kalpana Mehra. 1996. "The Incidence of Social Spending in Côte d'Ivoire, 1986–95." Working Paper No. 65701, World Bank, Washington.

Higgins, Sean, and Nora Lustig. 2015. "Can a Poverty-Reducing and Progressive Tax and Transfer System Hurt the Poor?" CEQ Working Paper No. 33, Center for Inter-American Policy and Research and Department of Economics, Tulane University and Inter-American Dialogue.

Higgins, Sean, and Claudiney Pereira. 2014. "The Effects of Brazil's Taxation and Social Spending on the Distribution of Household Income." *Public Finance Review* 42 (3): 346–67.

Hill, Ruth, Eyasu Tsehaye, and Tassew Woldehanna. 2014. CEQ Master Workbook: Ethiopia, September 28, Tulane University and World Bank.

Inchauste, Gabriela, Nora Lustig, Mashekwa Maboshe, Catriona Purfield, and Ingrid Woolard. 2015. "The Distributional Impact of Fiscal Policy in South Africa." World Bank Policy Research Working Paper 7194, World Bank, Washington.

———, and Precious Zikhali. 2014. CEQ Master Workbook: South Africa, August 25, Tulane University and World Bank.

Jaramillo, Miguel. 2014. "The Incidence of Social Spending and Taxes in Peru." *Public Finance Review* 42 (3): 391–412.

Lambert, Peter. 2001. *The Distribution and Redistribution of Income*, third edition. Manchester, U.K.: Manchester University Press.

Leibbrandt, Murray, Ingrid Woolard, Arden Finn, and Jonathan Argent. 2010. "Trends in South African Income Distribution and Poverty since the Fall of Apartheid." OECD Social, Employment and Migration Working Paper No. 101, OECD Publishing, Paris.

Lindert, Peter H. 1994. "The Rise of Social Spending, 1880–1930." *Explorations in Economic History* 31 (1): 1–37.

———. 2004. *Social Spending and Economic Growth since the Eighteenth Century*. Cambridge, U.K.: Cambridge University Press.

Luebker, Malte. 2014. "Income Inequality, Redistribution, and Poverty: Contrasting Rational Choice and Behavioral Perspectives." *Review of Income and Wealth* 60 (1): 133–54.

Lustig, Nora. Forthcoming. "Fiscal Policy, Inequality and the Poor in the Developing World." CEQ Working Paper No. 23, Center for Inter-American Policy and Research and Department of Economics, Tulane University and Inter-American Dialogue.

———, and Sean Higgins. 2013. "Commitment to Equity Assessment (CEQ): Estimating the Incidence of Social Spending, Subsidies and Taxes. Handbook." CEQ Working Paper No. 1, July 2011; revised January 2013, Center for Inter-American Policy and Research and Department of Economics, Tulane University and Inter-American Dialogue.

Lustig, Nora, Carola Pessino, and John Scott, eds. 2014. *The Redistributive Impact of Taxes and Social Spending in Latin America. Special Issue. Public Finance Review* 42 (3).

Maddison, Angus. 2010. *Historical Statistics of the World Economy: 1–2008 AD*. Downloadable spreadsheet http://www.google.com/url?sa=t&rct=j&q=&esrc=s&source=web&cd=4&ved=0CDEQFjAD&rl=http%3A%2F%2Fwww.ggdc.net%2Fmaddison%2FHistorical_Statistics%2Fhorizontal-file_022010.xls&ei=nFJSVav0MaHfsASYioGYBg&usg=AFQjCNFFKKZ1UysTOutlY4NsZF9qwdu2H&sig2=qCggv807s4eQm-wZvPINeQ&bvm=bv.92885102,d.cWc.

Meerman, Jacob. 1979. *Public Expenditure in Malaysia: Who Benefits and Why*. New York: Oxford University Press.

Melendez, Marcela. 2014. CEQ Master Workbook: Colombia, November 21, Center for Inter-American Policy and Research and Department of Economics, Tulane University and Inter-American Dialogue.

Meltzer, A. H., and S. F. Richard. 1981. "A Rational Theory of the Size of Government." *Journal of Political Economy* 89 (5): 914–27.

Paz Arauco, Verónica, George Gray Molina, Wilson Jiménez Pozo, and Ernesto Yáñez Aguilar. 2014. "Explaining Low Redistributive Impact in Bolivia." *Public Finance Review* 42 (3): 326–45.

Ruiz-Tagle, Jaime, and Dante Contreras. 2014. CEQ Master Workbook: Chile, August, Center for Inter-American Policy and Research and Department of Economics, Tulane University and Inter-American Dialogue.

Sahn, David, and Stephen Younger. 2000. "Expenditure Incidence in Africa: Microeconomic Evidence." *Fiscal Studies* 21 (3): 329–47.

Scott, John. 2014. "Redistributive Impact and Efficiency of Mexico's Fiscal System." *Public Finance Review* 42 (3): 368–90.

Selowsky, Marcelo. 1979. *Who Benefits from Government Expenditures?* Washington: Oxford University Press for the World Bank.

Tanzi, Vito. 2008. "The Role of the State and Public Finance in the Next Generation." *OECD Journal on Budgeting* 8 (2): 1–27.

Younger, Stephen, and Artsvi Khachatryan. 2014. CEQ Master Workbook: Armenia, May 31, Tulane University and World Bank.

CHAPTER 17

Income Inequality, Fiscal Decentralization, and Transfer Dependency

CAROLINE-ANTONIA HUMMEL AND MIKE SEIFERLING

INTRODUCTION

Within the context of reigniting postcrisis macroeconomic growth, income inequality has emerged as a topic of significant interest for both academics and policymakers (Bastagli, Coady, and Gupta 2012). Fiscal decentralization has also gained considerable attention in many countries because of its potential ability to raise the efficiency of government (Oates 2005; OECD 2006, 2009a, 2009b). Where state and local governments do gain a significant degree of autonomy in the formation of redistributive policies (Bahl, Martinez-Vazquez, and Wallace 2000), the question arises as to if, and how, this decentralization might interact with income inequality. The purpose of this chapter is to provide some initial empirical evidence regarding this link, mainly (1) whether income inequality is systematically associated with the decentralization of government finances, and (2) whether greater fiscal autonomy, or lower revenue dependency, at the state and local levels could potentially improve a country's income distribution.

The relationship between redistributive fiscal policy and income distribution has a long history in the literature, suggesting that differences in the progressivity of tax and spending policies account for much of the observed variation in inequality of average disposable income within countries (for example, Bastagli, Coady, and Gupta 2012). A smaller collection of interregional literature on fiscal decentralization and income inequality suggests the two should be related, particularly if government redistribution is decentralized and subnational governments are not highly dependent on transfers to finance their expenditures. Taking advantage of the intertemporal variation in posttax income inequality, along with variation in the degree to which state and local governments engage in redistributive policies, allows the way in which they interact to be analyzed empirically.

This chapter tests for these potential links using macro-level data for a globally representative, multisector sample of countries for a 30-year period. In addition to previous studies, this chapter examines decentralization patterns using an aggregate measure of decentralization along with redistributive spending subaggregates to achieve a better fit with theoretical expectations. On the revenue side, the analysis also tests for potential effects from the decentralization of income taxation and the level of subnational transfer dependency. The results are generally consistent with past findings, suggesting that the decentralization of government expenditure can help achieve a more equal distribution of income. However, several conditions need to be fulfilled. First, the government sector needs to be sufficiently large. Second, decentralization should be comprehensive and should include redistributive government spending. Third, decentralization on the expenditure side should be accompanied by adequate decentralization on the *revenue* side, such that subnational governments rely primarily on their own revenue sources instead of relying on intergovernmental transfers.

FISCAL DECENTRALIZATION AND INEQUALITY, A LITERATURE REVIEW

In the large body of literature on income inequality, government redistribution plays a pivotal role in explaining both interregional and cross-country variance (Gustafsson and Johansson 1999; Li, Xie, and Zou 2000; Chu, Davoodi, and Gupta 2000; Galli and van der Hoeven 2001; Dollar and Kraay 2002; Lundberg and Squire 2003). At the same time, the literature on fiscal federalism suggests that fiscal decentralization can affect redistributive efficiency within an economy. The existing empirical literature has generally confirmed the existence of a relationship between these two strands; however, the theoretical connection between fiscal decentralization and income inequality remains somewhat less clear.

The first wave, or "first-generation theory," of fiscal federalism argued that state and local governments should not engage in income redistribution (see Oates 2008). According to this literature, decentralized redistribution creates incentives for "poor" households to migrate into alternative jurisdictions that provide more generous redistribution schemes, while "rich" households could, in turn, move to areas with minimal tax and transfer schemes (Stigler 1957; Musgrave 1959; Oates 1972). This "voting by feet" phenomenon would make redistribution at subcentral levels of government, or in economic unions with full mobility of labor, self-defeating and unsustainable (Tiebout 1956; Prud'homme 1995). In this case, income inequality within each homogeneous income region might decrease because of in-migration of the poor and out-migration of the rich, but national income inequality would be left unaffected. Because local authorities would be severely constrained in their capacity to alter the existing national income distribution, they would likely not engage in extensive redistribution (Oates 1972). According to this strand of literature, a system of decentralized redistribution should lead to lower levels of redistribution than are socially desirable (Tiebout 1956; Prud'homme 1995). In other words, local government attempts at redistribution through decentralization would be both too little and ineffective at altering the national income distribution. Therefore, less redistribution and more inequality should be expected when redistributive policies are decentralized.

The "second generation of fiscal federalism" challenged this claim. McKinnon (1995, 1997) and Qian and Weingast (1997) suggest that jurisdictional competition triggered by comprehensive decentralization, including varying degrees of welfare provision, could be more effective in reducing regional inequality than centrally mandated redistribution. Local governments of poorer regions could take advantage of less generous welfare provisions and lower taxes to attract investment and increase growth (McKinnon 1997). The resulting factor movements could therefore reduce regional income differentials, which would also lower income inequality on a national basis. Transfers from central to subcentral governments are also highlighted in the second generation literature as a potential source of distortions in the spending priorities of recipient governments. Transfer dependency could hinder the adjustment and convergence processes where reliance on own-source revenue would otherwise induce equalization.

Padovano (2007) presents a political economy model in which redistribution is more efficiently carried out by subcentral entities. In this model, regions must finance redistributive policies with own resources in decentralized fiscal systems. In contrast, centralized redistribution allows regions to access revenues from other regions, which produces distortions that impede the relocation of factors of production that would normally lead to long-term income convergence. Because these forces more than offset the initial direction of redistribution, Padovano (2007, 42) concludes that "centralizing income redistribution, rather than being a means to reduce income inequalities of less developed regions, tends to perpetuate the very problems that it is meant to solve." Using the cases of Italy and the United States, his contribution provides suggestive evidence that centralized systems may lead to "more" redistribution, while decentralized systems achieve greater effective incidence and stability of redistributive flows. In sum, the second-generation authors maintain that broad fiscal decentralization, encompassing redistribution, is likely to achieve more income equality when it is financed primarily by own revenues.

Empirical work examining the effects of fiscal decentralization on income inequality has generally shown a conditional negative relationship between income inequality and fiscal decentralization. For example, Sepulveda and Martinez-Vazquez (2011) test the relationship between decentralization and inequality using five-year-averages over the 1971–2000 period for a sample of 56 countries. Measuring fiscal decentralization as the share of subnational expenditure in total government expenditures, they estimate the effect of fiscal decentralization on income inequality conditional on the size of government, with findings suggesting that fiscal decentralization reduces income inequality, conditional on the general government representing at least 20 percent of the economy.

Other related empirical work examines the effect of decentralization on inequality within regions. Tselios and others (2012) investigate this relationship using a panel of 102 European Union regions for the 1995–2000 period. They find that greater fiscal decentralization, proxied by the subnational share in total government expenditure, reduces regional inequality. This effect, however, declines with rising levels of regional per capita income. Lessmann (2012) examines the impact of decentralization on inequality within regions using a panel of 54 developed and developing countries from 1980 to 2009. The general findings are consistent with those of Tselios and others, suggesting that fiscal decentralization, measured either through the degree of "vertical imbalance" (Eyraud and Lusinyan 2013; Aldasoro and Seiferling 2014) or subcentral shares of overall expenditure, revenue, or taxes, tends to decrease regional inequality contingent on regional development. In other words, decentralization increases inequality at low levels of development.

All of the above empirical work constructs decentralization ratios covering either aggregate expenditure or revenue, but not both. Such measures may be too broad to capture the channels through which decentralization affects inequality. If decentralization can help reduce income inequality, for example, does it matter whether subnational governments are given greater responsibility over health care or defense? Does redistributive expenditure decentralization have a separate relationship from the decentralization of total expenditure with income inequality? The remainder of this chapter provides some initial empirical evidence regarding the relationship between decentralization of redistributive expenditure subaggregates, progressive revenues, transfer dependency, and income inequality.

WHAT DO THE DATA TELL US?

Income Inequality

Over the past 40 years, income inequality has undergone significant dynamic and cross-regional changes in several parts of the world. Figure 17.1 shows annual Gini coefficient averages for posttax-and-transfer income by regional country groups for 150 countries.[1] Despite significant changes in average Gini coefficients over time in some regions or country groups, differences in disposable income inequality across regions tend to exceed variation within country groups over time.[2]

---

[1] Income inequality data are based on disposable income where possible, and are otherwise based on consumption or expenditure. Posttax Gini coefficient data are obtained from Bastagli, Coady, and Gupta 2012, covering 150 advanced and developing economies drawing data from five data sources: European Union Statistics on Income and Living Conditions; Luxembourg Income Study; Organisation for Economic Co-operation and Development; Socio-Economic Database for Latin America and the Caribbean; and the World Bank World Development Indicators. Country groups are defined following the classification of the IMF *World Economic Outlook*.

[2] Because of a small number of missing observations for some country-years and the slow-moving nature of income inequality over short periods, missing values for a small group of countries with sufficient data are linearly interpolated to derive meaningful estimates. This approach appears to be justified because the degree of income inequality as measured by the Gini coefficient typically evolves slowly and steadily over time, which is also reflected in the available data. Linear interpolation is a cautious approach because it assumes that Gini coefficients do not fluctuate beyond the range defined by the given data points. The extent of variation in income inequality will thus be understated because of the interpolation.

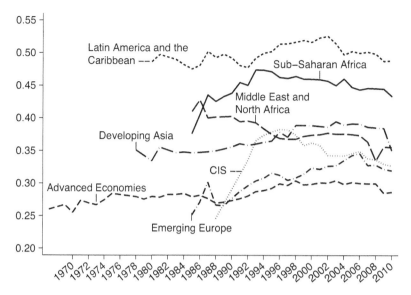

Figure 17.1   Average Gini Coefficients by Country Group, 1970–2010

Sources: Bastagli, Coady, and Gupta (2012); and World Bank, *World Development Indicators*.
Note: CIS = Commonwealth of Independent States.

Although variation within these regional groupings exists, income inequality appears to be somewhat clustered over time.[3] Latin America and the Caribbean countries have, on average, consistently experienced the highest levels of income inequality, with Gini coefficients ranging around the 0.5 mark since the early 1980s. Since the early 2000s, income inequality reductions seem to have been following a progressive trend. Sub-Saharan Africa, the second most unequal region, closely followed the dynamic path of Latin American and the Caribbean in the 1980s, but average inequality began a gradual downward trend beginning in the early 1990s. Moving to the other end of the y-axis, the income distribution in advanced economies has consistently been, on average, the most equal, but has also experienced a slow trend toward more inequality since the 1980s, with Gini coefficients increasing from an average of 0.27 to more than 0.3 in the early 2000s.

Some of these dynamics may be attributable to movement along the Kuznets curve (Kuznets 1955), where rising inequality in many emerging market regions could be viewed as a side effect of the high economic growth experienced during a period of market liberalization. For example, average Gini coefficients rose steadily in developing Asia during periods of high growth. A sharp increase in income inequality also occurred in the countries of the former Soviet Union and emerging Europe following the breakup of the Soviet Union. Average Gini coefficients in the Commonwealth of Independent States have, however, decreased since reaching a peak above 0.38 in 1996, but they continue to rise in emerging Europe.

As noted, much of the observed differences in inequality between regions from Figure 17.1 can be explained by the level and progressivity of a country's redistributive systems (see Bastagli,

---

[3] Standard deviations within regional groupings are as follows: Latin America and the Caribbean = 0.06; sub-Saharan Africa = 0.08; Middle East and North Africa = 0.04; developing Asia = 0.06; Commonwealth of Independent States = 0.05; advanced economies = 0.04; emerging Europe = 0.05.

Coady, and Gupta 2012). For example, while the generous tax and transfer system reduced the average Gini coefficient in 15 European countries by about 15 percentage points in the mid-2000s, government redistribution in six Latin American countries achieved only a 2 percentage point reduction (Goñi, López, and Servén 2008). Given the significant role of the volume and effectiveness of government redistribution in explaining variation in income inequality, it is important to consider who holds fiscal authority over these redistributive functions.

Fiscal Decentralization and Transfer Dependency

For the majority of countries, a reduction in inequality of market income is achieved mainly through the expenditure side of the budget. Not all government expenditures are equally redistributive or decentralized, so it may be helpful to divide these expenditures into functions. On the revenue side, progressive tax structures—in particular, income taxes—should be expected to play a significant role in shaping the income distribution. As noted, the degree to which such redistributive spending is financed by own-source revenues or intergovernmental transfers may also be an important factor in determining any potential effects on income inequality.

Decentralized Redistributive Expenditure

Government spending usually leads to redistribution, but certain government activities have more pronounced or explicit redistributive roles and achieve higher levels of income redistribution. The assignment of these functions to different levels of government is what fiscal federalism theories saw as crucial in triggering factor movements, which would be key in determining income inequality. Decentralization ratios do not imply that subcentral governments have full autonomy over the entirety of their spending share given that a significant amount of state and local expenditure can still be mandated by higher levels of government and can thus be constrained by central government legislation or directives. However, it has been shown that even devolving the administrative responsibility for redistributive programs to subcentral levels of government creates substantial within-country differences in the efficiency and generosity of welfare systems (Padovano 2007).

Non-means-tested and means-tested cash transfers make up the majority of redistribution across countries. However, in-kind transfers have also been shown to significantly decrease inequality, with health and education achieving almost all of the redistributive impact. The Classification of Functions of Government (COFOG) data contained in the IMF *Government Finance Statistics Yearbook* (GFSY) provide the necessary disaggregation of expenditure to isolate these spending categories. COFOG classifies government outlays into 10 divisions.[4] Among these, social protection, health, and education correspond closely to the types of redistributive expenditure.

To measure expenditure decentralization, this analysis constructs an index of decentralization (γ) for each area of functional expenditure j by calculating the share of subcentral, that is, state and local, government expenditure as a percentage of total government expenditure in country i in year t.[5] The

---

[4]The 10 divisions are general public services; defense; public order and safety; economic affairs; environmental protection; housing and community amenities; health; recreation, culture, and religion; education; and social protection.

[5]This is computed using consolidated general government in the denominator for total expenditure. In the case of functional expenditures, the analysis is run on both consolidated and unconsolidated data to maximize the number of observations. Although local and state governments in the numerator cannot be consolidated, transfers between these levels of government are not likely to be extensive and, in most countries, a state government subsector does not exist. Data source is *Government Finance Statistics Yearbook*.

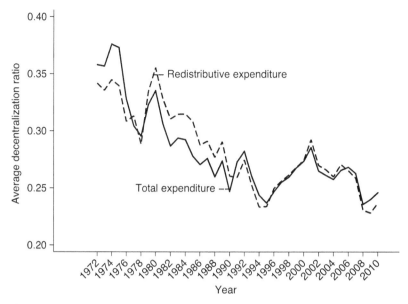

Figure 17.2 Average Decentralization Ratio of Total and Redistributive Expenditure, 1972–2010

Source: IMF, *Government Finance Statistics Yearbook* (1972–2011).
Note: Based on a maximum sample size of 59 countries. Decentralization ratios range from 0 (no decentralization) to 1 (full decentralization).

index can range from 0 (decentralization does not exist or there are no state and local governments) to 1 (all expenditure is executed by state and local governments).

$$\gamma_{ijt} = \frac{exp_{ijt}^{LG} + exp_{ijt}^{SG}}{exp_{ijt}^{CG} + exp_{ijt}^{LG} + exp_{ijt}^{SG}} \tag{17.1}$$

An additional index of decentralization is also calculated for total expenditure and redistributive spending (the sum of the three selected COFOG areas). Cross-country averages for decentralization of total and redistributive expenditure are depicted in Figure 17.2. Although the two measures generally appear to have moved in parallel during the past 40 years, substantial differences of up to 40 percentage points exist within this sample of countries, suggesting that decentralization of total expenditure can be quite different from decentralization of redistributive expenditure.

A more detailed breakdown of decentralization and government expenditure is shown in Figure 17.3, which depicts the extent of, and correlation between, decentralization ratios for eight categories of functional expenditure.[6] Areas such as public services, public order and safety, and social protection tend to be highly centralized (clustered around 0), but a much larger degree of decentralization can be observed in economic affairs, housing, health, education, and recreation and culture. There also appears to be a positive correlation between all areas of functional

---

[6] Defense, which is very highly centralized in all countries, is excluded, as is environmental protection because of the small sample of data for this category.

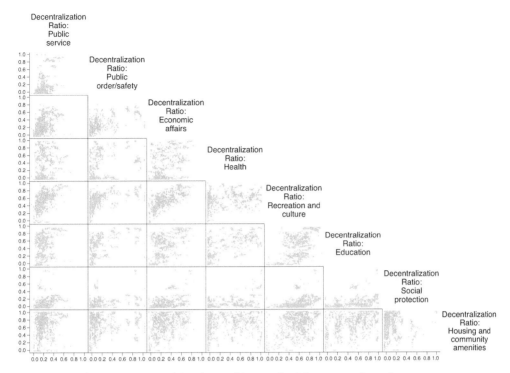

Figure 17.3 The Composition and Correlation of Decentralized Government Expenditure

Source: IMF, *Government Finance Statistics Yearbook* (1972–2012).
Note: Sample of 77 countries. Decentralization ratios range from 0 (highly centralized) to 1 (highly decentralized). Each data point corresponds to one country in one year.

expenditure, however, a significant variance exists around them suggesting a potential loss of information from aggregation. For example, some degree of positive correlation is discernible for the redistributive categories of social protection, education, and health, but the decentralization ratios do not appear to form a single underlying dimension.

Isolating redistributive spending categories, Figure 17.4 shows dynamic trends in average decentralization ratios during the period 1976–2010.[7] The general trend suggests that these functions have become more centralized since the 1970s, with some interesting movement in the late 1990s and early 2000s. Until the late 1980s, the majority of education spending occurred at the subnational level—decentralization ratios frequently exceeded 50 percent. However, the degree of decentralization in education spending exhibits a downward trend, most recently seen since the mid-2000s. The cross-country average decentralization ratio has also fallen for health expenditure, with about 38 percent of spending taking place at the subnational level in 1999 falling to about 26 percent in 2010. Social protection expenditure appears to have a relatively stable and highly centralized history for the entire 1976–2010 period. Finally, the solid line in Figure 17.4 shows

---

[7]The figure is based on 65 advanced, emerging, and developing economies in which a local government level or a local and state government level exist in addition to the central government, thus excluding completely centralized countries for which decentralization ratios are always equal to zero. For most countries, data are not available for all years.

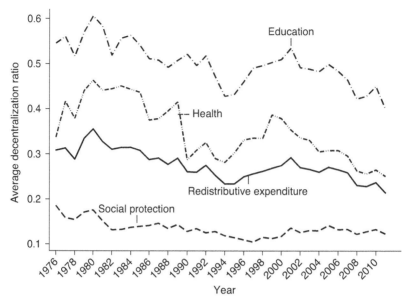

Figure 17.4 Evolution of Average Decentralization Ratio by Redistributive Function

Source: IMF, *Government Finance Statistics Yearbook* (1976–2011).

the aggregate measure of decentralization for the three redistributive spending areas; it has, on average, ranged between 20 and 30 percent since the 1970s.

The higher average degree of decentralization in health and education spending compared with social protection can also be interpreted as a reflection of the fiscal federalism theory: these two areas—while also contributing to an equitable income distribution—contain a mixture of local and national public goods, and should therefore involve subnational government participation.

Transfer Dependency and Decentralized Redistributive Revenue

Transfers to subnational government are frequently designed to perform an equalizing role and reduce differences in fiscal capacity across jurisdictions (OECD 2009b) but can also reduce their policy autonomy. As noted, second-generation fiscal federalism advocates decentralized redistribution in a setting of jurisdictional competition that is financed primarily by own-source revenues as opposed to intergovernmental transfers (Qian and Weingast 1997; Padovano 2007). Following this line of argument, this analysis measures the extent to which state and local governments rely on transfers from other government units to fund their redistributive and other expenditures.

The GFSY database provides information on "grants from other general government units" for all subsectors of general government, allowing an indicator of transfer dependency to be constructed. Transfer dependency is calculated as the share of total subnational expenditure $\left(exp_{it}^{LG} + exp_{it}^{SG}\right)$ that is financed by transfers from other levels of government $(grant\_rev_{it}^{LG} + grant\_rev_{it}^{SG})$:

$$trans\_dep_{it} = \frac{grant\_rev_{it}^{LG} + grant\_rev_{it}^{SG}}{exp_{it}^{LG} + exp_{it}^{SG}}. \tag{17.2}$$

An additional important ingredient on the revenue side is the progressivity of the tax system. For theoretical and empirical reasons, an analysis of decentralized redistribution and its

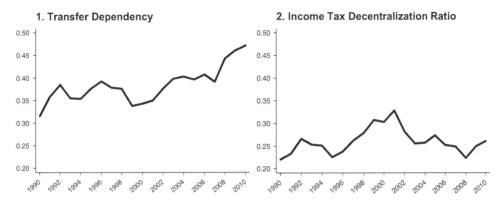

Figure 17.5 Average Transfer Dependency and Average Income Tax Decentralization Ratios, 1990–2011

Source: IMF, *Government Finance Statistics Yearbook* (1990–2011).
Note: Figures are based on a maximum sample size of 62 for transfer dependency and 68 for income tax decentralization. "Transfer dependency" measures the share of state and local government expenditure financed from transfers from other levels of government. "Income tax decentralization ratio" measures the share of state and local income tax revenue relative to total income tax revenue.

impact on inequality should also consider redistributive revenues—in particular, progressive taxation—raised by government. As the main counterpart of transfers, tax revenues are as much a part of the motivation for household and factor mobility in the theoretical models of both generations of fiscal federalism as the transfers and public services that they help to finance.

Income taxes generally achieve the greatest amount of redistribution (Bastagli, Coady, and Gupta 2012). Given their important role, this analysis calculates an index of income tax decentralization using the GFSY revenue category "taxes on income, profits and capital gains" broken down by subsector (central, state, local).[8] Similar to the spending decentralization ratios, this index is calculated as local and state income tax revenue ($inctax_{it}^{LG} + inctax_{it}^{SG}$) relative to total income tax revenue ($inctax_{it}^{CG} + inctax_{it}^{LG} + inctax_{it}^{SG}$):

$$inctax\_dec_{it} = \frac{inctax_{it}^{LG} + inctax_{it}^{SG}}{inctax_{it}^{CG} + inctax_{it}^{LG} + inctax_{it}^{SG}} . \tag{17.3}$$

Figure 17.5 plots average movements in the transfer dependency and income tax decentralization indices. Since the mid- to late 1990s, subnational governments' reliance on intergovernmental transfers has steadily increased, reaching about half of their total expenditure by 2010. Average expenditure decentralization remained relatively constant during the same period, suggesting a relative increase of transfers in the revenue mix of state and local governments. Rising transfer dependency is accompanied by falling shares in income tax revenues since the early 2000s. Income taxes appear to have become less important revenue sources for subnational governments.

---

[8] Under the Government Finance Statistics (GFS) classification, taxes are attributed to the government unit that "(i) exercises the authority to impose the tax…; and (ii) has final discretion to set and vary the rate of the tax" (IMF 2014, 90). Consequently, income tax revenues that are collected by state and local governments under tax-sharing arrangements, where they have no authority to impose the tax or vary its rate, should not be classified as tax revenue under GFS. Such revenues should be recorded as current grants. Thus, the income tax decentralization ratio is a useful measure for subnational engagement in income redistribution through taxation.

TABLE 17.1

Summary Statistics of Gini Coefficients and Independent Variables

Variable	Observations	Mean	Standard Deviation	Minimum	Maximum	Source
Gini Coefficient	602	0.32	0.08	0.20	0.67	Bastagli, Coady, and Gupta (2012); World Bank WDI
Decentralization Ratio, Social Protection	577	0.14	0.13	0	0.96	Computed from IMF GFSY
Decentralization Ratio, Education	577	0.51	0.28	0	0.96	Computed from IMF GFSY
Decentralization Ratio, Health	569	0.34	0.33	0	0.98	Computed from IMF GFSY
Decentralization Ratio, Redistributive Expenditure	569	0.27	0.18	0	0.75	Computed from IMF GFSY
Decentralization Ratio, Total Expenditure	602	0.28	0.14	0	0.62	Computed from IMF GFSY
Transfer Dependency	602	0.39	0.18	0	0.79	Computed from IMF GFSY
Income Tax Decentralization Ratio	602	0.28	0.26	0	1.00	Computed from IMF GFSY
GDP per capita (log)	602	9.44	1.15	6.31	11.46	IMF IFS
Size of General Government (% of GDP)	602	0.41	0.10	0.12	0.64	Computed from IMF GFSY
Openness Ratio	602	0.87	0.39	0.21	2.79	World Bank WDI

Source: Authors' calculations.

Note: GFSY = *Government Finance Statistics Yearbook;* IFS = International Finance Statistics; WDI = World Development Indicators.

ESTIMATION

Building on past findings, this analysis estimates the impact of decentralized redistributive expenditure on income inequality using equation (17.4):

$$
\begin{aligned}
gini_{it} = \alpha_i + \delta_1 \gamma_{j,it} + \delta_2 \gamma_{j,it}^2 + \delta_3 \left(size_{it}\right) + \delta_4 \left(size_{it}\right)^2 \\
+ \delta_5 \gamma_{j,it} \times size_{it} + \delta_6 trans\_dep_{it} + \delta_7 inctax\_dec_{it} + \boldsymbol{X}\beta + \varepsilon_{it},
\end{aligned}
\tag{17.4}
$$

in which

α_i are country fixed effects.

$\gamma_{j,it}$ is the decentralization ratio for functional expenditure on j (social protection, health, education, aggregate redistributive spending) in country i at time t.

$size_{it}$ is the size of the general government in country i at time t, measured as general government expenditures as a percentage of GDP.

$trans\_dep_{it}$ is subnational government transfer dependency for country i at time t.

$inctax\_dec_{it}$ is income tax decentralization for country i at time t.

Following theoretical expectations and past specifications, $\boldsymbol{X}$ is a matrix containing GDP per capita (log) and openness (exports plus imports as a percentage of GDP); and δ_k ($k = 1,...,4$) and β are unknown parameters to be estimated.[9] A "baseline" specification from past literature is also estimated using $\gamma_{j,it}$ in which $j =$ total government expenditure. Table 17.1 shows summary statistics and sources of Gini coefficients and independent variables. Table 17.2 lists the countries included in the sample.

---

[9] GDP per capita and data on exports and imports are taken from the World Bank's World Development Indicators. General government expenditure is taken from the IMF GFSY.

TABLE 17.2

List of Countries	
Country Group	**Countries**
Advanced Economies	Australia, Austria, Belgium, Canada, Czech Republic, Denmark, Estonia, Finland, France, Germany, Greece, Ireland, Israel, Italy, Luxembourg, Netherlands, New Zealand, Norway, Portugal, Slovak Republic, Slovenia, Spain, Sweden, Switzerland, United Kingdom, United States
Emerging and Developing Economies	Belarus, Bhutan, Bolivia, Bulgaria, Egypt, El Salvador, Georgia, Hungary, Iran, Kazakhstan, Latvia, Maldives, Moldova, Poland, Romania, Russia, Serbia, Seychelles, South Africa, Thailand, Turkey, Ukraine

Because of serial correlation and the unbalanced nature of the panel, the analysis uses the estimator proposed by Baltagi and Wu (1999) in which the disturbance term ε_{it} in equation (17.4) follows a stationary AR(1) process ($\varepsilon_{it} = \rho\varepsilon_{i,t-1} + \upsilon_{it}$) in which $|\rho| < 1$, $\varepsilon_{it} \sim \left(0, \sigma_\upsilon^2 / \left(1 - \rho^2\right)\right)$, $\upsilon_{it} \sim N\left(0, \sigma_\upsilon^2\right)$, and $cov(\alpha_i, \upsilon_{it}) = 0$. This estimator is a modification of the Prais-Winsten transformation, which accounts for the unbalanced nature of the panel.[10] This analysis also deviates from the standard approach by focusing exclusively on within-country effects.

This exercise focuses on within-country effects for three reasons. First, because the theoretical literature is based on within-country income distributions, changes in national income distribution as they relate to within-country circumstance are at the core of the examination. Second, focusing on the relationship between fiscal decentralization and income inequality over time, the relatively large static cross-country variance in Gini coefficients, and difficulty in explaining this variance, makes the parametric results potentially misleading. Isolating the estimates to within-country effects avoids any ecological fallacy (Simpson's paradox) problems—especially in the presence of omitted variable bias. Third, country-constant information that is important in cross-country analysis (region, federal or nonfederal structure of government, culture, and so on) can be ignored because it is captured by country fixed effects. This allows the number of explanatory factors to be contained to a small subset of what is necessary to correctly specify a cross-country equation.

A potential reverse causality argument may also be present, stemming from the seminal work of Meltzer and Richard (1981). Meltzer and Richard's results indicate that the size of government, or level of government redistribution, within a country is a function of the distance between mean and median income (income inequality) within that country. In contrast to Meltzer and Richard's model, this chapter's specification focuses on net and not gross inequality. Reverse causality between Gini coefficients of post-tax-and-transfer income and the size of government should not pose a concern because this measure nets out government income redistribution. Although it is difficult to provide clearer insight into causality using lags or Granger causality tests, with slow-moving series (income inequality and size of government) we run a series of government size lagged specifications (one, two, and three period) and still cautiously report parametric results as correlative.

A related reverse causality issue concerns the type of inequality found in an economy and the degree of decentralization of redistribution. One might argue along the lines of Beramendi (2007) that preferences for decentralization of redistribution are a function of the degree of regional inequality within a country. The specification employed in this chapter focuses on national inequality and not regional inequality, so reverse causality of this form seems less likely.

---

[10] For balanced panels this is equivalent to the Prais-Winsten transformation.

RESULTS

The results in Table 17.3 show estimates from five specifications. The first column of results breaks down the decentralization of redistributive expenditures into three categories (education, health, social protection). The second and third columns of Table 17.3 show estimates from an aggregate redistributive decentralization measure for a full sample and subsample of countries (those with at least 10 years of observations). The fourth and fifth columns of Table 17.3 show estimates from an aggregate expenditure decentralization measure for a full sample and subsample of countries (those with at least 10 years of observations).

These results are largely consistent with past findings. GDP per capita and relative economic openness have a significant and robust relationship with income inequality (log-linear for GDP per capita). This finding is consistent with a complex and well-developed history on the

TABLE 17.3

Econometric Results

Variables	Income Inequality (1)	Income Inequality (2)	Income Inequality (3)	Income Inequality (4)	Income Inequality (5)
Income Tax Decentralization Ratio	0.023*	0.023*	0.042**	0.014	0.033**
	(0.014)	(0.014)	(0.016)	(0.014)	(0.016)
Size	0.253***	0.292***	0.409***	0.332***	0.414***
	(0.097)	(0.097)	(0.109)	(0.097)	(0.118)
Size Squared	−0.278**	−0.267**	−0.393***	−0.267**	−0.338***
	(0.113)	(0.113)	(0.124)	(0.109)	(0.129)
GDP per Capita (log)	0.015***	0.015***	0.014***	0.014***	0.014***
	(0.003)	(0.003)	(0.003)	(0.003)	(0.003)
Openness	0.017**	0.015*	0.021**	0.012	0.020**
	(0.008)	(0.008)	(0.009)	(0.008)	(0.009)
Transfer Dependency	0.031**	0.025*	0.026*	0.025**	0.026*
	(0.013)	(0.013)	(0.015)	(0.012)	(0.014)
Ratio, Health	−0.012				
	(0.008)				
Ratio, Education	0.010				
	(0.012)				
Ratio, Social Protection	0.006				
	(0.026)				
Ratio, Redistribution		0.108*	0.116		
		(0.063)	(0.077)		
Ratio, Redistribution Squared		−0.074	−0.062		
		(0.084)	(0.112)		
Ratio, Redistribution × Size		−0.222**	−0.283**		
		(0.110)	(0.119)		
Ratio, Total Expenditure				0.326***	0.381***
				(0.117)	(0.134)
Ratio, Total Expenditure Squared				−0.288*	−0.347**
				(0.156)	(0.171)
Ratio, Total Expenditure × Size				−0.374***	−0.473***
				(0.140)	(0.164)
Country Sample	48	48	27	48	27
Sample Size	521	521	416	554	430
ρ (AR(1))	0.72	0.71	0.64	0.77	0.73
R^2 (within)	0.20	0.21	0.31	0.34	0.43

Source: Authors' calculations.

Note: Standard errors in parentheses. Column 1: decentralization ratios for three redistributive expenditure categories (health, education, social protection), full sample. Column 2: decentralization ratio for redistributive expenditure, full sample. Column 3: decentralization ratio for redistributive expenditure, subsample of countries with at least 10 years of observations. Column 4: decentralization ratio of aggregate expenditure, full sample. Column 5: decentralization ratio of aggregate expenditure, subsample of countries with at least 10 years of observations.

* $p < .10$; ** $p < .05$; *** $p < .01$.

relationship between economic growth and income inequality (see, for example, Persson and Tabellini 1994; Barro 2000, 2008).

With respect to the variables of interest, despite a battery of specifications, there appears to be no significant relationship between redistributive expenditure and income inequality for any of the redistributive spending categories (see the first column of results in Table 17.3). There does appear to be a significant relationship between income inequality and both aggregate redistributive and total expenditure. This finding is also robust to the inclusion of a time trend (not reported). It suggests that expenditure decentralization can have a significant effect on income inequality only when aggregate expenditure rather than a select area of expenditure is decentralized. It is clear from Figure 17.3 that some areas are more likely targets for decentralization, but an aggregate increase (regardless of its dispersion) is the only way to achieve greater income equality.

Taking the first derivative of equation (17.4) with respect to the measure of expenditure decentralization breaks the marginal effect of fiscal decentralization down into the following:

$$\frac{\partial gini}{\partial \gamma_j} = \delta_1 + 2\delta_2 + \gamma_j \delta_5 \left(size\right) \Rightarrow \gamma_j^* = \frac{-\left(\delta_1 + \delta_5 \left(size\right)\right)}{2\delta_2}. \tag{17.5}$$

In equation (17.5), from Table 17.3, δ_1 is consistently positive, while δ_5 and δ_2 are consistently negative, and γ_j^* (from equation (17.5)) is the threshold at which the quadratic effect of decentralization begins to negatively affect income inequality.

Because of the significant interaction between the size of general government and degrees of decentralization, the relationship with income inequality is mutually dependent. Figure 17.6 plots this relationship with fiscal decentralization (redistributive and total expenditure) on the x-axis and predicted Gini coefficient from equation (17.4) on the y-axis. This relationship is plotted for three discrete levels of government size (20 percent, 30 percent, and 40 percent of GDP). As the estimates from Table 17.3 suggest, the effect of decentralization of redistributive expenditure has a significantly softer slope than that of total expenditure.

Looking more closely at the continuous effect of government expansion (measured as total general government expenditure as a percentage of GDP), the results are relatively consistent with those of Sepulveda and Martinez-Vazquez (2011). Again, taking the first derivative of

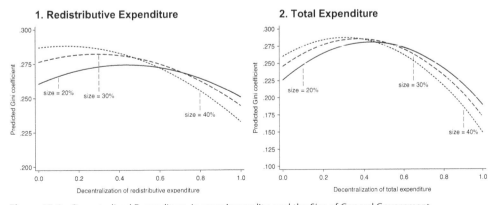

Figure 17.6 Decentralized Expenditure, Income Inequality, and the Size of General Government

Source: Authors' calculations.
Note: Size refers to general government expenditure as a percentage of GDP. Predicted effect holds all other control variables at their mean values.

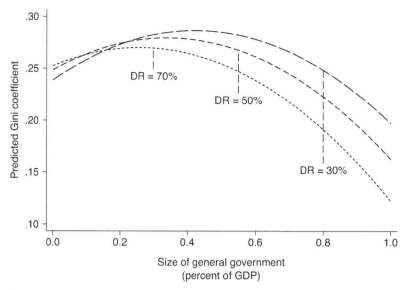

Figure 17.7   Decentralized Redistribution and Size of General Government

Source: Authors' calculations.
Note: DR = decentralization ratio. Size refers to general government expenditure as a percentage of GDP. Predicted effect holds all other control variables at their mean values.

equation (17.4), the marginal effect of a change in government size can be shown as in equation (17.6):

$$\frac{\partial gini}{\partial size} = \delta_3 + 2\delta_4 \left(size\right) + \delta_5 \gamma_j \; ; \Rightarrow size^* = \frac{-\left(\delta_3 + \delta_5 \gamma_j\right)}{2\delta_4} \, , \tag{17.6}$$

in which, from Table 17.3, δ_3 is positive, and δ_4 and δ_5 are both negative. As in Sepulveda and Martinez-Vazquez 2011, the marginal effect of government expansion on income inequality is positive at low levels; however, it significantly decreases income inequality once past a threshold (where $size = \frac{-\left(\delta_3 + \delta_5 \gamma_j\right)}{2\delta_4}$). The magnitude of this effect, and location of the threshold, is dependent on what proportion of an increase in general government is at the subnational level γ_j. For example, plugging the results from column three of Table 17.3 into equation (17.6) gives $size^* = 0.51 - 0.36\gamma_j$ implying that, for a fully decentralized government ($\gamma_j = 1$), this "threshold" government size is 15 percent of GDP, whereas for a fully centralized government, the threshold is 51 percent.

Figure 17.7 illustrates this dependence, plotting the predicted relationship between income inequality and the size of general government for three fixed levels of decentralization (as measured by decentralization ratios of 30, 50, and 70 percent).

Consistent with the expectations of Padovano (2007) and Qian and Weingast (1997), transfer dependency also appears to have a significant relationship with income inequality. Where subcentral revenues are less dependent on intergovernmental transfers, lower levels of income inequality within countries should be expected. This result is fairly robust across specifications. Figure 17.8 plots this relationship with transfer dependency on the x-axis (0 = no transfer dependency; 1 = full transfer dependency).

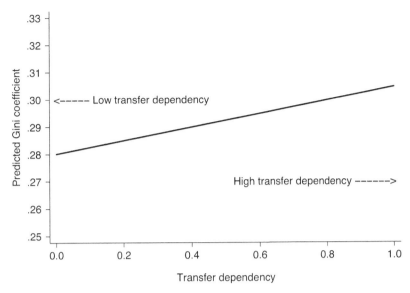

Figure 17.8 Income Inequality and Transfer Dependency

Source: Authors' calculations.
Note: Predicted effect holds all other variables at their mean values.

At the same time, Table 17.3 shows that income tax decentralization is associated with higher inequality in this sample. Although it is not significant in all specifications, this result suggests that although own revenue sources for subnational governments are important, they need to be chosen with care. In view of income inequality, income taxes may not be the best choice.

These empirical results are generally consistent with past analytical work, and with the second generation of fiscal federalism, regarding the relationship between income inequality and fiscal decentralization. The results provide further evidence that the effect of an expansion of government on income inequality depends on the extent to which the expansion takes place at the subnational level. The analysis also confirms past approaches that measure redistribution at the aggregate level. If only selected expenditures are decentralized, without any increase in total decentralization, the results suggest that income inequality will be unaffected. Consistent with the second-generation literature of fiscal federalism, the extent to which subnational governments are more dependent on transfers from other government levels appears to have a negative effect on income inequality within countries. These results should be interpreted carefully as interesting correlations that require further work on a micro level to validate the path of causation. For instance, a high degree of transfer dependency might also be the result of inequality and regional disparities. Central governments might increase transfers to relatively poor jurisdictions to enable them to provide a more adequate amount of local public goods.

CONCLUSION

The purpose of this chapter is to empirically test the relationship between fiscal decentralization and income inequality within countries. Past research on interregional income inequality and fiscal decentralization suggests that the two should be related, particularly when government redistribution is decentralized and subnational governments are not highly dependent on transfers to finance their expenditures. The macro-level results in this chapter lend support to these findings, as well as to the tenets of the second generation of fiscal federalism, which recommends redistribution in a setting of comprehensive fiscal decentralization in which subnational governments have sufficient access to own resources (as opposed to transfers).

The decentralization of specific categories of redistributive spending appears to have no significant impact on income inequality, suggesting that decentralization should occur on an aggregate level to reduce income inequality. A significant quadratic relationship only emerges once we move to a higher level of aggregation by jointly considering all redistributive, or total, spending items. In all cases, the effect of expenditure decentralization is also contingent on the total size of government, consistent with evidence in past empirical literature.

The degree to which subnational governments rely on grants from other government levels to finance their expenditure is an important mediating factor: other things being equal, income inequality is more pronounced when transfer dependency is high. However, decentralization of redistribution on the revenue side of the budget, measured by the subnational share of income tax revenues, is found to increase rather than decrease inequality. This, in turn, reflects expectations from the first-generation fiscal federalism literature more so than from the second.

In sum, the decentralization of government expenditure can help achieve a more equal distribution of income. However, several conditions need to be fulfilled. First, the government sector needs to be sufficiently large. Second, decentralization should be comprehensive, including redistributive government spending. Given the softer slope associated with decentralizing redistributive expenditure, such expenditure may be a good target for an initial move toward greater decentralization. Third, decentralization on the expenditure side should be accompanied by adequate decentralization on the revenue side, so that subnational governments rely primarily on their own revenue sources as opposed to intergovernmental transfers. Fourth, when assigning revenue sources to subnational governments, preference should be given to revenue categories that do not have strong redistributive implications. Given limited empirical work in this area and growing interest in achieving inclusive growth, further evidence and qualitative case studies would be beneficial to clarify policy conclusions for achieving a more equal income distribution.

REFERENCES

Aldasoro, Iñaki, and Mike Seiferling. 2014. "Vertical Fiscal Imbalances and the Accumulation of Government Debt." IMF Working Paper No. 14/209, International Monetary Fund, Washington.

Bahl, Roy, Jorge Martinez-Vazquez, and Sally Wallace. 2000. "State and Local Government Choices in Fiscal Redistribution." Fiscal Research Program Report No. 49, Georgia State University, Atlanta, Georgia.

Baltagi, Badi H., and Ping X. Wu. 1999. "Spaced Panel Data Regressions with AR(1) Disturbances." *Econometric Theory* 15 (December): 814–23.

Barro, Robert. 2000. "Inequality and Growth in a Panel of Countries." *Journal of Economic Growth* 5 (1): 5–32.

———. 2008. "Inequality and Growth Revisited." Working Paper on Regional Economic Integration No. 11, Asian Development Bank, Manila.

Bastagli, Francesca, David Coady, and Sanjeev Gupta. 2012. "Income Inequality and Fiscal Policy." IMF Staff Discussion Note No. 12/08 (Revised), International Monetary Fund, Washington.

Beramendi, Pablo. 2007. "Inequality and the Territorial Fragmentation of Solidarity." *International Organization* 61 (October): 783–820.

Chu, Ke-young, Hamid Davoodi, and Sanjeev Gupta. 2000. "Income Distribution and Tax and Government Social Spending Policies in Developing Countries." IMF Working Paper No. 00/62, International Monetary Fund, Washington.

Dollar, David, and Aart Kraay. 2002. "Growth Is Good for the Poor." *Journal of Economic Growth* 7: 195–225.

Eyraud, Luc, and Lusine Lusinyan. 2013. "Vertical Fiscal Imbalances and Fiscal Performance in Advanced Economies." *Journal of Monetary Economics* 60 (July): 571–87.

Galli, Rossana, and Rolph van der Hoeven. 2001. "Is Inflation Bad for Income Inequality?" ILO Employment Paper No. 29, International Labour Organization, Geneva.

Goñi, Edwin, J. Humberto López, and Luis Servén. 2008. "Fiscal Redistribution and Income Inequality in Latin America." Policy Research Working Paper No. 4487, World Bank, Washington.

Gustafsson, Björn, and Mats Johansson. 1999. "In Search of Smoking Guns: What Makes Income Inequality Vary over Time in Different Countries?" *American Sociological Review* 64 (4): 585–608.

International Monetary Fund (IMF). 2001. *Government Finance Statistics Manual.* Washington.

———. 2014. *Government Finance Statistics Manual: Pre-Publication Draft.* Washington.

———. various years. *Government Finance Statistics Yearbook.* Washington.

Kuznets, Simon. 1955. "Economic Growth and Income Inequality." *American Economic Review* 45 (March): 1–28.

Lessmann, Christian. 2012. "Regional Inequality and Decentralization: An Empirical Analysis." *Environment and Planning A* 44 (6): 1363–88.

Li, Hongyi, Danyang Xie, and Heng-Fu Zou. 2000. "Dynamics of Income Distribution." *Canadian Journal of Economics* 33 (November): 937–61.

Lundberg, Mattias, and Lyn Squire. 2003. "The Simultaneous Evolution of Growth and Inequality." *Economic Journal* 113 (April): 326–44.

McKinnon, Ronald I. 1995. "Intergovernmental Competition in Europe with and without a Common Currency." *Journal of Policy Modeling* 17 (5): 463–78.

———. 1997. "Market-Preserving Fiscal Federalism in the American Monetary Union." In *Macroeconomic Dimensions of Public Finance: Essays in Honour of Vito Tanzi*, edited by Mario I. Blejer and Teresa Ter-Minassian. London: Routledge.

Meltzer, Allan H., and Scott F. Richard. 1981. "A Rational Theory of the Size of Government." *Journal of Political Economy* 89 (October): 914–27.

Musgrave, Richard A. 1959. *The Theory of Public Finance: A Study in Public Economy.* New York: McGraw-Hill.

Oates, Wallace E. 1972. *Fiscal Federalism.* New York: Harcourt Brace Jovanovich.

———. 2005. "Toward a Second-Generation Theory of Fiscal Federalism." *International Tax and Public Finance* 12: 349–73.

———. 2008. "On the Evolution of Fiscal Federalism: Theory and Institutions." *National Tax Journal* 61 (June): 313–34.

Organisation for Economic Co-operation and Development (OECD). 2006. "Intergovernmental Transfers and Decentralised Public Spending." Working Paper No. 3, Paris.

———. 2009a. "The Fiscal Autonomy of Sub-Central Governments: An Update." Working Paper No. 9, Paris.

———. 2009b. "Taxes and Grants: On the Revenue Mix of Sub-Central Governments." Working Paper No. 7, Paris.

Padovano, Fabio. 2007. *The Politics and Economics of Regional Transfers: Decentralization, Interregional Redistribution and Income Convergence.* Cheltenham, U.K.: Edward Elgar.

Persson, T., and G. Tabellini. 1994. "Is Inequality Harmful for Growth? Theory and Evidence." *American Economic Review* 84 (3): 600–21.

Prud'homme, Rémy. 1995. "The Dangers of Decentralization." *World Bank Research Observer* 10 (2): 201–20.

Qian, Yingyi, and Barry R. Weingast. 1997. "Federalism as a Commitment to Preserving Market Incentives." *Journal of Economic Perspectives* 11 (4): 83–92.

Sepulveda, Cristian F., and Jorge Martinez-Vazquez. 2011. "The Consequences of Fiscal Decentralization on Poverty and Income Equality." *Environment and Planning C: Government and Policy* 29 (2): 321–43.

Stigler, George J. 1957. "The Tenable Range of Functions of Local Government." In *Federal Expenditure Policy for Economic Growth and Stability*, 213–19. Washington: U.S. Congress Joint Economic Committee.

Tiebout, Charles M. 1956. "A Pure Theory of Local Expenditures." *Journal of Political Economy* 64 (October): 416–24.

Tselios, Vassilis, Andrés Rodríguez-Pose, Andy Pike, John Tomaney, and Torrisi Gianpiero. 2012. "Income Inequality, Decentralisation, and Regional Development in Western Europe." *Environment and Planning A* 44 (6): 1278–301.

PART VI

Country Case Studies

Reinventing the Dutch Tax-Benefit System: Exploring the Frontier of the Equity-Efficiency Trade-Off

RUUD DE MOOIJ

INTRODUCTION

Increasing employment is a top priority for European governments. The aim is especially to better integrate particular groups in labor market, such as the low-skilled, women, elderly and social benefit recipients. To achieve this goal, countries are now restructuring their welfare states. At the same time, however, European governments want to preserve social cohesion that is traditionally a major objective of these welfare states. Achieving these twin objectives ignores the fundamental trade-off between equity and efficiency, however, which seems inherent in the design of tax-benefit systems. It raises the question whether reforms are feasible that improve the equity-efficiency possibility frontier. This chapter analyzes the opportunities for such reforms.

The chapter starts by reviewing key insights from optimal tax theory to identify the factors determining the equity-efficiency possibility frontier. We discuss important results from applied optimal tax analyses, which gives guidance to potentially promising directions for reform. The optimal tax models, however, usually contain only one or two distortions, apply aggregate income distributions for the total population, and do not differentiate between agents. Moreover, most studies apply data for the United States, which has a more dispersed income distribution than is common in Europe and a smaller share of part-time work. This chapter analyzes reforms in the Dutch tax-benefit system by using an applied general equilibrium model for the Netherlands. The model is comprehensive in describing various distortions induced by redistributive taxation. In particular, it encompasses decisions at the intensive margin of labor supply of males and females, the participation decision of secondary earners in couples, and the job acceptance decision of the unemployed. The elasticities at various decision margins are calibrated on the basis of existing empirical evidence. For various household types and decision margins, population densities are calibrated on the basis of Dutch income distributions.

The model simulations yield a number of policy conclusions. Selective in-work tax credits for low labor incomes and secondary earners in couples have the potential to raise employment without sacrificing equality. These selective tax credits should be targeted at decision margins with the highest elasticities and with the highest population densities. If they shift the marginal tax burden onto more densely populated groups, for example, just above the minimum wage in the Netherlands, they tend to reduce employment. Flat tax reforms aimed to reduce top marginal income tax rates turn out to worsen the equity-efficiency trade-off. The reason is that they shift the marginal tax burden towards more elastic secondary earners. Removing the poverty trap by switching from means-tested income

---

This chapter originally appeared as Ruud A. de Mooij, "Reinventing the Dutch Tax-Benefit System: Exploring the Frontier of the Equity-Efficiency Trade-Off," *International Tax and Public Finance*, Vol. 15 (2008), pp. 87–103; © Springer Science+Business Media, LLC 2007. Reprinted with the kind permission of Springer Science+Business Media.

transfers to a general basic income exacerbates the distortionary impact of the tax-benefit system by raising the marginal tax burden on the densely populated middle income groups.

The rest of this chapter is organized as follows. The second section discusses the potential for efficiency-enhancing reforms in the tax-benefit system on the basis of optimal tax theory. The third section demonstrates the main features of our applied general equilibrium model. The fourth section presents model simulations of concrete reforms in the Netherlands to see which reforms improve efficiency. Finally, the fifth section concludes.

OPTIMAL TAX THEORY AS A GUIDE FOR REFORM

Optimal tax theory provides a good starting point for an analysis of the equity-efficiency trade-off. The theory reveals that the optimal marginal tax schedule—that is, the tax structure that achieves equity goals with minimal distortions in the labor market—is found to depend on at least five factors.[1] First, there are two factors that determine the benefits from redistribution, namely:

1. pre-tax income inequality;

2. social preference for redistribution;

If pre-tax inequality is large and society features much aversion against inequality, the government should put much effort in the redistribution of incomes from high- to low-ability agents. In this chapter, we make no attempt to measure the social benefits from equality.

The social benefits from equality should be weighed against the efficiency losses induced by redistribution. These efficiency costs are determined by the following three factors:

3. elasticity of labor supply of various agents;

4. elasticities at other decision margins;

5. population density at various decision margins.

The elasticity of labor supply (3) determines the classical distortionary impact of marginal tax rates on the consumption/leisure choice. This distortion was already present in the original analysis of Mirrlees (1971). The larger is the elasticity, the bigger is the distortionary impact of redistributive taxation and the less redistribution is optimal. Redistributive policies may also distort other decision margins, such as the extensive margin of labor supply or the search and acceptance behavior of the unemployed (4). Finally, the optimal tax depends on the population density at various margins (5). If density is higher at some point in the income distribution, a marginal tax creates larger aggregate distortions so that the optimal tax rate is lower.

The optimal-tax literature reports a variety of results with respect to the optimal marginal tax schedule. In general, these findings can be understood by the variation in assumptions on the factors (1)–(5). The optimal tax schedule reported in applied optimal tax studies will thus depend on, for example, the calibration of the income distribution, the choice of decision margins, the corresponding elasticities at these margins, and the disaggregation with respect to agents and households. Overall, optimal tax theory reveals that distortions can best be avoided if elasticities are high and if the density in the income distribution is high. Below, we summarize some of the main policy lessons from applied optimal tax models.

A Linear Tax Structure

Mirrlees (1971) simulates the optimal marginal tax schedule for a utilitarian social welfare function, Cobb-Douglas preferences in consumption and leisure, and a log-normal distribution of

---

[1] The seminal contribution to this literature is Mirrlees (1971). A recent review of subsequent literature and its policy relevance can be found in Sorensen (2007).

abilities. He concludes that "the most striking feature of the results is the closeness to linearity of the optimal tax schedules" (p. 206). This result provides efficiency grounds for a flat income tax structure. This flat tax has considerable appeal to policy makers. Recently, a number of Eastern European countries have introduced flat income tax systems with a single rate on labor income (see Keen and others 2006 for a review and discussion of these reforms). Also other European countries consider reforms in this direction.

Subsequent contributions in the optimal tax literature have raised doubts on the optimality of the linear income tax schedule. Tuomala (1990) finds that the optimal marginal tax schedule is sensitive to the underlying assumptions. In fact, the optimal structure is non-linear if social welfare functions feature relatively high inequality aversion and if labor supply responses are different between agents. The non-linear structure is more efficient because it employs more information on individual earnings so that it can achieve the same redistribution with less dead weight loss.

With respect to the shape of the non-linearities, early contributions to the literature conclude that the optimal marginal income tax features an inverse-U shape, that is, high for middle incomes and low for low and high incomes. If abilities are bounded above, the optimal marginal tax on the highest ability agent even goes down to zero (Seade 1977, 1982). Intuitively, a positive marginal tax would not contribute to redistribution but does distort labor supply of this person. Tuomala (1990) shows, however, that these results are very local and of little practical relevance.

More recently, Diamond (1998) and Saez (2001) have used pre-tax income distributions for the United States and a uniform positive labor supply elasticity to show that the optimal marginal tax structure typically features a U-shaped pattern: high at the bottom and top of the distribution and low for middle incomes. This result is driven by population densities. Intuitively, a negative average tax for the poor is necessary to redistribute income. It should be phased out with income in a range where the population density is not so high. In the United States, this is just above the minimum income. Beyond this level, the optimal marginal tax falls as population density increases and marginal taxes create large aggregate distortions in labor supply. It may rise again for higher incomes if inequality aversion is sufficiently large.[2]

Still, high marginal tax rates at the bottom and top of the income distribution are often criticized in European policy debates. High marginal income tax rates at the top are often held responsible for severe distortions in labor supply (see, for example, Prescott 2004). Reducing these rates has therefore been advocated in many European countries. During the 1980s and 1990s, countries have indeed substantially reduced their top marginal tax rates. High marginal tax rates at the bottom of the labor market—known as the poverty trap—are held responsible for severe labor market distortions in Europe. Indeed, unemployment in Europe is concentrated at the bottom of the labor market. In this connection, some have proposed to replace means-tested transfer schemes by a negative income tax or basic income (see, for example, Atkinson 1995). It provides an effective floor in the income distribution and avoids complexities and administrative difficulties in gathering information about eligibility to means-tested social transfers. Moreover, non-compliance and moral hazard would disappear. The abolishment of means-tested benefits would reduce marginal tax rates at the bottom of the income distribution and thus alleviate the poverty trap. Yet, it does not comply with the U-shaped form of the optimal marginal tax schedule emphasized by empirically simulated optimal tax models.

Taxation of Couples

Empirical evidence reveals that female labor supply is more elastic than male labor supply. Optimal-tax principles then imply that labor income of females should be taxed at a lower

---

[2] The U-shaped pattern obtained from empirical income distributions opposes the zero marginal tax rate at the top of the income distribution found by Seade (1977, 1982). The reason is that the empirical income distribution is thicker at the top than the assumed log-normal distributions in the earlier studies.

marginal rate than labor income of males, see, for example, Rosen (1977). However, laws typically do not permit such discrimination on the basis of gender. Hence, the government should look for indicators that are correlated with it. As argued by Boskin and Sheshinski (1983), females are often secondary earners in families. They suggest that an optimal income tax should therefore differentiate marginal tax rates between primary and secondary earners. This requires selective taxation measures for secondary earners (Kleven and others 2006).

The responsiveness of secondary earners also matters for the taxation of couples (Apps and Rees 2003; Kleven and others 2006). Here, we can distinguish between joint taxation and individual taxation. Under individual taxation, each family member is taxed separately, independent of the income of other household members. Under joint taxation, the tax liability is determined by total family income. In progressive tax systems, the two principles score differently with respect to labor-market incentives for secondary earners. Indeed, compared to joint taxation, individual taxation imposes a lower marginal tax burden on the labor income of secondary earners. Individual taxation is therefore more efficient if secondary earners feature a relatively high elasticity. It is adopted in Denmark, Sweden, Finland, United Kingdom, Belgium, Austria and the Netherlands. Joint taxation is adopted in United States, Germany, France, Portugal and Spain.

In-Work Tax Credits

Empirical studies on labor supply elasticities emphasize that the extensive margin of participation tends to be more elastic than the intensive margin of hours worked (Evers and others 2005). Efficiency concerns thus call for smaller distortions at the participation margin (Boone and Bovenberg 2004). In light of this, Saez (2002) advocates in-work tax credits for low income workers. Such credits have gained popularity during recent decades in a number of countries. For instance, the United States has introduced the earned income tax credit and the United Kingdom the working family tax credit. These credits aim at alleviating poverty among the working poor, but also have important implications for labor-market incentives. On the one hand, the credits encourage labor-market participation of low-skilled people by raising the income gap between those inside and outside the labor market. On the other hand, they make the tax system more progressive by benefiting workers with low incomes compared to those with high incomes. Tax progression reduces labor-supply incentives at the intensive margin.

Several empirical studies have analyzed the labor-market implications of in-work tax credits. Eissa and Liebman (1996) and Meyer and Rosenbaum (2001) find positive effects of the American earned income tax credit on the participation margin. Blundell and others (2000) find that the working families' tax credit has raised aggregate participation in the United Kingdom. Moreover, Keane and Mofit (1996) and Meyer (2002) conclude that there is no significant adverse effect of earned income tax credits on the intensive margin of labor supply, that is, hours worked. Hence, the aggregate impact of these credits on employment is likely to be positive. Note, however, that none of these studies considers a balanced budget reform where in-work tax credits are financed by general tax increases.

MIMIC: AN AGE MODEL FOR THE NETHERLANDS

This section presents an applied general equilibrium model—MIMIC—that is used to explore potentially promising reforms in the Dutch tax-benefit system. The model is comprehensive in modeling various decision margins, it contains a high degree of disaggregation in the household sector, and it is calibrated for a typical European country: the Netherlands.[3]

---

[3] See Bovenberg and others 2000 for a core version of MIMIC. A description of the full model and its calibration can be found in Graafland and others 2001.

Households

MIMIC contains a disaggregated household model aimed at describing the impact of the tax-benefit system on labor supply and the income distribution. Table 18.1 gives a quick overview of this disaggregation. First, the model accounts for heterogeneity in various dimensions, including skill, cohabitation, the presence of children, whether household members participate or are eligible for social benefits, and age (see panel 1 of Table 18.1). Overall, the model distinguishes 40 different household types.

Within each type, we make a further distinction with respect to discrete options for labor supply (see panel 2 of Table 18.1). For instance, primary earners can choose their optimal working time between the options 80 percent, 100 percent and 120 percent of a full-time equivalent. Secondary earners and singles face more options. Secondary earners in couples can also opt for voluntary non-participation. The option that an individual chooses is derived from utility maximization, with consumption and leisure as arguments, subject to a household budget constraint. The preference for leisure is heterogeneous across agents. We use a uniform distribution of this preference parameter to calibrate the high share of part-time work of secondary earners and single persons in the Netherlands. Hence, part-timers feature a relatively high marginal utility of leisure. In determining labor supply of couples, we assume that each partner makes an individual decision, given an average income from his or her spouse.

In interpreting the labor supply responses to changes in prices and incomes, the traditional income and substitution effects are at work. Hence, if the marginal tax rate declines, labor supply increases on account of the substitution effect. A lower average tax exerts a positive income effect, which reduces labor supply. Based on a meta analysis of labor-supply elasticities by Evers and others (2005), we set utility parameters such that the uncompensated labor-supply elasticity equals 0.5 for secondary earners, 0.1 for primary earners and 0.25 for singles.

Within each combination of household-hours type, we employ a wage distribution based on Dutch microdata (panel 3 of Table 18.1). We distinguish 10 income classes for each group and base the density of each class on the data for 1992. The average wage levels in the model are updated on the basis of realized wage growth in the Netherlands until 2006. For each income class, we derive disposable income by applying the Dutch tax-benefit system to the gross incomes. The after-tax disposable incomes and the marginal tax burdens determine labor supply behavior.

Firms

Labor demand for high-skilled and low-skilled workers is derived from firms that maximize profits subject to a constant elasticity of substitution (CES) production technology. The first-order

TABLE 18.1

Structure of the Household Model in MIMIC

1. Types: Individual characteristics	
Skill	Low skilled or high skilled agents
Cohabitation	Single or in couple
Children	With or without children
Labor-market status	Working or receiving a social benefit (unemployment, disability or welfare)
Age	Students > 18; workers < 55; workers 55–64; or pensioners > 65
2. Options: Choice of working time per individual	
Primary earner in couple	80 - 100 - 120 percent of full-time equivalent
Secondary earner in couple	0 - 30 - 50 - 80 - 100 percent of full-time equivalent
Singles	50 - 80 - 100 - 120 percent of full-time equivalent
3. Wage distribution	
Each type and option	Population density in 10 different income classes based on micro data

conditions reveal that labor demand depends on the relative wage costs for the respective types of labor. Based on time series estimates for the Netherlands, the substitution elasticity between high-skilled and low-skilled workers is set at 1.15. The substitution elasticity between capital and labor is set at 0.25.[4] Economic profits originate from monopolistic competition without free entry. Hence, firms set prices as a mark-up over marginal production costs.[5] This setting allows for endogenous terms-of-trade effects. As the export elasticity is set at a high value of –5 for this small open economy, these effects are of minor importance for our simulations.

Union Bargaining

Wages are obtained from a right-to-manage model. In bargaining over wages, trade unions exploit their monopsony power to reap part of the rents earned in production. However, by setting wages above the market clearing level, trade unions create unemployment which they value negatively. Unions thus face a trade off between high wages and low unemployment. An important specification in the right-to-manage model is the fall-back position of the trade union. In our model, it depends on unemployment benefits and an untaxed informal wage. The latter is modeled as a function of labor productivity and the price of consumption. Labor productivity is a proxy for the wage rate in the black market, while the price of consumption reflects the value of household production. This specification yields a non-linear wage equation in which several institutional variables enter. The non-linear equation has been estimated using Dutch time-series data (see Graafland and Huizinga 1999). In linearized form and evaluated in the initial equilibrium of MIMIC, it reads as follows (where only parameters are presented that are relevant for our analysis):

$$\log W = \log h + 0.3 \log RR - 0.6 \log(1 - Ta) + 0.1 \log(1 - Tm) - 0.1 \log U \tag{18.1}$$

where W is the real producer wage and h stands for labor productivity. The positive coefficient for the replacement rate (RR) reflects larger bargaining power of the union if social benefits increase. Higher benefits thus raise wage demands. The average tax rate enters the wage equation via $(1 - Ta)$. This is because the untaxed informal wage is part of the outside option of the union. Higher average labor taxes therefore strengthen the relative bargaining position of the union and increase wage demands. The marginal tax rate enters the wage equation via $(1 - Tm)$. This term exerts a positive effect on wages. With a low marginal tax rate, the trade union will find it more attractive to bid for higher wages since a larger part of additional wage increases are absorbed by government in the form of taxes. The elasticity of 0.1 for the unemployment rate (U) is consistent with a consensus estimate from empirical studies reported by Blanchflower and Oswald (2005).

Wages for low skilled and high skilled workers are determined as a weighted average of a macro wage equation and a skill-specific wage equation (with weights of ½). This is based on empirical findings of sectoral wages in the Netherlands by Graafland and Lever (1996). In the macro wage equation, the institutional variables, Ta, Tm and RR are computed as averages for all workers. In the skill-specific wage equation, the variables reflect averages for respective skill groups.

MIMIC uses a non-linear version of the wage equation (18.1); see Graafland and Huizinga (1999). One non-linear effect deserves special attention, as it plays an important role in our

---

[4] This may seem small compared to the calibration of other applied general equilibrium models. It is, however, consistent with the majority of empirical findings; see for example Chirinko (2002).

[5] We do not consider taxes on rents. The reason for introducing economic profits is that employers and unions negotiate over this rent, which explains involuntary unemployment. Rents could alternatively be modeled as the return from a fixed factor in production.

simulations. This is the positive interaction between the replacement rate and the unemployment rate. Intuitively, a high unemployment rate makes it more important for trade unions to care about the outside option since more union members face the fall-back income. Accordingly, the elasticity of the replacement rate rises in the rate of unemployment. As the unemployment rate is higher for low-skilled workers than for high-skilled workers, the replacement rate of the low-skilled causes relatively large increases in the wages of the low skilled.

Search-Matching

In addition to structural unemployment caused by unions, MIMIC also captures frictional unemployment due to imperfect matching on the labor market. Frictional unemployment is specified separately for low-skilled and high-skilled workers.

The model assumes an exogenous rate of job quits that leads to vacancies. At the same time, there is an exogenous rate of job lay-offs that cause unemployment. We model the steady state of a matching process between these vacancies and the unemployed searching for work. The more efficient job matching becomes, the lower are the search costs for employers to fill vacancies and the higher is number of vacancies posted. Thus, more efficient matching reduces the frictional rate of unemployment.

Matching efficiency depends on the net benefit replacement rate in two ways. First, the unemployed endogenously determine their search effort by trading off leisure against job search. A high replacement rate reduces the incentives for job search and thus reduces the efficiency of job matching. Second, a higher replacement rate raises the reservation wage of the unemployed in deciding about accepting a job offer or continue searching. The unemployed are thus less willing to accept an offer if the replacement rate is higher.

ANALYZING REFORMS IN THE DUTCH TAX-BENEFIT SYSTEM

We perform various simulations with MIMIC. They can be interpreted as an analysis of comparative statics. All simulations represent balanced-budget reforms. Personal income tax rates are always adjusted (each with the same percentage points) to maintain the public budget balanced ex-post, that is, after behavioral responses have been taken into account.

In presenting simulation outcomes, we concentrate on two types of variables reflecting equity and efficiency. The equity effects are presented by means of net disposable income ratios for different groups. For instance, the ratio of average incomes of high-skilled/low-skilled workers represents equality in the income distribution among workers. We also present the replacement ratio, which involves a weighted average of the net benefit/net wage ratio for various workers and where weights are based on populations in employment. Regarding efficiency, we present the effects on hours worked for various groups, the participation rate of secondary earners (labeled "female participation rate"), the unemployment rate, and aggregate employment.

The first subsection analyzes two flat tax proposals and a basic income. The flat tax reforms replace the current progressive tax structure with increasing marginal tax rates. In 2006, tax rates on labor income range from 34 percent for incomes up to €17,000, 41 percent for incomes between €17,000 and €30,000, 42 percent for incomes between €30,000 and €53,000 and 52 percent for incomes above €53,000. The system contains a general tax credit of €2,000. The basic income replaces means-tested benefits and subsidies that are provided to the poor.

The second subsection analyzes two reforms in the taxation of couples. First, while the Dutch tax system is largely individualized, partners in single-earner couples can still transfer their general tax credit of €2,000 to the primary earner. We consider the individualization of this credit. Second, the Dutch system contains a tax credit for secondary earners in couples, which is conditional on having children under 12, both partners working, and a partner income of at least

TABLE 18.2

Effects of Two Budgetary Neutral Flat Tax Proposals (Percent changes unless indicated)

	Flat Tax 37.5 Percent	Flat Tax 43.5 Percent and Higher General Tax Credit	Flat Tax 53.5 Percent and Basic Income
1. Effects on Distribution			
Ratio High Skilled/Low Skilled	1.5	0.0	−7.6
Mean of Marginal Tax Rates (abs. dif.)	−2.9	0.3	7.8
Mean of Replacement Rates (abs. dif.)	−1.7	0.1	−2.6
2. Effects on Labor Market			
Labor supply (hours)	1.0	−0.3	−5.3
Primary Earners	1.2	0.1	−1.4
Secondary Earners	0.0	−0.2	−8.8
Single Persons	1.0	−1.2	−7.4
Female Participation Rate	−1.7	1.5	−10.0
Employment	1.4	−0.3	−3.8
Unemployment Rate (abs. dif.)	−0.1	−0.1	−1.9

Source: MIMIC simulations.

€4,500. In that case, the partner with the lowest income in the family receives a credit of €600 per year. We consider an extension of this selective tax relief for secondary earners.

The third subsection explores selective in-work tax credits for low incomes. Today, the Dutch system contains an earned income tax credit with a maximum of €1,350. It features a linear phase-in range between €8,000 and €16,000 and no phase-out range. We explore various extensions of this credit.

Flat Tax Reforms

We explore three flat income tax reforms. The first two aim to cut the top marginal tax rate. In the first version, we replace the current rate structure by a flat tax rate of 37.5 percent. This rate keeps the government budget balanced. The general tax credit remains unchanged. In the second flat-tax reform, we increase the general tax credit by €1,400. At the same time, we raise the flat tax rate to 43.5 percent to keep the government budget balanced. The extra tax credit applies only to people with a positive income and cannot be transferred by a non-participating partner to its spouse.[6] The third simulation is the introduction of a basic income of €550 per month for all individuals above the age of 18. The basic income replaces existing income transfers, such as welfare benefits, basic pensions, student grants, the general tax credit and the labor tax credit.[7] To finance the basic income, we replace the current progressive tax system by a flat tax of 53.5 percent on all income to keep the government budget balanced. Hence, the top marginal tax rate increases, rather than falls. The effects of the three reforms are presented in Table 18.2.

The 37.5 percent flat tax raises the income differential between high-skilled and low-skilled workers. This is reflected in a 1.5 percent increase in the ratio of income between high and low skilled workers. The 43.5 percent flat tax yields smaller effects on the income distribution as people earning low incomes are compensated by the higher tax credit. This benefits lower incomes more than higher incomes. The middle income groups typically lose. Hence, the 43.5 percent flat tax redistributes the tax burden from low and high incomes towards the middle

---

[6] In both reforms, we maintain a lower rate in the first two brackets for the elderly above 65 as they do not pay premiums for the pay-as-you-go pension system. Hence, the tax structure for the elderly is not flat.

[7] Single persons and single parents maintain to receive supplementary welfare benefits. We reduce the level of unemployment benefits and disability benefits with the basic income. Hence, there remains only a top-up insurance for unemployment and disability.

income groups. Overall, the ratio of high and low skilled labor incomes remains unchanged. The basic income benefits low-skilled workers more than high-skilled workers and reduces the income ratio by 7.6 percent.

The 37.5 percent flat tax reduces the marginal tax rates for many workers. On average, the decline is 2.9 percent. This increases labor supply incentives due to substitution from leisure to consumption. Overall, labor supply expands by 1 percent. The increase in hours worked does not apply to all individuals. Most primary earners and single persons face lower marginal tax rates as they are taxed at the margin in the higher tax brackets. Hence, these groups work longer hours. Many secondary earners in couples hold part-time jobs where they are taxed at the margin in the first bracket. The increase in the tax rate from 34 percent to 37.5 percent discourages them to work longer hours or to occupy small part-time jobs. Accordingly, the female participation rate drops by 1.7 percent. Working females who work longer hours increase their hours worked due to lower marginal tax rates in the higher tax brackets. On balance, the effect on partner labor supply in hours is negligible. Overall, the simulations suggest that the 37.5 percent flat tax causes more inequality in the income distribution, but it reduces distortions in labor supply. It thus illustrates the classical trade-off between equity and efficiency.

Under the 43.5 percent flat tax, labor supply distortions become larger, rather than smaller: labor supply falls by 0.3 percent. The reason is that the marginal tax burden is shifted from people at the bottom and top of the income distribution towards the middle incomes. The lower tax at the bottom encourages non-working partners to participate in small part-time jobs. Female participation thus expands by 1.5 percent. Also high-skilled primary earners, who face a lower marginal tax rate, raise their hours worked. The higher marginal tax on middle incomes exerts negative effects on labor supply. This effect is relatively sizable for two reasons. First, it raises the marginal tax for the more densely populated group, which renders the distortions larger. Second, it raises the marginal tax primarily for secondary earners and singles who feature larger elasticities than male breadwinners. Labor supply of partners and singles fall by, respectively 0.2 percent and 1.2 percent, while male breadwinner labor supply rises by only 0.1 percent. Hence, a flat tax yields less efficient redistribution than the current progressive rate structure in the Netherlands.

The third column of Table 18.2 shows the effects of the basic income proposal. This reform reduces the replacement rate for low incomes. On average over the population, the replacement rate falls by 2.6 percentage points. The lower replacement rate induces wage moderation, encourages job search and job acceptance and thus reduces the unemployment rate by 1.9 percent. The downside of the basic income is a higher marginal tax burden. Indeed, a 53.5 percent tax is necessary to finance the basic income, which increases the marginal tax burden on average by 7.8 percent. This reinforces the wage moderating impact of the reform and contributes to the reduction in equilibrium unemployment. However, the higher marginal tax burden reduces the incentives for labor supply across the board. Overall, labor supply falls by 5.3 percent and the female participation rate drops by 10 percent. On balance, aggregate employment falls by 3.8 percent. The negative income tax thus tends to fail in improving the equity-efficiency trade-off. Removing the poverty trap while maintaining the minimum income guarantee will exacerbate the overall distortionary impact of the tax system on labor supply as it hurts labor supply incentives of the densely populated group of middle incomes. This is why the optimal marginal tax schedule features high marginal taxes for low income groups. The poverty trap thus tends to be part of an optimal tax schedule and minimizes the distortionary cost associated with redistribution to the poor.

Taxation of Couples

Selective marginal tax relief for secondary earners in couples is explored in two forms: an extension of the selective earned income tax credit for secondary earners with children and an individualization of the general tax credit. The proposed selective tax credit is linearly phased in

TABLE 18.3

Effects of Reforms in the Taxation of Couples *(Percent changes unless indicated)*

	Secondary Earner Tax Credit	Individualized General Tax Credit
1. Effects on Distribution		
Ratio High Skilled/Low Skilled	−0.0	1.8
Ratio Single Earner/Two Earner	−2.7	−5.5
Mean of Marginal Tax Burdens (abs. dif.)	0.5	−0.6
Mean of Replacement Rates (abs. dif.)	0.0	−0.1
2. Labor Market Effects		
Labor Supply (hours)	0.1	1.0
Primary Earners	−0.3	0.1
Secondary Earners	2.2	4.8
Single Persons	−0.3	0.4
Female Participation Rate	4.7	9.5
Aggregate Employment	0.4	1.2
Unemployment Rate (abs. dif.)	−0.2	0.1

Source: MIMIC simulations.

between 0 and €12,000 and that has a maximum of €2,700. It features no phase-out range. The government budget is balanced by an increase in all personal income tax rates by approximately 1 percent age point. Individualization is analyzed by abolishing the right to transfer the general tax credit to the working spouse.[8] This saves 1.75 billion euros. It is used to cut income tax rates by 0.75 percentage point. The effects of both reforms are presented in Table 18.3.

The selective credit for secondary earners raises the marginal tax burden for most workers due to a higher personal income tax rate. This reduces hours worked by primary earners and singles. The credit reduces the tax burden at the extensive margin of secondary earners. Accordingly, the female participation rate rises by 4.7 percent. This primarily consists of part-time jobs. Female labor supply in hours expands by 2.2 percent. On balance, the higher female participation rate dominates the decline in hours by males and singles so that aggregate labor supply expands by 0.1 percent. The unemployment rate falls because the credit is conditional on both partners working. Hence, the credit encourages unemployed males and females to search for work and accept jobs. This improves the efficiency of job matching and reduces unemployment. Overall, aggregate employment rises by 0.4 percent. We conclude that selective tax relief for the elastic group of secondary earners has the potential to raise labor-market participation, both in terms of persons and in terms of total labor hours. It comes at the expense of a lower disposable income for single-earner couples. The income ratio between high-skilled and low-skilled workers does not change, on average.

Individualization of the general tax credit raises the tax burden on single-earner couples, while it reduces it on other households. Accordingly, the ratio of net income for single-earner couples and two-earner couples falls by 5.5 percent. Singles and primary earners substitute consumption for leisure and raise labor supply due to a lower marginal tax burden. Secondary earners respond more. Table 18.3 shows that the female participation rate increases by 9.5 percent while hours worked expands by 4.8 percent. The reason is that the substantial increase in the after-tax income difference between one-earner and two-earner couples makes it attractive for partners to enter the labor market. These partners primarily occupy part-time jobs. As the replacement rate remains virtually

---

[8]This reform will reduce the net social minimum income in the Netherlands for couples. A number of social benefits are indexed by this level of social minimum. To prevent this, we raise the gross social minimum to compensate for this effect of the reform.

unchanged and marginal tax rates fall, there is a small upward effect on wages, which exacerbates the imperfections in the right-to-manage model. This raises equilibrium unemployment. Overall, we find an expansion of total employment by 1.2 percent. Individualizing the Dutch tax system will thus raise employment. It comes at the expense of single-earner families, especially those with low skills. In that respect, the reform does not fully escape the equity-efficiency trade-off.

In-Work Tax Credits

We simulate seven alternative in-work tax credits in the Netherlands. They differ with respect to the phase-in range, the flat range and the phase-out range. Each credit costs 2.5 billion euro ex-ante. The government budget is closed by means of an increase in the income tax rates by approximately 1 percentage point. The reforms thus make the tax system more progressive. The different designs of the credit are illustrated in panel 1 of Table 18.4. The first credit is a fixed amount of €360 for each worker. The other credits feature a phase-in range between an annual earned income of €8,000 and €16,000. The second credit of €390 features no phase-out range. Other credits differ with respect to their flat and phase-out ranges. The third and fourth credits are very much targeted on low incomes: they feature no flat range and are rapidly phased out with annual incomes between €16,000 and €20,000 or €24,000. The last three credits feature a flat range and a phase-out range for successively higher annual incomes.

Table 18.4 reveals that all in-work tax credits reduce inequality. This is reflected in a smaller ratio of high-skilled and low-skilled labor income. The reason is that the value of a credit is fixed for all eligible workers. The higher tax rate, in contrast, hurts higher incomes more than lower incomes. Therefore, even the fixed in-work tax credit shifts the tax burden from low to high incomes. Targeted credits that only apply to people collecting lower incomes reduce inequality much more.

In-work tax credits reduce the replacement rate because only workers are eligible, not social benefit recipients. The latter group actually faces a decline in income due to higher income tax rates. Hence, the incomes between people inside and outside the labor market becomes more dispersed.

The marginal tax burden rises for two reasons. First, higher tax rates are necessary to finance the in-work tax credit. Second, marginal tax rates rise in the phase-out range of the credit. Yet, the

TABLE 18.4

Effects of In-Work Tax Credits, Financed by Higher Income Tax Rates *(Percent changes unless indicated)*

1. Design of the Credit							
Credit	€360	€390	€2,600	€1,800	€1,600	€800	€-560
Phase-In Range (€1,000)	—	8 – 16	8 – 16	8 – 16	8 – 16	8 – 16	8 – 16
Flat Range (€1,000)	0 – ∞	16 – ∞	—	—	16 – 20	16 – 24	16 – 32
Phase-Out Range (€1,000)	—	—	16 – 20	16 – 24	20 – 24	24 – 32	32 – 40
2. Effects on Distribution							
Ratio High Skilled/Low Skilled	−0.7	−0.5	−2.1	−2.2	−2.5	−1.6	−1.0
Mean of Marginal Tax Burdens (abs. dif.)	0.6	0.4	2.9	1.7	2.3	1.8	1.1
Mean of Replacement Rate (abs. dif.)	−0.8	−0.8	−0.1	−0.2	−0.1	−0.5	−0.7
3. Labor Market Effects							
Labor Supply in Hours	−0.2	0.1	−1.2	−0.9	−0.7	−0.4	−0.2
Primary Earners	−0.2	−0.2	−0.8	−0.7	−0.6	−0.5	−0.5
Secondary Earners	0.5	0.4	0.4	0.1	−0.2	0.1	0.6
Single Persons	−0.5	0.2	−2.6	−1.7	−1.0	−0.4	−0.1
Female Participation Rate	1.5	0.3	3.6	2.4	1.4	1.1	0.6
Aggregate Employment	0.1	0.5	−1.0	−0.6	−0.3	0.0	0.3
Unemployment Rate (abs. dif.)	−0.27	−0.27	−0.37	−0.34	−0.32	−0.35	−0.31
Low Skilled (abs. dif.)	−0.6	−0.6	−0.9	−0.7	−0.6	−0.7	−0.6
High Skilled (abs. dif.)	−0.2	−0.2	−0.2	−0.2	−0.3	−0.3	−0.3

Source: MIMIC simulations.

marginal tax in the phase-in range declines. On balance, the marginal tax burden rises for the majority of workers, especially under the targeted credits.

The simulations reveal that the unemployment rate falls by between 0.27 percent and 0.37 percent, depending on the precise design of the credit. The lower replacement rate encourages the unemployed to search for work and to accept jobs, thereby improving matching efficiency and reducing frictional unemployment. Moreover, the lower replacement rate, together with the higher marginal tax burden, moderates wage demands by trade unions. This further reduces unemployment. The decline in unemployment is concentrated among the low skilled, especially under the more targeted credits. This is caused by the positive interaction between the replacement rate and the unemployment rate in the wage equation (18.1). It implies that the reduction in the replacement rate for low-skilled workers causes a relatively strong reduction in wages and, therefore, in the unemployment rate.

In-work tax credits stimulate the participation of secondary earners. Indeed, non-participating partners find it more attractive to participate in part-time jobs. This is reflected in the positive effect on the female participation rate in Table 18.4: it rises by between 0.3 percent and 3.6 percent. Credits that reduce the marginal burden in the phase-in range may further encourage female labor supply by reducing the marginal tax burden on small part-time jobs.

Others, like primary earners and singles, reduce their hours worked as higher marginal taxes induce substitution into leisure. Labor supply of primary earners falls between 0.2 and 0.8 percent. Labor supply of singles falls in most simulations, especially when the most targeted credits are introduced with rapid phase-out ranges. The reason is that the population of singles in the Netherlands is dense in the range between €16,000 and €20,000. Hence, distortions imposed by marginal tax rates in this range are large. A more gradual phasing out of the credit at higher incomes mitigates the adverse labor supply effects on singles.

The labor supply effect for secondary earners is the balance of positive participation effects (and hours effects for partners in the phase-in range) and negative hours effects for partners in the phase-out range. On balance, secondary workers increase labor supply with most credits. If the credit is phased out between €16,000 and €32,000, however, the negative effect on hours worked dominates. Overall, Table 18.4 shows that aggregate labor supply drops in most reforms, but not all. For the credit of €390 with a phase-in range but no phase-out, aggregate labor supply expands by 0.1 percent. Other credits reduce labor supply by between 0.2 percent when least targeted to 1.2 percent when most targeted.

Our simulations thus reveal that in-work tax credits for low labor incomes are effective to raise participation at the extensive margin of labor supply. Thereby, more targeting reinforces the positive impact at the participation margin, that is, in reducing unemployment and raising the female participation rate. However, targeted in-work credits also cause larger disincentives to work longer hours as they increase marginal tax rates elsewhere. Hence, we face a trade-off between stimulating participation at the extensive margin and encouraging hours worked at the intensive margin of labor supply. It appears that phasing out just above the minimum wage is counterproductive in the Netherlands since it induces large adverse labor supply effects on singles who often occupy part-time jobs. Phasing out higher in the income distribution is less distortionary. On balance, selective in-work tax credits can then raise aggregate employment. Depending on their design, in-work tax credits thus have the potential to improve the equity-efficiency trade off.

CONCLUSIONS

This chapter explores reforms in the tax-benefit system with the potential to improve the equity-efficiency trade-off. Optimal tax theory provides guidance to this. In particular, efficient redistribution calls for low marginal tax rates at decision margins that are relatively elastic and where population densities are high. We identify reforms in the Dutch tax-benefit system that meet these conditions by using an applied general equilibrium model for the Netherlands. In the model various decision margins and population densities are calibrated.

We find that flat tax reforms do not raise employment if aggregate income inequality is maintained. If a flat tax is combined with a basic income, it can remove the poverty trap and reduces low-skilled unemployment. However, it hurts overall labor-market performance by reducing labor supply. Hence, a high marginal tax rate at the bottom seems an inevitable consequence of efficient redistribution: it comes along with the lowest possible efficiency cost associated with fiscal policy to reduce inequality.

Shifting the tax burden away from elastic secondary earners may help to raise aggregate employment levels. In case of the Netherlands—which features a high share of part-time work—this may be achieved by a progressive tax rate structure, a completion of the individualization of the income tax, and an extension of selective in-work tax credits for secondary earners.

Reforms that reduce the tax burden at the extensive margin of labor supply also have the potential to raise employment. In-work tax credits for low incomes may reduce involuntary unemployment and boost female labor-market participation rates. The risk of these credits is, however, to exacerbate distortions at the intensive margin of labor supply, which can more than offset the positive participation effects of the marginal tax rate increases for the densely populated groups. We find that phasing out in-work tax credits just above the minimum wage (where density is high in the Netherlands) reinforces these adverse labor-supply distortions and renders the system less efficient.

REFERENCES

Apps, P., and R. Rees. 2003. "The Taxation of Couples." Unpublished, University of Munich.

Atkinson, A. B. 1995. *Public Economics in Action: the Basic Income/Flat Tax Proposal*. Oxford: Clarendon Press.

Blanchflower, D. G., and A. J. Oswald. 2005. "The Wage Curve Reloaded." IZA Discussion Paper No. 1665, Institute for the Study of Labor, Bonn.

Blundell, R., A. Duncan, J. McCrae, and C. Meghir. 2000. "The Labour Market Impact of the Working Families' Tax Credit." *Fiscal Studies* 21 (1): 75–104.

Boone, J., and A. L. Bovenberg. 2004. "The Optimal Taxation of Unskilled Labor with Job Search and Social Assistance." *Journal of Public Economics* 88 (11): 2227–58.

Boskin, M., and E. Sheshinski. 1983. "Optimal Tax Treatment of the Family: Married Couples." *Journal of Public Economics* 20 (3): 281–97.

Bovenberg, A. L., J. J. Graafland, and R. A. de Mooij. 2000. "Tax Reform and the Dutch Labor Market: An Applied General Equilibrium Approach." *Journal of Public Economics* 78 (1–2): 193–214.

Chirinko, R .S. 2002. "Corporate Taxation, Capital Formation, and the Substitution Elasticity between Labor and Capital." CESifo Working Paper No. 707.

Diamond, P. A. 1998. "Optimal Income Taxation: An Example with a U-Shaped Pattern of Optimal Marginal Tax Rates." *American Economic Review* 88 (1): 83–95.

Eissa, N., and J. B. Liebman. 1996. "Labor Supply Response to the Earned Income Tax Credit." *Quarterly Journal of Economics* 111 (2): 605–37.

Evers, M., R. A. de Mooij, and D. J. van Vuuren. 2005. "What Explains the Variation in Estimates of Labour Supply Elasticities?" CPB Discussion Paper 51, The Hague.

Graafland, J. J., R. A. de Mooij, A. G. H. Nibbelink, and A. Nieuwenhuis. 2001. *MIMICing Tax Policies and the Labour Market*. Contributions to Economic Analysis 251. Amsterdam: North Holland.

Graafland, J. J., and F. H. Huizinga. 1999. "Taxes and Benefits in a Non-Linear Wage Equation." *De Economist* 147 (1): 39–54.

Graafland, J. J., and M. H. C. Lever. 1996. "Internal and External Forces in Sectoral Wage Formation: Evidence from the Netherlands." *Oxford Bulletin of Economics and Statistics* 58 (2): 241–52.

Keane, M., and R. Moffitt. 1996. "A Structural Model of Multiple Welfare Program Participation and Labour Supply." *International Economic Review* 39 (3): 553–89.

Keen, M., Y. Kim, and R. Varsano. 2006. "The 'Flat Tax(es)': Principles and Evidence." IMF Working Paper No. 06/218, International Monetary Fund, Washington.

Kleven, H. J., C. T. Kreiner, and E. Saez. 2006. "The Optimal Taxation of Couples." NBER Working Paper No. 12685, National Bureau of Economic Research, Cambridge, Massachusetts.

Meyer, B. D. 2002. "Labor Supply at the Extensive and Intensive Margins: The EITC, Welfare, and Hours Worked." *American Economic Review* 92 (May): 373–79.

———, and D. T. Rosenbaum. 2001. "Welfare, the Earned Income Tax Credit, and the Labor Supply of Single Mothers." *Quarterly Journal of Economics* 116 (3): 1063–114.

Mirrlees, J. A. 1971. "An Exploration in the Theory of Optimum Income Taxation." *Review of Economic Studies* 38 (2): 175–208.

Prescott, E. C. 2004. "Why Do Americans Work So Much More than Europeans?" NBER Working Paper No. 10316, National Bureau of Economic Research, Cambridge, Massachusetts.

Rosen, H. 1977. "Is It Time to Abandon Joint Filing?" *National Tax Journal* 30 (4): 423–28.

Saez, E. 2001. "Using Elasticities to Derive Optimal Income Tax Rates." *Review of Economic Studies* 68 (234): 205–30.

———. 2002. "Optimal Income Transfer Programs: Intensive Versus Extensive Labor Supply Responses." *Quarterly Journal of Economics* 117 (3): 1039–73.

Seade, J. K. 1977. "On the Shape of the Optimal Tax Schedules." *Journal of Public Economics* 7 (2): 203–35.

———. 1982. "On the Sign of the Optimum Marginal Income Tax." *Review of Economic Studies* 49 (4): 637–43.

Sorensen, P. B. 2007. "The Theory of Optimal Taxation: What Is the Policy Relevance? *International Tax and Public Finance* 14 (4): 383–406.

Tuomala, M. 1990. *Optimal Income Tax and Redistribution*. Oxford: Clarendon Press.

CHAPTER 19

Growing (Un)equal: Fiscal Policy and Income Inequality in China and BRIC+

SERHAN CEVIK AND CAROLINA CORREA-CARO

INTRODUCTION

China provides an important case for analyzing the long-term evolution of household income inequality. Since the first wave of economic liberalization in the late 1970s, China has grown at an astonishing rate of almost 10 percent per year, raising 660 million people out of poverty. Per capita income increased from $320 in 1980 to about $5,500 in 2012, and the number of people living on less than $1.25 a day declined from 85 percent of the population in 1980 to 11 percent by 2012, according to the World Bank's World Development Indicators database. But the fruits of the transition from a system of centrally planned socialism to a market-oriented economy are not being widely shared across the society. Income inequality—as measured by the Gini coefficient for pretax market income—has exhibited an increasing trend from 0.28 in 1980 to 0.44 in 2000 and 0.52 by 2013. Income inequality also varies significantly within China at the regional level. This widening in the gap between rich and poor demonstrates China's transition from a relatively egalitarian society to one of the most unequal countries in the world.[1]

The sharp increase in income inequality since 1985 appears to be a result of China's investment- and export-led development model.[2] The growth incidence curve—the extent to which each quintile of households benefits from growth in real terms—shows a cumulative increase of 331 percent for the lowest income quintile between 1980 and 2012, but 1,042 percent for the highest income quintile. As a result, the top quintile now captures 47 percent of total income (up from 38 percent in 1980), whereas the lowest quintile accounts for only 4.7 percent (down from 8.7 percent).[3] In other words, China's widening income inequality is largely a reflection of faster income growth among the rich rather than stagnant living standards among the poor. Reforms to the Chinese economy (*gaige kaifang*) started in 1978 by decollectivizing agricultural land and allocating it to individual households and then expanded in the early 1980s to industrial development in coastal urban areas with greater openness to international trade and finance. This reform strategy ultimately aimed for high aggregate growth rates at the expense of an increase in income inequality.[4]

This paper benefited from helpful comments and suggestions by Santiago Acosta-Ormaechea, Andrew Berg, Benedict Clements, Mark De Broeck, Maura Francese, Sanjeev Gupta, Takuji Komatsuzaki, Bin Grace Li, Leandro Medina, Philippe Wingender, and participants at a seminar at the Fiscal Affairs Department of the International Monetary Fund.
[1] There are various methods of estimating the Gini coefficient, resulting in significant differences. For example, the China Household Finance Survey conducted by Texas A&M University and Southwestern University of Finance and Economics in Chengdu estimated that the overall Gini coefficient was 0.61 in 2010.

[2] Lee, Syed, and Wang (2013) provide a detailed account of China's development model and its potential effects on income distribution.

[3] According to the Chinese Family Panel Studies, conducted by Peking University and covering 14,960 households in five province-level areas, the top 5 percent bracket earned 23 percent of total household income, whereas the households in the lowest 5 percent bracket accounted for just 0.1 percent of total income.

[4] At the beginning of gaige kaifang, Deng Xiaoping's popular slogan was "We should let some people get rich first, both in the countryside and in the urban areas" (Shawki 1997).

However, mounting evidence suggests that income disparities become detrimental to economic growth in the long term, with significant social consequences, especially in a country like China, which is aiming to move beyond its "middle-income" status. Berg and Ostry (2011), among others, show that income inequality is a key determinant of the pace and sustainability of economic growth, even after taking into account other economic and institutional factors.

Income distribution depends on a complex array of factors, including the design of fiscal policy instruments. According to the Standardized World Income Inequality Database (SWIID), the *market-income* Gini coefficient (before taxes and transfers) in China increased by 82 percent between 1980 and 2013, whereas the *net* Gini coefficient (after taxes and transfers) increased by 90 percent (Figure 19.1). This difference indicates that the redistributive impact of fiscal policy is eroding. Fiscal redistribution—defined as the difference between market-income and net Gini coefficients—amounted to an average of 1.7 Gini-index points in the 1990s, but it turned negative during the period 2000–13, averaging –1.1 Gini-index points. Fiscal policy, however, can matter not just for redistribution, but also for market-income inequality. Redistribution is, of course, a function of the level and composition of taxation and spending as well as their distribution across income groups. The distribution of taxes in China, for example, remains regressive, with taxes accounting for 10.8 percent of annual income among the bottom decile of households (and 13.3 percent among the bottom 5 percent) compared with 8.7 percent among the top decile of households.

The aim of this chapter is to isolate the distributional effects of fiscal policy in China during the period 1980–2013. The empirical objective is to identify the proximate determinants of income inequality, with a focus on the distributional effects of fiscal policy. From an econometric point of view, there are two significant challenges. First, potential endogeneity (or reverse causality) between inequality and growth is a problem. Second, time-series analysis based on a small sample may degrade the quality of the estimations and result in misleading conclusions. To deal with the potential endogeneity of economic growth to income inequality, the analysis uses the number of international tourist arrivals as an instrumental variable (IV) for real GDP per capita and uses the IV estimation via the two-stage least squares and the generalized method of moments (GMM) estimators. To overcome the data constraint of a time-series approach in a single-country case, this investigation undertakes a panel data analysis of income inequality for BRIC+ countries (Brazil, Russia, India, and China, plus 30 other emerging market economies) using the IV-GMM estimator. This approach allows for a more vigorous empirical analysis, including a broader set of explanatory variables.

The empirical results support the hypothesis of an inverted U-shaped relationship between income inequality and growth. For China, government spending and taxation are found to have opposing effects on income inequality in the short term as well as in the long term. Whereas government spending appears to be associated with worsening income inequality, taxation improves the distribution of household income. The results of the panel data analysis of the BRIC+ countries are broadly consistent with the China-specific findings, with one important exception. Both government spending and taxation have the desired redistributive effect, but it is statistically insignificant. Although the redistributive impact of fiscal policy in China appears to be stronger, the combined effect is still not sufficient to compensate for the adverse impact of other influential factors identified in the analysis.

Appropriate fiscal redistribution can bring about balanced and sustainable growth by reducing net income inequality.[5] The empirical findings presented in this chapter have important policy implications. Fiscal policy in China and in BRIC+ countries can be redesigned to foster inclusive

---

[5] Ostry, Berg, and Tsangarides (2014) find that lower net income inequality is robustly correlated with faster and more durable growth.

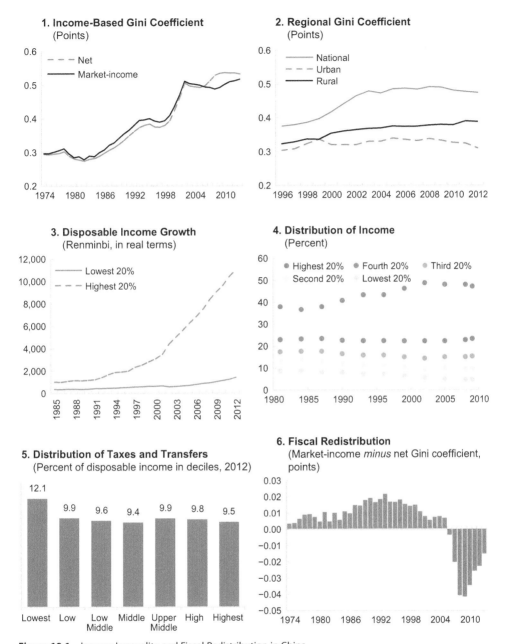

Figure 19.1   Income Inequality and Fiscal Redistribution in China

Sources: Standardized World Income Inequality Database (panel 1); OECD Economic Surveys, China, 2013 (panel 2); CEIC China database (panel 3); World Bank, World Development Indicators database (panel 4); National Bureau of Statistics (panel 5); Standardized World Income Inequality Database and authors' calculations (panel 6).

growth and to reverse the pattern of widening income inequality without undermining fiscal sustainability and causing distortions and efficiency losses. First, the tax base needs to be broadened and the tax system made more progressive with a shift from indirect to direct taxation to help narrow income inequality. Second, there is great scope for improving progressivity through well-targeted spending programs that champion greater access for the poor to education, health care, and other social services, particularly in rural areas, which account for more than 95 percent of poor households in China.

The remainder of this chapter is organized as follows: First, China's experience is put in a comparative perspective. A brief overview of the literature on income inequality is then provided, followed by an outline of China's fiscal policy space. The data sources and the salient features of this chapter's empirical strategy are then described. The econometric results are presented, followed by concluding remarks that focus on broad fiscal policy implications.

CHINA'S EXPERIENCE IN THE GLOBAL CONTEXT

How does China's experience look from a comparative perspective? Across the world, intracountry income inequality has widened since the 1980s to levels unprecedented in the postwar period, with some exceptions in Latin America and sub-Saharan Africa (Figure 19.2). The gap between rich and poor

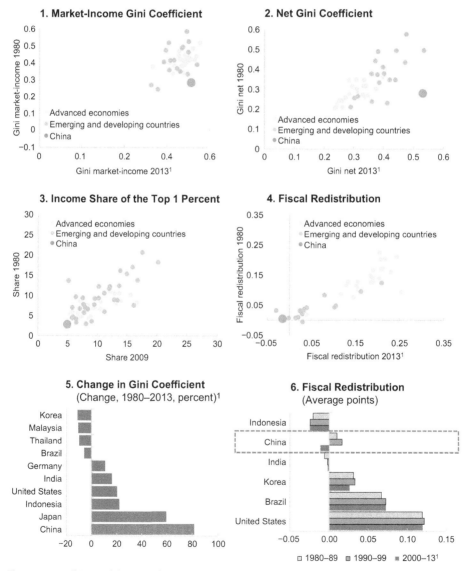

Figure 19.2 China and the Rest of the World

Sources: Standardized World Income Inequality Database and authors' calculations.
[1] Or latest data point available between 2009 and 2013.

households within countries has widened despite a significant degree of convergence in per capita income levels between countries. The unweighted world average market Gini coefficient increased from 0.41 in the 1980s to 0.43 by 2007 and, after the recent global crisis, to 0.45 in 2013. Even after accounting for taxes and social transfers, income inequality followed a similar widening trend, with the unweighted "world average" net Gini coefficient increasing from 0.36 in the 1980s to 0.38 by 2013.

These averages, however, mask significant differences in inequality across countries and over time. They reflect country-specific demographic, institutional, and economic characteristics and varying degrees of progressivity in taxation and expenditure policies. At one end of the spectrum are countries such as Bulgaria and Belgium with traditionally low levels of income inequality. At the other end are countries such as Kenya and Indonesia with income inequality significantly above the average. Within this global context, although having achieved an exceptionally high rate of economic growth and remarkable progress in poverty reduction, China has recorded a significant deterioration in income inequality, with the market and net Gini coefficients rising from an average of 0.30 and 0.29 in the 1980s, respectively, to 0.52 and 0.53 by 2013. Similarly, the income share of the top 1 percent of households in China increased from 2.8 percent in 1980 to 4.9 percent in 2009. This ratio is relatively low compared with that in many other countries (such as 7.2 percent in Korea and 19 percent in the United States), but it is still significantly higher than the total income share of the lowest quintile of households in China.

Fiscal policy has contributed to changes in income inequality in most countries. On average, the decrease in income inequality brought about by tax and transfer policies was greater in economies with higher inequality of pretax income. The redistributive effect of fiscal policy, as measured by the difference between market and net Gini coefficients, diminished from an unweighted world average of 7.1 Gini-index points in the 1980s to 6.3 Gini-index points in the 1990s, but recovered to an average of 6.9 Gini-index points in the 2000s. Against this global background, fiscal policy in China has been much less effective at decreasing income inequality. The extent of fiscal redistribution declined from an average of 1 Gini-index point in the 1980s and 1.7 Gini-index points in the 1990s to −1.1 Gini-index points during the period 2000–13.

AN OVERVIEW OF THE LITERATURE

There is a vast literature on income inequality, but most of these studies focus on the relationship between income inequality and economic development. In a seminal paper, Kuznets (1955) conjectured that a country's income distribution becomes less egalitarian as its level of economic development increases, and that growth brings about more equality only after the level of income reaches a threshold. In other words, the income distribution evolves along an inverted U-shaped curve: growth results in relatively more inequality in the initial stages of economic development and greater equality at advanced stages. Greenwood and Jovanovic (1990), Banerjee and Newman (1993), Galor and Zeira (1993), Perotti (1993), and Barro (2000) find a positive correlation between growth and income inequality in a cross-section of international data. This hypothesis, however, has been challenged by other studies. Adelman and Robinson (1989), Anand and Kanbur (1993), and Ravallion (1995), among others, show that there is no empirical support for Kuznets' conjecture.

A strand of the literature has looked beyond Kuznets' hypothesis, aiming to identify the fundamental determinants of income inequality. Extensive evidence suggests that high inflation tends to depress income growth for the poor and lead to greater income inequality (Datt and Ravallion 1998; Ferreira, Leite, and Litchfield 2007). However, one of the most debated issues is the role of globalization—the increased openness to foreign trade and investment. From a theoretical point of view, the impact of trade openness on income inequality depends on factor endowments—countries with higher (lower) levels of human capital experience increases (decreases) in inequality. In the empirical literature, however, some scholars, such as Dollar and Kraay (2004), argue that globalization benefits the poor, while others, such as Barro (2000) and

Milanovic (2005) show that greater openness leads to an increase in inequality, especially in countries with higher income levels. Similarly, the relationship between foreign direct investment (FDI) and income inequality has been extensively investigated and found to be positive. While Evans and Timberlake (1980) argue that dependence on FDI tends to exacerbate income inequality by altering the occupational structure of developing economies and producing both a highly paid elite and large groups of marginalized workers, Alderson and Nielson (1999) show an inverted U-shaped relationship between income inequality and the stock of FDI per capita.

Financial development has been shown to affect the distribution of income through multiple channels. A plethora of studies show that financial development affects income equality by enhancing human capital accumulation, improving the access to capital for entrepreneurial activity, and changing the sectoral composition of employment (Beck, Demirgüç-Kunt, and Levine 2007; Demirgüç-Kunt and Levine 2009). Most of the empirical literature reaches the conclusion that financial development lowers income inequality in the long term (Galor and Zeira 1993; Banerjee and Newman 1993; Clarke, Xu, and Zou 2006), except at the very early stages of development (Greenwood and Jovanovic 1990). However, because the distribution of capital income is significantly more unequal than the distribution of labor income, the concentration of wealth could become one of the root causes of income inequality over time (McKenzie and Woodruff 2006; Rajan 2010).[6]

The literature has also focused on the relationship between demographic and social characteristics and income inequality. Population growth is found to be critical, mainly through its effect on the demographic composition. First, while an increase in the supply of unskilled young workers may depress income growth (Alderson and Nielsen 1999), an increase in the share of the population older than 65 years tends to worsen income inequality (Deaton and Paxson 1997). Second, as pointed out by Kuznets (1955), the urbanization process becomes decisive, especially in the initial stage of economic development, because the evolution from an agrarian economy to industrialization leads to significant income disparities between and within rural and urban areas. Third, education forms a vital link between the pace and quality of growth and income distribution, although the relationship is not straightforward. Although cross-country studies indicate that a higher level of educational attainment brings about greater equality in the distribution of income, the type, quality, and distribution of education result in an intricate effect on income inequality, particularly in connection with skill-biased technological change (Barro 2000; Checci 2000).

Another critical dimension of income inequality is related to the distributional effects of fiscal policy. Although fiscal policy is traditionally assigned a limited role that focuses on the provision of public goods and services and long-term fiscal sustainability without directly taking into account distributional considerations, Musgrave (1959), among others, shows that fiscal policy can have an activist role in achieving an equitable distribution of income among households. The large variation in net income inequality across countries indicates that fiscal policy can influence the distribution of income (Feenberg and Poterba 1993; Auten and Carroll 1999; Benabou 2000; Muinelo-Gallo and Roca-Sagales 2011). The key consideration is the level and progressivity of taxation and expenditure policies. Well-targeted public spending can improve income distribution by providing greater equality of access to education and health care, thereby redistributing ownership of the factors of production.[7] Taxation plays an important role in attaining greater equity in the distribution of income through the progressivity of the tax system and by generating sufficient revenues to fund

---

[6]This chapter does not explore wealth inequality because of data constraints. Cross-country data, however, indicate that wealth inequality tends to be worse than income inequality and has a significant bearing on income inequality through nonlabor income accrued to the asset-rich bracket of households. For China, available data based on the China Household Income Project surveys show that the share of asset income increased from 8 percent of total household income in 2002 to 15 percent in 2007, contributing 13–19 percent of income inequality (Li and Sicular 2014).

[7]In general, social spending such as pensions and unemployment benefits transfer resources to groups of the population who do not earn labor income and whose risk of falling into poverty would otherwise be large.

public spending on social programs. Although taxation, especially of the top earning bracket, is presented as an obstacle to growth and an ineffective tool for fiscal redistribution (Bird and Zolt 2005), Bastagli, Coady, and Gupta (2012) show that direct income taxes and cash transfer schemes reduced the average Gini coefficient by about one-third in Organisation for Economic Co-operation and Development (OECD) countries during the period 1985–2005.

In China, uneven educational attainment and large geographical disparities are shown to be the primary causes of inequality.[8] Ping (1997), Knight and Song (1999), Sicular and others (2006), and Whyte (2010) identify the rural-urban income gap—driven by a secular decline in agricultural prices and rapid urbanization—as the key determinant of income inequality. In particular, the *hukou* (household registration) system contributed to rural-urban income inequality by restricting internal migration (Herd, Koen, and Reutersward 2010). Walsh and Yu (2012) find that inflation exacerbates income inequality; Xu and Zou (2000) show that the increase in income inequality is associated with, besides high inflation, the decline in the share of state-owned enterprises and, to a lesser extent, trade openness. With regard to the relationship between financial development and income distribution in China, the empirical evidence is not conclusive. Although most studies identify an adverse effect, Deng and Su (2012) find that financial deepening contributes to income growth among the poor and thereby to reducing income inequality. Taken together, the findings in the literature suggest that income inequality in China appears to be intimately linked to the state-engineered, export-led development model that has reshaped the opportunity landscape and the rates of return on human, financial, and physical capital.

A SYNOPSIS OF CHINA'S FISCAL POLICY

China has reformed its fiscal policy framework to improve revenue collection and enhance the effectiveness of public spending. One of the key components of fiscal reform is the devolution of authority for fiscal policymaking from the central government to provincial governments, which now account for 53 percent of general government revenues and 85 percent of expenditures. Another strategic development has been the enactment of a range of tax policy and administration reforms, including the introduction of the value-added tax (VAT) regime that replaced the wholesale turnover tax. Although the VAT still suffers from a narrow tax base that is confined to goods and a few services, the system has helped remove tax-induced distortions and provided a significant and stable source of revenue.

China's tax-to-GDP ratio doubled from less than 10 percent in the early 1990s to 19 percent in 2013. It is, however, still significantly below the average of about 35 percent in the OECD countries. Furthermore, China collects more than half of its revenues from indirect taxes. Personal income taxes amount to 6 percent of total tax revenues (and 1.1 percent of GDP), whereas indirect taxes on goods and services account for more than 50 percent of total tax revenues (and about 10 percent of GDP). Even though China has a progressive personal income tax rate schedule with a top rate of 45 percent, its broad tax brackets and generous allowance schedule result in a very low ratio of personal income taxes to indirect taxes, which is a rough measure of the overall progressivity of taxation.[9]

China's government spending has grown steadily from 18 percent of GDP in 1990 to 29 percent in 2013, but it remains below the OECD average of 45 percent. Off-budget spending by local governments, however, is substantial and amounts to about 15 percent of GDP.[10] This increase in government spending is largely due to higher outlays for infrastructure investment and public administration, while social spending accounts for about 6 percent of GDP. The government has recently expanded the minimum subsistence allowance (*dibao*) system and introduced a new pension scheme in rural

---

[8] Knight (2014) provides a comprehensive overview of the literature on income inequality in China.

[9] The effective number of personal income tax payers in China is less than 3 percent of the working population.

[10] Zhang and Barnett (2014) provide an extensive analysis of off-budget activity in China.

1. General Government Gross Debt
(Percent of GDP)

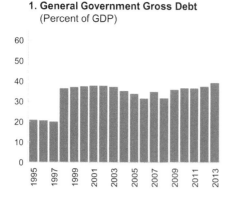

2. General Government Expenditure and Tax Revenue (Percent of GDP)

3. Extrabudgetary Expenditure and Revenue
(Percent of GDP)

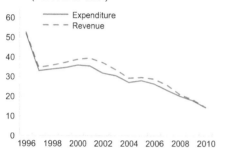

4. Fiscal Decentralization
(Percent of general government)

5. Composition of Expenditure
(Percent of total expenditure)

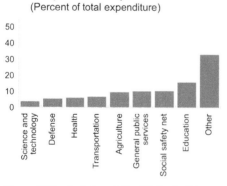

6. Composition of Taxes
(Percent of general government total taxes)

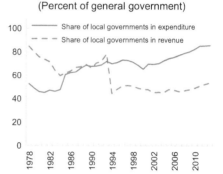

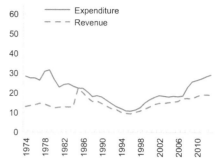

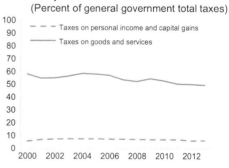

Figure 19.3   Evolution of Fiscal Policy in China

Sources: IMF, *World Economic Outlook* (panels 1, 2, and 6); National Bureau of Statistics and authors' calculations (panel 3); National Bureau of Statistics (panels 4 and 5).

areas, but these programs have limited coverage and provide a low level of income compared with what urban workers earn.[11] An additional complication is the existing system of fiscal relations between the central government and subnational governments. Although subnational governments are responsible for more than half of total spending, they have limited revenue-raising capacity and experience substantial differences in per capita allocations for basic public services (Figure 19.3).

---

[11] According to the China Household Finance Survey in 2010, retirement insurance coverage was 34.5 percent in rural areas, compared with 87 percent in urban areas; annual pension income was 12,000 yuan for rural households, compared with 33,000 yuan for urban households.

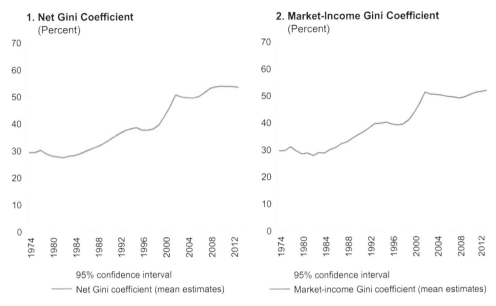

Figure 19.4 Confidence Intervals of Gini Coefficients in China

Source: Standardized World Income Inequality Database.

DATA DESCRIPTION

The empirical analysis is based on annual data spanning 1980–2013, covering a panel of 33 countries along with China. The dependent variable is income inequality as measured by the net Gini coefficients for China and the panel of BRIC+ countries, which are drawn from the SWIID, constructed by Solt (2009) using the Luxembourg Income Study as the harmonized benchmark for comparable estimates. The SWIID provides two definitions of the Gini coefficient—the first based on market income and the second net of taxes and transfers—on an annual basis, using a custom missing-data multiple-imputation algorithm to standardize observations collected from various sources.[12] The SWIID is the preferred source of data on income inequality for this analysis because it provides comparable figures across countries and for a longer span of time. Nevertheless, although these series allow for better identification of the sources of income inequality and the redistributive impact of fiscal policy, they are still subject to measurement uncertainty as depicted in Figure 19.4. This is why the analysis is limited to the *net* Gini coefficient, which describes income distribution across size-adjusted households after taxes and transfers are taken into account.

Drawing on the literature and facing data constraints, the analysis focuses on a list of key explanatory variables. In China-specific regressions, the exercise includes real GDP per capita (instrumented by the number of international tourist arrivals), tax revenues as a share of GDP, and government spending as a share of GDP as the variables of interest. In BRIC+ panel data estimations, the list of explanatory variables is broadened to include real GDP per capita (instrumented by the number of international tourist arrivals), tax revenues as a share of GDP, government spending as a share of GDP, trade openness, financial development, an index of human capital, urbanization, and old-age dependency. Economic and financial statistics are compiled from the IMF's Government Finance Statistics, International Financial Statistics, and World Economic Outlook databases; the World Bank's World Development Indicators database; and the

---

[12]The latest version (5.0) of the SWIID database is available at http://thedata.harvard.edu/dvn/dv/fsolt.

TABLE 19.1

Descriptive Statistics: China

Variable	Observations	Mean	Median	Standard Deviation	Minimum	Maximum
Net Gini Coefficient	34	40.3	37.9	9.5	27.3	53.6
Real GDP per Capita (yuan)	34	4,440.3	3,229.0	3,640.9	806.6	13,164.4
International Tourist Arrivals (millions)	34	27.8	23.3	18.2	5.7	57.7
Government Spending (percent of GDP)	34	19.4	18.4	5.2	10.7	29.1
Tax Revenue (percent GDP)	34	14.6	14.6	3.2	9.3	22.2

Source: Authors' calculations.

TABLE 19.2

Descriptive Statistics: BRIC+ Countries

Variable	Observations	Mean	Median	Standard Deviation	Minimum	Maximum
Net Gini Coefficient	1,012	40.0	40.8	9.2	19.2	62.6
Real GDP per Capita (U.S. dollars)	1,073	3,492.6	2,867.4	2,443.4	221.7	11,533.8
International Tourist Arrivals (millions)	792	6.8	3.3	8.8	0.0	57.7
Government Spending (percent of GDP)	665	28.1	26.6	9.7	0.0	55.4
Tax Revenue (percent of GDP)	563	18.5	17.9	7.9	3.9	50.0
Trade Openness (percent of GDP)	963	62.1	53.4	37.8	11.5	321.1
Domestic Credit to Private Sector (percent of GDP)	1,031	39.8	28.0	32.3	1.2	167.5
Index of Human Capital per Person	920	2.3	2.4	0.5	1.3	3.3
Urban Population (percent of total)	1,156	57.5	57.6	18.7	18.3	95.0

Source: Authors' calculations.

Note: A country is classified as BRIC+ if it belongs to the IMF's "Emerging Market and Middle-Income Economies" country group classification, which includes Algeria, Angola, Argentina, Azerbaijan, Belarus, Brazil, Chile, China, Colombia, Croatia, the Dominican Republic, Ecuador, Egypt, Hungary, India, Indonesia, Iran, Kazakhstan, Malaysia, Mexico, Morocco, Pakistan, Peru, the Philippines, Poland, Romania, Russia, South Africa, Sri Lanka, Thailand, Turkey, Ukraine, Uruguay, and Venezuela.

National Bureau of Statistics of China. Descriptive statistics for the key variables of interest are presented in Table 19.1 for China and in Table 19.2 for the panel data set for BRIC+ countries.

Before proceeding with the estimations, it is important to analyze the time-series properties of the data to avoid spurious results. The Augmented Dickey-Fuller (ADF) test is commonly used in the literature to investigate the integration order, but it may suffer from size distortions and fail to differentiate between a highly persistent stationary series and a nonstationary process. Accordingly, the Ng-Perron (Ng-P) test is also performed to ensure the robustness of the empirical results.[13] The unit-root results, available upon request, indicate that the variables used in the analysis are stationary after logarithmic transformation.

---

[13] Regarding the optimal lag order selection for the ADF test, we use the modified Schwarz information criteria. For the Ng-P test, we use the Quadratic Spectral kernel–Andrews bandwidth combination to take into account the sample characteristics such as size and possible existence of structural breaks.

EMPIRICAL STRATEGY AND RESULTS

The analysis investigates the determinants of income inequality in China, with a particular focus on the redistributive contribution of fiscal policy. In view of data constraints and the need to have sufficient degrees of freedom, only a limited number of explanatory variables can be considered in the specification. Accordingly, using the IV regression via the two-stage least squares and GMM estimators, the following equation is estimated:

$$ln(GINI_t) = \beta_0 + \beta_1 ln(GDPPC_t) + \beta_2 (ln\,GDPPC_t)^2 + \beta_3 ln(EXP_t)$$
$$+ \beta_4 ln(TAX_t) + \varepsilon_t,$$

(19.1)

in which $GINI_t$ is the net Gini coefficient at time t; β_0 is the intercept term; $GDPPC_t$ is real GDP per capita; EXP_t and TAX_t are government spending and tax revenues as a share of GDP, respectively; and ε_t is the error term.

To control for potential reverse causality, international tourist arrivals are used as an instrument for real GDP per capita. The relationship between economic growth and income inequality may exhibit contemporaneous reverse causation, given that income inequality influences the pace of growth. The challenge is to find a robust, time-varying IV, which needs to be correlated with real GDP per capita and needs to be exogenous with respect to real GDP per capita, but will have no effect on income inequality, except through its effect on per capita income. Although several empirical studies have used variations in rainfall and international commodity prices as IVs for economic growth, these may not be plausible for China and for most of the sample of BRIC+ countries. First, these countries are no longer highly dependent on the agriculture sector. Second, economic developments in these countries may likely influence the behavior of international commodity prices. As an alternative, the number of international tourist arrivals is introduced as the IV for real GDP per capita. According to the test statistics, this is a robust IV for per capita income with no direct effect on income inequality for China. However, although the number of international tourist arrivals is also a plausible IV for BRIC+ countries as a group, it should be noted that the strict exogeneity assumption may not hold in some countries where tourism plays a more significant role in economic activity.

The panel data analysis in the context of BRIC+ countries allows the analysis to overcome data constraints and include a broader set of control variables. The cross-country analysis for a panel of BRIC+ countries for the period 1980–2013 is conducted with the following specification:

$$ln(GINI_{i,t}) = \beta_0 + \beta_1 ln(GINI_{i,t-1}) + \beta_2 ln(GDPPC_{i,t}) + \beta_3 (ln\,GDPPC_{i,t})^2 + \beta_4 ln(EXP_{i,t})$$
$$+ \beta_5 ln(TAX_{i,t}) + \alpha_i X_{i,t} + \eta_i + \nu_t + \varepsilon_{i,t},$$

(19.2)

in which $GINI_{i,t}$ is the net Gini coefficient in country i at time t; $GDPPC_{i,t}$ is real GDP per capita instrumented by the number of international tourist arrivals; and $EXP_{i,t}$ and $TAX_{i,t}$ are government expenditures and tax revenues as a share of GDP, respectively. The term $X_{i,t}$ is a vector of control variables including trade openness, financial development, human capital accumulation, and urbanization. The η_i and ν_t coefficients denote country- and time-specific effects, and $\varepsilon_{i,t}$ is an idiosyncratic error term that satisfies the standard assumptions of zero mean and constant variance.

Because panel data tend to have complex error structures, standard estimation techniques are likely to yield inefficient estimates with biased standard errors. The Wooldridge-Drukker test is performed and indeed detects the presence of first-order serial correlation in the panel data used in this analysis.[14] To account for the persistence of income inequality, the IV-GMM estimator

---

[14] Implementing an idea originally proposed by Wooldridge (2002), Drukker (2003) developed an easy-to-use test for serial correlation in panel data based on the ordinary least squares residuals of the first-differenced model.

TABLE 19.3

China: Instrumental Variables Estimation		
	Log (net Gini coefficient)	
Variable	(1)	(2)
Log (real GDP per capita)	0.682***	1.396***
	(0.208)	(0.461)
Log (real GDP per capita) (squared)	−0.025*	−0.069**
	(0.013)	(0.028)
Log (government spending as percent of GDP)		0.152**
		(0.070)
Log (tax revenue as percent of GDP)		−0.085*
		(0.043)
Adjusted R^2	0.959	0.963
HAC score Chi^2	5.058*	6.197**
HAC regression F	27.084***	39.810***

Source: Authors' calculations.
Note: Real GDP per capita is instrumented using the number of international tourist arrivals. The sample period is
   1980–2013. Heteroscedasticity and autocorrelation consistent (HAC) standard errors are reported in parentheses.
*** $p < 0.01$; ** $p < 0.05$; * $p < 0.1$.

is applied in a dynamic model that includes lagged values of the dependent variable as a regressor. The GMM approach takes into account unobserved country effects and possible endogeneity of the explanatory variables, providing more robust and consistent parameter estimates. This method also allows a dynamic specification with the lagged dependent variable as an explanatory variable to be used, thereby taking into account the persistence of income inequality over time.

Instrumental Variable Models—China

Table 19.3 presents the IV estimation results for China, relating income inequality to the principal explanatory variables. Below each coefficient are reported the robust standard errors that account for heteroscedasticity and first-order autocorrelation in the error terms.[15] Model (1) regresses the net Gini coefficient on real GDP per capita—instrumented by the number of international tourist arrivals—and its square term. Model (2) incorporates government spending and taxation as a share of GDP.[16] The results indicate that an increase in per capita income leads to a worsening of income inequality, while its square term lowers inequality. The coefficients on both real GDP per capita and its square term are highly statistically significant, and support the hypothesis of the existence of a Kuznets curve—an inverted U-shaped relationship between income inequality and economic development.

Government spending is found to be a statistically significant factor with a worsening effect on the distribution of household income. This outcome reflects the fact that government spending in China is low and dominated by infrastructure investment and public administration.

[15] The results presented in Table 19.3 are based on the two-stage least squares approach. The IV estimator using the GMM yields similar findings, which are available upon request.
[16] Although collinearity between government spending and tax revenue is a potential problem that may lead to unstable parameter estimates, collinearity diagnostics yield a variance inflation factor of 1.24, which is significantly less than the critical threshold of 10.

Conversely, taxation appears to have the desired negative coefficient and comes out to be statistically significant. This suggests that taxation has a redistributive effect in China, where the tax-to-GDP ratio almost doubled during the past two decades, even though it still remains significantly below the OECD average. The adjusted R^2 of this model is slightly higher, and the coefficients on per capita income and its square term are larger, than when the impact of economic development is considered separately.

Instrumental Variable Panel Data Analysis—BRIC+

The results of the BRIC+ panel estimations, presented in Table 19.4, are broadly consistent with the findings of the time-series analysis of China. The IV-GMM estimations indicate a high degree of persistence in income inequality. The coefficient on the lagged net Gini coefficient is positive and statistically significant across all specifications, although it becomes marginally smaller with the inclusion of other explanatory variables. The exercise finds that the level of per capita income, instrumented by the number of international tourist arrivals, widens income inequality, while its square term has a narrowing effect. Both of the estimated coefficients are statistically significant across all specifications, confirming the existence of the Kuznets curve in the BRIC+ panel. With regard to the impact of fiscal policy on inequality, the estimation finds that the coefficient on government spending has the desired negative sign, indicating that higher government spending lowers the net Gini coefficient. The magnitude of this effect, however, is small and statistically insignificant. Similarly, taxation appears to have a redistributive impact but comes out to be a statistically insignificant factor.

TABLE 19.4

BRIC+ Panel: IV-GMM Estimation

	Log (net Gini coefficient)		
Variable	(1)	(2)	(3)
Log (net Gini coefficient)$_{t-1}$	0.919***	0.874***	0.894***
	(0.010)	(0.050)	(0.031)
Log (real GDP per capita)	0.194***	0.322*	0.210***
	(0.027)	(0.177)	(0.070)
Log (real GDP per capita) (squared)	−0.013**	−0.020*	−0.014***
	(0.002)	(0.010)	(0.005)
Log (government spending as percent of GDP)		−0.009	−0.001
		(0.014)	(0.015)
Log (tax revenue as percent of GDP)		−0.004	−0.013
		(0.016)	(0.018)
Log (trade openness as percent of GDP)			−0.003
			(0.008)
Log (domestic credit to private sector as percent of GDP)			0.005
			(0.005)
Index of Human Capital per Person			−0.034
			(0.036)
Log (urban population as percent of total)			0.064
			(0.040)
Wald χ²	10,352.73***	3,429.81***	3,408.46***

Source: Authors' calculations.

Note: Real GDP per capita is instrumented using the number of international tourist arrivals. The sample period is 1980–2013. Heteroscedasticity and autocorrelation consistent standard errors are reported in parentheses.

*** $p < 0.01$; ** $p < 0.05$; * $p < 0.1$.

The empirical findings of the baseline IV-GMM model remain robust to the inclusion of various control variables. In line with the literature, the analysis finds that trade openness and human capital accumulation improve the distribution of household income in the BRIC+ panel, but the estimated coefficients do not reach the threshold of statistical significance. However, financial development has a worsening effect on income inequality, as expected, but it is statistically insignificant. The results suggest that an increase in the share of urban population worsens income distribution, but this effect is not statistically significant in the panel of BRIC+ countries.

CONCLUDING REMARKS AND POLICY ISSUES

China has made remarkable progress in reducing poverty, but this achievement has been accompanied by widening income disparities across the society. Although this situation reflects an intricate array of developments, including the country's investment- and export-led growth model as well as socioeconomic, financial, and institutional undercurrents, fiscal policy appears to have played an important role through the impact of taxes and transfers on income distribution. The market and net Gini coefficients increased by 82 percent and 90 percent, respectively, during the period 1974–2013. In other words, the egalitarian effects of fiscal policy fell from an average of 1.7 Gini-index points in the 1990s to –1.1 Gini-index points during the period 2000–13.

China's tax-to-GDP ratio has almost doubled since 1995 to 19 percent, but it remains significantly below the OECD average of about 35 percent. This low level of tax support effectively sets a limit on public expenditures, including redistributive measures. Furthermore, China's system of taxation distributes the tax burden in a regressive manner across income groups, largely because China collects more than half of its revenues from indirect taxes. Personal income taxes amount to 6 percent of total tax revenues, whereas indirect taxes on goods and services account for more than 50 percent of total tax revenues. Although China has a progressive personal income tax rate schedule with a top rate of 45 percent, its broad tax brackets and generous allowance schedule diminish the effective progressivity of the tax regime, resulting in a very low ratio of personal income taxes to indirect taxes.

Although government spending has grown from 18 percent of GDP in 1990 to 29 percent in 2013, it is still significantly below the OECD average of 45 percent. This increase in government spending is largely due to higher outlays for infrastructure investment and public administration, while social protection and health care account for only about 6 percent of GDP (compared with an average of 15 percent in OECD countries and 9 percent in upper-middle-income countries). In other words, excluding social protection and health care, China's nonredistributive government spending is comparable to that in OECD countries. Furthermore, the incidence of benefits from public services and transfers is shown to favor high-income groups in urban areas.[17] For example, the top quartile of households receives about 80 percent of pension spending, compared with only 2 percent for the bottom quartile. As a part of the "harmonious society" strategy, the government has expanded the minimum subsistence allowance system and introduced a new pension scheme in rural areas, but these programs have limited coverage and provide a low level of income compared with what urban workers receive. An additional complication is the existing system of fiscal relations between the central government and subnational governments. Although

---

[17] Using the framework of the National Transfer Accounts Project and household-level data, Shen and Lee (2014) provide an analysis of the benefit incidence of public spending across socioeconomic groups in 2009 and conclude that (1) education spending was equally distributed at the primary and secondary level, but favored high-income urban households at the tertiary level; (2) health care spending skewed toward high-income urban households; and (3) pension spending was far more favorable to high-income urban households.

subnational governments are responsible for more than half of total spending, they have limited revenue-raising capacity and experience substantial differences in per capita allocations for basic public services.

The empirical findings presented in this chapter are consistent with the stylized facts about China. First, the analysis shows that an increase in real GDP per capita—instrumented by the number of international tourist arrivals—leads to an increase in the net Gini coefficient, while its square term lowers income inequality. This confirms the existence of an inverted U-shaped relationship between income inequality and economic growth. Second, the exercise shows that government spending and taxation have opposing effects on income inequality. Whereas government spending appears to worsen inequality, taxation improves the distribution of household income. The results of the panel data analysis are broadly consistent with the findings of the time-series analysis for China, with one important exception—both government spending and taxation have the desired redistributive effect, although it is statistically insignificant. Altogether the redistributive impact of fiscal policy in China appears to be stronger than what is identified in the BRIC+ panel, the "net" effect is still not sufficient to compensate for the adverse impact of other influential factors identified in the analysis.

Fiscal policy can be redesigned to have a greater redistributive effect, especially in the long term. On the taxation front, the system needs to be broadened in a more progressive way to help narrow income inequality. The effective number of personal income tax payers is less than 3 percent of the working population, indicating a high degree of informality and tax avoidance. Strengthening tax administration and broadening the personal income tax, including capital gains—thus increasing effective taxation of the rich—and imposing VAT on services, which tend to be consumed more by the rich, would make the tax regime more progressive and also create additional fiscal space. In particular, China has room to lower high labor taxation that hurts the low- and middle-income brackets more than the rich, while increasing direct taxes on capital and wealth, especially through more effective land and property taxation. The planned extension of a recurrent property tax from pilot implementation to the rest of the country is a step in the right direction to generate additional revenues and improve the progressivity of the tax regime.

On the expenditure side, there is scope for making public spending a more effective tool by improving progressivity through well-targeted programs that champion greater access for the poor, particularly in rural areas, where more than 95 percent of poor households in China reside. To this end, given the decentralized nature of China's fiscal system, expenditure assignments need to be realigned with revenue sources across all layers of government. Expanding the social safety net, including means-tested income support to the poor and unemployment insurance, is critical, and untargeted energy subsidies, which tend to benefit the rich more than the poor, should be reduced.[18] Reforming the pension system, including redesigning the eligibility criteria for the basic retirement pension, could have a positive redistributive impact, but it needs to be accompanied by structural and parametric changes (that is, pooling of provincial-level pension funds and adjusting the retirement age and replacement rates) to ensure long-term sustainability, especially in view of China's rising old-age dependency ratio.[19]

The distributional effects of fiscal policy should be taken into account, but redistributive measures need to be consistent with the objective of fiscal sustainability. In particular, the expansion of social assistance programs needs to take into account the fiscal cost of rapid population

---

[18] As of 2011, posttax subsidies for petroleum products, electricity, natural gas, and coal accounted for more than 3.8 percent of GDP in China—almost four times the amount of health care spending.

[19] Dunaway and Arora (2007) provide an approach to strengthening the pension system and dealing with the "legacy costs" associated with the relatively more generous benefits provided under the old system.

aging. Ultimately, fiscal policy is only one aspect of an inclusive growth strategy that requires a comprehensive range of structural reforms aiming to sustain economic growth as well as to provide every segment of the society with greater access to emerging opportunities.

REFERENCES

Adelman, I., and S. Robinson. 1989. "Income Distribution and Development." In *Handbook of Development Economics*, edited by H. Chenery and T. Srinivasan. Amsterdam: North-Holland.

Alderson, A., and F. Nielsen. 1999. "Income Inequality, Development, and Dependence." *American Sociological Review* 64 (4): 606–31.

Anand, S., and S. Kanbur. 1993. "Inequality and Development: A Critique." *Journal of Development Economics* 41 (1): 19–43.

Auten, G., and R. Carroll. 1999. "The Effects of Income Taxes on Household Income." *Review of Economics and Statistics* 81 (4): 681–93.

Banerjee, A., and A. Newman. 1993. "Occupational Choice and the Process of Development." *Journal of Political Economy* 101 (2): 274–98.

Barro, R. 2000. "Inequality and Growth in a Panel of Countries." *Journal of Economic Growth* 5 (1): 5–32.

Bastagli, F., D. Coady, and S. Gupta. 2012. "Income Inequality and Fiscal Policy." IMF Staff Discussion Note No. 12/08, International Monetary Fund, Washington.

Beck, T., A. Demirgüç-Kunt, and R. Levine. 2007. "Finance, Inequality and the Poor." *Journal of Economic Growth* 12 (1): 27–49.

Benabou, R. 2000. "Unequal Societies: Income Distribution and the Social Contract." *American Economic Review* 90 (1): 96–129.

Berg, A., and J. Ostry. 2011. "Inequality and Unsustainable Growth: Two Sides of the Same Coin?" IMF Staff Discussion Note No. 11/08, International Monetary Fund, Washington.

Bird, R., and E. Zolt. 2005. "Redistribution via Taxation: The Limited Role of the Personal Income Tax in Developing Countries." *UCLA Law Review* 52: 1–71.

Checci, D. 2000. "Does Educational Achievement Help to Explain Income Inequality?" UNU-WIDER Research Paper No. 2000/208, United Nations University–World Institute for Development Economics Research, Helsinki.

Clarke, G., L. Xu, and H. Zou. 2006. "Finance and Income Inequality: What Do the Data Tell Us?" *Southern Economic Journal* 72 (3): 578–96.

Datt, G., and M. Ravallion. 1998. "Farm Productivity and Rural Poverty in India." *Journal of Development Studies* 34 (4): 62–85.

Deaton, A., and C. Paxson. 1997. "The Effects of Economic and Population Growth on National Saving and Inequality." *Demography* 34 (1): 97–114.

Demirgüç-Kunt, A., and R. Levine. 2009. "Finance and Inequality: Theory and Evidence." World Bank Policy Research Working Paper No. 4967, World Bank, Washington.

Deng, H., and J. Su. 2012. "Influence of Financial Development on the Income Distribution in China." *Social Science Letters* 1 (1): 73–79.

Dollar, D., and A. Kraay. 2004. "Trade, Growth, and Poverty." *Economic Journal* 114 (493): F22–F49.

Drukker, D. 2003. "Testing for Serial Correlation in Linear Panel-Data Models." *Stata Journal* 3 (3): 168–77.

Dunaway, S., and V. Arora. 2007. "Pension Reform in China: The Need for a New Approach." IMF Working Paper No. 07/109, International Monetary Fund, Washington.

Evans, Peter B., and Michael Timberlake. 1980. "Dependence, Inequality, and the Growth of the Tertiary: A Comparative Analysis of Less Developed Countries." *American Sociological Review* 45 (4): 531–52.

Feenberg, D., and J. Poterba. 1993. "Income Inequality and the Incomes of Very High Income Taxpayers." *Tax Policy and the Economy* 7: 145–77.

Ferreira, F., P. Leite, and J. Litchfield. 2007. "The Rise and Fall of Brazilian Inequality: 1981–2004." *Macroeconomic Dynamics* 12 (September): 199–250.

Galor, O., and J. Zeira. 1993. "Income Distribution and Macroeconomics." *Review of Economic Studies* 60 (1): 35–52.

Greenwood, J., and B. Jovanovic. 1990. "Financial Development, Growth, and the Distribution of Income." *Journal of Political Economy* 98 (5): 1076–107.

Herd, R., V. Koen, and A. Reutersward. 2010. "China's Labor Market in Transition: Job Creation, Migration and Regulation." OECD Working Paper No. 749, Organisation for Economic Co-operation and Development, Paris.

Knight, J. 2014. "Inequality in China: An Overview." *World Bank Research Observer* 29: 1–19.

———, and L. Song. 1999. *The Rural-Urban Divide: Economic Disparities and Interactions in China*. New York: Oxford University Press.

Kuznets, S. 1955. "Economic Growth and Income Inequality." *American Economic Review* 45 (1): 1–28.

Lee, I., M. Syed, and X. Wang. 2013. "Two Sides of the Same Coin? Rebalancing and Inclusive Growth in China." IMF Working Paper No. 13/185, International Monetary Fund, Washington.

Li, S., and T. Sicular. 2014. "The Distribution of Household Income in China: Inequality, Poverty and Policies." *China Quarterly* 217 (March): 1–41.

McKenzie, D., and C. Woodruff. 2006. "Do Entry Costs Provide an Empirical Basis for Poverty Traps? Evidence from Mexican Microenterprises." *Economic Development and Cultural Change* 55 (1): 3–42.

Milanovic, B. 2005. *Worlds Apart: Measuring International and Global Inequality, 1950–2000*. Princeton, New Jersey: Princeton University Press.

Muinelo-Gallo, L., and O. Roca-Sagales. 2011. "Economic Growth and Inequality: The Role of Fiscal Policies." *Australian Economic Papers* 50 (2–3): 74–97.

Musgrave, R. 1959. *The Theory of Public Finance*. New York: McGraw Hill.

Ostry, J., A. Berg, and C. Tsangarides. 2014. "Redistribution, Inequality, and Growth." IMF Staff Discussion Note No. 14/02, International Monetary Fund, Washington.

Perotti, R. 1993. "Political Equilibrium, Income Distribution and Growth." *Review of Economic Studies* 60 (4): 755–76.

Ping, Z. 1997. "Income Distribution during the Transition in China." UNU-WIDER Research Paper No. 1997/138, United Nations University-World Institute for Development Economics Research, Helsinki.

Rajan, R. 2010. *Fault Lines: How Hidden Fractures Still Threaten the World Economy*. Princeton, New Jersey: Princeton University Press.

Ravallion, M. 1995. "Growth and Poverty: Evidence for Developing Countries in the 1980s." *Economics Letters* 48 (3–4): 411–17.

Shawki, A. 1997. "China: From Mao to Deng." *International Socialist Review* 1 (Summer).

Shen, K., and S.-H. Lee. 2014. "Benefit Incidence of Public Transfers: Evidence from the People's Republic of China." ADB Working Paper No. 413, Asian Development Bank, Manila.

Sicular, T., X. Yue, B. Gustafsson, and S. Li. 2006. "The Urban-Rural Income Gap and Inequality in China." UNU-WIDER Research Paper No. 2006/135, United Nations University-World Institute for Development Economics Research, Helsinki.

Solt, F. 2009. "Standardizing the World Income Inequality Database." *Social Science Quarterly* 90 (2): 231–42.

Walsh, J., and J. Yu. 2012. "Inflation and Income Inequality: Is Food Inflation Different?" IMF Working Paper No. 12/147, International Monetary Fund, Washington.

Whyte, M. 2010. *One Country, Two Societies: Rural Urban Inequality in Contemporary China*. Cambridge, Massachusetts: Harvard University Press.

Wooldridge, J. 2002. *Econometric Analysis of Cross section and Panel Data*. Cambridge, Massachusetts: MIT Press.

Xu, L., and H. Zou. 2000. "Explaining the Changes of Income Distribution in China." *China Economic Review* 11 (2): 149–70.

Zhang, Y., and S. Barnett. 2014. "Fiscal Vulnerabilities and Risks from Local Government Finance in China." IMF Working Paper No. 14/4, International Monetary Fund, Washington.

CHAPTER 20

The Quest for the Holy Grail: Efficient and Equitable Fiscal Consolidation in India

CHADI ABDALLAH, DAVID COADY, SANJEEV GUPTA, AND EMINE HANEDAR

INTRODUCTION

The need for continued fiscal consolidation in India is widely recognized (Kelkar, Rajaraman, and Misra 2012). However, a key challenge facing Indian policymakers is how to achieve fiscal consolidation objectives without undermining growth and poverty-reduction efforts. Reflecting these concerns, various authors have emphasized that fiscal consolidation needs to be achieved through expansion of the consumption tax base and accompanied by a reallocation of public spending toward public investment and social spending (Mundle, Bhanumurthy, and Das 2011; Tapsoba 2014).

This chapter demonstrates the potential for achieving efficient and growth-friendly fiscal consolidation in India while simultaneously reinforcing efforts to alleviate poverty and reduce inequality. It shows that although higher consumption taxes result in the classical trade-off between efficient fiscal consolidation and equity objectives, this trade-off can be substantially mitigated, or even reversed, by reallocating some of the increased consumption tax revenues to finance expansion of well-targeted social spending.

The chapter is structured as follows: The next section provides a brief overview of the existing tax and transfer system in India. On the tax side, it highlights the potential for efficiently expanding the consumption tax base through the reduction of tax subsidies for consumption items with negative environmental and health externalities, that is, fuel, alcohol, and tobacco. On the spending side, it focuses on two of the key social programs in India—the Public Distribution System and the Employment Guarantee Scheme. The subsequent sections discuss the impact of tax and transfer reforms on households and how these impacts are distributed across household income groups. The analysis demonstrates how the design of taxes and transfers can generate fiscal space in support of fiscal consolidation as well as reinforce equity objectives, especially when the efficiency of social spending is further improved. The final section summarizes the main findings and concludes.

The analysis presented below is solely intended to be illustrative of the potential for designing tax and transfer reforms that can simultaneously increase fiscal space, improve the efficiency of the tax system, and contribute to lowering poverty and income inequality. In this respect, some caveats should be borne in mind. First, for the most part, the discussion abstracts from the important distinction in India between central and state revenues when analyzing taxes. Second, the choice of social programs examined in the chapter reflects as much the availability of household survey data to analyze the distributional impact of transfers as it does their relative importance in

The authors thank Volodymir Tulin, Kavita Rao, and Charan Singh for comments and suggestions on an earlier draft, and Louis Sears for excellent research assistance.

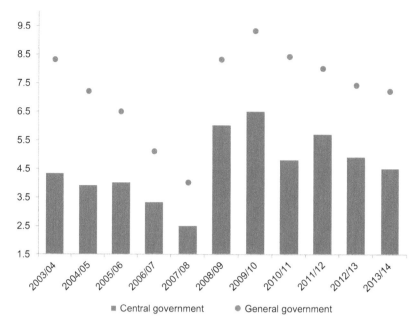

Figure 20.1 Evolution of Fiscal Deficits in India, 2003–14 *(Percent of GDP)*

Sources: IMF, Article IV Staff Reports (various years); and IMF staff calculations.

the overall social safety net. For these reasons, care needs to be taken before translating these findings into specific policy recommendations, which would also need to consider the implications for the distribution of revenues between the center and states, the importance of other important components of the safety net, and the institutional capacity to implement these reforms.

RECENT FISCAL POLICY IN INDIA

The need for fiscal consolidation has been a recurring theme in India over the last two decades. In fiscal year 2003/04, the central government fiscal deficit reached nearly 4.5 percent of GDP, and the general government deficit was almost 8.5 percent of GDP (Figure 20.1). These deficit levels prompted the government to adopt the Fiscal Responsibility and Budget Management (FRBM) Act, which set a target ceiling of 3 percent of GDP for the central government budget deficit.[1] The deficit subsequently declined, with the central government deficit falling below 2.5 percent of GDP in 2007/08.

Countercyclical fiscal policy responses aimed at mitigating the adverse impact of the global financial crisis quickly reversed the decline in the fiscal deficit. Following the implementation of fiscal stimulus measures in 2008, comprising both increases in spending and cuts in taxes, the central deficit more than doubled and reached a peak of 6.5 percent of GDP in 2009/10. Indian states, however, have had more success in containing their deficits to within the 3 percent ceiling. Although renewed fiscal consolidation efforts lowered the central deficit during subsequent years so that it reached about 4.5 percent of GDP in 2013/14, it is still well above the FRBM ceiling of 3 percent of GDP. In addition, much of the fiscal consolidation has been achieved by cutting

---

[1] States have also successfully enacted their own FRBM legislation to benefit from the "debt write-off package" that was put in place by the Twelfth Finance Commission for the period 2005/06 to 2009/10.

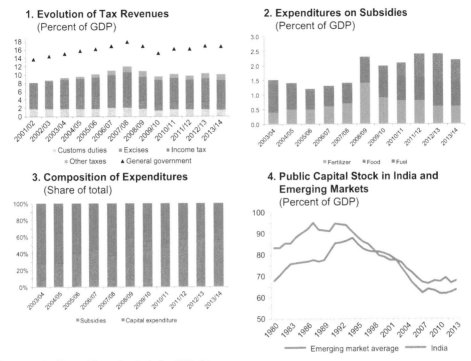

Figure 20.2 Tax and Spending in India, 2001–14

Sources: IMF, Article IV Staff Reports (various years); Fiscal Monitor database; India's Economic Survey (various years); and IMF staff calculations.

capital spending. Therefore, substantial additional fiscal consolidation is still required to attain the fiscal deficit target, create the fiscal space necessary to increase growth-enhancing public investment, and rebuild fiscal buffers.

India's tax-to-GDP ratio has been declining in recent years. After peaking at about 12 percent of GDP in 2007/08, the central government tax ratio declined to about 10 percent of GDP in 2013/14 (Figure 20.2). Although the general government tax ratio similarly declined, its upward trend was renewed beginning in 2010/11. The decline in the central government tax ratio reflects the decline in excise tax revenues, partly due to the sizable reduction in indirect tax rates as a component of the 2009/10 stimulus package. India's general government tax ratio is well below levels observed in many countries with similar levels of income.

A notable feature of India's public expenditures is the large and increasing share absorbed by subsidies and the decline in public capital spending. Spending on subsidies has increased substantially since the mid-2000s, from 1.2 percent of GDP in 2005/06 to 2.4 percent of GDP in 2012/13. This increase has been largely driven by increasing fuel subsidies, reflecting a reluctance to pass through rising international oil prices to controlled retail fuel prices (Anand and others 2014). At the same time, public capital expenditures have declined and stagnated, as reflected in a declining stock of public capital as a share of output, a fall much sharper than that observed in other emerging market economies.

SIN TAXES AND SOCIAL TRANSFERS IN INDIA

Sin Taxes in India

There is ample room in India to generate more revenue from higher taxation of consumption that generates large negative externalities. This study focuses on three such consumption items: fuel, alcohol, and tobacco.

Fuel Product Taxation

The government in India has traditionally controlled the retail prices for key fuel products: petrol, kerosene, diesel, and liquefied petroleum gas (LPG). These products are consumed directly by households for cooking, lighting, and personal transport (Anand and others 2014). They are also consumed indirectly through the use of public transportation and the consumption of other goods and services that use fuel in their production and distribution. Consumption of these fuels is widely recognized to cause considerable environmental and health damage, both locally and globally.

Reforms have recently been implemented to help reduce energy subsidies and prevent their recurrence. Gasoline and diesel prices were deregulated in 2010 and 2014, respectively, and now move in line with international prices. The excise duties on petrol and diesel have been raised on four occasions (most recently in January 2015). The formula for fixing the price of natural gas has also been revised and gas prices have been raised with a provision to revise prices every six months. LPG subsidies have been reduced and fixed on a per cylinder basis. In January 2015, the government also relaunched the modified Direct Benefit Transfer Scheme in LPG, which covers all 676 districts of the country.

However, energy prices are still substantially below levels that would fully internalize their associated negative externalities. For example, based on estimates provided by Parry and others (2014), the optimal corrective (or "Pigouvian") taxes for diesel and gasoline in India are 36 rupees (Rs) and Rs 50 per liter, respectively, both of which are substantially above the currently prevailing levels. The drop in international oil prices in 2014–15 presents an opportunity to increase fuel taxation levels to generate additional indirect tax revenues and to raise the overall tax ratio. At domestic international prices as of mid-2015, eliminating tax subsidies (including levying Pigouvian taxes) on diesel and gasoline would require almost a doubling of the tax on gasoline and a more than fivefold increase in the diesel tax, resulting in approximately a doubling of both of their domestic retail prices.

Although increasing fuel taxation is an efficient way of generating additional tax revenues, the resulting higher prices will have an adverse impact on households, including poor households. The magnitude of this impact, as well as how it varies across income groups, will depend on the importance of these consumption items in household budgets. On average, households in India spend about 3.8 percent of their total consumption on direct consumption of these fuel products, ranging from 2.1 percent for the poorest income decile to 6.7 percent for the richest decile (Table 20.1)—these budget shares also represent the percentage decrease in real incomes from a doubling of retail prices, absent any demand response. The relatively large budget share for the highest income groups reflects the relatively high share of total spending they allocate to transport

TABLE 20.1

Household Budget Shares for Fuel Products *(Percent of total household consumption)*

Decile	Kerosene	LPG	Petrol	Diesel	Total
1	1.54	0.37	0.15	0.02	2.08
2	1.24	0.63	0.39	0.01	2.28
3	1.17	0.69	0.49	0.02	2.37
4	1.05	0.90	0.78	0.02	2.75
5	0.92	1.13	0.96	0.03	3.04
6	0.80	1.38	1.39	0.04	3.62
7	0.72	1.57	1.94	0.07	4.31
8	0.59	1.88	2.60	0.10	5.17
9	0.47	2.08	3.25	0.16	5.97
10	0.24	1.72	4.33	0.40	6.70
Total	**0.88**	**1.24**	**1.63**	**0.09**	**3.83**

Source: IMF staff estimates based on the 2011/12 Indian National Sample Survey.
Note: Kerosene consumption includes purchases from Fair Price Shops and from the open market. LPG = liquefied petroleum gas.

fuels (that is, diesel and petrol) as well as to LPG for cooking. Kerosene, in contrast, absorbs a relatively higher share of expenditures for low-income households. The impact of fuel price increases will be substantially higher if the indirect impact of higher prices for other goods and services due to higher fuel and distribution costs are included. Typically the indirect impact accounts for more than half of the total impact on households, with the percentage impact being similar across income groups (see Chapter 14).

Alcohol and Tobacco Taxation

The taxation of alcohol and tobacco differs according to the level of government responsible for determining rates and collecting revenues.[2] Alcohol is subject to taxation at the state level with an excise duty typically levied at a rate of 10.3 percent.[3] In addition, some states levy sales taxes on both the intrastate and interstate sale of alcohol. For tobacco, the central government levies and collects a central sales tax. In addition, states impose sales taxes on tobacco products, and some have also experimented with imposing penalty tax rates (for example, 67 percent in Rajasthan).

Smoking is a key driver of the recent dramatic rise in annual deaths from noncommunicable diseases in low- and middle-income countries, and the age-adjusted mortality rate for these diseases is higher than in high-income countries (Jamison and others 2013). In India, one in five adult male deaths and one in twenty adult female deaths at ages 30–69 are due to smoking and this is only expected to worsen over time (Jha and others 2008). Tobacco taxation is widely viewed as the single most effective policy tool for reducing tobacco consumption (Jamison and others 2013). However, in India, the share of the retail price accounted for by excises is especially low compared with other countries of a similar level of development and is well below the 70 percent recommended target level (WHO 2013). Tax increases are also a highly cost-effective approach for reducing total alcohol consumption and the number of episodes of heavy drinking, especially in young people.[4] In addition, since smoking and drinking are often highly complementary, the public health benefits from taxing both alcohol and tobacco are magnified (Young-Wolff and others 2014).

On average, households allocate nearly 1.9 percent of total consumption expenditures to alcohol and tobacco consumption (Table 20.2). Across most income groups, consumption expenditures on tobacco exceed those on alcohol. The share of total consumption absorbed by alcohol is similar across income groups, ranging from 0.66 to 0.84 percent. However, the share of total consumption absorbed by tobacco is higher for lower-income groups, ranging from about 1.3 percent for the bottom income quintile to 0.75 percent for the top quintile.

Transfer Programs in India

India has a range of social programs aimed at supporting the income and consumption levels of lower-income households (World Bank 2011). Two of the most prominent of these programs are the Public Distribution System (PDS) and the Mahatma Gandhi National Rural Employment Guarantee Act (MGNREGA) public works program. At their peak in 2009/10 the budget cost of these programs reached around 1.2 percent of GDP (Figure 20.3).

---

[2] The Indian Constitution distributes legislative powers over taxation between the Parliament of India and the state legislatures according to three commodity lists. List I relates to commodities for which only the parliament is competent to determine tax rates; List II relates to commodities for which only the state legislatures are competent to determine tax rates; and List III relates to commodities for which both the parliament and state legislatures are competent to determine tax rates.

[3] Customs duties are levied on imported alcoholic products, but no central tax applies to domestic manufacturing and sales.

[4] The appropriate taxation of alcohol and tobacco should also take account of the existence of often very low-quality substitutes that fall outside of the tax system. To realize the revenue and health benefits of alcohol and tobacco taxation, it is important that consumption of low-quality substitutes be properly regulated.

TABLE 20.2

Household Budget Shares for Alcohol and Tobacco *(Percent of total household consumption)*

Decile	Tobacco	Alcohol	Total
1	1.27	0.78	2.05
2	1.31	0.69	1.99
3	1.29	0.68	1.97
4	1.29	0.71	2.00
5	1.24	0.71	1.95
6	1.26	0.79	2.05
7	1.17	0.84	2.01
8	1.05	0.71	1.76
9	0.94	0.73	1.67
10	0.57	0.66	1.23
Total	**1.14**	**0.73**	**1.87**

Source: IMF staff estimates based on the 2011/12 Indian National Sample Survey.
Note: The tobacco category includes bidi, cigarettes, leaf tobacco, snuff, hookah, tobacco, cheroot, zarda, kimam, surti, and other tobacco products. The alcohol category includes ganja, toddy, country liquor, beer, foreign or refined liquor or wine, and other intoxicants.

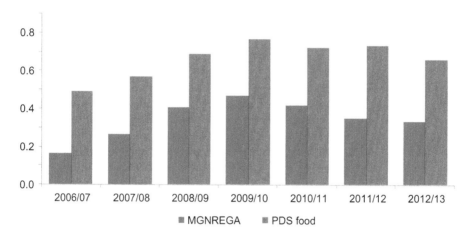

Figure 20.3   Fiscal Cost for Transfer Programs, 2006–13 *(Percent of GDP)*

Sources: Indian Institute of Management; and India's Economic Survey (various years).
Note: MGNREGA = Mahatma Gandhi National Rural Employment Guarantee Act; PDS = Public Distribution System.

Public Distribution System

The PDS has a long history. It was introduced initially in urban areas of India in the 1960s to protect consumers from food shortages and producers from price fluctuations. Since then it has gone through a number of reforms to expand coverage to rural areas and improve its performance, especially since the early 1990s. The current version of the program, the Targeted Public Distribution System (TPDS), was launched in June 1997 with a greater emphasis on providing better support to lower-income groups and increasing state-level responsibility.

The TPDS is operated under the joint responsibility of the central and the state governments. The central government, through Food Corporation of India, is responsible for the procurement, storage, transportation, and bulk allocation of food grains to state governments. States are responsible for allocation, identification of eligible families, issuance of ration cards, and supervision of Fair Price Shops. The main commodities distributed at subsidized prices under the program are wheat, rice, sugar, and kerosene.

TABLE 20.3

Targeting Performance of PDS Food Program

	Current Program			
Decile	Possession of a ration card (percent)	Coverage (percent)	Benefit level (percentage of household consumption)	Benefit share (percent)
1	85.1	74.5	60.0	17.5
2	85.9	73.4	41.2	14.2
3	85.6	76.0	33.6	12.4
4	85.9	70.2	28.9	10.2
5	88.0	69.1	25.4	10.6
6	86.0	62.5	22.4	8.8
7	86.1	61.6	19.3	8.2
8	84.7	56.8	17.1	8.1
9	81.2	49.1	12.6	6.1
10	72.8	38.2	7.3	3.8
Total	**84.1**	**63.5**	**29.6**	**100**

Source: IMF staff estimates based on the 2011/12 Indian National Sample Survey.
Note: Coverage refers to "using a card." PDS = Public Distribution System.

Eligibility for PDS food subsidies is determined by comparing monthly household income to the income level constituting the poverty line. Entitlement is based on three categories with corresponding ration cards—a below the poverty line card (BPL card), an above the poverty line card (APL card), and an Antyodaya Anna Yojana card (AAY card) introduced in 2000 to reduce hunger among the poorest segments of the BPL population. An APL card entitles a household to 15 kilograms of food grains every month, a BPL card to 35 kilograms, and an AAY card to 50 kilograms. Subsidized "issue prices" for food grains vary across states and cardholders, with the lowest prices being for AAY cardholders.

Despite reform efforts, the current PDS program suffers from poor performance in a number of respects.[5] Household data show that coverage of ration cards is very high, with 84 percent of the total population reporting having a ration card (Table 20.3); 57 percent of all cardholders have an APL card, 37 percent have a BPL card, and only 6 percent have an AAY card. However, only about two-thirds of all households report using their cards. Extensive coverage results in significant leakage of subsidy benefits to non-poor households with the top half of the income distribution receiving about one-third of all benefits. At the same time, coverage of lower-income groups is incomplete, with about one-quarter of the poorest three income deciles not purchasing subsidized items. But for those who do receive benefits, these benefits are very important; for example, the benefits are equivalent, on average, to half of total household consumption for the poorest income quintile.

Public Works (MGNREGA)

Public works programs also have a long history in India. The current public works program, MGNREGA, was enacted by parliament in September 2005 and became operational in February 2006. In an important departure from past programs, it focuses on providing a legislatively backed employment guarantee rather than the provision of rural works. It was initially rolled out in 200

---

[5] It should be noted that performance varies substantially across states as do ration prices and eligibility rules (Drèze and Khera 2013). For instance, subsidy levels (the difference between issue and market prices) are substantial in Tamil Nadu and West Bengal, but much smaller in Bihar and Arunachal Pradesh. Evaluations of the program have also found substantial illegal leakage of food from the system, including through nonexistent "ghost" beneficiaries and families with duplicate cards (World Bank 2011).

TABLE 20.4

Targeting Performance of the MGNREGA Program

	Current Program			
Decile	Rural (percent)	Coverage (percent)	Benefit level (percent of HH consumption)	Benefit share (percent)
1	85.2	33.7	16.0	12.1
2	81.7	31.0	12.2	11.6
3	82.7	29.5	11.6	12.1
4	80.5	26.9	11.0	11.8
5	80.2	25.7	9.9	11.2
6	77.1	24.9	10.1	11.8
7	72.6	23.8	9.5	11.2
8	65.9	19.4	8.5	8.7
9	55.1	16.6	7.4	6.7
10	34.9	9.8	5.2	2.8
Total	**68.8**	**24.4**	**10.8**	**100**

Source: IMF staff estimates based on the 2011/12 Employment and Unemployment Survey.
Note: MGNREGA = Mahatma Gandhi National Rural Employment Guarantee Act.

marginal districts, expanded to an additional 130 districts starting in 2007, and then finally expanded to cover the remaining districts as of April 2008. The program now covers all rural districts.

In principle, MGNREGA is a rights-based and demand-driven approach to public works provision, guaranteeing all rural households up to 100 days unskilled employment per year on public works projects, with a heavy focus on irrigation and communication activities. The work is supposed to be provided on demand, so it is self-targeted, and should be provided locally within five kilometers of one's residence. However, in practice, opening a worksite requires "enough" people expressing demand for work. Under the program, each rural household receives upon registration a free job card and has discretion as to how the 100 guaranteed days are to be distributed among the household's adult members. The job card contains photographs of all the adult household members listed on it. The holder of the card may then apply for employment, which the government is required to provide within 15 days. If the government fails to provide employment, a daily unemployment allowance is to be paid to the applicant.

Benefits under MGNREGA are paid on a piece-rate basis at the agricultural minimum wage rate, which can vary significantly across states. Wages are based on a Schedule of Rates that depends on the amount of work done by a person. Wages are paid fully in cash and are required to be directly deposited into the post office or bank account of the household. Administrative data indicate that employment generated under MGNREGA is less than the 100 day guarantee, although much higher than under past public works programs, and varies significantly across states. This variation could reflect either demand-side factors (for example, lower demand for the program in richer states) or supply-side factors (for example, limited state budgets). Program expenditures amounted to about 0.35 percent of GDP in 2012/13, with the central government bearing 90 percent of all the costs. Costs include wage disbursements (0.25 percent of GDP), as well as the cost of materials and the administrative structure (0.1 percent of GDP).

Household survey data indicate that a quarter of rural households participated in MGNREGA in 2011/12, ranging from about one-third of households in the poorest three income deciles to less than a fifth of households in the top three deciles (Table 20.4). The large coverage of higher-income groups results in substantial leakage of benefits to non-poor households, for example, the richest half of the national population receives slightly more than 40 percent of total benefits.[6] Although

---

[6]The broader performance of MGNREGA has been much debated in recent years (for example, Sheahan and others 2014; Bhagwati and Panagaryia 2014; Abreu and others 2014).

benefits are less than those received under the PDS they are still substantial, being equivalent to 10–15 percent of annual household consumption for lower-income groups. However, because participants self-select into the program, employment and income can, in principle, be received when households need them most (for example, in the agricultural off-season or after receiving an income shock) so that the program can be expected to have an important insurance value.

DISTRIBUTIONAL IMPACT OF TAX AND TRANSFER REFORMS

The above-noted taxes and programs are now used to illustrate the impact of reforms in India. This type of analysis can be extended to other taxes and programs as well. The impact of reforms and how that impact is distributed across income groups will depend on both the magnitude and composition of these reforms. These factors are discussed below, first for tax reform and transfer reform separately, and then for the two combined. Throughout the chapter the term *progressivity* is used to mean that the transfer benefit (tax burden) as a share of household total income decreases (increases) with the level of household income, and vice versa for the term *regressivity* (see Box 20.1 for more discussion).

BOX 20.1 Progressivity, Regressivity, and Targeting Effectiveness

The terms progressivity, regressivity, and targeting are used extensively in this chapter to describe the distributional impact of taxes and transfers and their reform. These terms are defined as follows:

Progressivity and Regressivity: A transfer is progressively (regressively) distributed across households if, as a share of household income, it increases (decreases) with the level of household income. Similarly, a tax is progressively (regressively) distributed across households if, as a share of household income, it decreases (increases) with the level of household income.

This definition of progressivity essentially compares the distribution of benefits and taxes with the underlying distribution of household income. For example, transfers are progressive (regressive) if the share of lower-income groups in total transfers is greater (lower) than their share in national income. For this reason, whether a tax or transfer is progressively or regressively distributed will differ across countries. For India, therefore, the reference in the chapter is taken as the distribution of income presented in Figure 20.1.1.

The term *targeting effectiveness* is intended to capture how effectively a transfer reaches the lowest income groups. For this reason, it is particularly relevant when evaluating social safety net programs that are intended to mainly benefit these groups. Targeting effectiveness is commonly evaluated by looking at the share of transfers that are received by lower-income groups (or, the corollary, the share "leaking" to higher-income groups). How well a transfer is targeted at lower-income groups is often gauged by looking at those groups' share of total benefits relative to the share of these groups in the population (Coady, Grosh, and Hoddinott 2004). The use of the population share reference reflects the idea that a universal and uniform untargeted (or randomly targeted, so-called helicopter drop) transfer program would accrue to income groups in direct proportion to their share of the population.

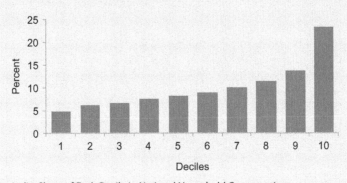

Figure 20.1.1 India: Share of Each Decile in National Household Consumption

Source: IMF staff estimates based on the 2011/12 Indian National Sample Survey.

Impact of Tax Reforms

Although decreasing tax subsidies for fuel products, alcohol, and tobacco is an efficient way of creating fiscal space, the resulting increase in consumer prices will have an adverse impact on household real incomes, including those of poor households.

The estimated impacts are based on data from the 2011/12 household survey. Therefore, for fuel products the domestic retail and international prices prevailing at the end of 2012 are used as the basis for simulating tax reforms aimed at eliminating fuel subsidies. This exercise involves increasing domestic prices to "reference" prices, defined as import prices plus distribution costs plus an element of taxation for revenue-raising purposes.[7] Raising retail prices to reference prices in 2012 is equivalent to increasing petrol prices by Rs 5 per liter (an 8 percent increase), diesel by Rs 12 per liter (a 29 percent increase), and LPG by Rs 21 per liter (a 70 percent increase). Since kerosene sold on the market is priced higher than that sold through the PDS, the required price increases differ, with PDS kerosene prices increasing by Rs 27 per liter (an increase of 181 percent) and market kerosene increasing by Rs 11 per liter (a 35 percent increase). Prices for alcohol and tobacco are both increased by 10 percent to reflect higher taxation.

The magnitude and distribution of these impacts are presented in Table 20.5. On average, fuel price increases result in a 3.5 percent decrease in household real incomes; this decline includes both the direct impact from higher prices for fuel consumed by households for cooking, lighting, and personal transport, and the indirect impacts from the pass-through of higher diesel prices to the prices of goods and services that use diesel as an input for their production and distribution. The impact is slightly regressive, ranging from 3.9 percent for the lowest income decile to 3 percent for the top decile. However, the burden share is higher for higher deciles, reflecting the underlying inequality of income; the top half of the income distribution bears about two-thirds of the total burden.

The impact of increases in alcohol and tobacco taxes by 10 percent is much smaller. For alcohol, the tax increase affects less than one-fifth of all households, and for tobacco it affects more than half of households. On average, these increases result in a less than 0.1 percent decrease in household real incomes from higher alcohol prices and a slightly more than 0.1 percent decrease from higher tobacco prices. For alcohol, the distribution of this impact is approximately neutral across income groups, so that the distribution of the total burden approximately reflects the distribution of consumption, with the top half of the income distribution bearing about two-thirds of the total burden. For tobacco, the impact is regressively distributed, ranging from 0.13 for the lowest income decile to 0.06 for the top decile, and the top half of the income distribution bears about 56 percent of the total burden.

The combined impact of all tax increases results, on average, in a 3.7 percent decrease in household real incomes. This impact is slightly regressively distributed, ranging from 4.1 percent for the lowest income decile to 3.1 percent for the highest income decile. The distribution of the overall tax burden is also concentrated among higher-income groups, with the top half of the income distribution bearing approximately two-thirds of the total burden. The tax increases result in a slight increase in the consumption Gini coefficient, from 0.355 to 0.357, and the poverty rate from 26.3 percent to 29.9 percent.

---

[7] Indeed, since 2012, increases in administered retail fuel prices and decreases in international oil prices (during the second half of 2014) have substantially decreased fuel subsidies. The simulations in the chapter are therefore intended to be illustrative of the impact of such reforms rather than to reflect the current situation in India. Currently, petrol and diesel prices are not subsidized, while kerosene and LPG prices are, although by less than in 2012. In addition, the tax component in petrol and diesel prices differs substantially from the optimal structure estimated by Parry and others (2014).

TABLE 20.5

Impact of Tax Reforms for Fuel, Alcohol, and Tobacco

Decile	Coverage (percent)	Impact (percent of HH consumption)	Burden Share (percent)	Coverage (percent)	Impact (percent of HH consumption)	Burden Share (percent)
	1. Energy subsidy reform			**2. Tobacco**		
1	100	3.93	5.4	69.8	0.13	6.5
2	100	3.59	6.4	70.2	0.13	8.2
3	100	3.50	6.7	65.6	0.13	8.6
4	100	3.51	7.7	65.0	0.13	10.0
5	100	3.50	8.3	61.9	0.12	10.1
6	100	3.53	9.2	59.3	0.13	11.0
7	100	3.54	10.4	55.6	0.12	11.1
8	100	3.57	12.1	50.4	0.10	11.7
9	100	3.52	14.0	43.8	0.09	12.1
10	100	3.02	19.9	29.5	0.06	10.7
Total	**100**	**3.52**	**100**	**57.1**	**0.11**	**100**
	3. Alcohol			**4. Total**		
1	19.7	0.08	5.2	100	4.13	5.4
2	18.8	0.07	6.0	100	3.79	6.4
3	18.3	0.07	6.4	100	3.69	6.8
4	16.5	0.07	7.7	100	3.71	7.7
5	17.6	0.07	8.0	100	3.69	8.4
6	17.6	0.08	10.3	100	3.73	9.2
7	16.7	0.08	11.5	100	3.74	10.4
8	15.9	0.07	11.3	100	3.74	12.0
9	15.4	0.07	13.5	100	3.69	13.9
10	15.3	0.07	20.0	100	3.14	19.6
Total	**17.2**	**0.07**	**100**	**100**	**3.71**	**100**

Source: IMF staff estimates based on the 2011/12 Indian National Sample Survey.

Note: Reform 1 is an increase in fuel prices to their reference levels, and its impact includes both direct and indirect effects. The price of Public Distribution System (PDS) kerosene is increased by Rs 27/liter (price gap of 181 percent), the price of non-PDS kerosene is increased by Rs 11/liter (price gap of 35 percent), the price of LPG is increased by Rs 21/liter (price gap of 70 percent), the price of petrol is increased by Rs 5/liter (price gap of 8 percent), and the price for diesel is increased by Rs 12/liter (price gap of 29 percent). Reforms 2 and 3 increase tobacco and alcohol prices by 10 percent. Coverage refers to the percentage of households affected by the reform.

Impact of Transfer Reforms

The impact of higher spending on transfer programs will depend on how these increases are designed. For food subsidies, the simulated reform involves a 20 percent increase in benefits for households holding AAY ration cards, and a 10 percent increase in benefits for both BPL and APL cardholders. For public works, the simulated reform involves increasing employment for all households that reported seeking work (whether they received it or not) to a minimum of 75 days per year.

Table 20.6 presents the impact of the increased spending on PDS food subsidies and the MGNREGA public works program, both separately and combined. The increase in food subsidies benefits nearly two-thirds of the population, with the share of households benefiting ranging from three-quarters for the lowest income decile to slightly more than one-third for the top income decile. The percentage increase in household incomes is also progressively distributed, with the increase ranging from 7.5 percent for the bottom income decile to less than 1 percent for the top decile. This progressivity also means that lower-income groups benefit most from the increased spending, with the bottom half of the income distribution receiving about two-thirds of the total increase in spending.

The increase in spending on the MGNREGA public works program benefits a much lower proportion of households, partly reflecting its rural focus. On average, about 7 percent of all households nationally benefit from increased benefits, ranging from 10 percent for the bottom

TABLE 20.6

Impact of Transfer Reforms: PDS Food Subsidies and MGNREGA

	PDS Food Program Reform			MGNREGA Program Reform			Combined	
Decile	coverage (percent)	Impact benefit (percent of HH consumption)	Impact burden share (percent)	coverage (percent)	Impact benefit (percent of HH consumption)	Impact benefit share (percent)	Impact benefit (percent of HH consumption)	Impact benefit share (percent)
1	74.5	7.5	17.7	10.2	37.1	14.0	5.3	17.8
2	73.4	4.7	14.1	9.2	27.1	12.3	3.2	13.6
3	76.0	3.8	12.4	8.3	23.7	12.1	2.7	12.4
4	70.2	3.2	10.2	9.4	23.4	12.3	2.1	10.9
5	69.1	2.8	10.6	7.8	21.0	11.5	1.9	10.7
6	62.5	2.4	8.7	7.8	20.3	11.4	1.5	9.4
7	61.6	2.1	8.2	7.2	18.6	10.6	1.3	8.8
8	56.8	1.8	8.1	5.8	16.2	7.8	1.0	7.7
9	49.1	1.3	6.1	4.5	13.1	5.7	0.6	5.6
10	38.2	0.7	3.8	3.1	9.1	2.4	0.2	3.1
Total	**63.5**	**3.4**	**100**	**7.4**	**22.8**	**100**	**1.4**	**100**

Source: IMF staff estimates based on the 2011/12 Indian National Sample Survey and the Employment Unemployment Survey.
Note: The reform consists of an increase in benefits for Antyodaya Anna Yojana cardholders of 20 percent, and for below poverty line and above poverty line cardholders of 10 percent. The MGNREGA reform involves (1) awarding employment to all those who sought it, and (2) increasing MGNREGA work days to 75 days per year (for those with fewer than 75 days). MGNREGA = Mahatma Gandhi National Rural Employment Guarantee Act; PDS = Public Distribution System.

income decile to 3 percent for the top decile. However, for those who do benefit, the impact on household incomes is much larger than is the impact of increased food subsidies, resulting, on average, in a nearly 23 percent increase in incomes for beneficiary households. In addition, the increase in benefits is progressively distributed, ranging from 37 percent for the bottom income decile to 9 percent for the top decile. As a result, the bottom half of the income distribution receives about two-thirds of the total increase in benefits.

The combined impact of the increase in spending on food subsidies and public works is also very progressively distributed. On average, the increase in spending results in a 1.4 percent increase in income for beneficiary households. This increase is progressively distributed, ranging from an increase of 5.3 percent for the bottom income decile to 0.2 percent for the top income decile. This results in the bottom half of the income distribution receiving about two-thirds of the total increase in spending. The transfers also result in a significant decrease in the consumption Gini coefficient, from 0.355 to 0.316, and the poverty rate from 26.3 percent to 7.8 percent.

Combined Impact of Tax and Transfer Reforms

The simulated increase in sin taxes for energy, alcohol, and tobacco underscores the classical trade-off between improving the efficiency of the tax system, and equity and poverty objectives. Although increasing taxes on consumption goods with negative consumption externalities provides incentives to households to better internalize the negative social effects associated with this type of consumption, the resulting impact on household incomes is regressively distributed. However, the resulting increase in tax revenues helps finance higher spending on key social programs, which disproportionately benefit lower-income groups. The net impact will depend on the relative average impact and distributional impact of taxes and transfers as well as the share of increased revenues allocated to increased social spending.

Figure 20.4 summarizes the net combined impact of the simulated tax and transfer reforms and their distribution across household income groups. On average, the tax increases result in a 3.7 percent decrease in household incomes while the increase in transfers results in a 1.4 percent increase. The difference reflects the net fiscal savings from the tax and transfer reforms, equivalent

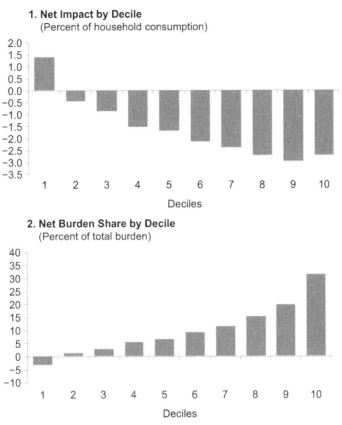

Figure 20.4 Net Impact of Combined Tax and Transfer Reforms

Source: IMF staff estimates based on the 2011/12 Indian National Sample Survey and the Employment Unemployment Survey.

to about 1.6 percent of GDP. On average, the net impact on households is a 2.3 percent decrease in income. However, this negative net impact is progressively distributed, with the percentage decrease in incomes being much higher for the top income deciles, which bear more than three-quarters of the total net burden. In fact, households in the bottom income decile are, on average, net gainers from the reforms. The reforms also decrease the consumption Gini from 0.355 to 0.317, and the poverty rate from 26.3 percent to 9.8 percent.

An unattractive feature of the simulated tax and transfer reforms is that they have a net negative impact on many poor households in the lower part of the household income distribution. This impact reflects not only the relative magnitude of the tax and transfer increases but also the inefficiency of transfer spending. Both of the transfer programs considered have substantial leakage of benefits to higher-income groups. Addressing these targeting inefficiencies can therefore help channel a greater proportion of program benefits to lower-income groups and better protect them from tax increases.

Table 20.7 shows how a more efficient transfer system can provide substantially more protection to lower-income groups. Under the simulated programs, eligibility for transfers is determined based on the commonly used approach of proxy means testing, which uses a statistical model that attaches weights to various household characteristics typically found to be highly correlated with poverty, and then calculates a score for each household reflecting its likelihood of being poor. Households are deemed eligible for cash transfers if they are among the 50 percent of households with the highest probability of being poor according to this score, and the cash transfer is set at a uniform level so as to cost exactly the same as the reform to the PDS program simulated above. A similar approach is applied to selecting rural beneficiaries of the MGNREGA, but the number of work days allowed is increased to 100 days, resulting in a slightly higher total expenditure.

The improved targeting of the transfer programs results in substantially greater protection for lower-income groups from the adverse impact of a tax increase. The more effective approach to targeting reallocates transfer program spending to lower-income groups and away from higher-income groups. This results in an increase in average household incomes in each of the bottom six income deciles, and losses for households in the top four deciles. More efficient targeting results in the bottom half of the income distribution now receiving roughly all transfers. It also results in the bottom four income deciles now being net beneficiaries from the tax and transfer reforms, while higher-income deciles are net losers.

In practice it may also be possible to improve transfer targeting even more by "tagging" benefits to demographic characteristics, such as family composition or number of family members. Under the second simulation presented in Table 20.7, a uniform transfer is given to all children under age of 16 years, starting with households with the highest probability of being poor

TABLE 20.7

Impact of Reforms for Proxy Means Targeting and Cash Transfer Programs

	1. PMT with Uniform Household Transfers			
	Cash Transfers and MGNREGA Reform		**All Reforms Combined**	
Decile	**Impact benefit (percent of HH consumption)**	**Impact benefit share (percent)**	**Impact benefit (percent of HH consumption)**	**Impact benefit share (percent)**
1	9.4	29.7	5.5	−13.8
2	9.3	36.6	5.6	−17.6
3	7.7	33.1	4.2	−14.1
4	6.8	33.0	3.2	−12.3
5	2.8	14.5	−0.8	3.4
6	1.3	7.6	−2.3	10.6
7	−0.6	−4.1	−4.3	22.0
8	−2.2	−16.5	−5.9	34.8
9	−2.1	−18.4	−5.7	39.6
10	−1.0	−15.5	−3.9	47.5
Total	**1.5**	**100**	**−1.9**	**100**
	2. PMT with Child Allowance			
	Cash Transfers and MGNREGA Reform		**All Reforms Combined**	
	Impact benefit (percent of HH consumption)	**Impact benefit share (percent)**	**Impact benefit (percent of HH consumption)**	**Impact benefit share (percent)**
1	15.4	48.1	11.5	−29.0
2	10.3	40.7	6.7	−21.2
3	6.7	28.5	3.1	−10.7
4	6.1	29.2	2.5	−9.5
5	2.3	12.0	−1.3	5.4
6	0.5	3.0	−3.1	14.3
7	−1.1	−7.3	−4.8	24.7
8	−2.6	−18.9	−6.2	37.0
9	−2.2	−19.4	−5.8	40.7
10	−1.1	−15.9	−4.0	48.2
Total	**1.5**	**100**	**−1.9**	**100**

Source: IMF staff estimates based on the 2011/12 Indian National Sample Survey and the Employment Unemployment Survey.
Note: The program allocates the same amount of total benefits as under the reform program in Table 20.6, through cash transfers based on PMT eligibility (panel 1) as well as PMT eligibility and child allowance (panel 2). The MGNREGA reform involves (1) awarding employment to all those who sought it, and (2) increasing MGNREGA work days to 100 per year (for those with fewer than 100 days). Under the proxy means test, all households with predicted consumption equal to or below the 50th percentile cutoff are eligible for benefits. MGNREGA = Mahatma Gandhi National Rural Employment Guarantee Act; PMT = proxy means test.

according to their predicted score and incorporating more households until the budget is exhausted. This method substantially increases the progressivity of the transfers and the share of benefits going to lower-income groups. As a result, it also provides even greater protection to these households against tax increases.

SUMMARY AND CONCLUSIONS

A key challenge facing policymakers in India is determining how to achieve fiscal consolidation objectives without undermining growth and poverty-reduction efforts. This chapter discusses how appropriate design of tax and transfer reforms can help achieve fiscal consolidation objectives while also creating fiscal space to finance higher growth-enhancing public investment and poverty-reducing social transfers. On the tax side, the analysis focuses on increasing consumption taxes on items that generate negative consumption externalities—fuel products, alcohol, and tobacco. On the spending side, the analysis focuses on increasing spending on two key social programs, the PDS subsidized ration program and the rural MGNREGA public works program.

The analysis clearly demonstrates the regressive impact of increasing consumption taxes. Although higher-income households bear a disproportionate share of the total additional tax burden, the impact on household income as a share of their total income is higher for the lowest-income groups. This outcome is especially true for fuel and tobacco consumption.

However, reallocating some of the fiscal resources generated by tax increases to the financing of higher social spending can significantly offset the regressive impact of higher taxes. The results demonstrate that expansion of the PDS and MGNREGA programs under existing design parameters transfers sufficient resources to lower-income households to make the net incidence of tax and transfer reforms progressive, reflecting the strong progressivity of transfers. However, even more substantial gains are possible if increased social spending can be accompanied by improved transfer targeting efficiency. Under the targeting reforms simulation, the efficiency gains are sufficient to render the lowest-income groups *net gainers* from net revenue-enhancing tax and transfer reforms.

REFERENCES

Abreu, D., P. Bardhan, M. Ghatak, A. Kotwal, D. Mookherjee, and D. Ray. 2014. "Wrong Numbers: Attack on NREGA Misleading." *Times of India*, November 9. http://timesofindia.indiatimes.com/home/sunday-times/all-that-matters/Wrong-numbers-Attack-on-NREGA-is-misleading/articleshow/45085301.cms.

Anand, R., D. Coady, A. Mohammad, V. Thakoor, and J. Walsh. 2014. "Fiscal and Welfare Effects of Fuel Subsidy Reform in India." *Economic and Political Weekly* 49 (28): 141–47.

Bhagwati, J., and A. Panagaryia. 2014. "Rural Inefficiency Act: Despite Protests about Diluting NREGA, the PM Is Right to Confine It to 200 Poorest Districts." *Times of India*, October 23. http://blogs.timesofindia.indiatimes.com/toi-edit-page/rural-inefficiency-act-despite-protests-about-diluting-nrega-the-pm-is-right-to-confine-it-to-200-poorest-districts/.

Coady, D., M. Grosh, and J. Hoddinott. 2004. "Targeting Outcomes, Redux." *World Bank Research Observer* 19 (1): 61–85.

Drèze, J., and R. Khera. 2013. "Rural Poverty and the Public Distribution System." *Economic and Political Weekly* 48 (45–46): 55–60.

Jamison, Dean T., Lawrence H. Summers, George Alleyne, Kenneth J. Arrow, Seth Berkley, Agnes Binagwaho, Flavia Bustreo, and others. 2013. "Global Health 2035: A World Converging Within a Generation." *The Lancet* 382 (9908): 1898–955.

Jha, P., B. Jacob, V. Gajalakshmi, P. C. Gupta, N. Dhingra, R. Kumar, D. N. Sinha, R. P. Dikshit, D. K. Parida, R. Kamadod, J. Boreham, and R. Peto. 2008. "A Nationally Representative Case-control Study of Smoking and Death in India." *New England Journal of Medicine* 358: 1137–47.

Kelkar, V., I. Rajaraman, and S. Misra. 2012. "Report of the Committee on Roadmap for Fiscal Consolidation." Government of India, Ministry of Finance, New Delhi.

Mundle, S., N. Bhanumurthy, and S. Das. 2011. "Fiscal Consolidation with High Growth: A Policy Simulation Model for India." *Economic Modelling* 28 (6): 2657–68.

Parry, I., D. Heine, E. Lis, and S. Li. 2014. *Getting Energy Prices Right: From Principle to Practice*. Washington: International Monetary Fund.

Sheahan, M., Y. Liu, C. Barrett, and S. Narayanan. 2014. "Preferential Resource Allocation? Mahatma Ghandi National Rural Employment Guarantee Scheme in Andhra Pradesh." Project Note 03, International Food Policy Research Institute, Washington.

Tapsoba, S. 2014. "Options and Strategies for Fiscal Consolidation in India." *Economic Modelling* 43 (December): 225–37.

World Bank. 2011. *Social Protection for a Challenging India*, Volumes I and II. Washington: World Bank.

World Health Organization. 2013. *World Health Report: Research for Universal Health Coverage*. Geneva: World Health Organization.

Young-Wolff, C., K. Kasza, A. Hyland, and S. McKee. 2014. "Increased Cigarette Tax Is Associated with Reductions in Alcohol Consumption in a Longitudinal U.S. Sample." *Alcoholism: Clinical and Experimental Research* 38: 241–48. doi: 10.1111/acer.12226.

CHAPTER 21

A Path to Equitable Fiscal Consolidation in the Republic of Congo

MAXIMILIEN QUEYRANNE, DALIA HAKURA, AND CAMERON MCLOUGHLIN

INTRODUCTION

This chapter addresses the issue of fiscal consolidation design in an oil-dependent country, the Republic of Congo, with a limited remaining lifetime of oil reserves and high income inequality and poverty. The scarcity of statistical data makes the analysis, as well as the formulation of policy recommendations, especially challenging. Within these constraints, the chapter presents a narrative of fiscal policy in Congo, including comparisons with similar countries, and its potential impact on poverty alleviation.

The Republic of Congo's economy faces short-term upside risks with the sharp decline in oil prices since mid-2014, and significant challenges in the medium term associated with the expected depletion of oil reserves. Therefore, room for active fiscal policy to reduce poverty and inequality has already narrowed, and is expected to drastically diminish in the coming years. So far, fiscal policy has proven excessively accommodative, with a limited impact on poverty and inequality. In 2013, the overall fiscal balance on a cash basis was in surplus (13.9 percent of non-oil GDP), but major adjustment is required in the medium term because the country runs a very large non-oil primary fiscal deficit (–61.2 percent of non-oil GDP).[1] Ensuring an orderly fiscal adjustment, while simultaneously reducing poverty and inequality, will prove particularly challenging given that income inequality tends to rise significantly during periods of fiscal consolidation (Agnello and Sousa 2012).

This chapter is structured as follows: First, an overview of inequality and poverty in Congo is provided and compared with that in similar countries. The current composition of the public budget in Congo is then discussed; this budget is insufficiently geared toward the reduction of inequalities and poverty. The need for fiscal consolidation going forward in Congo is examined, and a strategy that could mitigate its adverse effect on inequality and poverty is proposed.

OVERVIEW OF INEQUALITY AND POVERTY IN CONGO

In 2011, poverty in Congo was significantly higher than that in countries with similar GDP per capita[2] (Figure 21.1), and Congo's poverty scores are similar to or higher than those of other sub-Saharan African countries with significantly lower incomes. Although the poverty rate declined from 50.7 percent in 2005 to 46.5 percent in 2011, the number of poor people increased from 1.8 million to 1.9 million.[3] In addition, poverty is widespread in rural areas (75.6 percent)

---

[1] Defined as total revenue (excluding investment loans and grants) minus total expenditure (excluding interest payments and foreign-financed investments). In 2013, non-oil nominal GDP (CFAF 2,796 billion) represented about 42 percent of nominal GDP (CFAF 6,657 billion).

[2] This analysis considers all countries whose per capita GDP (in purchasing-power-parity U.S. dollars) is between 25 percent above and 25 percent below that of the Republic of Congo. The analysis is based on internationally comparable data, for which the latest observations are 2011 or 2012.

[3] The Republic of Congo's population grew at an annual average rate of 3 percent during the same period.

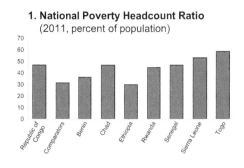

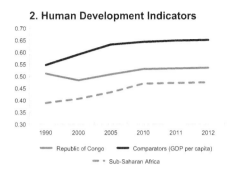

Figure 21.1   Republic of Congo: Selected Poverty and Human Development Indicators

Sources: World Bank, World Development Indicators database (panel 1); United Nations Development Program, Human Development Index (panel 2).
Note: Comparators are developing countries whose per capita GDP (in purchasing-power-parity U.S. dollars) is between 25 percent above and 25 percent below that of the Republic of Congo.

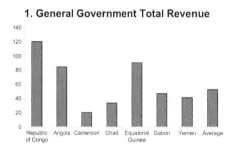

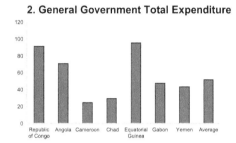

Figure 21.2   Fiscal Aggregates in 2013 *(Percent of non-oil GDP)*

Source: IMF staff estimates.

compared with urban areas (29.4 percent in Brazzaville). With regard to income inequality, the Gini coefficient for disposable income declined in Congo between 2005 and 2011 and is now equivalent to the average for sub-Saharan Africa countries (0.44).[4] But the Gini remains higher than that of countries with similar income levels (0.39). And Congo's United Nations Human Development Index score is significantly below the average of countries with similar GDP per capita and has improved more slowly since 2005.

COMPOSITION OF PUBLIC EXPENDITURE AND REVENUE

Total government revenue and spending are particularly high in the Republic of Congo. Total government revenue represented 120.5 percent of non-oil GDP in 2013, significantly higher than in most oil-exporting low-income countries (Figure 21.2). Oil revenue accounted for almost 75 percent of total government revenues. As a result, total government spending was also significantly higher than for comparators, with the exception of Equatorial Guinea.[5]

However, the low level of tax revenue significantly reduces the redistributive role of tax policy. Tax revenue accounted for only 6.7 percent of GDP in 2010, much lower than the average

---

[4]The latest available international Gini coefficient is for 2005. For comparison purposes, the 2011 figure was estimated by applying the percentage point improvement between 2005 and 2011 from the national household survey, in which the Gini coefficient went down from 0.42 to 0.39 over this period.

[5]Part of the oil revenues generated by the proceeds of the Republic of Congo's oil sales to China (equivalent to more than one-third of the Republic of Congo's total annual oil exports) is kept in an escrow account in the Export-Import Bank of China as a guarantee for the concessional loans granted by that bank to the Republic of Congo.

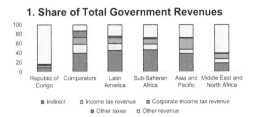

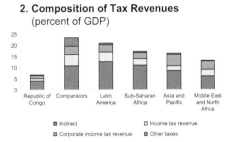

Figure 21.3   Composition of Government Revenues

Source: IMF staff estimates.

TABLE 21.1

Decrease in the Average Tax Rate Due to the 2013 Personal Income Tax Reform *(Percentage points)*

Taxable Income Levels (CFAF)	Change in the Average Tax Rate for a Single Person	Change in the Average Tax Rate for a Family with Two Children	Change in the Average Tax Rate for a Family with Four Children
232,000	0	0	0
732,000	5.8	0	0
2,000,000	6.2	6.1	5.6
5,500,000	6.2	6.4	7.2
15,000,000	4.8	6.4	7.2

Source: IMF staff estimates.
Note: CFAF = Communauté Financière Africaine Franc.

for sub-Saharan Africa countries (17.9 percent) and countries with comparable income levels (23.4 percent). Tax policy can, therefore, play only a marginal role in achieving redistributive goals in Congo. In addition, the tax structure favors consumption taxes, which are less progressive than income and wealth-related taxes. Income tax and property tax revenues (classified as "other taxes") are particularly limited, even compared with other sub-Saharan Africa countries (Figure 21.3).

Recent personal income tax reforms have not strengthened progressivity. The government reformed the personal income tax system in 2011 and 2013 by reducing the rate applicable to each bracket by 5 percentage points (except the first bracket, which was maintained at 1 percent) and increasing the size of the four lowest brackets.[6] The IMF staff estimates that this reform is mostly regressive because its benefits accrue more to higher-income families and single people with intermediate incomes (Table 21.1). These results reflect that (1) the impact of the tax rate reduction will be larger than the impact of the widening of the lowest brackets, which benefits more low-income households; and (2) the large tax deductions on salary income and the family tax system benefit higher-income taxpayers more, because they are proportional to income.

Social spending was marginal in 2010 and was largely crowded out by significant energy subsidies. Social spending was much lower than in most sub-Saharan Africa countries and countries with similar income levels (Figure 21.4). In Congo, fuel subsidies were higher in 2010 (3.6 percent GDP) than aggregate spending on education, health, and social protection (2.5 percent GDP) and significantly larger than in the sub-Saharan Africa region as a whole (1.4 percent). Large fuel subsidies may reflect the desire to share the country's oil wealth through the provision of petroleum products at prices below those in the international market (Arze del Granado,

---

[6] Tax brackets are as follows (2014 Budget Act): 1 percent (below CFAF 0.46 million), 10 percent (CFAF 0.46–1 million), 25 percent (CFAF 1–3 million), 40 percent (CFAF 3–8 million), and 45 percent (more than CFAF 8 million).

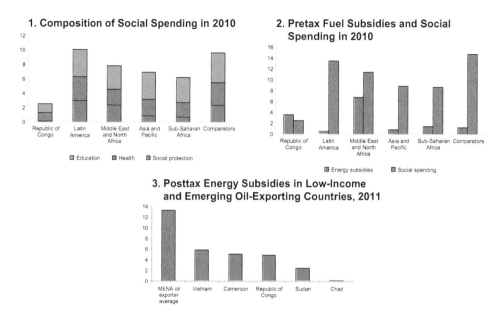

Figure 21.4 Composition of Spending *(Percent of GDP)*

Source: IMF staff estimates.
Note: In panel 2, pretax consumer subsidies are estimated as the difference between international prices, adjusted upward for transportation and distribution margins, and domestic consumer prices. MENA = Middle East and North Africa.

Coady, and Gillingham 2010), even if refined oil is imported.[7] Posttax subsidies, which take into account both revenue needs and negative consumption externalities, are among the highest for oil-exporting low-income countries, but remain below those of the Middle East and North Africa oil-exporting countries.

Fuel subsidies distort market incentives, lead to overconsumption of petroleum products, and favor higher-income groups. In the Republic of Congo, domestic petroleum prices are fixed by ministerial decree below supply costs. As a consequence, market participants consume more petroleum products, reducing the overall efficiency of the economy. And the overconsumption adds to the total cost of the subsidies. Moreover, low prices relative to neighboring countries create incentives to smuggle petroleum products out of the country. Finally, fuel subsidies are usually poorly targeted, and benefits accrue mostly to higher-income groups because they consume the most. Except for kerosene, the distribution of fuel subsidies is skewed toward the top two quintiles, which receive, on average, 62–81 percent of the benefits.[8]

The government has stepped up its investment sharply to address infrastructure gaps. Public capital spending rose from 6.1 percent of GDP in 2006 to 18.8 percent in 2010 (Figure 21.5). As a result, public capital stock in the Republic of Congo has increased since 2006 and was significantly higher than in comparators in 2011, including oil-exporting low-income countries[9] (Figure 21.5). According to the National Development Plan, the vast majority of capital spending for the period 2012–16 is to be allocated to infrastructure (51.7 percent in 2014) and economic development (16.7 percent). However, the share of capital expenditure allocated to social development was expected to increase from 11.7 percent to 16.7 in 2014. According to the 2014 Budget Act, social ministries are to receive about 14 percent of government capital expenditure.

---

[7]Only about 5 percent of domestic production is processed for domestic consumption by the national refinery; this amount meets about 70 percent of domestic demand for petroleum products. As a result, the national oil company imports additional refined products.
[8]IMF staff estimates based on the 2005 household survey.
[9]Cameroon, Chad, Sudan, Vietnam, Yemen.

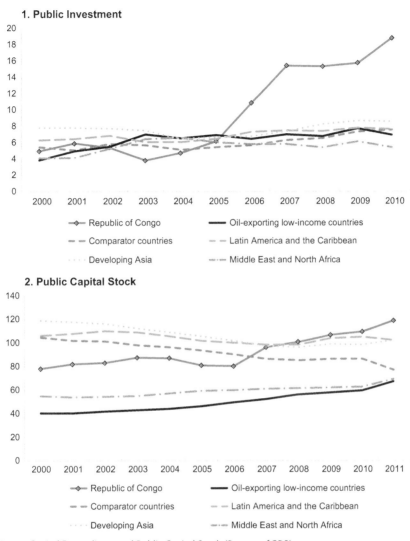

Figure 21.5   Capital Expenditure and Public Capital Stock *(Percent of GDP)*

Sources: Center for International Comparisons; OECD; and IMF staff calculations.

Education spending and service provision have recently increased significantly. Public resources allocated to the education sector were limited in 2010 compared with other sub-Saharan Africa countries and countries in the same income range (Figure 21.6). In addition, the composition of education spending was somewhat regressive. Primary education tends to be more progressive, because lower-income groups have greater access to this level of education. But the share of expenditure allocated to secondary and tertiary education in the Republic of Congo was higher than in countries with comparable income levels. In addition, although Congo was performing comparatively well according to the gross enrollment rate, the average class size in 2010 was significantly higher than in countries with comparable GDP per capita, raising questions about service quality. In recognition of these weaknesses, the government has progressively increased its education spending. The share of the budget allocated to the education ministries rose from 6.1 percent in 2012 to 8.9 percent in 2014, with a nominal increase of 57 percent during the same period, but the impact on education headline indicators is yet to be measured.

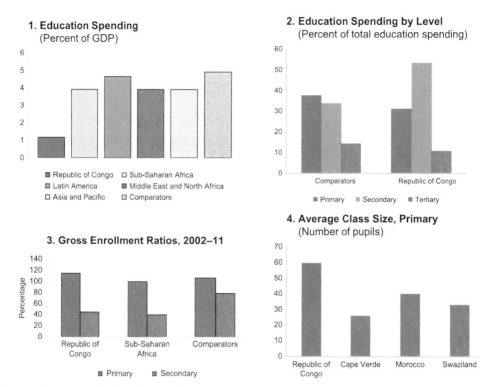

Figure 21.6   Education Spending and Outcomes, 2010

Source: World Bank.

Health spending and in-kind services have not compensated for large income and geographic inequalities. In 2010, health spending in Congo was among the lowest in sub-Saharan Africa (Figure 21.7). As a result, the country's reliance on out-of-pocket spending, at 64 percent of total health financing, was among the highest in sub-Saharan Africa. Service provision is insufficient and access to health care professionals limited, particularly in rural areas, which are also the poorest. Health inequality is high, with households in the lowest 20 percent of the income distribution suffering from significantly higher child mortality than the richest 20 percent.

The government has committed to implementing a system of universal health care insurance. Whereas budget allocations have increased for the education sector, they decreased for the Ministry of Health between 2012 and 2014, both in nominal terms (by 1.6 percent) and as a share of total budget spending (by 1.3 percentage points). However, with World Bank support, the government is expected to spend US$100 million between 2015 and 2020, with the aim of implementing universal health coverage. This program would include fee waivers for the poorest households, as well as free service provision. How it will be financed has not yet been determined and will depend on funding from household contributions and government subsidies to the poorest households.

The Republic of Congo has also started implementing social safety net programs. With increased donor support, safety net spending in Africa has increased since 2005, following food and financial crises (Monchuk 2014). Congo got a late start compared with other sub-Saharan Africa countries, but is preparing temporary income-generating activities for unemployed youth and labor-intensive, self-employment, and rural employment programs. In addition, a pilot conditional cash transfer program (the LISUNGI project) is being rolled out for 5,000 poor households and 1,000 elderly people. The cost of expanding this program on a national scale is estimated to be about 1 percent of GDP (Box 21.1).

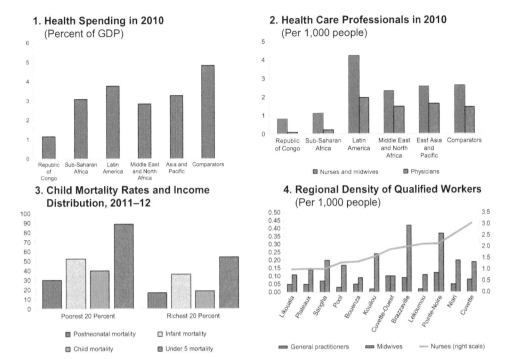

Figure 21.7   Health Spending, Service Provision, and Inequalities

Sources: World Health Organization (panels 1 and 2); Government of the Republic of Congo, Demographic and Health Survey, 2012 (panels 3 and 4).

BOX 21.1   Initiating a Social Safety Net through Cash Transfers

To address the challenges of high poverty and inequality, the government of the Republic of Congo is focusing on the development of a social safety net for poor and vulnerable groups. In its initial phase, the four-year social safety net program (the LISUNGI project) will make conditional cash transfers to 5,000 poor families and 1,000 people older than age 60 in three areas (Brazzaville, Pointe-Noire, and Cuvette). Eligible households are those living below the food poverty line and with at least one child (between the ages of 0 and 14 years) or an elderly person. Transfers to the households will be conditional on continuous schooling of children and regular health checks for all household members. The program will be monitored and evaluated regularly. Depending on its effectiveness, the program's coverage will be expanded to all eligible households in 2016.

The conditional cash transfer program is expected to improve the Republic of Congo's social and economic indicators in three ways. First, the transfers are expected to reduce current poverty, reaching families that do not directly benefit from economic growth. Second, because they are conditional on education and health access, the transfers should have a positive impact on school enrollment rates and on child nutrition, thereby improving human capital. Finally, household productivity should improve because the collateral provided by the cash transfers will help families invest in economic activities and gain access to microcredit. Higher employment and social cohesion should ensue.

The LISUNGI project mimics similar programs in other countries, such as Brazil, Colombia, Ghana, Kenya, Mexico, and Niger. The success of these programs is directly related to the quality of the management information system and direct and regular payments to recipients.

An impact analysis carried out by the World Bank suggests that the cash transfer program could have a significant impact on poverty and inequality. It is expected that the poverty rate would decline from 46.5 percent in 2011 to 38.9 percent—3.9 percentage points higher than the Millennium Development Goals Initiative target (35 percent by 2015)—if the program were to operate nationwide. The Gini index of inequality would also drop between 8.0 and 11.8 percent. Implementing the program on a national scale—with payments of CFAF 20,000–25,000 on average a month to the poorest households with children or elderly members (or both)—would cost about 1 percent of GDP or about 2 percent of public expenditure.

TABLE 21.2

Medium-Term Fiscal Consolidation *(Percent of non-oil GDP)*							
	2013	2014	2015	2019	2025	2033	2034
Revenue and Grants	111.7	102.6	94.2	67.4	45.2	32.5	31.8
Oil Revenue	82.1	72.3	64.2	36.2	13.4	2.2	1.9
Non-oil Revenue	28.6	28.8	29.1	30.3	31.3	30	29.7
Total Expenditure	91.4	91	83.7	62.3	38.2	31.2	30.5
Capital Expenditure	57.7	56.4	49.4	32.6	15.7	13.2	12.9
Non-oil Primary Balance	−61.2	−60.5	−53.6	−31.1	−6.5	−2.2	−1.5
Debt-to-GDP Ratio	38.2	38.7	37.3	35.2	31.4	18.8	17.4

STRATEGY FOR EQUITABLE FISCAL CONSOLIDATION

Estimates of proven oil reserves suggest that oil production is to peak in 2017 and will then decline decisively after 15 years.[10] This pattern will have a major impact on government revenues, which are expected to decline by about 80 percentage points of non-oil GDP during the next 20 years (Table 21.2). As a consequence, spending will have to be sharply reduced, by about 60 percentage points of non-oil GDP during the same period, to cut the non-oil primary deficit to about 30 percent of non-oil GDP by 2019, with a further reduction in the medium to long term (IMF 2014c). This reduction in the non-oil deficit should be achieved by decreasing and reallocating spending, while progressively raising tax revenues and increasing the progressivity of the tax system.

Fiscal consolidation should be based on progressive tax and spending measures to protect vulnerable households during adjustment. In low-income countries, fiscal adjustment can have an adverse effect on employment and inequality in the short term, but this effect may be reversed in the long term. Inequality and unemployment may even decline in the longer term if fiscal adjustment helps bring down inflation—which is damaging to the poor—or corrects macroeconomic imbalances that are hindering growth. And because spending in developing economies is generally not progressive, cutting such spending can ensure fiscal consolidation while avoiding a surge in inequality (IMF 2014a). Hence, fiscal policy should aim to balance the provision of much-needed public services with fiscal sustainability, through tax revenue mobilization and prioritization of spending. The government should not resort to across-the-board spending cuts, which can hurt low-income groups. It should instead focus on improving the composition and efficiency of spending to prevent spending restraint from affecting the quantity or quality of basic services.

A better-functioning personal income tax system would enhance tax progressivity. Strengthening the personal income tax yield can raise the tax ratio while strengthening progressivity (OECD 2006). Implementing a zero bracket for the lowest-income brackets would both simplify revenue administration and enhance tax progressivity. Tax deductions must also be reduced because they accrue disproportionately to the rich and lead to significant revenue losses. Large tax deductions on salary income should be eliminated and further reduced for professional expenses. The family tax system benefits based on the number of dependents (*quotient familial*) is a major hindrance to income tax equity because it favors large, high-income families; it should be replaced by a fixed tax credit that is the same for all taxpayers. In addition, there is no need for a tax incentive to increase the fertility rate in the Republic of Congo, which is among the highest in the world. Deductions for mortgage interest and capital income should also be eliminated: only high-income households are able to borrow from banks and receive financial earnings.

---

[10] Average production in 2012 and 2013 was 93 million barrels a year. After peaking at 118 million barrels in 2017, oil production is estimated to decline to about 18 million barrels by 2030.

Property taxes should be developed. Taxes on residential property and on excess returns or rents, particularly in resource-rich economies, are considered the least distortive for growth (IMF 2014b). There is large scope for increasing the residential property tax in the Republic of Congo. This reform could have a significant redistributive impact. To make it progressive, the tax could exclude the permanent residences of those below a certain threshold to prevent taxation of low-income households. A property tax could be implemented gradually given that it requires a reliable land registry and the administrative capacity to manage it.

The use of reduced value-added tax (VAT) rates and exemptions should be minimized. Achieving redistributive objectives through consumption taxes usually proves to be costly. The rich generally spend more in absolute terms, so they tend to benefit more from exemptions or reduced VAT rates. The Republic of Congo uses these instruments extensively for necessities, in particular on a large variety of food products and agricultural inputs. There is also an exemption for electricity and water consumption, which is particularly regressive given that only 37.8 percent of the population had access to electricity in 2011. Reducing the list of goods exempt or benefiting from reduced VAT rates would help raise revenues that could be used to increase targeted social transfers, administrative capacity permitting.

With regard to expenditure efficiency, the government should aim to cut fuel subsidies to scale up social spending. Reducing or eliminating fuel subsidies would create fiscal space for social spending. It would improve the progressivity of public spending, since higher-income households consume more petroleum products. However, it would have a negative impact on the poorest households, because energy consumption represents a large share of their total consumption. Implementing this reform gradually and compensating vulnerable households would be critical to its success (Alleyne and Hussain 2013). In particular, interventions targeted to vulnerable households through conditional cash transfers would be needed. But designing such programs requires significantly improved data transparency and reliability for informed policy decision making. Other mitigating measures could, for example, take the form of subsidies for public transportation.

Containing the public wage bill and spending on goods and services could provide additional fiscal space for social spending. Purchases of goods and services (9.2 percent of non-oil GDP) are much higher in the Republic of Congo than the average for oil-exporting low-income countries (6.9 percent) and other Central African Economic and Monetary Community (CEMAC) countries (excluding Gabon). Some expenditure reform is needed in this area (Figure 21.8). The wage

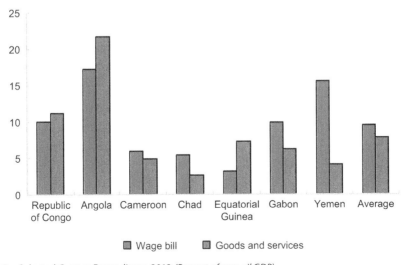

Figure 21.8   Selected Current Expenditure, 2013 *(Percent of non-oil GDP)*

Source: IMF staff estimates.

bill in the Republic of Congo (9.8 percent of non-oil GDP) is also higher than in most other CEMAC countries. Progressive containment of the wage bill would help create fiscal space for social spending. The strategy should aim for adequate recruitment in the health and education sectors and reduced hiring in nonpriority sectors through natural attrition.

A reduction and a change of the composition of public investment would also provide room for additional pro-poor and pro-growth infrastructure spending as well as social spending. The capital stock accumulated in the Republic of Congo by 2011 was significantly higher than in countries with similar income levels and almost twice the average of oil-exporting low-income countries. In addition, capital spending pressures will increase with the organization of the 2015 All Africa Games in the Republic of Congo. The proposed long-term path aims at stabilizing the capital-stock-to-GDP ratio at its 2011 level. The composition of public investment could be improved to maximize the impact on growth and human development. This applies particularly to public investment in infrastructure. Through better prioritization of public investment, space can be created to expand government social sector spending to improve service provision. This approach will require evaluating current expenditure needs associated with the increase in education and health infrastructure.

Improving access to in-kind services by low-income groups would help reduce poverty and inequality in the medium term and boost growth in the long term. In the education sector, the government should prioritize spending on primary schools and improve service quality, in particular through recruitment of additional teachers to close large staffing gaps (estimated to be 14,000 teachers by the Primary National Education Council). In the health sector, the fiscal costs of the introduction of universal health coverage should be carefully assessed. The implementation should be sequenced to increase household coverage progressively while mitigating the impact on fiscal aggregates. Plans should be made in particular to determine the level of noncontributory coverage to protect population groups unable to afford insurance, while containing fiscal costs. Progressivity should also be embedded in the design of social taxes to finance the health care system—a flat price would weigh disproportionately on those who are less well off. And to reduce poverty and inequality, the system should focus on expanding access to a broad package of essential health services for poor households; reducing health copayment and user charges for low-income households; and ensuring access to health care facilities and professionals, particularly in rural areas.

New social safety nets should be adequately designed. The Republic of Congo is in the initial steps of designing new safety net programs, so it should be mindful of design and implementation shortcomings that have been observed in other low-income countries. In particular, the Republic of Congo should avoid fragmenting and duplicating small social programs and guard against bad targeting, which can cause substantial leakage for non-poor households and result in insufficient benefits for the most vulnerable people.

CONCLUSION

Government spending in the Republic of Congo is comparatively high, benefiting from very large resource revenue. However, it is poorly targeted, with large fuel subsidies that crowd out social spending and ambitious investment plans that may prove to be unsustainable and inefficient.

The expected decline in oil revenue in the medium term is a major challenge to the Republic of Congo's fiscal policy stance. Compensating for the shortfall in oil revenue through tax revenue mobilization will be difficult even in the medium to long term and may negatively affect the poorest, given the current low level of the tax-to-GDP ratio. Reducing the non-oil deficit will also require a significant reduction in spending, which may affect pro-poor spending.

To ensure that the fiscal consolidation is equitable, the government should aim to increase progressive taxation, sharply reduce fuel subsidies, and improve the efficiency and quality of capital spending by prioritizing public sector infrastructure investment that maximizes the growth and human development impact to create space to reallocate spending toward social sectors.

REFERENCES

Agnello, L., and R. M. Sousa. 2012. "How Does Fiscal Consolidation Impact on Income Inequality?" Banque de France Working Paper No. 382, Paris.

Alleyne, T., and M. Hussain. 2013. "Energy Subsidy Reform in Sub-Saharan Africa: Experience and Lessons." African Departmental Paper No. 13/2, International Monetary Fund, Washington.

Arze del Granado, J., D. Coady, and R. Gillingham. 2010. "The Unequal Benefits of Fuel Subsidies: A Review of Evidence for Developing Countries." IMF Working Paper No. 10/202, International Monetary Fund, Washington.

International Monetary Fund. 2014a. "Fiscal Policy and Income Inequality." Washington. http://www.imf.org/external/np/pp/eng/2014/012314.pdf.

———. 2014b. "Growth-Friendly Fiscal Policy." Washington.

———. 2014c. "Republic of Congo: Staff Report for the 2014 Article IV Consultation." IMF Country Report No. 14/272, Washington.

Monchuk, Victoria. 2014. *Reducing Poverty and Investing in People: The New Role of Safety Nets in Africa.* Washington: World Bank.

Organisation for Economic Co-operation and Development (OECD). 2006. "Fundamental Reform of Personal Income Tax." OECD Tax Policy Studies, Paris.

———. 2010. "Tax Policy Reform and Economic Growth." Paris.

World Bank. 2013. "Congo, Republic of—LISUNGI Safety Nets Project." World Bank, Washington. http://documents.worldbank.org/curated/en/2013/12/18794003/congo-republic-lisungi-safety-nets-project.

CHAPTER 22

Fiscal Adjustment and Income Inequality in Brazilian States

João Pedro Azevedo, Antonio C. David, and Fabiano Rodrigues Bastos

INTRODUCTION

This chapter assesses the links between fiscal policy and income inequality in Brazil for the period 1995–2011 by combining fiscal data with household survey information at the state level.[1] The period under analysis is marked by important changes in subnational fiscal policy and institutions because states had to increase their primary balances to comply with debt renegotiation programs that they agreed to with the federal government in the late 1990s. Even those states that did not have significantly large debt levels were bound by new fiscal rules designed to mitigate long-standing fiscal risks stemming from subnational entities.

This fiscally constrained environment has profoundly reshaped revenue and expenditure policies at the subnational level since 2000. Against this backdrop, income inequality decreased significantly. The Gini coefficient declined from 57.7 in 1995 to 52.2 percent in 2011, although it remains among the highest in the world. Microeconomic studies have linked inequality reduction in Brazil to changes in labor income, including changes in both the supply of and demand for skilled workers, and to the emergence of effective social transfer programs at the federal level (Azevedo and others 2013; Pecora and Menezes 2013; Lopez-Calva and Rocha 2012). Azevedo and others (2013) show that approximately 40 percent of the reduction of inequality in Brazil between 2001 and 2011 can be attributed to changes in the labor markets, in particular to higher hourly earnings of low-skilled workers. Transfers (public and private) and noncontributory pensions contributed 20 percent and 18 percent, respectively, to the reduction of inequality. Demographic factors are one last important component in the reduction of inequality in this period.

This chapter examines to what extent subnational fiscal policy is associated with inequality dynamics, after controlling for a number of determinants of inequality already established in the literature. The results indicate that a tighter fiscal stance in Brazilian states, measured by changes in their cyclically adjusted primary balances, is not linked to a deterioration in inequality. This conclusion differs from the results of several papers that analyze the impact of fiscal consolidation on inequality at the national level for Organisation for Economic Co-operation and Development (OECD) countries, which typically conclude that fiscal consolidation is associated with increases

This chapter is largely based on the analysis presented in Azevedo and others 2014. The views expressed in this chapter are those of the authors and do not necessarily represent those of the IMF or IMF policy or those of the World Bank and World Bank policy. The authors thank Benedict Clements and Maura Francese for excellent comments and suggestions.
[1] Brazil is organized politically and administratively as a federal system consisting of 26 states and 1 federal district. The states are characterized by heterogeneous levels of inequality and fiscal outcomes, but share common institutions and federal regulations.

in inequality. The findings in this chapter caution against extrapolating policy implications of the literature focusing on advanced economies to other settings.

A BRIEF SURVEY OF THE LITERATURE

The recent empirical literature on the effects of the fiscal policy stance on inequality has focused mostly on OECD or advanced economies and uses data at the national level. Agnello and Sousa (2012) look at the impact of fiscal consolidation on inequality in a panel of 18 industrial countries and find that inequality increases during periods of fiscal consolidation. In addition, consolidation is particularly detrimental to inequality if led by expenditure cuts. In contrast, fiscal consolidation driven by revenue increases is associated with reductions in inequality.

Ball and others (2013) find that both expenditure- and taxed-based fiscal consolidations at the national level have typically raised inequality for a panel of OECD countries, even if the distributional effects of spending-based adjustments tend to be larger relative to tax-based adjustments. These conclusions are largely confirmed for a broader panel of countries that also includes emerging markets in a study by Woo and others (2013). These authors find positive and statistically significant elasticities of spending-based consolidations on inequality (of about 1.5 to 2), but the coefficients for tax-based consolidations are not statistically significant.

These findings are likely to differ for developing economies, where the impact of fiscal policy on inequality is shaped by lower levels of taxes and transfers relative to advanced economies. This differential impact is compounded by greater reliance on regressive taxes (such as consumption taxes) and low coverage and benefit levels of transfer programs (Bastagli, Coady, and Gupta 2012). Furthermore, overall in-kind public expenditures (on health and education, for example) have been found to be regressive in several developing countries, reflecting lower-income households' lack of access to public services (Bastagli, Coady, and Gupta 2012).

The literature on fiscal policy and inequality in Brazil has mainly concentrated on static incidence analysis. Lustig, Pessino, and Scott (2012), using data from the 2009 household budget survey (Pesquisa de Orçamento Familiar, POF) conclude that direct taxes (such as personal income taxes) in Brazil appear to be progressive, but their impact on inequality is relatively small because of their small size relative to GDP, whereas indirect taxes are regressive. Lustig, Pessino, and Scott (2012) also examine the incidence of direct cash transfers and conclude that it varies significantly depending on the program. Bolsa Familia is well targeted to the poor, but other programs such as the Special Circumstances Pensions (SCP) benefit the top quintile relatively more.

Ferreira, Leite, and Ravallion (2010) examine the importance of macroeconomic and redistributive policies on poverty dynamics in Brazil for the period 1985–2004, focusing on state-level data, as does this chapter. They find that state and municipal "social" public expenditures have had an adverse effect on poverty (regressive incidence), whereas state-level investment spending had no significant effect.

FISCAL INSTITUTIONS AND FISCAL STRUCTURE IN BRAZIL

Brazil's current fiscal federalism arrangements were shaped by the 1988 Constitution, which created an environment of fiscal decentralization with revenue-sharing transfer mechanisms inspired by equity concerns among states. Fiscal policy among different levels of government (federal government, states, and municipalities) is not formally coordinated. A sequence of subnational fiscal crises occurred during the first 10 years after the 1988 Constitution was adopted. These crises originated in great part from a lack of fiscal discipline and the existence of moral hazard associated with federal bail-out packages. High subnational indebtedness turned into a macroeconomic risk factor at the country level.

In 1997, the federal government and the states engaged in a debt-restructuring agreement, whereby the center would take on most of the states' debt stock and the states would be given 30 years to repay, under special conditions. The debt-restructuring agreement introduced binding constraints on the fiscal behavior of the states and required hard commitments to fiscal goals. These changes were reinforced by the 2000 Fiscal Responsibility Law, which is considered to be a landmark of fiscal reform in Brazil and an essential part of broader macroeconomic reforms (the country's move toward inflation targeting and floating exchange rates). Among other features, the 2000 Fiscal Responsibility Law imposed quantitative restrictions such as caps on payroll expenditure, as well as limits on the debt level as a share of tax revenue (Sturzenegger and Werneck 2006).

Hence, since 2000 fiscal decentralization has been accompanied by constraints on subnational debt growth. States' and municipalities' fiscal performance improved quickly in this new environment. However, the subnational fiscal adjustment was not without cost. States and municipalities faced sizable current expenditures with considerable downward rigidity, so the limitation on new borrowing meant that public investment became the main adjustment variable in many instances. This situation led to the accumulation of infrastructure weaknesses as well as other repressed investment needs. From the revenue side, states began to compete with each other and offer tax exemptions to attract firms, which further compressed fiscal space.

The regressive nature of the overall tax system in Brazil is emphasized by Soares and others (2009). As of 2007, based on national accounts data, these authors estimate that indirect taxes accounted for more than 40 percent of the total gross tax burden (excluding government transfers), whereas income and property taxes accounted for less than 30 percent.[2] Most of the taxation of income and property can be decomposed into corporate income taxes (close to 39 percent of the total taxation of income and property); property taxes, including the financial transactions tax (close to 27 percent); and personal income taxes (21 percent). In addition, these authors estimate that income and property taxes accounted for close to 44 percent of the increase in tax buoyancy (tax-to-GDP ratio) between 1997 and 2007, whereas indirect taxes accounted for about 33 percent of the increase.

The main state-level tax is a value-added tax on the consumption of goods and services (Imposto sobre a Circulação de Mercadorias e Prestação de Serviços, ICMS). Moreover, as discussed in Sturzenegger and Werneck 2006, most federal revenue transfers to state governments stem from the sharing of the revenue from a tax on manufactured products (Imposto sobre Produtos Industrializados, IPI). Thus, Brazilian states rely mostly on tax revenue from so-called indirect taxes rather than taxes on income or property. However, the relative importance of the ICMS and federal revenue transfers varies widely across states. The median ICMS-to-state-GDP ratio in 2012 was about 8 percent. For richer states, the ICMS corresponds to more than 50 percent of total revenue, while federal revenue transfers amount to very little. The opposite is true for states with less developed economic bases. On the expenditure side, the median public-investment-to-state-GDP ratio is about 1.5 percent with strong variation as well; for instance, in 2012, the lowest investment-to-GDP ratio was 0.3 percent while the highest was 8.2 percent. Another important expenditure category is compensation of employees, which reached about 9 percent of GDP in 2012 for the median state.

---

[2] Indirect taxes are estimated by Soares and others (2009) to amount to about 10 percent of GDP.

A FIRST LOOK AT INEQUALITY AND FISCAL POLICY AT THE SUBNATIONAL LEVEL IN BRAZIL

The Data

Annex 22.1 presents data definitions and sources and Annex 22.2 provides descriptive statistics for selected variables.[3] The income per capita inequality measure and the employment rate variable were constructed using data from an annual household survey (Pesquisa Nacional por Amostra de Domicilios, PNAD) undertaken by Brazil's Institute of Geography and Statistics (IBGE) and compiled by the Socio-Economic Database for Latin America and the Caribbean. PNAD is a representative survey at both the national and state levels.

Because of data availability, the measures of inequality in this analysis are based on income per capita after transfers, but before taxes. The PNAD contains information on household market income and transfers (both public and private). In this context, one could argue that this chapter is focusing on the "macroeconomic" effects of fiscal adjustments. It might have been of interest to use measures of inequality on a net-of-taxes basis to also pick up the effect of fiscal adjustment on direct taxes, but this information is not available from the PNAD.

Lustig, Pessino, and Scott (2012) attempt to infer the disposable income of Brazilian households based on current tax legislation. These authors also try to impute other in-kind transfers, such as public expenditure on health and education, using a different data set, the household budget survey (Pesquisa de Orçamento Familiar, POF). However, the POF is published every five years, not annually as is the PNAD.

Lustig, Pessino, and Scott's (2012) approach could not be implemented to obtain disposable incomes in this analysis for several reasons. In addition to the limitations in the time dimension of the POF data, the imputations performed by these authors are only available for one year. More generally, the use of disposable income as a dependent variable would hinge on the assumption that the tax legislation is actually binding. Furthermore, any attempt to apply Lustig and colleagues' methodology to other POFs would still encounter the problem of geographical representativeness, since the 1994/95 and 2002/03 POFs are not representative at the state level (they are only representative at a broader geographical level for the five macro regions).

State-level fiscal indicators are constructed based on a data set compiled by the National Treasury Department at the Ministry of Finance. The data set provides comprehensive information on revenue, expenditures, assets, and liabilities for the Brazilian states. The exercise also uses additional Treasury data for information on "social" public expenditures at both the state and municipal levels. These expenditures are defined as spending on education and culture, health and sanitation, and social security and social assistance (similar to the categories used in Ferreira, Leite, and Ravallion 2010).

In addition, this analysis also uses Regional National Accounts Statistics from IBGE to obtain a series for state-level GDP and the respective deflators. Finally, it uses information on federal social transfers at the state level obtained from the Institute for Applied Economic Research (Instituto de Pesquisa Economica Aplicada, IPEA). This comprises information on three main federal social programs—Bolsa Família, Benefício de Prestação Continuada, and Renda Mensal Vitalícia—all of which are direct cash transfers to households.

---

[3] See Azevedo and others 2014 for a richer and more detailed description of the data and of the construction of the variables.

1. Inequality at the national level has decreased over the period ...

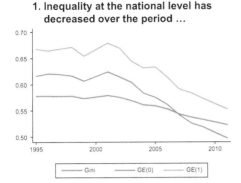

2. ... and so have median (across states) inequality measures

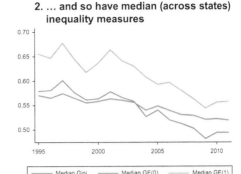

Figure 22.1   Income Inequality in Brazil, 1995–2011

Source: Authors' calculations.

Note: GE refers to the generalized entropy index of inequality. GE(0) and GE(1) are measures of the index taking the parameter alpha to be 0 and 1, respectively.

Recent Trends and Stylized Facts

Figure 22.1 depicts trends in a number of inequality measures during the period of interest. As panel 1 illustrates, overall per capita income inequality at the national level has declined significantly irrespective of the measure considered (the Gini coefficient, as well as the GE(0) and GE(1) measures[4] are shown). Median inequality across states has also fallen during the period. Moreover, Azevedo and others (2014) show that for the GE(0), GE(1), and GE(2) indicators, the "between states dimension" accounts for only 3–8 percent of total inequality in Brazil and remains relatively constant over time. Therefore, the analysis presented in subsequent sections of this chapter focuses on within-state inequality.

As mentioned, the first decade of the 2000s was a time of fiscal adjustment for Brazilian states. The median primary balance moved to surplus in the late 1990s, and hovered around 1 percent of state GDP for most of the subsequent decade, before falling to near zero after the global financial crisis (Figure 22.2, panel 2). In contrast, the federal government primary balance has been in surplus since 1995 (Figure 22.2, panel 1).

An emerging literature links the cyclicality of fiscal policy to social outcomes. Vegh and Vuletin (2014) use evidence from a number of Latin American and European countries to show a causal link from countercyclical (procyclical) fiscal policy at the national level and improvement (deterioration) in social indicators, including inequality indicators; that is, countercyclical policies are expected to reduce inequality.

This chapter follows their approach and finds that the overall correlation between the cyclical component of real government expenditure at the state level and the output gap is very weak, pointing to an essentially acyclical fiscal policy at the state level during the period (Figure 22.2, panel 3). However, considerable variation in the cyclicality of policies can be discovered by looking at the state-by-state correlation between the cyclical component of real government expenditures and the output gap (Figure 22.2, panel 4). In fact, 14 of the 27 states demonstrate a positive correlation between expenditures and the output gap, suggesting procyclical policies.

Figure 22.3 presents simple scatter plots including the log of the Gini coefficient, the level of the primary fiscal balance at the state level, and changes in the cyclically adjusted primary

---

[4] GE refers to the generalized entropy index of inequality. We present two measures of the index taking the parameter alpha to be 0 and 1, respectively. GE(1) is the so-called Theil index.

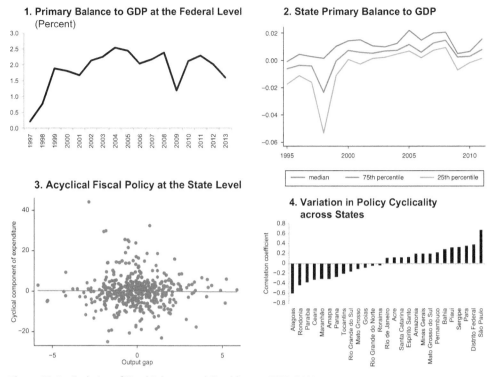

Figure 22.2   Evolution of Fiscal Balances and Fiscal Stance, 1995–2011

Source: Authors' calculations.

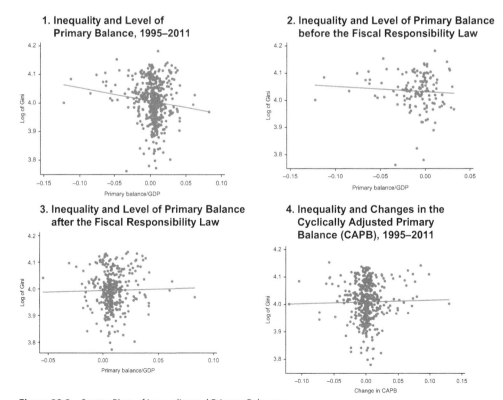

Figure 22.3   Scatter Plots of Inequality and Primary Balances

Source: Authors' calculations.

balance, which is the preferred measure of the fiscal stance in this analysis (see discussion in the next section). Note the negative correlation between the level of the primary balance and the Gini for the entire sample. This negative link seems to be stronger before the enactment of the Fiscal Responsibility Law (in a comparison of panels 2 and 3 of Figure 22.3). In fact, the association between the level of the primary balance and the Gini practically disappears if only the period after 2000 is considered. Finally, the simple correlation between the Gini and changes in the cyclically adjusted primary balance (the measure of fiscal adjustment in this analysis) is also weak; there is no indication that fiscal adjustment is associated with increases in inequality at the subnational level.

MODELING APPROACH AND RESULTS

This investigation follows an empirical specification summarized in equation (22.1) for $i = 1, \ldots,$ N states, $t = 1, \ldots, T$ time periods, and $m = 1, \ldots M$ control variables. The variable y_{it} represents the log of the Gini index at the state level; Δpb are changes in the cyclically adjusted primary balance as a share of state GDP (a measure of the fiscal stance); X is a set of controls; α_i are state-specific fixed effects; and ε_{it} is the error term, assumed to be white noise. The estimation of equation (22.1) also includes time dummies and a time trend in the specification.

$$
y_{i,t} = \rho y_{i,t-1} + \psi \Delta pb_{i,t-1} + \sum_{m=1}^{M} \beta_m X_{m,i,t-1} + u_{i,t},
$$

$$
u_{i,t} = \alpha_i + \lambda_t + \varepsilon_{i,t}.
$$

(22.1)

The following macroeconomic and fiscal variables are considered as controls in the baseline regressions: the employment rate, the state-level GDP per capita growth rate, inflation (measured by changes in the state GDP deflator), state and municipal social expenditure as a share of state GDP, and federal social transfers as a share of state GDP. To mitigate possible endogeneity problems, lagged values of the control variables are used and these control variables are therefore assumed to be weakly exogenous. Cross-sectional dependence problems are addressed by including time effects in the regressions and by using Driscoll and Kraay (1998) corrected standard errors.

When constructing the cyclically adjusted primary balance we focus on adjustments of revenue and expenditure to the output gap and do not consider the impact of asset or commodity price fluctuations. This is justified given the results discussed in IMF 2011 that suggest that, at the national level, revenue elasticities relative to cycles in equity and commodity prices appear to be very small. The analysis follows the "aggregated method" described in Bornhorst and others 2011 and focuses on the sensitivity of aggregate revenues and expenditures to the output gap at the state level. The revenue and expenditure elasticities estimated by Arena and Revilla (2009) for Brazilian states for the period 1991–2006 are used. These authors estimate a total revenue elasticity of about 1.7 and total expenditure elasticity of 1.3.

This chapter's measure of the fiscal stance differs from the action-based fiscal consolidation measures constructed by Devries and others (2011) and used in several papers in the literature on fiscal consolidation and inequality for OECD economies (Ball and others 2013). The construction of a similar action-based measure for Brazilian states is more difficult given that historical policy documents providing information on discretionary changes in taxes and expenditures are not readily available at the subnational level. Furthermore, this examination also considers the effects of gradual continuous adjustment rather than focusing on large consolidation episodes, as is frequently done in the literature (Alesina and Ardagna 2012).

A structurally adjusted primary balance (that is, the primary balance adjusted not only for cyclical fluctuations but also for one-off fiscal operations) would provide a better measure of the fiscal stance. However, lack of information and accounting challenges make it impossible to remove one-off fiscal operations at the state level in a consistent and systematic way.

Results for the Baseline Specification

The results presented in Table 22.1 indicate that the employment rate is an important factor in explaining inequality for the period. Furthermore, both real GDP per capita growth and the inflation rate are linked to increases in inequality, but only the coefficients obtained for the inflation rate are statistically significant, mirroring some of the results of the literature. These findings highlight the importance of macroeconomic stabilization in inequality reduction, a well-established result in the Brazilian context.

More important for the purposes of this volume, fiscal variables seem to matter. Somewhat intriguingly, a tighter fiscal stance is associated with less inequality. In addition, as expected, the highly progressive social transfers at the federal level are strongly linked to reductions in inequality with economically large coefficients. Social expenditures at the state and municipal levels appear to be associated with higher inequality, with positive and statistically significant coefficients for all specifications, in line with the results obtained by Lim and McNelis (2014)[5] for Latin American countries and with results by Ferreira, Leite, and Ravallion (2010) for Brazil.

The link between the cyclically adjusted primary balance and inequality remains statistically significant when average years of education and average returns to education at the state level are controlled for (specifications 7 and 8 in Table 22.1). The short-term coefficients for the effects of changes in the primary surplus as a share of GDP on inequality range from –0.18 to –0.15 (the long-term effects are about –0.4). These coefficients can be interpreted as semi-elasticities.

It is possible that the results obtained with fixed effects specifications are due to shortcomings in statistical techniques. Hence, the models are reestimated using generalized method of moments (GMM) techniques, namely the system (Blundell-Bond) GMM estimator,[6] which allow the potential endogeneity of some regressors to be handled by using lagged values of these variables as instruments. We transform instruments using forward orthogonal deviations and present robust standard errors, which are consistent in the presence of heteroscedasticity and autocorrelation. The bias introduced by high instrument count is mitigated by replacing instruments with their principal components.

The results obtained (Table 22.2) confirm the association between inequality measures, the employment rate, and federal social transfers, as well as the link between the cyclically adjusted primary balance and reductions in inequality. However, the coefficient for the inflation rate is no longer statistically significant. The estimated coefficient (semi-elasticity) for changes in the primary balance continues to be statistically significant and is larger than what was obtained in the fixed effects regressions, ranging from about –0.26 to –0.51.

Diagnostic tests reject the null of cross-sectional independence in the residuals for most specifications, despite the inclusion of time dummies; therefore, the results should be interpreted with caution. In addition, autoregression tests do not indicate the presence of serial correlation of the residuals. As far as the validity of instruments is concerned, the Hansen test suggests that overidentifying restrictions are valid, but the Sargan test rejects the validity of these restrictions. However, one should bear in mind that the Sargan test statistic is not robust to heteroscedasticity or serial correlation.

---

[5] Note that Lim and McNelis (2014) focus on overall spending rather than social spending, and they use country-level data.

[6] See Roodman 2009 for a discussion.

TABLE 22.1

Fixed Effects Regressions, 1995–2011

	1 Gini	2 Gini	3 Gini	4 Gini	5 Gini	6 Gini	7 Gini	8 Gini
Lagged Dependent Variable	0.455*** [0.100]	0.455*** [0.100]	0.430*** [0.096]	0.433*** [0.096]	0.425*** [0.098]	0.422*** [0.094]	0.420*** [0.098]	0.415*** [0.099]
Δ(Cyclically Adjusted Primary Surplus/GDP)$_{t-1}$	-0.181** [0.067]	-0.182** [0.066]	-0.179** [0.071]	-0.176** [0.068]	-0.162** [0.064]	-0.153** [0.060]	-0.153** [0.061]	-0.157** [0.062]
(GDP Growth per Capita)$_{t-1}$		0.025 [0.071]	0.021 [0.074]	0.037 [0.078]	0.035 [0.076]	0.049 [0.074]	0.050 [0.074]	0.044 [0.077]
(Employment Rate)$_{t-1}$			-0.284** [0.102]	-0.294** [0.105]	-0.251* [0.118]	-0.307** [0.119]	-0.301** [0.117]	-0.272** [0.118]
(Inflation)$_{t-1}$				0.073** [0.028]	0.076** [0.027]	0.076** [0.028]	0.076** [0.028]	0.078*** [0.026]
(Subnational Social Expenditure)$_{t-1}$					0.217** [0.077]	0.348*** [0.073]	0.345*** [0.074]	0.348*** [0.074]
(Federal Social Transfers/GDP)$_{t-1}$						-1.073*** [0.344]	-1.036** [0.369]	-0.915** [0.388]
(Years of Education)$_{t-1}$							-0.007 [0.018]	0.027 [0.020]
(Returns to Education)$_{t-1}$								-0.094 [0.070]
Constant	0.000 [0.000]	0.000 [0.000]	0.000 [0.000]	0.000 [0.000]	0.000 [0.000]	0.000 [0.000]	0.000 [0.000]	0.000 [0.000]
Time Dummies	Yes	Yes	Yes	Yes	Yes	Yes	Yes	Yes
Time Trend	Yes	Yes	Yes	Yes	Yes	Yes	Yes	Yes
Pesaran (2004) Cross-Sectional Dependence Test	-1.87*	-1.89*	-2.05**	-2.04**	-2.19**	-2.28**	-2.28**	-2.30**
Number of Observations	405	405	405	405	405	405	405	405
Number of Groups	27	27	27	27	27	27	27	27
R^2	0.589	0.589	0.606	0.609	0.614	0.621	0.621	0.622

Source: Azevedo and others (2014).

Note: Driscoll-Kraay standard errors in brackets. Null hypothesis of Pesaran (2004) test for regression residuals is cross-sectional independence. Time effects coefficients not reported to save space.

*** $p < 0.01$, ** $p < 0.05$, * $p < 0.1$.

TABLE 22.2

System (Blundell-Bond) Generalized Method of Moments Regressions, 1995–2011

	Gini	Gini	Gini	Gini	Gini	Gini	Gini	Gini
Lagged Dependent Variable	0.595***	0.670***	0.648***	0.654***	0.543***	0.624***	0.565***	0.593***
	[0.096]	[0.093]	[0.081]	[0.077]	[0.107]	[0.094]	[0.122]	[0.120]
Δ(Cyclically Adjusted Primary Surplus/GDP)$_{t-1}$	−0.512***	−0.390***	−0.442***	−0.392***	−0.256**	−0.309**	−0.257**	−0.292**
	[0.098]	[0.117]	[0.100]	[0.110]	[0.103]	[0.111]	[0.119]	[0.116]
(GDP Growth per Capita)$_{t-1}$		0.015	0.033	−0.086	−0.119	−0.099	−0.072	−0.065
		[0.107]	[0.118]	[0.096]	[0.081]	[0.090]	[0.095]	[0.090]
(Employment Rate)$_{t-1}$			−0.329**	−0.283*	−0.206**	−0.316***	−0.294***	−0.288***
			[0.155]	[0.149]	[0.091]	[0.085]	[0.071]	[0.078]
(Inflation)$_{t-1}$				0.021	0.018	0.020	0.012	0.027
				[0.058]	[0.061]	[0.064]	[0.057]	[0.058]
(Subnational Social Expenditure)$_{t-1}$					0.286**	0.337**	0.368**	0.377***
					[0.125]	[0.136]	[0.140]	[0.135]
(Federal Social Transfers/GDP)$_{t-1}$						−0.761**	−1.108**	−1.109***
						[0.358]	[0.403]	[0.381]
(Years of Education)$_{t-1}$							−0.001	−0.008
							[0.029]	[0.029]
(Returns to Education)$_{t-1}$								0.016
								[0.057]
Constant	−5.302	−5.172	−5.924	12.538	25.931**	19.519	18.859	13.879
	[8.187]	[15.363]	[16.386]	[14.812]	[11.323]	[12.777]	[14.220]	[17.910]
Time Dummies	Yes	Yes	Yes	Yes	Yes	Yes	Yes	Yes
Time Trend	Yes	Yes	Yes	Yes	Yes	Yes	Yes	Yes
Pesaran (2004) Cross-Sectional Dependence Test	−1.99**	−1.90*	−2.00**	−1.91*	−2.08**	−2.08**	−2.16**	−2.16**
Sargan Test	98.24***	153.3***	159.9***	171.8***	165.1***	181.7***	173.1***	177.0***
Hansen Test	10.70	12.33	16.41	14.73	8.519	2.873	2.142	1.627
Arellano-Bond AR(2) Test	0.354	0.563	0.547	0.837	0.657	0.603	0.499	0.515
Number of Observations	405	405	405	405	405	405	405	405
Number of Groups	27	27	27	27	27	27	27	27

Source: Azevedo and others (2014).

Note: Heteroscedasticity and autocorrelation consistent (HAC) robust standard errors in brackets. Null hypothesis of Pesaran (2004) test for regression residuals is cross-sectional independence. Null of Arellano-Bond test is that first-differenced errors exhibit no second-order serial correlation. Sargan and Hansen tests of the validity of overidentifying restrictions. GMM = generalized method of moments.

*** $p < 0.01$, ** $p < 0.05$, * $p < 0.1$.

Azevedo and others (2014) also present a number of robustness checks on the baseline speci-fication. The authors start by considering additional control variables, including the share of prime-age workers in the informal sector, the share of employment in agriculture, the share of employment in manufacturing, as well as some demographic variables (the dependency ratio and the average household size), and the share of employment in all sectors (excluding manufac-turing). None of the additional control variables present statistically significant coefficients, but otherwise the results are broadly similar to the ones obtained previously.

Moreover, Azevedo and others (2014) also consider specifications that include the log of the average labor income of low-skilled workers (defined as workers with eight years of education or less), the log of average labor income of high-skilled workers, and the total labor income of low- and high-skilled workers as control variables. As expected, the coefficient for average earnings of high-skilled workers is positive and significant, and the earnings for low-skilled workers present a negative coefficient. More important for the purposes of this chapter, the coefficient for the primary balance continues to be negative and significant in all specifications, although its statisti-cal significance is reduced to the 10 percent level in fixed effects regressions (but not in GMM ones).

Finally, alternative estimation methods and different modeling of deterministic components were also tried. Random effects models do not perform well (in the sense that most variables are not statistically significant), but the link between changes in the cyclically adjusted primary balance and inequality remains negative and statistically significant. Models that allow both the intercept and slope coefficients to vary across panel members were also considered, following the random coeffi-cient model proposed by Swamy (1970). For these models, the coefficient for the primary balance continues to be negative, but is no longer statistically significant.

Specifications that model deterministic components (that is, time trends and time effects) in a different way were also tried. Regressions were estimated including national, regional, and state-level polynomial time trends, and results are qualitatively similar to those already presented. Overall, the robustness checks confirm that there is no evidence that fiscal adjustment at the subnational level is positively linked to inequality in Brazil.

Disentangling the Effects of Changes in Expenditures and Changes in Revenue

A number of papers in the literature on fiscal consolidation at the national level tend to find dif-ferent effects on inequality depending on whether the consolidation is expenditure based or revenue based (Agnello and Sousa 2012). This section explores these differential channels for the Brazilian case by separately including changes in revenues and changes in primary expenditures in the regressions.

The evidence at the national level for Brazil and other Latin American countries points to a greater reliance on indirect (regressive) taxes relative to income taxes, which would suggest that higher primary surpluses driven by higher tax revenues would tend to be associated with increases in inequality (Bastagli, Coady, and Gupta 2012; Goñi, López, and Servén 2011). However, the evidence at the national level also indicates that a large share of social spending is captured by the better off, and thus reductions of these expenditures would not necessarily lead to increases in inequality.

Before the regression results are presented, it is important to note that revenues played an important relative role in those years in which the state-level primary surpluses experienced a positive change. Expenditures, however, have been relatively more relevant in those years in which the state-level primary surpluses experienced negative changes. Hence, fluctuations of the overall fiscal adjustment process have embedded in them changing roles for revenue and expenditure. Also, from a descriptive perspective, the fiscal adjustment process at the state level appears to have had a relatively stronger revenue-side component in aggregate, though this pattern can vary significantly by state.

The regression results are presented in Table 22.3. As before, aggregate revenues and expenditures are adjusted to the cycle using the elasticities estimated by Arena and Revilla (2009), but because of the considerable uncertainty regarding these disaggregated elasticity estimates specific revenue and expenditure items are not adjusted. In fixed effects regressions (specification 1 in Table 22.3), changes in revenues are negatively associated with inequality, whereas changes in primary expenditures show a positive association. Further disaggregation of revenues and expenditures

TABLE 22.3

Effects of Changes in Expenditures and Changes in Revenue, 1995–2011

	1 Fixed Effects	2 Fixed Effects	3 System GMM	4 System GMM
	Gini	Gini	Gini	Gini
Lagged Dependent Variable	0.421***	0.423***	0.642***	0.774***
	[0.091]	[0.093]	[0.126]	[0.097]
Δ(Primary Revenues)$_{t-1}$	−0.184***		−0.260	
	[0.058]		[0.162]	
Δ(Primary Expenditure)$_{t-1}$	0.149**		0.350***	
	[0.068]		[0.124]	
Δ(Tax Revenue)$_{t-1}$		−0.037		−0.262
		[0.242]		[0.268]
Δ(Revenue Transfers)$_{t-1}$		−0.293**		−0.314
		[0.104]		[0.223]
Δ(Other Revenue)$_{t-1}$		0.049		0.101
		[0.114]		[0.258]
Δ(Current Expenditure)$_{t-1}$		0.078		0.407*
		[0.115]		[0.232]
Δ(Investment Expenditure)$_{t-1}$		0.215***		0.263**
		[0.057]		[0.117]
Δ(Other Expenditure)$_{t-1}$		0.197		0.194
		[0.158]		[0.365]
(GDP Growth per Capita)$_{t-1}$	0.042	0.049	−0.027	−0.039
	[0.068]	[0.075]	[0.082]	[0.095]
(Employment Rate)$_{t-1}$	−0.309**	−0.311**	−0.182**	−0.103
	[0.120]	[0.112]	[0.077]	[0.086]
(Inflation)$_{t-1}$	0.074**	0.064*	0.051	0.065
	[0.025]	[0.031]	[0.058]	[0.066]
(Subnational Social Expenditure)$_{t-1}$	0.356***	0.346***	0.251	0.133
	[0.076]	[0.082]	[0.161]	[0.136]
(Federal Social Transfers/GDP)$_{t-1}$	−1.083***	−1.091***	−0.386	−0.104
	[0.349]	[0.354]	[0.350]	[0.273]
Constant	0.000	0.000	9.560	7.317
	[0.000]	[0.000]	[12.738]	[16.464]
Time Trend	Yes	Yes	Yes	Yes
Time Dummies	Yes	Yes	Yes	Yes
Pesaran (2004) Cross-Sectional Dependence Test	−2.29**	−2.26**	−2.07**	−1.84*
Sargan Test			210.3***	293.0***
Hansen Test			1.642	8.002
Arellano-Bond AR(2) Test			0.728	0.792
Number of Observations	405	405	405	405
Number of Groups	27	27	27	27
R^2	0.621	0.626		

Source: Authors' calculations.

Note: Heteroscedasticity and autocorrelation consistent (HAC) robust (GMM regressions) or Driscoll-Kraay (fixed effects regressions) standard errors in brackets. Null hypothesis of Pesaran (2004) test for regression residuals is cross-sectional independence. Null of Arellano-Bond test is that first-differenced errors exhibit no second-order serial correlation. Sargan and Hansen tests of the validity of overidentifying restrictions. GMM = generalized method of moments.

*** $p < 0.01$, ** $p < 0.05$, * $p < 0.1$.

suggests that these results are driven by changes in revenues linked to revenue transfers to states[7] and by changes in investment expenditure (specification 2), with coefficients for these variables being significant at the 1 percent level. These relationships are robust in GMM regressions as well; however, only changes in primary expenditures are statistically significant.

In this context, it can be concluded that revenue increases in Brazilian states were not typically linked to increases in inequality during the period of analysis. Furthermore, reductions in primary expenditures also do not seem to have had deleterious impacts on inequality measures. The behavior of revenue transfers to states and investment expenditure seems to be particularly important in explaining these results. Changes in revenues linked to revenue transfers are associated with reductions in within-state income inequality, though between-state inequality has remained broadly stable (as discussed previously). The rules that govern federal revenue transfers to states in Brazil favor poorer states (as measured by GDP per capita), which tend to present higher inequality indicators as well.

Changes in investment expenditure also seem to have played a role in inequality dynamics, but in the direction of increasing inequality. As argued by Lim and McNelis (2014), capital spending (especially infrastructure spending) enhances the returns to capital and might contribute to an increase in inequality. In Brazil, public investment does appear to have an infrastructure bias.

Finally, it is important to note that the scope for efficiency gains in revenue mobilization at the state level a decade ago was substantial, so it would have been plausible for states to raise revenues without necessarily exacerbating existing inefficiencies. In addition, current public spending could also have been captured by the better off, and thus controlling the growth of these expenditures would not necessarily lead to increases in inequality. Overall, the results of this analysis are consistent with the view that the observed fiscal adjustment process has contributed to a more judicious and efficient use of public resources.

One important caveat regarding the disaggregated results is that the quality of the fiscal information deteriorates as one moves into a higher degree of desegregation of revenues and expenditures. This arises from the potential misclassification of data and lack of harmonized classification practices across states, an issue that is difficult for the federal government to resolve alone.

CONCLUSION

This chapter finds that a tighter fiscal stance in Brazilian states, measured by changes in the cyclically adjusted primary balance, is not associated with an increase in inequality during the period 1995–2011. This conclusion is in contrast to the results of several papers that analyze the impact of fiscal consolidations at the national level for OECD countries (Ball and others 2013). The results also suggest that revenue increases in Brazilian states were not associated with increases in inequality. Similarly, reductions in primary expenditures do not seem to have had deleterious impacts on inequality measures. Further disaggregation indicates that revenue increases due to revenue transfers to states are linked to decreases in inequality, whereas changes in investment expenditure are positively linked to inequality measures.

The different conclusions obtained in this chapter with respect to the rest of the literature could be explained by the fact that several of these studies employ measures of fiscal adjustment

---

[7] Note that the federal revenue transfers go to state governments, whereas federal social transfers also considered in the regressions are direct cash transfers to households; thus, these components have very different implications for inequality. Revenue transfers from the federal government to states are made according to revenue-sharing mechanisms. The bulk of revenue transfers originate from the "States' Participation Fund," which comprises revenues from income taxes and the IPI tax on manufactured products (21.5 percent of the revenues linked to these taxes is allocated to the Fund). States with lower GDP per capita receive a relatively larger share of the transfers.

that are different from the ones used here. The differences could also be linked to the definition of income used to measure inequality. Some studies use measures based on disposable income, while income after transfers and before taxes is used for Brazil.

Nevertheless, the bulk of the difference in the results is likely to be explained by differences in structural characteristics (fiscal, social, and economic) of Brazilian states compared with OECD economies. The chapter does not attempt to establish the precise mechanism linking fiscal policy and inequality, but possible differences driving the result include higher initial levels of inequality, lesser reliance on progressive taxation, the absence of extensive social safety nets and other automatic stabilizers, scope to significantly improve the efficiency of public spending and the quality of public services, and the regressive nature of some forms of public expenditure at the state level. Furthermore, fiscal adjustment at the state level might also have been achieved through efficiency gains in revenue collection with no discernible impact on inequality.

Finally, it is worth noting that all measures of inequality used in this chapter came from the same survey, which is conducted using the exact same questionnaire, with the same field work protocols, and using the same period of reference. As Beegle and others (2012) rigorously demonstrate, survey design and implementation effects can have significant impacts on the final indicators, which can confound any cross-country analysis in this field.

Future research could focus on drilling down on the mechanisms linking the fiscal stance and inequality dynamics. This would be important to ascertaining how the relationship is expected to evolve as the country's macroeconomic and social conditions change, thus more precisely informing policymaking. A central message, however, is that the results linking fiscal adjustment to an increase in inequality in advanced economies cannot be easily generalized to developing countries, given the Brazilian experience.

ANNEX 22.1 VARIABLE DEFINITIONS AND SOURCES

Variable	Description and Notes	Source
Income Inequality	Comprises different measures of inequality in household income per capita (after transfers, but before taxes) including the log of the Gini coefficient and the generalized entropy indices GE(0) and GE(1)	Authors' calculations based on PNAD data
Employment Rate	Share of employed population at prime working age (25–65 years) by state	Authors' calculations based on PNAD data
State GDP Growth per Capita	Log of change in real GDP per capita at the state level	Authors' calculations based on IBGE data
Inflation	Change in GDP deflator at the state level; log of (1 + (state inflation)/100).	Authors' calculations based on IBGE data
Cyclically Adjusted Primary Balance	See main text for details of variable construction. State-level primary balance (revenues minus expenditures net of interest payments) as a share of state GDP	Authors' calculations based on Treasury Department's database
Subnational Social Expenditures	Sum of state and municipal expenditures on education and culture; health and sanitation; and social security and social assistance as a share of state GDP	Authors' calculations based on Treasury Department's database
Federal Social Transfers	Comprises information at the state level on three main federal social programs: Bolsa Familia, Beneficio de Prestacao Continuada, and Renda Mensal Vitalicia; values in the data set are for December of each year and have been multiplied by 12 to obtain annual figures	IPEADATA (www.IPEADATA. org)
Years of Education	Log of average years of education of prime working-age individuals (25–65 years) by state	Authors' calculations based on PNAD data
Returns to Education	Returns to education at prime working age	Authors' calculations based on PNAD data

Note: IBGE = Institute of Geography and Statistics; PNAD = Pesquisa Nacional por Amostra de Domicilios.

ANNEX 22.2 DESCRIPTIVE STATISTICS FOR SELECTED VARIABLES

Variable		Mean	Standard Deviation	Minimum	Maximum	Observations
Log of Gini Coefficient	overall	4.006	0.072	3.762	4.182	N = 459
	between		0.055	3.867	4.105	n = 27
	within		0.048	3.835	4.109	T = 17
GE(0)	overall	0.555	0.088	0.326	0.807	N = 459
	between		0.070	0.403	0.712	n = 27
	within		0.054	0.397	0.710	T = 17
Shared Prosperity	overall	0.097	0.101	−0.433	0.526	N = 432
	between		0.017	0.047	0.123	n = 27
	within		0.099	−0.384	0.554	T = 16
GDP per Capita Growth	overall	0.013	0.040	−0.144	0.144	N = 405
	between		0.007	0.000	0.033	n = 27
	within		0.039	−0.149	0.140	T = 15
Employment Rate	overall	0.657	0.042	0.519	0.765	N = 459
	between		0.035	0.569	0.710	n = 27
	within		0.024	0.522	0.731	T = 17
Inflation	overall	0.083	0.046	−0.078	0.269	N = 405
	between		0.009	0.063	0.099	n = 27
	within		0.045	−0.061	0.254	T = 15
Subnational Social Expenditure/GDP	overall	0.123	0.047	0.035	0.258	N = 459
	between		0.040	0.052	0.204	n = 27
	within		0.026	0.033	0.188	T = 17
Cyclically Adjusted Primary Balance	overall	0.002	0.020	−0.125	0.079	N = 432
	between		0.006	−0.008	0.017	n = 27
	within		0.019	−0.118	0.066	T = 16
Federal Social Transfers/GDP	overall	0.011	0.011	0.000	0.054	N = 459
	between		0.008	0.002	0.026	n = 27
	within		0.008	−0.007	0.039	T = 17
Years of Education	overall	1.840	0.213	1.280	2.911	N = 459
	between		0.163	1.553	2.193	n = 27
	within		0.140	1.435	2.941	T = 17
Returns to Education	overall	0.733	0.133	0.434	1.143	N = 459
	between		0.123	0.541	1.052	n = 27
	within		0.057	0.527	0.969	T = 17

Source: Authors' calculations.

REFERENCES

Agnello, L., and R. M. Sousa. 2012. "How Does Fiscal Consolidation Impact on Income Inequality." Banque de France Working Paper No. 382, Paris.

Alesina, A., and S. Ardagna. 2012. "The Design of Fiscal Adjustments." NBER Working Paper No. 18423, National Bureau of Economic Research, Cambridge, Massachusetts.

Arena, M., and J. E. Revilla. 2009. "Pro-Cyclical Fiscal Policy in Brazil: Evidence from the States." World Bank Policy Research Working Paper No. 5144, World Bank, Washington.

Azevedo, J. P., M. E. Davalos, C. Diaz-Bonilla, B. Atuesta, and R. Castaneda. 2013. "Fifteen Years of Inequality in Latin America: How Have Labor Markets Helped?" World Bank Policy Research Working Paper No. 6384, World Bank, Washington.

Azevedo, J. P., A. C. David, F. Rodrigues Bastos, and E. Pineda. 2014. "Fiscal Adjustment and Income Inequality: Sub-National Evidence from Brazil." IMF Working Paper No. 14/85, International Monetary Fund, Washington.

Ball, L., D. Furceri, D. Leigh, and P. Loungani. 2013. "The Distributional Effects of Fiscal Consolidation." IMF Working Paper No. 13/151, International Monetary Fund, Washington.

Bastagli, F., D. Coady, and S. Gupta. 2012. "Income Inequality and Fiscal Policy." IMF Staff Discussion Note No. 12/08, International Monetary Fund, Washington.

Beegle, K., J. De Weerdt, J. Friedman, and J. Gibson. 2012. "Methods of Household Consumption Measurement through Surveys: Experimental Results from Tanzania." *Journal of Development Economics* 98 (1): 3–18.

Bornhorst, F., G. Dobrescu, A. Fedelino, J. Gottschalk, and T. Nakata. 2011. "When and How to Adjust beyond the Business Cycle? A Guide to Structural Fiscal Balances." IMF Technical Note and Manuals No. 11/02, International Monetary Fund, Washington.

Devries, P., J. Guajardo, D. Leigh, and A. Pescatori. 2011. "A New Action-Based Dataset of Fiscal Consolidation." IMF Working Paper No. 11/128, International Monetary Fund, Washington.

Driscoll, J. C., and A. C. Kraay. 1998. "Consistent Covariance Matrix Estimation with Spatially Dependent Panel Data." *Review of Economics and Statistics* 80 (4): 549–60.

Ferreira, F., P. G. Leite, and M. Ravallion. 2010. "Poverty Reduction without Economic Growth? Explaining Brazil's Poverty Dynamics, 1985–1994." *Journal of Development Economics* 93 (1): 20–36.

Goñi, E., H. López, and L. Servén. 2011. "Fiscal Redistribution and Income Inequality in Latin America." *World Development* 39 (9): 1558–69.

International Monetary Fund (IMF). 2011. "Brazil: Selected Issues Paper." International Monetary Fund, Washington.

Lim, G. C., and P. D. McNelis. 2014. "Income Inequality, Trade and Financial Openness." Paper presented at the conference "Macroeconomic Challenges Facing Low-Income Countries," Washington, January 30–31.

Lopez-Calva, L. F., and S. Rocha. 2012. "Exiting Belindia? Lessons from the Recent Decline in Income Inequality in Brazil." Poverty, Equity and Gender Unit, Latin America and the Caribbean, World Bank, Washington.

Lustig, N., Carola Pessino, and John Scott. 2012. "The Impact of Taxes and Social Spending on Inequality and Poverty in Argentina, Bolivia, Brazil, Mexico, and Peru: A Synthesis of Results." Working Paper No. 1313, Tulane University, New Orleans, Louisiana.

Pecora, A. R., and N. Menezes. 2013. "O Papel Da Oferta E Da Demanda Por Qualificação Na Evolução Do Diferencial De Salários Por Nível Educacional No Brasil." Texto para Discussão USP. São Paulo.

Pesaran, H. 2004. "General Diagnostic Tests for Cross Section Dependence in Panels." Cambridge Working Papers in Economics No. 0435, University of Cambridge.

Roodman, D. 2009. "How to Do xtabond2: An Introduction to 'Difference' and 'System' GMM in Stata." *Stata Journal* 9 (1): 86–136.

Soares, S., F. G. Silveira, C. H. dos Santos, F. M. Vaz, and A. L. Souza. 2009. "O Potencial Distributivo do Imposto de Renda-Pessoa Física (IRPF)." IPEA Texto para Discussão (Working Paper) No. 1433, Rio de Janeiro.

Sturzenegger, F., and R. L. F. Werneck. 2006. "Fiscal Federalism and Procyclical Spending: The Cases of Argentina and Brazil." *Económica* 52 (1–2): 151–94.

Swamy, P. 1970. "Efficient Inference in a Random Coefficient Regression Model." *Econometrica* 38 (2): 311–23.

Vegh, C. A., and G. Vuletin. 2014. "Social Implications of Fiscal Policy Responses during Crises." NBER Working Paper No. 19828, National Bureau of Economic Research, Cambridge, Massachusetts.

Woo, J., E. Bova, T. Kinda, and Y. S. Zhang. 2013. "Distributional Consequences of Fiscal Consolidation and the Role of Fiscal Policy: What Do the Data Say?" IMF Working Paper No. 13/195, International Monetary Fund, Washington.

Contributors

Chadi Abdallah is an Economist in the Expenditure Policy Division of the IMF's Fiscal Affairs Department. He joined the IMF in 2012. Prior to his current position, he was an Assistant Professor of Economics at Miami University. He has published several studies on fiscal and macroeconomic issues, including in peer-reviewed journals such as the *Journal of Money, Credit and Banking* and the *American Economic Journal: Macroeconomics*.

João Pedro Azevedo is a Lead Economist at the World Bank. He currently works for the Poverty Global Practice in the Europe & Central Asia region, focusing on Central Asia and Turkey and leading the region's Statistics Team. He also leads the Global Solutions Group on Welfare Measurement and Statistical Capacity for Results in the Poverty Global Practice. Before joining the Bank, he led the Monitoring and Evaluation Unit in the Secretary of Finance for the State of Rio de Janeiro and was a Research Fellow at the Institute of Applied Economic Research in the Brazilian Ministry of Planning. He is a former Chairman of the Latin American and Caribbean Network on Inequality and Poverty and holds a Ph.D. in economics.

Francesca Bastagli is the Head of Social Protection at the Overseas Development Institute and a Senior Visiting Fellow at the Centre for Analysis of Social Exclusion at the London School of Economics and Political Science. She specializes in the analysis of social policy, poverty and inequality, employment, and gender. Her recent research examines trends in the distribution of wealth and the extension of social protection to informal sector workers. She holds a *laurea* in economics from Bocconi University and a Ph.D. in social policy from the London School of Economics and Political Science.

Serhan Cevik is a Senior Economist in the IMF's Fiscal Affairs Department. Prior to joining the IMF in 2009, he worked at Morgan Stanley and Nomura as Chief Emerging Markets Economist. He completed his graduate studies in economic history at the London School of Economics and Political Science and in economics at American University.

Benedict Clements is the Chief of the Fiscal Policy and Surveillance Division in the IMF's Fiscal Affairs Department. He has worked at the IMF since 1991. He was previously the Chief of the department's Expenditure Policy Division as well as a Division Chief in the Western Hemisphere Department, where he led IMF teams working on Brazil and Colombia. He has published extensively on public finance and macroeconomic issues.

David Coady is the Chief of the Expenditure Policy Division in the IMF's Fiscal Affairs Department. Prior to that, he was Lead Social Spending Expert in the department, the Deputy Chief of its Expenditure Policy Division, a Research Fellow at the International Food Policy Research Institute, and a Lecturer in economics in the University of London. He earned his Ph.D. in economics from the London School of Economics and Political Science. His research interests include development and public economics, and he has worked extensively on policy issues related to the efficiency and distributional implications of public policies. He recently coedited *The Economics of Public Health Care Reform in Advanced and Emerging Economies* and

Energy Subsidy Reform: Lessons and Implications. His research has been published in leading economic journals.

Carolina Correa-Caro is a Research Analyst in the IMF's Fiscal Affairs Department. She previously worked with governmental organizations in Colombia as a Research Assistant.

Antonio C. David is an Economist in the IMF's Institute for Capacity Development. Before joining the institute's staff, he worked in the IMF's African Department, and prior to that, he was an Economist at the World Bank and a Lecturer at the University of Essex. He received a Ph.D. in economics from the University of Cambridge and has published research on a wide range of topics in macroeconomics, including international capital flows, international integration and financial development, fiscal policy and inequality, and postconflict economic recovery.

Ruud de Mooij is the Deputy Chief in the Tax Policy Division of the IMF's Fiscal Affairs Department. Before joining the IMF in 2010, he was Professor of Public Economics at Erasmus University Rotterdam. He has published extensively on taxation issues, including in the *American Economic Review* and the *Journal of Public Economics*. His recent work deals with taxation and inequality, international tax spillovers, and corporate debt bias. He is also a Research Fellow at the Universities of Oxford, Bergen, and Mannheim and a member of the CESifo (Ifo Institute for Economic Research, Center for Economic Studies) network. He serves on the boards of the International Institute of Public Finance and the National Tax Association.

Luc Eyraud is a Senior Economist in the IMF's Western Hemisphere Department. He previously worked in the IMF's Fiscal Affairs Department and at the French Treasury.

Stefania Fabrizio is the Deputy Chief of the Low-Income Countries Strategy Unit in the IMF's Strategy, Policy, and Review Department. Previously she has worked in the IMF's Fiscal Affairs Department, European Department, and African Department. Her research interests include public expenditure, fiscal institutions, macroeconomic risks and vulnerabilities, external competitiveness, unemployment, and inequality. Prior to joining the IMF, she was a Visiting Professor at the University of Salamanca.

Csaba Feher is a Technical Assistance Advisor in the IMF's Fiscal Affairs Department. Prior to joining the IMF, he worked at the World Bank as a Senior Economist and Senior Financial Sector Specialist, covering public and private pension issues, including multipillar reforms, private pension scheme regulations, supervision and guarantees, disability insurance, and other social insurance expenditures. Between his earlier and current assignments in the United States, he worked as a Lead Analyst at the National Bank of Hungary, where he was involved in fiscal forecasting and long-term pension modeling and was also responsible for the country's first sustainability report. As a Lead Economist at the Fiscal Council of Hungary, he was in charge of the Social Expenditures Unit. His private sector experience includes being the first Managing Director of the Private Pensions Guarantee Fund (Hungary) and working as an Investment Officer at the International Finance Corporation.

Valentina Flamini is an Economist in the Expenditure Policy Division of the IMF's Fiscal Affairs Department. She has worked at the IMF since 2009, previously in the European Department. She holds a doctoral degree in economics and finance. Prior to joining the IMF, she worked as an Economist in the Treasury Department of Italy's Ministry of Economy and Finance.

Maura Francese is a Technical Assistance Advisor in the IMF's Fiscal Affairs Department. Prior to that she worked as a Senior Economist in the Fiscal Policy Division of Banca d'Italia, as a Research Fellow at the University of Ancona, and as a Lecturer at the University of York. She holds a doctorate in economics from the University of Ancona and a master's from the University of York. Her work to date and publications cover a wide range of public economics and fiscal policies issues related in particular to the area of public spending and debt.

Davide Furceri is an Economist in the IMF's Research Department. He holds a Ph.D. in economics from the University of Illinois and a doctoral degree in regional economics from the University of Palermo. He previously worked as an Economist in the Fiscal Policy Division of the European Central Bank, in the Macroeconomic Analysis Division of the Organisation for Economic Co-operation and Development, and in the IMF's Middle East and Central Asia Department. He has published extensively in international journals in the areas of macroeconomics, public finance, and international macroeconomics.

Vitor Gaspar, a Portuguese national, is the Director of the IMF's Fiscal Affairs Department. Prior to joining the IMF, he held a variety of senior policy positions at Banco de Portugal, including, most recently, Special Adviser. He served as Portugal's Minister of State and Finance during 2011–13. He was head of the European Commission's Bureau of European Policy Advisers during 2007–10 and Director-General of Research at the European Central Bank from 1998 to 2004. He holds a Ph.D. and a postdoctoral *agregado* in economics from Universidade Nova de Lisboa; he also studied at Universidade Católica Portuguesa.

Sanjeev Gupta is a Deputy Director in the IMF's Fiscal Affairs Department. He has also worked in the IMF's African Department and European Department. He has authored or coauthored more than 150 papers on macroeconomic and fiscal issues and authored, coauthored, or coedited eleven books; the most recent books, all published by the IMF, are *The Economics of Public Health Care Reform in Advanced and Emerging Economies* (2012), *Energy Subsidy Reform: Lessons and Implications* (2013), and *Equitable and Sustainable Pensions: Challenges and Experiences* (2014).

Dalia Hakura is a Deputy Chief and Mission Chief for the Republic of Congo in the IMF's African Department; she has worked at the IMF since 1995. She was previously a Deputy Chief in the IMF's Institute for Capacity Development, where she worked on regional training strategies and led training courses for government officials. She has also worked for the IMF's Executive Board, Middle East and Central Asia Department, and Research Department. She holds a doctorate from the University of Michigan, Ann Arbor. She has published extensively on various macroeconomic issues.

Emine Hanedar is a Technical Assistance Advisor in the Expenditure Policy Division of the IMF's Fiscal Affairs Department. Prior to that she worked as a Senior Economist in the Strategy and Economic Policy Department and the European Department of the Dutch Ministry of Finance. Her work to date covers a wide range of macro and fiscal policy issues, in particular in the areas of fiscal adjustment, public debt (sustainability), public spending, tax policy, inequality, and the European Monetary Union. She has contributed to several (research) publications of the Dutch Ministry of Finance.

Caroline-Antonia Hummel is a Researcher at the Finanzwissenschaftliches Forschungsinstitut (FiFo) Institute for Public Economics. Her research focuses on fiscal federalism, local public finance, and fiscal sustainability. She has worked as a Policy Consultant for numerous governments from the local to the federal level in Germany. She holds master's degrees from the London

School of Economics and Political Science and Sciences Po and is currently pursuing her Ph.D. at the University of Cologne.

Ravi Kanbur is T. H. Lee Professor of World Affairs, International Professor of Applied Economics and Management, and Professor of Economics at Cornell University. He is ranked in the top 0.5% of academic economists in the world. He is President-Elect of the Human and Development Capabilities Association and a member of the Organisation for Economic Co-operation and Development's High-Level Expert Group on the Measurement of Economic Performance. He has served on the senior staff of the World Bank, including as Chief Economist of the Africa Region and as Director of the Bank's *World Development Report*.

Michael Keen is a Deputy Director in the IMF's Fiscal Affairs Department, where he was previously head of the Tax Policy and Tax Coordination Divisions. Before joining the IMF, he was Professor of Economics at the University of Essex and Visiting Professor at Kyoto University. He was awarded the Ifo Institute for Economic Research, Center for Economic Studies (CESifo)– International Institute of Public Finance (IIPF) Musgrave Prize in 2010, delivered the 2012 Chelliah lecture at the National Institute of Public Finance and Policy (NIPFP), and is Honorary President of the IIPF. He has led technical assistance missions to more than thirty countries on a wide range of issues in tax policy and consulted for the World Bank, European Commission, and private sector. He has served on the editorial boards of several leading journals and published extensively on tax policy and public finance issues.

Tidiane Kinda is an Economist in the IMF's Fiscal Affairs Department. He has contributed to the IMF's multilateral surveillance analyses such as the *Fiscal Monitor* and the Vulnerability Exercise for Advanced Economies, as well as other cross-country work, including on fiscal rules and institutions and sovereign debt stabilization. At the IMF, he has worked on several countries, including Canada and Croatia, as well as the euro area. He holds a doctorate from the School of Economics of the University of Clermont-Ferrand. He has published numerous papers on public finance.

Prakash Loungani is an Advisor in the IMF's Research Department. He has worked at the IMF since 1998. He is also Adjunct Professor of Management at Vanderbilt University's Owen Graduate School of Management. He has also worked in the Federal Reserve System (1992–98) and at the University of Florida (1986–90).

Nora Lustig is Samuel Z. Stone Professor of Latin American Economics at Tulane University and the Director of the Commitment to Equity Institute, an initiative designed to analyze the impact of taxation and social spending on inequality and poverty in developing countries. She is also a Nonresident Fellow at the Center for Global Development and the Inter-American Dialogue. Her main research interests are the analytics of fiscal redistribution, applied fiscal incidence analysis, and the determinants of income distribution. She is a founding member and Past President of the Latin American and Caribbean Economic Association and codirected the World Bank's *World Development Report 2000–01, Attacking Poverty*. She has a Ph.D. from the University of California, Berkeley.

Thornton Matheson is a Senior Economist in the IMF's Fiscal Affairs Department. An expert in taxation of financial services, she previously worked at the U.S. Department of the Treasury and holds degrees from the University of Maryland, the Johns Hopkins University, and Yale.

Cameron McLoughlin is an Economist in the IMF's African Department. Prior to joining the IMF, he worked as an Economist in the International Monetary Division of Banque de France. He holds a doctorate from the Graduate Institute of International Studies, Geneva.

Carlos Mulas-Granados is a tenured Professor of Applied Economics at Madrid's Complutense University. He is currently on secondment to the IMF's Fiscal Affairs Department. Since he arrived at the IMF in late 2012, he has worked on fiscal adjustments, growth, inequality, and public investment. He holds a Ph.D. from the University of Cambridge and a master's degree from Columbia University.

John Norregaard is the Deputy Chief in the Tax Policy Division of the IMF's Fiscal Affairs Department. He has worked at the IMF since 1992. Previously he worked at the Organisation for Economic Co-operation and Development (the Committee on Fiscal Affairs' Working Party on Tax Policy and Tax Statistics) and in the Danish central administration, focusing on tax policy and intergovernmental public finance issues. He has published extensively on tax policy and fiscal decentralization issues.

Ian Parry is a Principal Environmental Fiscal Policy Expert in the IMF's Fiscal Affairs Department, where he leads environment, climate, and energy tax work. Prior to joining the IMF in 2010, he was at Resources for the Future for 15 years, where he was the first appointee to the Allen V. Kneese Chair in Environmental Economics. He holds a Ph.D. in economics from the University of Chicago. His research focuses on analytical models to quantify, for various countries, the economic impacts and efficient levels of a wide range of environmental, energy, and transportation policies. His work emphasizes the critical role of fiscal instruments in addressing externalities and raising revenue.

Maximilien Queyranne is an Economist in the Expenditure Policy Division of the IMF's Fiscal Affairs Department. Prior to joining the IMF, he worked as an Auditor in the French government and as a Public Sector Specialist at the World Bank. He is an alumnus of the French National School of Administration (ENA, École National d'Administration).

Fabiano Rodrigues Bastos is an Economist in the Regional Studies Division of the IMF's Western Hemisphere Department. Previously he worked in the IMF's African Department. He has also worked at the Inter-American Development Bank, World Bank, and Bank of England. He has a Ph.D. from the University of Maryland.

Roberto Schatan has been a Technical Assistance Advisor in the IMF's Fiscal Affairs Department since 2011. He was previously with the Centre for Tax Policy and Administration at the Organisation for Economic Co-operation and Development and with Mexico's Ministry of Finance, specializing in the taxation of multinational enterprises. He holds a doctorate in economics from the National University of Mexico.

Louis Sears is a doctoral student at the University of California, Davis. His research interests are in the field of natural resource economics. He previously worked in the IMF's Fiscal Affairs Department from 2012 to 2015.

Mike Seiferling is a Lecturer in Public Finance at University College of London. He spent three and a half years working at the IMF and has since worked with several international organizations on public finance and statistical issues, including as a Visiting Scholar at the IMF. His research interests include public finance, fiscal transparency, quantitative methods, public sector accounting, and balance sheet analysis.

Baoping Shang is an Economist in the Expenditure Policy Division of the IMF's Fiscal Affairs Department. Prior to his current position, he worked at several leading research institutions, including RAND, the National Bureau of Economic Research, and the Urban Institute. His work to date has covered a wide range of fiscal policy issues, in particular in the area of expenditure policy, including health, pensions, employment, subsidies, and social assistance.

João Tovar Jalles is an Economist in the IMF's Fiscal Affairs Department. Previously, he was an Economist at the Organisation for Economic Co-operation and Development and before that a Fiscal Economist at the European Central Bank. He was also a Visiting Scholar in the IMF's and Bank of Portugal's Research Departments. He has been an Invited Lecturer at Sciences Po and an Assistant Professor at the University of Aberdeen, and he also taught at the University of Cambridge and Universidade Nova de Lisboa. He has worked mainly on fiscal policy and has published more than 35 papers in academic journals. He holds a B.Sc., M.Sc., and Ph.D., all in economics, from Universidade Nova de Lisboa, the University of Warwick, and the University of Cambridge, respectively.

Index

[Page numbers followed by *b, f, n,* or *t* refer to boxed text, figures, footnotes or tables, respectively.]

CPSIA information can be obtained at www.ICGtesting.com
Printed in the USA
BVOW07*0032061015

420217BV00001B/1/P